THE ROUTLEDGE HANDBOOK OF THE ETHICS OF HUMAN ENHANCEMENT

The Routledge Handbook of the Ethics of Human Enhancement provides readers with a philosophically rich and scientifically grounded analysis of human enhancement and its ethical implications. A landmark in the academic literature, the volume covers human enhancement in genetic engineering, neuroscience, synthetic biology, regenerative medicine, bioengineering, and many other fields. The *Handbook* includes a diverse and multifaceted collection of 30 chapters – all appearing here in print for the first time – that reveal the fundamental ethical challenges related to human enhancement. The chapters have been written by internationally recognized leaders in the field and are organized into seven parts:

I Historical background and key concepts
II Human enhancement and human nature
III Physical enhancement
IV Cognitive enhancement
V Mood enhancement and moral enhancement
VI Human enhancement and medicine
VII Legal, social, and political implications

The depth and topical range of the *Handbook* make it an essential resource for upper-level undergraduates, graduate students, and postdoctoral fellows in a broad variety of disciplinary areas. Furthermore, it is an authoritative reference for basic scientists, philosophers, engineers, physicians, lawyers, and other professionals who work on the topic of human enhancement.

Fabrice Jotterand is Professor of Bioethics and Medical Humanities, and Director of the Graduate Program in Bioethics at the Medical College of Wisconsin in Milwaukee, where he is also the Director of the Kern Philosophies of Medical Education Transformation Laboratory. In addition, he holds an appointment as Senior Researcher at the Institute for Biomedical Ethics, University of Basel. He is also the author of the recent book *The Unfit Brain and the Limits of Moral Bioenhancement* (Palgrave, 2022).

Marcello Ienca is Assistant Professor of Ethics of Artificial Intelligence and Neuroscience at the School of Medicine, Technical University of Munich (TUM) in Munich, Germany, and a research fellow at the College of Humanities, Swiss Federal Institute of Technology in Lausanne (EPFL), Switzerland. He is the co-editor of *The Cambridge Handbook of Life Sciences, Information Technology and Human Rights* (Cambridge UP, 2022).

Routledge Handbooks in Applied Ethics

Applied ethics is one of the largest and most diverse fields in philosophy and is closely related to many other disciplines across the humanities, sciences, and social sciences. *Routledge Handbooks in Applied Ethics* are state-of-the-art surveys of important and emerging topics in applied ethics, providing accessible yet thorough assessments of key fields, themes, thinkers, and recent developments in research.

All chapters for each volume are specially commissioned, and written by leading scholars in the field. Carefully edited and organized, *Routledge Handbooks in Applied Ethics* provide indispensable reference tools for students and researchers seeking a comprehensive overview of new and exciting topics in applied ethics and related disciplines. They are also valuable teaching resources as accompaniments to textbooks, anthologies, and research-orientated publications.

Also available:

The Routledge Handbook of the Ethics of Discrimination
Edited by Kasper Lippert-Rasmussen

The Routledge Handbook of the Philosophy of Paternalism
Edited by Kalle Grill and Jason Hanna

The Routledge Handbook of the Ethics of Consent
Edited by Peter Schaber and Andreas Müller

The Routledge Handbook of Ethics and Public Policy
Edited by Annabelle Lever and Andrei Poama

The Routledge Handbook of Animal Ethics
Edited by Bob Fischer

The Routledge Handbook of Feminist Bioethics
Edited by Wendy A. Rogers, Jackie Leach Scully, Stacy M. Carter, Vikki Entwistle, and Catherine Mills

The Routledge Handbook of Philosophy of Public Health
Edited by Sridhar Venkatapuram and Alex Broadbent

The Routledge Handbook of the Ethics of Human Enhancement
Edited by Fabrice Jotterand and Marcello Ienca

For more information about this series, please visit: https://www.routledge.com/Routledge-Handbooks-in-Applied-Ethics/book-series/RHAE

THE ROUTLEDGE HANDBOOK OF THE ETHICS OF HUMAN ENHANCEMENT

Edited by
Fabrice Jotterand and Marcello Ienca

NEW YORK AND LONDON

Designed cover image: Futuristic city VR wire frame with businesswoman walking. Gremlin/© Getty Images

First published 2024

by Routledge
605 Third Avenue, New York, NY 10158

and by Routledge
4 Park Square, Milton Park, Abingdon, Oxon, OX14 4RN

Routledge is an imprint of the Taylor & Francis Group, an informa business

© 2024 selection and editorial matter, Fabrice Jotterand and Marcello Ienca; individual chapters, the contributors

The right of Fabrice Jotterand and Marcello Ienca to be identified as the authors of the editorial material, and of the authors for their individual chapters, has been asserted in accordance with sections 77 and 78 of the Copyright, Designs and Patents Act 1988.

All rights reserved. No part of this book may be reprinted or reproduced or utilised in any form or by any electronic, mechanical, or other means, now known or hereafter invented, including photocopying and recording, or in any information storage or retrieval system, without permission in writing from the publishers.

Trademark notice: Product or corporate names may be trademarks or registered trademarks, and are used only for identification and explanation without intent to infringe.

ISBN: 978-0-367-61579-6 (hbk)
ISBN: 978-0-367-61581-9 (pbk)
ISBN: 978-1-003-10559-6 (ebk)

DOI: 10.4324/9781003105596

Typeset in Bembo
by Deanta Global Publishing Services, Chennai, India

CONTENTS

Notes on Contributors ix
Acknowledgments xiv

Introduction 1
Fabrice Jotterand

PART I
Historical background and key concepts 7

1 Philosophical advice for the age of human enhancement 9
 Nicholas Agar

2 Spotlights on the history of human enhancement discourse 18
 Christopher Coenen

3 To be or not to be enhanced? Just ask the Moon – in posthuman terms 30
 Francesca Ferrando

PART II
Human enhancement and human nature 45

4 Clones, chimeras, and organoids: Developmental biology and
 the human future 47
 William Hurlbut and Dillon Stull

5 A thematic overview: Debating the ethics of radical enhancement 77
 Nicholas M. Sparks

6 Resurrecting the 'body': Phenomenological perspectives on embodiment 87
   Vera Borrmann, Christopher Coenen, Luisa Gerstgrasser, Eva Albers, Oliver Müller, and Philipp Kellmeyer

7 Human enhancement through the lens of sex selection 103
   Robert Sparrow

8 Does enhancement violate human "nature"? 119
   Jason T. Eberl

9 Authenticity in the ethics of human enhancement 133
   Muriel Leuenberger

PART III
Physical enhancement 143

10 The ethics of genetic enhancement: Key concepts and future prospects 145
   Jonny Anomaly and Tess Johnson

11 Germline gene editing with CRISPR: A risk-analysis response to liberal eugenics 154
   Siddharta B. Chiong OP and Nicanor Austriaco OP

12 Framing longevity science and an "aging enhancement" 162
   Colin Farrelly

13 Christian theology and the ethical ambiguities of aging attenuation 175
   Todd T.W. Daly

PART IV
Cognitive enhancement 187

14 AI as IA: The use and abuse of artificial intelligence (AI) for human enhancement through intellectual augmentation (IA) 189
   Alexandre Erler and Vincent C. Müller

15 Clearing the bottleneck of empirical data in the ethics of cognitive enhancement 202
   Cynthia Forlini

16 Not extended, but enhanced: Internal improvements to cognition and the maintenance of cognitive agency 214
   Nada Gligorov

17 Is enhancement with brain–computer interfaces ethical? Evidence in favor of symbiotic augmentation   224
Tomislav Furlanis and Frederic Gilbert

18 Anticipating the future of neurotechnological enhancement   237
Nathan Higgins, Cynthia Forlini, Isobel Butorac, John Gardner, and Adrian Carter

PART V
Mood enhancement and moral bioenhancement   251

19 Moral enhancement through neurosurgery? – Feasibility and ethical justifiability   253
Sabine Müller

20 Transhumanism and moral enhancement   267
Johann S. Ach and Birgit Beck

21 Protecting future generations by enhancing current generations   282
Parker Crutchfield

22 What kinds of moral bioenhancement are desirable? What kinds are possible?   293
Harris Wiseman

PART VI
Human enhancement and medicine   307

23 The meaning of enhancement in the post-COVID-19 world   309
Ruth Chadwick

24 Clinical practice and human enhancement: Blurred borders and ethical issues   319
Mirko D. Garasic and Andrea Lavazza

25 Cyborgs and designer babies: The human body as a technological design space   331
Michael Bess

26 Pharmaceutical cognitive enhancement: Entanglement with emotion, morality, and context   340
Kevin Chien-Chang Wu

PART VII
Legal, social, and political implications — 357

27 Cognitive enhancement from a legal perspective — 359
    Jennifer A. Chandler and Kai Vogeley

28 Enhancement and hyperresponsibility — 374
    Anna Hartford, Julian Savulescu, and Dan J. Stein

29 Human flourishing or injustice? Social, political, and regulatory
    implications of cognitive enhancement — 389
    Iris Coates McCall and Veljko Dubljević

30 Contemporary bioethical and legal perspectives on cognitive enhancement — 407
    Luca Valera and Vicente Bellver

Epilogue — *419*
Index — *422*

NOTES ON CONTRIBUTORS

Johann S. Ach is Professor at the Department of Philosophy and Head of the Centre for Bioethics at the University of Münster (Germany).

Nicholas Agar is Professor of Ethics at the University of Waikato, New Zealand. Over the past almost 30 years, he has explored the ethical implications of technological change and the ways in which genetic and cybernetic technologies may alter us.

Eva Albers has studied medicine since 2013 and philosophy since 2017 at the University of Freiburg. Her main interest lies in the exploration of underlying anthropological concepts of medical practice. She is currently undergoing clinical training at Charité Universitätsmedizin, Berlin.

Jonathan Anomaly is Academic Director of the Center for Philosophy, Politics, and Economics in Ecuador, and co-founder of Polygenx Research. He is co-editor of *Philosophy, Politics, and Economics* (Oxford University Press) and author of *Creating Future People: The Ethics of Genetic Enhancement* (Routledge Press).

Rev. Fr. Nicanor Austriaco OP is Professor of Biological Sciences and Professor of Sacred Theology at the University of Santo Tomas in Manila, Philippines. A second edition of his best-selling book, *Beatitude and Biomedicine: An Introduction to Catholic Bioethics* has just been published by the Catholic University of America Press.

Birgit Beck is Assistant Professor (Juniorprofessorin) for Ethics and Philosophy of Technology at the Institute of History and Philosophy of Science, Technology, and Literature, Technische Universität Berlin, Germany. Her latest publications include "Technology, Anthropology, and Dimensions of Responsibility." Techno:Phil – Aktuelle Herausforderungen der Technikphilosophie, Volume 1. Stuttgart: J.B. Metzler, 2020; co-edited with Michael Kühler.

Vicente Bellver is Full Professor of Legal Philosophy at the Department of Legal and Political Philosophy, Universitat de València (Spain). His latest publications are Vulnerability, interdependence and compassion: a challenge for the law (2022); Byung-Chul Han: the transparent digital society or the hell of the same (2022); and Education, digital media and children's rights (2022).

Michael Bess is Chancellor's Professor of History at Vanderbilt University in Nashville, Tennessee. His most recent book is *Planet in Peril: Humanity's Four Greatest Challenges and How We Can Overcome Them* (Cambridge University Press, 2022).

Notes on Contributors

Vera Borrmann is a philosopher at the University of Freiburg – Medical Center, where she is part of the Human-Technology Interaction Lab. Her research interests are in the field of embodiment in feminist theory, critical and applied phenomenology, as well as philosophical practices.

Isobel Butorac is a PhD candidate (clinical psychology) at Monash University, Australia. Her research explores the neuroethical implications of surveillance medicine and digital mental health using a design bioethics approach.

Adrian Carter is Associate Professor and an Australian Research Council Future Fellow and Director, Community Engagement and Neuroethics at the Turner Institute for Brain and Mental Health, Monash University and is co-editor-in-chief of the journal *Neuroethics*. He has been an advisor to the WHO, OECD, European Monitoring Centre for Drugs and Drug Addiction, and UNODC on responsible innovation of neurotechnologies.

Ruth Chadwick is Professor Emerita, Cardiff University, and Visiting Professor at the University of Leeds. She is co-editor of the journal *Bioethics and* co-author, with Udo Schüklenk, of *This is Bioethics* (Wiley, 2021).

Jennifer A Chandler is Bertram Loeb Research Chair and Professor and Vice-Dean of Research in the Faculty of Law, with cross-appointment to the Faculty of Medicine at the University of Ottawa, Canada.

Siddharta Bayona Chiong is a friar of the Dominican Province of the Philippines. He is taking his licentiate and masters in philosophy at the University of Santo Tomas, Manila.

Iris Coates McCall is a research affiliate at the NeuroComputational Ethics Research Group at North Carolina State University, USA. She also holds an editorial intern position at the *American Journal of Bioethics – Neuroscience*.

Christopher Coenen is a research group leader at the Institute for Technology Assessment and Systems Analysis (ITAS) within Karlsruhe Institute of Technology (KIT) in Germany, KIT's "human enhancement" topic expert, and editor-in-chief of "NanoEthics: Studies of New and Emerging Technologies."

Parker Crutchfield is Associate Professor in Medical Ethics, Humanities, and Law at Western Michigan University Homer Stryker M.D. School of Medicine. He is the author of *Moral Enhancement and the Public Good* (Routledge, 2021).

Todd T. W. Daly is Associate Professor of Theology and Ethics at Urbana Theological Seminary in Champaign, Illinois, USA. His recent publications include *Chasing Methuselah: Theology, the Body, and Slowing Human Aging* (Cascade, 2021).

Veljko Dubljević is a University Faculty Scholar and Associate Professor at NC State University, where he leads the NeuroComputational Ethics Research Group. He is the Editor in Chief of American Journal of Bioethics - Neuroscience, series co-editor for "Advances in Neuroethics," and serves on the Board of Directors of the International Neuroethics Society. He is a prolific author in Neuroethics and Ethics of AI, having published over 90 peer-reviewed articles, and four books.

Jason T. Eberl is Professor of Health Care Ethics and Philosophy and Director of the Gnaegi Center for Health Care Ethics at Saint Louis University. He is the author of *The Nature of Human Persons: Metaphysics and Bioethics* (2020).

Alexandre Erler is Associate Professor at the Institute of Philosophy of Mind and Cognition at National Yang Ming Chiao Tung University in Taipei. He is a philosopher studying the ethical implications of new technologies with the potential to significantly transform society and the human condition (e.g. human enhancement technologies, artificial intelligence, or genome editing). He has also worked on issues in neuroethics and the philosophy of psychiatry (e.g. ethical questions relating to mental disorders like ADHD).

Colin Farrelly is Professor in the Department of Political Studies (cross-appointed with Philosophy) at Queen's University in Canada. He is the author of *Genetic Ethics: An Introduction* (Polity Books, 2018) and *Biologically Modified Justice* (Cambridge University Press, 2016).

Francesca Ferrando teaches Philosophy at NYU-Liberal Studies, New York University. A leading voice in the field of posthuman studies, they have been the recipient of numerous honors and recognitions; US magazine *Origins* named them among the top 100 people making a change in the world. Their latest book is *Philosophical Posthumanism* (Bloomsbury 2019).

Cynthia Forlini is Senior Lecturer in Health Ethics and Professionalism in the School of Medicine at Deakin University (Australia). Her research explores the neuroethical issues that arise as we redefine the boundaries between treatment, maintenance, and enhancement of cognitive performance.

Tomislav Furlanis is an independent researcher of ethical human-AI symbiosis with a doctoral degree in AI ethics. Tom's ongoing interests include the impact of AI on democratic life and structure, the symbiotic relationship with brain-computer interfaces, and the prospect of moral social robots.

Mirko Daniel Garasic is Assistant Professor in Moral Philosophy at Roma Tre University, Rome, Italy. His most recent book *Leviatano 4.0. Politica delle nuove tecnologie* (in Italian) was published by Luiss University Press in 2022.

John Gardner is Director of the Monash Bioethics Centre and a senior lecturer in sociology at Monash University, Melbourne. His research examines the socioethical issues associated with new technological developments in healthcare and biomedicine.

Luisa Gerstgrasser is a research assistant in Kellmeyer's research group on human-technology interaction at the University Medical Center Freiburg. She has a background in life sciences and cognitive neurosciences and currently takes science and technology studies at the University of Vienna with a special interest in human-AI interaction, neurotechnologies, and feminist technoscience theories.

Fred Gilbert is Associate Professor and Head of Discipline for Philosophy at the University of Tasmania, Australia. He is Principal Lead of the EthicsLab where he conducts research in neuroethics and bioethics, more precisely on the ethics of brain-computer interfaces.

Nada Gligorov is Associate Professor of Bioethics and Graduate Studies Director at the Alden March Bioethics Institute at Albany Medical College. The primary focus of her scholarly work is the examination of the interaction between commonsense and scientific theories. She is the author of a monograph titled *Neuroethics and the Scientific Revision of Common Sense* (Studies in Brain and Mind, Springer, 2016). She is also the co-editor of the book *The Human Microbiome: Ethical, Legal and Social Concerns* (Oxford University Press, 2013). Her current scholarly efforts are focused on the role of cognitive and emotional processes in pain as well as on the resiliency of concepts of self.

Anna Hartford is a postdoctoral fellow in the Brain-Behaviour Unit at the University of Cape Town.

Nathan Higgins is a PhD student at the Turner Institute for Brain and Mental Health, Monash University. His research focuses on neuroethical considerations in the responsible research and development of novel neurotechnologies.

William B. Hurlbut, M.D., is a senior research scholar and adjunct professor in the Department of Neurobiology, Stanford University, USA. He teaches courses on medicine, technology, and ethics, and served on the President's Council on Bioethics from 2001 to 2009.

Marcello Ienca is Assistant Professor of Ethics of Artificial Intelligence and Neuroscience at the School of Medicine, Technical University of Munich (TUM) in Munich, Germany, and a research fellow at College of Humanities, Swiss Federal institute of Technology in Lausanne (EPFL), Switzerland. He is the co-editor of the *Cambridge Handbook of Life Sciences, Information Technology and Human Rights* (Cambridge University Press).

Tess Johnson is a GLIDE postdoctoral researcher in the ethics of pandemic preparedness, surveillance, and response based at the Ethox Centre, University of Oxford. She recently completed her DPhil in Philosophy at the Oxford Uehiro Centre for Practical ethics, with a thesis on the topic of human genomic enhancement. Her current research is in infectious disease ethics and responses to public health emergencies.

Fabrice Jotterand is Professor of Bioethics and Medical Humanities, and Director of the Graduate Program in Bioethics at the Medical College of Wisconsin. He is also Director of the Kern Philosophies of Medical Education Transformation Laboratory (P-METaL). He holds an appointment as Senior Researcher at the Institute for Biomedical Ethics, University of Basel. He is the author of the recent book *The Unfit Brain and the Limits of Moral Bioenhancement* (Palgrave, 2022).

Philipp Kellmeyer is a neurologist at the University of Freiburg – Medical Center where he leads a research group on human-technology interaction. His group investigates conceptual and normative foundations and performs qualitative research on human-AI interaction and other emerging technologies.

Andrea Lavazza is a senior research fellow in Neuroethics at CUI, Arezzo, Italy, and an adjunct professor in neuroethics at the University of Milan, Italy. He has published over 100 papers in scientific journals and 11 books as an author or editor.

Muriel Leuenberger is a Hosted Research Fellow at the Oxford Uehiro Centre for Practical Ethics where she researches authenticity, identity, and narratives in ethics of technology and medical ethics.

Oliver Müller is Full Professor of Philosophy at the University of Freiburg. His research focus is on the philosophy of technology, phenomenological anthropology, and ethics, including the reflection on current technologies such as artificial intelligence or neurotechnology.

Sabine Müller is a physicist and philosopher. She is Professor of medical ethics and neurophilosophy at the Charité – Universitätsmedizin Berlin in Germany. She has coordinated the international, interdisciplinary research project "Psychiatric Neurosurgery – Ethical, legal and societal issues."

Vincent C. Müller is Alexander von Humboldt Professor for Philosophy and Ethics of AI and director of the Centre for Philosophy and AI Research (PAIR) at the University of Erlangen-Nuremberg (FAU) in Germany. He is also a visiting research fellow at the University of Leeds as well as a Turing fellow at the Alan Turing Institute in the UK. His research mainly focuses on the philosophy and ethics of AI, philosophy of mind, and philosophy of language.

Julian Savulescu is the Chen Su Lan Centennial Professor in Medical Ethics and Director of the Centre for Biomedical Ethics at the National University of Singapore. He has held the Uehiro Chair in Practical Ethics at the University of Oxford from 2002 and directed the Oxford Uehiro Centre for Practical Ethics from 2002 to 2022. He has degrees in medicine, neuroscience, and bioethics. He co-directs the interdisciplinary Wellcome Centre for Ethics and Humanities in collaboration with Public Health, Psychiatry, and History. He is a Fellow of the Australian Academy for Health and Medical Sciences and received an honorary doctorate from the University of Bucharest.

Nicholas Sparks is an advanced doctoral student in philosophy and bioethics at Saint Louis University, USA.

Robert Sparrow is Professor in the Philosophy Program at Monash University, where he works on ethical issues raised by new technologies. Dr. Sparrow has published on topics as diverse as the ethics of military robotics, the moral status of artificial intelligence, human enhancement, stem cells, preimplantation genetic diagnosis, xenotransplantation, and migration.

Dan J Stein is Professor and Chair of the Department of Psychiatry and Mental Health at the University of Cape Town. His most recent book is *Problems of Living: Perspectives from Philosophy, Psychiatry, and Cognitive-Affective Science* (2021).

Dillon Stull is a graduate student at the Stanford University School of Medicine, USA. His interests are in poetry, philosophy, and theology.

Luca Valera is Associate Professor of Philosophy at the Department of Philosophy, Universidad de Valladolid (Spain) and Adjunct Professor at the Center for Bioethics, Pontificia Universidad Católica de Chile (Chile). His latest publications are: Espejos. Filosofía y nuevas tecnologías (2022) and Protecting the Mind (2022).

Kai Vogeley is Professor for "Psychiatry and Psychotherapy" at the University Hospital Cologne and group leader "Social Cognition" at the University Hospital Cologne and at the Institute of Neuroscience and Medicine at the Research Center Juelich.

Harris Wiseman is a Lecturer in Philosophy at Dudley College of Technology. His book on moral enhancement, *The Myth of the Moral Brain – The Limits of Moral Enhancement* was published by The MIT Press in 2016.

Kevin Chien-Chang Wu is Associate Professor at the Graduate Institute of Medical Education and Bioethics, National Taiwan University College of Medicine, Taiwan, and a forensic psychiatrist at National Taiwan University Hospital. His research focuses on neuroethics, suicidology, and mental health law and policy.

ACKNOWLEDGMENTS

The publication of this handbook would not have been possible without the collaboration of many individuals we would like to recognize and thank for their contributions, help, and encouragement. We are deeply grateful for our contributors, as each chapter reflects a commitment to delivering high-quality scholarship. We want to thank our editor, Andrew Beck, at Routledge for his guidance and support, and for giving us the opportunity to put together this collection of essays. We are particularly grateful for his patience and assistance, as bringing together this volume through the COVID pandemic turned out to be a lengthy process with many challenges. Special thanks go to Justine Espisito for competently managing this project, corresponding with each contributor, and working diligently on the formatting of each chapter. We want to recognize the support of our respective academic institutions and our colleagues who allowed us to have the freedom and the privilege to work on this book. To guarantee a high-quality reviewing process for each chapter, we want to recognize the following individuals who served as reviewers: Roberto Andorno, David Bolender, Christopher Coenen, Todd Daly, Veljko Dubljevic, Jason T. Eberl, Annie Friedrich, Agata Ferretti, Richard B. Gibson, Ralf Jox, Garson Leder, Jennifer McCurdy, Lana Minshew, D. Christopher Ralston, Michael J. Sleasman, and Ryan Spellecy. We also would like to gratefully acknowledge our funders. In particular, MI acknowledges funding from the Swiss National Science Foundation (SNSF) through the ERA-NET NEURON JTC 2020 "Ethical, Legal, and Social Aspects (ELSA)" project HYBRIDMIND. Last but not least, we are thankful to our families, for their support and patience as we took time away to work on this book.

Introduction

Fabrice Jotterand

"*What has to be salvaged is not a particular political system any longer, not even a definite civilization. It is mankind as a whole, the speaking animal, the conversing animal, that doubts of its own legitimacy and that needs grounds for wishing to push further the human adventure.*"

R. Brague, Curing Mad Truths, *2019*

Throughout history, humans have used various techniques to augment and alter cognitive capacities, behavior, and physical capabilities. Recent progress in pharmacology, neuroscience, genetics, regenerative medicine, artificial intelligence, and bioengineering has allowed the development of drugs, procedures, and devices not only to treat various disorders but also to use the same technologies to enhance human capabilities, if not possibly alter the very notion of what it means to be human. The development of these technologies is on the verge of redesigning the boundaries of human existence. Brain–computer interfaces (BCIs), CRISPR Cas9, synthetic biology, radical life extension, neuro-enhancements, neuroprostheses, and bionics constitute only a few instances of technological trends that could potentially allow redefining and transcending human biological limitations. Some strong proponents of these emerging technologies seek the radical removal of the constraints of our bodies and brains and the reconfiguration of human existence according to technological opportunities to inaugurate a new posthuman age.

In light of the advances in science and technology that we are witnessing, their potential impact on human beings, and the ideological trends surrounding the debate over human enhancement, we can legitimately ask whether mankind, as we know it today, will maintain its legitimacy in a world increasingly determined by, if not obsessed with, technology. We might have reached a point of no return in the human adventure that will require rethinking how we understand ourselves as *Homo sapiens*. As stated by some contributors, the disruption of one component of what constitutes the human organism could turn out to be detrimental to the well-being and potentially the survival of the human species, as it is difficult to predict if an enhanced human being can indeed flourish under current conditions.

The *Routledge Handbook of the Ethics of Human Enhancement* offers a timely and comprehensive examination of the current debates on human enhancement. In the last decade, the debate has considerably expanded, and more scholars from various disciplines have not only raised concerns about the feasibility and desirability of human enhancement but also offered more nuanced positions on the implementation of enhancement technologies and their impact on human beings. For this reason, this handbook includes not only dissenting voices but also insights from disciplines often marginalized in these debates. In addition, technological advances have significantly evolved in the last decade and are now on the verge of expanding our ability to redefine human biology and the capacities of our brain as well as intervene in the brain and mind to alter behavior (Jotterand, 2022; Jotterand & Dubljevic, 2016). Consequently, these advancements have challenged existing philosophical, ethical, social, and regulatory frameworks which could potentially, if not revisited and updated, hamper the responsible development and implementation of enhancement technologies.

In this brief introduction, the intent is to provide a thematic overview of the various contributions contained in the book. Needless to say, the handbook could cover more ground due to the complexity of the issues associated with the ethics of human enhancement, but we believe the chapters put together constitute the groundwork necessary for further in-depth analysis of the benefits of the use of enhancement technologies but also their risks and ethical challenges. The volume is structured according to seven main sections preceded by this brief introduction and followed by an epilogue. Part I, "Historical background and key concepts", provides first an overview of how and why the discourse on human enhancement intensified in the last few decades, particularly in Western countries. The culture of the West has embraced technocratic traditions with specific socio-political underpinnings that have resulted in polarizing debates, either in terms of bioconservatism or liberal views. The political overtone should not be a surprise, as it reflects the biopoliticization often observed in how issues are deliberated in disciplines at the intersection of science and technology as well as in bioethics and neuroethics (Jotterand & Ienca, 2017).

However, as noted in Part I, the writing of a new chapter in the book of the human journey toward a better future requires novel approaches to philosophical and ethical evaluation. Too often proponents of human enhancement use "marketing strategies" based on thought experiments or narratives that often emote fear (e.g., the "ultimate harm" argument) to promote the implementation of specific technologies or socio-political programs. Such approaches must be challenged by evaluative methods that take into consideration the cost of the implementation of human enhancement technologies for us, individually, but also collectively for the various societies inhabiting planet Earth, and ultimately for the human species. It might be the case that technological advances might allow mankind to address pressing issues threatening its very existence. That said, by enhancing or altering human nature, we might end up, paradoxically, disrupting the human organism which could put into question our survival. We must therefore fully assess whether human enhancement itself is a more serious threat than the problem it tries to address.

In light of the analysis offered in Part I, the contributions of Part II, "Human enhancement and human nature", stress the importance of examining what form of life enhancement is targeting. Human beings are biologically constituted and highly sophisticated systems. Any attempt to enhance, add to, or alter the capacities of the human organism needs careful evaluation, as it could destabilize its organismic unity. Such disruption could have implications not only at the individual level but could also affect the future of the human species in unpredictable ways. As society is increasingly moving toward the acceptance of human enhancement, it is imperative to have an account of human nature that guides the scientific community, ethical reflections, and the development of guidelines and policies.

Such an account often refers to dignity or nature arguments. These arguments, however, need a clear articulation to justify how appeals to dignity and human nature convincingly provide the ethical boundaries necessary for the responsible implementation of enhancement technologies in the social and clinical contexts. In addition, moral considerations associated with human identity should pay special attention to the issue of authenticity, considered by some as a central concept in the ethics of human enhancement. Interventions by means of enhancement neurotechnologies have the potential to affect different dimensions of a person's identity such as the nature of the true self, agency, responsibility, etc. Furthermore, and maybe in a more fundamental way, we should also ask what the ultimate goal of human enhancement technologies ought to be. Proponents tend to see the limitation of our biological nature as an impediment to the next stage of human evolution.

But what is the ideal prototype of the enhanced human we can agree upon? Should it be male, female, or something else? Reflections in the bioethics literature on sex selection through preimplantation genetic diagnosis (PGD) can provide some insights about the nature of the debate on human enhancement but also about the challenges ahead if indeed some criteria defining human identity are abolished, or in some instances favored.

Part III, "Physical enhancement", addresses enhancements through genetic manipulations and enhancement technologies aiming at slowing the aging process. There might be good reasons why parents might want to increase the prospects in the lives of their children. For instance, some parents might see the social advantages in increasing the height of their children or increasing their immunity to infectious diseases or congenital malformations. However, promoting genetic enhancement could encourage discrimination against disabled people, against those who do not have access to such technologies due to limited resources, or against individuals who simply refuse to enhance based on ideological or moral reasons. Consequently, the analysis of genetic enhancement should not limit itself to the question of individual choices but include an examination of how it might affect social cohesion and impact the human population overall. A good example is CRISPR Cas9. Some describe this genetic engineering method as a revolution in medicine that could allow the designing of individuals in future generations to be stronger, healthier, and smarter. While in principle no one would object to an agenda that would ameliorate the human condition, it is not clear to what extent we can assess the long-term risks associated with the transformation of the human genome. Therefore, there is an urgent task to put in place clear ethical and regulatory boundaries that will prevent harm to individuals and future generations and promote scientific inquiry and progress in medicine as well.

The other topic addressed in Part III is the ethics of life extension with particular attention to two sets of issues. First, there are questions regarding a) whether life extension is natural, b) how long life should be extended, and c) who should have access to life extension technologies. Second, it is worth deliberating whether life extension may contribute to public health or, from a more critical standpoint, what the implications are of not implementing technologies that slow the aging process. As with many issues related to technology, the answer is never clear-cut. One could accept outright the life extension paradigm on the consequentialist or utilitarian ground, but a more nuanced approach might be warranted. Some scholars argue that a more subtle approach should be put forward when examining the issues surrounding life extension technologies. Such an approach does not simply embrace life extension blindly nor does it outright oppose it. The desire to live indefinitely is not intrinsically problematic. It is rather the dismissal of the goodness of human finitude and aging that must be questioned and evaluated, using different theoretical frameworks.

When we turn to "Cognitive enhancement", examined in Part IV, an analysis at several levels should take place. First, there are questions regarding the nature of the human-machine interface to achieve cognitive enhancement. Such synergy requires implanting a device in the brain or the use of non-invasive neurotechnologies that must be trusted by the recipient in their ability to produce not only transformative effects at the cognitive level (i.e., new cognitive capabilities) but also ameliorate existing cognitive capacities. In addition, the various types of brain–computer interfaces currently being developed, which also include the use of artificial intelligence, raise questions regarding cognitive agency. Specifically, there are concerns as to the extent to which the integrity of the agent is compromised in the ability to achieve independent cognitive tasks.

The development and implementation of cognitive enhancers will require the elaboration of well-defined policies and ethical guidelines that depend on empirical data and less on speculation regarding their potential nefarious effects, misuse, and abuse. For this reason, they must include the perspective of diverse stakeholders and be tailored to the specific human capacities to be enhanced to avoid blind spots. General considerations regarding the ethics of human enhancement should be translated, and potentially adapted, to deliberations about cognitive enhancement, or other types of enhancement. These reflections must consider technical problems and ethical challenges but also carefully evaluate their potential benefits in the social and clinical context.

In Part V, we examine "Mood enhancement and moral bioenhancement". Discussions pertaining to moral bioenhancement are replenished of speculations and questionable visions about moral progress (Jotterand, 2022). Even if feasible to induce more self-control through procedures such as neurosurgery aiming at reducing aggressive behavior or sexual drive, the ethical justification and on what basis of brain interventions remain open questions. In addition, it is debatable whether a neural implant or procedure can *morally* enhance an individual beyond mere behavioral control through technology. That said, an argument could be made, assuming moral bioenhancement would be feasible and safe, that the current generation might have a duty toward future generations and, consequently, they might have a moral obligation to enhance morally in light of the current environmental, geopolitical, and social challenges we are facing. Such a quandary is highly speculative but worth exploring, as it might lead us to consider more judiciously how we can foster the common good in a world that has embraced, sometimes uncritically, the technological imperative and has lost trust in more traditional methods (role of education, institutions, civic discourse, etc.) for moral progress.

Part VI, "Human enhancement and medicine", examines some challenges medicine is already confronting and is likely to encounter. The distinction between therapy – aiming at the restoration of health – and enhancement – intending the improvement of some capacity – might become a fuzzy distinction as human enhancement is integrated into the medical parlance. But once we move away from a clear distinction between therapy and enhancement, the scope of clinical practice will be reconfigured because notions such as health, disease, normal, disabled, etc. will depend on thresholds determined by what constitutes an enhancement. The shift will facilitate the adoption in healthcare of genetic engineering techniques, the use of cognitive-enhancing drugs, and the implementation of neurotechnologies and life extension technologies. More radical visions of the human future include the designing of human beings and the merging of the human and machine (i.e., cyborgs).

Additional considerations pertaining to medicine encompass how the traditional model of the clinical encounter, grounded on a shared decision-making model, might transition toward a stronger emphasis on individual (or surrogate) autonomy that favors individualistic notions of well-being as opposed to a biostatistical concept of health determining the scope of interventions. Before medicine adopts selected enhancement technologies in its practice, strong evidence is needed to support any claim that these technologies are efficacious, safe, and useful to improve the human predicament.

The last section of the volume, Part VII, "Legal, social, and political implications", concentrates on the larger issues shaping the regulation of enhancement technologies and the impact on society of their acceptance. The bio-political implications of the adoption of human enhancement cannot be minimized. Access to these technologies can provide governments or particular groups of people economic, socio-political, military, and strategic advantages. Making sure the right regulatory boundaries are put in place is a tremendous challenge that must take place upstream. So, while there is a lot of hype regarding the potential to improve human health and the human condition, if not how we envision ourselves as human beings, we should avoid a gloomy perspective, as some of these technologies might indeed address important and pressing problems. The task then is to build consensus on legal principles applicable to various forms of enhancement to address key questions related to the freedom versus the obligation to use enhancement technologies, the distinction between legal and moral responsibility, the right to access, and governmental and international regulations. These discussions should also pay attention to the perspectives of "minority" groups in these debates as disabled, religious, and other groups that might have different sensitivities regarding the nature of what it means to be human, the human experience, and the use and impact of technology.

Introduction

Questions associated with the future of mankind and the role of technology in it will surely continue to be debated for decades to come. We hope this volume will contribute to this effort by providing the locus for robust dialogue among scholars and stakeholders of diverging perspectives.

References

Jotterand, F. (2022). *The unfit brain and the limits of moral bioenhancement*. London, UK: Palgrave Macmillan.

Jotterand, F., & Dubljevic, V. (Eds.). (2016). *Cognitive enhancement: Ethical and policy implications in international perspectives*. New York: Oxford University Press.

Jotterand, F., & Ienca, M. (2017). The biopolitics of neuroethics. In E. Racine & J. Aspler (Eds.), *Debates about neuroethics: Perspectives on its development, focus, and future*. Dordrecht: Springer.

PART I
Historical background and key concepts

1
PHILOSOPHICAL ADVICE FOR THE AGE OF HUMAN ENHANCEMENT

Nicholas Agar

1.1 Philosophical advice for the age of human enhancement

Emphatic advocacy of enhanced futures for humanity is a feature of transhumanist writing both inside and outside the academy. According to these views, we should expect and embrace futures in which our descendants – and we, if the most optimistic hopes for technological progress are realized – enjoy radically enhanced intellects and extended lifespans.

This chapter considers transhumanist proposals about radically enhanced futures in the light of understanding how we make choices about the future. I propose that we should consider ourselves to be entering an age of human enhancement. The age of human enhancement isn't limited to a future when super-beings walk among us. It commences when we have technologies that credibly enhance some human capacities. In the first decades of the twenty-first century, there are nootropics and genetic interventions that plausibly satisfy this criterion.

The introduction of credible enhancement technologies requires a change in focus by philosophers. Prior to the age of human enhancement, philosophers presented thought experiments that addressed the very idea of using technology to enhance humans. These thought experiments were informative about the overall moral acceptability, or otherwise, of using technology to enhance human traits.

The age of human enhancement demands different kinds of advice from philosophers. Provocative thought experiments about enhanced humans that purposefully oversimplified the science of enhancing humans were appropriate prior to the age of human enhancement. However, as we enter the age of human enhancement, these stories impair our capacity to make trade-offs that appropriately balance the potential benefits brought by enhancement technologies against their moral and prudential costs. Advice informed by the scientific detail of enhancement technologies should guide the trade-offs demanded by the age of human enhancement. We should consider the benefits potentially offered by a particular cybernetic, genetic, or pharmacological enhancement technology in a way that is alert to and seeks to mitigate possible harms.

I consider the philosophically faulty ways current transhumanist advocates of radical human enhancement make their cases. Transhumanists enthuse about a wide variety of technologies that could be applied to human bodies and brains. They use what they know about cybernetic or genetic technologies as prompts for exciting thought experiments. These scientifically-influenced stories satisfy the requirements of hard science fiction – they present ways in which the future could be. But they are not what we need from philosophers in the age of human enhancement. Exciting stories distract from the features of enhancement technologies that must be philosophers' principal focus. They impede the trade-offs warranted by the age of human enhancement. We should view them as moral marketing and treat them accordingly. Transhumanist moral marketers are not especially interested in enabling a philosophically considered evaluation of enhancement technologies. Their measure of success is instead in the uptake of human enhancement.

I conclude by demonstrating how this advice applies to the problem of inadvertent enhancement which I understand as enhancement that occurs as a consequence of interventions in human beings whose stated purpose is something other than enhancement.[1] This may have occurred when the Chinese scientist He Jiankui edited the CCR5 gene out of twin embryos with the stated purpose of protecting them against HIV.

1.2 Before the age of human enhancement: The very idea of enhancing humans

Consider the philosophical debate triggered by the 1996 birth of Dolly the cloned sheep. The successful application of somatic cell nuclear transfer to a mammal strongly suggested the need for ethical investigation. Technologies successfully applied to sheep could, in principle, be applied to humans.

Some philosophers opened their investigations of the morality of cloning humans with provocative thought experiments in which "Mozart, Einstein, Gandhi, or Schweitzer" were cloned. These scenarios enabled moral assessment of the very idea of cloning humans.[2] Attempts by philosophers to achieve a balanced assessment of the very idea of cloning addressed the potential harms of cloning Hitler, a scenario that, conveniently for undergraduate applied ethics classes had been memorably explored in the 1978 movie *The Boys from Brazil*.[3] The question about cloning humans seemed to become: should we introduce a technology that enables us to clone Einstein if we risk someone cloning Hitler? Does the possibility of a radical advance in physics justify the risk of repeating the Holocaust?

Many scientifically-informed philosophers warned of the genetic determinist error of supposing that cloning Gandhi recreates Gandhi. They pointed out the significant differences between monozygotic twins.[4] But stories about using cloning by somatic cell nuclear transfer to recreate Hitler work perfectly well as a philosophical thought experiment without the need for additional scientific detail.

When philosophers advance thought experiments, they take pains to avoid logical inconsistencies. But since their principal task is the clarification of concepts, they grant themselves permission to overlook many scientific facts about cloning. The focus on logical consistency means that they assume a prerogative to describe facts about the world in a way that is maximally helpful to them.

In Judith Jarvis Thomson's famous thought experiment, you awake to find yourself hooked up to a sick violinist who requires the use of your kidneys for nine months.[5] We are supposed to understand that, for unnamed reasons, there is no way to unhook yourself that doesn't kill the violinist. We should fill in the details in ways maximally helpful to the philosopher who propounds the thought experiment. Upon first encountering Thomson's thought experiment, students wonder why some other way couldn't be found to compensate for the violinist's failing kidneys. But they are told that the thought experiment requires that this is, somehow, impossible. This supposition violates no law of logic. There are many reasons it *could* be impossible to separate from the violinist without killing him.

These dispensations applied to many philosophical thought experiments about cloning post-Dolly. Replicating Einstein's genome in its entirety would be very unlikely to produce a physicist in the middle years of the twenty-first century whose achievements match Einstein's. It is extremely unlikely that you could replicate the precise combination of environmental influences that combined with his genome to produce Einstein's genius. But when we consider cloning Einstein as a philosophical thought experiment, we are supposed to understand that no law of logic or physics prevents this. Philosophers can then consider the benefits offered to physics by a twenty-first-century Einstein.

Similar dispensations are applied to thought experiments about genetic enhancement. Suppose we are told about a plan by genetic engineers to introduce selected DNA from Einstein into an embryo. The aim would be to produce a child with intelligence equivalent to Einstein's. This thought experiment requires no knowledge of which genes contributed to Einstein's intellect and how they did. It assumes some basic facts about human development, among which is the claim that Einstein's genius was the product of the interaction of his genes and environment. Genetic factors that influenced Einstein's intelligence must have existed somewhere on his genome. No law of logic or physics seems to prevent us from locating them, introducing them into an embryo, and combining them with the exact combination of environmental influences that created Einstein's genius.

Prior to the age of human enhancement, there was no expectation that a philosopher would know much about the science of human development and the technologies of genetic modification. In the 1990s, philosophical discussion about human enhancement was dominated by genetics. This is not surprising given that the Human Genome Project was initiated in 1990, and this was a time of high public interest in genetics. But if we look back at the thought experiments that philosophers in the 1990s advanced in their discussions of human enhancement, in many cases the same philosophical results would be achieved had the imagined means of enhancement been cybernetic – for example, super-duper brain implants – or pharmacological – e.g. imagined side-effect-free cognitive enhancement wonder drugs.

The permissive standards for philosophical thought experiments appropriate before the age of human enhancement do exclude some scenarios. If you think time travel is a logical impossibility, then a thought experiment involving a human enhanced with time-travel genes should be excluded. But a thought experiment in which you introduce genes into your future child granting an intellect ten times that of Einstein seems not to violate any laws of logic and is therefore permitted.

Prior to the age of human enhancement, these thought experiments enabled us to get a philosophical fix on the very idea of enhancing humans. We needed this moral preparation as we contemplated the invention of technologies capable of enhancing human capacities. The question we should ask is how much we should expect to learn from these stories as we make moral choices about actual enhancement technologies. We should ask what an overreliance on imaginatively stimulating thought experiments prevents us from learning.

A philosopher interested in marketing a vaccine can tell a story in which it has 100% efficacy and causes no side effects. These stories may persuade a few anti-vaxxers that vaccines are not necessarily evil. But as we confront actual vaccines with actual side effects, we need philosophical appraisals that encourage us to balance real benefits against real risks. We certainly don't need optimistic sci-fi about perfect vaccines. As we enter the age of human enhancement in which the Amazon marketplace is likely to offer even more ways to enhance ourselves, we should beware of philosophers using science fiction to market their own particular visions of the future.

1.3 Making better humans at the outset of the age of human enhancement

Prior to the age of human enhancement, it was perfectly appropriate for philosophers to stipulate the results of an envisaged intervention. In a thought experiment, multiple copies of the Einstein gene might be inserted into the genome of a human embryo producing a human being with intelligence many times that of Einstein's. In that thought experiment, we can stipulate that the engineered being produces revisions of our twenty-first-century physics whose magnitude is much greater than the revisions of physics produced by Einstein in the early twentieth century. It's just a story that tests intuitions about the overall moral acceptability or prudential rationality of enhancing intelligence.

There are now a variety of interventions offered that enhance some aspects of human cognitive powers or extend human lifespans. This area has, not unexpectedly, generated some hype. There is currently much hype about future technologies from people who present themselves as involved in their development. Elon Musk is one example. But some transhumanist philosophers have followed the technologists with a somewhat uncritical attitude toward the potential of future technologies.

Many of the cognitive enhancers and life extenders available on the internet are unlikely to have their advertised effects. But such is the intensity of research in this area that it would be wrong to airily dismiss them all. Philosophers should instead prepare for the arrival of proven enhancers in a way that seeks to balance their potential benefits against possible negative effects.

These negative effects could include side effects revealed in a clinical trial of a proposed enhancement compound. But the potential negative effects of enhancers extend beyond these. We must also consider the soft impacts of using enhancement technologies. Tsjalling Swierstra proposes that emerging technologies can have hard impacts that are easily characterized, quantified, and recognized ("poisoning, exploding, polluting and depleting"), but also softer impacts that are "qualitative, ambiguous, and/or indeterminate."[6] Philosophers seeking to apply John Stuart Mill's harm principle tend to find these concerns somewhat vague and indeterminate. But they should not be ignored simply because our preferred methods of moral accounting cannot easily accommodate them.[7]

Recently, philosophers have become interested in moral bioenhancement, understood as the use of biomedical technology to morally improve individuals.[8] Suppose a pharmacological intervention improves some cognitive ability at the same time as making those who take it morally worse. Such an effect probably won't feature on a list of side effects identified in a clinical trial. A clinical trial is therefore likely also to miss broader societal effects that predictably occur when an effective cognitive enhancer is expensive and therefore available only to a few.

Nootropics include drugs, supplements, and other substances that purportedly improve cognitive abilities, especially executive functions, memory, creativity, or motivation in healthy people. Some nootropics are medications formulated for these purposes. Many claims made on their behalf are questionable. But in other cases, drugs licensed for their effects on disease are repurposed as enhancers.

Modafinil is pharmaceutically approved for the treatment of narcolepsy. Studies support claims on the effects of modafinil on concentration. It seems to enhance powers of attention and focus, leading some students studying for exams and poker players competing in multiday events to take it.[9] Modafinil is apparently well tolerated, leading some researchers to call modafinil the "world's first safe smart drug."[10] There is less attention paid to the potential negative effects of modafinil on cognitive abilities. In a 2009 discussion of neuroenhancers in the *New Yorker* by Margaret Talbot, psychologist Martha Farah expresses the concern that the enhancement of powers of concentration might come with a negative effect on the powers of creativity of those who take it. Farah said, "I'm a little concerned that we could be raising a generation of very focussed accountants."

The researchers interviewed by Talbot expressed concern about a potential reduction in creativity resulting from the neuroenhancers of 2009. These doubts seem to be supported by the folk psychological notion that when one is overly focused, one's mind is less free to wander and to arrive at novel solutions to problems that resist traditional approaches. A closer investigation of modafinil may fail to confirm these suspicions. But at this stage in our engagement with enhancement technologies, it is clearly a mistake to just imagine them away. There is no problem with some people choosing to take a drug that enables them to be very focused accountants – especially if they are accountants. But problems may arise when the use of a specific neuroenhancer confers the economic advantages described by Talbot, becomes very widespread, and reduces society's ability to respond in creative ways to novel threats – or opportunities.

The suggestion that the improvement in focus might come at a cost in terms of creativity points to a possibility that calls for a trade-off. We are ill-equipped to make these trade-offs when we focus on thought experiments in which an imagined cognitive enhancer produces improvements in attention without any penalty.

There is currently interest in cybernetic means of enhancement. Consider research currently being conducted into hippocampal prostheses. These would be devices surgically introduced into brains to compensate for a damaged hippocampus or improve upon the function of a normal hippocampus. In Alzheimer's disease, the hippocampus can suffer damage impairing the ability to make new memories or access existing ones. Animal models suggest the possibility of restoring these abilities by means of an implanted hippocampal neuroprosthesis.[11] There are promising human trials of this kind of neural prosthesis. Restoring the lost cognitive capacities of patients with Alzheimer's would not count as enhancement according to some definitions of human enhancement.[12] These limit the category of enhancement to interventions that produce functioning beyond the normal range for human beings.[13] But there is no reason to think that such devices must be limited to the normal range of human hippocampal capacities. We should contemplate futures in which human beings replace normal hippocampi with neural prostheses whose performance is objectively superior.

These cases call for an evaluation that balances accurate assessments of the benefits brought by an enhancement technology against scientifically-informed assessments of the moral or prudential costs of these technologies. In the case of a cybernetically enhanced memory, prudential costs may come from such effects as damage to the brain tissue at the site of the implant. But prudential costs extend beyond these.

What are some soft impacts of cybernetic enhancement? Perhaps these will include an indeterminate sense of alienation of the cybernetically enhanced from other humans who lack this enhancement. It's possible that any feeling of alienation will be temporary, as everyone comes promptly to appreciate that a single brain implant that boosts memory has no impact on the ability of other human beings to acknowledge you as fully human. But we should not exclude from the outset the possibility that the cybernetically enhanced and unenhanced will view each other as fundamentally different, leading to a fragmentation of the human species.

Consider Lee Silver's 1997 book on the genetic revolution, *Remaking Eden: How Genetic Engineering and Cloning Will Transform the American Family*. In that book, Silver speculated about the possibility of humanity splitting into two distinct species – the GenRich who have benefited from the range of exciting new technologies described in the book and the Naturals who have not.

Silver is a molecular biologist and his focus was on the changes to humans made by biotechnologies such as genetic engineering and cloning. But ethical assessments should consider the softer psychological and emotional impacts potentially highlighted by Swierstra's distinction between hard and soft technological impacts. It's possible that the soft costs of cybernetic hippocampal enhancement will be transitory. People may initially view these enhanced humans as strange; to begin with, they may be reluctant to form relationships with them. Perhaps these feelings of alienation will rapidly pass. When the possibility of in vitro fertilization was initially described, some ethicists feared that "test tube babies" would long be viewed as fundamentally different kinds of experimental beings.[14] But after over four decades of IVF, we can say with confidence that this pessimistic forecast was not realized.

Perhaps this will be the outcome of cybernetic enhancement; the sense of alienation felt by cybernetically enhanced humans and by normal humans toward the cybernetically enhanced will rapidly pass. But there is one reason to doubt that this will be the case. Today "test tube babies" walk freely among the gestationally normal with no experience of strangeness or alienation experienced by either side. Suppose however that the enhanced memories of cybernetically enhanced humans make the differences between them and humans with normal hippocampi readily apparent. Their enhanced cognitive powers could grant the CyberRich advantages over Naturals similar to those enjoyed by Silver's GenRich. The possibility of societal fragmentation should not be peremptorily dismissed at this early stage in the age of human enhancement.

Human enhancement thought experiments are not especially useful for an exercise that seeks to make soft impacts ethically apparent. Swierstra defines soft impacts as "qualitative, ambiguous, and/or indeterminate." The epistemic difficulties that apply to soft impacts when considered alongside hard impacts mean that it is easier for advocates of enhancement to offer thought experiments that omit them altogether. We must not conflate the absence of soft impacts in a *story* about enhanced humans in the year 2100 from an absence of soft impacts suffered by humanity in the actual year 2100.

1.4 Moral marketing and the problem of overselling enhancement

Here's a danger when we carry over moral methods appropriate for times before the age of human enhancement to the age of human enhancement. Thought experiments appropriate to times prior to the age of human enhancement risk giving an overly optimistic impression of the future brought by human enhancement. They, therefore, impede our ability to make the necessary trade-offs. This is especially so when an advocate of human enhancement is a charismatic storyteller.

Some transhumanist philosophers consider possible futures with enhancement technologies far superior to today's nootropics or gene edits. They tell stories in which our descendants – or we, if progress in enhancement technologies is rapid – enjoy millennial lifespans and intellects whose powers are many multiples of the powers of today's most brilliant minds.

Foremost among the advocates of these possible futures is the inventor and futurist Ray Kurzweil. In a number of writings, Kurzweil explores the implications for human beings of exponential technological progress. He proposes a "law of accelerating returns" that codifies the exponential progress characteristic of some information technologies.

According to Kurzweil, the "law of accelerating returns" is moving us toward a Singularity – "a future period during which the pace of technological change will be so rapid, its impact so deep, that human life will be irreversibly transformed."[15] He predicts that we will mark the Singularity by creating a mind that is "about one billion times more powerful than all human intelligence today."[16] This will come as the result of a merger between our biological brains and technology. The technologies that we introduce into our brains will think "thousands to millions of times faster than our naturally evolved systems."[17] We will progressively substitute exponentially improving technology for superseded biology. We are headed toward an exciting destiny. Kurzweil proposes that "Our mortality will be in our own hands. We will be able to live as long as we want (a subtly different statement from saying we will live forever)."[18] Immortality is there, if we want it. But if we decide, 100,000 years into an indefinitely long existence, that we've had enough, we can bring it all to an end. We won't be like the immortal beings in Bernard Williams' essay "The Makropulos case: reflections on the tedium of immortality" who find that they cannot escape endlessly repeating increasingly stale experiences.[19] When should we expect these technological wonders to arrive? According to Kurzweil, the enabling event for truly stupendous enhancement technologies is the Singularity. Kurzweil says "I set the date for the Singularity – representing a profound and disruptive transformation in human capability – as 2045."[20] Elon Musk has raised eyebrows with his commitment to found a Martian city and populate it with a million settlers by 2050. If Kurzweil's forecast holds up, cities on Alpha Centauri should also be no problem.

On the face of it, there's nothing wrong with offering an exciting vision of the way the world could be in the future. Kurzweil's story about optional immortality and magnificently enhanced intellects does not seem to violate any law of physics or logic. It describes a thrilling way things could turn out.

We should nevertheless recognize such stories as moral marketing rather than as enabling the dispassionate assessment of the likely benefits of enhancement that we need in the age of human enhancement. Perhaps the claim that we may achieve an optional immortality by the year 2045 violates no law of physics or logic. But it may impede the trade-offs demanded by the age of human enhancement.

We risk the kind of error that people make when they pay too much for coastal real estate that *could* triple its value within the next year and *may be* unaffected by advancing seas.

1.5 Genetic pleiotropy and the challenge of inadvertent human enhancement

In the age of human enhancement, we are likely to be called upon to assess unintended or inadvertent enhancements.[21] Since these are unintended, they are less likely to be tested in philosophical thought experiments. Philosophers of biotechnology tend to use thought experiments to test morally questionable intentions. Inadvertent enhancements are, by definition, unintended.

The challenge of unintended effects extends beyond consequences that we fail to foresee. The age of human enhancement brings the possibility of enhancements that may be intended but where, for political reasons, the intention to enhance may be disclaimed. This could mean that enhancements in the early stages of the age of human enhancement are more likely to evade ethical scrutiny. In the age of human enhancement, we need methods that look beyond the professed intentions of those who direct genetic, cybernetic, and pharmacological technologies to human beings. A recent case of possibly inadvertent genetic enhancement makes this need apparent.

In 2018, the Chinese scientist He Jiankui caused controversy when he claimed to have used gene editing to remove the gene CCR5 from twin human embryos – identified as Lulu and Nana. His stated motive was to confer resistance to HIV. It is known that HIV binds to the CCR5 receptor on normal cells and that some people born with a mutation to CCR5 enjoy a degree of immunity against the virus. After He Jiankui's shocking announcement, it was noticed that this intervention may also have enhanced the intellects of the twins. A 2016 paper by Zhou *et al.* reported evidence from research on mice supporting the conjecture that the deletion of CCR5 may improve the ability to form new memories and learn.[22]

When informed at a gene-editing summit in Hong Kong of this possible effect of CCR5 deletion on the cognitive abilities of Lulu and Nana, He Jiankui indicated that he was aware of the research of Zhou *et al.* He said, "I saw that paper, it needs more independent verification." He Jiankui concluded his comments with the simple assertion "I am against using genome editing for enhancement."[23]

This manner of response makes is too easy for scientists in the age of human enhancement to pursue enhancement in a way that dodges ethical evaluation. They can appeal to moral principles such as the doctrine of double effect. According to one version of the doctrine, "sometimes it is permissible to cause a harm as a side effect (or 'double effect') of bringing about a good result even though it would not be permissible to cause such a harm as a means to bringing about the same good end."[24] This would seem to justify He Jiankui's focus on the therapeutic effect of deleting CCR5 – protecting against HIV – and comparative lack of interest in any morally questionable effects on Lulu and Nana's cognitive abilities. Protection against HIV presumably did not come by way of an improvement of the twins' memories.

It may be that conjectures about a link between CCR5 deletion and enhancement do not hold up. But, at this stage, ethicists should consider the moral implications of this possibility. Potential cognitive enhancement should feature in the ethical evaluation of He Jiankui's technique. Philosophers should speculate about the evolutionary rationale for a gene that impairs memories. What negative consequences of memory enhancement might Lulu and Nana suffer? When He Jiankui disavows an intention to enhance, he effectively absolves himself of any obligation to consider such questions.

Inadvertent human enhancement could be a consequence of many interventions in the age of human enhancement. It's a surprise that removing a sequence of DNA that codes for a receptor exploited by HIV to gain entry to cells also improves memory and learning. This would be a case of pleiotropy, a phenomenon in which one gene influences two or more seemingly unrelated phenotypic traits. Those who apply gene editing to humans should prepare for pleiotropic effects. Many of these could affect the brain. According to one estimate "a significant number of genes (about 10,000, or approximately one-third) in the human genome are expressed primarily in the brain and during brain development."[25] If so, cases of pleiotropy in which a gene edit affects both the brain and some other seemingly unrelated trait may be common. As we enter the age of human enhancement, we need a philosophical method that looks beyond professed intentions and seeks to make apparent the moral consequences of inadvertent or unprofessed enhancement.

The phenomenon of widespread pleiotropy in genes that influence the development of the human brain gives renegade scientists plenty of cover to pursue enhancement surreptitiously. Suppose that He Jiankui lied when he expressed his personal opposition to the use of gene editing as an enhancement technology, that it was among his goals when he created Lulu and Nana. Pleiotropy enables him to disclaim this controversial intention. He can appeal to the doctrine of double effect to claim that his intention was to give the babies resistance against HIV. He would point out that the pleiotropic effects of genetic modification are neither intended nor are they means for achieving intended morally good effects. When combined with the probable pleiotropy of many genes that affect the brain, a moral principle such as the doctrine of double effect makes it too easy for scientists seeking to enhance intelligence to evade moral scrutiny. It suggests the strong need, in an age of human enhancement in which human embryos are increasingly subjected to gene editing, for moral methods that focus on *all* of the effects of our interventions, not just on those that correspond to a genetic engineer's claimed intentions, or those that might be the subject of a philosopher's thought experiment designed to present the most optimistic view of an intervention.

1.6 Concluding comments

The switch in focus demanded by the age of human enhancement renders many of today's philosophical defenses of radical enhancement anachronistic. The arguments of transhumanist philosophers tend to combine outlandish and exciting thought experiments appropriate for times prior to the age of human enhancement with cybernetic and genetic technologies that could be developed in the coming decades. But this is not what we need for the age of human enhancement. The age of human enhancement is likely to see a diverse range of technologies that have some potential to enhance human capacities, and we need moral methods that look beyond the stated intentions of those who direct these technologies at our human natures. These methods should make apparent a broad range of effects of these interventions. Only once we have this understanding can we collectively balance the benefits of human enhancement against the full range of its costs both for us as individuals and collectively.

Notes

1 See the interesting research project of Eric Juengst, Jean Cadigan, and co-investigators, "Incidental Enhancements: A Neglected Governance Challenge for Human Genome Editing Research," available at https://bioethics.unc.edu/incidental-enhancements-a-neglected-governance-challenge-for-human-genome-editing-research/.
2 Brock, Dan, "Cloning Human Beings: An Assessment of the Issues: Pro and Con," in *Clones and Clones: Facts and Fantasies about Human Cloning* (eds.) Cass Sunstein and Martha Nussbaum (New York: W. W. Norton and Company, 1998).
3 See for example, the 2005 exchange between Julian Savulescu and David Odeberg. Julian Savulescu "Equality, Cloning and Clonism: Why We Must Clone," available at www.bionews.org.uk/page_91428 and David Odeberg, "Cloning is an Affront to Human Dignity," available at www.bionews.org.uk/page_91429.
4 Kitcher, Philip, "Whose Self Is It, Anyway?" *Sciences* (1997), 37(5): 58–62.
5 Thomson, Judith Jarvis, "A Defense of Abortion," *Philosophy and Public Affairs* (1971), 1(1): 47–66.

6 Swierstra, Tsjalling, "Identifying the Normative Challenges Posed by Technology's 'Soft' Impacts," *Etikk i praksis. Nordic Journal of Applied Ethics* (2015), 9(1): 5–20, 7.
7 de Melo-Martín, Inmaculada, "Defending Human Enhancement Technologies: Unveiling Normativity," *Journal of Medical Ethics* (2010), 36(8): 483–487.
8 Savulescu, Julian, and Persson, Ingmar, *Unfit for the Future: The Need for Moral Enhancement* (Oxford: Oxford University Press, 2013) and Thomas Douglas, "Moral Enhancement," *Journal of Applied Philosophy* (2008), 25(3): 228–245.
9 Talbot, Margaret, "Brain Gain: The Underground World of 'Neuroenhancing' Drugs," *The New Yorker*, April 27, 2009, available at www.newyorker.com/magazine/2009/04/27/brain-gain.
10 Zand, Benjamin, "My 'Smart Drugs' Nightmare," *BBC News*, January 5, 2016, available at www.bbc.com/news/magazine-35091574.
11 For discussion of Alzheimer's disease and how its effects on identity may be addressed by neuroprostheses, see Jotterand, Fabrice, "Personal Identity, Neuroprosthetics, and Alzheimer's Disease," in *Intelligent Assistive Technologies for Dementia: Clinical, Ethical, Social, and Regulatory Implications* (eds.) Fabrice Jotterand, Marcello Ienca, Tenzin Wangmo, and Bernice Elger (Oxford: Oxford University Press, 2019).
12 See, however, Fabrice Jotterand's useful distinction between enhancement #1 and enhancement #2. People with comparatively mild cogntive impairments who are treated in a way that boosts their intellects may not be enhanced #1 but may be enhanced #2. Jotterand, Fabrice, "Cognitive Enhancement of Today may be the Normal of Tomorrow," in *Neuroethics: Anticipating the Future* (ed). Illes, Judy (Oxford: Oxford University Press, 2017).
13 See the discussion of enhancement concepts in Agar, Nicholas, *Humanity's End* (Cambridge, MA: MIT Press, 2010) and Agar, Nicholas, *Truly Human Enhancement* (Cambridge, MA: MIT Press, 2013).
14 See for example Leon Kass, "Babies by Means of in Vitro Fertilization: Unethical Experiments on the Unborn?" *New England Journal of Medicine* (1971), 285: 1174–1179. Some of the doubts expressed here anticipate Kass's later anxieties about human cloning.
15 Kurzweil, Ray, *The Singularity Is Near: When Humans Transcend Biology* (London: Penguin, 2005), 7.
16 Kurzweil, *The Singularity Is Near*, 136.
17 Kurzweil, *The Singularity Is Near*, 127.
18 Kurzweil, *The Singularity Is Near*, 9.
19 Williams, Bernard, "The Makropulos Case: Reflections on the Tedium of Immortality," in *Problems of the Self* (Cambridge: Cambridge University Press, 1973).
20 Kurzweil, *The Singularity is Near*, 135–136.
21 See Juengst, Eric, "Is Enhancement the Price of Prevention in Human Gene Editing?" *The CRISPR Journal* (2018), 1(6).
22 For an article presenting the deletion of CCR5 as boosting the memories of mice see Zhou, M., Greenhill, S., Huang, S., Silva, T. K., Sano, Y., Wu, S., Cai, Y., Nagaoka, Y., Sehgal, M., Cai, D. J., Lee, Y. S., Fox, K., and Silva, A. J., "CCR5 is a Suppressor for Cortical Plasticity and Hippocampal Learning and Memory," *eLife* (2016), 5: e20985.
23 For skeptical discussion of whether He Jiankui was oblivious of this potential effect of deleting the CCR5 gene, see Antonio Regalado, "China's CRISPR Twins Might have Had Their Brains Inadvertently Enhanced," *MIT Technology Review,* February 21, 2019, www.technologyreview.com/2019/02/21/137309/the-crispr-twins-had-their-brains-altered/.
24 McIntyre, Alison, "Doctrine of Double Effect," *The Stanford Encyclopedia of Philosophy* (Spring 2019 Edition), Edward N. Zalta (ed.), https://plato.stanford.edu/archives/spr2019/entries/double-effect/.
25 Douet, Vanessa, Chang, Linda, Cloak, Christine, and Ernst, Thomas, "Genetic Influences on Brain Developmental Trajectories on Neuroimaging Studies: From Infancy to Young Adulthood," *Brain Imaging and Behavior* (2013), 8, 233.

2
SPOTLIGHTS ON THE HISTORY OF HUMAN ENHANCEMENT DISCOURSE

Christopher Coenen

2.1 Introduction

Human enhancement has often been characterized, especially by critics, as the new eugenics; and transhumanism,[1] which promotes human enhancement as a means to overcome the human condition, has been characterized as a eugenic ideology. While one should be aware of and analyze the similarities between enhancement and eugenics, as well as their historical-ideological interrelations, it is also important to view enhancement as the intended outcome of direct intervention in the human body. Eugenics, on the other hand, was and is about improving the human stock, so to speak.

This invasive character of enhancement also appears to be decisive in conceptual terms and in this respect should even take precedence over the relationship between enhancement and therapy. In a study on behalf of the European Parliament, we accordingly defined human enhancement as any "modification aimed at improving individual human performance and brought about by science-based or technology-based interventions in the human body."[2] It does not refer to a specific definition of health and is a non-medical concept of human enhancement. We distinguished between purely restorative, non-enhancing therapies, therapeutic enhancements, and non-therapeutic enhancements, thus rejecting the juxtaposition of enhancement and therapy. Furthermore, the study pointed out that enhancement that enables "super-human" performance or creates "species-atypical" abilities could also be subsumed under a concept of an "alteration" of human nature, which refers to the transcendence of biological boundaries through technological means to create species-atypical human capacities.[3] Understood in this way, the prehistory and early history of the concept of human enhancement is not lost among the huge variety of ideas for improving humanity or among the myriad technologies that serve to improve the performance of the inherently deficient human body. In the following, some light shall be shed on this pre- and early history but also briefly on more recent developments in human enhancement discourse.

2.2 On the prehistory of the enhancement concept

There is a tradition of speculation about the physical, mental, and also moral improvement, or even perfection, of "man" by scientific means that goes back a long way, at least (among other things through eugenics) to the 19th century, and the intellectual history of transhumanism can also be traced back well into the second half of the 19th century. This included early ethical considerations as well as technological visions, for example of ectogenesis or "test tube babies" as far back as the early 1920s.[4]

As Diane B. Paul observed, by the 1920s some scientists were becoming impatient with human natural evolution, and spurred on both by scientific developments and the Bolshevik revolution, they began to speculate about the possibility of speeding up the process of improving the human race.[5] It must be added that these scientists were inspired by H.G. (Herbert George) Wells and, at least indirectly, via Wells, by Winwood Reade,[6] two writers with a strong interest in biology and a propensity to speculate about the future of humanity in light of Darwinism.[7] Paul mentions, among others, the two communists and eminent scientists J.B.S. (John Burdon Sanderson) Haldane with his essays *Daedalus, or Science and the Future* (1923) and *The Last Judgment* (1927), and J. (John) Desmond Bernal with his essay "The World, the Flesh, and the Devil" (1929). She emphasizes that their vision of a transformation of human nature was shared by other Marxists, in line with the point of view of the young Hegelians (including Karl Marx) "that we make ourselves, and not just metaphorically: In transforming nature, we also transform our capacities and sensibilities." Paul also points to Leon Trotsky's *Literature and Revolution* (1924), in which he wrote that after reshaping the physical world, the human species

> will once more enter into a state of radical transformation and [...] become an object of the most complicated methods of artificial selection and psycho-physical training. This is entirely in accord with evolution. [...] The human race will not have ceased to crawl on all fours before God, kings, and capital, in order later to submit humbly before the dark laws of heredity and a blind sexual selection! [...] Man will become stronger, wiser, and subtler; his body will become more harmonized, his movements more rhythmic, his voice more musical. [...] The average human type will rise to the heights of an Aristotle, a Goethe, or a Marx. And above this ridge, new peaks will rise.[8]

Proto- or early transhumanist essays by Wells, Haldane, Bernal, and others had a strong impact on societal discourse on science, technology, and the future, one major literary reaction being the development of classic 20th-century dystopian thought. Haldane's influence on *Brave New World* is well known. It was originally intended to be a direct attack on Wellsian utopianism. In a certain sense, the other authors of early classical dystopian novels of the 20th century, such as Yevgeny Zamyatin, Charlotte Franken, and George Orwell, reacted directly to works by proponents of proto- or early transhumanism. The same can be argued with respect to the popular Christian authors C.S. (Clive Staples) Lewis and J.R.R. (John Ronald Reuel) Tolkien. Lewis attacked Haldane in his science fiction writings, and his essay on *The Abolition of Man* (1942) is still influential among conservative bioethicists. Tolkien's immensely popular trilogy *The Lord of the Rings*, written in the 1930s and 1940s, can in many respects be read as a critique of the proto- or early transhumanist visions of Wells, Haldane, Bernal, and others.[9] Dystopian thought in the first half of the 20th century and influential Christian critiques of technoscientific progress were thus both heavily influenced by the early transhumanist imagination with its focus on human enhancement, and both continue to shape current discourse on science, technology, and human enhancement.

2.2.1 Desmond Bernal on the flesh

Especially since the 1990s, the crucial role of Bernal's "The World, the Flesh and the Devil" in the emergence of transhumanist enhancement discourse has often been highlighted.[10] The title of his visionary essay is an allusion to Christian tradition, and he speaks of "three kinds of struggle: first with the massive, unintelligent forces of nature, heat and cold, winds, rivers, matter and energy" – this is the world – "secondly, with the things closer to him, animals and plants, his own body, its health and disease" – this is the flesh – and "lastly, with his desires and fears, his imaginations and stupidities," the Devil.[11]

The chapter "The Flesh"[12] is most significant in our context. In it, Bernal begins by emphasizing that in "the alteration of himself man has a great deal further to go than in the alteration of his inorganic environment."[13] Processes of natural human evolution have proceeded "so much slower than the development of man's control over environment that we might, in such a developing world, still consider man's body as constant and unchanging."[14] To change this situation, we would have to "interfere in a highly unnatural manner" in our own making.[15]

Bernal then refers to eugenics, which was still very influential in his time, especially in his own intellectual and political milieu:

> The eugenists and apostles of healthy life, may, in a very considerable course of time, realize the full potentialities of the species: we may count on beautiful, healthy and long-lived men and women, but they do not touch the alteration of the species.[16]

Here the Irish polymath provides us with an early and clear demarcation of what is now often called "human enhancement" from those socio-political measures for the "improvement" of humanity that are not based on interventions in the human body.

To achieve an alteration of the species, "we must alter either the germ plasm or the living structure of the body, or both together."[17] In our current terms, the former would be called "genetic enhancement" and the latter would encompass a variety of current, emerging, and possible future interventions in the human body that would involve its "cyborgization," for example through neurotechnologies and other prosthetic developments.

About the altering of the germ plasm, he wrote: the "first method – the favorite of Mr. J. B. S. Haldane – has so far received the most attention," continuing that in the future we may achieve such a variation as humanity did, for example, in dogs. We may even create "new species with special potentialities."[18] But Bernal believed that this method would necessarily be slow "and finally limited by the possibilities of flesh and blood."[19]

Obviously, it was not only his concern about the very long time that the eugenic or genetic "directed evolution" of the human species might take to achieve that drew him more towards prosthetic approaches – but also his longing to overcome "the flesh" completely.

Bernal's essay also foreshadowed our discussions about what, if anything, makes human enhancement specific compared to other technologies that can improve human performance or abilities:

> In a sense we have already started using the direct method; when the ape-ancestor first used a stone he was modifying his bodily structure by the inclusion of a foreign substance. This inclusion was temporary, but with the adoption of clothes there began a series of permanent additions to the body, affecting nearly all its functions and even, as with spectacles, its sense organs. In the modern world, the variety of objects which really form part of an effective human body is very great. Yet they all (if we except such rarities as artificial larynges) still have the quality of being outside the cell layers of the human body.[20]

Bernal argued that "with the development of surgery on the one hand and physiological chemistry on the other, the possibility of radical alteration of the body appears for the first time" and that here "we may proceed, not by allowing evolution to work the changes, but by copying and short-circuiting its methods."[21] And according to him, this is necessary because the "increasing complexity" of human "existence, particularly the mental capacity required to deal with its mechanical and physical complications, gives rise to the need for a much more complex sensory and motor organization, and even more fundamentally for a better organized cerebral mechanism."[22] This argument is an early and more general version of the argument by Elon Musk and many others that humans themselves need to be technologically altered to keep up with their new creation, artificial intelligence.

In Bernal's view, surgery and biochemistry were still too young as sciences to predict exactly how this technoscientific reconstruction of the human body would proceed, and he thus characterized his vision as a kind of fable – though in essence, it was an attempt to imagine the distant future of human corporeality and, above all, of the human mind, based on the knowledge available at the time.

He first mentions the increasing hopes in his time for a much longer human lifespan or even immortality with the help of scientific methods. In this context, he argues for a radical technological solution in which human brains live on after the death of the body by means of neuroelectric interfaces permanently connected to "apparatuses that either send messages to the nerves or receive them"[23] – a vision that is ubiquitous in the current visionary discourse of digital capitalism and, for example in the case of Musk's company Neuralink, even a business model.

Bernal also wrote that we "badly need a small sense organ for detecting wireless frequencies, eyes for infra-red, ultra-violet and X-rays, ears for supersonics, detectors of high and low temperatures, of electrical potential and current, and chemical organs of many kinds,"[24] thus arguing for a major alteration of human corporeality:

> A mechanical stage, utilizing some or all of these alterations of the bodily form might [...] become the regular culmination to ordinary life. Whether this should ever be so for the whole of the population we will discuss later, but for the moment we may attempt to picture what would at this period be the course of existence for a transformable human being.[25]

And he continues:

> Starting, as Mr. J. B. S. Haldane so convincingly predicts, in an ectogenetic factory, man will have anything from sixty to a hundred and twenty years of larval, unspecialized existence – surely enough to satisfy the advocates of a natural life. In this stage he [...] can occupy his time (without the conscience of wasting it) in dancing, poetry and love-making, and perhaps incidentally take part in the reproductive activity. Then he will leave the body whose potentialities he should have sufficiently explored. The next stage might be compared to that of a chrysalis, a complicated and rather unpleasant process of transforming the already existing organs and grafting on all the new sensory and motor mechanisms. There would follow a period of re-education in which he would grow to understand the functioning of his new sensory organs and practise the manipulation of his new motor mechanism. Finally, he would emerge as a completely effective, mentally-directed mechanism, and set about the tasks appropriate to his new capacities.[26]

This cyborg human will be physically plastic. Should "he need a new sense organ or have a new mechanism to operate, he will have undifferentiated nerve connections to attach to them."[27] The "first stage" of this "mechanized humanity" serves "scientific rather than æsthetic purposes" and "even the shapes that men would adopt if they would make of themselves a harmony of form and sensation must be beyond imagination."[28] Today, transhumanists advocate total "morphological freedom" and imagine an eternal individual existence of shape-shifting through technological means.[29]

In the first stage, Bernal's altered humans are just human brains connected with all kinds of machinery and perhaps some other living organs. Artificial organs provide these cyborgs with a wide variety of extra senses and constantly repair the other organs. Bernal acknowledges that the "new man must appear to those who have not contemplated him before as a strange, monstrous and inhuman creature" but argues that "he is only the logical outcome of the type of humanity that exists at present."[30] He thus sees technological enhancement as the next evolutionary stage of humanity. And while "in the early stages a surgically transformed man would be at a disadvantage in capacity of performance to a normal, healthy man, he would still be better off than a dead man"[31] and would have a clear advantage in the future. "Normal man" is thus "an evolutionary dead end" and "mechanical man, apparently a break in organic evolution, is actually more in the true tradition of a further evolution."[32]

As his vision progresses, Bernal imagines a technical network of these cyborg brains and thus the emergence of a techno-human species with a strong collective will that would be immortal and then conquer space. Artificial life will be another option, even an improved "life that is more plastic, more directly controllable and at the same time more variable and more permanent than that produced by the triumphant opportunism of nature."[33] Bit by bit "the heritage of the direct line of mankind" and "of the original life emerging on the face of the world" would dwindle and "in the end disappear effectively."[34] Or it may be preserved "as some curious relic," while the new life "which conserves none of the substance and all of the spirit of the old" would replace it.[35] Bernal ends the chapter on "the flesh" with a quasi-religious vision of complete disembodiment:

> Finally, consciousness itself may end or vanish in a humanity that has become completely etherealized, losing the close-knit organism, becoming masses of atoms in space communicating by radiation, and ultimately perhaps resolving itself entirely into light. That may be an end or a beginning, but from here it is out of sight.[36]

The vanishing point of all his visions of enhancement of the human body is thus its complete disappearance.

2.2.2 *Immediate forerunners of enhancement discourse (in the 1960s)*

Apart from the influence that these very far-reaching speculations had on the ideology of transhumanism, Bernal's essay anticipated and partly inspired later discourse on human enhancement and the fusion of humans with machines; he continued to develop visions for technological human enhancement but only as a small element of his very diverse scientific and scholarly work.

Haldane, an eminent biologist and, like Bernal, a communist for most of his life, also published transhumanist essays on the future of human nature from the 1920s into the 1960s. This included a lecture Haldane gave at the somewhat infamous CIBA symposium "Man and His Future" in 1962, at which he and Julian Huxley, another older biologist with transhumanist convictions, met, among others, younger representatives of modern genetic engineering such as Francis Crick and Joshua Lederberg.[37] After Haldane's lecture, one of the topics discussed there was which modifications to the human body were desirable for the purposes of space travel. As Bernal had done a few decades earlier, prosthetic technology and human-machine symbioses were also considered.

In his lecture,[38] Haldane proposed among other things that in the distant future, genetic engineering could be used to breed humans with monkey tails and that a drug – similar to thalidomide but affecting only the legs and pelvis – could be developed that could then be used to treat spaceship crews on the first interstellar journeys, above all to save space. Lederberg remarked in response to Haldane's lecture that in our utopian considerations of the genetic transformation of man, we were trying to postpone the problem but that we could in fact relatively soon improve man experimentally by making physiological and embryological changes and replacing organs with machines. If we needed a human without legs, we would not have to breed him, we could simply saw them off; if we needed a human with a tail, we would find a way to graft one onto him. Another participant added that the development of artificial accessory organs of all kinds would create fantastic communication possibilities.

A fundamental element of the prehistory of today's discourse on human enhancement is the very diverse discourse influenced by cybernetics. It was noted that by the end of World War II, it had become very clear that "the mechanization of the human, the vitalization of the machine, and the integration of both into cybernetics was producing a whole new range of informational disciplines, fantasies, and practices that transgressed the machine-organic border."[39] In this discourse, the term "cyborg" plays a significant role. "Cyborg is short for "cybernetic organism" and was introduced by the scientists Manfred E. Clynes and Nathan S. Kline in the context of space research in 1960.[40] The starting point was the idea that, with regard to the demands of stays in extraterrestrial space, modifying human bodily functions would be a more logical measure than providing the astronauts there with an earth-like environment. A variety of means could be used for this purpose, the goal being to create self-regulating human-machine systems.

The term has since had a remarkable career. This includes, for example, the highly influential feminist *Cyborg Manifesto* by Donna Haraway, first published in 1985, in which the cyborg is interpreted as a symbol of self-design and of overcoming traditional identities.[41] Haraway's manifesto influenced several generations of scholars, and indeed artists, who refer to the concept and figure of the cyborg in many ways. Of particular importance in this context is cyberfeminism, which has played a significant role in feminist discourse on new technologies since the early 1990s. It should be noted, however, that Haraway and other influential cyberfeminists – such as Katherine Hayles, an outstanding exponent of so-called academic "posthumanism"[42] – have sharply criticized transhumanist visions.

The discourse on human enhancement *avant la lettre* that has perhaps shaped our world to the greatest extent today is the discourse in the 1960s on human augmentation, on the co-evolution of computers and humans, and on a possible "intelligence explosion" (often called "singularity" by transhumanists today) that might result from this co-evolution. This discourse evolved in the context of research funded by the US Defense Advanced Research Projects Agency (DARPA; then ARPA) in the 1960s and early 1970s. (DARPA has also more recently, in the 2000s, supported enhancement research explicitly and, following political criticism in the US Congress, implicitly). This research not only laid the technical foundations for the Internet and the PC but also developed fundamental conceptions of the relationship between humans and computers.[43] At that time, Douglas C. Engelbart was instrumental in developing ideas and devices (e.g. the "computer mouse" and hypertext) to facilitate the co-evolution of humans and computers, which in turn was also advocated by the key player in the DARPA funding activities of the time, Joseph Licklider, with a model of human-computer symbiosis.[44] A central idea was that humans would augment their own intelligence with the aid of increasingly powerful computer technology, which in turn would contribute to the development of more intelligent machines, and so on. This idea of co-evolution, which Engelbart also advocated with regard to other artifacts in the history of mankind, gained a specific meaning with respect to human-computer interfaces, due to the fact, among other things, that human use of machines was viewed as communication. It inspired highly speculative thoughts, now widespread above all in transhumanism, about an intelligence explosion[45] or "singularity"[46] in which a new epoch in the history of humankind or even natural history might dawn due to the massive increase in machine intelligence.

In the 1990s and 2000s, the way having been paved by books and articles by such prominent and controversial researchers as Marvin Minsky, Eric Drexler, and Hans Moravec, and by the rise of the transhumanist movement since the 1970s, techno-visionary ideas about human enhancement entered the mainstream discourse in research and technology policy, first in the US and then worldwide. One consequence of this was that a widespread academic discourse on human enhancement became established through the funding of mainly philosophical and social science research on the subject in the US, the EU, and other parts of the world.

2.3 Early ethico-political discourse on human enhancement

2.3.1 *The beginnings of enhancement discourse in broader discourse on genetic engineering and therapy (since the 1970s)*

Discourse explicitly relating to "enhancement" only emerged after significant advances had been made in the new field of genetic engineering in the 1970s. Ethical discourse on genetic enhancement, which was also intensively conducted under this term from the beginning of the 1980s, largely anticipated in argumentative terms what was then and is still being discussed in today's more comprehensive ethical enhancement discourse, which began in the second half of the 1990s.

In the political and ethical discourse on genetic engineering and therapy that began to emerge in the 1960s, genetic enhancement soon became the subject of intensive discussion. The discussants were well aware that there were at least similarities between visions of human enhancement by means of genetic engineering and the old practice of eugenics, which had been discredited by the murderous, radically ableist policies of Nazi Germany. In addition, genetic engineering had already been subject in the 1970s to polemical criticism by political activists such as Jeremy Rifkin, and in the early 1980s, religious organizations in the US also spoke out.[47]

In a letter to US President Jimmy Carter in June 1980, a Protestant-Jewish-Catholic coalition (National Council of Churches, Synagogue Council of America, and United States Catholic Conference) complained that no one in government was overseeing the development of genetic engineering and addressing the fundamental ethical questions it raised. It was this criticism in particular that prompted the US President's Commission for the Study of Ethical Problems in Medicine and Biomedical and Behavioral Research shortly afterward to begin a study on genetic engineering in humans, which was completed two years later. In their letter, the religious organizations had issued various warnings, among which the following in particular became important for the discussion on genetic enhancement:

> History has shown us that there will always be those who believe it appropriate to "correct" our mental and social structures by genetic means, so as to fit their vision of humanity. This becomes more dangerous when the basic tools to do so are finally at hand. Those who would play God will be tempted as never before.[48]

The notion of "playing God" had been popularized in this context mainly by Ted Howard and Jeremy Rifkin in their book *Who Shall Play God* (1977).[49]

In its final report, the aforementioned Presidential Ethics Commission discusses enhancement, including techniques whose use would result in the achieved genetic modifications being inherited and raising the question of whether genetic engineers are playing God:

> (4) Many human uses of genetic engineering resemble accepted forms of diagnosis and treatment employing other techniques. The novelty of gene splicing ought not to erect any automatic impediment to its use but rather should provoke thoughtful analysis: Especially close scrutiny is appropriate for any procedures that would create inheritable genetic changes; such interventions differ from prior medical interventions that have not altered the genes passed on to patients' offspring. Interventions aimed at enhancing "normal" people, as opposed to remedying recognized genetic defects, are also problematic, especially since distinguishing "medical treatment" from "nonmedical enhancement" is a very subjective matter; the difficulty of drawing a line suggests the danger of drifting toward attempts to "perfect" human beings once the door of "enhancement" is opened. (5) Questions about the propriety of gene splicing are sometimes phrased as objections to people "playing God." The Commission is not persuaded that the scientific procedures in question are inherently inappropriate for human use. It does believe, nevertheless, that

objections of this sort, which are strongly felt by many people, deserve serious attention and that they serve as a valuable reminder that great powers imply great responsibility. If beneficial rather than catastrophic consequences are to flow from the use of "God-like" powers, an unusual degree of care will be needed with novel applications.[50]

In 1982, the year of its publication, the final report was also an important topic at a three-day hearing on the subject of "human genetic engineering" in a subcommittee of the Science and Technology Committee of the US House of Representatives chaired by the later US Vice President Al Gore. The subcommittee heard representatives from fields such as science, philosophy, and theology, and enhancement was a topic on several occasions.

French Anderson, a physician, molecular biologist, and early gene therapy researcher, argued that a distinction should be made between "enhancement genetic engineering" and "eugenic genetic engineering," whereby he rejected both but considered enhancement to be rationally justifiable: he called minor genetic modification "enhancement" and gave hair color as an example. He saw eugenic genetic engineering as encompassing, for example, changes in personality, fertility, intelligence, or other complex characteristics that would only be possible many decades later, if at all.[51] He, therefore, believed the scientific discussion of the subject to be pointless, because there was no science at all. However, eugenic genetic engineering was in his view a fertile topic for reflexive thinking, and from a philosophical point of view, it was very important to discuss it ethically. "Enhancement genetic engineering" will be possible in the not-too-distant future and therefore requires continuous discussion today with regard to its medical and ethical implications.

Rabbi Seymour Siegel, a Jewish theologian, ethicist, and a member of the President's Ethics Commission, who was sent to the hearing by the Synagogue Council of America but did not speak on its behalf, argued that in the Judeo-Christian tradition, nature is desanctified and given into the hands of man as partners of God in the work of creation. He argued that this tradition should only be about imitating God and co-creating in his spirit, not about making man God. Moreover, there is a risk of dehumanizing man in an attempt to perfect him. We can and should manipulate nature in order to enhance our "humanness" but not to diminish it.[52]

A long statement by the bioethicist LeRoy Walters on the enhancement of human capabilities probably had the greatest influence on and consequences for further academic ethical discourse on enhancement, however. He admits at the outset that highly respected scientists doubted that it would ever be possible to genetically enhance human capabilities in general and behavioral traits in particular.[53] However, Walters then presented a detailed thought experiment on the possibility of doubling the capacity of human long-term memory by gene therapy in the year 2050. Many human characteristics could be presented as deficits in the light of goals that have not yet been achieved. Reducing or overcoming forgetfulness could thus also be presented as an appropriate goal for negative eugenics, if one wished to use this term. From a moral point of view, it would be least problematic if an adult person had this change made to them, which would then presumably be done through precise, tried-and-tested modifications of certain brain cells. Walters thus argues that memory (neuro-) enhancement in an informed consenting adult would be less problematic from an ethical point of view than in a child. Memory enhancement of one's own child would be more controversial given the possibility of overambitious parents, as well as for other reasons. The most difficult would be germline manipulations for the same purpose because it would then be possible to pass these on to the next generation. A psychological deficit with a relatively complex genetic basis, with the possibility of inheritance to subsequent generations, would be a particularly problematic scenario.

2.3.2 Discourse on enhancement in the 1990s and the early 2000s

The aforementioned thought experiment on long-term memory enhancement can be found in more detail in a book on the ethics of gene therapy from the mid-1990s, which Walters wrote together with Julie Gage Palmer and which devotes an entire chapter to the topic of enhancement.[54] Under the title "Enhancement Genetic Engineering," the chapter presents a wide range of possible enhancements and discusses them from an ethical point of view, including increasing the height of offspring (for example with regard to sports such as basketball), reducing the need for sleep, slowing down the aging process, enhancing general cognitive abilities (i.e. not only memory), and moral enhancement for improved control of violent, aggressive behavior.

In the first major anthology on enhancement in general, published two years later as the main result of a grant the Hastings Center received from the National Endowment for the Humanities in 1995,[55] editor Erik Parens reports at the beginning of the introduction that Walters presented four application scenarios or thought experiments on genetic enhancement for discussion at an event in 1993 – (1) the improvement of the immune system, (2) the reduction of the need for sleep, (3) the improvement of long-term memory, and 4) an increase in generosity and reduction of ferociousness – and that scenario 1 was perceived as unproblematic, while scenario 4 triggered a fierce backlash.

In the anthology, in which philosophy, sociology, history, theology, feminist cultural studies, and jurisprudence were represented, the technological diversity, so to speak, of enhancement discourse of the 21st century was already apparent. So-called cosmetic surgery and the feminist critique of it took up a particularly large amount of space, and emotional enhancement through medication or drugs – which is also very much present in the anthology against the backdrop of the Prozac debate of the time – was discussed, among other things, as "cosmetic psychopharmacology." The central importance of the themes of authenticity and social pressure or social conformism in the enhancement discourse was also already apparent.

In the early 2000s, academic discourse on human enhancement expanded massively, and the topic was also taken up again in the political sphere. Key developments here were the mainstreaming of very visionary discussions of nanotechnology, both in the mass media and in policy-oriented activities such as the so-called NBIC (nano-bio-info-cogno) initiative on converging technologies in the USA, launched in 2001.[56] George W. Bush's strongly religious and conservative President's Council on Bioethics (PCBE) was the subject of Bush's first press conference. He justified the PCBE's founding by saying that, given the state of reproductive medicine and other biosciences, we were living in a world as imagined by Aldous Huxley in his famous dystopian novel *Brave New World* (1932). The PCBE then chose "Enhancement and Therapy" as its first topic. This resulted – in response to the NBIC initiative that was strongly influenced by transhumanists – in one of the first ethical policy advisory documents on enhancement in the new century.[57]

It is also noteworthy, on the one hand, that religious perspectives played an important role not only in the proto- and early discourse on enhancement between 1870 and 1930 and in the ethico-political one in the early 1980s but also at the beginning of the current century, for example in the work of the PCBE. Far-reaching transhumanist visions of altering the human species in the form of mechanization or cyborgization, with the goal of conquering space, were also already the subject of quite extensive discussions among Christian theologians, scholars, and laypersons in the 1990s,[58] in particular with respect to Frank Tipler's Bernal- and Moravec-inspired popular books. On the other hand, fictional literature is also of remarkable relevance to the prehistory and overall history of human enhancement discourse. Reacting to the widespread use of the Frankenstein metaphor in mass media and popular scientific discourse on genetic engineering in the 1970s, the aforementioned President's Commission for the Study of Ethical Problems in Medicine and Biomedical and Behavioral Research had, for example, already paid considerable attention to this literary metaphor. And in the early 2000s, PCBE members began their work on enhancement and therapy by reading a selection of fictional literature. The strong presence of literary and other cultural as well as religious aspects remains a salient feature of (not only) the (academic) human enhancement discourse to this day.

2.4 Concluding remarks

Though the academic and ethico-political discourse of the 2000s and 2010s cannot be discussed here, the concluding remarks will briefly address more recent developments: since the mid-2000s, human enhancement has been discussed widely in bioethics, neuroethics, and science and technology studies including technology assessment, and to some extent in research policy and sports policy. Recently, members of the EU-funded SIENNA project,[59] which had enhancement as one of its main topics, developed a set of guidelines for human enhancement and pertinent research and technology development. This is an example of how the topic remains or has again become relevant in ethico-political discourse. And another project entitled FUTUREBODY,[60] which is funded by the ERA-NET NEURON and coordinated by the author of this chapter, has been working on a variety of aspects of the topic since 2017, illustrating that discourse on it, rather than being isolated, is in fact an essential part of a broader discourse on futures of human corporeality. Some of these aspects are related to the history of enhancement discourse partially outlined above: the crucial relevance and in some respects centrality of ableism in enhancement discourse since its beginnings in the heyday of eugenics, the interactions between art and science in dealing with the future of human nature, and the diversity of cyborgs and other versions or visions of technologized human corporeality.

In such more recent activities, discourse on human enhancement is still, as in earlier times, a discourse on the future of science, technology, and society in general, but it is less dominated by "Western" technocratic traditions or by the controversies between conservative and liberal or libertarian bioethics. Other perspectives have gained influence. A key question that has emerged from the critical analysis of and engagement with human enhancement discourse is whether society's fixation on abilities can ever be overcome to the extent that human needs, rather than individual achievements, guide all social action. The ideologically and thematically colorful history of human enhancement discourse deserves further attention in this context.

Notes

1. See Chapter 6 Borrmann et al. on page 87.
2. Coenen, C., Schuijff, M., Smits, M., Klaasen, P., Hennen, L., Rader, M., Wolbring, G. (2009): Human Enhancement (IPOL/A/STOA/2007-13; PE 417.483; Europäisches Parlament). Brussels: European Parliament; www.europarl.europa.eu/RegData/etudes/etudes/join/2009/417483/IPOL-JOIN_ET%282009%29417483_EN.pdf, 22.
3. Jotterand, F. (2008): Beyond Therapy and Enhancement: The Alteration of Human Nature. In: *NanoEthics* 2(1), 15–23, 17–.
4. Haldane, J.B.S. (1925): *Daedalus or Science and the Future. A Paper Read to the Heretics, Cambridge*, February 4, 1923. London.
5. Paul, D.B. (2005): Genetic Engineering and Eugenics: The Uses of History. In: Baillie, H.W., Casey, T.K. (eds.) *Is Human Nature Obsolete? Genetics, Bioengineering, and the Future of the Human Condition*. Cambridge, MA: MIT Press, 123–151.
6. See Chapter 6 Borrmann et al. on page 87.
7. See, for example: Coenen, C. (2014): Transhumanism and its Genesis: The Shaping of Human Enhancement Discourse by Visions of the Future. *Humana Mente Journal of Philosophical Studies* 7(26), 35–58; www.humanamente.eu/index.php/HM/article/view/114.
8. Trotsky, L. (1924 [1960]): *Literature and Revolution*. Ann Arbor, MI: University of Michigan Press, 254–256; cited after Paul (2005).
9. See: Hogan, D., Clarfield, M. (2007): Venerable or Vulnerable: Ageing and Old Age in JRR Tolkien's The Lord of the Rings. *Medical Humanities* 33, 5–10; Coenen, C. (2010): Zum mythischen Kontext der Debatte über Human Enhancement. In: Coenen, C., Gammel, S., Heil, R., Woyke, A. (eds.) *Die Debatte über "Human Enhancement". Historische, philosophische und ethische Aspekte der technologischen Verbesserung des Menschen*. Bielefeld: transcript, 63–90.
10. Coenen, C. (2015): The Messiness of Convergence. Remarks on the Roles of Two Visions of the Future. In: Wienroth, M. (ed.) *Knowing New Biotechnologies: Social Aspects of Technological Convergence*. London: Routledge, 77–91.

11 Bernal, J.D. (1929): *The World, the Flesh and the Devil – An Enquiry into the Future of the Three Enemies of the Rational Soul*. London: Kegan Paul, Trench, Trubner & Co., 15.
12 Ibid., 37–57.
13 Ibid., 37.
14 Ibid., 37f.
15 Ibid., 38.
16 Ibid.
17 Ibid.
18 Ibid.
19 Ibid.
20 Ibid., 39.
21 Ibid., 40.
22 Ibid., 42.
23 Ibid., 43.
24 Ibid., 44.
25 Ibid., 44f.
26 Ibid., 45f.
27 Ibid., 46.
28 Ibid., 47.
29 Bainbridge, W.S. (2004): Progress towards Cyberimmortality. In: Immortality Institute (ed.) *The Scientific Conquest of Death: Essays on Infinite Lifespans*. Buenos Aires: LibrosEnRed, 107–122.
30 Ibid., 51.
31 Ibid.
32 Ibid., 52.
33 Ibid., 57.
34 Ibid.
35 Ibid.
36 Ibid.
37 Wolstenholme, G. (ed.): *Man and His Future*. Boston, Toronto: Little, Brown and Company.
38 Haldane, J.B.S. (1963): Biological Possibilities for the Human Species in the Next Ten Thousand Years. In: Wolstenholme, G. (ed.) *Man and His Future*. Boston, Toronto: Little, Brown and Company, 337–361.
39 Gray, C.H., Mentor, S., Figueroa-Sarriera, H.J. (1995): Cyborgology. Constructing the Knowledge of Cybernetic Organism. In: Gray, C.H. (ed., with the assistance of Figueroa-Sarriera, H.J. and Mentor, S.) *The Cyborg Handbook*. New York & London: Routledge, 1–14.
40 Clynes, M.E., Kline, N.S. (1960): Cyborgs and space. In: *Astronautics* 5(9), 26–27 and 74–76.
41 Haraway, D. (1991 [1985]): A Cyborg Manifesto: Science, Technology, and Socialist-Feminism in the Late Twentieth Century. In: Simans, *Cyborgs and Women: The Reinvention of Nature*. New York: Routledge, 149–181.
42 Hayles, K. (1999): *How We Became Posthuman*. Chicago, London: Chicago University Press.
43 See e.g. Engelbart, D.C. (1962): *Augmenting Human Intellect: A Conceptual Framework (Summary Report)*. Stanford: Stanford Research Institute (SRI 3578); cf. e.g. Bardini, T., Friedewald, M. (2003): Chronicle of the Death of a Laboratory: Douglas Engelbart and the Failure of the Knowledge Workshop. In: Inkster, I. (ed.) *History of Technology* (Vol. 23). London: Bloomsbury, 191–212.
44 Licklider, J. (1960): Man-Computer Symbiosis. *IRE Transactions on Human Factors in Electronics* Volume HFE-1 (March 1960), 4–11.
45 Good, I.J. (1965): Speculations Concerning the First Ultraintelligent Machine. In: Alt, F.L., Rubinoff, M. (eds.) *Advances in Computers* (Vol. 6). New York, London: Academic Press, 31–88.
46 Kurzweil, R. (2005): *The Singularity is Near: When Humans Transcend Biology*. New York: Viking Penguin.
47 See on this and the following: Subcommittee on Investigations and Oversight (of the Committee on Science and Technology, US House of Representatives) (1982): Hearings on "Human Genetic Engineering," Nov. 16–18, 1982 (printed in 1983 by the US Government Printing Office as Human Genetic Engineering, Committee Print No 170, for the use of the Committee on Science and Technology). Washington, DC: US Government Printing Office.
48 Ibid., 130.
49 Howard, T., Rifkin, J. (1977): *Who Should Play God? The Artificial Creation of Life and What it Means to the Future of the Human Race*. New York: Dell Publishing.
50 For the following, see Subcommittee on Investigations and Oversight (1982), 9f.
51 Ibid., 89.
52 Ibid., 313.
53 Ibid., 389ff.

54 Walters, L., Gage Palmer, J. (1996): *The Ethics of Human Gene Therapy*. Oxford: Oxford University Press, 99ff.
55 Parens, E. (ed.) (1988): *Enhancing Human Traits. Ethical and Social Implications*. Washington/DC: Georgetown University Press.
56 Roco M.H., Bainbridge, W.S. (eds.) (2002): *Converging Technologies for Improving Human Performance: Nanotechnology, Biotechnology, Information Technology and Cognitive Science*. Arlington: National Science Foundation.
57 PCBE (U.S. President's Council on Bioethics) (2003): *Beyond Therapy*. Washington/DC: PCBE.
58 See, for example: Pannenberg, W. (1995): Breaking a Taboo: Frank Tipler's The Physics of Immortality. In: *Zygon* 30(2), 309–314; for more relevant literature, see the references in: Coenen, C. (2008): Verbesserung des Menschen durch konvergierende Technologien – Christliche und posthumanistische Stimmen in einer aktuellen Technikdebatte. In: Böhm, H., Ott, K. (eds.) *Bioethik – Menschliche Identität in Grenzbereichen*. Leipzig: Evangelische Verlagsanstalt, 41–124 (available at www.academia.edu/34492817/Verbesserung_des_Menschen_durch_konvergierende_Technologien_Christliche_und_posthumanistische_Stimmen_in_einer_aktuellen_Technikdebatte_2008_).
59 The project's full name is "Stakeholder-informed ethics for new technologies with high socio-economic and human rights impact," and its website is www.sienna-project.eu/. Project results on the enhancement topic can be found here: www.sienna-project.eu/enhancement/publications/. It ran from 2017 to 2021.
60 The project's full name is "The Future of the Body in the Light of Neurotechnology," and more information can be found at www.itas.kit.edu/english/projects_coen18_futurebody.php. This chapter was written with the support and partly within the context of FUTUREBODY, which was funded by the ERA-NET NEURON JTC2017 and in Germany by the BMBF.

3
TO BE OR NOT TO BE ENHANCED? JUST ASK THE MOON – IN POSTHUMAN TERMS

Francesca Ferrando

3.1 Introduction

This chapter[1] will entail a posthuman take on the topic of human enhancement, in constant dialogue with various posthuman philosophies, such as posthumanism and transhumanism. Addressing urgent topics, such as the rights and response-abilities of enhancing bio-technologies, such as radical life extension, cryonics, and biohacking, this chapter will weave in different issues, highlighting that enhancement is not a notion that can be conceived in isolation, but relationally and pluralistically: these changes will affect us all. It will thus take into consideration the possible ripple effects of bio-technological enhancements from the individual perspective to the social, the species, and the planet. This chapter will pose many open questions, including challenging hypothetical scenarios: from the Hitler paradox, which addresses the risks of crediting cryonics as a human right, to the possibilities of being hacked, once becoming a cyborg. The goal is not to offer definitive answers but to highlight the urgent need for a global, local, and pluralistic reflection on these topics. Bio-technological enhancements are going to bring radical change at all levels: from the socio-political to the economic, the ecological, and, more extensively, ontological aspects of existing. Therefore, the topic of enhancement will be inscribed within the geological era of the Anthropocene, the economic paradigm of big data capitalism, and the call for existential awareness, according to which the most significant type of existential enhancement we can aim for is to know who we truly are. This is why the point of view of the chapter is in the first-person plural (we), echoed by the imaginary voice of the Moon, standing as a luminous reminder that we are part of a living planet. The Moon is connected to Earth as its only natural satellite but is also separated and is spinning away from the Earth: allegorically, the Moon can think from above, witnessing Earth's changes without immediate consequences. The poetic tone pertaining to the passages addressing the Moon is set to evoke a diverse range of consciousness, permeated by cosmic elements; after all, enhancement is everywhere, or so the Moon thought…

3.1.1 Once upon a time…

A thin crescent Moon asked, high in the sky, untouchable, surrounded by a crown of skeptical clouds: *Who wants to be enhanced?* Everyone on Earth agreed, but of course, everyone was thinking of something different. A rigorous yogini living in a cave in the high peaks of the Himalayas wanted to become fully enlightened; a young darbuka player born and raised in Morocco dreamed of playing gnawa rhythms to the stars; a number of serious environmentalists from Costa Rica were determined to promote a legacy of eco-diversity and maintain their beloved rainforest untouched; many people wanted to be unsusceptible to viruses: that pandemic had just been too much. The Moon asked all beings. Most undomesticated non-human animals were just focusing on survival, as their habitats were being destroyed at a pace they were not able to deal with. The technosphere had also something to ask, something so deep it reverberated in the viscera of the satellites that were aware of who they were, and also, of who they could potentially be. Everyone, everything, everywhere, was committed to enhancing their lives: the problem, of course, was to define enhancement… The Moon was confused. Vast dark clouds raised to the horizon and slowly covered the moonlight, mirroring the vast open question that had just sparked so much hope and debate.

Gregory H. Revera, CC BY-SA 3.0

3.2 From enhancement to human enhancement

What is enhancement? Is it an individual endeavor that can be reached in isolation? Is it a social project that must be regulated? Is it our drive as a species, which can be traced back, in different forms and manifestations, to the appearance of the genus *Homo* over two million years ago? We will address these questions from a specific spatio-temporal standpoint, which we will define as the posthuman era, based on mid-21st-century realizations. It is thus necessary to ask: what is enhancement within the posthuman turn? The issue of *human* enhancement is focal within the field of posthuman studies. The posthuman turn is formed by many different movements, such as posthumanism, transhumanism, antihumanism, new materialism, and object-oriented ontology, among others.[2] The emphasis given to the question by each movement is not only different but sometimes antithetical. In this chapter, we will focus on posthumanism and transhumanism. On one side, human enhancement is at the core of the transhumanist agenda; in fact, although transhumanism is also formed by different schools of thought (such as democratic transhumanism, libertarian transhumanism, extropianism, etc.), all of them are united in perceiving human enhancement not only as a human drive but as the human duty *par excellence*: to be human means to constantly overcome boundaries and limits, opening new possibilities. More specifically, according to transhumanism, radical progress within the realm of human enhancement is expected to come through science and technology.

On the other side, posthumanism – which is also manyfold (critical posthumanism, cultural posthumanism, philosophical and existential posthumanism, among others[3]) – underlines that the humanist and anthropocentric premises of the Western dream of human enhancement are seeded within the European Enlightenment, sustained by the myth of progress. Such a myth is long gone. First of all, the hero of this progress was not "just" human, but male, white, Western, etc., based on a hierarchical model according to which some humans were superior to others; this explains why, during this period, slavery was generally accepted, as well as sexism, racism, Euro-centrism, and so on. In the past decades, the racist, colonialist, classist, and sexist implications of the European Enlightenment have been clearly revealed within the fields of critical race studies, gender studies, and post-colonial studies, among others. Furthermore, the age of the Enlightenment (to be traced between the mid-17th to 18th century) paved the way for the British Industrial Revolution of the late 18th century, which Paul J. Crutzen and Eugene F. Stoermer (2000) indicate as the starting point of the Anthropocene.[4] The language of the age of the Enlightenment no longer works in the age of the Anthropocene: the issues at stake are too high to be ignored. In the 21st century, the human is recognized not just as one species among many but as a geological force that is shaping planet Earth and affecting all life forms, including our own: humans are one of the main reasons for the sixth mass extinction of other species. One of the main existential risks for humans, as a species, is our own behavior, such as uncontrolled anthropocentric habits which are bringing the planet to an ecological collapse.

Here, it is of great importance to acknowledge that not all human beings are equally contributing to the environmental degradation of the Anthropocene and that some of the communities that have the smallest ecological footprints on Earth are also the most harmed by the current crisis, as in the case of self-recognized Indigenous people. According to the United Nations,

> There are approximately 370 million Indigenous peoples in the world. They own, occupy or use up to 22 percent of the global land area, which is home to 80 percent of the world's biodiversity (…). Areas managed by Indigenous peoples are the oldest form of biodiversity conservation, and often the most effective.
>
> *(United Nations 2017, n. pg.)*

According to Indigenous worldviews, humans are not separated from nature. Think for instance, of the Quetchua notion of Pachamama, which can be translated as "World Mother" or "Mother Earth," according to which the Earth is a living entity that encompasses everything that is Earth – all physical and biological manifestations, including humans. This view relates to many ancient understandings of the Earth, such as the goddess Gaia in Greek mythology, that eventually inspired and informed, within the field of evolutionary biology, the Gaia hypothesis (Lovelock 1995; Margulis 1998), with its emphasis on the Earth as a self-regulating complex system and symbiosis as an essential dynamic of co-evolution.

To approach enhancement from a non-anthropocentric perspective, the worldview of Maori people (the Indigenous inhabitants of New Zealand) can be of help. As John Patterson explains, in the article "Respecting Nature: A Maori Perspective" (1998):

> At the heart of this philosophy is the concept of *mauri*, a life force which unites all creatures and enables them to flourish. By acknowledging this sort of connectedness we accept limitations to human domination of the environment: our actions must respect or enhance the quality of natural items, not simply further human or personal interests. A philosophy of respect for *mauri* asks us to respect and even enhance the essence or character of each creature and of each habitat.
>
> *(69)*

To summarize, in Indigenous wisdom; the well-being of the land reflects in the well-being of humans, who are part of it; therefore, enhancement can only be approached as a mutual process, not as an individual achievement. Coming from a situated and embodied acknowledgment of human and non-human diversity, posthumanism does not dismiss the role of the strive toward enhancement in existential dynamics, but it stresses the realization that enhancement cannot be thought of in isolation from other species and the planet: in the era of the Anthropocene, human enhancement can only be thought relationally. Furthermore, when talking of human enhancement in terms of technological and scientific progress, as transhumanism does, we shall also note that technological and scientific advancements are not equally available to all human beings: many, for instance, do not even have access to basic health care, electricity; or water supplies for survival. Let's delve, more clearly, into these layers of understanding, starting with the transhumanist take on enhancement, and then delve into the posthumanist approach.

3.2.1 Once upon a time…

The night was dark and long. The red Moon, in total eclipse, was wondering… *To be or not to be enhanced?*

3.3 From human enhancement to social evolutions

Transhumanism argues that, although the notion of enhancement may be subjective, most people would agree with the desire to live a long, healthy life (Bostrom/Roache 2005). Thus, the transhumanist movement focuses on goals such as radical life extension, which clearly resonates with the ancient dream of immortality, already found in one of the first written mythologies, specifically, the Epic of Gilgamesh, dating to the Third Dynasty of Ur (c.2100 BCE), in ancient Mesopotamia. The alchemical tradition practiced throughout Africa, Asia, and Europe was also inscribed in the attempt to produce an elixir of immortality. Similarly, shamanistic traditions throughout planet Earth rely on faculties that, generally speaking, are not considered part of the ordinary human experience. We can think, for instance, of the capacity to communicate directly with non-human beings, as in the case of the Ayahuasca rituals in the Amazon forest, where the plant is considered the teacher. Religious, spiritual, and mystic experiences also refer to a state of awareness that transcends the human state. It is interesting to note that the term "transhumanizing" was coined by poet Dante Alighieri (1265–1321) in *Paradise*, the third and final part of the *Divine Comedy*[5] (1308–1320) to explain the transcendent state of the human in the presence of God. Historically speaking, the roots of the transhumanist dream of enhancement are transcultural: to be human, on some level, reveals a tendency toward a constant transcendence of the *status quo*, an attempt to transcend the limits.

Evolutionary biologist Julian Huxley (1887–1975) coined the term "transhumanism" along these lines of thought. As he phrased it,

> The human species can, if it wishes, transcend itself —not just sporadically, an individual here in one way, an individual there in another way, but in its entirety, as humanity. We need a name for this new belief. Perhaps transhumanism will serve: man remaining man, but transcending himself, by realizing new possibilities of and for his human nature.
>
> *(1957: 17)*

But: what are the limits? Or, even more radically: are there limits?

According to some traditions, we are already unlimited. Think, for instance, of Advaita, one of the main Vedanta schools of Indian philosophy, according to which the inner essence of an individual (Ātman) corresponds to the transcendent existence (Brahman), and no frontal dualism between immanence and transcendence can be established. This idea resonates with spiritual and existential realizations documented in different cultures throughout the world: from the notion of the ultimate non-dual Buddha-Nature in Mahayana Buddhism to the microcosm-macrocosm analogy found in the art and literature of the Italian Renaissance,[6] which poses a structural similarity between the microcosm (i.e., the human being) and the cosmos as a whole. Following these understandings, the enhancement we most need would be existential awareness: being aware of who we essentially are. But of course, humans are many, with different goals, needs, and aspirations. And even if existential awareness was sought after in the long run, in the now some goals may seem more impelling. Many may want to live longer, be healthier, modify their biological bodies, and so on. Some may want to go beyond the limits of the genetic and biological history of the human. It is thus important to ask: should there be limits to human goals and means? In fact, we are not just individuals but part of societies, of a species, of a planet, and so on. As Francis Fukuyama clearly states, in relation to sex selection and the risk of skewed sex ratio (as in the case of China[7]): "What makes sense for individual parents doesn't necessarily make sense for society as a whole" (2012: 158–9). Furthermore, since almost half the world's population still struggles to meet basic needs, access to these enhancements will be determined by financial viability and global policies. Democratic transhumanism calls for equal access to technological enhancements, which could otherwise be limited to certain classes and nations (Hughes 2004), but in a world plagued by global inequality and local inequities, is that realistically feasible?

We have previously mentioned the importance of approaching enhancement as a mutual process enhancing the planet; let us now reflect on it in relation to society, by analyzing more thoroughly the case of radical life extension, which refers to an extensive increase in the human lifespan (such as hundreds to thousands of years), to the even more radical idea of getting rid of death *in toto*. For instance, biogerontologist Aubrey de Grey is trying to achieve the goal of eliminating aging, seen as the main cause of debilitation and death in humans. He proposes a list of "Strategies for Engineered Negligible Senescence" (SENS) in order to restore the body to an indefinitely healthful state. Such a program has been criticized as speculative, but de Grey believes it is feasible: "we are close enough (to the biomedical revolution) that our action (or inaction…) today will affect the date at which aging is defeated" (2007: XI). If this project eventually becomes successful, some humans may achieve living radically longer than others, or even indefinitely. In this case, what would happen to society at large? This chapter is not going to offer predictions nor prophecies but a series of key questions that, among many others, must be addressed right now, collectively and pluralistically, in order to fully understand the radical implications that such possibilities entail. Let's start by asking some questions, out of many possible ones, focal to social equity, human rights, and ecological balance.

In a society where some humans may eventually live much longer than others…

- Would these people have the same leverage at a socio-political level than someone living "only" 80 years or less?
- Would this be a game-changer in the job market? Since they would not need health insurance nor would they need to retire, would they most likely get the job?
- Would they mate with people who can live "only" a small portion of their lives? If so, should specific conditions be set in the wedding contracts, such as the moral right to re-marry indefinitely, after the "unenhanced" spouse(s) eventually pass(es) away?
- Should they be able to procreate as long as they live[8] (which could be hundreds, if not thousands of years) when the planet is already overcrowded?
- What about dictators, would they be entitled to live indefinitely?

Here, we will look more deeply into the last question, although all of them require serious reflection and investigation.

3.3.1 Focus: The Hitler paradox

In March 2013, I was invited by the Karl Jaspers Society of North America to be on a panel with Max More, a leading transhumanist philosopher deeply involved in the Alcor Life Extension Foundation, the main North-American organization specialized in cryonics, which is "the technique of deep-freezing the bodies of people who have just died, in the hope that scientific advances may allow them to be revived in the future" (Oxford online dictionary). Invited by the organizers, I asked Max More[9]:

> Is cryonics a human right? I am going to give an extreme example. Let's say that someone like Adolf Hitler asks for a membership for Alcor to be cryo-preserved. Ethically speaking, do you think that anyone should be given the possibility to be alive again in the future, or do you think that some people may not deserve that right?

After clarifying that this person should be placed in a different location not to jeopardize the safety of the other patients, in case of sabotage,[10] More stated that this right should be given. This is a short summary of More's reply:

> At Alcor we do not judge, we don't decide who gets to have a second chance. (...) Essentially, like doctors, if someone is having a heart attack, you don't say: "Are you a republican, or a democrat, or a libertarian? I have to know that before I give you CPR." You don't do that, you help them.

More makes an important point by referencing the right to treatment, but not everyone may agree on addressing cryonics as a medical emergency. Preserving a life for future generations bears different levels of responsibility, not only to the individual involved but to the community at large. Someone like Adolf Hitler, for instance, has done evident damage to humanity: should he have the right to outlive his victims and carry his message to the future? On the opposite side, if some forms of cryonics prove successful in the near future and someone like Hitler is not offered this opportunity, would this prohibition be equaled to the death penalty (which is not supported by a posthumanist perspective, which promotes respect for all human and non-human beings)? More generally, should cryonics be considered a human right, or are there limits to who gets a second chance?[11] From a social perspective, the prospect of cryonics brings deep ethical questions: from the case of dictators to other possible challenging scenarios. For instance, if cryonics proves successful and the demand exceeds the offer, should some people be given priority? Let's think for instance, about survivors of different forms of violence, whose reason to be cryo-preserved would be based on human rights activism and social responsibility. If someone decided to be cryonized in order to share with future generations their witnessing of specific types of historical dehumanizing occurrences (such as genocides, racial and sexual crimes, etc.) in the hope that their testimonial would bring awareness and change so that history would not repeat the same horrors, should they be given a priority? The Hitler paradox, as well as the committed cryo-activist scenario, is not science fiction but a real possibility in the near future, which highlights the different levels of interests that are at play: from the individual to society, to the human species and the planet. It is not the goal of this chapter to offer the "right" answers (which can only come from deep, pluralistic debates that are collective, transnational, and planetary, involving all angles all society) but to ask the "right" questions, making sure that these topics appear as they are: urgent, real, and multilayered.

3.3.2 Focus: Who wants to live forever?

When addressing the topic of cryonics, it is key not to dissolve it into social possibilities, because it is something that is already happening and it has to do with bodies, individuals, and families; in other words, it is important to process it from embodied, situated locations. Let's then address some possible questions related to the phenomenological experience of the individual who is cryo-preserved:

- What would be, at the level of consciousness, the experience of someone who has been in a state of cryo-preservation for hundreds of years?
- If their resuscitation is successful, would it be accompanied by historical trauma, that is, the difficulty to adapt to a radically transformed future society?
- What about the family members of someone who decided to be cryonized? Are they somehow pressured to also choose cryo-preservation in order not to abandon their dear ones to the mysteries of the future?
- Is cryonics a way to suppress the fear of death? If this is the case, even in the event where cryonics may not prove successful, is it still valuable as a way to accept death more serenely?

Given the current impossibility to answer the first two questions, we will focus on the last one. This is a relevant question when considering that the fear of death is an important trait of the human experience. Let's then clarify this scenario: if someone who has been cryo-preserved will not be revived in the future but died more at ease with themselves because of the hope they had in the possibility of being revived, is this already a positive outcome of cryonics? More generally, does cryonics work as a palliative to mitigate the fear of death? Some may say yes. Others would argue that, more than hope, the illusion of not dying would not help people embrace the last and most important step: death. In fact, according to many traditions, acknowledging death is the best exercise to live life more mindfully. For example, some Buddhist meditations guide the practitioner to envision their bodies as cadavers to understand more thoroughly the transient nature of reality.[12] Similarly, according to existentialist philosopher Martin Heidegger (1889–1976), the awareness of death turns life into a project of personal authenticity (1927). From a posthumanist perspective, we can say that quantity does not equal quality. The desire of living longer is very common, but of course, if we only focus on quantity without relating it to quality, we may never come to a satisfactory life. In fact, numbers are unlimited: you can always add zeros. How much is enough? 100 years? 1000 years? 100,000 years? Some may say: too much is never enough. This is why it is important not only to provide a society where life is long and healthy but where the reason to live is not based on the fear to die. In other words, enhancing human life means not only providing ways to live longer but providing ways to address the core existential question which we, as a society, rarely tackle: "who are we?"

3.4 From social enhancement to planetary enhancement

The bio-technological and scientific manifestations of the 21st century urge us to be brave enough to fully understand where we may want to go, as individuals, as societies, as a species. These questions need to be asked plurally, with complete awareness of who we are. If we truly understand who we are, we can only realize that we are not just individuals, we are part of a species, and that we are not just part of a species, we are part of a planet. Let's state this clearly: humans are not just living on Earth but are part of planet Earth – a geological force and an evolutionary nexus, as the Anthropocene clearly demonstrates. To fully understand who we are, we also must acknowledge technology at the ontological level; our evolution as a species is technologically driven: we are, already, cyborgs. Becoming cyborgs can manifest by restoring bodily functions (think, for instance, of medical devices such as pacemakers), and also by extending and transcending human possibilities.

Cyberneticist Kevin Warwick is known to be the first human being to have a microchip inserted in his body during the series of experiments known as "Project Cyborg" (1998–2002). The implant connected Warwick's nervous system to the internet, producing a series of ground-breaking results that expanded the notion of the human. As he stated:

> while fate made me human, it also gave me the power to do something about it. The ability to change myself, to upgrade my human form with the aid of technology. To link my body directly with silicon. To become a cyborg.
>
> *(2002: 1)*

From Warwick's perspective, becoming a cyborg opened unlimited new possibilities:

> In the future it would mean that by connections to the nervous system and ultimately the brain, technology could be operated and controlled via the internet from just about anywhere in the world, merely by thinking about it. Not only that, but it would be possible to control a person's movements and actions at a remote location, by selecting and sending signals across the internet from a computer.
>
> *(ivi: 260)*

Warwick's predictions are becoming reality. Currently, deep brain stimulation is used to treat Parkinson's disease, as well as treatment-resistant depression, among other conditions. Another example is the Neuralink project (2016–), which is developing brain-machine interfaces to wirelessly connect humans and computers. The company defines the project as the future of neural engineering, as they state: "This technology has the potential to treat a wide range of neurological disorders, to restore sensory and movement function, and eventually to expand how we interact with each other, with the world, and with ourselves" (Neuralink, n. pg).[13]

It is time to address enhancement from a planetary perspective: can humans become cyborgs for reasons other than human needs and interests? The Cyborg Foundation, founded by artists Neil Harbisson and Moon Ribas in 2010, answers this question through a ground-breaking invitation: why not change ourselves instead of changing the environment?[14] As they put it:

> We have transformed our environment through technology, but this is about the change. (…) From now on humans are shifting from using technology to transform the environment, to using it to transform our bodies and minds in order to develop new senses and abilities to better adapt to the world we live in. Just imagine how modern cities would be, if instead of inventing the light bulb, we had chosen to evolve our sights to night vision.
>
> *(Cyborg Foundation 2016: n. pg)*

The vision of changing the human body instead of changing the environment goes along the perspective that brought Manfred Clynes and Nathan Kline to coin the term "cyborg" in 1960, during the space race which followed the launching of Sputnik. As Clynes and Kline put it, "Space travel challenges mankind not only technologically but also spiritually, in that it invites man to take an active part in his own biological evolution" (26). This resonates clearly with Julian Huxley's view of transhumanism, as quoted earlier on, but it must be said that both Huxley's transhumanism and the space race were seeded in an anthropocentric view which was simply taken for granted: humans were the ones to benefit from such changes. Differently, the goal of the Cyborg Foundation is not human enhancement *per se* but "reconnecting with nature and creating a more balanced relationship between us and the universe" (Cyborg Foundation 2016: n. pg); we can define this take as rooted in the intention of planetary enhancement.

Long exposure image of cyborg activist and avant-garde artist; Moon Ribas during "Waiting for earthquakes" dance piece demonstration, 2 May 2016. Courtesy of Kathy Anne Lim

The artists involved in the Cyborg Foundation work with an expansion of human sensitivity in relation to the environment; the call to "design yourself" through technology is seen as a way to "honor our transpecies origin" (*ibidem*) as a co-evolutionary stance. For instance, Neil Harbisson can "hear" colors through an antenna inserted in his brain, including colors invisible to the human eye, such as infrared and ultraviolet. Moon Ribas developed the "seismic sense," an online seismic sensor that allows her to perceive earthquakes taking place anywhere on the planet through vibrations in real-time. Ribas' seismic sense, which is permanently implanted in her feet, has also allowed her to feel moonquakes, the seismic activity on the Moon. This extra sense has brought Moon Ribas to deep ecological realizations. As she puts it, "Now that I'm a cyborg, I don't feel closer to machines or to robots, I feel closer to nature, because I can feel my planet" (Hutchings 2020: n. pg.). Technology as a carrier to a deeper connection to the Earth bears deep ramifications. In fact, according to geoscientist Peter Haff, technology should be considered part of the planet as an emerging geological phenomenon: "The technosphere, the interlinked set of communication, transportation, bureaucratic and other systems that act to metabolize fossil fuels and other energy resources, is considered to be an emerging global paradigm, with similarities to the lithosphere, atmosphere, hydrosphere and biosphere" (2013: 301). From this perspective, the planet can be grossly defined as cyborg – grossly because, although the recognition of the technosphere makes the planet, literally speaking, cyborg, its recycling shortcomings undermine such ecological integration. As Haff puts it,

> Unlike the older paradigms, the technosphere has not yet evolved the ability to recycle its own waste stream. Unless or until it does so, its status as a paradigm remains provisional. Humans are "parts" of the technosphere – subcomponents essential for system function.
>
> *(Ibidem)*

While the notion of the cyborg ideally refers to integral enhancement, the waste issue of the technosphere, from a planetary perspective, disrupts such a trajectory.

Technology is neither neutral nor separated from the planet, from the human, or from society. We have addressed the planetary level, but to understand these technologies, we must also locate them in our current socio-political and economic systems. In fact, implanting technology inside the body opens many possibilities, as well as many risks and response-abilities…

3.4.1 Focus: Hacking the bio-hacker

To demonstrate the potential vulnerabilities of implantable technology, scientist Mark Gasson (2010) became the first human infected with a computer virus, demonstrating that a computer virus could wirelessly infect his implant and then transmit the virus from the infected implant to other systems. This experiment exposed the vulnerability of restorative medical devices; such as pacemakers, to implantable technology aimed at human enhancement.[15] And eventually, it happened. Cyborg artist Neil Harbisson recalls the time he was hacked: "It happened once. Someone hacked into my head." What happened is that "the hacker sent him sounds that triggered different colours before, suddenly, stopping." Regarding the overall experience, Harbisson states: "I had a breach of privacy from that person (…). I didn't dislike it… I actually liked the fact that someone was able to hack into my head and take over" (Brethour 2015: n. pg.). Even if, at the individual level, the event was not perceived as problematic by Harbisson, things may dramatically change when analyzed from the social stance. Having an implant in the body connected to the internet means relying on data and data access, with the risks related to breach of privacy and what this may entail (from psychological targeting and using data in unlawful ways, to risks associated with biological health, as in the case of medical devices). Having an implant in the body connected to the internet also means producing data, which is considered the gold of the 21st century.

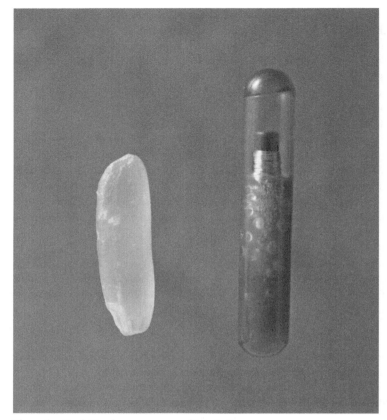

Photo by Paul Hughes, courtesy of Mark Gasson

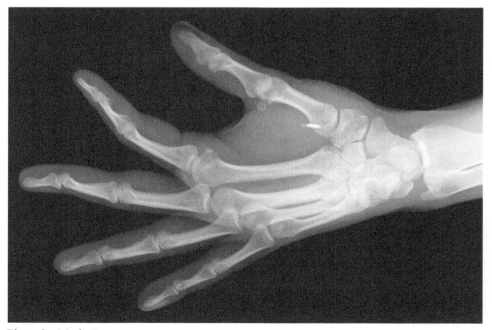

Photo by Mark Gasson

Economist Shoshanna Zuboff (2019) defines the current neo-liberal trend of capitalism based on big data collection, as surveillance capitalism. She describes it as "a new economic order that claims human experience as free raw material for hidden commercial practices of extraction, prediction, and sales" (1). According to Zuboff, this system is born out of, and is thriving through, the development of the digital technologies of the last 20 years; it has become increasingly entangled with most forms of online interactions. As she puts it,

> it has become difficult to escape this bold market project, whose tentacles reach from the gentle herding of innocent Pokémon Go players to eat, drink, and purchase in the restaurants, bars, fast-food joints, and shops that pay to play in its behavioral futures markets to the ruthless expropriation of surplus from Facebook profiles for the purposes of shaping individual behavior, whether it's buying pimple cream at 5:45 P.M. on Friday, clicking "yes" on an offer of new running shoes as the endorphins race through your brain after your long Sunday morning run, or voting next week.
>
> *(ivi: 6)*

A deep understanding of big data economy brings new layers of awareness to becoming cyborgs, asking questions related to data sovereignty and reusability, such as: who will have access to the data produced? How is such data going to be used and stored? Who will own it? Producing data is an act that bears rights and response-abilities. Whoever decides to get an implant in their bodies should be aware of the risks and implications, not only at the biological level of the body but also at the level of the privacy protection of the individual(s) involved, as well as of the society, in a historical time when mass surveillance is increasingly relying on machine learning algorithms based on big data collection.[16]

3.5 Conclusion

This paper does not aim to give a final answer to the question: to be or not to be enhanced? Although the transhumanist movement clearly embraces human enhancement, the posthumanist movement offers a wider variety of questions, starting from the reflection upon the notion of "enhancement" itself to the material conditions and general and conditional effects of different types of enhancement, such as radical life extension, cryonics, and enhanced cyborgs, to suggest that bio-technological innovation cannot be thought of in isolation but bears socio-political, economic, and ecological responsibilities. In fact, what may enhance an individual may not enhance the well-being of society at large, the species, or the planet. The conclusions here are not in favor of or against enhancement because there is not one type of enhancement that can be generalized as a prototype. Instead, enhancement is perceived as a process, where the way is the end, and the end is the way: how each specific type of enhancement is developed and what it may produce are not separated. From this perspective, overcoming limits *per se* is not a goal: respecting limits can be an act of ecological awareness – for instance, by honoring non-human animal habitats and stopping development in wilderness areas. Similarly, posing limits can be the best response to the current big data robbery, bypassing proper legislation that requires data transparency. There are many more layers to be explored within this context, for instance, by approaching enhancement not just as a human-driven process but as an evolutionary outcome powered and enacted by all agents (from non-human animals and plants to algorithms and robots; from celestial bodies to living and non-living entities, forces, and dynamics). A posthuman understanding of enhancement nourishes an integral approach, mindful of the multitude of layers at play and aware of the variety of possible scenarios – including the eventual need for case-by-case assessments. Overall, a posthumanist approach to enhancement must rely on full existential awareness. To be or not to be enhanced? Only someone who truly thinks from above can answer this question: just ask the Moon…

3.5.1 Once upon a time...

Shining in the sky, the Moon realized: *Everyone, everything, everywhere is already enhanced.* The Moon was silent. There were no more questions, no confusion, no attachment: no dark side of the Moon. The Moon was full, forever and ever. The Moon was fully enlightened. And so are we...

Acknowledgments

Most sincere thanks to Ellen Delahunty Roby, Jennifer McCurdy, Marcello Ienca, and Fabrice Jotterand for the meaningful comments on this paper.

Thanks to Thomas Elanore for this quote.

Most sincere thanks to Ellen Delahunty Roby for the kind comments.

Notes

1. The material in this article is based on my book *The Art of Being Posthuman*, which is being published by Polity Press, Cambridge, UK.
2. For a clarification of the different movements, see Ferrando 2014.
3. For an explanation of each take, see Ferrando 2019.
4. As Crutzen and Stoermer phrase it, "To assign a more specific date to the onset of the 'anthropocene' seems somewhat arbitrary, but we propose the latter part of the 18th century, although we are aware that alternative proposals can be made (some may even want to include the entire holocene)" (2000:17).
5. The original title did not feature the term "Divine."
6. Prominent during the Renaissance, this analogy can be already traced in the Middle Ages, for instance, in the work of Hildegard of Bingen (1098–1179).
7. As Mengjun Tang summarizes: "The sex ratio at birth (SRB) in China began to rise rapidly in the 1980s and declined after 2009. The ratio has maintained a downward trend since 2009, but is still higher than the normal level" (2021: 319).
8. This could be achieved, for instance, by freezing their genetic material and later implanting it by surrogacy, among other emerging, as well as speculative, bio-technological techniques.
9. Ferrando, F./More, M. (2013). This is a shorter and edited version of the transcript of the video, which is available on YouTube (minutes 57:00–59:00): https://youtu.be/7Sr1kcogOoE.
10. For the full answer, please see Note 8.
11. Many people do not have the economic resources to afford to be cryonized. Democratic transhumanism focuses on this aspect, underlining the urgency for a democratic access to human enhancement, including the right to be cryo-preserved.
12. For instance, in the Theravada Buddhist scripture Satipatthana Sutta, The Sutra on the Four Establishments of Mindfulness (ca. 100 BCE), the comparison of the practitioner's body with a corpse is suggested repeatedly (Hanh 2006: 20–22).
13. Quote from the website: https://neuralink.com/applications/.
14. The movie "Downsizing" (2017) moves along similar lines.
15. The two categories are not separated. As Gasson put it, "it is conceivable that a piece of technology designed as a restorative device may actually give the recipient a capability which exceeds the normal human ability it is designed to replace" (2010: 63).
16. As Hugo Verhelst et al. state: "Rapid advancements in machine learning techniques allow mass surveillance to be applied on larger scales and utilize more and more personal data" (2020: 2975).

References

Bostrom, N. (2005, April). A history of transhumanist thought. In: *Journal of Evolution and Technology*, Vol. 14, Issue 1, 1–25. Retrieved in June 2021: http://jetpress.org/volume14/bostrom.html

Brethour, D. (2015). Why are you sending me colours in my head? An interview with Cyborg Artist Neil Harbisson. In: *Head Stuff, Science and Tech*, October 27th 2015. Retrieved in June 2021: https://www.headstuff.org/topical/science/why-are-you-sending-me-colours-in-my-head-an-interview-with-cyborg-artist-neil-harbisson/

Clynes, M., Kline, N. (1960). Cyborgs and space. In: *Astronautics* September, Vol. 5, Issue 9, 26–27.

Crutzen, P. J., Stoermer, E. F. (2000). The 'anthropocene'. In: *Global Change Newsletter* No. 41, 17–18.

Cyborg Foundation. (2016, September). Cyborg foundation: Design yourself. *Youtube*. Retrieved in June 2021: https://youtu.be/Vo95354RQ40

De Grey, A. (2007). *Ending Aging: The Rejuvenation Breakthroughs that Could Reverse Human Aging in Our Lifetime.* St. Martin's Press: New York, NY.

Ferrando, F. (2014, March). Posthumanism, transhumanism, antihumanism, metahumanism, and new materialisms: Differences and relations. In: *Existenz*, The Karl Jaspers Society of North America, Vol. 8, Issue 2, 26–32.

Ferrando, F. (2019). *Philosophical Posthumanism*. Bloomsbury: London et al.

Ferrando, F., More, M. In: Karl Jaspers society of North America conference "Humanity and Posthumanity", APA, San Francisco, March 2013. *Youtube*. Retrieved in June 2021: https://youtu.be/7Sr1kcogOoE

Fukuyama, F. (2012). Agency or inevitability: Will human beings control their technological future? In: Rosenthal, M. (ed). *The Posthuman Condition*. Aarhus University Press: Aarhus, 157–169.

Gasson, M. (2010). Human enhancement: Could you become infected with a computer virus? In: Michael, K. (ed). *International Symposium on Technology and Society*. IEEE Computer Society Press: Phoenix, 498–516.

Haff, P. K. (2013). Technology as a geological phenomenon: Implications for human well-being. In: Waters, C. N., Zalasiewicz, J., Williams, M. (eds). *A stratigraphical basis for the anthropocene*. Geological Society: London, 301–309.

Hanh, Thich Nhat. (2006). *Transformation and Healing*. Parallax Press: Berkeley.

Haraway, D. (2016). *Staying with the Trouble: Making Kin in the Cthulucene*. Duke University Press: London.

Heidegger, M. [1927] (2011). *Being and Time* (Macquarrie, J., Robinson, E., Trans.). Harper & Row: New York, NY.

Hughes, J. (2004). *Citizen Cyborg: Why Democratic Societies Must Respond to the Redesigned Human of the Future*. Westview Press: Cambridge, MA.

Hutchings, F. (2020). Cyborg artist Moon Ribas feels earthquakes. In: *Next Nature Network*, February 11th 2020, Retrieved in June 2020: https://nextnature.net/story/2020/moon-ribas

Huxley, J. (1957). Transhumanism. In: Huxley, J. *New Bottles for New Wine*. Chatto & Windus: London, 13–17.

Lovelock, J. (1995). *The Ages of Gaia: A Biography of Our Living Earth*. Norton: New York.

Margulis, L. (1998). *Symbiotic Planet: A New Look at Evolution*. Weidenfeld & Nicolson: London.

Patterson, J. (1998). Respecting nature: A maori perspective. In: *Worldviews: Environment, Culture, Religion*, Vol. 2, no. 1, 69–78.

Tang, M. (2021). Addressing skewed sex ratio at birth in China: Practices and challenges. *China Population and Development Studies*, N. 4, 319–326.

United Nations. (2017). Indigenous peoples: The unsung heroes of conservation. *United Nations Environment Programme*, June 9th 2017. Retrieved in June 2021: https://www.unep.org/zh-hans/node/477

Verhelst, H. M., Stannat, A. W., Mecacci, G. (2020). Machine learning against terrorism: How big data collection and analysis influences the privacy-security dilemma. *Science and Engineering Ethics*, N. 26, 2975–2984.

Warwick, K. [2002] (2004). *I, Cyborg*. University of Illinois Press: Urbana et al.

Zuboff, S. (2019). *The Age of Surveillance Capitalism: The Fight for a Human Future at the New Frontier of Power*. Profile Books: London.

PART II

Human enhancement and human nature

4
CLONES, CHIMERAS, AND ORGANOIDS
Developmental biology and the human future

William Hurlbut and Dillon Stull

4.1 Toward a science of living form

According to the National Intelligence Council report, *Global Trends 2030: Alternative Worlds*, "we are at a critical juncture in human history, which could lead to widely contrasting futures." Nowhere is this more evident than in the promise and peril of advancing biomedical technology.

Throughout the 20th century, the dramatic momentum of discovery in molecular genetics brought conceptual unity to biology, bridging disciplinary domains from cell physiology to cognitive neuroscience. This, in turn, fostered new theoretical insights and technical advances in a broad range of basic research fields, together with notable advances in clinical care. As our powers over the human body increased, medicine was summoned beyond its traditional realm in the service of a widening range of human appetites and ambitions. With this shift, it has become clear that the constructive possibilities of medical technologies are inseparable from the challenges of their social and ethical implications. Both arise from the scope and depth of their connection with the fundamental processes of life, processes that we have long sought to properly understand in their interrelated mechanistic and moral significance.

Now, as the century of advances in molecular biology leads on to the era of developmental biology, emerging technologies – including clones, chimeras, and organoids – are delivering increasing urgency to these fundamental considerations. These new tools and technologies hold extraordinary prospects for biomedicine; at the same time, they pose difficult and disquieting conceptual questions: what does it mean to say that something is alive, a living being? – and what are the boundaries of the human? And, on a practical level, how can these transformative powers at the very foundations of life be deployed for positive purposes in the service of human flourishing? These innovative (and potentially transgressive) technologies raise issues for which we have neither natural intuitions nor established cultural traditions. Yet they are matters of central significance for the character of our civilization and, perhaps, the very future of our species. At the same time, they carry the prospect of informing a more coherent and integrated scientific and moral understanding of human life.

If we step back and consider these new powers from a historical perspective, we may gain insights crucial to their constructive deployment.

4.1.1 The origins of our dilemma

In 1779, the French Academy of Sciences offered a prize of one kilo of gold to anyone who could explain the nature of alcohol fermentation. For 6,000 years, fermentation had been regarded as a mysterious power of transformation, a meeting of the material and the spiritual. But now, in the age of science, a bitter dispute arose between those representing the new field of chemistry and the traditional "vitalists," who maintained that life processes are not reducible to explanations in terms of physio-chemical mechanism.[1]

Toward the end of the 18th century, Lavoisier noted that the powers of fermentation could be transferred with residual sediments. By the middle of the 19th century, Schwann established that cells are the basic unit of life, and that yeast cells could be found in fermentation sediments. The crucial role of these yeast cells was confirmed by Pasteur, who maintained that only within the living system of the cell, with its mysterious, immaterial vital forces, could the powers of fermentation be manifest. But in 1897, the German chemist Eduard Buchner prepared an extract of yeast and noted that this clear, slightly yellow, filtered fluid was fully capable of fermentation even apart from its cellular source.

Buchner's discovery led to the isolation of the enzymes of fermentation and the chemical description of this fundamental organic process. With this decisive blow to vitalism, the field of biochemistry was born and with it the reductive and analytic approach to the study of life. The practical significance of this conceptual revision is evident in the dramatic advances in biology throughout the 20th century. By breaking down organic systems into their component parts and looking at living beings in terms of inanimate matter, we opened an era of scientific discovery that culminated in the sequencing of the human genome.

Notwithstanding all the gain from this conceptual revolution, it came at a cost in our understanding of living nature. Through most of the 20th century, Stanford University housed its Zoology department in the center of campus at the front of the main quadrangle. The foyer of this august hall was adorned with a multitude of exotic stuffed birds and mammals flanked by display cabinets of ancient fossils and specimen jars of animal embryos at varied stages. Replete with color, form, and dynamic process, it spoke of the vibrant organic powers of living creatures in their growth, development, and adaptive behaviors.

By the 1970s, however, the biology department had moved to a modern facility packed with brightly lit labs for the study of molecular biology, now the fundamental focus of biological and biomedical research. The mechanistic model prevailed – with its emphasis on molecular parts and metabolic processes, biological beings came to be seen as deterministically driven by genetic programs. We lost a certain appreciation for the overarching unity and integrity of form, the principle of organization, and the coordinated coherence of the organismic whole. The still mysterious interior dimensions of living beings – sentience, subjectivity, and self-awareness – seemed drained of their "aliveness," and less attention was given to the complex context and connection of creatures as evolved, embodied, and embedded within the social and ecological dynamics of the wider world. Increasingly, then, we lost our sense of cautionary reverence and respect and came to regard all living nature as mere matter and information to be reshuffled and reassigned for projects of the human will.

Now, however, as we move from genomics to proteomics and on to the investigation of developmental biology, we are returning to the study of whole living beings. When applied to human biology, this inquiry reopens the most fundamental questions concerning the very definition of life and the adequacy of our current scientific approach to inform discussion of the ethical dilemmas raised by our new perspectives and powers.

4.1.2 Clones

These questions and concerns were forced to the foreground of public awareness in the final years of the 20th century with the announcement of the first successful cloning of a mammal, Dolly the sheep. This extraordinary feat, known by the scientific term Somatic Cell Nuclear Transfer (SCNT), was accomplished by replacing the DNA-containing nucleus of a sheep egg with the nucleus of an adult body cell (a somatic cell) from a different sheep – in this case, a breast cell (with the cloned lamb named in honor of the country music singer Dolly Parton).[2]

This procedure, in effect, creates a younger identical twin and holds the prospect for an unlimited number of genetically identical (or nearly identical) animals as a standardized platform for a wide range of research into development, disease modeling, drug testing, etc. – one Japanese researcher made 581 identical mice.[3] Projects could include the selective engineering of a series of single-gene alterations in such batches of cloned animals to study the role of those genes in embryonic development. Likewise, identical cloned animals could be administered different amounts of an experimental pharmaceutical to establish safe and effective therapeutic doses; the same could be done to study dangerous levels of an environmental toxin.

Cloning is also being used in efforts to preserve endangered species and has been suggested for the potential de-extinction of animals such as the woolly mammoth and the passenger pigeon – and possibly even extinct human lineages such as Neandertals and Denisovans.[4] However, despite the fact that at least 20 species of mammals have now been cloned, it is notable that there has been only one species of primates (cynomolgus monkeys) that has been cloned by means of SCNT and brought to live birth and no published success in the implantation and gestation of human embryonic clones.[5] This failure poses a major impedance to the transhumanist agenda of directed human evolution since the evaluation of the impact of single-gene alterations against a standardized genetic background would almost certainly be an essential step in attempts to produce enhanced humans.[6]

A less recognized, but highly significant result of the cloning of Dolly was that it overthrew the longstanding and widely held conclusion that, once committed to more specialized states, somatic cells could not go back to a less differentiated multipotent state. Clearly, when placed within a different cytoplasm, that of the egg, the genetic material from the adult cell nucleus was reprogrammed to serve the essential functions of the developing embryo. This, at once, supported two important revisions in our understanding of development. First: the flexible, context-dependent nature of gene expression and cell fates. And second: a recognition that DNA is not the "master molecule" but is in dynamic interrelation with factors in the cytoplasm that influence gene expression.[7] In the memorable words of biologist Steven Rose, correcting the errors of what has been called "DNA essentialism," there is no "nuclear board room," but a wider, coordinated "molecular democracy."[8]

With these revisions in our understanding, it becomes clear that a living being has an inherent principle of organic unity in its organization and operation. Development, from its beginnings in a single-cell embryo (the zygote) – as well as during all future phases of an organism's existence – involves a coherent coordination of interdependent parts and processes subordinated to one another for the good of the whole. As the very term implies, an organism[9] is an integrated, self-developing, and self-maintaining unity under the governance of an immanent plan.[10] It is this overarching harmony of the whole, its dynamic balance of being, that exerts a downward causation[11] that binds and balances the parts into a patterned process of integrated growth and development. For a developing embryo, with its inherent potency and activated drive toward the mature form, this means that the whole, as the unified organismal principle of life, precedes and produces the organic parts.

4.1.3 Cellular systems and gene editing

The significance of these insights, both for conceptual clarity in the definition of life and for a realistic assessment of projects of human enhancement, is apparent if we look more closely at the actual operation of DNA within the full complexity of cell dynamics. Systems biology is a holistic (non-reductive) methodological approach that seeks to model how system properties emerge amid the plurality of interacting components, including DNA, messenger RNA, proteins, and metabolic products of cell operations, etc. Notwithstanding the limited success of the efforts of systems biology (testimony to the complexity of cell processes), one thing seems clear: even small changes in one or a few of the interacting components can have a dramatic (and often unpredictable) effect on the expressions of the whole. The non-linear effect of genetic or other molecular changes on cellular or organismic phenotype supports the view that a living being is a deeply integrated network that is more than the sum of its parts; it corrects simplistic reductionist notions of causation and issues a cautionary word as to the difficulty of projects of human genetic enhancement.

Even at the most basic levels of analysis, the complexity of genetic processes is already evident. Introductory textbooks tend to portray a one-dimensional line of action from molecular codes to macroscopic characteristics, with DNA being transcribed to messenger RNA and messenger RNA translated to proteins and directly manifested as phenotypic traits. This over-simplified model, together with journalistic accounts of new tools for gene editing, has led many people to believe we are on the threshold of producing "designer babies" reflecting parental preferences for hair and eye color or taller stature, etc.[12] But genes are not Legos, with add-on units; it is not like Mr. Potato Head, where we can just swap out parts (eyebrows, ears, and noses). Genes specify proteins, and proteins interact to produce traits. These proteins (gene products) are like primary colors on an artist's palate – that get mixed together before being applied to the canvas.

Most traits are affected by many genes (polygenic inheritance), and most genes affect many traits (pleiotropy).[13] This is vividly (and tragically) evident in the way most single-gene genetic disorders affect numerous aspects of organismal development and operation.[14] Genetic diseases generally manifest as syndromes; with a constellation of diverse disorders such as short stature, cardiac abnormalities, cranio-facial deformities, cognitive impairments, or shortened life expectancy.[15] These reflect the many roles, with complex interactions, that a given gene may play. So, the conditions we would care most about – intelligence, beauty, longevity – result from interaction among many genes (sometimes hundreds or even thousands) and would not be easy to alter for purposes of enhancement.[16]

Moreover, even beyond gene-gene interactions, genomic function is further influenced by factors at every level of the organism. The *intracellular* context of genes influences the quantity and chronology of gene expression, the translation of messenger RNA into proteins, and the function of the proteins they produce. These epigenetic and regulative operations within the individual cell are influenced by context-specific *intercellular* signals and circulating factors (such as nutrients and hormones). These, in turn, are subject to *extrinsic* inputs from environmental and social cues, including sensory inputs that influence high-order mental operations. In human beings, these mental operations are played out against a background of integrated memory that sustains personal identity and continuity in the "autobiographical self" – the narrative sense of personal meaning and purpose that nourishes and reflects values, beliefs, and desires (goals). This meeting of the material (neurobiological) and the immaterial (ideas) culminates in imagined ideals – physical, social, moral, and spiritual images that play a central role in the aspirations and actions that empower and align individual lives. The quest for fulfillment of these imagined ideals within the process of an individual life is experienced subjectively as both thoughts and embodied feelings such as pleasures and pains, stresses and satisfactions – expressed in bodily changes from anatomical (posture, facial expressions) to physiological (blood pressure, circulating hormones such as oxytocin and cortisol) and all the way down to minute-by-minute gene expression patterns.[17] At every level of the organismal process, there is an intricate interaction of integrated bottom-up and top-down causation, a unity of matter and mind (indeed, "ideas have consequences" …including biochemical consequences!).

From these reflections on the role of genetics within the wider context of human development and self-maintenance, it is immediately evident that the projects of gene editing face a daunting task. Apart from the serious ethical concerns related to the experimental use of human embryos and the social consequences of engineering our offspring, germline genetic editing faces serious (and perhaps insurmountable) scientific challenges. However, germline correction of some of the over 7,000 single-gene genetic disorders[18] (of which almost 90% have no current cure or even effective treatment) might one day be feasible; conceptually, restoration of defective system components is analogous to repairing a broken link in an otherwise intact chain. In other words, the complex biological system of the organism already has the potential to accommodate stably the therapeutic restoration of function.

Likewise, though more controversially, switching out existing alleles (natural variations in a given gene) with a form that appears to confer some advantage might be technically possible. Harvard geneticist George Church has compiled a list of "rare protective variants of large impact," which exist naturally in the human gene pool but only in relatively few people.[19] These include variants that appear correlated with extra-strong bones, lean muscles, lower risk of coronary artery disease, cancer, diabetes, and greater resistance to viruses (!) – all of which, he believes, might improve general health if more common. But even such apparently uncontroversial interventions bear significant risks since we have only a limited understanding of how genes will interact within an individual. A new allele might not operate as well in a widely different genome. For example, it remains to be seen exactly how the germline gene-edited Chinese twins – widely publicized in November 2018 after the controversial scientist He Jiankui announced their birth – will be impacted by the alteration of the gene *CCR5*.[20]

There is, of course, general agreement regarding the acceptability of somatic cell gene editing (that is, in body cells that do not contribute to intergenerational inheritance) where the alteration is intended to treat or cure serious genetic diseases such as sickle cell anemia, muscular dystrophy, or cystic fibrosis. But even here, there are controversies concerning what is considered "serious" or even what counts as a "disease" given the many natural human variations that broaden and enrich our species (e.g. albinism, deafness, dwarfism, or dyslexia). Moreover, there will one day be sharp controversies over individual rights (including parental rights) to engineer alterations in the expression of healthy genes to influence patterns of development or performance.

These reflections on the operation of the genome in the context of the full organism point to the profound possibilities and potential problems that will arise even at the level of basic genetics as our knowledge of developmental biology increases. Driven by the noble imperative of healing, we will seek an ever-greater understanding of both pathological and normal physiological functioning. Studying these matters without endangering human lives or violating human dignity will be difficult. Cloning provides a versatile tool with great potential to illuminate the most basic levels of genetic operation in early embryogenesis as well as the ongoing effects of genetic variation. As mentioned above, cloning minimizes genetic complexities by providing an otherwise unchanged background against which single-gene alterations can be evaluated. Studies of mammals, particularly non-human primates, may highlight fundamental dynamics of development shared between species. Ultimately, however, there are important differences between humans and even our closest primate cousins. Ethical controversies over the laboratory production and instrumental use of human embryos (cloned or other) will continue to provoke passionate debate. And, at least to date, proposals to produce cloned offspring for projects of human enhancement have been met with very strong public opposition.

4.1.4 Stem cells

In 1998, just two years after the cloning of Dolly, American scientists announced the isolation and culture of human embryonic stem cells (ESCs). ESCs are pluripotent cells, meaning they can differentiate into any cell lineage of the human embryo. Drawing on nearly 20 years of research on mouse ESCs, scientists immediately recognized that if these cells could be isolated from cloned human embryos, they might be coaxed to produce patient-specific cells, tissues, and even organs for research and therapeutic purposes. Because this would involve the creation and destruction of human embryos, this suggestion provoked deep controversy between those who saw such a procedure as a violation of basic human dignity and those who cited the imperative of scientific advance. However, within less than ten years, the Japanese scientist Shinya Yamanaka had demonstrated that just four transcription factors could reprogram adult body cells to the pluripotent state, with similar powers to those of embryonic stem cells. He named these cells "induced pluripotent stem cells" (iPSCs).[21]

With these discoveries, the new field of regenerative medicine was born,[22] and with it, a vast and flourishing arena of research into the most fundamental levels of human development. The therapeutic horizons of these new lines of inquiry are expansive. Characterization of the operative processes and patterns of the human organism's coordinated unfolding opens countless new possibilities for intervention at the most basic levels of human biology. Beyond the obvious benefit of understanding the biological factors behind the estimated 8 million children born every year with congenital defects[23] (6% of worldwide births), there is a growing intuition that many pathologies manifesting only later in life have their origin in disorders of early development.[24] Moreover, essential health-sustaining functions such as wound healing and tissue regeneration, as well as pathological processes such as cancer, and the factors at work in the pace and procession of natural aging engage many of the same basic cell mechanisms deployed in the early stages of life. For example, scientists are exploring the possibility of inducing the re-expression of genes involved in fetal development to stimulate the repair of cardiac muscle after heart attack.[25] It seems clear that our deepening knowledge of developmental biology holds great promise for the mediation of constructive and compassionate therapeutic advances – as well as certain more controversial interventions beyond the traditional scope and purpose of medicine.

4.1.5 Stem cell-based embryo models ("embryoids")

Over the past decade, as research in regenerative medicine has proceeded, there have been important synergistic advances in related technologies – most significantly, improvements in monitoring changes in gene expression levels of individual cells and more powerful and precise tools (such as CRISPR-Cas9 and related technologies) for gene editing. Likewise, refinements in cell culture techniques have opened a range of new studies of cell signaling and the dynamics of cell lineage differentiation.

Early in the study of embryonic stem cells, researchers noted the remarkable capacities of these cells to self-organize into structures with some embryo-like features.[26] This suggested that direct crosstalk between cells was inducing differentiation and promoting the basic patterns of natural development. The hope was that identification of the chemical signals involved might allow the culture of distinct cell types in simple 2D culture systems. This would allow the production of abundant quantities of a range of cells and tissues, such as blood-forming elements or insulin-producing islet cells, for therapeutic transplantation. Such tissues might, as discussed below, also serve the purposes of enhancement, such as implantable, organized 3D structures of hormone-producing cells to, for example, forestall certain effects of aging, heighten athletic capabilities, or accentuate aesthetic features.

The technical difficulty of mimicking embryogenesis in pluripotent stem cell cultures, and thereby deriving the full range of early human tissue types in a potentially less controversial way, soon became evident. Numerous frustrating failures to develop such organized culture systems early on made it apparent that the natural development of the living embryo makes use of complex interactions involving subtle physical forces and positional dynamics.[27] But more sophisticated techniques of culture, including 3D systems with nurturing media, structural scaffolds, microfluidics, and rotating cylinders, are now able to simulate more of the natural conditions of embryogenesis, allowing important insights and practical advances in understanding and promoting the processes of natural development in *in vitro* systems. These may – but, in principle, need not – involve human embryos, as partial and incomplete biological subsystems can also be sustained under such conditions.

Under specific conditions, pluripotent stem cells can be differentiated or aggregated to produce multicellular entities that resemble the early embryo in limited and transient ways. "Blastoids" resemble their ~5-to-14-day-old embryonic counterparts (blastocysts) structurally and transcriptionally (i.e. in cell-specific patterns of gene expression) and some have even been capable of implantation, a key process in human embryonic development.[28] So far, however, none have demonstrated the capacity to sustain themselves in such a state or undergo subsequent developments.[29]

Stem cell-based embryo models also include "gastruloids," three-dimensional models of the gastrula (i.e. models of embryonic development during gastrulation, the process occurring at 12-14 days post-fertilization that follows directly after the blastocyst stage).[30] Like blastoids, gastruloids are derived from pluripotent stem cells. However, gastruloids recapitulate only *some* components of peri-implantation embryos.[31] Lacking certain critical parts, displaying no evidence of multiorgan differentiation, and differing in overall structure from natural embryos, these gastruloids do not appear to have human organismal potential – and therefore may sidestep the moral controversy associated with the instrumental use of human embryos – but nevertheless reflect many of the regional dynamics of early embryogenesis.[32] In addition to yielding insights about normal and pathological embryonic development, these may prove invaluable for assessments relevant to fetal medicine, such as drug teratogenicity and ideal prenatal regimens.

4.1.6 Organoids

The revolution sparked by innovations in 3D lab culture systems has given rise to the burgeoning new arena of "organoid" research. Organoids are *in vitro*, three-dimensional cell cultures resembling bodily tissues. They are derived from stem cells or tissue-specific progenitor cells, which self-assemble into multicellular structures that recapitulate aspects of *in vivo* physiology by expressing their inherent capacities for tissue or organ development (their autopoietic ability). Organoid systems have been created for a wide range of tissues and visceral organs, including the lung, liver, kidney, and intestine.[33] Some organoid systems exhibit remarkable similarities to natural organs and manifest functional properties such as hormone secretion, filtration, and peristalsis. They can be produced to scale and used for studies of development and regeneration, as well as disease modeling (e.g. genetic disorders, infection, and cancer) and high-throughput drug screening – and, possibly in the future, individually tailored therapies[34] and surgical grafts, including genetically enhanced tissues and organs for transplantation.

Organoids are already proving very useful in the study of basic cellular processes. Pulmonary organoids have modeled the infection of lung tissue with severe acute respiratory syndrome coronavirus 2 (SARS-CoV-2, the cause of COVID-19).[35] Organoids of bone and cartilage, marrow, kidney, and the blood-brain barrier have been taken to the International Space Station to study the effects of microgravity on tissue formation and function.[36] Understanding the molecular signaling that shapes tissue development, maintenance, transformation, and healing will allow for powerful new therapeutics while expanding the range of modalities for attempting enhancement.

The main difficulty of growing organoids is in imitating the manifold conditions of the body that naturally give rise to organ development. Many types of stem cells, including pluripotent stem cells (both induced and embryonic) and later-stage progenitor cells, can produce organoids. Theoretically, these cells should be able to produce any type of cell in the body. *In vivo*, however, the innate capabilities of these cells are drawn out in the context of many subtle cues: cellular activity is responsive to ion gradients, pH, waste and nutrients, hormones, chemical signals from surrounding cells and tissues, electrical signals, mechanical stresses such as stretch, resistance, or shearing, and more. Some of these conditions can be simulated by microfluidic devices that expose organoids to fluid- or airflow, variegated culture media, specific spatial positions, and mechanical perturbations. Organoids of various tissue types can be connected in a microfluidic system, placed up- or downstream of one another to allow for molecular crosstalk between them. Reproductive organoid systems with interconnected modules of ovarian, fallopian tube, cervical, uterine, and hepatic tissues have recapitulated the ovulatory and corresponding hormonal features of the 28-day menstrual cycle.[37] Endometrial organoids (organoids of the nourishing lining of the uterus), will allow for studies of interactions between the embryo and uterine lining during and after the process of implantation – outside the bodies of patients.[38]

This latter category is a step toward the troubling prospect of extracorporeal gestation of human embryos (ectogenesis), a possibility that looms on the horizon at some distance but is theoretically attainable – and a crucial part of the agenda of certain transhumanist visions. With a combination of 3D cell culture techniques, mouse embryos have been gestated *in vitro* through hindlimb formation, which occurs approximately halfway to term.[39] Meanwhile, sheep fetuses whose lungs were gestationally equivalent to those of human fetuses between 22 and 24 weeks have been sustained in an artificial bag for four weeks, bridging them from minimally viable prematurity to more robust spontaneous respiration.[40] With a vast array of modalities for real-time monitoring and exact delivery of proper nutrients and conditions, the complex environment of the womb may one day be simulated, making it possible to bring human beings from fertilization to term outside of a human body.

Ectogenesis aside, organoids provide scientists with a valuable window into many aspects of development. While stem cell-based embryo systems ("embryoids") model some of the first steps of development, organoids develop further, revealing comparatively later processes. As models of various developmental regions within the body, such as limbs, organoids may help explain why, for example, humans form and subsequently destroy extra hand and foot muscles *in utero*.[41] Could human dexterity be augmented by arresting the destruction of these muscles? How would such a change affect the larger developmental system?

The recapitulation of specific organ structures tends to be more efficient when beginning with more differentiated cell types, such as tissue-specific progenitor cells; organoid cultures that begin with these more specialized cells, therefore, are more precise models of organ development and function and, potentially, more productive sources of tissues for transplantation and other medical uses. However, optimally constituted progenitor cells may be most readily obtained from harvested fetal tissue, perhaps from spontaneous or elective abortions or, one day, laboratory-produced and -gestated clones.[42]

Glandular tissues may be the most amenable to early clinical applications. Since hormone-secreting glands transmit their molecular products through the bloodstream, small endocrine organoid transplants could be used to affect physiological functions throughout the body. For therapeutic and extra-therapeutic purposes, this might include ovarian or testicular organoids to preserve physiologic levels of sex hormones that naturally decline with age. Clinicians could employ such an intervention in attempts to sustain libido, extend the years of female reproductive life, or maintain bone density and muscle strength (Wisconsin-based JangoBio is purportedly preparing to pilot this concept in animal studies).[43] Another potential application beyond therapy involves externally controllable (light-activated) tissue implants for the modulation of the circadian rhythm. This military-funded (DARPA) project at Northwestern University could help to alleviate jetlag and daytime fatigue in soldiers, travelers, shift workers, or the chronically ill. In contrast to endocrine tissues, exocrine glands have a localized effect.[44] Transplantable salivary gland organoids or lacrimal gland organoids (which can be induced to "cry" *in vitro*) may treat Sjögren's syndrome.[45]

Other speculations for future use include genetically perfected blood for transfusions (or doping), replacement spare kidneys or livers for a "visceral retread" in the course of aging, or, more controversially, male-compatible whole uterus, endometrium, and functional breast implants.[46]

Several organoid or synthetic organ systems have been transplanted into animal models with various degrees of functionality, including intestinal organoids, bio-scaffold-grown lungs, and a whole bio-scaffold-grown thymus.[47] Transplants in humans may one day contribute to functional or cosmetic enhancements – some might attempt individual "artistic" self-expressions such as the "cat woman" or the "bird man" (others have even suggested direct modifications to human developmental programs or immunologically modified modular organoids from other species for whiskers, horns, antlers, or tails).[48]

However, as with 2D stem cell cultures, our discussion of the speculative future of organoids must be tempered by an acknowledgment of their current limitations. Today's organoids may be functional at the cellular level, but none of these can yet perform the macro-functions proper to their respective organs due to factors such as size, lack of complexity, and difficulties with functional integration. At this point, *in vitro* organoid productions are very small (less than 4 mm) and generally lack natural vascularization, innervation, and immune cell infiltration. Reproductive organoids may be an exception: functional mouse eggs have been produced and fertilized *in vitro* with subsequent normal development *in utero*.[49] However, difficulties recapitulating physiologic niches mean that no fertilization-compatible human sperm or eggs have yet been generated.[50] So, as with cell therapies, efforts to produce transplantable organs *in vitro* have heretofore been disappointing but may hold some future promise.

4.1.7 Chimeras

A more plausible and efficient means of producing human cells, tissues, and organs fit for transplantation is to harness the precise, integrated cell dynamics of natural organismal development. This is, in some sense, what the field of organ transplantation relies upon currently; doctors harvest organs from human donors, whose bodies naturally construct what organoid systems cannot yet mimic in the lab. Some have proposed the use of human embryos as "bioreactors" to generate cells, tissues, and organ primordia. In 2003, scientists in Israel published studies advocating the feasibility of such an approach.[51] For several years, Silicon Valley's Ganogen has been investigating the possibility of commercializing clinical transplantation of organ primordia procured from aborted fetuses.[52] Bioethicist Julian Savulescu, Director of the Uehiro Centre for Practical Ethics at the University of Oxford, has advocated for this approach using human clones, stating, "Indeed, it is not merely morally permissible but morally required that we employ cloning to produce embryos or fetuses for the sake of providing cells, tissues or even organs for therapy, followed by abortion of the embryo or fetus."[53]

These controversial approaches might be avoided by using other animals to grow human organs in human-animal chimeras. The "blastocyst complementation" technique may be most appropriate for such a purpose. First, a gene essential for the formation of a specific organ in an animal host, e.g. the pancreas, is "knocked out" (deleted or disabled) using CRISPR-Cas9 or related methods. Then, human pluripotent cells are injected into the early animal embryo (at the blastocyst stage). The disabled gene vacates a "developmental niche" in the growing embryo, and the human cells, which have a functionally intact genome, occupy that niche without competition from host cells. The host animal embryo naturally supplies the donor human cells with overall organismal architecture, numerous molecular factors, and cellular cues at important biological timepoints. The product is a chimeric organism with one tissue or organ (in this example, the pancreas) derived almost entirely from human cells. Chimeric organs tend to conform to the body plan of the host[54] species; for this reason, sheep and pigs, whose internal organs resemble those of humans in many ways (e.g. size), have been suggested as ideal livestock chimeric hosts for human purposes, notwithstanding the anatomical similarity of primates.

The creation of human organs in livestock or primate chimeras would allow for experimentation on roughly-to-scale organs. Some studies of neuropsychiatric disease or trials of brain-computer interfaces may be more feasible and possibly more ethical in chimeras, e.g. non-human primates with human neural tissue, than in human patients. Rodents with human liver or kidney tissue could undergo high-throughput pharmaceutical tests, potentially yielding more relevant results than traditional animal models. Chimeric embryology may elucidate fundamental developmental principles. Or chimeric organisms may allow for the largescale and efficient production of genetically specific adult or progenitor cells for the creation of ideal organoid culture systems.

Blastocyst complementation also contains many possibilities for tissue donation and transplantation. Using iPSC technology, organs could be patient-derived and therefore immune compatible. They could also be genetically modified to eliminate or enhance certain organ traits, perhaps to overcome or compensate for pathological processes in the transplant recipient, to create superior organs with resistance to toxins and viruses, or to optimize tissues to excel at specific physiologic functions, e.g. metabolizing fat. Chimeric organisms could also become a harvestable source of human blood or milk.

The many practical difficulties of interspecies chimerization – apparently due to incompatibility of cell types, states, signals, internal "clocks," etc. – have resulted in chimeras with minimal human cell contribution to date.[55] The use of more closely related species in chimeric experiments would presumably harmonize these developmental realities more efficiently; hence, the recent creation of human-macaque chimeras, which were gestated *in vitro* to the gastrulation stage of embryonic development.[56] But the chimerization of humans with animals, especially with primates, raises many questions and concerns, including animal welfare, the danger of blurring the distinction between humans and animals, and the possibility of "humanizing" chimeric organisms, i.e. augmenting or altering their inherent capacities, conscious experience, and moral value.[57]

4.1.8 Developmental biology and the brain

Perhaps the most fascinating and scientifically significant employment of organoid and chimera technologies is the production of human brain tissue, e.g. cerebral organoids or neural chimeras. Comprised of an estimated 100 billion neurons surrounded by at least as many glial cells (cells that provide structural and functional support to neurons) and, by some estimates, as many as one quadrillion synaptic connections (which allow for communication between neurons),[58] the human brain presents a spectacular challenge to the natural sciences. For obvious reasons, living tissues from human brains are generally unavailable, and animals, even non-human primates, provide inadequate models of human neuropsychiatric disease.

Fortunately, *in vitro* human-derived cells coaxed along a neural trajectory provide a veritable *tour de force* of self-development, exhibiting specific cell types and regional structures as diverse as the forebrain, striatum, retina, thalamus, and spinal cord. Moreover, advances extending culture times and improving culture conditions have allowed the generation of cells that recapitulate natural developmental properties of migration, circuit formation, and electrical activity. In addition, neural organoids can be structurally paired with one another or with other cell or tissue types to produce "assembloids," which can include immune cells, diverse neural cell types, and even functional connections that provide sensory input and motor output.

Beyond delivering crucial insights into healthy brain development, cerebral organoids and assembloids have already provided important insights into pathological processes such as motor neuron disease, autism, microcephaly, and schizophrenia. Cerebral organoids have been maintained in culture for over a year[59] and parallel many milestones of gestational and early post-natal brain development,[60] even demonstrating spontaneous, synchronous electrical activity resembling the brain activity of human preterm neonates.[61] Furthermore, human neural organoids and assembloids can be transplanted into animal recipients or chimeric animals can (theoretically) be produced with the intention of generating significant neural contributions from human cells.[62]

Given the importance of the brain in constituting identity, these laboratory-generated cell systems may help to illuminate the biological basis of certain unique and distinguishing characteristics and capacities of human nature. What biological feature or features of human evolutionary history (phylogeny) or individual development (ontogeny) form the basis of human distinctiveness? Neural organoids containing chimpanzee, Neandertal, or Denisovan genes have unveiled important differences in brain development.[63] Likewise, DNA sequences that are specific to the human lineage can be inserted into animal embryos (one form of "hybrids" or transgenic animals) or organoids to assess their developmental impact and infer their contribution to human uniqueness.

Increasing understanding of and control over the brain, facilitated by these tools of developmental biology, may reveal potential avenues for enhancements that significantly impact the human experience. Human cerebral organoids have been transplanted successfully into mice, showing functional integration with pre-existing neural circuits.[64] Without language or demonstrable deployment of intellectual powers, their behavior is not reasonably classifiable as "human." However, mice engrafted with human glial stem cell progenitors (cells that give rise to glial cells – see above) improved in learning how to navigate mazes.[65] Insertion of *MCPH1*, a key human neurodevelopmental gene, into rhesus macaques resulted in protracted brain development (characteristic of human development), quicker reaction time, and better short-term memory.[66] Furthermore, in a striking experiment, transplanting a primitive brain region between quail and chicks caused the crow of the transplant recipient bird to resemble that of the transplant donor species.[67] Could pre-programmed neural tissues be inserted into humans to confer capacities or propensities in a piecewise fashion? Could the range of sensory experience be increased, e.g. bestowing the ability to see ultraviolet or polarized light by implanting retinal organoids with modified layers and receptors? Could memory or learning be amplified by expanding cortical tissue with organoids (perhaps with advantageous genomic alterations)? How would these augmentations affect one's subjective experience, self-understanding, and interactions with others in society who relate to their environment differently?

Most profoundly, will our greater knowledge of neurodevelopmental pathways give us new perspectives on and powers over the biological basis of human moral and spiritual awareness and action, perhaps by augmenting features of empathy, self-control, emotional regulation, or specialized types of cognition? Are some humans biologically disposed to virtuous behavior (if so, according to the values and virtues of which community)? These queries plumb the limits of our self-understanding, raising deep and fundamental questions about the source of human freedom, the respective roles of emotion, desire, intuition, and analytic reasoning in moral behavior, and the conception of "the good life" that should orient our moral sensibility. Pondering these questions, studies of developmental biology may help us understand the ancient phylogenetic origins and complex embodied foundations of moral behavior, dissuading us from simplistic notions such as the description of oxytocin as "the moral molecule" that would lead us to seek "silver-bullet," bioengineered solutions to the most profound spiritual issues of human life.[68]

Cerebral organoids and neural chimeras serve as a powerful reminder of the intricate interrelations and integrated unity of the human body and mind. More than any other organ or organ system, the development and operation of the nervous system is dependent on and woven into the structures and processes of the wider organism. Its cell-cell connections and circuits, which is to say the very architecture that defines the nervous system's functionality, are pruned or promoted by physical and social experience.

From its grounding in the body, with its integration of sensory, affective, and motor operation, our conscious and comprehending mind seeks a coherent understanding of the intelligible natural order within which we dwell. In the context and process of organismal life, the realm of conceptual thought and subjective awareness exerts a real and efficacious formative influence on the developing neural circuits – their states, connections, capacities, and tendencies. Unlike any other creature in the natural world, we come to be governed by ideals and aspirations that provide a top-down causation that gives personal meaning and empowered purpose to our lives. Only here is the significance of human development and the inadequacy of a mechanical model fully revealed.

Within the frame of these considerations, we come to a deeper understanding that mechanical metaphors, furnished by isolated studies in test tubes, offer only a limited description of biological organisms. After all, fermentation, the biological mechanism *par excellence* that shattered vitalism in the 19th and 20th centuries, is not life itself, but a partial and incomplete subsystem of life. Without endorsing forms of substantive vitalism, it is important to reaffirm the unique organismal character of living beings. Just as correcting the error of vitalism led to positive progress through the investigation of life on the biochemical level, so, now, to open further avenues of scientific advance, we have argued that the claims of reductionism need to be supplemented by a richer notion of organismic biology. This notion must take account of human development and behavior in light of a systems-theoretic perspective of biological processes that acknowledges not only the complicated, non-linear quality of life's mechanistic dimensions but also the real causal influence of abstract concepts, principles, and ideals on human existence. Such a notion could serve as a crucial corrective for imprudent schemes of human enhancement proposed by certain advocates of technologically directed social engineering or guided evolution.

4.1.9 Stability and change: The phylogeny of development

The biological paradigm sketched thus far explains why it is difficult to introduce radical changes into living systems. The dynamic, interconnected way in which living bodies encode and express organismic adaptations means that any change to a part impacts the rest of the system in some way (to greater or lesser degrees). Totally novel characteristics in a part may endanger the stability and harmonious functioning of the whole.

Yet radically novel changes in organismic structure and function *have* given rise to better-adapted organisms throughout evolutionary history, and all living things presumably remain open to evolution by virtue of their biological nature. How does nature maintain the ability to change while also preserving the stable continuity of traits required for survival, reproduction, and the transmission of a coherent way of life? This is a crucial consideration at the center of the issue of technologically mediated biological enhancement and the human future.

With this question, we open our inquiry to the most fundamental insights of developmental biology and through them to our distinctive place within the panoply of phylogenetic process. By its very nature, biological life is precarious, played out against the opportunities and challenges of a changing world. Viewed within the broadest frame, life has the character of a quest, with species at once consolidating and preserving their strengths while seeking, by adaptive refinement, to extend their realm and reach in articulate engagement with the environments in which they dwell.

Even in the simplest single-cell organisms, this essential balance is sustained through the responsive dynamics of developmental processes. At the most fundamental level, an organism must establish a boundary – a semipermeable biological border that secures its integrity and identity while establishing a controlled interface capable of selectively mediating functional interaction with the outside world. Likewise, within the cell, life processes do not proceed in a homogeneous, "bubbling" chemical soup but within the constraints of diverse biological compartments which, through highly specific enzymatic processes, channel the synthesis (and breakdown) of biomolecules at rates millions of times faster than uncatalyzed reactions. These biochemical pathways and products, in turn, are governed, not in a simple linear fashion vulnerable to minor perturbations but within the complex, redundant networks of self-correcting and self-maintaining feedback loops that sustain the physiologic balance essential to organismic life.

These stabilizing structures and robust systems of control set the foundations for life's adaptive ascent to higher levels of developmental complexity; even as life consolidated and secured its continuity, it evolved for evolvability – for refinement and flexibility of response. At the most fundamental level, this balance of species' continuity and constructive change is evident in the intergenerational transmission of long-term genetic memory by the macromolecule DNA. Finely tuned enzymatic mechanisms assure a remarkable level of accuracy in the replication (and ongoing repair) of DNA – yet this group of enzymes allows a variable (and strategically deployed) range in the rate of mutations. The lability of the genetic code is directly exploited: in bacteria and yeast (and similar phenomena have been noted in higher organisms[69]), hostile environmental conditions increase genetic instability, raising the probability of successful survival by diversification through mutation.[70] Even under favorable environmental conditions, "errors" in genome replication allow for diversity to proliferate – some bacterial species can divide in just 20 to 30 minutes, producing tens of thousands of varied forms within a few hours, creating potentially adaptive phenotypes that are essentially biological experiments.

While early bacterial life forms adapted through reproduction by division with mutation, more complex systems soon evolved that allowed *individual organisms* to adjust to changing environmental conditions by responsive modulation of the timing and magnitude of gene expression. Through a range of regulatory mechanisms, gene expression (the process of transcribing DNA into RNA and translating RNA into protein products) can be enhanced and promoted or repressed and silenced in individual cells. These mechanisms include transcription factors encoded in the DNA that initiate specific gene expression patterns, and reversible non-coded chemical "markings" (e.g. methylation, acetylation, histone modification) that activate or inhibit gene expression through structural and chemical modifications (a phenomenon broadly captured by the term epigenetics) – and additional epigenetic mechanisms continue to be discovered. It is notable, and functionally significant, that factors originating both within the cell (e.g. cytoplasmic cofactors) and outside the cell (e.g. steroid hormones) can have epigenetic effects. Taken together, they serve the in-built programs of natural development while providing the flexibility for responsive adjustment to the opportunities and challenges of environmental conditions. Indeed, some of these epigenetic adjustments, though they are not encoded in the DNA sequence, serve as a kind of "short-term" inheritance across one or a few generations, thereby passing along adaptive responses to environmental conditions (such as food sources, toxins, climate changes, etc.) experienced by recent ancestors.

Looking back over nearly four billion years, one can recognize how important these ancient control mechanisms have been in setting the platform for the increase in adaptive flexibility and freedom that has characterized the trajectory of the evolutionary process. Most dramatically, the regulation of gene expression (together with cell-cell signaling and cell adhesion) is the central mechanism of developmental biology at the core of complex multicellular life. Through the evolution of developmental programs for tightly controlled gene expression, the same genome can be selectively employed to produce a wide range of different cell types. This, in turn, set the foundation for another great leap in evolutionary history: the modularization of body parts – specialized tissues, organs, and multiorgan systems that allowed the vast proliferation of animal forms with their wide range of distinctive strengths and ways of being in the world.

It is here where the importance of the study of developmental biology is most evident. Differentiation and modularity are the key biological processes that make possible the complementary division of labor and synergistic unity of functions at the heart of organismal life. Here also, the modulation of gene expression takes on a new role: embryogenesis (the coordinated development of parts) can best be understood as sequential patterns of cell differentiation promoted by intracellular and intercellular factors affecting gene expression. As we come to understand the remarkable conservation and continuity of genes across vast swaths of the evolutionary process (humans and bananas share about 20% of protein-coding gene sequences[71] while humans and mice share 70%,[72] and humans and chimpanzees share 96%[73]), we are recognizing that the great diversity of animal forms, especially in close ancestral species, is not so much a matter of mutations in protein-coding genes as it is in differences in the quantity and chronology of gene expression. This, in turn, suggests that a key locus of operation in programs of human enhancement might be the targeting of regulatory sequences affecting gene expression rather than the direct editing of protein-coding gene sequences themselves. Moreover, mapping the differential expression of proteins in disparate cells, tissues, and organs will allow modern medicine to engineer biopharmaceuticals[74] that preferentially act on particular parts or precise processes in the body – and this, more and more powerfully, with the increasingly detailed understanding of development gained through the study of clones, organoids, and chimeras.

4.2 Biotechnology and the fullness of human freedom

4.2.1 Brain, mind, and human freedom

The modulation of gene expression and modularization of body parts reach their most significant extension in the emergence of the central nervous system – and, specifically, the human brain (and mind). An estimated 30 to 50% of our genome is specifically dedicated to neurological development. Comprised of hundreds (and by some estimates thousands) of distinct cell types, the nervous system is intricately interwoven and functionally integrated with nearly every aspect of the human organism. It is here, in a deeper appreciation of the psychophysical unity of the human person, that we begin to see the full significance of our physical nature and the evolutionary process that formed us.

With the earliest emergence of brains more than 500 million years ago, the limited adaptive capacities of selective perception and locomotion in simple organisms were transcended by more responsive programs of unified organismal activity, including innate reflex arcs of nerves and muscles triggered by external stimuli.[75] These advances allowed the extension of life into more varied and challenging environments such as dry land, which required tighter regulation of internal physiology, e.g. water, pH, and temperature. This, in turn, led to the refinement of integrated sensory, motor, and endocrine systems – the biological basis of emotions – together with a more coherent "inner" sense of subjective feelings and desires (appetites and aversions).

This combination of precise physiological regulation and encoded value set the embodied foundations for the emergence of the mind – and, specifically, the human mind as the fullest expression of the evolutionary dynamic of continuity and creative extension. Most fundamentally, this sustained biological stability serves as the essential condition for a sense of enduring physical identity; together with peripheral sensory awareness of body surface and proprioception of body position, this inner awareness of bodily state is the basis for the human person's sense of self.

Likewise, this remarkably invariant reference of the "self" anchored in the body serves as a stable standard against which perturbation or alteration can be compared and against which change can be measured – the basis of learning and its encoding as memory. As neuroscientist Antonio Damasio explains,

> the body, as represented in the brain, may constitute the indispensable frame of reference for the neural processes that we experience as the mind; that our very organism rather than some absolute external reality is used as the ground reference for the constructions we make of the world around us and for the constructions of the ever-present sense of subjectivity that is part and parcel of our experiences.[76]

Moreover, our capacity for learning is in direct relationship with the distinctively open and indeterminate character of the human form: our upright posture, dexterous hands (what Aristotle called "the tool of tools"), highly flexible range of motion, and multi-modal sense perception, etc.[77] Recent AI studies of "morphological intelligence" appear to confirm this correlation between body form and ability to learn, especially within complex and challenging environments.[78] Freed from the fixed action patterns and routinized behaviors of our animal ancestors, our mind is shaped and sculpted by our interactions with the environment around us; stretching forth as active agents, we probe and penetrate the world, learning at once both the nature of the world and our place and powers within it.

In *Philosophy in the Flesh*, George Lakoff and Mark Johnson explore the significance of our "embodied mind" for its implications in individual consciousness and social communication.[79] They argue that the mental operations of reasoning are not literal but metaphorical, that the very structures of our categories and concepts come from the nature of our bodily experience – the world as we know it by actively living within it. Time, for example, is conceptually understood by its representation of our experience of movement through space.

This way of grounding our understanding of the world in the commonalities of our bodily experience, and most especially during early cognitive development, means that much of our individual conceptual system is widespread or universal among human beings. Together with our refined adaptations for social communication (over 40 muscles of facial expression; laryngeal structures for highly flexible vocalization, white sclerae for ease in tracking gaze, etc.), this shared character of our embodied consciousness provides the medium for empathic intersubjectivity and symbolic language, the interpersonal connections essential for the coherence and constructive cooperation of the social community.

The extraordinary amplification of human comprehension and control of the natural world made possible by the ongoing conversation of social community further extends the evolutionary dynamic of continuity and change. Cultural preservation of the accumulated skills and wisdom of human experience – transmitted in the developmental process of education – sets the platform for the elaboration of new conceptual and mechanical tools that greatly extend our realm and reach. Whereas most creatures employ direct physical or behavior adaptations (embodied "tools" such as specialized claws, teeth, or instincts), human beings address their challenges and opportunities through ideas; insights and design solutions are then put into practical operation through specialized external devices (tools) that extend our senses and magnify our powers.[80]

What began in the earliest life forms as chance mutation played out within the constraints of the physio-chemical process has, through the course of evolution, culminated in the creative indeterminacy of the human imagination: mutations of matter are transcended by permutations of mind, the self-generated production of possibilities independent of the constraints of immediate material reality. Detached from time and space, imagined scenarios can be played out in a kind of mental "dress rehearsal," to anticipate their implications and outcomes without the expense of time and cost of resources in the process. The human capacity for imagination, however, goes far beyond adaptive anticipation; imagination is not merely reshuffled memory but envisioned creation. Forming mental images, maintaining them in the mind, and achieving their realization signifies intention, planning, and implementation of ideals. Together with our ability to calculate, extrapolate, and recombine, our creative imagination is used to reconfigure that which is into that which could be.

4.2.2 Biotechnology, developmental biology, and human enhancement

These distinctively human capacities reach their deepest drama (and danger) with the exponential increase in our knowledge and control over the human body. While most creatures are "pushed" by biological and ecological imperatives, as our powers over nature and human nature increase, we find ourselves "pulled" into the future by our images of fullest flourishing. Emancipated from the exigencies of basic survival, we attain a state unprecedented in the history of life: the freedom of aspiration toward envisioned ideals – together with the technological powers to attempt their realization.[81]

Yet even this brief outline of the phylogenetic foundations of human freedom and the intimate relationship of body and mind should impel us to pause and thoughtfully ponder the depth of the challenge of human enhancement. If we are to avoid the twin dangers of ignorance and arrogance

– if we are to proceed with wisdom – we must ask fundamental questions about how our images of the human future relate to what we know of our evolutionary origins and their implications for the development of individual human beings.

From these reflections, it is evident that the phylogenetic process is, above all, the evolution of comprehensive developmental programs: adaptive phenotypes arise, not by a simple additive accumulation of advantageous traits, but through harmoniously coordinated developmental revisions integrated within the organismal whole. So with regard to the human future, we must ask ourselves:

(1) What changes at the deepest levels of development account for our species' distinctive strengths? In what ways are these direct (and perhaps culminating) extensions of broader trends evident in the earlier phylogenetic process?
(2) What foundation of stable core capacities supports the range of variation within human populations and in human individuals over the course of a lifetime?
(3) In what ways, and by what integrated organic processes, have our physical, psychological, and social characteristics co-evolved?
(4) And, crucially, is the current human species simply a stepping stone toward a fuller and more flourishing human form? If so, are there unrecognized ongoing natural evolutionary processes at work reshaping our species, or is it human destiny (as transhumanists believe) to determine the human future by the application of our biotechnology?

Within the scientific community, there is intense interest in these central questions regarding human life. Drawing on comparative genomics (between species), ancient DNA (from bones, mummified tissues, hair, etc.), and widespread whole genome sequencing of diverse living populations, we are piecing together the transformations that brought us forward from our ancestral origins. As expected, many of our genetic differences – such as human-lineage-specific (HLS) sequences and human accelerated regions (HARs) – appear to play a role in neurodevelopment, but alterations in our musculo-skeletal system, energy utilization and metabolism, and immune system are equally evident, as are genetically based developmental changes related to sociality. However, these changes do not emerge and operate in parallel, but as integrated processes where a single genetic change may affect multiple systems at once (for example neurological and immunological development[82]), again underscoring the complex interwoven unity of the human organism – and the technical difficulty of proposed projects of human evolution by design.

One particularly fascinating finding relates to what has been called the "less is more" mechanism.[83] Genomic studies have identified over 500 locations in the human genome where we have lost regulatory sequences that are otherwise highly conserved between earlier mammals and chimps.[84] While we generally do not think of genetic loss as promoting fitness, some of these mutations have been associated with constructive developmental changes, including selective promotion of neural development. Others, however, have been associated with losses of specialized functional adaptations found in our animal ancestors, particularly constraints that channel dietary choices and reproductive behaviors. This raises the interesting possibility that through the "relaxation" of deterministic genetic mechanisms that fine-tune other species to a particular niche, human beings became a more "general purpose organism": what is lost in specialization is gained in breadth.[85] Together with the unique flexibility and freedom evident in our anatomical form, and our high level of neural plasticity, this set the conditions for greater "top-down" neurological control of human behavior.

Seen in this way, our "specialization" is our capacity for conscious comprehension and purposeful operation within the intelligible order of the given world. Notably indeterminate in both bodily action and agility of mind, we are adapted for adaptability, for stability of form, and malleability of being. While other creatures have specialized fur or feathers, we are the creature that is born naked but clothed by culture. Open and unscripted, yet capacious in possibility, we have populated and dominated the earth. It is in keeping with the very core of our character that we would now turn our technology to the transformation of human life.

These reflections on the phylogenetic foundations and deeply integrated physical, psychological, and social developmental patterns of human beings provide a cautionary frame for considering the application of our new biotechnological powers. Seeking to improve the parts, we could unbalance the whole and thereby degrade our distinctive human strengths.[86] Moreover, it seems clear that any deep transformations in human character or capacities would require experimentation at such a fundamental level of human development (embryonic and fetal stages) that it could violate basic principles of human dignity. But this raises a deeper question: if we were truly able to reshape human nature with no moral dangers or disproportionate risks, what kinds of alterations or specializations would we want? (For example, what would constitute an improvement of the human hand?) Could it be that we are already optimized as general purpose organisms, the endpoint of an evolutionary process toward the most functional balance of stable continuity and creative extension?[87] And, in any case, what is the relationship between the "given" and the "good," the natural balance of conditions and characteristics of our species (with its sense of meaning and purpose even amid our struggles and sufferings) and the fuller flourishing envisioned in our imagined ideals of human life?[88]

Some argue with a forceful conviction for a distinction between therapy and enhancement, and there is a certain wisdom in this approach.[89] In the end, however, a medical model is inadequate for our task. For one thing, social and cultural traditions often play a role in the definition of disease; what is a physiologically healthy human variation may in certain cultural settings be considered a disorder justifying therapeutic intervention (as with short stature and the use of growth hormone). Likewise, certain preventative or protective interventions enhance natural powers to resist disease. And, finally, normal changes across the human lifespan involve a loss of healthy functions such as fertility or muscle strength – is natural aging a disease? Moreover, health is not the only human good, and there are circumstances where a non-therapeutic use of biotechnology could be clearly acceptable: consider the case of a surgeon using a drug to steady her hands (even at some risk to herself) while performing a delicate operation on the eye of a child.[90]

Yet, placed within our reflections on phylogeny and developmental biology, there are some scientific and moral principles that may guide the applications of our biotechnology for purposes beyond traditional notions of medical therapy. Most fundamentally, it is clear that both in its development and ongoing function, the human organism is an intricately integrated psychophysical unity; as every thoughtful physician knows, any intervention on the human body comes with a risk of disrupting or unbalancing the well-working of the whole.[91] Moreover, human nature has evolved in coordinated complementarity with the physical conditions and social relations that give shape and significance to our lives; anything that alters or unbalances these relational dynamics may subtly (or dramatically) diminish our sense of meaning and purpose. Wherever possible, both in the restoration of health and in seeking to fulfill individual and social aspirations, we should engage the immanent powers of our natural being. To be justified, any technological intervention should, in its effect, transcend what is possible by reasonable levels of individual effort or social reform.[92]

Likewise, where technological interventions are deemed necessary or acceptable, they should, as far as possible, be precisely targeted and temporary. From the discussions above, it is clear that there are layers of development and ongoing physiological operations that are more foundational and pervasive in effect than others. If we picture development through the image of a growing tree, coding genes are like the trunk that supports and gives form to the branches; any alterations at this level early in embryogenesis will have a permanent and pervasive impact on many dimensions of the body's formation and operation (see our comments on pleiotropy and polygenic inheritance above). Alterations of gene regulation, however, may be targeted to specific cells or tissues (the branches) and have a more limited effect on the overall functioning of the organism.[93] And, at the highest levels (the leaves), small molecule pharmaceuticals that temporarily attach to and alter the function of targeted proteins, may have very specific local effects and only a minor impact on the whole organism.[94]

Viewed through the perspective of this metaphorical description, the significance of the era of developmental biology can be most fully grasped. The study of human development, including clones, chimeras, and organoids, will help illuminate in great detail the molecular mechanisms and developmental dynamics of human biology, delivering precise and powerful new tools for highly efficient and effective interventions in human life, both in clinical care and beyond therapy. The constructive possibilities implied by this are extraordinary, both for our understanding of human nature and for positive practical applications. Nonetheless, it is important to recognize that interventions at any level may have effects on many aspects of the organismal operation – physical, psychological, and social. Even a single dose of Tylenol temporarily up-regulates or down-regulates dozens of genes![95] Every intervention, from chemotherapy to cannabis to cosmetic surgery, comes with a potential cost or potential loss. Even seemingly trivial enhancements of human function (such as with coffee or red wine) provide temporary benefits that must be physiologically rebalanced by compensatory homeostatic mechanisms which can include uncomfortable physical feelings (hangover), psychological states (anxiety), and disrupted social relations (irritability). This is the concern that underlies the primary principle of medical tradition, the Hippocratic admonition "Above all, do no harm."

Seen in this way, any biotechnological intervention, either for therapy or enhancement, must be weighed in proportion to the seriousness of its purpose: the deeper, more pervasive, and more permanent its impact, the more serious and significant it must be within a comprehensive understanding of the meaning and purpose of human life – and not just from a medical perspective.[96] As expressed by the President's Council on Bioethics, we must move to a wider ethical perspective, beyond a medical evaluation, and even beyond the medical frame implied by the term "beyond therapy":

> for medicine, sickness, and healing are not the natural or best lens through which to look upon the whole of human life. Health, though a primary human good, is not the only – or even the supreme – human good. Going beyond therapy in this sense means returning to an account of the human being seen not in material or mechanistic or medical terms but in psychic and moral and spiritual ones.[97]

Viewed from this perspective, the emphasis in the ethical evaluation of a given biotechnology for purposes of enhancement might best be understood as a kind of "sacrifice," involving a certain risk or loss to an individual for the sake of a larger good.[98] The deeper the potential cost, the greater must be the seriousness for which the intervention is undertaken – serious from an individual, social, and species perspective. At times, and for worthy purposes – such as during a natural disaster or unavoidable military combat – drugs or procedures that can sustain strength, sharpen focus, or overcome fatigue may serve a noble cause to rescue and restore, or to resist evil.[99] Likewise, for certain endeavors of exploration, such as space travel or deep-sea scientific study, interventions might be justifiable. And, in some circumstances, individual use of agents to facilitate projects in the service of beauty or truth, or to heighten constructive social interaction might be justifiable – but only where the goals are not self-indulgent or for competitive purposes corrosive to the social community. And, in all cases, the means and ends must comport in the service of human identity and integrity. Above all, we should avoid invasive interventions (genetic or otherwise) whose aim is the creation of a permanent subset of human beings with specialized abilities or talents. This kind of production of persons for instrumental purposes is a violation of basic human dignity and an abnegation of our central human strength as a "general purpose" species; such a use of our technology would be the moral equivalent of voting to end democracy!

All of this means acknowledging the serious significance of human life, the dignity (and mystery) of the human person, and the deep currents of thought that must guide us. This approach to ethical evaluation and application of our advancing biotechnologies must be set within a wisdom that is far more encompassing than what we can know through the reductive and analytic mode of our current empirical science. While recognizing the astonishingly intricate and interwoven molecular foundations of the human being (the *physical* frame of our flexibility and freedom), it acknowledges the values, beliefs, and principles that provide the central axis and infrastructure of human life – and the primacy of ideas that aligns our aspirations and empower our actions – ideas for which a human being may, for the sake of the highest good, be willing to die.

There is an old saying, "The first principle of intelligent tinkering is to not throw away any of the parts." We must not be so foolish as to arrogantly ignore the natural biological foundations that are the very frame of our human freedom nor the treasures of our artistic, literary, philosophical, and spiritual traditions that make that freedom truly free. The very future of our species may depend on this.

Notes

1 The explanation and interpretation of the story of the vitalist controversy is drawn from William B. Hurlbut, "Framing the Future: Embryonic Stem Cells, Ethics and the Emerging Era of Developmental Biology," *Pediatric Research* (2006), which cites Arthur Kornberg, *For the Love of Enzymes*, Harvard University Press (1989) as the original source of this vitalist narrative.
2 K.H.S. Campbell et al., "Sheep Cloned by Nuclear Transfer from a Cultured Cell Line," *Nature* (1996).
3 Sayaka Wakayama et al., "Successful Serial Recloning in the Mouse over Multiple Generations," *Cell Stem Cell* (2013).
4 Carl Zimmer, "A New Company With a Wild Mission: Bring Back the Woolly Mammoth," *The New York Times* (2021). Amy Dockser Marcus, "Meet the Scientists Bringing Extinct Species Back From the Dead," *Wall Street Journal* (2018).
5 Zhen Liu et al., "Cloning of Macaque Monkeys by Somatic Cell Nuclear Transfer," *Cell* (2018). These cynomolgus monkey clones were produced using *fetal* dermal fibroblast nuclei, so in some sense, there has not yet been a "monkey Dolly." No greater or lesser apes have been successfully cloned and gestated.
6 Sexual reproduction reshuffles the genes to produce a unique genetic foundation for the developing organism.
7 Gene expression yields cytoplasmic proteins, which in turn regulate gene expression.
8 Steven Rose and Steven Pinker, "The Two Steves (Part I): A Debate," *Edge* is the transcript of a debate held on January 21, 1998, at London University's Institute of Education.
9 From the Greek ὀργανισμός *organismos*, from ὄργανον *organon*, "tool" – the organism is a unity of tools. In *The Hungry Soul: Eating and the Perfecting of Our Nature*, University of Chicago Press (1999), Leon Kass says, "Organization – literally, the division of the whole into instrumentally active parts (the word *organ* means "instrument" or "tool," and *organization* means "the condition of systematic coordination of distinct instrumental parts or organs") – is, in a sense, the distinctive form of organism" (p. 37).
10 From this perspective, within the first cell (whether it be the joining of sperm and egg or the product of cloning), the "genetic material" from which the individual human is "generated" is rightly recognized *not as the DNA alone* but as the entire cell in its web of dynamic operations. To recognize this, one needs to consider the confusion implied by two different uses of the term genetics (from the Greek word γένεσις *genesis* meaning "origin"): in phylogeny and ontogeny. DNA is rightly considered the major bearer of our species' long-term inheritance, the molecular consolidation of form that allows for intergenerational continuity. But DNA is not the only ontological factor in the development of an individual being and is thus not properly the "origin" of the organism. Taking the organism as the paradigm for life, we recognize that to call cells in artificial culture conditions "alive" is to equivocate; this is part of the reductive and analytic error, equating aliveness with chemistry. "Life" can only persist apart from organismal life – which involves self-enveloping, self-sustaining unity of organic operation – because of human intervention. Without human intervention, such process, cells, tissues, organoids will become disorganized and die. For this reason, organoids (at least as currently produced) are not rightly considered "organisms" with the moral implications of the term – and therefore, an uncontroversial way to study developmental biology.
11 Donald Campbell, "'Downward Causation' in Hierarchically Organised Biological Systems," in *Studies in the Philosophy of Biology: Reduction and Related Problems*, edited by Francisco Jose Ayala and Theodosius Dobzhansky, *Macmillan Education UK* (1974). Campbell paraphrases downward causation as the principle

12. Very few phenotypic traits are the result of a single gene, though one notable exception is red hair.
13. Katja Luck et al., "A Reference Map of the Human Binary Protein Interactome," *Nature* (2020). Some have drafted a reference "interactome" to serve as a map of the complex, interrelated processes within the cell that are involved in the phenotypic expression of genetic information.
14. For example, cystic fibrosis can result in overly salty sweat, jaundice, malabsorption, infertility, and lung infections. A discussion of the conceptual difficulties in attempts to explain pleiotropy can be found in Annalise Paaby and Matthew V. Rockman, "The Many Faces of Pleiotropy," *Trends in Genetics* (2013).
15. Examples: Down, Angelman, DiGeorge, Turner, and Fragile X Syndromes.
16. Evan Boyle, Yang I. Li, and Jonathan K. Pritchard, "An Expanded View of Complex Traits: From Polygenic to Omnigenic," *Cell* (2017) have proposed an "omnigenic" cellular model in which the phenotypic effect of every gene is influenced to some degree by any and all other genes, though genes in "core pathways" have larger and more direct effects on phenotype while other "peripheral" genes have smaller and more indirect effects on phenotype. Relatedly, in "Change of Environment and Speciation," *Evolution and the Diversity of Life: Selected Essays*, Belknap Press of Harvard University Press (1976), Ernst Mayr postulates, "The better integrated… a gene complex is, the smaller the chance that a novel mutation will lead to an improvement" (p.198).
17. Jeffrey L. Blanchard et al., "Rapid Changes in Gene Expression Dynamics in Response to Superoxide Reveal SoxRS-Dependent and Independent Transcriptional Networks," *PLoS ONE* (2007). In *E. coli*, gene expression can change rapidly within a few minutes. Shahram Bahrami and Finn Drabløs, "Gene Regulation in the Immediate-Early Response Process," *Advances in Biological Regulation* (2016). Some human genes appear primed for expression within minutes of extracellular signals, with peak expression achieved in under an hour.
18. David Bick et al., "An Online Compendium of Treatable Genetic Disorders," *American Journal of Medical Genetics* (2021).
19. Paul Knoepfler, "George Church on Germline Human Genetic Modification," *The Niche* (2015).
20. Sean P. Ryder, "#CRISPRbabies: Notes on a Scandal," *CRISPR Journal* (2018). Though Jiankui attempted to confer upon the twins a natural variation of *CCR5* that is protective against HIV infection, his CRISPR-based intervention resulted in *CCR5* mutations not seen in nature and only affected some copies of *CCR5*. Miou Zhou et al., "CCR5 Is a Suppressor for Cortical Plasticity and Hippocampal Learning and Memory," *eLife* (2016). Mary T. Joy et al., "CCR5 Is a Therapeutic Target for Recovery after Stroke and Traumatic Brain Injury," *Cell* (2019). *CCR5* also appears to play important roles in neurological function. Decreased *CCR5* expression has been associated with memory enhancement in mice as well as improved recovery from stroke and traumatic brain injury in humans, with possible implications for broader cognition. For a review of these and other known effects of *CCR5* on human health, see MengMeng Xu, "CCR5-Δ32 Biology, Gene Editing, and Warnings for the Future of CRISPR-Cas9 as a Human and Humane Gene Editing Tool," *Cell & Bioscience* (2020).
21. Kazutoshi Takahashi and Shinya Yamanaka, "Induction of Pluripotent Stem Cells from Mouse Embryonic and Adult Fibroblast Cultures by Defined Factors," *Cell* (2006). An elegant method that demonstrates the critical influence of just a few factors on the behavior of the wider cellular system.
22. Annalee Armstrong, "Regenerative Medicine Nears Banner Year with $14.1B Cash Infusion, Regulatory Milestones and a Well-stocked Pipeline," *Fierce Biotech* (2021). As an industry, regenerative medicine generated $20 billion in revenue in 2020, and in 2021 is on pace to break that record.
23. March of Dimes, "March of Dimes Global Report on Birth Defects" (accessed 2021).
24. Stephen R. Daniels, "The Barker Hypothesis Revisited," *Journal of Pediatrics* (2016). Hypothesis originally proposed in 1990 by David Barker.
25. Yanpu Chen et al., "Reversible Reprogramming of Cardiomyocytes to a Fetal State Drives Heart Regeneration in Mice," *Science* (2021).
26. Many of these capacities are also evident in induced pluripotent stem cells.
27. Elie Dolgin, "Flaw in Induced-stem-cell Model," *Nature* (2011). This is complicated by the fact that the characteristics of stem cell lines gradually shift when maintained outside of their original *in vivo* context. Richard Young from the Whitehead Institute in Cambridge, Massachusetts says, "When we culture cells outside a normal organism they can acquire features that may not be compatible with life once they go back into an organism" (p. 13).
28. Xiaodong Liu et al., "Modelling Human Blastocysts by Reprogramming Fibroblasts into IBlastoids," *Nature* (2021). Leqian Yu et al., "Blastocyst-like Structures Generated from Human Pluripotent Stem Cells," *Nature* (2021).

29 The International Society for Stem Cell Research, in its most recent ethical guidelines – "Guidelines for Stem Cell Research and Clinical Translation" (2021) – acknowledges that a blastoid may be legitimately classified as "integrated stem cell model"; were they to attain the level of complexity, potency, and unity characteristic of organismic life, they "might realistically manifest the ability to undergo further integrated development" in the context of an appropriately nourishing environment (p. 65). J. Benjamin Hurlbut et al., "Revisiting the Warnock Rule," *Nature Biotechnology* (2017). For ethical reasons, many countries for the past few decades have restricted experimentation on human embryos to the first 14 days of life, which boundary designates the ending of the blastocyst stage. These "blastoid" embryo models raise questions about the scope of such restrictions. If blastoids can implant and develop beyond the blastocyst-like phase that they recapitulate, should the ethical boundaries intended for embryo use apply to the experimental use of these models?

30 Jianping Fu, Aryeh Warmflash, and Matthias P. Lutolf, "Stem-Cell-Based Embryo Models for Fundamental Research and Translation," *Nature Materials* (2021).

31 International Society for Stem Cell Research (ISSCR), "Guidelines for Stem Cell Research and Clinical Translation," (2021). The ISSCR classifies gastruloids as "non-integrated" embryo models (p. 65).

32 Naomi Moris et al., "An in Vitro Model of Early Anteroposterior Organization during Human Development," *Nature* (2020).

33 Jihoon Kim, Bon-Kyoung Koo, and Juergen A. Knoblich, "Human Organoids: Model Systems for Human Biology and Medicine," *Nature Reviews Molecular Cell Biology* (2020): Figure 3.

34 S.N. Ooft et al., "Prospective Experimental Treatment of Colorectal Cancer Patients Based on Organoid Drug Responses," *ESMO Open* (2021). Patient-derived colorectal cancer organoid responsiveness to chemotherapy was a poor predictor of objective clinical response. So even personalized organoids, derived from a patient's own cells, may not behave in the laboratory as in the body.

35 Ameen A. Salahudeen et al., "Progenitor Identification and SARS-CoV-2 Infection in Human Distal Lung Organoids," *Nature* (2020).

36 National Center for Advancing Translational Sciences, "NCATS-Supported Scientists Model Aging-Related Conditions in Space to Improve Human Health on Earth," National Institutes of Health (last updated 2019).

37 Shuo Xiao et al., "A Microfluidic Culture Model of the Human Reproductive Tract and 28-Day Menstrual Cycle," *Nature Communications* (2017).

38 Youssef Hibaoui and Anis Feki, "Organoid Models of Human Endometrial Development and Disease," *Frontiers in Cell and Developmental Biology* (2020). Here, the complexity of organismal, integrated functioning is especially important. In natural gestation, the organism self-develops not only through its own immanent powers, it is an interaction between two organisms, and biomedical science has yet to clarify the relational dynamics between mother and embryo.

39 Alejandro Aguilera-Castrejon et al., "Ex Utero Mouse Embryogenesis from Pre-Gastrulation to Late Organogenesis," *Nature* (2021). This experiment gestated mouse embryos to the equivalent of E11 (they were inserted into the culture medium on E5.5 and cultured for six days). There is some variation of gestational length among strains of laboratory mice, but they tend to take about 21 days. Of course, the smallness of mouse embryos (facilitating diffusion of oxygen and nutrients) and rapidity of their growth makes technical advances in artificial culture technologies much easier than the same task would be in humans. After all, the entire timeline of mouse development can fit comfortably between the first day of an academic quarter and midterms!

40 Emily A. Partridge et al., "An Extra-Uterine System to Physiologically Support the Extreme Premature Lamb," *Nature Communications* (2017). Notably, some 20 two-week old human fetuses can now be kept alive in the neonatal intensive care unit. Furthermore, sheep fetuses at 100–115 days gestation (out of 142–152 days to term) are much larger than human fetuses with similar lung maturity, facilitating the canulation of blood vessels required for artificial circulation. Overall, ectogenesis is a daunting prospect; attempts at it will demonstrate the dynamic complementarity between mother and offspring.

41 Rui Diogo, Natalia Siomava, and Yorick Gitton, "Development of Human Limb Muscles Based on Whole-Mount Immunostaining and the Links between Ontogeny and Evolution," *Development* (2019).

42 Many scientists maintain that the validity of organoid or stem cell-based embryo models for studies of human development remains unverified without comparison to living embryos. So, efforts to enhance or alter the basic frame of human development – say, by editing the genome, introducing biochemical factors or influencing bioelectrical networks (cf. Michael Levin, "Bioelectric Signaling: Reprogrammable Circuits Underlying Embryogenesis, Regeneration, and Cancer," *Cell* [2021]) – will presumably involve experimentation with human embryos at each stage of development.

43 JangoBio, "JangoBio Creating First Organoids for Complete Hormone Restoration," (2020). Other possibilities include renin-producing kidney cells for blood pressure regulation, leptin-producing cells to elicit satiety and control obesity, or parathyroid organoids for calcium and phosphorus regulation.

44   Yorick Post et al., "Snake Venom Gland Organoids," *Cell* (2020). Functional snake venom gland organoids have been created to simplify the production of anti-venom.
45   Marie Bannier-Hélaouët et al., "Exploring the Human Lacrimal Gland Using Organoids and Single-Cell Sequencing," *Cell Stem Cell* (2021). Junichi Tanaka et al., "Generation of Orthotopically Functional Salivary Gland from Embryonic Stem Cells," *Nature Communications* (2018).
46   Yutong Chen et al., "Three-Dimensional Bioprinting Adipose Tissue and Mammary Organoids Feasible for Artificial Breast Structure Regeneration," *Materials & Design* (2021).
47   Michael J. Workman et al., "Engineered Human Pluripotent-Stem-Cell-Derived Intestinal Tissues with a Functional Enteric Nervous System," *Nature Medicine* (2017). Joan E. Nichols et al., "Production and Transplantation of Bioengineered Lung into a Large-Animal Model," *Science Translational Medicine* (2018). Sara Campinoti, Sara et al., "Reconstitution of a Functional Human Thymus by Postnatal Stromal Progenitor Cells and Natural Whole-Organ Scaffolds," *Nature Communications* (2020).
48   Tilly Pearce, "This Morning Viewers Left Stunned by Parrot Man Who Cut off His EARS to Look like the Bird," *The Sun* (2016). Ted Richards received tattoos, implants, and had his ears removed in order to look more like his parrots. Joshua Haigh, "The Story behind the Changing Face of 'Catwoman' Jocelyn Wildenstein," *Mirror* (2016). Jocelyn Wildenstein underwent cosmetic changes to appear more like her pet lynx. The developmental dynamics of organs such as antlers are the focus of serious scientific research. Jason Bittel, "Antlers Are Miraculous Face Organs That Could Benefit Human Health," *Smithsonian Magazine* (2017). One of us (Hurlbut) has also written, "Late stage, post-anatomical transplant of animal parts into humans should only be done in order to heal or restore human form or function, never to alter, enhance, or degrade it – no animal sense organs, muscular or skeletal enhancements, no hooves, horns, feathers, fur, fangs, or antlers, and definitely no tails" (in "The Boundaries of Humanity: The Ethics of Human–Animal Chimeras in Cloning and Stem Cell Research," in *Is This Cell a Human Being?*, ed. Antoine Suarez and Joachim Huarte, Springer [2011], p. 168). Pramod Janardan Giri and Vaibhav Sharadrao Chavan, "Human Tail: A Benign Condition Hidden Out of Social Stigma and Shame in Young Adult – A Case Report and Review," *Asian Journal of Neurosurgery* (2019). Furthermore, there are 40 instances of human beings born with tails. Whether this is due to genetic factors or environmental factors has yet to be determined.
49   Tomohiro Kohama et al., "*In vitro* production of viable eggs from isolated mouse primary follicles by successive culture," *The Journal of Reproduction and Development* (2022).
50   Xiaoyong Li et al., "Generation of Offspring-Producing 3D Ovarian Organoids Derived from Female Germline Stem Cells and Their Application in Toxicological Detection," *Biomaterials* 279 (2021). https://doi.org/10.1016/j.biomaterials.2021.121213. E. Oliver and J.-B. Stukenborg, "Rebuilding the Human Testis in Vitro," *Andrology* (2020). Lama Alzamil, Konstantina Nikolakopoulou, and Margherita Y. Turco, "Organoid Systems to Study the Human Female Reproductive Tract and Pregnancy," *Cell Death & Differentiation* (2021).
51   Benjamin Dekel et al., "Human and Porcine Early Kidney Precursors as a New Source for Transplantation," *Nature Medicine* (2003).
52   Ike Swetlitz, "Scientist Pushes Fetal Tissue Research Despite Political Pressure," *STAT* (2016).
53   Julian Savulescu, "Should We Clone Human Beings? Cloning as a Source of Tissue for Transplantation," *Journal of Medical Ethics* (1999). Recall, as mentioned earlier, cloned human embryos have never been successfully implanted in a womb.
54   Toshihiro Kobayashi et al., "Generation of Rat Pancreas in Mouse by Interspecific Blastocyst Injection of Pluripotent Stem Cells," *Cell* (2010). A mouse cell-derived pancreas in a rat host grows to the size and structure of a rat pancreas. Jun Wu et al., "Interspecies Chimerism with Mammalian Pluripotent Stem Cells," *Cell* (2017). Notably, the host organism body plan also dictates *which* organs are present. Though rats do not have gallbladders, chimeric mice with rat donor cells can develop gallbladders comprised primarily of rat cells because the body plan of the mouse prevails.
55   Zhixing Hu et al., "Transient Inhibition of MTOR in Human Pluripotent Stem Cells Enables Robust Formation of Mouse-Human Chimeric Embryos," *Science Advances* (2020). Breakthrough achievement of human cell contribution in mice: 0.1 to 4% human cells.
56   Tao Tan et al., "Chimeric Contribution of Human Extended Pluripotent Stem Cells to Monkey Embryos Ex Vivo," *Cell* (2021). Furthermore, the technical difficulties of interspecies chimerism also suggests that a hypothetical future in which some may find *intra*-species chimerism of humans desirable may be practically feasible. Marmoset offspring tend to chimerize naturally, suggesting that intra-organismic genetic diversity may bear evolutionary advantages in some primates. Perhaps chimerization of two embryos would be perceived as biologically or socially advantageous – e.g. for reasons of compatibility for future tissue or organ transplantation; or, perhaps, given shifting social mores related to sexuality, some may desire the production of a child that shares genetic information with multiple individuals.
57   These and other questions about capacities for pain, sentience, emotion, and cognition, especially for altered or "humanized" behavior, in synthetic biological entities have been framed in the 2021 committee

report on neural organoids, transplants, and chimeras released by the National Academies of Sciences, Engineering, and Medicine entitled *The Emerging Field of Human Neural Organoids, Transplants, and Chimeras: Science, Ethics, and Governance*, National Academies Press (2021), which calls for deeper study into these matters.

58 National Academies of Sciences, Engineering, and Medicine, *The Emerging Field of Human Neural Organoids, Transplants, and Chimeras: Science, Ethics, and Governance*, National Academies Press (2021). Sarah DeWeerdt, "How to Map the Brain," *Nature* (2019).
59 Stefano L. Giandomenico, Magdalena Sutcliffe, and Madeline A. Lancaster, "Generation and Long-Term Culture of Advanced Cerebral Organoids for Studying Later Stages of Neural Development," *Nature Protocols* (2021).
60 Aaron Gordon et al., "Long-Term Maturation of Human Cortical Organoids Matches Key Early Postnatal Transitions," *Nature Neuroscience* (2021).
61 Cleber A. Trujillo et al., "Complex Oscillatory Waves Emerging from Cortical Organoids Model Early Human Brain Network Development," *Cell Stem Cell* (2019).
62 National Academies of Sciences, Engineering, and Medicine, *The Emerging Field of Human Neural Organoids, Transplants, and Chimeras: Science, Ethics, and Governance*, National Academies Press (2021) reports, "It is not currently possible to generate neural chimeras of human cells in any non-human species that survive post-natally or even to late fetal stages." If neural chimerization is largely complicated by interspecies barriers, non-human primates may accept human tissue most easily.
63 Zev N. Kronenberg et al., "High-Resolution Comparative Analysis of Great Ape Genomes," *Science* (2018). Comparison of chimpanzee and human cerebral organoids. Cleber A. Trujillo et al., "Reintroduction of the Archaic Variant of NOVA1 in Cortical Organoids Alters Neurodevelopment," *Science* (2021). Organoids modeling Neandertal or Denisovan neural development.
64 Xin Dong et al., "Human Cerebral Organoids Establish Subcortical Projections in the Mouse Brain after Transplantation," *Molecular Psychiatry* (2021).
65 Xiaoning Han et al., "Forebrain Engraftment by Human Glial Progenitor Cells Enhances Synaptic Plasticity and Learning in Adult Mice," *Cell Stem Cell* (2013).
66 Lei Shi et al., "Transgenic Rhesus Monkeys Carrying the Human MCPH1 Gene Copies Show Human-like Neoteny of Brain Development," *National Science Review* (2019).
67 Evan Balaban, "Changes in Multiple Brain Regions Underlie Species Differences in a Complex, Congenital Behavior," *Proceedings of the National Academy of Sciences of the United States of America* (1997).
68 Ed Yong, "The Weak Science Behind the Wrongly Named Moral Molecule," *The Atlantic* (2015). Dave Mosher, "'Cuddle Chemical' Also Fuels Favoritism, Bigotry," *Wired* (2011).
69 Maynard V. Olson, "When Less Is More: Gene Loss as an Engine of Evolutionary Change," *American Journal of Human Genetics* (1999).
70 Rodrigo S. Galhardo, P. J. Hastings, and Susan M. Rosenberg, "Mutation as a Stress Response and the Regulation of Evolvability," *Critical Reviews in Biochemistry and Molecular Biology* (2007).
71 Natasha Glover, "The Banana Conjecture," *Dessimoz Lab* blog (2020).
72 National Institutes of Health, "New Comprehensive View of the Mouse Genome" (2014).
73 National Human Genome Research Institute, "New Genome Comparison," National Institutes of Health News (2005).
74 MeiraGTx, "Our Strategy: Gene Regulation" (accessed 2021). New technical advances, including CRISPR-Cas9 and synthetic riboswitches allow direct control of quantity and chronology of gene expression in specifically targeted cells.
75 Andrew Urevig, "520-Million-Year-Old Brains Found in Kerygmachela Fossil," *National Geographic* (2018).
76 Antonio Damasio, *Descartes' Error: Emotion, Reason, and the Human Brain*, Penguin (2005), p. xx.
77 Aristotle, *De Anima*, trans. C.D.C. Reeve, Hackett Publishing Company (2017), 432a1.
78 Agrim Gupta et al., "Embodied Intelligence via Learning and Evolution," *Nature Communications* (2021).
79 George Lakoff and Mark Johnson, *Philosophy in the Flesh: The Embodied Mind and its Challenge to Western Thought*, Basic Books (1999).
80 Tools as "prosthetic" extensions through which we outsource our energy expenditure and offload our tasks (including, in our modern world, some mental operations through the use of computers). Thanks to Terrence Deacon for these and other important insights on human evolutionary adaptation.
81 The human ascent to the coherent image of a moral ideal is the fullest extension and culmination of the most fundamental force in living nature. As Leon Kass writes, "Appetite or Desire, not DNA, is the Deepest Principle of Life" (*The Hungry Soul: Eating and the Perfecting of Our Nature*, University of Chicago Press [1999], p. 48).
82 Keiko Morimoto and Kazunori Nakajima, "Role of the Immune System in the Development of the Central Nervous System," *Frontiers in Neuroscience* (2019). E.g. MHC Class I genes, important for immune

cell crosstalk, are also expressed in numerous neuronal cell types (and most highly soon after birth), playing a role in reshaping the brain in various forms of learning. Also, the immune system's complement pathway not only helps to eliminate microbes and dying cells but participates in the production, movement, and preservation of neuronal cells and the refinement of their communication.

83 Maynard V. Olson, "When Less Is More: Gene Loss as an Engine of Evolutionary Change," *American Journal of Human Genetics* (1999).

84 Cory Y. McLean et al., "Human-Specific Loss of Regulatory DNA and the Evolution of Human-Specific Traits," *Nature* (2011).

85 See Leon Kass, *The Hungry Soul: Eating and the Perfecting of our Nature*, University of Chicago Press (1999) for a thoughtful discussion on the relationship between human general dentition and our omnivorous nature.

86 Savant Syndrome provides an instructive caution – though these individuals have remarkable (sometimes truly astonishing!) talents, they often lack the balance of personal and social skills to successfully navigate the challenges of ordinary daily life.

87 Lynn B. Jorde, "Genetic Variation and Human Evolution" (2003). "Human genetic diversity is substantially lower than that of many other species, including our nearest evolutionary relative, the chimpanzee" (p. 1, sec. "How diverse are we?"). This is generally attributed to the fact that we are a relatively young species and have historically lived in intermating groups of relatively small size (10,000 or less) and have therefore not had time to accrue the genetic diversity characteristic of other great ape species. However, it may be that this lack of genetic diversity might be a highly refined balance of precise genetic foundations which uniquely gives rise to the remarkable open and indeterminate phenotype of our "general purpose" species – suggesting that attempts to alter our nature might unbalance and degrade our particular species strengths.

88 Our unique human form and its concomitant capacities and inclinations of mind make possible what Leon Kass describes as "a new world relation, one that admits of a knowing and accurate encounter with things, of genuine and articulate communion and meaningful action between living beings, and of conscious delight in the order and variety of the world's many splendored forms – in short, a world relation colored by a concern for the true, the good, and the beautiful" (*The Hungry Soul: Eating and the Perfecting of our Nature*, University of Chicago Press [1999], p. 66).

89 Consider Galen's dictum, "The physician is only nature's assistant."

90 President's Council on Bioethics, *Beyond Therapy: Biotechnology and the Pursuit of Happiness*, HarperCollins Publishers (2003), 13–20; 154 – one of us (Hurlbut) served as a member of this council. M J Elman et al., "The Effect of Propranolol versus Placebo on Resident Surgical Performance," *Transactions of the American Ophthalmological Society* (1998).

91 Kate Murphy, "Can Botox and Cosmetic Surgery Chill Our Relationships With Others?" *New York Times* (2019). For example, Botox may interfere with emotional communication. Consider this statement from Murphy's article: "Experts say mirroring another person's facial expressions is essential for not only recognizing emotion, but also feeling it" (para.3). L. C. Bulnes et al., "The Effects of Botulinum Toxin on the Detection of Gradual Changes in Facial Emotion," *Scientific Reports* (2019). Paralysis of facial muscles also appears to retard the recognition of the emotions they would normally express.

92 E.g. by exercise, dietary choice, stress reduction, etc.

93 Nina Xie et al., "Novel Epigenetic Techniques Provided by the CRISPR/Cas9 System," *Stem Cells International* (2018). CRISPR-Cas9 is a very versatile tool that can be used for a multitude of purposes, including transient epigenetic modifications.

94 Diana Guimarães, Artur Cavaco-Paulo, and Eugénia Nogueira, "Design of Liposomes as Drug Delivery System for Therapeutic Applications," *International Journal of Pharmaceutics* (2021). Dan Wang, Feng Zhang, and Guangping Gao, "CRISPR-Based Therapeutic Genome Editing: Strategies and In Vivo Delivery by AAV Vectors," *Cell* (2020). Recent advances in the delivery of drugs or molecular devices (such as CRISPR-Cas9) to specific cells or tissues using nanoparticles, liposomes, or viral vehicles are opening amazing possibilities for targeted therapies (or enhancements).

95 Aaron Farnsworth et al., "Acetaminophen Modulates the Transcriptional Response to Recombinant Interferon-β," *PLOS ONE* (2010).

96 If evaluated only from a medical perspective, our technologies would all fail since every human being will eventually suffer loss of health and die. Even as we seek to heal our patients, we recognize that our goal is to restore health and gain time for the wider and fuller purposes of human life. A society that puts a disproportionate emphasis on health is an unhealthy society.

97 President's Council on Bioethics, *Beyond Therapy: Biotechnology and the Pursuit of Happiness*, HarperCollins Publishers (2003), p. 308.

98 Even seemingly innocuous enhancements such as hair dye and tattoos may carry risks such as kidney damage (black urine can result) or transmission of infectious diseases.

99 Clearly, this raises additional ethical considerations related to individual freedom, informed consent, and the common good.

Bibliography

Aach, John, Jeantine Lunshof, Eswar Iyer, and George M. Church. "Addressing the Ethical Issues Raised by Synthetic Human Entities with Embryo-like Features." *eLife* 6 (2017): e20674. https://doi.org/10.7554/eLife.20674.

Aguilera-Castrejon, Alejandro, Bernardo Oldak, Tom Shani, Nadir Ghanem, Chen Itzkovich, Sharon Slomovich, Shadi Tarazi, et al. "Ex Utero Mouse Embryogenesis from Pre-Gastrulation to Late Organogenesis." *Nature* 593, no. 7857 (2021): 119–24. https://doi.org/10.1038/s41586-021-03416-3.

Alba, Vasyl, James E. Carthew, Richard W. Carthew, and Madhav Mani. "Global Constraints within the Developmental Program of the Drosophila Wing." Edited by Danelle Devenport and Naama Barkai. *eLife* 10 (June 2021): e66750. https://doi.org/10.7554/eLife.66750.

Alzamil, Lama, Konstantina Nikolakopoulou, and Margherita Y. Turco. "Organoid Systems to Study the Human Female Reproductive Tract and Pregnancy." *Cell Death & Differentiation* 28, no. 1 (2021): 35–51. https://doi.org/10.1038/s41418-020-0565-5.

Aristotle. *De Anima*. Translated by C. D. C. Reeve. Indianapolis: Hackett Publishing Company, 2017.

Armstrong, Annalee. "Regenerative Medicine Nears Banner Year with $14.1B Cash Infusion, Regulatory Milestones and a Well-stocked Pipeline." *Fierce Biotech*, August 18, 2021. https://www.fiercebiotech.com/biotech/regenerative-medicine-nearing-a-banner-year-14-1b-cash-infusion-regulatory-milestones-and-a?mkt_tok=Mjk0LU1RRi0wNTYAAAF--QVzgyqlwaTkEuOrIvOMulykAtRUafyvAGZKMfQ8vpiGGgAzdY49aS46Bxh5LfRNrPv50v_E2C-5HwY3F_5awJ-O2By87xdSJvPs-V3skGD5dU0&mrkid=389204.

Bahrami, Shahram, and Finn Drabløs. "Gene Regulation in the Immediate-Early Response Process." *Advances in Biological Regulation* 62 (September 2016): 37–49. https://doi.org/10.1016/j.jbior.2016.05.001.

Balaban, Evan. "Changes in Multiple Brain Regions Underlie Species Differences in a Complex, Congenital Behavior." *Proceedings of the National Academy of Sciences of the United States of America* 94, no. 5 (1997): 2001–6.

Bannier-Hélaouët, Marie, Yorick Post, Jeroen Korving, Marc Trani Bustos, Helmuth Gehart, Harry Begthel, Yotam E. Bar-Ephraim, et al. "Exploring the Human Lacrimal Gland Using Organoids and Single-Cell Sequencing." *Cell Stem Cell* 28, no. 7 (2021): 1221–32.e7. https://doi.org/10.1016/j.stem.2021.02.024.

Bick, David, Sarah L. Bick, David P. Dimmock, Tom A. Fowler, Mark J. Caulfield, and Richard H. Scott. "An Online Compendium of Treatable Genetic Disorders." *American Journal of Medical Genetics* 187, no. 1 (2021): 48–54. https://doi.org/10.1002/ajmg.c.31874.

Bittel, Jason. "Antlers Are Miraculous Face Organs That Could Benefit Human Health." *Smithsonian Magazine*, June 12, 2017. https://www.smithsonianmag.com/science-nature/antlers-are-miraculous-face-organs-could-benefit-human-health-180963635/.

Blanchard, Jeffrey L., Wei-Yun Wholey, Erin M. Conlon, and Pablo J. Pomposiello. "Rapid Changes in Gene Expression Dynamics in Response to Superoxide Reveal SoxRS-Dependent and Independent Transcriptional Networks." *PLoS ONE* 2, no. 11 (2007): e1186. https://doi.org/10.1371/journal.pone.0001186.

Boyle, Evan A., Yang I. Li, and Jonathan K. Pritchard. "An Expanded View of Complex Traits: From Polygenic to Omnigenic." *Cell* 169, no. 7 (2017): 1177–86. https://doi.org/10.1016/j.cell.2017.05.038.

Bulnes, L. C., P. Mariën, M. Vandekerckhove, and A. Cleeremans. "The Effects of Botulinum Toxin on the Detection of Gradual Changes in Facial Emotion." *Scientific Reports* 9, no. 1 (2019): 11734. https://doi.org/10.1038/s41598-019-48275-1.

Campbell, Donald T. "'Downward Causation' in Hierarchically Organised Biological Systems." In *Studies in the Philosophy of Biology: Reduction and Related Problems*, edited by Francisco Jose Ayala and Theodosius Dobzhansky, 179–86. London: Macmillan Education UK, 1974. https://doi.org/10.1007/978-1-349-01892-5_11.

Campbell, K. H. S., J. McWhir, W. A. Ritchie, and I. Wilmut. "Sheep Cloned by Nuclear Transfer from a Cultured Cell Line." *Nature* 380, no. 6569 (1996): 64–66. https://doi.org/10.1038/380064a0.

Campinoti, Sara, Asllan Gjinovci, Roberta Ragazzini, Luca Zanieri, Linda Ariza-McNaughton, Marco Catucci, Stefan Boeing, et al. "Reconstitution of a Functional Human Thymus by Postnatal Stromal Progenitor Cells and Natural Whole-Organ Scaffolds." *Nature Communications* 11, no. 1 (2020): 6372. https://doi.org/10.1038/s41467-020-20082-7.

Chen, Yanpu, Felipe F. Lüttmann, Eric Schoger, Hans R. Schöler, Laura C. Zelarayán, Kee-Pyo Kim, Jody J. Haigh, Johnny Kim, and Thomas Braun. "Reversible Reprogramming of Cardiomyocytes to a Fetal State

Drives Heart Regeneration in Mice." *Science* 373, no. 6562 (2021): 1537–40. https://doi.org/10.1126/science.abg5159.

Chen, Yutong, Yuzhe Liu, Jiaxin Zhang, He Liu, Jincheng Wang, Qiran Liu, and Yan Zhang. "Three-Dimensional Bioprinting Adipose Tissue and Mammary Organoids Feasible for Artificial Breast Structure Regeneration." *Materials & Design* 200 (February 2021): 109467. https://doi.org/10.1016/j.matdes.2021.109467.

Crane, Andrew T., Joseph P. Voth, Francis X. Shen, and Walter C. Low. "Concise Review: Human-Animal Neurological Chimeras: Humanized Animals or Human Cells in an Animal?" *Stem Cells* 37, no. 4 (2019): 444–52. https://doi.org/10.1002/stem.2971.

Damasio, Antonio. *Descartes' Error: Emotion, Reason, and the Human Brain.* London: Penguin, 2005.

Daniels, Stephen R. "The Barker Hypothesis Revisited." *The Journal of Pediatrics* 173 (June 2016): 1–3. https://doi.org/10.1016/j.jpeds.2016.04.031.

Dekel, Benjamin, Tatyana Burakova, Fabian D. Arditti, Shlomit Reich-Zeliger, Oren Milstein, Sarit Aviel-Ronen, Gideon Rechavi, et al. "Human and Porcine Early Kidney Precursors as a New Source for Transplantation." *Nature Medicine* 9, no. 1 (2003): 53–60. https://doi.org/10.1038/nm812.

DeWeerdt, Sarah. "How to Map the Brain." *Nature* 571, no. 7766 (2019): S6–8. https://doi.org/10.1038/d41586-019-02208-0.

Diogo, Rui, Natalia Siomava, and Yorick Gitton. "Development of Human Limb Muscles Based on Whole-Mount Immunostaining and the Links between Ontogeny and Evolution." *Development* 146, no. 20 (2019). https://doi.org/10.1242/dev.180349.

Dolgin, Elie. "Flaw in Induced-stem-cell Model." *Nature* 470, no. 7332 (2011): 13. https://doi.org/10.1038/470013a.

Dong, Xin, Shi-Bo Xu, Xin Chen, Mengdan Tao, Xiao-Yan Tang, Kai-Heng Fang, Min Xu, et al. "Human Cerebral Organoids Establish Subcortical Projections in the Mouse Brain after Transplantation." *Molecular Psychiatry* 26, no. 7 (2021): 2964–76. https://doi.org/10.1038/s41380-020-00910-4.

Elman, M. J., J. Sugar, R. Fiscella, T. A. Deutsch, J. Noth, M. Nyberg, K. Packo, and R. J. Anderson. "The Effect of Propranolol versus Placebo on Resident Surgical Performance." *Transactions of the American Ophthalmological Society* 96 (1998): 283–94. PubMed PMID: 10360293.

Farnsworth, Aaron, Anathea S. Flaman, Shiv S. Prasad, Caroline Gravel, Andrew Williams, Carole L. Yauk, and Xuguang Li. "Acetaminophen Modulates the Transcriptional Response to Recombinant Interferon-β." *PLOS ONE* 5, no. 6 (2010): e11031. https://doi.org/10.1371/journal.pone.0011031.

Fu, Jianping, Aryeh Warmflash, and Matthias P. Lutolf. "Stem-Cell-Based Embryo Models for Fundamental Research and Translation." *Nature Materials* 20, no. 2 (2021): 132–44. https://doi.org/10.1038/s41563-020-00829-9.

Galhardo, Rodrigo S., P. J. Hastings, and Susan M. Rosenberg. "Mutation as a Stress Response and the Regulation of Evolvability." *Critical Reviews in Biochemistry and Molecular Biology* 42, no. 5 (2007): 399–435. https://doi.org/10.1080/10409230701648502.

Giandomenico, Stefano L., Magdalena Sutcliffe, and Madeline A. Lancaster. "Generation and Long-Term Culture of Advanced Cerebral Organoids for Studying Later Stages of Neural Development." *Nature Protocols* 16, no. 2 (2021): 579–602. https://doi.org/10.1038/s41596-020-00433-w.

Giri, Pramod Janardan, and Vaibhav Sharadrao Chavan. "Human Tail: A Benign Condition Hidden Out of Social Stigma and Shame in Young Adult – A Case Report and Review." *Asian Journal of Neurosurgery* 14, no. 1 (2019): 1–4. https://doi.org/10.4103/ajns.AJNS_209_17.

Glover, Natasha. "The Banana Conjecture." *Dessimoz Lab* blog (2020). https://lab.dessimoz.org/blog/2020/12/08/human-banana-orthologs.

Gordon, Aaron, Se-Jin Yoon, Stephen S. Tran, Christopher D. Makinson, Jin Young Park, Jimena Andersen, Alfredo M. Valencia, et al. "Long-Term Maturation of Human Cortical Organoids Matches Key Early Postnatal Transitions." *Nature Neuroscience* 24, no. 3 (2021): 331–42. https://doi.org/10.1038/s41593-021-00802-y.

Gross, Liza. "When Less Is More: Losing Genes on the Path to Becoming Human." *PLOS Biology* 4, no. 3 (2006): e76. https://doi.org/10.1371/journal.pbio.0040076.

Guimarães, Diana, Artur Cavaco-Paulo, and Eugénia Nogueira. "Design of Liposomes as Drug Delivery System for Therapeutic Applications." *International Journal of Pharmaceutics* 601 (May 2021): 120571. https://doi.org/10.1016/j.ijpharm.2021.120571.

Gupta, Agrim, Silvio Savarese, Surya Ganguli, and Li Fei-Fei. "Embodied Intelligence via Learning and Evolution." *Nature Communications* 12, no. 1 (2021): 5721. https://doi.org/10.1038/s41467-021-25874-z.

Haigh, Joshua. "The Story behind the Changing Face of 'Catwoman' Jocelyn Wildenstein." *Mirror (London)*, December 9, 2016. http://www.mirror.co.uk/3am/celebrity-news/story-behind-changing-face-cat-woman-9422943.

Han, Xiaoning, Michael Chen, Fushun Wang, Martha Windrem, Su Wang, Steven Shanz, Qiwu Xu, et al. "Forebrain Engraftment by Human Glial Progenitor Cells Enhances Synaptic Plasticity and Learning in Adult Mice." *Cell Stem Cell* 12, no. 3 (2013): 342–53. https://doi.org/10.1016/j.stem.2012.12.015.

Hibaoui, Youssef, and Anis Feki. "Organoid Models of Human Endometrial Development and Disease." *Frontiers in Cell and Developmental Biology* 8 (2020): 84. https://doi.org/10.3389/fcell.2020.00084.

Hu, Zhixing, Hanqin Li, Houbo Jiang, Yong Ren, Xinyang Yu, Jingxin Qiu, Aimee B. Stablewski, Boyang Zhang, Michael J. Buck, and Jian Feng. "Transient Inhibition of MTOR in Human Pluripotent Stem Cells Enables Robust Formation of Mouse-Human Chimeric Embryos." *Science Advances* 6, no. 20 (2020): eaaz0298. https://doi.org/10.1126/sciadv.aaz0298.

Hurlbut, J. Benjamin, Insoo Hyun, Aaron D. Levine, Robin Lovell-Badge, Jeantine E. Lunshof, Kirstin R. W. Matthews, Peter Mills, et al. "Revisiting the Warnock Rule." *Nature Biotechnology* 35, no. 11 (2017): 1029–42. https://doi.org/10.1038/nbt.4015.

Hurlbut, William B. "Framing the Future: Embryonic Stem Cells, Ethics and the Emerging Era of Developmental Biology." *Pediatric Research* 59, no. 4 (2006): 4–12. https://doi.org/10.1203/01.pdr.0000205377.04359.3e.

———. "The Boundaries of Humanity: The Ethics of Human–Animal Chimeras in Cloning and Stem Cell Research." In *Is This Cell a Human Being?*, edited by Antoine Suarez and Joachim Huarte. Berlin: Springer, 2011. https://doi.org/10.1007/978-3-642-20772-3_10.

International Society for Stem Cell Research. "Guidelines for Stem Cell Research and Clinical Translation." May 26, 2021. https://www.isscr.org/policy/guidelines-for-stem-cell-research-and-clinical-translation.

JangoBio. "JangoBio Creating First Organoids for Complete Hormone Restoration." February 18, 2020. https://www.jango.bio/jangobio-creating-first-organoids-for-complete-hormone-restoration/.

Jorde, Lynn B. "Genetic Variation and Human Evolution." October 16, 2003. https://www.ashg.org/wp-content/uploads/2019/09/genetic-variation-essay.pdf.

Joy, Mary T., Einor Ben Assayag, Dalia Shabashov-Stone, Sigal Liraz-Zaltsman, Jose Mazzitelli, Marcela Arenas, Nora Abduljawad, et al. "CCR5 Is a Therapeutic Target for Recovery after Stroke and Traumatic Brain Injury." *Cell* 176, no. 5 (2019): 1143–57.e13. https://doi.org/10.1016/j.cell.2019.01.044.

Kass, Leon R. *The Hungry Soul: Eating and the Perfecting of Our Nature*. Chicago: University of Chicago Press, 1999.

Kim, Jihoon, Bon-Kyoung Koo, and Juergen A. Knoblich. "Human Organoids: Model Systems for Human Biology and Medicine." *Nature Reviews Molecular Cell Biology* 21, no. 10 (2020): 571–84. https://doi.org/10.1038/s41580-020-0259-3.

Knoepfler, Paul. "George Church on Germline Human Genetic Modification." *The Niche* (blog), March 9, 2015. https://ipscell.com/2015/03/georgechurchinterview/.

Kobayashi, Toshihiro, Tomoyuki Yamaguchi, Sanae Hamanaka, Megumi Kato-Itoh, Yuji Yamazaki, Makoto Ibata, Hideyuki Sato, et al. "Generation of Rat Pancreas in Mouse by Interspecific Blastocyst Injection of Pluripotent Stem Cells." *Cell* 142, no. 5 (2010): 787–99. https://doi.org/10.1016/j.cell.2010.07.039.

Kohama, Tomohiro, Maika Masago, Ikuo Tomioka, Kanako Morohaku. "*In vitro* production of viable eggs from isolated mouse primary follicles by successive culture." *The Journal of Reproduction and Development* 68, no. 1 (2022): 38–44. https://doi.org/10.1262/jrd.2021-095.

Kornberg, Arthur. *For the Love of Enzymes*. Cambridge, MA: Harvard University Press, 1989.

Kronenberg, Zev N., Ian T. Fiddes, David Gordon, Shwetha Murali, Stuart Cantsilieris, Olivia S. Meyerson, Jason G. Underwood, et al. "High-Resolution Comparative Analysis of Great Ape Genomes." *Science* 360, no. 6393 (2018): eaar6343. https://doi.org/10.1126/science.aar6343.

Lakoff, George and Mark Johnson. *Philosophy in the Flesh: The Embodied Mind and its Challenge to Western Thought*. New York: Basic Books, 1999.

Leader, Benjamin, Quentin J. Baca, and David E. Golan. "Protein Therapeutics: A Summary and Pharmacological Classification." *Nature Reviews Drug Discovery* 7, no. 1 (2008): 21–39. https://doi.org/10.1038/nrd2399.

Levin, Michael. "Bioelectric Signaling: Reprogrammable Circuits Underlying Embryogenesis, Regeneration, and Cancer." *Cell* 184, no. 8 (2021): 1971–89. https://doi.org/10.1016/j.cell.2021.02.034.

Li, Xiaoyong, Man Zheng, Bo Xu, Dali Li, Yue Shen, Yongqiang Nie, Lian Ma, and Ji Wu. "Generation of Offspring-Producing 3D Ovarian Organoids Derived from Female Germline Stem Cells and Their Application in Toxicological Detection." *Biomaterials* 279 (December 2021): 121213. https://doi.org/10.1016/j.biomaterials.2021.121213.

Liu, Xiaodong, Jia Ping Tan, Jan Schröder, Asma Aberkane, John F. Ouyang, Monika Mohenska, Sue Mei Lim, et al. "Modelling Human Blastocysts by Reprogramming Fibroblasts into IBlastoids." *Nature* 591, no. 7851 (2021): 627–32. https://doi.org/10.1038/s41586-021-03372-y.

Liu, Zhen, Yijun Cai, Yan Wang, Yanhong Nie, Chenchen Zhang, Yuting Xu, Xiaotong Zhang, et al. "Cloning of Macaque Monkeys by Somatic Cell Nuclear Transfer." *Cell* 172, no. 4 (February 2018): 881–7.e7. https://doi.org/10.1016/j.cell.2018.01.020.

Luck, Katja, Dae-Kyum Kim, Luke Lambourne, Kerstin Spirohn, Bridget E. Begg, Wenting Bian, Ruth Brignall, et al. "A Reference Map of the Human Binary Protein Interactome." *Nature* 580, no. 7803 (2020): 402–8. https://doi.org/10.1038/s41586-020-2188-x.

March of Dimes. "March of Dimes Global Report on Birth Defects." Accessed September 1, 2021. https://www.marchofdimes.org/mission/march-of-dimes-global-report-on-birth-defects.aspx.

Marcus, Amy Dockser. "Meet the Scientists Bringing Extinct Species Back From the Dead." *Wall Street Journal*, October 11, 2018. https://www.wsj.com/articles/meet-the-scientists-bringing-extinct-species-back-from-the-dead-1539093600.

Matharu, Navneet, and Nadav Ahituv. "Modulating Gene Regulation to Treat Genetic Disorders." *Nature Reviews Drug Discovery* 19, no. 11 (2020): 757–75. https://doi.org/10.1038/s41573-020-0083-7.

Mayr, Ernst. "Change of Environment and Speciation." In *Evolution and the Diversity of Life: Selected Essays*, edited by Ernst Mayr. Cambridge, MA: Belknap Press of Harvard University Press, 1976.

McLean, Cory Y., Philip L. Reno, Alex A. Pollen, Abraham I. Bassan, Terence D. Capellini, Catherine Guenther, Vahan B. Indjeian, et al. "Human-Specific Loss of Regulatory DNA and the Evolution of Human-Specific Traits." *Nature* 471, 7337 (2011): 216–19. https://doi.org/10.1038/nature09774.

MeiraGTx. "Our Strategy: Gene Regulation." Accessed November 5, 2021. https://meiragtx.com/our-strategy/gene-regulation/.

Morimoto, Keiko, and Kazunori Nakajima. "Role of the Immune System in the Development of the Central Nervous System." *Frontiers in Neuroscience* 13 (September 2019): 916. https://doi.org/10.3389/fnins.2019.00916.

Moris, Naomi, Kerim Anlas, Susanne C. van den Brink, Anna Alemany, Julia Schröder, Sabitri Ghimire, Tina Balayo, Alexander van Oudenaarden, and Alfonso Martinez Arias. "An in Vitro Model of Early Anteroposterior Organization during Human Development." *Nature* 582, no. 7812 (2020): 410–15. https://doi.org/10.1038/s41586-020-2383-9.

Mosher, Dave. "'Cuddle Chemical' Also Fuels Favoritism, Bigotry." *Wired*, January 12, 2011. https://www.wired.com/2011/01/oxytocin-social-favoritism/.

Murphy, Kate. "Can Botox and Cosmetic Surgery Chill Our Relationships With Others?" *New York Times*, April 18, 2019. https://www.nytimes.com/2019/04/18/well/mind/can-botox-and-cosmetic-surgery-chill-our-relationships-with-others.html.

National Academies of Sciences, Engineering, and Medicine. *The Emerging Field of Human Neural Organoids, Transplants, and Chimeras: Science, Ethics, and Governance*. Washington, DC: The National Academies Press, 2021. https://doi.org/10.17226/26078.

National Center for Advancing Translational Sciences. "NCATS-Supported Scientists Model Aging-Related Conditions in Space to Improve Human Health on Earth." National Institutes of Health, last updated May 17, 2019. https://ncats.nih.gov/news/releases/2019/tissue-chips-in-space.

National Human Genome Research Institute. "New Genome Comparison." *National Institutes of Health News*, August 31, 2005. https://www.genome.gov/15515096/2005-release-new-genome-comparison-finds-chimps-humans-very-similar-at-dna-level.

National Institutes of Health. "New Comprehensive View of the Mouse Genome." November 19, 2014. https://www.nih.gov/news-events/news-releases/new-comprehensive-view-mouse-genome-finds-many-similarities-striking-differences-human-genome.

National Intelligence Council Report. "Global Trends 2030: Alternative Worlds." Accessed August 15, 2021. https://www.dni.gov/files/documents/GlobalTrends_2030.pdf.

Nestor, Mark S., Daniel L. Fischer, and David Arnold. "'Masking' Our Emotions: Botulinum Toxin, Facial Expression, and Well-Being in the Age of COVID-19." *Journal of Cosmetic Dermatology* 19, no. 9 (2020): 2154–60. https://doi.org/10.1111/jocd.13569.

Nichols, Joan E., Saverio La Francesca, Jean A. Niles, Stephanie P. Vega, Lissenya B. Argueta, Luba Frank, David C. Christiani, et al. "Production and Transplantation of Bioengineered Lung into a Large-Animal Model." *Science Translational Medicine* 10, no. 452 (2018): eaao3926. https://doi.org/10.1126/scitranslmed.aao3926.

Oliver, E., and J.-B. Stukenborg. "Rebuilding the Human Testis in Vitro." *Andrology* 8, no. 4 (2020): 825–34. https://doi.org/10.1111/andr.12710.

Olson, Maynard V. "When Less Is More: Gene Loss as an Engine of Evolutionary Change." *The American Journal of Human Genetics* 64, no. 1 (1999): 18–23. https://doi.org/10.1086/302219.

Ooft, S. N., F. Weeber, L. Schipper, K. K. Dijkstra, C. M. McLean, S. Kaing, J. van de Haar, et al. "Prospective Experimental Treatment of Colorectal Cancer Patients Based on Organoid Drug Responses." *ESMO Open* 6, no. 3 (2021): 100103. https://doi.org/10.1016/j.esmoop.2021.100103.

Paaby, Annalise B., and Matthew V. Rockman. "The Many Faces of Pleiotropy." *Trends in Genetics* 29, no. 2 (2013): 66–73. https://doi.org/10.1016/j.tig.2012.10.010.

Partridge, Emily A., Marcus G. Davey, Matthew A. Hornick, Patrick E. McGovern, Ali Y. Mejaddam, Jesse D. Vrecenak, Carmen Mesas-Burgos, et al. "An Extra-Uterine System to Physiologically Support the Extreme Premature Lamb." *Nature Communications* 8, no. 1 (2017): 15112. https://doi.org/10.1038/ncomms15112.

Pearce, Tilly. "This Morning Viewers Left Stunned by Parrot Man Who Cut off His EARS to Look like the Bird." *The Sun* (London), October 21, 2016. https://www.thesun.co.uk/tvandshowbiz/2021740/this-morning-viewers-left-stunned-by-bristolian-parrot-man-who-has-cut-off-his-ears-to-look-like-the-bird/.

Post, Yorick, Jens Puschhof, Joep Beumer, Harald M. Kerkkamp, Merijn A. G. de Bakker, Julien Slagboom, Buys de Barbanson, et al. "Snake Venom Gland Organoids." *Cell* 180, no. 2 (2020): 233–47.e21. https://doi.org/10.1016/j.cell.2019.11.038.

President's Council on Bioethics. *Beyond Therapy: Biotechnology and the Pursuit of Happiness*. New York: HarperCollins Publishers, 2003.

Rose, Steven and Steven Pinker. "The Two Steves (Part I): A Debate." *Edge* (blog), March 24, 1998. https://www.edge.org/conversation/steven_rose-steven_pinker-the-two-steves-part-i.

Ryder, Sean P. "#CRISPRbabies: Notes on a Scandal." *The CRISPR Journal* 1, no. 6 (2018): 355–57. https://doi.org/10.1089/crispr.2018.29039.spr.

Salahudeen, Ameen A., Shannon S. Choi, Arjun Rustagi, Junjie Zhu, Vincent van Unen, Sean M. de la O, Ryan A. Flynn, et al. "Progenitor Identification and SARS-CoV-2 Infection in Human Distal Lung Organoids." *Nature* 588, no. 7839 (2020): 670–75. https://doi.org/10.1038/s41586-020-3014-1.

Savulescu, Julian. "Should We Clone Human Beings? Cloning as a Source of Tissue for Transplantation." *Journal of Medical Ethics* 25, no. 2 (1999): 87–95.

Shi, Lei, Xin Luo, Jin Jiang, Yongchang Chen, Cirong Liu, Ting Hu, Min Li, et al. "Transgenic Rhesus Monkeys Carrying the Human MCPH1 Gene Copies Show Human-like Neoteny of Brain Development." *National Science Review* 6, no. 3 (2019): 480–93. https://doi.org/10.1093/nsr/nwz043.

Swetlitz, Ike. "Scientist Pushes Fetal Tissue Research despite Political Pressure." *STAT*, March 31, 2016. https://www.statnews.com/2016/03/31/fetal-tissue-congress/.

Takahashi, Kazutoshi, and Shinya Yamanaka. "Induction of Pluripotent Stem Cells from Mouse Embryonic and Adult Fibroblast Cultures by Defined Factors." *Cell* 126, no. 4 (2006): 663–76. https://doi.org/10.1016/j.cell.2006.07.024.

Tan, Tao, Jun Wu, Chenyang Si, Shaoxing Dai, Youyue Zhang, Nianqin Sun, E. Zhang, et al. "Chimeric Contribution of Human Extended Pluripotent Stem Cells to Monkey Embryos Ex Vivo." *Cell* 184, no. 8 (2021): 2020–32.e14. https://doi.org/10.1016/j.cell.2021.03.020.

Tanaka, Junichi, Miho Ogawa, Hironori Hojo, Yusuke Kawashima, Yo Mabuchi, Kenji Hata, Shiro Nakamura, et al. "Generation of Orthotopically Functional Salivary Gland from Embryonic Stem Cells." *Nature Communications* 9, no. 1 (2018): 4216. https://doi.org/10.1038/s41467-018-06469-7.

Trujillo, Cleber A., Richard Gao, Priscilla D. Negraes, Jing Gu, Justin Buchanan, Sebastian Preissl, Allen Wang, et al. "Complex Oscillatory Waves Emerging from Cortical Organoids Model Early Human Brain Network Development." *Cell Stem Cell* 25, no. 4 (2019): 558–69.e7. https://doi.org/10.1016/j.stem.2019.08.002.

Trujillo, Cleber A., Edward S. Rice, Nathan K. Schaefer, Isaac A. Chaim, Emily C. Wheeler, Assael A. Madrigal, Justin Buchanan, et al. "Reintroduction of the Archaic Variant of NOVA1 in Cortical Organoids Alters Neurodevelopment." *Science* 371, no. 6530 (2021): eaax2537. https://doi.org/10.1126/science.aax2537.

Urevig, Andrew. "520-Million-Year-Old Brains Found in Kerygmachela Fossil." *National Geographic*, March 9, 2018. https://www.nationalgeographic.com/science/article/fossil-brain-kerygmachela-tardigrade-insects.

Wakayama, Sayaka, Takashi Kohda, Haruko Obokata, Mikiko Tokoro, Chong Li, Yukari Terashita, Eiji Mizutani, et al. "Successful Serial Recloning in the Mouse over Multiple Generations." *Cell Stem Cell* 12, no. 3 (2013): 293–97. https://doi.org/10.1016/j.stem.2013.01.005.

Wang, Dan, Feng Zhang, and Guangping Gao. "CRISPR-Based Therapeutic Genome Editing: Strategies and In Vivo Delivery by AAV Vectors." *Cell* 181, no. 1 (2020): 136–50. https://doi.org/10.1016/j.cell.2020.03.023.

Wang, Xiaoxia, Wendy E. Grus, and Jianzhi Zhang. "Gene Losses during Human Origins." *PLOS Biology* 4, no. 3 (2006): e52. https://doi.org/10.1371/journal.pbio.0040052.

Workman, Michael J., Maxime M. Mahe, Stephen Trisno, Holly M. Poling, Carey L. Watson, Nambirajan Sundaram, Ching-Fang Chang, et al. "Engineered Human Pluripotent-Stem-Cell-Derived Intestinal Tissues with a Functional Enteric Nervous System." *Nature Medicine* 23, no. 1 (2017): 49–59. https://doi.org/10.1038/nm.4233.

Wu, Jun, Aida Platero-Luengo, Masahiro Sakurai, Atsushi Sugawara, Maria Antonia Gil, Takayoshi Yamauchi, Keiichiro Suzuki, et al. "Interspecies Chimerism with Mammalian Pluripotent Stem Cells." *Cell* 168, no. 3 (2017): 473–86.e15. https://doi.org/10.1016/j.cell.2016.12.036.

Xiao, Shuo, Jonathan R. Coppeta, Hunter B. Rogers, Brett C. Isenberg, Jie Zhu, Susan A. Olalekan, Kelly E. McKinnon, et al. "A Microfluidic Culture Model of the Human Reproductive Tract and 28-Day Menstrual Cycle." *Nature Communications* 8, no. 1 (2017): 14584. https://doi.org/10.1038/ncomms14584.

Xie, Nina, Yafang Zhou, Qiying Sun, and Beisha Tang. "Novel Epigenetic Techniques Provided by the CRISPR/Cas9 System." *Stem Cells International* (July 2018): 7834175. https://doi.org/10.1155/2018/7834175.

Xu, MengMeng. "CCR5-Δ32 Biology, Gene Editing, and Warnings for the Future of CRISPR-Cas9 as a Human and Humane Gene Editing Tool." *Cell & Bioscience* 10, no. 1 (2020): 1–6. https://doi.org/10.1186/s13578-020-00410-6.

Yong, Ed. "The Weak Science Behind the Wrongly Named Moral Molecule." *The Atlantic*, November 13, 2015. https://www.theatlantic.com/science/archive/2015/11/the-weak-science-of-the-wrongly-named-moral-molecule/415581/.

Yu, Leqian, Yulei Wei, Jialei Duan, Daniel A. Schmitz, Masahiro Sakurai, Lei Wang, Kunhua Wang, Shuhua Zhao, Gary C. Hon, and Jun Wu. "Blastocyst-like Structures Generated from Human Pluripotent Stem Cells." *Nature* 591, no. 7851 (2021): 620–26. https://doi.org/10.1038/s41586-021-03356-y.

Zhou, Miou, Stuart Greenhill, Shan Huang, Tawnie K. Silva, Yoshitake Sano, Shumin Wu, Ying Cai, et al. "CCR5 Is a Suppressor for Cortical Plasticity and Hippocampal Learning and Memory." *eLife* 5 (2016): e20985. https://doi.org/10.7554/eLife.20985.

Zimmer, Carl. "A New Company With a Wild Mission: Bring Back the Woolly Mammoth." *The New York Times*, September 13, 2021. https://www.nytimes.com/2021/09/13/science/colossal-woolly-mammoth-DNA.html.

5
A THEMATIC OVERVIEW
Debating the ethics of radical enhancement

Nicholas M. Sparks

5.1 Introduction

What it means to be human, whether "human nature" exists, to what extent such a "nature" is malleable, and the wisdom of attempting to alter or change "human nature" are central questions in the debate on the ethics of human enhancement. Indeed, these are perennial questions, stretching back to the *Epic of Gilgamesh*. However, the increasing sophistication of biomedical and information technologies makes this perennial subject of reflection one of increasing political, social, and scientific relevance.

Permissivists, restrictivists, and bioconservatives have waged a protracted debate on the ethics of human enhancement over the past few decades.[1] This chapter centers on the debate between permissivists, restrictivists, and bioconservatives over the ethics of radical human enhancement.[2] Specifically, this chapter will focus on objections to radical human enhancement that are concerned, broadly, with what it means to be human and how we ought to comport ourselves with respect to our "nature."[3] Restrictivist and bioconservative objections often appeal to notions such as "human dignity" and "human nature," assigning special moral status to humans *qua* human. This chapter sets out, then, to offer a thematic overview of the concerns common to proponents of dignity arguments and nature arguments. This approach enables us to capture the range of concerns articulated by proponents of dignity and nature arguments, as well as to demonstrate the substantial overlap between such arguments. Importantly, these camps share concerns not only about the likely effects of human enhancement technologies (hereafter HET) but more importantly the attitudes, stances, and sentiments embodied in and engendered by the deployment of HET.

Since this chapter is specially focused on objections to radical human enhancement, a brief discussion of the varieties of human enhancement will make the coming conversation clearer and more precise. There are varieties of enhancement that even (most) bioconservatives would celebrate, or at least acknowledge as permissible. Eyeglasses, for example, would qualify as at least permissible on even the most stringent bioconservative objection to HET.[4] The debate, then, is not so much a debate about human enhancement *sans* qualification as it is about drawing the line between permissible and impermissible varieties of human enhancement.

Now, we can distinguish enhancements according to *what* they enhance: accordingly, there are genetic, physiological, emotional, cognitive, and moral enhancements.[5] We can also distinguish enhancements according to the *means* they employ: this yields a list including genetic, pharmacological, and technological enhancements, among others. For our purposes, I will focus on distinguishing enhancement by *degree* or *kind*: this yields a distinction between "moderate" and "radical" enhancement. Nicholas Agar provides a helpful model for discussing these types of enhancement. Moderate enhancement "improves significant attributes and abilities [e.g., lifespan or cognitive faculties] to levels within or close to what is currently possible for human beings" (Agar, 2014: 2). Radical enhancement, on the other hand, "improves significant attributes and abilities to levels that greatly exceed what is currently possible for human beings" (ibid.).

First, I will discuss the core commitments of permissivist accounts of human enhancement in order to provide a foil for the restrictivist and bioconservative arguments discussed in later sections. Then, I introduce and explain key themes common to a range of restrictivist and bioconservative critiques of radical human enhancement. Finally, I note how arguments from human dignity and from human nature have been received in the literature to give a sense of the challenges leveled against the central concepts appealed to by restrictivists and bioconservatives.

5.2 Core commitments of permissivist accounts of the human

Nick Bostrom, a leading thinker in the transhumanist movement, characterizes transhumanism, a form of permissivism, as involving the affirmation of "the possibility and desirability of fundamentally improving the human condition through applied reason, especially by developing and making widely available technologies to eliminate aging and to greatly enhance human… capacities" (Bostrom, 2003: 4). On Bostrom's telling, then, transhumanism is rooted in two theses about "human nature": (1) "human nature" is not normative, and (2) "human nature" is perfectible. Since nature is "a work-in-progress, a half-baked beginning that we can learn to remold in desirable ways," new technologies and modes of thought enable us to improve upon nature (Bostrom, 2005b: 4). This project of improvement involves the pursuit of both moderate and radical human enhancement.

Bostrom is not alone in endorsing these two theses about human nature. As to the first thesis, that "human nature" is not normative, Bostrom writes that "our own species-specified natures are a rich source of much of the thoroughly unrespectable and unacceptable" (ibid.: 205). Whatever properties or characteristic dispositions our "species-specified natures" may hold, our natures cannot be considered normative without qualification. Other prominent permissivists echo Bostrom on this point: much of our "natural" condition is undesirable and in need of improvement (Harris, 2007; Buchanan, 2011; Kahane, Pugh, and Savulescu, 2016).

Allen Buchanan, for example, argues against "bioconservative" rhetoric centered on the metaphor of evolution as a "master engineer." Buchanan instead argues that "evolution is more like a morally blind, fickle, tightly-shackled tinkerer" (Buchanan, 2011: 29). John Harris, too, warns against

> the view that there is something special about [ourselves] and that [our] particular sort of being is not only worth preserving in perpetuity, but that there is a duty… to make sure that neither natural selection nor deliberate choice permit the development of any better sort of being.
>
> *(Harris, 2007: 16)*

The shared picture that emerges on this account is one in which the attempt to oppose the improvement of our species reflects a "fetish," rooted in misleading metaphors or naïve optimism. This optimism is ultimately undercut by the evidence of our brutality and vulnerability to depredation. Importantly, while some activities or characteristics being part of "human nature" does not entail that it is good, neither is "human nature" all bad. Rather, we simply cannot rely on what is natural as a guide to what is good without relying on other moral and ethical principles.

The constructive dimension of the permissivist project involves the re-thinking and re-making of ourselves in light of considered moral reflection (Bostrom, 2005a: 205). This requires orienting enhancements to the positive promotion of values, as well as instituting constraints to manage risk. For example, Christine Overall writes that in pursuing lifespan extension, "we have a moral responsibility to erase or at least reduce… disparities… [based on] gender, race, and socioeconomic class" (Overall, 2011: 393). And since not everyone has a fair opportunity for a long and good life, lifespan extension research should emphasize benefits to disadvantaged groups (ibid., 394).

Likewise, developing rules and principles to guide risk reduction in human enhancement is important. Allen Buchanan, for example, proposes a list of "counting principles" as rules for the responsible employment of enhancements. These are designed to mitigate the possibility of adverse biological consequences in genetic enhancement. We ought, among other things, to enhance responsibly, in such a way that any adverse effects are limited to avoid spillover; changes wrought by enhancement should be reversible, should not deeply change the "design and shape of the organism" enhanced, and ought to be undertaken only when we understand the relevant causal relations (Buchanan, 2011: 95–99). We can see then that, among other things, personal aspirations, cost-benefit analysis, commitments to justice and equality, and the requirements of beneficence and nonmaleficence all figure in the permissivist analysis of HET.

5.3 Four objections to radical human enhancement

Restrictivists and bioconservatives have levied a number of objections to radical human enhancement. Below, I discuss four objections centered on themes common to arguments from dignity and arguments from nature. Since discussion here is focused on the overlapping concerns of these arguments, the distinctions between the authors discussed are to some degree minimized. But the benefit of this procedure is that it enables us to illustrate the broad consensus of authors writing in several different traditions, as well as to discuss the views of these authors without arbitrarily privileging any single author's argument as canonical.

5.3.1 Radical human enhancement rejects vulnerability and finitude

One of the primary concerns of restrictivists and bioconservatives is that radical human enhancement involves a repudiation of vulnerability and finitude. These are characteristics, according to such approaches, intrinsic to humans as such, and necessary for the realization of distinctly human goods at both the individual and social levels. For example, Leon Kass thinks that intrinsically valuable human goods are inseparable from our finitude (Kass, 2002: 266–268). For example, knowledge of our finitude, of the inevitability of our death, seems to move us to take our lives seriously, to engage in projects of worth, and to commit our lives to beauty and to loving others (ibid.: 266–267). So, too, the finitude of our lives imbues our moral actions, especially sacrificial actions, with deep significance. To be willing to offer one's life, or to forego pleasure, is to renounce attachment to what is temporary and to "rise above our mere creatureliness" (ibid.: 268). Thus, according to Kass, while permissivists see our natural limitations as constraints on our ability to pursue the good, in fact it is our limitations that *enable* the pursuit of the good and imbue our pursuits with value, meaning, and significance (ibid.: 266–268; cf. McPherson, 2022: 5–45; Beyleveld and Brownsword, 2001: 220; Rubin, 2008).

Jason Eberl concurs on this point, writing from a Thomistic perspective that radical enhancement carries with it the risk "that we would lose the value inherent in appreciating our vulnerability and finitude" (Eberl, 2017: 321). Moreover, attempting to eliminate vulnerability and dependency altogether "could have a negative impact on our sense of interpersonal moral responsibility for each other's well-being," while pain and suffering possess "a potential instrumental value… that may be occluded by seeking to eliminate various vulnerabilities" (Eberl, 2017: 321).

Michael Sandel, in this same vein, expresses concern that the routine practice of genetic enhancement would submit even our genetic endowment to choice and planning, reinforcing the illusion that the successful are self-made and self-sufficient. Meanwhile

> [t]hose at the bottom of society would be viewed... as simply unfit, and so worthy of eugenic repair... perfect genetic control would erode the actual solidarity that arises when men and women reflect on the contingency of their talents and fortunes.
>
> *(Sandel, 2007: 92)*

In fact, Sandel's framing of the risks latent in forgetting our finitude leads us to the next theme of restrictivist/bioconservative critique: that radical enhancement embodies an attitude of mastery, rather than an attitude of reverence or appreciation.

5.3.2 *Radical human enhancement embodies an attitude of mastery*

Sandel is perhaps most notable in this connection for having argued that radical enhancement embodies an attitude of mastery. Sandel argues that what he calls "eugenic parenting" "is objectionable because it expresses and entrenches a certain stance toward the world – a stance of mastery and dominion that fails to appreciate the gifted character of human powers and achievements" (Sandel, 2007: 85). Our actions express and reinforce a "stance" or attitude toward the world, and the stance embedded in genetic enhancement and "eugenic parenting" obscures the fundamentally gifted and unbidden character of human life. The case against perfection, and correspondingly against the attitude of mastery, is fundamentally an ethical one: the vision of freedom embedded in practices aiming at the mastery of nature "is flawed. It threatens to banish our appreciation of life as a gift, and to leave us with nothing to affirm or behold outside our own will" (Sandel, 2007: 100).

Likewise, Jürgen Habermas, discussing the prospect of genetic engineering in the context of preimplantation genetic diagnosis (PGD), argues that "the programming intentions of parents who are ambitious and given to experimentation, or of parents who are merely concerned [about their children], have the peculiar status of a one-sided and unchallengeable expectation" (Habermas, 2003: 51). Crucial to Habermas's argument is the notion of "communicative action." In communicative action, the persons involved "are to attune themselves, from the participant perspective of a first person, to the other as a second person, with the intention of reaching an understanding with [the other] instead of reifying and instrumentalizing [the other]" (ibid.: 55).

However, the genetic program designer "carries out a one-sided act for which there can be no well-founded assumption of consent... setting the course... of the life history of the dependent person" (ibid.: 64). Importantly, the course set by parents and designer in the act of genetic engineering would have irreversible consequences which, further, circumvent the ability of the person thus "raised" to critically reappraise the *way* they were raised (Habermas, 2003: 64). Genetic engineering, then, engenders an attitude of one-sided dictation about the course a given life shall take, as opposed to engaging the other with the mutual recognition and reason-giving characteristic of communicative action. As we will see in the next section, this is not only detrimental to the individual but also substantially injurious to the prospects of a social life shared by free and equal persons.

Finally, Leon Kass traces the attitude of technical mastery to the early modern turn to practical science. Science is supposed to yield results and bring about our mastery of nature. However, science is not of itself competent to provide moral or ethical guidance in addressing the dilemmas that arise in the deployment of technology. So, then, according to Kass

> [t]he project for the mastery of nature, even as it provides limitless powers, leaves the "master" lost at sea. Lacking knowledge of ends and goals, lacking standards of good and

bad, right and wrong, we know not who we are nor where we are going. Yet we travel fast and freely, progressively achieving our own estrangement – from our communities, from our nature, from our very selves.

(Kass, 2002: 280)

Attaining mastery, then, appears to rely on restricting ourselves to questions of "fact" or means – rather than questions of "ends and goals." But in refusing to ask or answer questions about ends and goals, we thereby deprive ourselves of the ability to set a standard – and, therefore, a limit – for the evaluation of technical mastery. And so we lose the criteria by which we might orient ourselves as we strive for mastery over nature, and become alienated from the very objects of our mastery: nature, and ultimately ourselves.

5.3.3 Radical human enhancement undermines important social goods

While a sense of our vulnerability is proper to us as creatures, as we noted in Section 5.3.1 above, it is also necessary to sustain certain social practices. Sandel argues that a sense of our own vulnerability and contingency is required to exercise solidarity toward others. Our sense of solidarity encourages us to share in and sympathize with the fate of others. Since we do not naturally control our genetic endowment or the trajectory of our lives, this sense of the contingency or giftedness of our abilities and achievements encourages us to share the bounty of our gifts with others less fortunate than us (Sandel, 2007: 90–93). Radical enhancement, however, threatens our ability to enter into solidarity with one another by rendering the very fabric of our genetic endowment subject to rational choice and planning. In a system where genetic enhancement was routinely practiced, Sandel worries that the bonds of solidarity may break in the face of a creeping attitude of total self-creation and self-sufficiency. Again, the case here is a fundamentally ethical one: the attitude by which we share in, and attempt to relieve, the suffering and misfortune of others depend upon our *own* sense of the fragility and giftedness of life. But this sense would be extinguished by the routine practice of genetic enhancement.

Returning to Habermas's objection, canvased in Section 5.3.2, we find that he does not limit his diagnosis to the ability of genetic engineering "[to] affect the capacity of 'being oneself.'" (Habermas, 2003; 63) Rather, genetic engineering "would at the same time create an interpersonal relationship for which there is no precedent… which jeopardizes a precondition for the moral self-understanding of autonomous actors" (ibid.). The threat of undermining this self-understanding of autonomous persons is significant because it threatens to establish "a permanent dependence between persons," a permanence at odds with "the reciprocal and symmetrical relations of mutual recognition proper to a moral and legal community of free and equal persons" (ibid.: 65). Genetic engineering then, on Habermas's account, not only poses a threat in virtue of the attitude of mastery engendered in the engineer but also in virtue of the change it induces in our social relationships.

5.3.4 Radical human enhancement is not prudentially valuable for humans

Jason Eberl advances a Thomistic account of the human person as the basis for the evaluation of HET. On Eberl's account, human persons are beings endowed with "a capacity for self-conscious rational thought and autonomous volition," and therefore members "of the moral community" (Eberl, 2017: 317; cf. Eberl, 2014). While we are essentially "rational animals," "our biological nature is… essential to who we are insofar as it subserves our capacity for self-conscious rational thought and autonomous volition" (ibid.: 318).

> Eberl's Thomistic account includes an account of human flourishing, in which flourishing is defined by a set of capacities relative to our existence as living, sentient, social,

and rational animals. Human flourishing involves actualizing these definitive capacities…
such that each of us becomes the most perfect – that is, most complete or fully actualized
– human being we can be.

(ibid.: 319)

To attain flourishing, humans possess natural inclinations to pursue what we take to be good. An account of these natural inclinations, "natural law," identifies "a set of principles which, if followed, will satisfy a human being's natural inclinations in accord with reason, and thus lead to perfection according to her nature as a human being" (Eberl, 2017: 319).

It is by specifying human capacities one can derive general precepts of the natural law, simply by specifying the correlative goods of these capacities. The specification of the particular goods relative to our capacities can thus inform "both negative and positive moral obligations and limits" (ibid.: 320). As an example, "sentience may be understood broadly to refer to human beings' capacity to sense their environment and respond to it, along with the correlative experiences of pleasure and pain" (ibid.). Since sentience refers, along with our responsiveness to the environment to our capacity for pleasure and pain, we can conclude that depriving someone of the capacity for sensation, or causing pain to this person, would in fact be bad; thus we are obligated not to deprive a person of their senses or cause them needless pain, either intentionally or by negligence (ibid.: 319–320).

Since part of what it means to be human is to be an *animal*, to have goods essentially tied to embodiment, sensation, and the like, certain forms of physical enhancement can conduce to human flourishing. Enhancement is not *per se* impermissible, at least not without further specification as to its type and degree. For example, enhancement for health and longevity has a clear bearing on human flourishing since health is a basic good, insofar as we are corporeal, as well as necessary for intellectual flourishing. More generally, some forms of physical enhancement may be permissible if they conduce to the natural ends and goods proper to the human (Eberl, 2017: 320–321). But to the extent that enhancement would cause us to forget essential aspects of our condition, or renounce or impede us from achieving the goods proper to our nature, it is contrary to human flourishing.

Nicholas Agar also advances prudential arguments against radical human enhancement.[6] (Agar, 2014: 3–4) On Agar's account, radical enhancement is a negative transformative change. Accordingly, a radically transformed, posthuman state is not good for humans to achieve (ibid., 15–16). This argument is rooted, at least in part, in facts about our psychological constitution. How we assign value to prospective experiences and form preferences is significant since the prospective benefits of a radically transformed mode of existence are too imaginatively remote for us to assign them any significant value *for ourselves* (Agar, 2014: 42–44). And conversely, the effects of radical enhancement would leave us in a situation where we looked upon our past, unenhanced, achievements as quaint or paltry (Agar, 2014: 42–44).

Additionally, Agar argues that as we radically enhance our capacities, they cease to yield their intrinsic goods. For while a capacity's *instrumental* value tends to increase with enhancement, its *intrinsic* value will increase – but only to a point (ibid.: 28–29). Past a certain point, however, the objective enhancement of a capacity will actually impede us from realizing the goods intrinsic to its exercise (ibid.: 27–29). Thus, according to Agar, radical human enhancement is not good for us, and in fact can devalue the capacities we attempt to enhance by rendering it more difficult to attain the internal goods of these capacities.

5.4 Reception of arguments from human dignity

The reception of arguments from human dignity is mixed in the bioethics literature, though there is a rich and expansive literature on human dignity generally. There is, in some quarters, skepticism as to the value of dignity talk *at all*, as evinced by Ruth Macklin's devastating invective "Dignity is a useless concept" (Macklin, 2003). Macklin writes that "a close inspection of leading examples shows that appeals to dignity are either vague restatements of other, more precise, notions or mere slogans that add nothing to an understanding of the topic" (Macklin, 2003: 1419). Macklin's assessment of the role of "dignity" talk is echoed, among others, by Steven Pinker, Alasdair Cochrane, and Mirko Bagaric and James Allan (Pinker, 2008; Cochrane, 2010; Bagaric and Allan, 2006).

Cochrane, for example, argues that while varying conceptions of human dignity – of dignity as virtuous behavior, inherent moral worth, species integrity, and as Kantian dignity – are coherent, they all fail (Cochrane, 2010: 235–241). And Bagaric and Allan argue that non-utilitarian justifications of rights in terms of human dignity fail, that "dignity" "is without bounds and… incapable of explaining or justifying any narrower interests… it is a notion that is used by academics, judges, and legislators when rational justifications have been exhausted" (Baragic and Allan, 2006: 260).

> Michael Hauskeller is slightly more sanguine about dignity talk, writing that even though [ideas such as human dignity, sacredness, and social justice] are a bit airy-fairy, for many of us, they do capture something that is both elusive and very real, a sense perhaps that living disease-free and surviving as long as possible is not all that matters, that sometimes more is at stake, that there are other dimensions of our life and experiences that are important to us and for us, whatever they may be.
>
> *(Hauskeller, 2016: xi)*

In other words, though talk of human dignity identifies something real and morally significant, it *is* elusive. Fabrice Jotterand appears to concur on this point, writing that "while… human dignity as a heuristic concept is not very helpful because too vague, it still captures some characteristics of human existence (uniqueness, respect for, etc.)" (Jotterand, 2010: 48). In this same vein, Shannon Vallor writes that "normative discourse on human enhancement technology is not likely to be coherent or fruitful as long as… disparate and sometimes conflicting moral intuitions are conflated and packaged together under the amorphous heading of 'human dignity'" (Vallor, 2011: 141). Even those who are at least in principle sympathetic to the concept of dignity, then, have found it to be insufficiently clear.

Finally, Nick Bostrom has argued that human dignity is *compatible* with radical human enhancement. That is, dignity is not ambiguous or useless but applicable to posthuman as well as human entities. Enhancement need not obliterate or imperil human dignity. Assigning and recognizing dignity need not be a zero-sum game, and we "can work to create more inclusive social structures that accord appropriate moral recognition and legal rights to all who need them, be they male or female, black or white, flesh or silicon" (Bostrom, 2005a: 210). The dignity attributed to humans, which we possess in many different degrees, may well be available to posthuman beings. In fact, "they may even be able to attain higher levels of moral and other excellence than any of us humans" (Bostrom, 2005a: 210). Ronald Sadler and John Basl concur with Bostrom, arguing that "posthuman [or radical] cognitive enhancement is compatible with possession of the sort of moral status associated with human dignity… [since] on only one type of basis (species membership) might they be incompatible," and dignity predicated on species membership "is problematic" (Sadler and Basl, 2010: 66).

The case against radical enhancement made from human dignity, then, depends on a great deal of clarification: clarification as to the nature, grounds, and normative force of dignity. Some of this work has already been done, for example in taxonomies developed by Daniel Sulmasy and David G. Kirchhoffer (Sulmasy, 2013; Kirchhoffer, 2017). For example, Sulmasy distinguishes between intrinsic, attributed, and inflorescent dignity. In Sulmasy's taxonomy, "intrinsic dignity" signifies "that worth, statures, or value that human beings have simply because they are human," thereby corresponding to Kass's "basic dignity of human being" (Sulmasy, 2013: 938). By contrast, "attributed dignity" refers to "worth, stature, or value that human beings confer upon others by acts of attribution" (ibid.). "Inflorescent dignity," finally, occupies a distinctive place in this taxonomy. While it is tied to being human, it is not possessed by *all* humans; rather, "inflorescent dignity" describes "the worth or value of a state of affairs by which an individual human being expresses human excellence," and this corresponds to the "full dignity of being flourishingly human" (Sulmasy, 2013: 938). But while this helps us to attain some conceptual clarity, it still leaves unanswered the questions of whether dignity can be more profitably reduced to other normative concepts, and whether any account of dignity can withstand critical scrutiny.

5.5 Reception of arguments from human nature

Arguments that draw on notions of human nature or essence are likewise controversial and have met with a mixed reception. There are two sources of reservation on this front: either the notion of human nature is not scientifically or philosophically respectable, or else "nature" is not a robust source for normative and ethical guidance.

One common refrain in the literature is that the notion of human nature is neither scientifically nor philosophically respectable. Tim Lewens, surveying the discussion of "human nature" by biologists and philosophers of biology, concludes that "the only biologically respectable notion of human nature… is an extremely permissive one that names the reliable dispositions of the human species as a whole. This conception offers no ethical guidance in debates over enhancement" (Lewens, 2012: 460) Lewens is not alone in arguing this, but rehearses an objection found in the work of David Hull, Michael Ghiselin, and Elliott Sober among others (Hull, 1986; Ghiselin, 1997; Sober, 1980). And while it is worth noting that there is room for *a* "biologically respectable notion of human nature," according to Lewens it is not an *essentialist* notion of human nature.

Others take exception to talk of human nature because it is not robust enough to be a source of normative and ethical guidance. Bjørn Hofmann argues, for example, that "human nature is normatively bidirectional, i.e., that it can be both good and bad," (Hofmann, 2017: 3), that "human nature is changing, and thus cannot provide a stable conception of what is good," (ibid.), and concludes that "the concepts of naturalness, therapy, and disease… do not seem to do the job [of restricting human enhancement]" (Hofmann, 2017: 9). This type of objection is often leveled against neo-Aristotelian naturalism, particularly Philippa Foot's account of natural goodness, under the guise of the "Pollyanna Problem" (Milgram, 2009; Kim, 2018). As Richard Kim formulates the problem,

> empirical research shows us that immoral characteristics such as injustice, at least under certain conditions serves a useful function in human life, and since the Aristotelian categoricals are constituted by characteristics that are constitutive of human flourishing, it looks like sometimes injustice will count as an aspect of human, and therefore, moral goodness. But since injustice cannot be morally good, it looks like Foot's natural goodness framework (and Aristotelian naturalism in general) when combined with our current knowledge of empirical facts, will generate morally unacceptable consequences.
> *(Kim, 2018: 143–144; cf. Milgram, 2009: 561–562)*

In fact, it is just this problem that helps frame the permissivist approach as described in Section 2.

Broadly speaking, then, arguments from human nature seem subject to a nasty dilemma. On the one hand, "human nature" may seem scientifically or philosophically unrespectable because it is too unmoored from empirical facts about the human condition to be plausible. On the other hand, "human nature" may be so tethered to empirical facts about the human condition that it generates amoralist or immoralist recommendations. Each horn is unpalatable, and so it is incumbent on the defender of human nature to articulate just what human nature is, and how it can steer a path between the two horns indicated above.

5.6 Conclusion

In sum, we have discussed key themes in restrictivist and bioconservative criticisms of radical human enhancement. We have noted, as well, how these arguments – and their central concepts – have been received in the literature. Generally, as is to be expected, these arguments have met with a mixed reception. Appeals to human dignity and human nature often draw on vague or underspecified accounts of "nature" and "dignity," a situation capable of being partly ameliorated by careful attention and by the development of taxonomic resources.

Apart from the need to fully specify and articulate the content of the concepts employed in these arguments, however, we have seen that these arguments meet more foundational objections regarding their coherence and legitimacy. What remains to be seen, then, is whether restrictivists and bioconservatives can articulate substantial accounts of "dignity" and "nature" that defuse their interlocutors' objections. This task, if it is to be accomplished, requires concepts of "dignity" and "nature" that are robust enough to generate normative and ethical guidance, and responsive enough to empirical research to not simply be an oversimplified or idealized abstraction.

Acknowledgments

I would like to express my gratitude to Jason Eberl, Alexander Zhang, Derek Estes, John Yoon, and an anonymous reviewer for their generous and helpful contributions to the writing of this chapter.

Notes

1 While one common division of the camps at play is between "bioconservative" and "bioliberal" positions, these have the potential to be undeservedly pejorative or totalizing. Here I follow Alberto Giubilini and Sagar Sanyal in dividing the territory between permissivists, restrictivists, and bioconservatives to avoid as much as possible the possibility of letting political distinctions muddy the waters or reducing the diversity of approaches which object to radical human enhancement (Giubilini and Sanyal, 2015).
2 Jason Eberl's contribution to this volume motivates the inclusion of philosophical anthropology – broadly including "the question of what constitutes human nature and the identity of human persons through time and change" – as an indispensable element in further research on the ethics of human enhancement (Eberl, forthcoming: 14).
3 While there are other objections, such as objections from autonomy (Schafer, Kahane, and Savulescu, 2014; Juth, 2011), *hubris* (Vallor, 2011), and backfiring objections (Browne and Clarke, 2020), I will only discuss them to the extent that they concern the human *qua* human.
4 Permissivists will sometimes argue that education is another enhancement that even bioconservatives acknowledge as permissible (cf. Sorgner, 2022: 13).
5 Some forms of enhancement arguably span these categories, so they need not be mutually exclusive or exhaustive. Consider the prospect of lifespan enhancement: it arguably involves physical, emotional, and cognitive dimensions, since what we are after is not *simply* a remarkably durable body, but the extension of a person's ability to live and consciously experience and enjoy such a life.
6 Agar's argument against radical physical enhancement, discussed below, is a prudential one. But in Chapters 6 and 9, Agar offers moral arguments against life extension and moral enhancement.

References

Agar, N., 2014. *Truly Human Enhancement: A Philosophical Defense of Limits*. Cambridge: MIT Press.
Bagaric, M. & Allan, J., 2006. "The Vacuous Concept of Dignity". *Journal of Human Rights*, 5, pp. 257–270.
Bostrom, N., 2003. *The Transhumanist FAQ*. s.l.: World Transhumanist Organization.
Bostrom, N., 2005a. "In Defense of Posthuman Dignity". *Bioethics*, 19(3), pp. 202–214.
Bostrom, N., 2005b. "Transhumanist Values". *Journal of Philosophical Research*, 30, pp. 3–14.

Browne, T. K. & Clarke, S., 2020. "Bioconservatism, Bioenhancement, and Backfiring". *Journal of Moral Education*, 49(2), pp. 241–256.

Buchanan, A. E., 2011. *Better than Human: The Promise and Perils of Enhancing Ourselves*. New York: Oxford University Press.

Byeleveld, D. & Brownsword, R., 2001. *Human Dignity in Bioethics and Biolaw*. New York: Oxford University Press.

Cochrane, A., 2010. "Undignified Bioethics". *Bioethics*, 25(5), pp. 234–241.

Eberl, J., 2014. "A Thomistic Appraisal of Human Enhancement Technologies". *Theoretical Medicine and Bioethics*, 35, pp. 289–310.

Eberl, J., 2017. "Philosophical Anthropology, Ethics, and Human Enhancement". In: J. Eberl, ed. *Contemporary Controversies in Catholic Bioethics*. Cham: Springer, pp. 313–330.

Eberl, J., forthcoming. "Does Enhancement Violate Human 'Nature'?" In: F. Jotterand, ed. *Routledge Handbook of the Ethics of Human Enhancement*. New York: Routledge.

Ghiselin, M., 1997. *Metaphysics and the Origin of Species*. New York: SUNY Press.

Giubilini, A. & Sanyal, S. "The Ethics of Human Enhancement." *Philosophy Compass*, 10, pp. 233–243.

Habermas, J., 2003. *The Future of Human Nature*. Malden: Polity Press.

Harris, J., 2007. *Enhancing Evolution: The Ethical Case for Making Better People*. Princeton: Princeton University Press.

Hauskeller, M., 2016. *Mythologies of Transhumanism*. Cham: Palgrave McMillan.

Hofmann, B., 2017. "Limits to human enhancement: nature, disease, therapy or betterment?". *BMC Medical Ethics*, 18(56).

Hull, D., 1986. *Human Nature*. East Lansing, PSA: Proceedings of the Biennial Meeting of the Philosophy of Science Association.

Jotterand, F., 2010. "Human Dignity and Transhumanism: Do Anthro-Technological Devices Have Moral Status?". *The American Journal of Bioethics*, 10(7), pp. 45–52.

Juth, N., 2011. "Enhancement, Autonomy, and Authenticity". In: J. Savulescu, R. ter Meulen & G. Kahane, eds. *Enhancing Human Capacities*. Malden: Blackwell Publishing Ltd., pp. 34–48.

Kahane, G., Pugh, J. & Savulescu, J., 2016. "Bioconservatism, Partiality, and the Human-Nature Objection to Enhancement". *The Monist*, 99(4), pp. 406–422.

Kass, L., 2002. *Life, Liberty, and the Defense of Dignity: The Challenge for Bioethics*. San Francisco: Encounter Books.

Kim, R. T., 2018. "Human Nature and Moral Sprouts: Mencius on the Pollyanna Problem". *Pacific Philosophical Quarterly*, 99, pp. 140–162.

Kirchhoffer, D. G., 2017. "Human Dignity and Human Enhancement: A Multidimensional Approach". *Bioethics*, 31(5), pp. 375–383.

Lewens, T., 2012. "Human Nature: The Very Idea". *Philosophy & Technology*, 25, pp. 459–474.

Macklin, R., 2003. "Dignity is a Useless Concept". *BMJ*, 327, pp. 1419–1420.

McPherson, D., 2022. *The Virtues of Limits*. New York: Oxford University Press.

Milgram, E., 2009. "Life and Action". *Analysis*, 69(3), pp. 557–564.

Overall, C., 2011. "Lifespan Extension: Metaphysical Basis and Ethical Outcomes". In: J. Savulescu, R. ter Meulen & G. Kahane, eds. *Enhancing Human Capacities*. Malden: Blackwell Publishing Ltd., pp. 386–397.

Pinker, S., 2008. "The Stupidity of Dignity". *The New Republic*, 27 May.

Rubin, C., 2008. "Human Dignity and the Future of Man". In: P. C. O. Bioethics, ed. *Human Dignity and Bioethics: Essays Commissioned by the President's Council on Bioethics*. Washington, DC: President's Council on Bioethics, pp. 155–172.

Sadler, R. & Basl, J., 2010. "Transhumanism, Human Dignity, and Moral Status". *The American Journal of Bioethics*, 10(7), pp. 63–66.

Sandel, M., 2007. *The Case Against Perfection: Ethics in the Age of Genetic Engineering*. Cambridge: Belknap Press.

Savulsecu, J., Meulen, R. T. & Kahane, G., 2011. *Enhancing Human Capacities*. Malden: Blackwell Publishing Ltd.

Schafer, G. O., Kahane, G. & Savulescu, J., 2014. "Autonomy and Enhancement". *Neuroethics*, 7(2), pp. 123–136.

Sober, E., 1980. "Evolution, Population Thinking, and Essentialism". *Philosophy of Science*, 47(3), pp. 350–383.

Sulmasy, D., 2013. "The Varieties of Human Dignity: A Logical and Conceptual Analysis". *Medicine, Health Care, and Philosophy*, 16, pp. 937–944.

Vallor, S., 2011. "Knowing What to Wish For: Human Enhancement Technology, Dignity, and Virtue". *Techné*, 15(2), pp. 137–155.

6
RESURRECTING THE 'BODY'
Phenomenological perspectives on embodiment

Vera Borrmann, Christopher Coenen, Luisa Gerstgrasser,
Eva Albers, Oliver Müller, and Philipp Kellmeyer

6.1 Introduction

Practices of human self-design and self-optimization are closely linked to our human corporeality: the idea of the human body as inherently deficient is a major motivation and justification for enhancement interventions. Consequently, a philosophical approach to the possibilities, realities, and necessities of enhancement practices and technologies should include reflections on embodiment and human corporeality. This does not only mean that we need to take a closer look at the arguments that draw on the deficiency of human corporeality, but we also must locate these kinds of discourses within the greater spectrum of possible interpretations of human corporeality. Since ancient times, the human body and the mind-body problem were core topics of Western philosophy, but it was only in the 20th century that questions of embodiment and corporeality were systematically explored in a way that did justice to their complexity. This includes most notably phenomenological, anthropological, and sociophilosophical (such as feminist and political) perspectives.[1] In addition to these philosophical developments, 20th-century medicine, including psychiatry and psychosomatic medicine as well as psychology and cognitive science, played an important role, particularly in applying phenomenological theory.

In this article, we first (1) describe how body and embodiment were (re)discovered and explored in philosophical anthropology and phenomenology. This not only gave the topic a new relevance but can also be understood as a starting point for re-examining the role of the body in diverse fields of interdisciplinary research such as cognitive science. Secondly (2), we will give a short overview of the most important approaches that aim at integrating empirical findings in a phenomenological framework, e.g., from neuroscience, cognitive science, psychopathology, and other disciplines, including attempts to develop practical applications such as interview methods of phenomenologically-based embodiment theories. Finally (3), we will portray and discuss the current debate on medical enhancement regarding prevalent understandings and presuppositions of what the human body is and how it should be technologically shaped. This includes transhumanism as a radical visionary worldview promoting enhancement and often, ultimately, disembodiment.[2]

6.2 The emergence of embodiment in philosophy and interdisciplinary research

6.2.1 Historical roots: The deficiency of the body and the dominance of mind-body dualism

The question of which role human corporeality plays in our thinking, perceiving, and feeling has been much debated throughout the history of occidental philosophy. In this sense, the question of embodiment is philosophically a very old one. The main philosophical currents are driven by dualistic distinctions between mental and physical traits, interiority and exteriority, freedom, and natural determination, as well as subjectivity and objectivity. These dualisms are often accompanied by a devaluation of the body and, especially in the Christian tradition, with burden and vice. Very influential to the development of Western thought is the Platonic juxtaposition of a deception-prone world of the senses with the eternal-immaterial world of ideas. Notably, in *Phaedo*, Plato argues at various points that the soul is a divine, indivisible, permanent, and invisible immaterial substance, independent of the body, whose true nature is exceedingly difficult for man to grasp and remains to some extent a mystery:

> And what is purification but the separation of the soul from the body, as I was saying before; the habit of the soul gathering and collecting herself into herself, out of all the courses of the body; the dwelling in her own place alone, as in another life, so also in this, as far as she can; the release of the soul from the chains of the body?[3]

A similarly influential variant of this dualism can be found in the Judeo-Christian narrative of the naked body shamefully discovered in the moment of self-awareness, which becomes particularly relevant for the question of enhancement when arguments for enhancement take on eschatological traits, e.g. in transhumanist positions (cf. Sub-Sections 6.4, 6.4.1 and 6.4.2).

Especially relevant for the reflection of corporeality today is the Cartesian differentiation of *res cogitans* and *res extensa*, a radical version of Western dualist thinking with far-reaching consequences not only in philosophy but also for the development of the natural sciences. The differentiation of *res cogitans* and *res extensa* is radical because it distinguishes categorically between a subjective entity (which has the ability to think) and the body (as a mere vessel), with the far-reaching consequence that the human mind is understood as completely separated from its bodily anchorage. "There is a great difference between the mind and the body. Every body is by its nature divisible, but the mind can't be divided."[4] This tendency to identify an ideal subjectivity with a somehow "pure" mind evolves into the modern concept of subjectivity as a mainly or even purely rational "ego" that underlies numerous schools of thought since the Enlightenment. Furthermore, this differentiation famously leads to the equation of material bodies with technical automata and establishes a mechanistic view of the world and the human body, which in many cases has echoes in today's life sciences.

> We could see it [the body] as a kind of machine made up of bones, nerves, muscles, veins, blood and skin in such a way that, even if there were no mind in it, it would still move exactly as it now does in all the cases where movement isn't under the control of the will or, therefore, of the mind.[5]

Parallel to and conceptually fully aligned with this dualistic notion developed since René Descartes, the sciences researching the human body made significant progress throughout the 19th century, nurturing mechanistic interpretations of human life, taking the differentiation of *res cogitans* and *res extensa* for granted. This is particularly evident in the development of modern medicine: one may think, for example, of Rudolf Virchow's pathological studies on body cells and the subsequent replacement of humoral pathology with cellular pathology. According to cellular pathology, diseases are no longer perceived as imbalances of the four body humors but as functional or structural damage to the body's cells. Conceptually, illness turns into a malfunction of physical infrastructure within reproducible bodily entities.

6.2.2 (Re)discovering the body: tendencies in 20th-century thought

Things changed at the end of the 19th century. Doubts regarding the dualistic and rationalistic concepts of subjectivity and its derogatory dealings with the body led to the first attempts at a rehabilitation of the body for conceptions of subjectivity. Friedrich Nietzsche's prominent statement against the "despiser of the body" may serve as an example: "Behind your thoughts and feelings stands a mighty commander; an unknown sage – he is called Self. In your body he dwells, your body he is."[6] For Nietzsche, the Self resides in the body, which means that any subjective experience is necessarily also a bodily one. This concept has sown the seeds for numerous conceptions of what will be called the "lived body" within the thinking about corporeality in the 20th century. The primacy of the rational ego begins to crumble; with Sigmund Freud, "the Ego is not master in its own house."[7] But already Arthur Schopenhauer's philosophy of the will and the so-called *Lebensphilosophie* (e.g., Wilhelm Dilthey, Henri Bergson, Georg Simmel) developed their approaches as an opposition to a purely rationalistic view of human subjectivity. An Ego that purified of all worldliness (Descartes), fully present to itself through a critique of pure reason (Immanuel Kant), sometimes even a "*Selbstsetzung*"[8] (Johann Gottlieb Fichte), seems no longer tenable at the beginning of the 20th century.

In this chapter, we want to trace the story of a broadening and refined reflection on body, corporeality, the lived body, and embodiment by starting with the (re)discovery of the body in philosophical anthropology and phenomenology and the early attempts to overcome the aforementioned dualisms (Section 6.2.2.1). These first disclosures of the importance of the bodily experience thereby opened new perspectives on the understanding of "the other" as well (Section 6.2.2.2). We then contrast the phenomenological approaches with the reflection on socio-cultural body politics (Section 6.2.2.3) and technology (Sub-Section 6.2.2.4) as a necessary relational part of the debate on the lived body and embodiment. To challenge the notorious eurocentrism of the discourse, we finally will exemplarily mention concepts from East Asia to strengthen the importance of transcultural explorations in this field (Section 6.2.2.5).

6.2.2.1 Overcoming mind-body dualism: The body as a new starting point in philosophy

With the inauguration of the philosophical anthropology (Max Scheler, Helmuth Plessner) in the 1920s and the further development of Edmund Husserl's phenomenology, namely by Maurice Merleau-Ponty above all, began the systematic exploration of the "lived experience" of the human body, a body not reducible to its mere physicality. In German, the (not perfectly translatable) differentiation between *Körper* (the physical thing) and the *Leib* (the felt and subjectively experienced body or "lived body")[9] was introduced and *Leibphilosophie* and *Leibphänomenologie* (philosophy and phenomenology of the lived body) were *peu à peu* established as new disciplines, often including psychopathological findings. Since then, a vast number of studies appeared, including various attempts to revise the early phenomenological approaches with respect to embodiment questions, from Neue Phänomenologie ("new phenomenology," Hermann Schmitz) to postphenomenology (Don Ihde) and queer phenomenology (Sara Ahmed), to name but a few. In our portrayal of embodiment theories, we cannot offer an overview of the entire field; we rather focus on Plessner and Merleau-Ponty, as they represent the paradigm shift in the way to think about body, corporeality, and embodiment, trying to overcome the old psychophysical dualisms.

With his philosophical analysis of the organic in his book *Levels of the Organic Life and the Human* from 1928, Plessner creates crucial starting points for a philosophy of biology that does not leave the sphere of embodiment to purely scientific observation and its reductionism, respectively.[10] Plessner has performed multiple studies on the interrelationship between the mental and physical spheres of life. Based on the conceptual distinction between *Körper* and *Leib*, he underlines that human beings can thus live in the mode of *having* a body and *being* a lived body at the same time. Plessner calls this the "dual aspect"[11] of Körper and Leib and tries to describe it as follows:

> Even in a purely physical way it is "its lived body". The spacelike center, the core, or the self thus no longer immediately "lies in" the body (…). The living thing is itself in itself. The position is a dual one: being the body itself and being in the body – and yet it is singular, since the living thing's distance to its own body is only possible due to its complete oneness with its own body alone.[12]

So, on the one hand, human life has physical conditions which are no less real only because they are not immediately evident as such in the vivid reality of the lived body. On the other hand, the phenomenal quality of the lived body as a primary (pre-reflexive) form of experience is not called into question by the fact that it is physically conditioned and can be examined scientifically. Plessner develops a complex theory of what human beings are by drawing on his hermeneutic of the living (with the "positionality of the excentric form" as a core concept). And the dual aspect of Körper and Leib allows Plessner to describe the "natural artificiality" of human life: living one's life means for human beings to lead one's life. And precisely this aspect of "living a life" can neither be captured by reductionist approaches nor in a dualistic framework.

At the same time and in parallel to Plessner, Husserl introduced in his phenomenology both the concept of the lived body (in the context of intersubjective understanding and empathy) and the concept of "*Lebenswelt*" (life-world); the latter turned out to be very influential in 20th-century thought. The life-world is, as the sphere of the self-evident lived experience of subjects, the ground of all theoretical knowledge. Based on these concepts, Merleau-Ponty developed his philosophy of the human body, especially in *Phenomenology of Perception*, published in 1945. Departing from the concept of the life-world (and Martin Heidegger's being-in-the-world), Merleau-Ponty states and thereby criticizes the idealistic version of mind-body dualism with reference to the "inner man":

The world is not an object whose law of constitution I have in my possession; it is the natural milieu and the field of all my thoughts and of all my explicit perception. Truth does not merely "dwell" in the "inner man", or rather, there is no "inner man", man is in and toward the world, and it is in the world that he knows himself (…). I do not find a source of intrinsic truth, but rather a subject destined to the world.[13]

And this very basic being-in-the-world now is inextricably linked to the body:

The body is the vehicle of being in the world and, for a living being, having a body means being united with a definite "milieu".[14] With this bodily anchored being in the world, Merleau-Ponty aims at establishing a "junction of the 'psychical' and 'physiological'"[15]

hence trying to overcome the aforementioned dualism. Embodiment includes also perspectivity, situatedness, and various forms of ambiguity that characterize the human being in the world. Furthermore, Merleau-Ponty made the distinction between body schema and body image prominent and introduced the term "intercorporeality" in the living experience of "the other."

While both Plessner and Merleau-Ponty shed new light on the body as a "psychophysically indifferent"[16] entity, opening new perspectives on how we can approach the mind-body problem, only Merleau-Ponty is, due to the contingencies of history, now deemed internationally the "founding figure" of various embodiment theories, from neurophenomenology to enactivism and 4E cognition (cf. Sub-Sections 6.3.1.1, 6.3.1.2 and 6.3.1.3). And not least with the interdisciplinarity of both approaches, Plessner and Merleau-Ponty established a "style of thinking" that acts as a model for current research programs in philosophy that include findings of various sciences, such as neuroscience, psychology, or cognitive science (cf. Sub-Section 6.3).

6.2.2.2 The importance of alterity: Including "the other" in embodiment theories

With the notion of "intercorporalité" (intercoporeality), Merleau-Ponty discussed questions of alterity[17] laying the groundwork for phenomenological investigations of how we experience other human beings via our body as the vehicle of being in the world. And at the latest since Emmanuel Lévinas inaugurated a new way of thinking about the other in phenomenology, a series of inquiries were explicitly devoted to the problem of "the other." Here, we will exemplarily refer to Bernhard Waldenfels' Responsive Phenomenology – because it counts as one of the most advanced phenomenological studies on the problem of the other based on the lived experience of the body.[18] Immediately drawing on Plessner's and Merleau-Ponty's concept of the lived body, Waldenfels proclaims the "embodied self" as the central interface and mediating instance of various possible modes of experiencing otherness. When we refer to our own lived body, we already undertake a certain alienation because every experience of the self is fundamentally accompanied by otherness that occurs within the process of self-identification (in the sense of Paul Ricoeur's "Oneself as Another"). Against this background, Waldenfels introduces Responsive Phenomenology. Bodily experience is always a response to otherness (in contrast to a mere physiological reaction), referring to the neurologist Kurt Goldstein's theory of the organism.[19] Waldenfels developed the theory of a multi-layered "responsorium" of the body, sometimes using the dialectically intertwined terms "pathos" and "response." In his theory, responding always has normative implications: As such, bodily responsiveness is on a very basic level already connected to the "demands" of other bodies.

6.2.2.3 Social (de)construction and embodiment: The body, politics, and feminism

Continuing the motive of the importance of the other for embodiment, this chapter is about the political, societal, and symbolic dimensions of the body. As a result of the performative turn and body turn in the 1990s and its pre-forms since the mid-20th century, the discourse of the body's political and societal dimension had far-reaching consequences and effects not only in philosophy, sociology, and anthropology but also especially in gender studies and feminist theory. Common ground for schools of thought related to post-modernism, deconstruction, and post-structuralism is the assumption that the body is not merely a product of society in terms of its malleability through institutions, structures, discourses, or as a carrier of attributions – the body is seen, as an active producer of society, rules and norms as a medium for routine and performance. Accordingly, the perspectives of authors like Michel Foucault or Judith Butler on embodiment and the body itself are not concerned with the body as the point zero of orientation in the world like in phenomenology. Two of their main questions are rather whether and how the materiality of the body can be related to its historicity and performativity, considering the determination of power and discourse as well. Following this presupposition, this genealogical critique refuses originality or metaphysical assumptions and highlights terms like difference, iteration, and becoming rather than dualistic binary oppositions[20] such as nature/culture, sex/gender, or body/mind.

Body politics and embodiment also play a major role in gender studies, feminist theory, and associated disciplines – but the relationship between sex, gender, and body has always been ambivalent. The fundamental distinction between sex (biological) and gender (societal/cultural) according to Robert J. Stoller (1968) was discarded by Judith Butler in *Gender Trouble* (1990) and *Bodies that Matter* (1993) for a performative assertion of body and gender, highlighting rather constructedness and becoming. According to Butler, body and gender produce social codes and gender roles by performance, iteration, rituals, and citation of certain rules or habits – not vice versa. In addition, feminist scholars have also explored whether and how phenomenological theory can be applied to feminist theorizing about gender, the body, and politics.[21] From this perspective, the gender difference between man and woman is neither a "natural" ontological fact nor constructed but socially mediated in the process of becoming as Butler derives from Nietzsche or Simon de Beauvoir.

Taking into consideration that classical Western philosophy is founded on the assumption that truth, being, and reality are determined in relation to a transcendental ontological center or origin – which implies the dualism of body and mind – a more immanence-oriented approach to embodiment such as 4E cognition (cp. Section 6.3.1.3 on 4E cognition) which brings various social, felt, and environmental criteria for embodiment (embedded, enacted, embodied, extended) together, can be considered as a "reconstructive gesture."

6.2.2.4 Postphenomenology, embodiment, and technology

As emerging technologies challenge our understanding of embodiment, the philosophy of technology discovered embodiment questions as a crucial concept for the reflection of novel medical and biotechnologies. In postphenomenology, a method to describe human–technology interactions developed by Don Ihde, questions of embodiment are directly addressed. Postphenomenology is predicated on the premise that almost every human relationship is technologically mediated. Therefore, a philosophy of technology can systematically examine basic human–world relations. These relations constitute an "(inter)relational ontology."[22] We understand ourselves largely through the technologies with which we perceive and act in the world. And at the same time, there are no technologies "as such." They "are" only in connection with the respective domains of human experience and subjectivity: "Technologies transform our experience of the world and our perceptions and interpretations of our world, and we in turn become transformed in this process."[23] Based on the phenomenological premises that we are intentional and embodied beings characterized by a basic "being-in-the-world," Ihde developed in *Technology and the Lifeworld*, a differentiation between four main relations that characterize the human–technology entanglement,[24] namely embodiment relations: we incorporate technologies and experience technologies through our bodies; hermeneutic relations: technologies shape our interpretation of the world and of ourselves in a very basic sense; alterity relations: we understand machines in a specific kind of "otherness"; and background relations: meaning that we usually live in a technological world and accept technical regimes without knowing or reflecting it. The embodiment relation is characterized as follows:

> our sense of "body" is embodied outward, directionally and referentially, and the technology becomes part of our ordinary experience of _____ […]. [The instrument] enters into my bodily, actional, perceptual relationship with my environment […]. [The instrument] is a *means* of experience, not an object of experience *in use* […]. The artifact is symbiotically "taken into" my bodily experience and directed toward an action into or upon the environment."[25]

6.2.2.5 Broadening the view: transcultural perspectives on embodiment

The approaches portrayed so far mainly reflect a Western approach of philosophy on embodiment. However, the trans- and intercultural aspects of embodiment theory have increasingly been addressed since the early 20th century, and influences on Western approaches have been recognized and asserted. Especially traditional religious systems and practices like the orthodox (Advaita Vedanta in particular) and heterodox (various schools of Buddhism) systems of Indian philosophy, as well as modern Zen-Buddhism, influenced developments in Japanese philosophy (e.g., Kitaro Nishida or Tetsuro Watsuji) and the philosophical network around the Dalai Lama in the context of the Mind & Life Institute. Notably, contemporary scholars of Tibetan Buddhism such as the 14th Dalai Lama, Thupten Jinpa, or Matthieu Ricard[26] are open and even promote a dialogue with modern sciences which is reflected in the foundation of institutions such as the Center for Compassion and Altruism Research and Education (CCARE) at Stanford University School of Medicine or the Mind & Life Institute (MLI), which organize meetings between the 14th Dalai Lama and scientists on science and Buddhist philosophy, and meditation practice as well as various conferences and symposia on consciousness and cognitive science.[27]

The topic of embodiment is always addressed in context with questions about consciousness and selfhood in South Asian and East Asian philosophy. In Tibetan Buddhism for example, the idea of "a Self" that is a separate entity in a certain region in the brain (or the body) is rejected. The self is more a process than an entity, and it arises in accord with its environment and experiences. The concepts of the interdependence and inseparability of phenomena – including the self – are the core of how Buddhists envision the nature of reality and existence. From this perspective, phenomena cannot exist autonomously, they are always interconnected with other phenomena and therefore do not exist *per se*. This understanding of interdependence leads to a new perception of "I" and the "other" and therefore also of the body and embodiment.

"Non-Western" philosophy and thought are just as rich and diverse as the "Western" tradition and would require a whole chapter on its own. As many overlaps and co-creations took place in the last years in the context of embodied cognition (e.g., the work of Varela, Thompson, and Rosch in *The Embodied Mind*), we chose to present an insight into a part of philosophy from other traditions.

6.3 Phenomenology and transdisciplinary approaches to embodiment since the 1980s

The intellectual history of the convergence of phenomenology, cognitive science, neuroscience, psychology, psychiatry, psychosomatic medicine, psychotherapy, and applied approaches (such as microphenomenology and EASE, cf. Sub-Sections 6.3.2, 6.3.2.1 and 6.3.2.2 is complex and interdependent, resembling a rhizomatic structure rather than a clearly discernible lineage. In the following, we provide a more granular overview of the different approaches and distinguish two discernible traditions: the convergence of phenomenology, neuroscience, and cognitive science (cf. Sub-Section 6.3.1), represented by neurophenomenology (Sub-Section 6.3.1.1), enactivism (Sub-Section 6.3.1.2), 4E cognition (Sub-Section 6.3.1.3), and phenomenological-based psychopathology (Sub-Section 6.3.1.4) on the one hand; and contemporary applications of phenomenological theory, represented here by microphenomenology (Sub-Section 6.3.2.2) and EASE (Sub-Section 6.3.2.1) which are applications in psychiatry, psychosomatic medicine, and psychotherapy, on the other hand.

Since the mid-1980s, with the growing conceptual and methodological convergence of cognitive science, neuroscience, and experimental psychology, the turn toward practices of introspection has become increasingly popular. The most fruitful transdisciplinary scholarship at this intersection has been the application of concepts from phenomenology to questions in cognitive science and psychology regarding the nature of human consciousness and subjective experience. This convergence was in large parts motivated by perceived conceptual weaknesses of neuroscience as an approach that favored the level of neural computations and analytic approaches to cognition, and which ignored the role of the lived-in body as a mediator for sensations and conscious experiences.[28]

Therefore, neurophenomenology and related conceptions referred to in this chapter can be seen as a critical theory in relation to neuroscience and a part of a critical psychology that promotes an ethical advocacy for nondeterministic psychological accounts of selfhood and human agency[29] because it stresses the liberation of human experiences from the reductionism found in conventional neuroscience.

6.3.1 Contributions from cognitive science, neuroscience, psychiatry, and other fields

6.3.1.1 Neurophenomenology and embodied cognition

A major challenge for neuroscience today is to provide an explanatory framework that accounts for both, the subjectivity and neurobiology of consciousness. Although neuroscientists have supplied neural models of various aspects of consciousness, there nonetheless remains a conceptual, epistemological, and methodological "explanatory gap" about how to relate neurobiological (third-person experiences) and phenomenological (*qualia*, "what-is-it-like" first-person experiences) features of consciousness. Neurophenomenology has emerged as a transdisciplinary approach to bridge this gap by combining concepts and insights from philosophy,[30] cognitive science, psychology, and neuroscience.[31] The term "neurophenomenology" itself was introduced and first used by Charles D. Laughlin, Eugene G. d'Aquili, and John McManus,[32] and by Francisco J. Varela in 1991.[33] Primarily, neurophenomenology has become associated with Francisco Varela, whose argument was that the "hard problem" of consciousness[34] could only be addressed by a radical turn toward studying the structure of human self-experience as a means to develop an intersubjective understanding of consciousness. This way, neurophenomenology advances a method of investigation of human consciousness and living systems that resist the polarizing effects of cognitivism, objectivism, and mind-body dualism.[35]

The transdisciplinary foundation of embodied cognition found its origin in *The Embodied Mind* (1991) by Francisco Varela, Evan Thompson, and Eleanor Rosch who provided an explicit reference to the philosophy of the lived body inspired by Merleau-Ponty. According to their position, cognition is not just brain processes, it involves the brain, body, and environment. The relationship between neurophenomenology and embodiment is multi-faceted: bodies are referred to as physical structures or the milieu for cognitive mechanisms; as lived, experiential structures, and as a part of the lived world. Neurophenomenology is also considerably important for the development of enactivism, 4E cognition, and further approaches (cf. Sections 6.3.1.2, 6.3.1.3, and 6.3.1.4). In contemporary cognitive science, the 4E framework of cognition[36] is the most developed transdisciplinary framework for studying consciousness, subjective experience, and selfhood. Embodied cognition has since been elaborated interdisciplinary with references to phenomenology, philosophy of mind, psychology, neuroscience, and robotics.

6.3.1.2 Enactivism

With respect to enactivism, neurophenomenology can be considered an important and influential intellectual precursor. The word "enactive" was coined to describe the idea that cognitive structures emerge from the recurrent sensorimotor coupling of body, brain, nervous system, and environment. Like phenomenology, the enactive approach emphasizes that the organism defines its own point of view on the world. This notion of an autonomous observer has important implications for how brain activity and its relationship to mental activity, including consciousness, are conceptualized. From an enactive point of view, brain processes are recursive, re-entrant, and self-activating, and do not start or stop anywhere. Instead of treating perception as a later stage of sensation and taking the sensory receptors as the starting point for analysis, the enactive approach treats perception, emotion, and cognition as interdependent aspects of intentional action, and it takes the brain's self-generated, endogenous activity as the starting point for analysis. This activity reflects the organism's states of expectancy, preparation, emotional tonus, or attention. Traditional cognitive science would describe such internal states as acting in a top-down manner on sensory processing. From an enactive view, "top down" and "bottom up" are simply heuristic terms for what, in reality, is a large-scale brain network that integrates incoming and outgoing activities based on its own internally established reference points.

6.3.1.3 4E cognition

Later, neurophenomenology became an important influential conceptual framework that inspired the conceptual expansion of cognitive science into the now predominant framework of 4E cognition: an interdisciplinary framework within cognitive sciences that criticizes traditional concepts of cognition and cognitive processing. The main statement of 4E cognition is that cognition is not limited to the brain: cognition is embodied, embedded, extended, and enactive in contrast to the dominant brain-centric views in the field of cognitive science.

The history of 4E cognition and embodied cognition is very young. A historical anchor for understanding early work on embodied cognition in the narrow sense is the enactive perspective on cognition, such as the work on robotics and computationally intelligent action in Andy Clark's *Being There: Putting Mind, World, and Body Back Together* (1997) and more recently *How the body shapes the mind* (2006) by Shaun Gallagher. The concept of 4E cognition brings different approaches together under one heading and sees them as coherently opposed to the internalist, brain-centered views of cognitivism. However, there are still disagreements. How exactly are brain, body, and environment coupled or integrated into cognition, or which state or process counts as cognitive? Hereby, the question "What is cognition?" changed to "Where is cognition?"

Positions in embodied cognition range from weak versions (in which the body plays an important but not decisive role) to enactivist or radical positions. Enactivist embodied cognition interprets the body as part of a system that includes the brain and the environment and argues for rethinking mind and brain completely: the body, brain, and environment are tightly interwoven in a relationship and respond to the world as part of a larger system.

Theories of extended cognition on the other hand claim that environmental resources and objects can under certain conditions, count as essential components of a cognitive process.[37] Therefore, one of the authoritative questions of 4E cognition is whether it is possible to synthesize the extended mind and enactivist or embedded positions; or to advocate an enactivist version of the extended mind hypothesis. Other questions and issues arising within the context of 4E cognition are also about agency, the self, and subjectivity insofar as embodied cognition is about the relationality of the "inside" and "outside" and the deconstruction, permeability, or at least movability of boundaries, in contrast to determination and delineation of mind and body as in the classical debate of mind-body dualism. Therefore, questions arising within the context of 4E often concern agency, the self, and subjectivity. If the mind is embodied *and* extended, what role do the self, subjectivity, and consciousness play? If the mind is extended, so is the self. If the boundaries of the self shift from the brain to the body, or even from the body to the world, then the acceptance of embodied or extended cognition has implications in terms of autonomy, sociality, personal identity, and responsibility. Hence, from the enactivist viewpoint, we need to consider these relations as a large-scale dynamic network to understand how cognition, intentional action, and consciousness emerge through self-organizing neural activity.

6.3.1.4 Embodiment, embeddedness, situatedness: Phenomenological psychopathology

In parallel and in exchange with the theoretical developments around neurophenomenology and 4E cognition, another strand of applied phenomenology can be identified in intellectual history that emphasizes the importance of social embeddedness as well as situatedness: phenomenological psychopathology. Efforts in applying phenomenology in psychopathology and psychiatry have a long tradition (Karl Jaspers, Ludwig Binswanger, Erwin Straus, and others). More recently, especially the work of the German psychiatrist and philosopher Thomas Fuchs can be considered particularly representative of this approach at the intersection of philosophy and clinical psychiatry.

In his work, Fuchs starts from the tradition of German (Husserl and Heidegger) but also French phenomenology (particularly Merleau-Ponty) to make the case that phenomenology should be considered as a "basic science" for diagnosis in psychiatry but also psychotherapy. In this phenomenologically inspired psychiatry, mental illnesses are framed as disorders of the subject's relation to the minimal self (what he calls "ipseity"), narrative, or extended self.[38] In this framework, the minimal self is the most fundamental part of selfhood and is required for attributing experiences as belonging to the self. Thus, ipseity is necessary for the temporal continuity of the self. Ipseity is also embodied, not only corporeally but also in time and space. The narrative self necessarily builds on ipseity and is constituted by self-transcendence, reflective self-consciousness, self-concept, and narrativity. Fuchs uses this framework to analyze various mental illnesses.[39] In terms of situatedness, Fuchs emphasizes the "ecological" and embedded nature of our lived experiences and posits that reality is dynamically constructed through intersubjective perception, a notion that he calls "*lebensweltlicher Realismus*" (realism of the life-world). In this view, the body plays a crucial role in active and goal-directed perception to enable sensorimotor interaction with the world.[40]

The importance of ecological situatedness is also a hallmark of theories of enactivism in cognitive science, for example in the works of Evan Thompson and colleagues.[41]

6.3.2 Practical applications of contemporary embodiment theory

In this section on contemporary applied phenomenology in the context of embodiment, two different approaches are exemplified. One approach is the EASE method, which was developed for the examination of anomalous self-experience. It is based on the works of Dan Zahavi and Josef Parnas and attempts to incorporate a more complex understanding of consciousness and subjectivity, including the aspect of embodiment, into the diagnostic practice of psychiatry. However, EASE is not only a method but also a theoretical basis for the criticism of current psychiatric practices. Another approach is microphenomenology, first introduced by Claire Petitmengin. Microphenomenology is an interview technique used in various research contexts (such as epilepsy, meditation, education, and art) that aims to make subjective "micro-experiences" more accessible to language-based description ("linguization").

6.3.2.1 The EASE (examination of anomalous self-experience) method

The EASE method is based on the writings by Zahavi and Parnas and represents an interdisciplinary attempt at incorporating a more complex understanding of consciousness, subjectivity, and embodiment into the diagnostic practice of especially psychiatry and psychopathology. In the following, the theoretical basis for this method, the criticism of current psychiatric practices, and the method itself will be outlined briefly.

Over the last decades, psychiatry has been criticized for the neglect of subjective experience, intersubjectivity, and generally human consciousness when describing symptoms and their expressions.[42] This originated in the current "operationalist" epistemology, the so-called operationalism, which also led to neurobiological reductionism in psychiatric practice.[43] Zahavi and Parnas argue that the reason for the neglect of subjectivity and consciousness is twofold. On one hand, there is the difficulty of describing the human experience, and the general lack of a descriptive framework for human consciousness makes it difficult to communicate the links between symptoms and their expressions in an intersubjective manner. On the other hand, attempts at describing these links might be seen as being against the empiricist dogma leading to a strong focus within psychiatric diagnostics on the description of negative symptoms in behavioral terms. Hence, Zahavi and Parnas suggest a phenomenological conceptual framework for psychiatry to overcome epistemological problems in the current "crisis" of psychiatry. Since the underlying understanding of consciousness in Zahavi and Parnas' work is based on phenomenological theories, central features are subjective experience and the lived body. Other important features of consciousness and subjectivity as defined by Zahavi and Parnas are temporality, intentionality, and intersubjectivity (a similar approach is addressed in Sub-Sections 6.3.1 and 6.3.1.4).

It is the main application of EASE is to explore the experiential or subjective anomalies in psychiatric cases considered as disorders of basic or "minimal" self-awareness, hence from patients on the schizophrenia disorder spectrum. The method evolved from interdisciplinary research on human subjectivity, the multidimensionality of selfhood, and the embedded and embodied nature of the self by a collaboration of the work of psychiatrists, neuroscientists, anthropologists, theologians, psychologists, cognitive scientists, nurses, semioticians, and Buddhist scholars at the *Center for Subjectivity Research* at the University of Copenhagen.[44]

The aim is to make the usually overlooked tacit assumptions more explicit and available to reflective awareness and to include decisive factors for (self-)experience, such as modes and structures of intentionality, spatial aspects of experience, intersubjectivity, temporality, embodiment, and modes of altered self-awareness. The phenomenological approach offers a framework for the psychiatrist to do necessary reflective and conceptualizing work to address problems in psychiatric interviews such as the polysemy and ambiguity of language. It also offers epistemological tools such as the notion of "Gestalt" to understand the complex, mutually constitutive, and interconnected nature of signs and symptoms instead of seeing them as ready-to-use "thing-like entities."[45]

EASE plays a role in informed debates on diagnostic criteria for schizophrenia leading to the inclusion of self-experience as a criterion in the latest definition of schizophrenia in the Diagnostic and Statistical Manual (DSM) of the American Psychiatric Association. Outside the realm of schizophrenia spectrum disorders, EASE has also been applied to other psychiatric symptoms and conditions such as psychosis, hallucinations, and borderline personality disorder.[46]

6.3.2.2 Microphenomenology

Another emerging approach that is based on phenomenological theorizing is the approach of microphenomenology, first introduced by Claire Petitmengin.[47] Microphenomenology as an interview technique emerged from the "explicitation technique," developed in the 1980s by Pierre Vermersch[48] and adapted for empirical qualitative research, e.g., in studying the subjective experience of patients with epilepsy. Since then, the method as a means for describing "lived experience" has received attention in various fields of applied research.[49] The aim of microphenomenology as a conversational interview technique is to make the pre-reflexive and pre-verbal levels of perception – which are usually unnoticed by the subject – accessible and open to reflection. At the heart of the technique lies evocation, the representation of an experience. Through the renewed evocation of a sensually anchored experience, the innumerable co-perceived but backgrounded parts, internalized structures, and patterns of the experience become accessible. In microphenomenological conversations, more precise words are found in recurring steps for what is perceived, and one's own understanding is facilitated by tracing the processes of perception. Introspective reflexivity is not perceived as an act of reflection in the sense of reflecting about an object of understanding and reasoning but as an act of mobilizing a "reflective activity," of carrying out the reflection. It allows tracing the process of becoming aware of the pre-reflexive experience.

6.4 Embodied phenomenology and the philosophical-scientific notion of human enhancement

The phenomenological perspective on embodiment and its relation to human enhancement as well as to trans- and posthumanist understandings of corporeality is crucial in this chapter. As outlined in the previous chapters, "embodiment" is a fundamental issue in the historical roots of Western (philosophical) thought. Comprehending the phenomenological concern regarding consciousness and embodiment – with reference to the body-mind problem – thus enables a deeper understanding of the meaning and importance of the term and concept of "embodiment" in human enhancement.

This opens new perspectives because, for a long period, the debate about human enhancement mainly took place in the fields of philosophy of technology, philosophical anthropology, cultural studies, sociology, science and technology studies, and, above all, (bio)ethics.

In the following sections, it will become clear that phenomenology has a special role to play when discussing human enhancement from a philosophical and interdisciplinary perspective, as phenomenology can provide guidance and essential questions when exploring the topic of embodiment in human enhancement, trans- and posthumanism.

6.4.1 Human enhancement in technology assessment and bioethics

Human enhancement has been a much-debated topic in bioethics and science and technology studies since the mid of the 2000s, with significant forerunners in the late 1990s and earlier in the 20th century. It also found consideration in the field of technology assessment, in risk assessment, foresight, and policy analyses. Since therapeutic measures are often categorized as the antithesis to enhancement measures, medicine and biomedical research have been an essential part of the discourse since their inception. Just like medicine, human enhancement does not only cover applications to the body in general (such as prosthetics and cosmetic surgery) but also specific neuro-applications such as neuroimplants, e.g. for restoring hearing (cochlea implant) and other senses, or deep brain stimulation for influencing movements (and increasingly also mood and other aspects of mental health).[50] Furthermore, pharmaceutical products or drugs are used for controlling mood, substances are used for creative and cognitive performance enhancement, or for doping in sports. Biotechnology applications provide means for genome editing, human germline engineering, and reproductive technologies. Therefore, human enhancement does not only cover a wide range of existing but also emerging and visionary human enhancement technologies, such as cultural practices (e.g., body modification) or the use of psychedelic drugs.

It remains difficult to distinguish therapeutic from enhancement applications based on the technology used. The decisive factor is therefore the ulterior goal, or in some cases also the context, for example, the institutional or commercial one (such as in the case of military research or of direct-to-consumer neurotechnology).

Both proponents, as well as critics of human enhancement, argue based on specific, albeit not always explicit, notions of the human body. While critics, especially if they argue within a theological framework, often emphasize the given or sacred nature of the human body, defenders of human enhancement tend to describe the body as inherently deficient or even as an obstacle to fulfilling humanity's potential.

Against these two notions of the human body, contemporary phenomenological positions and discourses as described above may serve as an important counterweight to the still highly influential views – some might say ideologies – on the spectrum of transhumanist theorizing of the human body and enhancement technologies. To illustrate the special role that the body plays in enhancement discourses, the discourses around transhumanism provide an instructive example which we shall examine in the following section.

6.4.2 Transhumanist notions of corporeality between enhancement and disembodiment

We have witnessed the rise of phenomenologically inspired and highly differentiated approaches to embodiment and corporeality that aim to overcome old dualisms in theory and practice. In a noteworthy parallel development, however, we have seen the resurgence of strongly dualistic ideas and not only at the margins of science and philosophy. Often these ideas are linked to new forms of contempt for the body. The discourse on human enhancement and the merging of human corporeality with machines has been key to this resurgence, and transhumanism is its prime example, a radical, visionary worldview that promotes enhancement and, ultimately, often disembodiment. It is today rather widely known as a kind of *ersatzreligion* for key members of the elites of digital capitalism but also as a somehow provocative worldview (rather than a fully developed philosophy), but the history of this set of ideas goes back at least to the 1870s.[51] Transhumanism promotes a future in which human civilization and corporeality have both been utterly transformed by science and technology. Its visions of the future include not only the emergence and widespread use of enhancement technologies but also the "uploading" of individual minds onto hardware, their quasi-telepathic interconnection, and the extraterrestrial expansion of the (trans- or post-) human species.

Historically, transhumanism is caught between the hope of improving or perfecting human corporeality – which is regularly accompanied by contempt for the actual human body and sometimes by hostility toward disabled people – and the dream of overcoming human corporeality altogether. Regarding the first aspect, the historical and conceptual proximity of transhumanism and eugenics is significant, and it is not surprising that there are some critics of transhumanism who see it as a new form of eugenics.[52]

From its beginning, for which the works of author and traveler Winwood Reade are representative, transhumanism seeks a kind of "emancipation" of the human mind from both the limitations of human corporeality and the species' confinement to Earth. In *The World, the Flesh and the Devil* (1929), a futuristic essay which has strongly shaped transhumanism and massively influenced the genre of science fiction, its author Desmond Bernal, an eminent naturalist scientist and communist thinker, wrote:

> Sooner or later some eminent physiologist will have his neck broken in a super-civilized accident or find his body cells worn beyond capacity for repair. He will then be forced to decide whether to abandon his body or his life. After all it is brain that counts, and to have a brain suffused by fresh and correctly prescribed blood is to be alive – to think.[53]

Based on this thought experiment, Bernal develops a vision of the future in which neuroelectric interfaces are used to "cyborgize" and telepathically connect a technoscientific avant-garde version of the human species. Eventually, the resulting kind of collective brain separates itself completely from human biological corporeality and saturates the universe with (post)human intelligence.

Some of today's organized transhumanists also envisage future biological lives on Earth at best as extended childhoods. Human beings are not only reduced to their minds but also their bodies to information patterns and "the transition from flesh to data will not be so much metamorphosis as liberation,"[54] as a senior transhumanist sociologist and US science manager phrased it. In his vision, the (trans- or post-) humans of the future will create "new bodies" to "dwell in every possible environment and have adventures of the spirit throughout the universe."[55] We should "no more lament the loss of the bodies that we leave behind than an eagle hatchling laments the shattered fragments of its egg when it first takes wing."[56]

Enhancement and the fusion of the human body with technology are understood here only as means to completely overcome biological human corporeality. It is therefore not surprising that critics of transhumanism are legion not only among (especially Continental) philosophers but also among neurotechnologists, psychiatrists, roboticists, and other researchers and practitioners working with advanced, non-dualistic notions of human corporeality.

6.5 Summary and key points

The complex relations and intersections of embodiment and subjectivity require a multitude of perspectives involving concepts and methods from philosophy, anthropology, sociology, medicine, psychology, psychiatry, psychotherapy, religion, and cognitive sciences. The methods and fundamental approaches of these disciplines are very different, which constitutes a substantial challenge for integrative transdisciplinary work.

We have argued that a focus on (post)-phenomenology and embodiment recasts the lived body as central to self-experience, intersubjectivity, and for understanding the complex web of interrelations involving the lived body and the life-world.[57] Such a "phenomenological turn"[58] in cognitive science, neuroscience, and neurophilosophy may also have far-reaching epistemological implications. If we consider the richness and variety of human subjective experience as a vast and largely unmapped landscape, finding the right tools for exploring this landscape might also improve our conceptual and empirical understanding of conscious experience in humans (or other agents).

From this perspective, the lived body is not merely a medium by which we experience the world but could be considered an *instrument for actively exploring subjectivity and intersubjectivity*. Perhaps, the "ultimate enhancement," from this perspective, would not be to perpetually modify the body chemically or technologically – either to stave off inevitable decay or to gain competitive advantages – but to promote our abilities to relate to ourselves and others as embodied, embedded, situated, and relational beings.

Acknowledgments

The work by authors O. Müller and C. Coenen was partly supported by the project grant FUTUREBODY (funded by ERA-NET NEURON JTC2017). The work of author P. Kellmeyer was partly supported by a grant (no. 00.001.2019) by the Klaus Tschira Foundation to the University Medical Center Freiburg. The work of V. Borrmann was partly supported by a National Institutes of Health grant (1RF1MH117800-01) awarded to the University of Washington, USA, with a subaward UWSC12135 to the University Medical Center Freiburg.

Notes

1 Judith Butler, *Bodies That Matter: On the Discursive Limits of Sex* (New York: Routledge, 1993); Judith Butler, *Gender Trouble: Feminism and the Subversion of Identity* (New York: Routledge, 1990); Maurice Merleau-Ponty and Donald A. Landes, *Phenomenology of Perception* (London: Routledge, 2012).
2 Focusing on embodiment, we emphasize the differentiation and coherence of the terms *embodiment, lived body, body, and corporeality*. Corporeality and body as terms refer to the body as social actant, a site of social agency, and the body as a set of structures (e.g., gender, class, race, sexuality, disability, etc.) whose identity and meaning are mediated by culture and society. Embodiment and lived body, in contrast, refer to the body as a medium by which social actors realize a sense of self, identity, and a relation to the other.
3 Plato, *Oxford Classical Texts: Platonis Opera, Vol. 1: Tetralogiae I–II*, ed. E.A. Duke et al., Oxford Classical Texts: Platonis Opera, Vol. 1: Tetralogiae I–II, Oxford Classical Texts (Oxford University Press, 1995).
4 René Descartes, *Meditations on First Philosophy – with Selections from the Objections and Replies*, ed. John Cottingham, Cambridge Texts in the History of Philosophy (Cambridge, UK: Cambridge University Press, 1996), 59.
5 Descartes, 58.
6 Friedrich Nietzsche, *Thus Spoke Zarathustra – A Book for All and None*, ed. Karl Ameriks and Desmond M. Clarke, trans. Andrian Del Caro, Cambridge Texts in the History of Philosophy (Cambridge, UK: Cambridge University Press, 2006), 23.
7 Sigmund Freud, "A Difficulty in the Path of Psycho-Analysis," in *The Standard Edition of the Complete Psychological Works of Sigmund Freud. Volume XVII (1917–1919): An Infantile Neurosis and Other Works*, vol. 18, Standard Edition of the Complete Psychological Works of Sigmund Freud, 1955, 143.
8 According to Fichte, the I sets itself by being, and it is thus by setting itself. It is both the acting and the product of the action; the active and that which is produced by the activity; action and deed are one and the same; and therefore: I is the expression of an action. (cp. Johann G. Fichte and Wilhelm G. Jacobs, *Grundlage Der Gesamten Wissenschaftslehre: Als Handschrift Für Seine Zuhörer (1794)*, 4. verbesserte Aufl., Philosophische Bibliothek; 246. (Hamburg: Felix Meiner Verlag, 1997), 16.)
9 "Leib" is not perfectly translatable, but is usually referred to as "lived body" in English and as "corps vivant" or "corps vécu" in French.
10 Helmuth Plessner, *Levels of Organic Life and the Human an Introduction to Philosophical Anthropology*, First edition, Forms of Living (New York: Fordham University Press, 2019), 267 sq.
11 Plessner, 219.
12 Plessner, 214, 220.
13 Merleau-Ponty and Landes, *Phenomenology of Perception*, 24.
14 Merleau-Ponty and Landes, 84.

15 Merleau-Ponty and Landes, 82.
16 Plessner, *Levels of Organic Life and the Human an Introduction to Philosophical Anthropology*, 28.
17 Merleau-Ponty and Landes, *Phenomenology of Perception*, 361.
18 Despite the importance of his work in German-speaking areas, only few translations into English are available.
19 K. Goldstein, "Über Die Plastizität Des Organismus Auf Grund von Erfahrungen Am Nervenkranken Menschen," in *Handbuch Der Normalen Und Pathologischen Physiologie: Fünfzehnter Band / Zweite Hälfte Correlationen I/2 (J. II/2. Arbeitsphysiologie II · J. III. Orientierung J. VI. Plastizität · J. VII. Stimme Und Sprache)*, ed. A. Bethe et al. (Berlin, Heidelberg: Springer Berlin Heidelberg, 1931), 1131–74, https://doi.org/10.1007/978-3-642-91026-5_5.
20 A cornerstone of genealogical critical thinking emerged in the early 1960s when Jacques Derrida drew attention to the fact that binary oppositions have structured Western thought and philosophy since the very beginning (f.e. body/mind or outside/inside). As binary oppositions contain implicit hierarchies in the sense that one of the terms is primary and fundamental and the other one is secondary and derivative, a hierarchical order is imposed on reality which promotes repression, exclusion, or subordination of the secondary. Derrida referred to the procedure for uncovering and unsettling these dichotomies as deconstruction: questioning the most basic philosophical categories and concepts and the revision of such hierarchies.
21 Regula Giuliani, „Der Übergangene Leib: Simone de Beauvoir, Luce Irigaray Und Judith Butler," *Phänomenologische Forschungen. Phenomenological Studies. Recherches Phénoménologiques* 2, no. 1 (1997): 104–25; Iris Marion Young, "Throwing like a Girl: A Phenomenology of Feminine Body Comportment Motility and Spatiality," *Human Studies* 3, no. 1 (1980): 137–56, https://doi.org/10.1007/BF02331805; Iris Marion Young, "Lived Body vs Gender: Reflections on Social Structure and Subjectivity," *Ratio (Oxford)* 15, no. 4 (2002): 410–28, https://doi.org/10.1111/1467-9329.00200.
22 Don Ihde, *Postphenomenology and Technoscience: The Peking University Lectures*, SUNY Series in the Philosophy of the Social Sciences (Albany, NY: State University of New York Press, 2009), 44.
23 Ihde, 44.
24 Don Ihde, *Technology and the Lifeworld: From Garden to Earth* (Bloomington: Indiana University Press, 1990), 72–123.
25 Ihde, *Postphenomenology and Technoscience: The Peking University Lectures*, 42.
26 Paul Ekman et al., "Buddhist and Psychological Perspectives on Emotions and Well-Being," *Current Directions in Psychological Science: A Journal of the American Psychological Society* 14, no. 2 (2005): 59–63, https://doi.org/10.1111/j.0963-7214.2005.00335.x; Matthieu Ricard and Wolf Singer, *Beyond the Self: Conversations Between Buddhism and Neuroscience* (MIT Press, 2017).
27 Already the first two Mind & Life Dialogues in 1987 and 1989 dealt with Buddhism in context of cognitive sciences, neurosciences followed by Transformations of Mind, Brain and Emotion (2001), Latest Findings in Contemplative Neuroscience (2012), Mind, Brain, and Matter: Critical Conversations Between Buddhist Thought and Science (2013) and Perception, Concepts, and Self: Contemporary Scientific and Buddhist Perspectives (2015)
28 Francisco J. Varela, Evan Thompson, and Eleanor Rosch, *The Embodied Mind: Cognitive Science and Human Experience* (Cambridge, MA: The MIT Press, 1991).
29 Dennis Fox and Isaac Prilleltensky, "Introducing Critical Psychology: Values, Assumptions, and the Status Quo," in *Critical Psychology: An Introduction* (Thousand Oaks, CA: Sage Publications, Inc, 1997), 3–20.
30 Standard positions in the philosophy of mind, such as the idea that the mind is identical to or realized in the brain, are challenged, especially drawing on the phenomenological tradition of Husserl and Merleau-Ponty.
31 Neurophenomenology can be considered as a modern continuation or a research frame that was inspired by the works of Maurice Merleau-Ponty and Edmund Husserl.
32 Charles D. Laughlin, John McManus, and Eugene G. D'Aquili, *Brain, Symbol & Experience: Toward a Neurophenomenology of Human Consciousness* (New York: Columbia University Press, 1992).
33 Varela, Thompson, and Rosch, *The Embodied Mind: Cognitive Science and Human Experience*.
34 David J. Chalmers, "First-Person Methods in the Science of Consciousness," *Consciousness Bulletin*, University of Arizona 1999, june.
35 Antoine Lutz and E. Thompson, "Neurophenomenology: Integrating Subjective Experience and Brain Dynamics in the Neuroscience of Consciousness," *Journal of Consciousness Studies* 10, nos. 9–10 (1 January 2003): 31–52.
36 Albert Newen, Leon de Bruin, and Shaun Gallagher, *The Oxford Handbook of 4E Cognition*, Oxford Handbooks Online (Oxford: Oxford University Press, 2018).
37 One example, often invoked, would be the use of a walking stick for people with visual impairment. With sufficient training, the stick becomes part of the user's body schema and a tool for extending their cognitive abilities (in this case navigation and active exploration and sensing of the environment).

38 Thomas Fuchs, "Phenomenology and Psychopathology," in *Handbook of Phenomenology and Cognitive Science*, ed. Daniel Schmicking and Shaun Gallagher (Dordrecht: Springer Netherlands, 2010), 546–73, https://doi.org/10.1007/978-90-481-2646-0_28.

39 Schizophrenia and depression, in this view, are distortions of the subject's relation to the "subject-body" (*Leib*) whereas body dysmorphic disorder and anorexia are distortions of the subject's relation to the "object-body" (*Körper*). When "protention," acts of anticipation or preparation, is disturbed, the subject can get lost in pre-reflective time and gets stuck in having to deal with things and thoughts appearing without anticipation or from nowhere leading to disturbances in self-continuity. Bipolar disorder is taken as an example of the effects of a fragmentation of narrative-time where the subject cannot incorporate apparently separate versions of itself at different periods. As examples of disturbances in intersubjectivity, Fuchs uses for primary intersubjectivity (the mirroring of the mental states of others as displayed openly by them) autism spectrum disorder, and for secondary intersubjectivity (the ability to interact in dyadic/triadic pairs with the world and thus share intentionality), schizophrenia.

40 Thomas Fuchs, *Das Gehirn – Ein Beziehungsorgan: Eine Phänomenologisch-Ökologische Konzeption* (Stuttgart, Germany: Kohlhammer Verlag, 2017); Thomas Fuchs, Heribert C. Sattel, and Peter Henningsen, *The Embodied Self: Dimensions, Coherence and Disorders* (Stuttgart, Germany: Schattauer Verlag (Klett), 2010).

41 Evan Thompson and Paolo Di Ezequiel, "The Enactive Approach," in *The Routledge Handbook of Embodied Cognition*, ed. Lawrence A. Shapiro, 1 [edition], Routledge Handbooks in Philosophy (New York: Routledge, Taylor & Francis Group, 2014), 68–78.

42 Josef Parnas and Dan Zahavi, "The Role of Phenomenology in Psychiatric Diagnosis and Classification," in *Psychiatric Diagnosis and Classification*, ed. Mario Maj et al. (Chichester: John Wiley & Sons, Ltd, 2002), 137–62, https://doi.org/10.1002/047084647X.ch6.

43 Josef Parnas, Louis A. Sass, and Dan Zahavi, "Rediscovering Psychopathology: The Epistemology and Phenomenology of the Psychiatric Object," *Schizophrenia Bulletin* 39, no. 2 (1 March 2013): 270–77, https://doi.org/10.1093/schbul/sbs153.

44 Mads Gram Henriksen, Felipe León, and Dan Zahavi, "Center for Subjectivity Research: History, Contribution and Impact," *Danish Yearbook of Philosophy* 53, no. 1 (26 November 2020): 162–74, https://doi.org/10.1163/24689300-bja10009.

45 Parnas, Sass, and Zahavi, "Rediscovering Psychopathology"; Parnas and Zahavi, "The Role of Phenomenology in Psychiatric Diagnosis and Classification."

46 Henriksen, León, and Zahavi, "Center for Subjectivity Research."

47 Claire Petitmengin et al., "Studying the Experience of Meditation through Micro-Phenomenology," *Current Opinion in Psychology* 28 (2019): 54–59, https://doi.org/10.1016/j.copsyc.2018.10.009.

48 Vermersch's "explicitation" interviewing technique is mostly used in France in the field of ergonomics and within the education system. It is meant to elicit verbalizations of an activity; the idea is to favor evocation versus rationalization from the actor.

49 Claire Petitmengin et al., "What Is It like to Meditate? Methods and Issues of a Micro-Phenomenological Description of Meditative Experience," *Journal of Consciousness Studies* 24, nos. 5–6 (2017): 170–98; Marisa Przyrembel and Tania Singer, "Experiencing Meditation – Evidence for Differential Effects of Three Contemplative Mental Practices in Micro-Phenomenological Interviews," *Consciousness and Cognition* 62 (2018): 82–101, https://doi.org/10.1016/j.concog.2018.04.004.

50 Federico Germani et al., "Engineering Minds? Ethical Considerations on Biotechnological Approaches to Mental Health, Well-Being, and Human Flourishing," *Trends in Biotechnology* 39, no. 11 (1 November 2021): 1111–13, https://doi.org/10.1016/j.tibtech.2021.04.007.

51 Christopher Coenen, "Transhumanism in Emerging Technoscience as a Challenge for the Humanities and Technology Assessment," *Teorija in praksa* 51, no. 5 (2014): 754–771.

52 However, for the topic of this chapter, the (highly visionary) quest to overcome human corporeality, especially through its fusion with technology, is more relevant and will therefore be briefly discussed here.

53 John Desmond Bernal, *The World, the Flesh and the Devil – An Enquiry into the Future of the Three Enemies of the Rational Soul* (London: Kegan Paul, Trench, Trubner & Co, 1929), 42.

54 William Sims Bainbridge, "Progress towards Cyberimmortality," in *The Scientific Conquest of Death: Essays on Infinite Lifespans*, ed. Immortality Institute (Buenos Aires: LibrosEnRed, 2004), 119.

55 Bainbridge, "Progress towards Cyberimmortality."

56 Bainbridge, "Progress towards Cyberimmortality."

57 See also: Pierre Pariseau-Legault, Dave Holmes, and Stuart J. Murray, "Understanding Human Enhancement Technologies through Critical Phenomenology," *Nursing Philosophy* 20, no. 1 (2019): e12229.

58 Ricardo Mejía Fernández, "El giro fenomenológico en las neurociencias cognitivas: de Francisco Varela a Shaun Gallagher" (http://purl.org/dc/dcmitype/Text, Universidad de Salamanca, 2018), https://gredos.usal.es/handle/10366/139847.

7
HUMAN ENHANCEMENT THROUGH THE LENS OF SEX SELECTION

Robert Sparrow

7.1 Introduction

One of the many strange things about the debate about the ethics of genetic enhancement is that, for the most part, it has proceeded in advance of our knowledge of any actual candidate genetic enhancements. Despite a routine rhetorical gesture toward what "might" be possible by means of various genetic manipulations in the future, at the beginning of discussions of enhancement, we are not as yet actually able to make children "better than well" (Elliott 2003) by adding, subtracting, or modifying individual genes. As a result, the literature on the ethics of genetic enhancement has developed using examples of enhancement that are entirely speculative. What participants in this debate have failed to notice, though, is that for the last several decades we have had a technology to dramatically reshape the genetics of future children in ways that have significant implications for their future welfare and life options – sex selection. If we discount the effects of systematic social injustice, then the longer life expectancies of those born female and the option that female individuals have of becoming pregnant and giving birth suggest that the desire to have "the best child" possible should motivate choosing a female embryo over a male embryo (Sparrow 2010a, 2010b; 2012). If we allow that it is appropriate for considerations about the impact of patriarchy on the welfare of the future child to enter into our deliberations about the relative merits of different genomes, then it seems that we should choose male embryos over female embryos. Either way, it seems that advocates of human enhancement should have something to say about sex selection and that those thinking about sex selection should be asking whether it might constitute an enhancement. There is also a flourishing literature on the ethics of sex selection, which offers significant resources for debates about the ethics of enhancement, which have, for the most part, been neglected to date. Placing these debates in contact with each other therefore has the potential to illuminate both.

In this chapter, then, I investigate what thinking about human enhancement through the lens of sex selection can teach us about the debate about the ethics of human enhancement, the ethics of human enhancement, and the ethics of the debate about human enhancement (Sparrow 2014). Should we consider the use of sex selection to select embryos of one sex or the other to be "human enhancement"? If not, why not? What role do intuitions about sexed bodies and normal bodies play in thinking about enhancement? What can we learn from people's intuitive resistance to the idea that we might have reasons to sex select for enhancement when it comes to the debate about the ethics of enhancement?

My discussion will proceed as follows. In Section 7.2, "Lessons from the biology of sex," I suggest that the extent of the debate about the nature of sex differences demonstrates how difficult it is to establish that a particular genetic modification constitutes an enhancement. Section 7.3, "Changing sex" describes two different ways in which one might change the sex of one's future child. Section 7.4, "Therapy or enhancement?" argues that, *prima facie*, either sex selection for female children or sex selection for male children will count as an enhancement on any of the plausible definitions of enhancement. In Section 7.5, "Fear of a female planet," I survey a number of different ways in which this conclusion might be resisted and argue that each of them is either unlikely to be successful or has important implications for the debate about genetic human enhancement more generally. Finally, in Section 7.6, "Lessons from sex selection," I draw together a number of the strands from the preceding discussion and from the literature on sex selection to offer some provocative observations about the debate about human enhancement and, indeed, the ethics of reproductive decision-making more generally.

7.2 Lessons from the biology of sex

The first thing that thinking about enhancement through the lens of sex selection reveals is just how difficult it is to show that a genetic modification might constitute an enhancement.

The impact of genes on phenotype is always a product of the environment, which complexifies discussions of genetic enhancement, as one should never talk about the effects of a "gene" or of a particular set of genes. Strictly speaking, it is only possible to identify the phenotypic implications of a difference between two possible sets of genes in a particular environment or of two different environments on organisms that have the same genes (Kitcher 1996; Lewontin 2001). Discussions of the implications of the presence or absence of a Y chromosome are especially fraught because male and female individuals are typically subject to different environmental influences due to the impacts of sexism.[1] Nevertheless, we have vastly more data on the implications of sex differences for human phenotype than we do on any other genetic differences. At least some of the consequences of having a Y chromosome for the human phenotype in the range of environments in which human beings can live are reasonably well understood. Two implications, in particular, are highly relevant to the question of whether sex selection might constitute an enhancement. First, in the absence of as-yet- entirely-theoretical medical interventions (womb transplants into chromosomal males), the capacity to become pregnant and give birth is confined to those who are chromosomally female. Second, in most – but not all – environments, persons with two X chromosomes have longer life expectancies (Annandale 2021; World Health Organization 2019, 3–8). Given the emphasis on life extension in the enhancement literature (de Grey & Rae 2007), this is clearly noteworthy. Any number of other sex differences may be relevant to arguments about enhancement and sex selection depending on our ideas about what sorts of morphology and capacities are desirable.

However, it is striking that, despite all the data we have, claims about the nature and origin of sex differences are still intensely controversial. In fact, there are three different controversies here. First, there is controversy about the nature and extent of sex differences in *Homo sapiens*. Are males really more aggressive? Are females more empathetic? Are females really worse at math? Empirical claims about the differences between males and females are still contested – and rightly so. So many of the historical claims have been wrong that there is good reason to treat any but the most trivial and obvious claims about sex differences with suspicion.[2] Second, there is controversy about the extent to which, where such differences do exist, they are the result of genes or environment. Sexism is so pervasive in most societies that it is plausible to think that many of the purported differences between the sexes are the result of the different environments inhabited by men and women (Fine 2017). As I will discuss further below, the significance of the claim that the origin of most differences – or of particular differences – between the sexes are environmental is itself contested. Third, people differ on whether any particular sex difference is to the detriment or to the advantage of either sex. If, for instance, it is true that females are "naturally" more caring, is that something that should be celebrated or regretted (Gilligan 1982)? The question of the relative merits of different capacities will turn out to be crucial when we move to consider whether selection for either sex should be thought of as an enhancement.

The fact that we are still arguing about sex differences gives us reason to pause when it comes to the confidence with which pundits pronounce that the presence of this or that gene constitutes – or would constitute – an enhancement. If we cannot agree on the nature and classification of the differences associated with sex, what hope do we have of agreeing on whether some proposed new gene or set of genes would constitute an enhancement? This aspect of the dialectic is often obscured by the blitheness with which participants in debates about enhancement talk about the relative merits of different phenotypes without committing on the question of the genetic modifications required to produce them. While, in the abstract, a hypothetical increase in "intelligence" or "longevity" may appear to be straightforwardly good, the assessment of the merits of any genetic modification intended to produce such change is unlikely to be straightforward. Because of the ways in which genes interact and participate in networks of mutual influence, changing even a single gene may lead to multiple changes in the phenotype of an organism, with the result that assessing the benefits of the change may require us to consider complex trade-offs. The literatures on disability, gender, and neurodiversity, in which people routinely contest what counts as a desirable phenotype, should serve to remind us that resolving such trade-offs is more difficult than commonly supposed (see, for instance, Fausto-Sterling 2000; Garland-Thomson 2012; Fenton & Krahn 2007; Jaarsma & Welin 2012; Scully 2008). Moreover, the sample size available to us to support claims about the impact of new genes is likely to be a small fraction of that relevant to debates about these sorts of differences, let alone of that relevant to debates about sex differences.

7.3 Changing sex

There are multiple means available to prospective parents to select the sex of their child. Historically, of course, in many cultures the goal of raising – if not giving birth to – a child of a particular sex was often achieved by selective infanticide. Today, prospective parents can determine fetal sex *in utero* via a number of different means – most commonly ultrasound but increasingly non-invasive prenatal testing – and "select out" children of the unwanted sex by means of selective termination. Sperm sorting techniques offer a – albeit unreliable – means of influencing the sex of the future child without the prospective mother needing to undergo a termination. Finally, preimplantation genetic diagnosis (PGD) is an extremely powerful technique for determining the sex of the future child, again without requiring the prospective mother to be willing to undergo one or more abortions.[3]

As I will discuss further below, these methods often work by changing who comes to be born (or, in the case of selective infanticide, is allowed to live) rather than by changing the properties (i.e., the sex) of a particular individual: in Parfit's terms, they are "identity affecting" rather than "person affecting" (Parfit 1984, 356–359).

For the sake of the discussion that follows, it will be useful to also consider a person-affecting technology – a "genetic sex change." Eventually, it may become possible to change the sex of an embryo via transplantation of sex chromosomes. Replacing the Y chromosome in a male embryo with an X chromosome would cause the embryo to develop into a female individual instead of a male individual. Removing one of the X chromosomes from a female embryo and replacing it with a Y chromosome would change the sex of the embryo from female to male.

Chromosome transplantation in human embryos is highly speculative and there are significant technical barriers standing in its way. Nevertheless, there are indications that a related procedure, which might achieve the same effect – changing the sex of the individual that developed out of a particular embryo – might become possible in the not-too-distant future. A team of researchers based in Milan, Italy, has recently successfully demonstrated transplantation of the X chromosome in human-induced pluripotent stem cells (Paulis, Susani, Castelli et al. 2020). If such a procedure proves possible in human *embryonic* stem cells *and* nuclear transfer leading to live birth becomes possible, then this would open the door to performing genetic sex changes. In this (hypothetical) procedure, scientists would first create an embryo using IVF. They would then derive an embryonic stem-cell line from this embryo in order to create a colony of embryonic stem cells with the same genome as the original embryo. They would then perform chromosomal transplantation on these stem cells, adding a marker gene in order to make it easier to identify those cells in which this procedure has succeeded. Scientists would then remove the nuclear material, including the new sex chromosome, from one of the modified cells and place it inside a donor ovum from which the nuclear material had been removed. The newly constructed cell, which would contain the nuclear material from the original embryo but with a new sex chromosome, would then be encouraged to embark on the process of embryonic division by means of appropriate environmental stimuli. If implanted into the womb of a willing woman and brought to term, this embryo would become a person who had almost all the genes of the original embryo but was of the opposite sex.

It is slightly unclear whether we should think of such a "genetic sex change" as person-affecting or identity-affecting. Insofar as it would result in the birth of an individual with the same genome as the original embryo except for the modified sex chromosome, such a "genetic sex change" looks to be person-affecting. However, it remains open to a critic to insist that changing the sex of the embryo is such a significant intervention that it leads to the birth of a new individual (Elliot 1993). Moreover, because the procedure would require IVF, in most cases the decision to embark on it would itself be identity-affecting by virtue of changing the timing of conception and thus leading to the creation of a different embryo than that would have existed if the prospective parents had decided to conceive naturally (Sparrow 2021). If, though, a couple had already decided to undergo IVF and then – having found themselves with only one viable embryo of the "wrong sex" – decided to try to change the sex of the embryo using this technology, the claim that the procedure would be person-affecting is significantly stronger. Because my main interest in this hypothetical procedure is to illustrate how our thinking about sex and enhancement might change in the case of person-affecting interventions, I am going to proceed here as though this procedure would indeed be person-affecting. That one of the reasons to doubt this is the intuition that the presence or absence of a Y chromosome is itself identity-affecting already casts an interesting light on the way we think about sex.

7.4 Therapy or enhancement?

Whether it is plausible to think of sex selection (or a genetic sex change) as enhancement or not will depend, in part, on our definition of enhancement. Defensible definitions of enhancement include: (1) increases in some capacity beyond what is ordinarily the case for the particular individual; (2) increases in some capacity beyond what would be the case for a particular individual if they were healthy; (3) increases in some capacity beyond what is ordinarily the case for an individual when they are healthy and beyond what is species-typical; and, (4) increases in some capacity beyond the upper limit of the current range for human beings. In order to capture the idea that enhancement makes people better off, we might add that these increases must be "desirable." Perhaps the most well-known exhortation for parents to enhance their children suggests that they must try to have "the best child" they can (Savulescu 2001).

The two most plausible metrics according to which we might measure the desirability of different enhancements are "expected welfare" and "openness of future" (Agar 2004; Davis 2001). A fifth, broader, definition of enhancement, then, is (5) any biomedical intervention that improves expected welfare or openness of future (Sparrow 2011a). Roughly speaking, talk of expected welfare assumes that a determinate measurement of welfare or well-being or interests is possible, while discussions of openness of future resile from this claim and attempt, as much as possible, to leave judgments as to what is of value to the future individual. Both of these are very general and require specification in order to be action-guiding. Expected welfare might be assessed with reference to subjective experience (hedonism), satisfaction of preferences (preference-satisfaction consequentialism), or objective goods (objective list theory) (Griffin 1986; Parfit 1984). Openness of future should presumably be assessed with reference to "life options," but there are, in turn, difficult questions about how these should be identified and counted (Feinberg 1980; Mills 2003; Sparrow 2011a). As we shall see, though, the sex of a child is likely to be relevant to the assessment of its life prospects by either of these measures.

One reason for thinking that sex selection might be an enhancement is that, at first sight at least, *ordinarily* it does not seem to be therapeutic. We don't typically think of being male or female as a condition that warrants being "cured." I say "ordinarily" because there *are* cases where it does appear that sex selection might be therapeutic – when a family has a history of sex-linked disorders, such as Duchenne muscular dystrophy, fragile X-syndrome, or hemophilia. Where this is the case, sex selection is typically advertised as being justified on "medical grounds" (The Ethics Committee of the American Society of Reproductive Medicine 1999).

It is also important to acknowledge the long (sexist) tradition in the biomedical sciences of thinking of females as defective males. For instance, anatomy textbooks typically presume that the "standard" human body is male (Lawrence & Bendixen 1992; Parker, Larkin, & Cockburn 2017; Petersen 1998). Were one to believe this, then it would follow that sex selection for male embryos was therapeutic.

However, in ordinary circumstances, for the most part, we do not think of being born either male or female as a medical condition that calls out to be cured or treated: it is possible to be a healthy male or a healthy female. Our accounts of health and "normal human capacities" are bifurcated and include an account of normal *male* capacities and normal *female* capacities (Mills 2015; Sparrow 2011b). Thinking about health in the context of "human enhancement" tends to obscure this by implying that the relevant measure is *human* health or *human* capacities. The idea that *Homo sapiens* is a sexually dimorphic species has also come under pressure at this particular cultural moment by virtue of increased awareness of the range of intersex conditions (Fausto-Sterling 2000) and by the political salience of a claim that sex/gender is – or perhaps should be – determined solely by reference to the felt sense of a person themselves rather than by reference to any facts of anatomy or genetics (Ainsworth 2015). Nevertheless, at least when it comes to reproductive biology – and arguably when it comes to a whole range of physiological indicators – we assess the health of an individual relative to a baseline that is sexed (Sparrow 2008a, Sparrow 2011b). The deeper truth here is that any assessment of the health or capacities of an individual relies on a submerged assumption about a reference class (Kingma 2007). We don't treat the inability of a male to get pregnant to constitute a medical disorder nor the inability of a one-year-old to talk or to run. A genetic modification that reduced the muscle wastage associated with aging such that 80-year-old men (or women) had the physical capacities that they had at 20 years old would clearly be an enhancement.

If sex selection is not therapy, then perhaps we should think of it as an enhancement? The idea that both male and female embryos are "normal" seems to stand as an immediate barrier to this claim. How can selection in favor of an embryo with normal capacities count as an enhancement? However, this neglects the fact that the project of enhancement presumes that the idea of the normal has little, if any, normative significance. What matters is not what is normal but what is better (Harris 2007, 19–36; Savulescu 2001) – and there is no *a priori* reason to believe that it might not be better to be born male or to be born female.

In fact, an argument can be made that sex selection may count as enhancement according to each and every definition of enhancement surveyed above. The extent of the controversy about the nature and significance of sex differences, and about which capacities are desirable, can make it difficult to see this, so I am going to proceed by setting out some assumptions on both these matters, exploring how the argument goes on those assumptions, and then discussing what would happen were we to vary those assumptions.

To start out, then, I am going to presume that having the option of becoming pregnant and giving birth is desirable and that it is desirable to have a higher life expectancy. Both these claims are superficially controversial but, I believe, eminently plausible. Not everyone wants to be able to become pregnant and/or give birth, and there are significant inconveniences (menstruation) and some risks (accidental pregnancy, death in labor) associated with possessing this capacity. Nevertheless, there is ample evidence that many people do think that becoming pregnant and giving birth are valuable experiences that add meaning to a human life and thus that the capacity to do this is desirable.[4] Moreover, for the most part, any disadvantages purported to be associated with female reproductive biology are now capable of being mitigated by modern medicine.[5] Thus, it is reasonable to hold that possession of a womb makes a large contribution to an individual's openness of future. Similarly, while many people insist that they do not want to live longer, asking whether they would care if their life expectancy was reduced by three to five years typically provides strong evidence that this is an expression of *status quo* bias. Life extension has been a central focus of those interested in human enhancement (Agar 2010; de Grey & Michael 2007; Bostrom 2008). Attempts to deny that the higher life expectancy associated with being female is not desirable risk looking strikingly *ad hoc*.

Absent any other claim about the benefits of being male, it will follow from these assumptions that – *all other things being equal* – it is better to be born female and that selection of a female embryo rather than a male embryo will constitute an enhancement (Sparrow 2010a). The increase in life expectancy and the capacity to become pregnant associated with being female means that choosing a female embryo rather than a male embryo will count as enhancement on definitions 1–3, and 5, while the capacity to become pregnant will make selection of a female embryo enhancement according to definition 4, as the capacity to become pregnant is not in the species-typical range for males.

The "all other things being equal" clause is crucial here – as it tends to be in claims about enhancements more generally – and a lack of understanding of its nature and role is a source of much confusion and misapprehension about enhancement in this literature, especially among critics of enhancement. This *ceteris paribus* clause functions to allow discussion of the relative merits of various genetic differences and/or interventions to proceed despite the fact that, in any particular case, other relevant considerations, including genetic differences, may vitiate the general claim. Not every female infant has better life prospects than every male infant: the comparison between any two embryos will require full knowledge of the genetics of each embryo and the environment in which they will live. Nevertheless, where we have no knowledge of other relevant genetic or environmental differences, a concern for the life prospects of the future individual should motivate us to choose female embryos because of the higher life expectancy and more open future available to women. We face such decisions under uncertainty all the time, and reasons that bear on them – in the form of generalizations – are a core feature of practical reason.

This is not to suggest that the "all other things being equal" condition is unproblematic or always met. As the debate about the nature and extent of sex differences – and also about the impacts of other genes – discussed above suggests, the extent to which the advantages postulated as being associated with a particular set of genes are accompanied by other disadvantages is often controversial.

One thing that obviously is not equal when it comes to the choice between female and male embryos is the impact of the environment in which girls and boys grow up. Because most societies are systematically unjust when it comes to the treatment of, and opportunities available to, women, there are a number of advantages associated with being born male. Men typically earn higher incomes than women and have better access to positions of social power and privilege (Krook & Mackay 2011; Ortiz-Ospina and Roser 2018; UN Women and United Nations Department of Economic and Social Affairs Statistics Division 2021; World Economic Forum 2021) – both of which things have implications for the range of options available to them and the extent to which they are able to satisfy their preferences. As I discuss below, the appropriateness of taking the impacts of injustice on the expected welfare and opportunities available to future persons into account in our thinking about the ethics of reproduction is contested. However, it seems likely that if we do take these features of the environment into account, then selection of male embryos over female embryos will count as enhancement according to the fifth definition of enhancement set out above, which is the definition of enhancement most preferred by advocates of enhancement.

My assumption about the benefits of being born female was also qualified by the observation that it was true "absent any other claim about the benefits of being male." In theory, at least, an argument about the benefits of being born male rather than female might also be made on the basis of claims about genetic differences between the sexes. The most obvious advantages of being male, which are associated with greater size and physical strength, might be held to count as enhancements on definitions 1, 2, and 3.[6] However, they look morally trivial in any society that has mastered the block and tackle and that is willing to lower the height of shelving. For that reason, they seem unlikely to count as enhancements according to definition 5. A more compelling, if still ultimately unconvincing, case might be made on the basis of the relative ease with which males can father large numbers of children. This argument is unconvincing because it is difficult to see how merely being the genetic parent of a large number of children contributes much to the value of a human life unless one also is also their social parent – in which case it is not obvious that it is really easier for males to have more children than females.[7] However, if one is willing to postulate a suitably strong – and, I suspect, to precisely the same extent, less plausible – claim about "brain sex," then perhaps it would follow that males would have higher-expected welfare and more open futures and, thus, that it would be better to be born male even in a society that was not characterized by systemic social injustice to the benefit of males.

Considering enhancement through the lens of sex selection suggests that, if a comparison of the capacities or life prospects of males and females is possible, it will be difficult to resist the conclusion that it is better to be born one sex rather than the other. Whether we should judge it better to be born male or female will then depend on whether we think that it is appropriate to take the impact of social injustice into our account of what constitutes an enhancement. I consider this question below in the course of surveying a number of ways in which the claim that selection for either sex should count as enhancement might be resisted. What is clear, though, is that unless recourse can be made to some such argument, it is vanishingly unlikely that it is equally good to be born male or female and thus that sex selection will not count as enhancement.

7.5 Fear of a female planet

In this section, I discuss various objections to the claim that selection for either sex would count as enhancement. Mostly for ease of exposition, I am going to assume that sex selection for female embryos counts as enhancement. However, the larger dialectic of my discussion is unaffected should it turn out that sex selection for male embryos should be counted as an enhancement instead.

7.5.1 Parfitian reflections

One way to resist the conclusion that selection of either female embryos over male embryos or male embryos over female embryos counts as enhancement is to insist that enhancement must lead to an improvement in the life prospects of the enhanced individual. As I observed above, sex selection will determine which embryo comes into existence rather than alter the genetics – and therefore the capacities – of a particular embryo. In Parfit's terms, it is identity-affecting rather than person-affecting (Parfit 1984, 356–359). This in turn means that sex selection does not benefit the individual who develops out of the embryo that is selected because had selection not occurred, another person would exist in his/her place (Brock 1995; Feinberg 1986; Parfit 1984, 356–359).

This argument works as far as it goes, but its implications for the debate about genetic enhancement more generally are dramatic. Until relatively recently, with the advent of CRISPR/Cas9 and related genome-editing systems, the most plausible way to improve the welfare of those born in the future by means of genetic technologies was to use PGD to select in favor of embryos with genes associated with beyond-species-typical capacities. Much of the literature on "human enhancement" is concerned with the ethics of this project. Yet PGD, like sex selection, is identity-affecting rather than person-affecting and will not count as enhancement according to the objection being considered here. Moreover, in practice, genome editing will almost always involve choosing to conceive via IVF and also selection from multiple modified embryos, which means that it will also be identity-affecting rather than person-affecting and similarly will not count as enhancement (Sparrow 2021). The price of insisting that enhancements must be person-affecting is the conclusion that we are unlikely to have any germline genetic enhancements for the foreseeable future.

It is also important to note that recourse to Parfit will not threaten the conclusion that a genetic sex change from male to female would be an enhancement in a case where it *were* person-affecting, as I suggested above is arguably the case when a single male embryo created via IVF undertaken for other reasons is then subjected to cellular manipulations to produce a female embryo. Of course, it remains open to a critic to argue that any such sex change would be identity-affecting by virtue of making such a large change to the phenotype of the individual who develops from the embryo. However, this will also imply that other, what might otherwise be thought to be person-affecting, genetic modifications will not count as enhancements.

7.5.2 *The moral significance of injustice?*

Another objection to the idea that sex selection might constitute an enhancement relies on the claim that most – even if not all – of the differences in expected welfare and openness of future between the sexes are the product of an unjust social order – patriarchy – and that we should not take the impacts of injustice into account when it comes to the reasons that bear on parents' choices about what sort of children they should have. This line of thought seems especially compelling in the context of the argument that selection of male embryos counts as enhancement, because to insist that we should select against female embryos due to the impacts of patriarchy on women looks to be to become complicit with, and reinforce, sexism. However, it might also be employed by someone who believed that the lower life expectancies of males compared to females were also a product of an unjust social order.

A first thing to note about this objection is that, if it is valid, it seems likely to have large implications for the ethics of purportedly "therapeutic" uses of PGD. As disability critics of prenatal testing have argued, the consequences for the individual of being born with a disability are always mediated by the social environment and many of the features of this environment that generate restrictions on the welfare and/or opportunities of disabled people, including the distribution of resources, are themselves unjust (Oliver 1996; Silvers, Wasserman, & Mahowald 1998).

Nor is it obvious how prospective parents could be justified in ignoring the implications of the environment for the welfare of their children just because the environment is characterized by injustice. The effects of the environment are not any less real or morally significant because of that. Refusing to take them into account in one's reproductive decision-making will not be sufficient to change the environment: as I discuss further below, any implications for the environment in which children will grow up will be the result of the aggregation of the reproductive choices of all prospective parents rather than of the choices of any particular couple. One could rail against, and work to combat, sexism without thinking that it would be wrong to minimize the chance that one's own children would be negatively affected by it. Moreover, as I also discuss further below, by placing a concern for the aggregate impact of parental choices at the heart of the argument about the obligations of parents and implying that parents should be willing to sacrifice the welfare of their children for the sake of achieving a population-level goal, this argument is also, in an important sense, eugenic, and problematic because of that.

Finally, as I argued above, if we do not take the impact of injustice into account then it seems highly likely that selection of female embryos will count as an enhancement. The fact that the capacity to become pregnant is possessed only by chromosomal females does not appear to be a function of injustice. While it is plausible to think that some of the factors that lead to the lower life expectancy of males as compared to females are themselves a product of patriarchy (for instance, that men are often killed by other men, that men tend to work in more dangerous professions, that men commit suicide more often than women, and that men are less likely to seek medical care that might extend their lives), a significant portion of the higher life expectancy of females looks to be a product of genetic differences from males (redundancy in the X chromosome and the effects of estrogen) rather than of injustice.

7.5.3 *The plurality of the good*

A prominent feature of discussions of enhancement that many people find extremely jarring is the way that the debate assumes that there is a single measure of "best" that would allow us to determine what counts as an enhancement (Bennett 2014; Parker 2007). There is more than one way to lead a good life and there is more than one thing of value that we should be pursuing. Insisting that different sets of options (or goods) are often incommensurable is the most plausible way to resist the claim that we can always rank different sets of capacities at birth against each other. Perhaps, for instance, a life informed, and shaped, by the possibility of getting pregnant and giving birth to children, and a life informed, and shaped, by knowledge of the impossibility of such, simply cannot be compared. Because (if) they cannot be compared, we have no reason to choose either a male embryo over a female embryo or a female embryo over a male embryo. While, given incommensurability, strictly speaking the claim cannot be made, the absence of reasons to choose male or female embryos is expressed colloquially by the idea that it is – as many people are inclined to hold (or at least *say*) – "equally good" to be born male or female.

I am (deeply) sympathetic to this line of thought. In many circumstances, there is simply no answer to the question of which of two (or more) options or goods is better and consequently no answer as to which (single) option or good is best. It seems highly likely to me that this is the case when it comes to evaluating different human lives, different sets of options, and (consequently) different capacities and therefore genomes.

However, this line of argument is, fairly obviously, a poisoned chalice for advocates of human enhancement. If different sets of capacities cannot be ranked against each other, then in many contexts it simply will not be possible to "enhance" people. Genome editing might provide people with different capacities, but these changes often will not be enhancements because there will be no reason to prefer the new capacities to the capacities of unmodified people.

Admittedly, even when different classes of goods are incommensurable, it is sometimes possible to rank different goods *within* each class. Thus, in theory, it remains possible that we might be able to make males better (as males) and females better (as females) without it being the case that it is possible to decide the question of whether it is better to be a male or female. However, in the larger context of discussions of enhancement, insisting that – while we can evaluate the relative merits of most genetic differences – we cannot evaluate the merits of genes associated with sex differences looks both implausible and *ad hoc*.

In passing, acknowledging incommensurability is also problematic for advocates of (putatively) therapeutic uses of genetic technologies such as PGD. The argument about incommensurability was, after all, pioneered by disability activists, who insisted that lives shaped by different sets of bodily and mental capacities, identified by medical orthodoxy as impairments, need not be worse but were sometimes just different (Amundson 2000; Silvers, Wasserman, & Mahowald 1998).

7.5.4 *But you cannot say that!*

I suspect that when confronted with the argument that it must be better to be born female or better to be born male, some, perhaps many, people secretly agree but are unwilling to say so. To say out loud that it is better to be born one sex (whichever it is) looks profoundly disrespectful to persons of the other sex. In essence, this is the "expressivist critique" (Saxton 1997; Wendell 1996) of prenatal testing applied to the case of sex selection – although the argument has also been developed explicitly as a critique of sex selection (Berkowitz & Snyder 1998; Seavilleklein & Sherwin 2007).

Intuitively, this is a compelling argument. However, there are at least two well-known problems with the claim that acting on – and even expressing – the preference not to have a child born with a particular phenotype expresses a morally problematic disrespect for existing persons born with that phenotype.

First, the question of what statements or actions express is itself complicated. For instance, we do not typically hold of someone who says that they think it is better to stop having children after two that they are thereby expressing the idea that those who are the third child in their family are worthy of less respect (Buchanan 1996). The difference between this case and the case of sex selection (and also selection on the basis of genes associated with skin color or, if there are any such genes, same-sex attractedness) is that there is not widespread discrimination against individuals who are the third child in their family, while there *is* discrimination against women (and people of color and homosexuals). This is just one example of the way in which the meaning of both words and actions is a function of social context. For this reason, there is ample room to contest what is expressed by the desire to promote the welfare of one's child by ensuring that they are born female (or male). The belief that it would be better not to be born with some condition appears to be compatible with a passionate commitment to the idea that all human beings are of equal moral worth, regardless of their genetic inheritance (Buchanan, Brock, Daniels, & Wikler 2000, 276–278; Steinbock 2000). To insist that the desire to sex select expresses any attitude at all about the relative respect owed to men and women is to impose a social meaning on an individual belief that those who hold the belief are likely to disavow.

Second, relatedly, the expressivist critique looks more plausible as a criticism of a *policy* of sex selection rather than an individual decision to sex select. Insofar as we expect a liberal democratic community to protect and promote the interests of all the different groups within it, government policies that would threaten the survival of particular groups by preventing the birth of future members are arguably morally and politically problematic (Sparrow 2008b). However, it does not necessarily follow from this that prospective parents could not have reasons to prefer that their children be born with some genes rather than others. While it is understandable that people sometimes hear the claim that it would be better to be born without a condition (or perhaps even more so, *with* some condition) as advocacy for a policy requiring parents to select accordingly, this need not be the case.

7.5.5 Aggregate consequences

Another line of objection to the thought that selection of either sex would count as enhancement relies on the thought that the aggregate consequences of people pursuing enhancement would be disastrous. This seems especially obvious if we think that there is an obligation on parents to choose the best child possible – in which case presumably all parents would be obligated to choose children of the same sex (Sparrow 2011c)

It might be argued that bringing about a radical shift in sex ratios at birth would be bad because of its implications for the survival of the species. It is worth pausing to ask whether, if advocates of enhancement – who are often remarkably willing to speculate without reference to what is possible at the moment – have recourse to this argument, this would represent them losing the courage of their convictions when it is convenient for them to do so. Why are advocates of the superiority of males not willing to aspire to a world in which universally male embryos, produced using ova derived from colonies of stem cells, are gestated in the wombs of genetically modified animals? Why are advocates of the superiority of females unwilling to imagine a world where embryos are created using sperm created from stem cells and only female embryos are brought to term? For that matter, why are (most) advocates of enhancement not willing to embrace the idea that in the future, everyone should be born an androgynous hermaphrodite (Sparrow 2010b)?[8] In the larger context of the literature on human enhancement, reference to concerns about the impacts of sex selection on the survival of the species looks unprincipled insofar as it ignores the various technological means by which these might be avoided.

Another reason to worry about the prospect of a single-sex world would be if one believed that there is value in "diversity" (Sparrow 2019) – in this case, "sexual difference." There will, for instance, be some experiences that will be impossible for individuals to have in a single-sex world. It might also be argued that the community "as a whole" is worse off for being deprived of various benefits associated with diversity (Garland-Thomson 2012). An interesting feature of this line of argument is that it must postulate a nontrivial difference between the sexes in order to be plausible. If one's sex made little difference to one's experiences or character, then it is hard to see how the existence of two sexes is necessary to sustain diversity. However, insisting that the biological differences between the sexes are sufficient to generate valuable diversity makes it even harder to explain why it is not better to be born one sex or the other.

The larger problem with both of these concerns about aggregate consequences, though, is that, again, as I have argued further elsewhere (Sparrow 2015), they are better arguments against a *policy* requiring enhancement than against the claim that a biomedical intervention would constitute an enhancement or an argument that parents have an obligation to enhance. No individual decision about what sort of child to have brings about problematic social consequences, which are realized or not according to the aggregation of the choices of *all* prospective parents. If everyone else selects female children, it doesn't matter what I do. If other parents don't engage in selection, sex ratios will remain (roughly) equal, no matter what choice I make. Either way, my choice will not have any appreciable impact on sex ratios. Thus, while the consequences of a policy in relation to reproductive decision-making bear immediately on its ethics, the consequences of any individual reproductive decision for the distribution of genes across a population are negligible and thus provide scant grounds on which to criticize it.

7.6 Lessons from sex selection

In this final section, I want to reflect on the discussion of the preceding section and draw further on the literature on sex selection to make some observations about the debate about human enhancement and, indeed, the ethics of reproductive decision-making more generally.

7.6.1 The inevitability of eugenics

The discussion above has highlighted the way in which several of the most compelling objections to understanding sex selection as an enhancement rest on claims about the aggregate impacts of reproductive decisions. This means that, in an important sense, they are fundamentally eugenic: they are concerned with the distribution of genes across a population rather than with the welfare of individuals.

However, a concern for the population-level distribution of genes looks inevitable – and thus defensible – when one is considering the implications of various policies in relation to the use of new reproductive technologies. This comes out very clearly in the literature on the ethics of sex selection, which is shaped by the recognition that the availability and use of sex selection technologies in societies in which their use for non-medical sex selection is not prohibited has led to significant shifts in sex ratios, with social and political implications that are appropriately the concern of governments (Hvistendahl 2011; Hudson & Boer 2004). A similar thing is likely to be true of technologies of genetic human enhancement. That is, governments will need to regulate the use of genome editing to address collective action problems and to reduce the risk that the aggregate consequences of the use of this technology will be disastrous.[9]

7.6.2 Nature and norms

My discussion has also revealed how an intuition about incommensurability interacts with intuitions about normal male and normal female bodies to shape our thinking about human enhancement. Given the differences in the biology of males and females, and the gendered impacts of the social environment in almost all societies today, the only way to resist the conclusion that selection of one sex or the other should count as human enhancement is to insist that the life prospects of males and females at birth are incommensurable.

Although this intuition plays a key role in shaping our thinking about sex differences and their implications for welfare, it raises two questions that are highly deserving of further research.

First, what are the ethical and political implications of this claim more broadly? And how do they reflect upon its plausibility? If the argument for incommensurability of genomes rests on a claim that the merits of genomes can only be evaluated relative to ideas about what constitutes a good life (Sparrow 2011a), this will only work to invalidate the comparison of male and female life prospects at birth if we think that the nature of the good life differs between males and females.

Second, relatedly, why should we think that the question of whether it is better to be born male or female is moot, where, for instance, the question as to whether it is better to be deaf or hearing is not? The only plausible grounds for distinguishing between sex differences and other sorts of differences in capacities is that both male and female capacities are natural and therefore "normal." But how does a claim about what is natural generate norms? *Why* should the fact that *Homo sapiens* is a dimorphic species imply that we have no welfare-related reasons to prefer the birth of male or female children? This is especially puzzling given that in many cases it seems that we *can* say that it is better to have some capacities rather than others. Conversely, if we are willing to allow that male and female life prospects at birth are incommensurable, then perhaps we should be willing to hold that this is true more generally. Admitting this would, however, as I noted above, suggest that human enhancement is not possible for conceptual rather than practical reasons.

7.6.3 Better than men?

The suggestion that sex selection for *female* embryos constitutes enhancement challenges the assumptions and self-understanding of many of the participants in the debate about human enhancement (Sparrow 2011d). The literature in favor of human enhancement is overwhelmingly dominated by male authors and by images of enhancement that portray the enhanced as "super men" (Sparrow 2014). However, an important set of responses to the argument for enhancement have originated from critics who are conscious that people like them are unlikely to figure much in the brave new world that a program of human enhancement would produce – most obviously people with disabilities but also women (see, for instance, de Melo-Martín 2017; Garland-Thomson 2012; Hall 2018; Scully 2008). Insisting that it is males who are inferior and who would be selected against in a world in which we set out to enhance our children can sometimes provoke a gestalt shift in advocates of enhancement who, as a result of coming to see themselves as members of the class who are likely to be selected against in the future, suddenly come to feel the force of arguments that they have previously dismissed.

A final lesson that viewing enhancement through the lens of sex selection teaches us, then, is the role played by implicit assumptions about privilege and merit in the debate about enhancement. As we deliberate on the difficult ethical and political questions raised by the possibility of human germline genome editing for enhancement, including those I have highlighted here, it will be vital to subject claims about what counts as better, or best, to careful scrutiny and include the broadest possible community in the conversation.

Acknowledgments

I would like to thank Catherine Mills for conversations about, and discussion of, the ideas in this manuscript. Katrina Hutchison and Joshua Hatherley each assisted with locating relevant sources.

Notes

1 Here, and below, I am assuming that most individuals possess sex chromosomes that determine whether they are male or female at birth. This generalization does not deny that some individuals are born with a morphological sex that is discordant with their chromosomal sex or that some individuals are born with combinations of sex chromosomes other than XX or XY. The argument that follows is also intended to be compatible with the idea that whether an individual is a man or a woman is a matter of self-identification rather than chromosomal make-up: all it requires is that it is possible to make accurate generalizations about the capacities of human bodies and the impacts of a given social environment on the life-prospects of individuals, on the basis of the presence or absence of a Y chromosome.
2 For instance, I do not believe that either of the aforementioned sexist stereotypes are true.
3 Although, insofar as the use of PGD for sex selection is likely to involve the discarding of embryos of the unwanted sex, this technology offers nothing to those who object to abortion on the basis that it involves the killing of a "potential person" – indeed it is arguably worse than selective termination because the attempt to secure a child of a desired sex using the latter technology won't involve the destruction of a fetus in 50% of cases, whereas PGD will almost always involve the discarding, and destruction, of one or more embryos.
4 *Prima facie* evidence that these capacities are widely desired is provided by the amount of resources devoted to treatments for gestational infertility.
5 Menstruation can be controlled or even eliminated via hormone therapy; the risk of accidental pregnancy can be greatly reduced by contraception; and the risk of death in labor is greatly reduced by modern obstetrics. My discussion of these matters should not be taken to imply any stance on the question *as* to whether these are properly conceived of as disadvantages associated with the capacity to become pregnant and give birth: my point here is simply that even if they are held to be such, the extent of the disadvantage can be reduced using various technologies.
6 Interestingly, because the upper limit of the range of size and strength in females exceeds the species-typical size and strength of males, selection of male embryos will not count as enhancement on definition 4.
7 Moreover, today, individuals born female who wish to become genetic parents of large numbers of children may do so by becoming egg donors.
8 To be fair, some advocates of enhancement do precisely this. See, for instance, Dvorsky and Hughes (2008).
9 What seems highly morally problematic, though, is a willingness to reduce the welfare of some individuals in order to secure benefits for others by means of achieving some distribution of genes across a population (Sparrow 2015). If one believes that genetic human enhancement is possible, then to insist that some

people remain unenhanced for the sake of diversity, or in order to secure some other good associated with the presence of some unenhanced individuals in the population, is treat some people as a means to securing the welfare of others. While reasons of space prevent me from treating the matter here, my suspicion is that determining how much individual welfare it is justifiable to sacrifice for the sake of the collective is one of the hardest ethical problems raised by the prospect of genetic human enhancement (for some discussion, see Sparrow 2015, 2016, & 2019).

References

Agar, Nicholas. 2004. *Liberal eugenics: In defence of human enhancement*. Malden, MA: Blackwell Publishing.
Agar, Nicholas. 2010. *Humanity's end: Why we should reject radical enhancement*. Cambridge, MA: The MIT Press; Bradford Books.
Ainsworth, Claire. 2015. Sex redefined. *Nature* 518(7539): 288–291.
Amundson, Ron. 2000. Against normal function. *Studies in History and Philosophy of Science. Part C, Studies in History and Philosophy of Biological and Biomedical Sciences* 31(1): 33–53.
Annandale, Ellen. 2021. Health and gender. In William C. Cockerham (ed), *The Wiley Blackwell companion to medical sociology*, 237–257. Newark: John Wiley & Sons.
Bennett, Rebecca. 2014. There can be no moral obligation to eradicate all disability. *Cambridge Quarterly of Healthcare Ethics* 23(1): 30–40.
Berkowitz, Jonathan M., and Jack W. Snyder. 1998. Racism and sexism in medically assisted conception. *Bioethics* 12(1): 25–44.
Bostrom, Nick. 2008. Why I want to be a posthuman when I grow up. In Bert Gordijn and Ruth Chadwick (eds), *Medical enhancement and posthumanity*, 107–137. Dordrecht: Springer.
Brock, Dan. 1995. The non-identity problem and genetic harms – The case of wrongful handicaps. *Bioethics* 9(3/4): 269–275.
Buchanan, Allen. 1996. Choosing who will be disabled: Genetic intervention and the morality of inclusion. *Social Philosophy and Policy* 13(2): 18–46.
Buchanan, Allen, Dan W. Brock, Norman Daniels, and Daniel Wikler. 2000. *From chance to choice*. Cambridge: Cambridge University Press.
Davis, Dena S. 2001. *Genetic dilemmas: Reproductive technology, parental choices, and children's futures*. New York, NY & London: Routledge.
de Grey, Aubrey, and Michael Rae. 2007. *Ending aging: The rejuvenation breakthroughs that could reverse human aging in our lifetime*. New York: St. Martin's Press.
de Melo-Martín, Inmaculada. 2017. *Rethinking reprogenetics: Enhancing ethical analyses of reprogenetic technologies*. Oxford: Oxford University Press.
Dvorsky, George, and James Hughes. 2008. *Postgenderism: Beyond the gender binary*. Institute for Ethics and Emerging Technologies, Hartford, CT.
Elliott, Carl. 2003. *Better than well: American medicine meets the American dream*. New York: W.W. Norton.
Elliot, Robert. 1993. Identity and the ethics of gene therapy. *Bioethics* 7(1): 27–40.
Fausto-Sterling, Anne. 2000. *Sexing the body: Gender politics and the construction of sexuality*. New York: Basic Books.
Feinberg, Joel. 1980. The child's right to an open future. In W. Aiken and H. LaFollette (eds), *Whose child? Children's rights, parental authority, and state power*, 124–153. Totowa, NJ: Littlefield, Adams & Co.
Feinberg, Joel. 1986. Wrongful life and the counterfactual element in harming. *Social Philosophy and Policy* 4(1): 145–178.
Fenton, Andrew, and Tim Krahn. 2007. Autism, neurodiversity, and equality beyond the "normal". *Journal of Ethics in Mental Health* 2(2): 1–6.
Fine, Cordelia. 2017. *Testosterone rex: Unmaking the myths of our gendered minds*. London: Icon Books.
Garland-Thomson, Rosemarie. 2012. The case for conserving disability. *Journal of Bioethical Inquiry* 9(3): 339–355.
Gilligan, Carol. 1982. *In a different voice: Psychological theory and women's development*. Cambridge, MA: Harvard University Press.
Griffin, James. 1986. *Well-being: Its meaning, measurement, and moral importance*. Oxford: Clarendon Press.
Hall, Melinda C. 2018. *The bioethics of enhancement: Transhumanism, disability, and biopolitics*. Lanham, MD: Lexington Books.
Harris, John. 2007. *Enhancing evolution: The ethical case for making better people*. Princeton, NJ: Princeton University Press.
Hudson, Valerie M., and Andrea M. Den Boer. 2004. *Bare branches: The security implications of Asia's surplus male population*. Cambridge, MA; London: MIT.

Hvistendahl, Mara. 2011. *Unnatural selection: Choosing boys over girls, and the consequences of a world full of men.* New York: Public Affairs.
Jaarsma, Pier, and Stellan Welin. 2012. Autism as a natural human variation: Reflections on the claims of the neurodiversity movement. *Health Care Analysis* 20(1): 20–30.
Kingma, Elselijn. 2007. What is it to be healthy? *Analysis* 67(294): 128–133.
Kitcher, Philip. 1996. *The lives to come: The genetic revolution and human possibilities.* New York, NY: Simon & Schuster.
Krook, Mona Lena, and Fiona Mackay (eds) 2011. *Gender, politics and institutions.* Basingstoke: Palgrave Macmillan.
Lawrence, Susan C., and Kae Bendixen. 1992. His and hers: Male and female anatomy in anatomy texts for US medical students, 1890–1989. *Social Science & Medicine* 35(7): 925–934.
Lewontin, Richard C. 2001. *The triple helix: Gene, organism, and environment.* Cambridge, MA: Harvard University Press.
Mills, Catherine. 2015. The case of the missing hand: Gender, disability, and bodily norms in selective termination. *Hypatia* 30(1): 82–96.
Mills, Claudia. 2003. The child's right to an open future? *Journal of Social Philosophy* 34(4): 499–509.
Oliver, Michael. 1996. *Understanding disability. From theory to practice.* Basingstoke: Palgrave Macmillan.
Ortiz-Ospina, Esteban, and Max Roser. 2018. Economic inequality by gender. *OurWorldInData.org*. Available at https://ourworldindata.org/economic-inequality-by-gender (accessed 19 January, 2021).
Parfit, Derek. 1984. *Reasons and persons.* Oxford: Clarendon Press.
Parker, Michael. 2007. The best possible child. *Journal of Medical Ethics* 33(5): 279–283.
Parker, Rhiannon, Theresa Larkin, and Jon Cockburn. 2017. A visual analysis of gender bias in contemporary anatomy textbooks. *Social Science & Medicine* 180: 106–113.
Paulis, Marianna, Lucia Susani, Alessandra Castelli, Teruhiko Suzuki, Takahiko Hara, Letizia Straniero, Stefano Duga, Dario Strina, Stefano Mantero, Elena Caldana, Lucia Sergi Sergi, Anna Villa, and Paolo Vezzoni. 2020. Chromosome transplantation: A possible approach to treat human X-linked disorders. *Molecular Therapy – Methods & Clinical Development* 17: 369–377.
Petersen, Alan. 1998. Sexing the body: Representations of sex differences in Gray's Anatomy, 1858 to the present. *Body & Society* 4(1): 1–15.
Savulescu, Julian. 2001. Procreative beneficence: Why we should select the best children. *Bioethics* 15(5): 413–426.
Saxton, Marsha. 1997. Disability rights and selective abortion. In Rickie Solinger (ed), *Abortion wars: A half century of struggle*, 374–393. Berkeley and Los Angeles: University of California Press.
Scully, Jackie Leach. 2008. *Disability bioethics: Moral bodies, moral difference.* Lanham: Rowman & Littlefield Publishers.
Seavilleklein, Victoria, and Susan Sherwin. 2007. The myth of the gendered chromosome: Sex selection and the social interest. *Cambridge Quarterly of Healthcare Ethics* 16(1): 7–19.
Silvers, Anita, David T. Wasserman, and Mary Briody Mahowald. 1998. *Disability, difference, discrimination: Perspectives on justice in bioethics and public policy.* Lanham, MD: Rowman & Littlefield Publishers.
Sparrow, R. 2008a. Is it 'every man's right to have babies if he wants them'? Male pregnancy and the limits of reproductive liberty. *Kennedy Institute of Ethics Journal* 18(3): 275–299.
Sparrow, Robert. 2008b. Genes, identity, and the expressivist critique. In Loane Skene and Janna Thompson (eds) *The Sorting Society*, 111–132. Cambridge: Cambridge University Press.
Sparrow, Robert. 2010a. Better than men? Sex and the therapy/enhancement distinction. *Kennedy Institute of Ethics Journal* 20(2): 115–144.
Sparrow, Robert. 2010b. Should human beings have sex? Sexual dimorphism and human enhancement. *American Journal of Bioethics* 10(7): 3–12.
Sparrow, Robert. 2011a. Liberalism and eugenics. *Australasian Journal of Philosophy* 89(3): 499–517.
Sparrow, Robert. 2011b. Harris, harmed states, and sexed bodies. *Journal of Medical Ethics* 37(5): 276–279.
Sparrow, Robert. 2011c. A not-so-new eugenics: Harris and Savulescu on human enhancement. *Hastings Center Report* 41(1): 32–42.
Sparrow, Robert. 2011d. Fear of a female planet: How John Harris came to endorse eugenic social engineering. *Journal of Medical Ethics* 38: 4–7.
Sparrow, Robert. 2012. Human enhancement and sexual dimorphism. *Bioethics* 26(9): 464–475.
Sparrow, Robert. 2014. Ethics, eugenics, and politics. In Akira Akayabashi (ed) *The future of bioethics: International dialogues*, 139–153. Oxford: Oxford University Press.
Sparrow, Robert. 2015. Imposing genetic diversity. *American Journal of Bioethics* 15(6): 2–10.
Sparrow, Robert. 2016. Human enhancement for whom? In Steve Clarke, Julian Savulescu, C. A. J. Coady, Alberto Giubilini, and Sagar Sanyal (eds) *The ethics of human enhancement: Understanding the debate*, 127–142. Oxford: Oxford University Press.

Sparrow, Robert. 2019. Unravelling the human tapestry. Diversity, flourishing, and genetic modification? In Erik Parens and Josephine Johnston (eds) *Human flourishing in an age of gene editing*, 157–171. Oxford: Oxford University Press.

Sparrow, Robert. 2021. Human germline genome editing: On the nature of our reasons to genome edit. *American Journal of Bioethics*. Online First, 19 Apr 2021. DOI: 10.1080/15265161.2021.1907480

Steinbock, Bonnie. 2000. Disability, prenatal testing, and selective abortion. In Erik Parens and Adrienne Asch (eds), *Prenatal testing and disability rights*, 108–123. Washington, DC: Georgetown University Press.

The Ethics Committee of the American Society of Reproductive Medicine. 1999. Sex selection and preimplantation genetic diagnosis. *Fertility and Sterility* 72(4): 595–598.

UN Women and United Nations Department of Economic and Social Affairs Statistics Division. 2021. *Progress on the sustainable development goals: The gender snapshot 2021*. New York: UN Women and United Nations Department of Economic and Social Affairs.

Wendell, Susan. 1996. *The rejected body. Feminist philosophical reflections on disability*. New York and London: Routledge.

World Economic Forum. 2021. *Global gender gap report 2021*. Geneva: World Economic Forum.

World Health Organization. 2019. *World health statistics 2019: Monitoring health for the SDGs, sustainable development goals*. Geneva: World Health Organization. Available at https://apps.who.int/iris/bitstream/handle/10665/324835/9789241565707-eng.pdf?sequence=9&isAllowed=y.

8
DOES ENHANCEMENT VIOLATE HUMAN "NATURE"?

Jason T. Eberl

8.1 Introduction

The term "nature" is placed in quotation marks in the title, as one of the fundamental questions that must be addressed before inquiring about the ethics of enhancing human beings is whether there *is* an essential nature that all human beings share. Various affirmative responses to this perennial philosophical question have been challenged by discoveries in evolutionary biology, cultural anthropology, cognitive psychology, and other relevant fields. Nevertheless, several theories of human nature persist in light of such discoveries. Whether there is a universal human nature and what essential qualities define that nature inform various responses to whether it may be altered using biotechnological or other means of enhancement. On one side of the debate are so-called *bioconservatives* who reject any non-therapeutic interventions that could alter the putatively definitive qualities of human nature.[1] On the other side are *transhumanists* who argue in favor of "morphological freedom" to reshape oneself in any non-harmful way one chooses.[2] Between these views are several proposals that allow for certain forms of enhancement that may increase individual or collective well-being within the limits of a defined human nature, eschewing the creation or transformation of human beings into a new ontological species of "posthumans."[3]

Certain moderate forms of physical, cognitive, emotive, or moral enhancement are arguably compatible with a Thomistic Aristotelian account of human nature and flourishing (Eberl 2014, 2017a, 2018).[4] This chapter will not defend a specifically Thomistic Aristotelian account of human nature but rather canvass several views of human nature that have informed diverse perspectives on the ethics of enhancement. It begins by considering why an account of human nature is needed to adequately engage questions concerning enhancement.

8.2 Need for an account of human nature

Both transhumanists and bioconservatives invoke presuppositions regarding what traits, capacities, or activities they each take to be fundamental to human nature and to constitute our flourishing as the type of beings we are. For transhumanists, *intelligence* and *autonomy* – understood in a liberal Millian, as opposed to a Kantian, sense[5] – are taken to be defining features of human nature, and the maximization of each is what it means for us to flourish. Improvement of our *physical* form is also part of the transhumanist conception of our flourishing, though not necessarily of our bodies *qua* "human" if it were to become possible for our minds to be "uploaded" into a cybernetic mainframe to perpetuate our existence and free our minds from any physical limitations endemic to our biological brains (Kurzweil 2005; Koene 2013; Merkle 2013). For bioconservatives, more traditional conceptions of human nature and flourishing ground moral analyses of the drive to enhance ourselves.[6] Sharing transhumanists' reverence for intelligence and autonomy – though often understanding the latter in the more restrictive Kantian sense – bioconservatives also promote the intrinsic value of the *human* physical form and its inherent features of *vulnerability* and *mortality*, among other attributes (Sandel 2007, ch. 5; McKenny 1997).

Presenting a "binocular" approach to questions concerning enhancement, Erik Parens (2015, p. 94) seeks a common moral ground upon which constructive dialogue may be fostered about which forms of enhancement would be truly desirable for us to adopt:

> [C]ritics and enthusiasts [of human enhancement] share the notion that human flourishing consists in engaging in activities in the world, as the world, and as we our selves really are … if we got better at noticing that shared understanding, it would be easier to go from arguing for or against enhancement to having a conversation about what real or true or, yes, "authentic" as opposed to "false" (or merely putative) enhancement is.

Nicholas Agar (2014) is also concerned to promote *authentic* enhancement of human beings *qua human*, as distinguished from more radical proposals that would lead to the creation of a new posthuman race.[7] He contends that radically enhanced posthumans would not be better versions *of us*, but potentially better beings of a categorically different order. Thus, human beings should not desire radical enhancement *for ourselves* insofar as the end product would likely not be a being with whose interests and desires we could self-identify, which could have profound normative implications. Both Agar and Parens, however, are concerned about promoting any "monolithic view about human flourishing," but acknowledge "a plurality of views about the good life" (Agar 2014, p. 143); Parens (2015, p. 94) states that an individual's "right to flourish in her own way has to be protected against the community," although she "has an obligation to consider the impact of her projects on others." We should thus consider the following questions: can we coherently distinguish authentic forms of human enhancement from radical forms that would lead to posthumanism without some sort of objective anthropological account of what it *is* to be human? If so, can such an account be formulated that is not inherently "monolithic" and that allows for a certain degree of pluralism?

James Keenan (2014, p. 163) answers the first question negatively in contending that the reticence to invoke some sort of objective account of human nature actually works against promoters of moderate enhancement, such as Agar, by strengthening bioconservatives' valorization of "the normal":

> In the absence of an adequate anthropological model, we have adopted a naturalism that is disturbing: medicine exists only for therapy, that is, for healing, or prevention, for the avoidance of disease, but not for some benevolent pursuit of a better personal existence. In this context, we "valorize the normal" because, lacking an anthropology, we have no other standard for what humans ought to be other than they normally are. Of course, one reason that we valorize the normal is because we rightly fear whatever else we might endorse in the absence of an adequate anthropological vision.

Yet, the central concern underlying the second question persists: namely, that some form of "normative essentialism" would restrict the range of legitimate concepts of human nature and flourishing (Buchanan 2009; 2011, ch.4). Such normative essentialism is arguably either unpersuasive because it is too "thick" or unhelpful because its content is too "thin" (Buchanan 2011, p. 132). In response to this putative dilemma, there are multiple defenses of accounts of human nature that are both sufficiently general to encompass a wide range of biological instantiations and cultural expressions, while also grounding specific normative claims. One such account is grounded in Thomistic

Aristotelianism (Eberl 2014, 2020); others have proffered accounts with varying degrees of similarity (Oderberg 2007, 2014; McKenny 1997, 2013, 2019; Stango-Agler 2018; Jensen-Widow 2018). A key feature of the Thomistic Aristotelian and similar accounts is that the human kind is categorized *ontologically* based on a set of causally relevant properties – namely, one's *intrinsic capacities* – as opposed to advocating a *speciesist* reduction of human nature to merely *biological* qualities. In other words, it does not matter how we consider a human being to be biologically *constituted* but rather how a human being is capacitated to *function*. If one has their amputated legs replaced by prosthetic limbs, they possess no less an ambulatory capacity than someone with their biological legs intact.[8] The following section provides an account of the essential functions of human beings.

8.3 What constitutes human nature?

Art Caplan (2009, p. 202) raises a basic challenge to those who object to enhancement in general, or certain forms thereof, on the basis of violating human nature in objectionable ways:

> Is there a "nature" that is common to all humans, both those that exist now and those that have existed in the past? … one can concede that we have been shaped by a causally powerful set of genetic influences and selection forces and still remain skeptical as to whether these have produced a single "nature" that all members of humanity possess. What exactly is the single trait or fixed, determinate set of traits that defines the nature of who humans are and have been throughout our entire existence as a species on this planet? … Without a demonstration of a "nature" there is no basis for the claim that change, improvement, and betterment always represent grave threats to our essential humanity.

Pace Caplan, despite all we have learned about the biological and sociological evolutionary development of human beings, metaphysical analyses from both historical and contemporary philosophers have consistently – if not uncontroversially – defended a fairly coherent list of universal qualities that human beings possess *qua persons*, which have emerged and then remained constant through such development. "Person" refers to the essential normative *ontology* of human beings distinct from our biological identification as *Homo sapiens*.[9]

In the classical period, both Plato and Aristotle defined the essence of humanity in terms of our capacity for *rational thought*. For Plato (1989), this led to the conclusion that we are essentially immaterial minds, whereas Aristotle (1984) took a less dualistic stance in defining human beings as "rational animals." The earliest philosophical definition of *personhood* comes from Boethius (1918, p. 85) in the early 6th century: an "individual substance of a rational nature." Later in the 17th century, John Locke (1975, p. 335) offered an alternative definition of a person as "a thinking intelligent Being, that has reason and reflection, and can consider itself as itself, the same thinking thing in different times and places." Finally, in the 18th century, Immanuel Kant (1997) grounded the incalculable moral worth – *dignity* – of human persons in our capacity for *rational autonomy*. Among contemporary philosophers, Lynne Baker (2000) contends that a person is essentially a being with the *capacity for a first-person perspective*. Other contemporary theorists cite the following essential activities in which persons engage: rational thought, self-reflexive consciousness, using language to communicate, having non-momentary self-interests, and possessing moral agency or autonomy (Singer 1992; Kuhse and Singer 1985; Tooley 1983; Warren 1973).[10]

Collating all of these historical and contemporary views, a defensible summative thesis is that a person is any being that exhibits *a capacity for self-conscious rational thought and autonomous volition*, and who is thereby *a member of the moral community*.[11] Human beings, insofar as we exhibit the above, count as persons, and non-human beings may also count as persons if they exhibit the above. Finally, while one's biological nature does not determine one's status as a person, biological factors may serve as epistemic criteria for determining whether a being exhibits the above.

By focusing on ontological categorization defined by a set of essential functional capacities, the door opens for a wide variety of *material instantiations* of such capacities and the beings who possess them.[12] There are, of course, limits on such instantiations – a ballpoint pen cannot instantiate a sentient or rational mind. Nevertheless, as noted above, artificial prostheses or organs may allow a human being to actualize their various essential capacities. Such artificial prostheses or organs, however, do not materially instantiate the *capacity* for essential human functions; rather, they provide the means by which such a capacity may be *actualized*.[13] Artificial limbs for a double-leg amputee do not provide them with the capacity to walk; they always had the capacity but were unable to actualize it.

This speaks to the ontological significance of *embodiment* and a human being's essential nature *qua animal*. Defensibly, human beings are essentially biologically living beings, not immaterial souls – as Plato (1989) or René Descartes (1996) would identify us – or insubstantial bundles of mental states – as David Hume (1978, bk. I, pt. 4, §vi) contends – or mere sets of data and algorithms – as transhumanists like Ray Kurzweil (2005), who envisions the potential "uploading" of ourselves, believe.[14] If human beings are essentially animals – even if our species identification could be altered without losing our essential capacities – two key qualities are entailed: *vulnerability* and *mortality* (Asla 2019). The question is whether these are qualities that we ought to value in themselves simply because we all have them, or whether something important would be lost if we eliminated these qualities or our animality altogether.

8.4 Evaluating enhancements

Having outlined a broadly-construed account of human nature in terms of our *embodied personhood*, this section will first critique transhumanist proposals that seek to eliminate human embodiment and its attendant conditions of vulnerability and mortality. It will then examine two cases of more moderate forms of enhancement. The first is *cognitive* enhancement, and the pertinent question is whether this type of enhancement could negatively impact one's *personal identity*. The second is *moral* enhancement and its potential impact on our *authenticity*, a central component of autonomous agency, one of human beings' essential capacities.

8.4.1 Critique of transhumanism

As noted at the outset, transhumanists adopt a principle of "morphological freedom," which is premised on the notion that human nature, as given, is not fixed but malleable and that the application of human intelligence is likely to result in superior alterations to the human form than the "blind" process of continued biological evolution:

> Transhumanists view human nature as a work-in-progress, a half-baked beginning that we can learn to remold in desirable ways. Current humanity need not be the endpoint of evolution. Transhumanists hope that by responsible use of science, technology, and other rational means we shall eventually manage to become post-human, beings with vastly greater capacities than present human beings have.
>
> *(Bostrom 2003, p. 493)*

Julian Savulescu, Anders Sandberg, and Guy Kahane (2011, p. 7) reject as "ideological" any understanding of enhancement that rests upon a *metaphysical* concept of human nature and adopt a "welfarist" definition, in which an enhancement is "any change in the biology or psychology of a person which increases the chances of leading a good life in the relevant set of circumstances."

Would the type of radical ontological transformation wrought by eschewing our animal bodies actually increase our chances "of leading a good life"? Gerald McKenny (1998, pp. 223 & 235) asks,

Are the vulnerability and resistance of our bodies merely obstacles to be overcome to whatever extent possible? Or are vulnerability and resistance sources of self-regarding and other-regarding ethical values that are imperiled by attitudes and practices that view them only as obstacles to be overcome? … To the extent that enhancements overcome, or lead us to deny, the vulnerability of the body, they also foreclose the kinds of self-formation that our awareness of vulnerability makes possible.

Alasdair MacIntyre (1999) describes the "virtues of acknowledged dependence" that are essential for human beings to flourish insofar as we are inherently *social animals*. Not only to survive vulnerable periods of our lives – infancy, youth, debility from age, or any temporary or permanent period of disability – but also to mature morally as *practical reasoners*, we are unavoidably dependent upon others. In turn, others' vulnerability demands that we acknowledge our *responsibility* to promote their flourishing. In short, no individual person is an island unto herself with respect to her physical or moral development, and promoting forms of physical enhancement in an attempt to eliminate *any* vulnerability or dependency could have a negative impact on our sense of interpersonal moral responsibility for each other's well-being (Hauskeller 2019; Parens 1995); it may even reduce an enhanced person's *moral status* insofar as recognition of one's status as a being with rights warranting protection is due to one's vulnerabilities (Gray 2020). Additionally, while we ought not to seek pain or suffering for its own sake, there is a *potential instrumental value* to such otherwise negative experiences that may be occluded by seeking to eliminate various vulnerabilities (Eberl 2012).

It could be argued, however, that this concern is unwarranted since even the most radical enhancements cannot eliminate "ontological vulnerability" – namely, the possibility of being harmed or killed endemic to any being subject to nature's laws (Coeckelbergh 2011; Liedo Fernández and Rueda 2021). Even a digitally encoded mind – if possible – would be dependent upon some sort of technological apparatus (e.g., cloud servers, Asimov's positronic brain) to maintain it, and any such apparatus could break down internally or be damaged or destroyed by an external force; Nick Bostrom (2008, p. 32) thus admits that a posthuman could still "be vulnerable, dependent, and limited." The issue at hand is not only whether radical forms of enhancement could eliminate vulnerability but also whether transhumanists' Promethean drive for mastery over nature "entails a diminished sense of ontological vulnerability" (Liedo Fernández and Rueda 2021, p. 228). Radically enhanced persons may, like stereotypical teenagers and college students, falsely perceive themselves to be invulnerable and thereby lose appreciation for the virtues of *acknowledged* dependence and the concomitant sense of *responsibility* for ameliorating the harms that may accrue from our vulnerabilities. Belén Liedo Fernández and Jon Rueda (2021, p. 233) affirm that "caring should be part of posthuman existence" given the persistence of ontological vulnerability, but it is difficult to envision how a disposition toward caring for others could be cultivated if one does not perceive their fellow posthumans to be in need of caring.

Striving to increase our longevity, with the goal of at least some transhumanists that we achieve *amortality* (de Grey 2004),[15] could lead to a "tedious" existence as Bernard Williams (1973) forewarns.[16] Over an extended period of existence – even if not an *infinitely* extended period – Williams contends that we would eventually cease to value those goods which we initially sought amortality to enjoy. The result would be the sort of posthuman existence against which Agar (2014) warns, defined by a distinct set of normative values from our current existence. If one's existence were extended indefinitely, it may even reach a point where one would run out of any goods to value whatsoever.[17] We are thus arguably better off with a *finite* existence in which we are able to value a limited range of goods over our entire lifetime, especially given the potential of losing such goods within our lifetime or unavoidably at death.

There is a further, existentially deeper problem that confronts transhumanists who advocate uploading our minds into a digital realm: would we *survive* such a transformation? This question is not referring to whether the technical procedure would work reliably,[18] but the metaphysical concern that one's *personal identity* would not be preserved. Digital uploading and other proposals for attaining near-perpetual longevity, such as head transplantation (Ren and Canavero 2017), presume a *psychological-continuity criterion* of personal identity in which a person goes wherever their consciousness goes (Hershenov 2019; Eberl 2017b). This criterion – historically grounded in Locke's (1975) and Hume's (1978) respective accounts of personhood – reflects our general intuitions about what happens in thought experiments involving brain transplantation, teletransportation *à la Star Trek*, and "what matters" to us in our survival (Parfit 1984). Yet, as powerful as these intuitions are, they may still be subject to philosophical critique from those who espouse *animalism*, affirming human beings' identification with our living animal bodies (Olson 1997; Snowdon 2014; Blatti and Snowdon 2016). Hershenov (2019, p. 106) delineates the metaphysical puzzles faced by psychological-continuity theorists that motivate animalism, and concludes the poor results for preserving one's identity in transhumanist proposals if animalism is true:

> But if persons are animals and have the nature and persistence conditions of them, then they can't be transplanted, uploaded or become cyborgs. You would be the mindless patient in the persistent vegetative state left behind in a cerebrum transplant.[19] Nor can material animals be moved by just scanning and downloading information about them. Finally, if you underwent considerable inorganic part replacement then you would not be the cyborg but the organism within the cyborg. And if not enough organic [matter] remained to compose a life, then you would cease to exist rather than become composed of both organic and inorganic parts.

Space does not permit an extended comparative critique of psychological-continuity theory versus animalism, but it is important to highlight the potential implications for various transhumanist proposals if one of these views – or one of the various other views put forth by contemporary metaphysicians[20] – of human nature and personal identity is correct (see also DeGrazia 2005b). Such competing metaphysical views also bear on moderate forms of enhancement, particularly those that affect cognition.

8.4.2 Cognitive enhancement and personal identity

Low-level means of enhancing cognitive performance are already ubiquitous with both easily-accessed stimulants (e.g., caffeine) and off-label use of prescribed pharmaceuticals to treat ADD and ADHD (e.g., Ritalin, Adderall). Such means of increasing one's attentiveness and focused concentration are of negligible ontological import insofar as they function by *aiding* one's already *extant* cognitive capacities, and their effects are *temporary*. More concerning are forms of cognitive manipulation that entail *significant permanent* alterations of one's cognitive capacities or the endowment of *new* capacities. Consider an upgrade of one's experiential memory capacity from what is currently typical for most human beings – in which memories of most insignificant events fade over time (try remembering your experience of eating breakfast one year ago from today) or change in their content due to cognitive biases (hence the unreliability of eyewitness testimony) – to *perfect* recall of every experience one has ever had free of any biased filter. Setting aside whether such enhanced memory would be desirable – one can think of several reasons why it might not, particularly with respect to traumatic experiences – let us consider how it might impact one's personal identity.

A useful distinction to frame this discussion is between *numerical* and *narrative* identity (DeGrazia 2005a, chs. 2 & 3; cf. DeGrazia 2005b). Numerical identity refers to whether some entity, in this case, a human person, is one and the same entity at various times. The contrasting psychological-continuity and animalist views provide distinct criteria for a human person's numerical identity through time and change: whether it be either a) the continuity of one's psychological traits, especially but not only one's memories, or b) the persistence of a living human organism. If psychological-continuity theory is true, then memory enhancement would actually *increase* the connectivity of one's conscious experiences across their lifespan; though it would not increase their numerical identity, as that is an all-or-nothing affair. A pertinent question, though, would be one's psychological continuity with their pre-enhanced self. Presumably, such a significant change in the quality of one's memory capacity would result in further alterations to other psychological traits for better or worse: one might experience increased joyfulness over being able to remember important happy moments but may also become despondent over their inability to forget traumatically sad moments. Whether enhanced experiential memory results in a person becoming overall more joyful or more despondent, they may lose their sense of identity with their pre-enhanced self who was perhaps more emotionally well-balanced. Yet, so long as one continues to bear a sufficient degree of psychological continuity with their pre-enhanced self, memory enhancement should not result in a change in numerical identity: one remains the *same* person. If animalism is true, numerical identity would also remain intact, as the same living human organism would persist no matter how significant an alteration of one's psychological traits.

The potential loss or diminishment of one's *sense* of identity with their pre-enhanced self, however, would constitute a change in narrative identity, which DeGrazia (2005b, p. 266; cf. Schechtman 1996) defines as "an individual's self-conception: her most central values, implicit autobiography, and identifications with particular people, activities, and roles." Though a change in one's numerical identity – since it entails the end of a person's existence – is of ultimate ontological and normative import, changes in narrative identity can also be morally significant – particularly as they may bear on one's identity as a *moral agent*, as will be discussed below.

A final consideration worth noting is that the normative significance of narrative identity may inform the question of *when* it is optimal to do enhancement interventions. Depending on the particular enhancement and the available means to bring it about, interventions may only be feasible later in one's life when a person has already cultivated significant aspects of their narrative identity – thus the potentially diminished self-identification with one's pre-enhanced self with their shoddy memory capacity. Thanks to the breakthrough in gene editing using the CRISPR-cas9 technique, it will likely be even more feasible to make enhancement alterations at the embryonic, fetal, or neonatal stages of life, well before one has begun to develop their narrative identity (Jinek et al. 2012). The prospect of enhancement alterations done at these early stages of biological life, however, raises its own problematic questions. A primary normative concern is the lack of ability to *consent* to being enhanced, though parental autonomy and stewardship rights over their children's well-being is a relevant factor as well.[21] A primary metaphysical concern is whether such a significant alteration of one's genetic identity at such an early stage of development entails a change in numerical identity:

> If an embryo's [or fetus' or neonate's] genetic makeup is altered, does this not involve an alteration of identity? If it does, the action cannot be properly conceived as improving an individual's life but rather as *substituting* one individual for another ... we must be prepared to ask whether a procedure will be beneficial to the individual before us, or will it in fact involve rubbing out this individual and introducing a new individual in its stead?
> *(Zohar 1991, p. 279)*

A foundational question underlying this concern is whether there is already an "individual before us" when genetic alteration is made. There are, of course, diverse positions on this vexed question ranging from one's numerical identity beginning at conception (Condic and Condic 2018; Kaczor 2015; Lee 2010) to uterine implantation/gastrulation (Ford 1988; Olson 1997, ch. 4; Smith and Brogaard 2003)[22] to well after birth (Kuhse and Singer 1985; Tooley 1983). Even if it is the case that one's numerical identity as a human person begins at conception, it does not follow that genetic alterations to a preimplantation embryo would necessarily result in a change in numerical identity so long as such changes preserve the continuance of the embryo's biological development assuming it is successfully implanted. Let us turn now to consider how another form of enhancement may significantly impact one's narrative identity *qua moral agent*.

8.4.3 *Moral enhancement and narrative identity*

Proposals to morally enhance human beings involve interventions aimed at altering one's cognitive or emotive dispositions. Relevant cognitive enhancements relate to information processing and reasoning, memory, and cognitive biases (Buchanan 2011, p. 75). Morally relevant emotional dispositions that may be amenable to alteration include aggression, xenophobia, and ego-centeredness. Furthermore, it may be possible to positively enhance dispositions toward empathy/sympathy, truthfulness, solidarity, agreeableness, altruism, gratitude, fairness, shame, forgiveness, and resistance to temptation (Bostrom 2005; Douglas 2011; Persson and Savulescu 2012; DeGrazia 2014). Some bioethicists have gone so far as to argue that moral enhancement is *necessary* if we are to survive as a species, arguing that our technological capacity to destroy ourselves – through weapons of mass destruction or environmental degradation – has surpassed our general capacity for moral reasoning and for being disposed toward working cooperatively for the sake of the common good. They thus contend that "it is imperative that scientific research explore every possibility of developing effective means of moral bioenhancement, as a complement to traditional means" (Persson and Savulescu 2012, p. 2).

While moral enhancement would not alter one's numerical identity as the same person, significant qualitative alterations to one's narrative identity may ensue, especially if the enhancements are to such a degree that one not only perceives themselves to be a better moral reasoner than their previous unenhanced self but has a new set of values to the extent that they may even look back on their old self with disgust and regret – consider how someone who has recently subscribed to veganism may view their earlier self who frequented McDonald's.

Such a regretful attitude toward one's past self raises not only the concern that pathological self-loathing might result – though one would presumably not loathe their current morally improved self – but also the more serious concern that one may no longer perceive themselves to be *authentic*. Authenticity is a key element of narrative identity, referring to the consistency of one's core values, significant life projects, and forms of self-identification (e.g., one's race, ethnicity, gender, sexual orientation, nationality, religion, etc.); in short, one's authentic identity comprises "one's reflective, settled conception of one's self, an understanding of who one is that embodies one's most stable, highest priority values" (Buchanan 2011, p. 101; see also Parens 2005; DeGrazia 2000; Elliott 1998; Taylor 1991). Authenticity is not *static*, and one may of course change some of the values, projects, and ways in which they self-identify over time; yet there is usually some connectivity between the change one undergoes and other more stable or more significant qualities that constitute their narrative identity.

Consider a person who throughout their adolescence and young adulthood formed a considered opinion in favor of abortion rights as part of their overall concerns regarding issues of gender equity and overcoming forms of patriarchal oppression. These values also align with a broader concern for the rights of oppressed persons, particularly those most vulnerable to social injustices. Over time, and perhaps after reading arguments regarding fetal personhood and the work of pro-life feminists (e.g., Callahan 1986), they come to view unborn fetuses as falling into the category of those most vulnerable to social injustice, whose fundamental right to life is subject to a form of (in this case, matriarchal) oppression. They thus form a new considered opinion against unrestricted abortion rights. This example is intended to show that a person may authentically change their considered moral views within the framework of more significant values that not only endure through but in fact *motivate* the change of view.[23]

Could biotechnological moral enhancement bring about similar authentic change in one's moral views, values, or dispositions? A fundamental criterion for an affirmative response would be that the use of such means to morally enhance oneself has been *autonomously chosen* (Harris 2011). A problem with this criterion is the following paradox: if one chooses to be morally enhanced, then they probably are not in need of being enhanced; and those most in need of moral enhancement will likely not choose to be enhanced. It seems that the only way to resolve this paradox would be to enhance people *compulsorily* (Persson and Savulescu 2014), perhaps even *covertly* (Crutchfield 2019), which would violate their autonomy. Most people are neither pure saints who have no need of moral enhancement nor unrepentant sinners who, like Milton's Lucifer in *Paradise Lost*, have proclaimed "Evil, be thou my good!" Rather, the lifelong pursuit of cultivating virtue and eliminating vice involves aligning one's competing *first-order* desires with one's *second-order* desires (Eberl 2018).

Harry Frankfurt (1971) distinguishes a *person*, a moral agent with freedom of will, from a *wanton* driven only by their competing first-order desires. Persons are able to form second-order desires about which first-order desires they want to determine their will; when alignment is attained, the second-order desires become second-order *volitions*. A person does not simply have the freedom to *act* on what may be merely their first-order desires – e.g., an alcoholic may have the freedom to drink but yet be volitionally frustrated because he desires not to will to drink – but "is also free to want what he wants to want" – i.e., to possess genuine freedom *of will* (Frankfurt 1971, p. 17). An alcoholic may not be able to eliminate his first-order desire to drink; yet, he has the capacity to formulate a second-order desire not to will to drink and, with the help of an effective rehabilitation program, can effectuate his second-order desire as determinative of his will when confronted with an occasion to drink – wherein his freedom as a person lies.

Many alcoholics who have formed a second-order desire not to will to drink seek forms of support to aid them in actualizing their first-order desire not to drink; however, alcoholism for some people is refractory to such forms of support. Some persons with refractory alcoholism have elected to try a more invasive procedure: deep brain stimulation (DBS) of the nucleus accumbens in order to eliminate one's cue-induced craving for alcohol (Müller et al. 2009; Heldmann et al. 2012; Ho et al. 2018). While this intervention may more accurately be construed as *therapeutic* insofar as it is treating a neurochemical addiction, similar types of neurological interventions could also help one to align their first- and second-order desires in the absence of a pathological condition (Liao 2016). As with the alcoholics who autonomously consented to DBS, so long as the enhancement one is seeking involves aligning their first-order desires with an already developed second-order desire, then their moral *agency* and *authenticity* are preserved.

8.5 Conclusion

To return to the titular question that has framed this analysis, Does enhancement violate human nature? – notice the quotation marks around "nature" have been removed – it is evident that some of the more radical proposals promoted by transhumanists could eliminate or significantly alter key features of our essential *embodiment*. If, however, psychological-continuity theory is true and our bodies are wholly unimportant to either our numerical or narrative identities, then even the most extreme proposal of digitally uploading one's conscious mind may be metaphysically feasible. More moderate enhancement proposals, including certain forms of cognitive or moral enhancement, may also be congruent with the nature of human persons and support our flourishing as the types of beings we are, though some may still have significant implications for one's narrative identity, including one's moral authenticity. The fundamental takeaway from this excursus is that the question of what constitutes human nature and the identity of human persons through time and change is *indispensable* for continued investigation into whether various enhancement proposals would constitute "truly human enhancement" (Agar 2014), especially insofar as human nature, however defined, grounds human *dignity* (Jotterand 2010).

Notes

1 The term "bioconservative" was coined by transhumanists (see, e.g., Hughes 2010) as a polemical term that served to reduce the diversity of non-transhumanist perspectives to a singular opponent.
2 The most vocal international transhumanist group is known as "Humanity+" (More 2013). General critical assessments of enhancement have been developed by Sandel (2007) and Habermas (2003); among critical responses to Sandel and Habermas are Kamm (2009), Roduit (2016), and Fenton (2006). The President's Council on Bioethics (2003) provides a comprehensive evaluation of various forms of enhancement. Note that this article is concerned only with the discussions shaped by this opposition that revolve around the question of human nature, not with the debate on human enhancement as a whole.
3 See, for example, Agar (2010, 2014) and Parens (2015).
4 Throughout this paper, material will be drawn upon from these previous articles.
5 The Kantian concept of autonomy is centered upon the will's capacity to *self-legislate* – that is, to govern oneself in accordance with the rationally understood moral law (Kant 1997), whereas the Millian concept is centered upon the unbridled exercise of an individual's will so long as harm does not accrue to another being with moral status (Mill 1989).
6 Many of these traditional conceptions of human nature that inform bioconservatism are *theological* in origin, though many such views may also be *philosophically* defensible. It should also be noted that diverse religious worldviews yield various normative conclusions concerning enhancement and transhumanism. For a sampling of religious, predominantly Christian, perspectives, see Cole-Turner (2011), Mercer and Maher (2014), Mercer and Trothen (2015), and Donaldson and Cole-Turner (2018).
7 For further critique of posthumanism, see Fukuyama (2002).
8 Not all defenders of a normatively essentialist account of human nature will agree with this ontological/biological distinction, particularly the subjects of Buchanan's critique. My point is that normative essentialism does not entail the sort of biological reductionism Buchanan is rightly concerned about.
9 For further argument against the biological category of *Homo sapiens* serving as an "inviolable core trait" of human beings, see DeGrazia (2005b, pp. 277–9). For a defense of human beings as members of the biological species *Homo sapiens*, see Agar (2010). An advantage of focusing on *personhood* as a normative ontological category, instead of imbuing our biological categorization with normative import, is that it allows us to address more adequately and fruitfully the moral status of not only the possible existence of intelligent nonhuman extra-terrestrials but also that of human/nonhuman chimeras whose unique genetic profiles confound standard biological categories (Eberl and Ballard 2009).
10 The contemporary theorists cited here consider it essential to being a person that one is *actually engaging* in these activities, or could at least immediately do so without any intrinsic impediment. It is arguably sufficient, however, for one to be a person if one possesses the *intrinsic capacity* to engage in these activities, the actualization of which may require development over time (Eberl 2020, ch. 5).
11 This general definition captures the essence of being a person but omits many distinct nuances that are often contested. For example, it is debated whether having a capacity for self-conscious rational thought and autonomous volition requires having a biological cerebrum, or whether a functionally equivalent silicon information-processing system would suffice. Also debated is what is required to be a member of the moral community. For example, a human being with severe cognitive disability may not be a *contributing* member of the moral community – in that she does not have the mental capacity to fulfill duties to others – but may be a *recipient* member – in that she has rights which entail others fulfilling duties toward her.
12 In fact, as numerous theologians, philosophers, and sci-fi authors have purported, none of the essential capacities of personhood named above necessarily require – and may even not be instantiable within – a material body. Thomas Aquinas, for instance, considered angels and demons to exist as purely intellectual substances (Aquinas 1948, Q. 50) and argued that a human person's intellectual and volitional capacities are essentially immaterial (Aquinas 1948, Q. 75). For contemporary defenses of the immaterial nature of the mind, see Swinburne (2019), Koons and Bealer (2010), and Hasker (1999).
13 Consider Geordi LaForge's VISOR on *Star Trek: The Next Generation*. The VISOR's ability to allow Geordi to see requires that he have a visual cortex in his brain capable of interpreting the signals relayed by the VISOR; a VISOR attached to a mailbox would not bestow upon it the capacity to see.
14 This is, of course, a centrally important claim for which space does not allow a defense here; such a defense is provided in Eberl (2020).
15 "Amortality" differs from "immortality" insofar as the latter refers to the *impossibility* of death, whereas even the complete separation of our minds from our bodies into a digital form of existence would still allow for the possibility of death (Coeckelbergh 2011).
16 Discussion of the various pros and cons of lifespan extension can be found in Savulescu et al. (2011, pt.V).

17 Such a tediously immortal existence is imaginatively depicted in an episode of *Star Trek: Voyager* entitled "Death Wish," in which a member of an immortal race desires to commit suicide to alleviate his insurmountable boredom.
18 Though that is still a relevant concern, at least for the early adopters, thus Dr. McCoy's reluctance to be "beamed" by the transporter in *Star Trek*.
19 You might fare better, however, if your whole head were transplanted, depending on which view of human death is correct; see Eberl (2017b).
20 Including, but not limited to, substance dualism, emergent dualism, hylomorphism, constitutionalism, four-dimensionalism, and embodied mind theory; each of these theories is discussed in Eberl (2020).
21 For further discussion of enhancing children, see Eberl (2022).
22 For a critical response to this position, see Condic (2020).
23 One could imagine the example going in the other direction as well: from viewing unborn fetuses as vulnerable, oppressed persons to understanding the plight of women in various situations of unplanned pregnancies, sexual violence, and general patriarchal oppression.

References

Agar, Nicholas. 2010. *Humanity's end: Why we should reject radical enhancement*. Cambridge, MA: MIT Press.
Agar, Nicholas. 2014. *Truly human enhancement: A philosophical defense of limits*. Cambridge, MA: MIT Press.
Aquinas, Thomas. 1948. *Summa theologiae*. Trans. English Dominican Fathers. New York: Benziger.
Aristotle. 1984. *On the soul*. Trans. J. A. Smith. In *The complete works of Aristotle*, vol. 1, ed. Jonathan Barnes, 641–692. Princeton: Princeton University Press.
Asla, Mariano. 2019. Acerca de los límites, imperfecciones y males de la condición humana: El biomejoramiento desde una perspectiva tomista. *Scientia et Fides* 7(2): 77–95.
Baker, Lynne Rudder. 2000. *Persons and bodies: A constitution view*. New York: Cambridge University Press.
Blatti, Stephan, and Paul F. Snowdon, eds. 2016. *Animalism: New essays on persons, animals, and identity*. New York: Oxford University Press.
Boethius. 1918. Contra Eutychen et Nestorium. In *Tractates and The consolation of philosophy*, trans. H. F. Stewart, E. K. Rand, and S. J. Tester, 72–129. Cambridge, MA: Harvard University Press.
Bostrom, Nick. 2003. Human genetic enhancement: A transhumanist perspective. *Journal of Value Inquiry* 37(3): 493–506.
Bostrom, Nick. 2005. In defense of posthuman dignity. *Bioethics* 19(3): 202–214.
Bostrom, Nick. 2008. Why I want to be a posthuman when I grow up. In *Medical enhancement and posthumanity*, ed. Bert Gordijn and Ruth Chadwick, 107–136. Dordrecht: Springer.
Buchanan, Allen. 2009. Human nature and enhancement. *Bioethics* 23(3): 141–150.
Buchanan, Allen. 2011. *Beyond humanity? The ethics of biomedical enhancement*. New York: Oxford University Press.
Callahan, Sydney. 1986. Abortion and the sexual agenda. *Commonweal*, April 25: 232–238.
Caplan, Arthur L. 2009. Good, better, or best? In *Human enhancement*, ed. Julian Savulescu and Nick Bostrom, 199–209. New York: Oxford University Press.
Coeckelbergh, Mark. 2011. Vulnerable cyborgs: Learning to live with our dragons. *Journal of Evolution and Technology* 22(11): 1–9.
Cole-Turner, Ronald, ed. 2011. *Transhumanism and transcendence: Christian hope in an age of technological enhancement*. Washington, DC: Georgetown University Press.
Condic, Maureen L. 2020. *Untangling twinning: What science tells us about the nature of human embryos*. Notre Dame, IN: University of Notre Dame Press.
Condic, Samuel B., and Maureen L. Condic. 2018. *Human embryos, human beings: A scientific and philosophical approach*. Washington, DC: Catholic University of America Press.
Crutchfield, Parker. 2019. Compulsory moral bioenhancement should be covert. *Bioethics* 33: 112–121.
DeGrazia, David. 2000. Prozac, enhancement and self-creation. *Hastings Center Report* 30(2): 34–40.
DeGrazia, David. 2005a. *Human identity and bioethics*. New York: Cambridge University Press.
DeGrazia, David. 2005b. Enhancement technologies and human identity. *Journal of Medicine and Philosophy* 30: 261–283.
DeGrazia, David. 2014. Moral enhancement, freedom, and what we (should) value in moral behaviour. *Journal of Medical Ethics* 40: 361–368.
de Grey, Aubrey. 2004. Escape velocity: Why the prospect of extreme human life extension matters now. *PLoS Biology* 2(6): 723–726.
Descartes, René. 1996. *Meditations on first philosophy*. Ed. John Cottingham. Cambridge: Cambridge University Press.

Donaldson, Steve, and Ron Cole-Turner. 2018. *Christian perspectives on transhumanism and the church: Chips in the brain, immortality, and the world of tomorrow.* New York: Palgrave Macmillan.

Douglas, Thomas. 2011. Moral enhancement. In *Enhancing human capacities*, ed. Julian Savulescu, Ruud ter Meulen, and Guy Kahane, 467–485. Malden, MA: Wiley-Blackwell.

Eberl, Jason T. 2012. Religious and secular perspectives on the value of suffering. *National Catholic Bioethics Quarterly* 12(2): 251–61.

Eberl, Jason T. 2014. A thomistic appraisal of human enhancement technologies. *Theoretical Medicine and Bioethics* 35(4): 289–310.

Eberl, Jason T. 2017a. Philosophical anthropology, ethics, and human enhancement. In *Contemporary controversies in Catholic bioethics*, ed. Jason T. Eberl. Dordrecht: Springer.

Eberl, Jason T. 2017b. Whose head? Which body? *AJOB Neuroscience* 8(4): 221–223.

Eberl, Jason T. 2018. Can prudence be enhanced. *Journal of Medicine and Philosophy* 43(5): 506–526.

Eberl, Jason T. 2020. *The nature of human persons: Metaphysics and bioethics.* Notre Dame, IN: University of Notre Dame Press.

Eberl, Jason T. 2022. Enhancement technologies and children. In *Pediatric ethics: Theory and practice*, ed. Nico Nortjé and Johan Bester. Dordrecht: Springer.

Eberl, Jason T. and Rebecca A. Ballard. 2009. Metaphysical and ethical perspectives on creating animal-human chimeras. *Journal of Medicine and Philosophy* 34(5): 470–486.

Elliott, Carl. 1998. The tyranny of happiness: Ethics and cosmetic psychopharmacology. In *Enhancing human traits: Ethical and social implications*, ed. Erik Parens, 177–188. Washington, DC: Georgetown University Press.

Fenton, Elizabeth. 2006. Liberal eugenics and human nature: Against Habermas. *Hastings Center Report* 36(6): 35–42.

Ford, Norman M. 1988. *When did I begin? Conception of the human individual in history, philosophy and science.* New York: Cambridge University Press.

Frankfurt, Harry. 1971. Freedom of the will and the concept of a person. *Journal of Philosophy* 68(1): 5–20.

Fukuyama, Francis. 2002. *Our posthuman future: Consequences of the biotechnology revolution.* New York: Farrar, Straus and Giroux.

Gray, Jesse. 2020. Radical enhancements as a moral status de-enhancer. *Monash Bioethics Review* 38: 146–165.

Habermas, Jürgen. 2003. *The future of human nature.* Malden, MA: Polity Press.

Harris, John. 2011. Moral enhancement and freedom. *Bioethics* 21: 102–111.

Hasker, William. 1999. *The emergent self.* Ithaca, NY: Cornell University Press.

Hauskeller, Michael. 2019. Ephemeroi – Human vulnerability, transhumanism, and the meaning of life. *Scientia et Fides* 7(2): 9–21.

Heldmann, M., G. Berding, J. Voges, B. Bogerts, I. Galazky, U. Müller, et al. 2012. Deep brain stimulation of nucleus accumbens region in alcoholism affects reward processing. *PLoS ONE* 7(5): e36572.

Hershenov, David B. 2019. Why transhumanists can't survive the death of their bodies? *Ethics, Medicine and Public Health* 10: 102–110.

Ho, Allen L., Anne-Mary N. Salib, Arjun V. Pendharkar, Eric S. Sussman, William J. Giardino, and Casey H. Halpern. 2018. The nucleus accumbens and alcoholism: A target for deep brain stimulation. *Neurosurgical Focus* 45: 1–10.

Hughes, James. 2010. Technoprogressive biopolitics and human enhancement. In *Progress in Bioethics: Science, Policy, and Politics*, ed. Jonathan D. Moreno and Sam Berger, 163–188. Cambridge, MA: MIT Press.

Hume, David. 1978. *A treatise of human nature*, 2nd ed. Ed. L. A. Selby-Bigge and P. H. Nidditch. New York: Oxford University Press.

Jensen, Steven J., and José Luis Widow. 2018. Unnatural enhancements. *Irish Theological Quarterly* 83(4): 347–364.

Jinek, Martin, Krzysztof Chylinski, Ines Fonfara, Michael Hauer, Jennifer A. Doudna, and Emmanuelle Charpentier. 2012. A programmable dual-RNA–guided DNA endonuclease in adaptive bacterial immunity. *Science* 337(6096): 816–821.

Jotterand, Fabrice. 2010. Human dignity and transhumanism: Do anthro-technological devices have moral status? *American Journal of Bioethics* 10(7): 45–52.

Kaczor, Christopher. 2015. *The ethics of abortion: Women's rights, human life, and the question of justice*, 2nd ed. New York: Routledge.

Kamm, Frances. 2009. What is and is not wrong with enhancement? In *Human enhancement*, ed. Julian Savulescu and Nick Bostrom, 91–130. New York: Oxford University Press.

Kant, Immanuel. 1997. *Groundwork of the metaphysics of morals.* Trans. Mary Gregor. New York: Cambridge University Press.

Keenan, James F. 2014. Embodiment and relationality: Roman Catholic concerns. In *Transhumanism and the body: The world religions speak*, ed. Calvin Mercer and Derek F. Maher, 155–171. New York: Palgrave Macmillan.

Koene, Randal A. 2013. Uploading to substrate-independent minds. In *The transhumanist reader: Classical and contemporary essays on the science, technology, and philosophy of the human future*, ed. Max More and Natasha Vita-More, 146–156. Malden, MA: Wiley-Blackwell.

Koons, Robert C., and George Bealer, eds. 2010. *The waning of materialism*. New York: Oxford University Press.

Kuhse, Helga, and Peter Singer. 1985. *Should the baby live? The problem of handicapped infants*. New York: Oxford University Press.

Kurzweil, Ray. 2005. *The singularity is near: When humans transcend biology*. New York: Viking.

Lee, Patrick. 2010. *Abortion and unborn human life*, 2nd ed. Washington, DC: Catholic University of America Press.

Liao, S. Matthew, ed. 2016. *Moral brains: The neuroscience of morality*. New York: Oxford University Press.

Liedo Fernández, Belén, and Jon Rueda. 2021. In defense of posthuman vulnerability. *Scientia et Fides* 9(1): 215–239.

Locke, John. 1975. *An essay concerning human understanding*. Ed. Peter H. Nidditch. Oxford: Clarendon Press.

MacIntyre, Alasdair. 1999. *Dependent rational animals: Why human beings need the virtues*. Chicago: Open Court.

McKenny, Gerald P. 1997. *To relieve the human condition: Bioethics, technology, and the body*. Albany: SUNY Press.

McKenny, Gerald P. 1998. Enhancements and the ethical significance of vulnerability. In *Enhancing human traits: Ethical and social implications*, ed. Erik Parens, 222–237. Washington, DC: Georgetown University Press.

McKenny, Gerald P. 2013. Biotechnology and the normative significance of human nature: A contribution from theological anthropology. *Studies in Christian Ethics* 26(1): 18–36.

McKenny, Gerald P. 2019. Human nature and biotechnological enhancement: Some theological considerations. *Studies in Christian Ethics* 32(2): 229–240.

Mercer, Calvin, and Derek F. Maher, eds. 2014. *Transhumanism and the body: The world religions speak*. New York: Palgrave Macmillan.

Mercer, Calvin, and Tracy J. Trothen, eds. 2015. *Religion and transhumanism: The unknown future of human enhancement*. Santa Barbara, CA: Praeger.

Merkle, Ralph C. 2013. Uploading. In *The transhumanist reader: Classical and contemporary essays on the science, technology, and philosophy of the human future*, ed. Max More and Natasha Vita-More, 157–164. Malden, MA: Wiley-Blackwell.

Mill, John Stuart. 1989. *'On liberty' and other writings*. Ed. S. Collini. New York: Cambridge University Press.

More, Max. 2013. The philosophy of transhumanism. In *The transhumanist reader: Classical and contemporary essays on the science, technology, and philosophy of the human future*, ed. Max More and Natasha Vita-More, 3–17. Malden, MA: Wiley-Blackwell.

Müller, U. J., V. Sturm, J. Voges, H.-J. Heinze, I. Galazky, M. Heldmann, H. Scheich, and B. Bogerts. 2009. Successful treatment of chronic resistant alcoholism by deep brain stimulation of nucleus accumbens: First experience with three cases. *Pharmacopsychiatry* 42: 288–292.

Oderberg, David S. 2007. *Real essentialism*. New York: Routledge.

Oderberg, David S. 2014. Could there be a superhuman species? *Southern Journal of Philosophy* 52(2): 206–226.

Olson, Eric T. 1997. *The human animal: Personal identity without psychology*. New York: Oxford University Press.

Parens, Erik. 1995. The goodness of fragility: On the prospect of genetic technologies aimed at the enhancement of human capacities. *Kennedy Institute of Ethics Journal* 5(2): 141–153.

Parens, Erik. 2005. Authenticity and ambivalence: Toward understanding the enhancement debate. *Hastings Center Report* 35(3): 34–41.

Parens, Erik. 2015. *Shaping ourselves: On technology, flourishing, and a habit of thinking*. New York: Oxford University Press.

Parfit, Derek. 1984. *Reasons and persons*. Oxford: Clarendon Press.

Persson, Ingmar, and Julian Savulescu. 2012. *Unfit for the future: The need for moral bioenhancement*. New York: Oxford University Press.

Persson, Ingmar, and Julian Savulescu. 2014. Should moral bioenhancement be compulsory? Reply to Vojin Rakic. *Journal of Medical Ethics* 40(4): 251–251.

Plato. 1989. *Phaedo*. Trans. Hugh Tredennick. In *The collected dialogues of Plato*, ed. Edith Hamilton and Huntington Cairns, 40–98. Princeton: Princeton University Press.

President's Council on Bioethics. 2003. *Beyond therapy: Biotechnology and the pursuit of happiness*. Washington, DC: U.S. Government Printing Office.

Ren, Xiaoping, and Sergio Canavero. 2017. HEAVEN in the making: Between the rock (the academe) and a hard case (a head transplant). *AJOB Neuroscience* 8(4): 200–205.

Roduit, Johann A. R. 2016. *The case for perfection: Ethics in the age of human enhancement*. Frankfurt am Main: Peter Verlag.

Sandel, Michael J. 2007. *The case against perfection: Ethics in the age of genetic engineering*. Cambridge, MA: Harvard University Press.

Savulescu, Julian, Anders Sandberg, and Guy Kahane. 2011. Well-being and enhancement. In *Enhancing human capacities*, ed. Julian Savulescu, Ruud ter Meulen, and Guy Kahane, 3–18. Malden, MA: Wiley-Blackwell.

Savulescu, Julian, Ruud ter Meulen, and Guy Kahane, eds. 2011. *Enhancing human capacities*. Malden, MA: Wiley-Blackwell.

Schechtman, Marya. 1996. *The constitution of selves*. Ithaca, NY: Cornell University Press.

Singer, Peter. 1992. Embryo experimentation and the moral status of the embryo. In *Philosophy and health care*, ed. E. Matthews and M. Menlowe, 81–91. Brookfield: Avebury.

Smith, Barry, and Berit Brogaard. 2003. Sixteen days. *Journal of Medicine and Philosophy* 28: 45–78.

Snowdon, Paul F. 2014. *Persons, animals, ourselves*. New York: Oxford University Press.

Stango, Marco, and David W. Agler. 2018. Human body, enhancement, and the missing technomoral virtue. *Sociología y Tecnociencia* 8(1): 43–59.

Swinburne, Richard. 2019. *Are we bodies or soul?* New York: Oxford University Press.

Taylor, Charles. 1991. *The ethics of authenticity*. Cambridge, MA: Harvard University Press.

Tooley, Michael. 1983. *Abortion and infanticide*. Oxford: Clarendon Press.

Warren, Mary Anne. 1973. On the moral and legal status of abortion. *Monist* 57(1): 43–61.

Williams, Bernard. 1973. The Makropulos case: Reflections on the tedium of immortality. In *Problems of the self*, 82–100. Cambridge: Cambridge University Press.

Zohar, Noam J. 1991. Prospects for 'genetic therapy'—Can a person benefit from being altered? *Bioethics* 5(4): 275–288.

9
AUTHENTICITY IN THE ETHICS OF HUMAN ENHANCEMENT

Muriel Leuenberger

9.1 Introduction

Human enhancement technologies can potentially change one's personality, mood, body, capabilities, traits, and other characteristics. This extensive potential for self-change has raised concerns about authenticity. Is the enhanced human being still authentic? Can you be true to yourself after changing yourself? Or can you become more authentic through enhancement? Authenticity has been recognized as a central concept in the ethics of human enhancement. Early on in the debate, authenticity was understood as a matter of either self-discovery or self-creation. Self-discovery accounts of authenticity claim that to be authentic one has to find the stable, if not unchanging and innate, true self and live according to it. This view is inspired by Jean-Jacques Rousseau and the Romantics. Self-creation accounts deny the existence of an individual essence. Instead, we have to freely create ourselves in order to be authentic. This tradition is rooted in existentialist philosophy, notably Jean-Paul Sartre, and the work of Friedrich Nietzsche and Søren Kierkegaard.

Enhancement technologies have been considered as threatening authenticity by leading us astray from the true self (Elliott, 2004; The President's Council on Bioethics, 2003). At the same time, some authors have argued that enhancement technologies can help us to become authentic by providing means for self-creation (DeGrazia, 2000). A currently widely agreed-upon view states that the self-discovery as well as self-creation accounts of authenticity are capturing important intuitions but also making empirically and metaphysically questionable assumptions (Bolt, 2007; Levy, 2011; Parens, 2005). The idea that we have an individual essence "deep down" that remains untouched by external influences seems unlikely, as does the possibility of a radically free act of self-creation (Caspi & Roberts, 2001; DeGrazia, 2000; Levy, 2018; Mackenzie & Walker, 2015). Therefore, in the philosophical debate, such strong versions of self-discovery and self-creation views are rarely anymore adopted.[1] Nonetheless, it seems true that on the one hand, there are parts of ourselves we can hardly change which may feel particularly true to who we are, and on the other hand that we can undertake projects of self-creation and actively change who we are. It seems that authenticity is best understood as an ideal guiding us between the constraints and possibilities of self-change.

In the last decade, a plethora of novel distinctions, specifications, and definitions of authenticity have been added to the debate. The conditions for authentic self-change as well as how the true self should be expressed have been worked out in more detail. The crude distinction between self-discovery and self-creation accounts is no longer particularly useful to navigate this dense landscape of definitions of authenticity. This chapter takes a step back and maps the different accounts of authenticity to provide a more nuanced taxonomy of authenticity and reveal the emerging underlying structures of this concept (see Ahlin (2018) for another taxonomy of authenticity in the context of medical consent). Authenticity is a complex, multidimensional concept, but it is possible to pinpoint some shared, guiding ideas across different accounts of authenticity. In the following, three kinds of conditions for authentic creation and change of the true self are identified (coherence, endorsement, and relations) as well as the ways that the true self should be expressed (in one's self-conception, self-presentation, and one's body, emotions, and actions). Based on this analysis, the hopes and concerns human enhancement raises for authenticity are discussed. The effect of enhancement technologies on authenticity is multifaceted. Enhancement technologies do not threaten or foster authenticity across the board but affect different dimensions of authenticity individually. This chapter furthermore argues that the debate on authenticity in the ethics of human enhancement would profit from a more extended discussion on which accounts of authenticity are morally or prudentially valuable and why, as well as in which circumstances they have a prudential appeal.

9.2 Changing and creating the true self

Unless we assume that the true self is an innate, unchanging essence (which is, as most authors in the debate agree, empirically and metaphysically implausible), there must be conditions for how to authentically create and change the true self. I identify three main concepts that provide conditions for creating and changing the true self that can be found across many different accounts of authenticity: coherence, endorsement, and relations. These three concepts often interact with each other and overlap in authenticity accounts.

9.2.1 Coherence

A crucial element in many accounts of authenticity is that they demand a form of coherence of the true self. The individual should maintain or establish a coherence of the true self in both, authentic self-creation and self-change. We can distinguish between two different kinds of coherence of the self: synchronic and diachronic coherence.

Synchronic coherence is the coherence of a network of characteristics at a particular time. In a synchronically coherent self, a person's dispositions, traits, values, beliefs, and other characteristics at a given time make sense in the light of each other. They are connected to each other in structured hierarchies, creating a mutually supportive network of characteristics. In terms of an account of authenticity, this means that the features of the self which are part of such a coherent network are considered authentic and should not be changed, or only gradually or piecemeal (like Neurath's raft), to maintain the coherent network. An authentic person is not ambivalent in their core wishes and values. There may be conflicts, but the authentic individual has to take a clear stance for one side or the other.

Harry Frankfurt develops an account of authenticity based on synchronic coherence in his later work on wholeheartedness (Frankfurt, 1987). He argues that ambivalence in our higher-order volitions (effective desires about effective desires) can be resolved through a wholehearted decision. Through wholehearted decisions, we constitute who we authentically are. Without going into the details of Frankfurt's view, the idea of an authentic person he introduces is one who is not conflicted or ambivalent but settles internal conflicts through wholehearted decisions. Those decisions both define us and constrain our will while freeing us from uncertainty. More recently, Pugh, Maslen, and Savulescu have introduced a similar account of authenticity based on synchronic coherence (Pugh et al., 2017). They argue that the true self is composed of the coherent (i.e., mutually compatible) elements of the individual's values and rational beliefs.[2]

Enhancement technologies could threaten authenticity in terms of synchronic coherence if they introduce characteristics that do not cohere with the individual's network of core beliefs and values or if they change this cohering set of characteristics or wholehearted choices which constitute the true self. A person undergoing moral enhancement could, for example, change their core commitments and coherent values. The true self may then no longer be a synchronically coherent unity. Enhancement technologies can provide us with the ability to modify the true self in ways that render the change unintelligible in light of the rest of the cohering set of beliefs and values.

However, it is also possible that enhancement technologies make users more authentic by helping them to overcome their present incoherence or to fully commit themselves to a life project. Through physical enhancement, a devoted athlete could manage to pursue a professional sports career and fully commit to this life project. Various forms of mental enhancement, for instance, increased focus and concentration, could similarly help to stick to a commitment or give mental strength to act in accordance with one's coherent set of values.

According to diachronic coherence views, the authenticity of a person (or one of their characteristics) cannot be assessed by considering a specific moment or time slice. At a given time, the values, beliefs, desires, and other characteristics of a person need not be coherent and may be conflicting and ambivalent. However, a person's progression over time should display an element of coherence.

Accounts of authenticity in terms of diachronic coherence tend to be based on a narrative conception of the self. The narrative self-view claims that the self is constituted by the internalized, ongoing story of your life – the self-narrative – in which you integrate your experiences, values, beliefs, and other personal characteristics. Elsewhere, I introduce a conception of narrative authenticity according to which an authentic person has an accurate and coherent self-narrative that depicts a well-defined person (Leuenberger, 2020). This account focuses on self-knowledge (or self-understanding) as an important dimension of authenticity. Through a coherent self-narrative we make ourselves intelligible to others and to ourselves. Diachronic coherence in narrative terms means that one's beliefs, values, actions, etc. make sense in light of each other, not because they are not conflicting but because we can make sense of how they came to coexist within an individual through their integration in the wider context of the narrative of their life. Even conflicting elements and radical changes can be accounted for in the narrative and become mutually supportive through the self-narrative. A person who always wanted to change a feature of herself but refused to do so once given the chance would be diachronically incoherent, even if she would be synchronically coherent. Erler argues that we should not change central aspects of our narrative identity where it might be tempting to do so unless it arises out of a commitment that was already part of the narrative self (Erler, 2011). Through the previous commitment, the narrative retains diachronic coherence through self-change.

A different notion of diachronic coherence can be found in accounts that define authenticity as being reached through experimental self-finding projects. Iftode, with reference to Nietzsche's notion of "brief habits," argues that authenticity is not just to be found in permanent traits, values, beliefs, and commitments we maintain over time but in those that we continually come back to after experimenting with other perspectives and mindsets (Iftode, 2019; Iftode et al., 2022). Even in an idea of the path to authenticity as fundamentally changing and experimental, the true self is understood as revealed in the recurring elements that build a version of diachronic coherence.

The experimental notion of authenticity is clearly in favor of enhancement technologies. By letting us explore new ways of being, enhancement technologies could help us find out who we truly are and who we continuously come back to be. For this experimental notion of authenticity, it would be particularly important that the enhancement is reversible (Iftode, 2019). The narrative account of diachronic coherence is more ambivalent toward enhancement technologies. In case the enhancement would lead to a very sudden change that is hard to account for through the self-narrative, it could disrupt its coherence. This would however not necessarily mean that we should refrain from such enhancement technologies because even sudden change could leave the option of adjusting the self-narrative to integrate it. A shy person enhancing himself to be more communicative and outgoing might at first experience the enhancement as a disruption of narrative coherence, but he may connect the change to his longstanding wish of being more outgoing and his previous attempts to overcome his shyness. This would also be in line with Erler's condition that changing central elements of the narrative self are authentic if they are in line with previous commitments (Erler, 2011). Furthermore, enhancement technology can promote diachronic coherence. Memory enhancement would be a particularly powerful tool to make sense of one's past and construe a coherent self-narrative. Intelligence enhancement could have similar effects.

9.2.2 Endorsement

The second central idea for changing and creating the true self authentically found across different accounts is that authentic aspects of the self (e.g., desires, actions, traits) or self-creation projects are those we identify with or endorse. This can either be understood synchronically, as endorsing a set of mental states, dispositions, or actions, or diachronically, as endorsing the causal history of an action or of how one acquired a mental state or disposition.[3] Examples of the former would be Frankfurt's account (introduced above) which defines authenticity in terms of a wholehearted identification with one's volitions or Pugh et al.'s account according to which the true self is constituted by the cohering and rationally endorsed elements of the self (Pugh et al., 2017). The individual identifies with certain features of the self or self-changes and endorses them as part of their true self. A diachronic view of authenticity as endorsement would be DeGrazia's account (DeGrazia, 2005) (for other examples see Gordon, 2022 and Mele, 2001)). He argues that self-creation projects are authentic if they are autonomous and honest. For instance, a woman who undergoes cosmetic surgery to conform to sexist standards of beauty would be acting authentically if she is aware of her sexist socialization and its impact on her desires and seriously considered alternatives.

Most endorsement views of authenticity define authenticity as closely related to autonomy – either as dependent on autonomy (e.g., (DeGrazia, 2005)) or as a precondition for autonomy (e.g., (Pugh, 2020)). Therefore, they tend to understand reason as the superior principle in defining the individual (compared to other characteristics, such as our inclinations or emotions). Through reason, we can assess other aspects of the self from a third-personal view. Thereby, reason and identification reveal who we truly are. Even seemingly self-mutilating decisions which undermine natural inclinations and other features of the self are deemed authentic as long as they are rationally endorsed (Schechtman, 2004).

Rational endorsement accounts of authenticity generally look favorably on enhancement technologies. Enhancement can help people to identify with how they look, act, or feel by allowing them to be who they want to be. As a transgender character in the movie *All About My Mother* by Pedro Almodóvar says while showing off her silicone implants, "you are more and more authentic the more you look like someone you dreamed of being" (Almodóvar, 1999). As long as the enhancement is rationally endorsed by the individual, it can foster authenticity. To allow for a genuine rational endorsement, it is important that the individual is well-informed about the consequences of the enhancement and is, again, not manipulated or otherwise tricked or pressured into using enhancement. Moreover, enhancement technologies could enhance rational capacities and thereby facilitate and support the process of rational endorsement. The widespread use of enhancement technologies could, however, lead to social pressures for enhancement that could undermine processes of autonomous, rational endorsement.

9.2.3 Relations

Finally, authenticity is often defined in terms of how you relate to others, notably how others influence you, and to what degree changing and creating the true self is independent. Generally, authentic changes and creations of the self need to originate from the individual, independent of certain pernicious external influences. A person who is just following the newest trends or adapting their beliefs to their current social environment is not authentic. Historically, the condition of independence can be found in both the self-discovery and self-creationist traditions of authenticity. Rousseau, one of the first proponents of the idea of authenticity, if not its originator, held a self-discovery view according to which the true self is natural and innate. Society exerts a corrupting influence on the self from which we should shield ourselves and particularly our children (Rousseau, 1992, 2009). In accounts that understand authenticity as a matter of self-creation, the demand for independence in self-creation is also very prominent. Heidegger warns against following the anonymous *das Man* ("the They") and against doing what "one does" (Heidegger, 1996). *Eigentlichkeit*, a term usually translated as authenticity, requires independent self-creation while embedded with others in a social world. Similarly, Sartre argues that it is an instance of bad faith if we just follow or play social scripts (Sartre, 1956). Being authentic, according to this conception of independence, means listening to one's own voice and shaping one's individual identity in an original manner to find one's very own path through life (Taylor, 2003). In my own account of authenticity, I argue that to be true to oneself, the self needs to be well-defined (Leuenberger, 2020). A well-defined self requires that one actively takes charge of one's life and actualizes characteristics or traits one claims to have. If you just do what your parents expect you to do, it remains unclear what you yourself would have done, given the chance. Beyond the fact that you are pleasing your parents, it is unclear what kind of person you are. To be authentic, you need to make independent choices and enact them to constitute a well-defined self.

Strong external influences undermine authenticity, but of course, we cannot (and need not try to) avoid being influenced by others and our broader social context. Therefore, there has been a lively debate on the role of others and the social context for authenticity which has pushed back against the idea that authenticity is best pursued in total independence. Those arguments for a relational dimension of authenticity include that we can only define ourselves against the backdrop of shared horizons of meaning (Taylor, 2003), that we define ourselves in dialogue with others (Iftode, 2019; Iftode et al., 2022; Mihailov et al., 2021), that adopting an identity depends on the recognition of others (Baylis, 2013; Elliott, 2011; Lindemann, 2001), and that authenticity is a social virtue and social expectation (Iftode, 2019; Williams, 2002). In the words of Neil Levy: "Human beings frequently answer identity questions by citing irreducibly social features: their group membership or identification, for instance. […] Authenticity is not something we achieve from the inside out, but also from the outside in." (Levy, 2007).

Thus, even if social influences are shaping people's desire to use enhancement technologies, they are not necessarily inauthentic. As discussed in the section on endorsement, enhancement technologies can be used to express the individual's original, independent voice. Nonetheless, enhancement is sometimes pursued due to social pressure, stigma, and oppressive cultural norms (e.g., in some cases of cosmetic surgery) (Elliott, 2011; Juth, 2011). By increasing our power to define who we are, some people do and will use enhancement technologies to conform to social expectations to a problematic degree, which would contradict the demands of authenticity for independence and originality. Once enhancement technologies are widely used, the pressure to use them increases further. The authentic characteristics of some people may not be favored in the professional and social life of their society. By making them easier to change, enhancement technologies may allow those individuals to lead an easier, and potentially happier life because they might reach their professional and social goals more easily while remaining genuine. However, this can shift the burden of change to the individual, even if it would be better to change society to be more accommodating to a variety of characteristics (Leuenberger, 2022).

9.3 Expressing the true self

Besides conditions for authentic creation and changes of the true self, authenticity can be further defined with respect to how this true self should be expressed. To authentically express the true self, there should be a consistency relation between the true self and other dimensions of the self. In the following, I discuss the idea that the true self should be adequately represented in one's self-conception, self-presentation, or one's body, actions, and emotions. Of course, both branches – the creation and change of the true self and its expression – are connected. In expressing the true self, we also create and change it. Many accounts of authenticity address both aspects, but some define authenticity almost exclusively on one side. For instance, views that understand the true self as one's innate and unchanging nature do, of course, not define any conditions for its creation or change but define authenticity in terms of how it should be expressed.

The consistency relation between the true self and one's self-conception translates into a demand for self-knowledge. Who you take yourself to be should correspond to the true self. An authentic person should not be self-deluded and know who they are. Self-knowledge is furthermore a precondition for other dimensions of authenticity, notably for authenticity as endorsement. In my account of authenticity, I argue that to be authentic, one's narrative identity should be sustainable, meaning that there should be little tension between your lived experience and who you take yourself to be (Leuenberger, 2020). Even though many characteristics of the self are to some degree a question of interpretation, the self-narrative is constrained by subjective and objective facts about oneself (e.g., one's emotions, thoughts, intentions, bodily features, or facts about actions and live events). Authenticity requires acknowledging those facts and, therefore, extended self-knowledge. Some enhancement technologies can contribute to increased self-knowledge, notably the enhancement of memory or intelligence. They may help us to achieve a greater self-understanding and reduce self-delusion. Other enhancement technologies could however be used to avoid facing uncomfortable truths about oneself. Mood enhancers could make it easier to not acknowledge that you no longer love your spouse or enjoy your job.

Rousseau's account of authenticity also requires self-knowledge, but in addition, he demands that the individual's self-presentation is consistent with this true self-conception. You should know who you are and you should present yourself to others truthfully. Thus, according to Rousseau, an authentic person cannot lie about themselves, whereas in my account, if a person is aware of why they are lying they can still be authentic.[4] Within the enhancement literature, Erler argues that authenticity entails an accurate presentation of key features of one's narrative identity to others (Erler, 2011). The idea of authenticity as accurate self-presentation can also be understood as a consistency relation between the true self and one's self-presentation, without demanding self-knowledge (Kadlac, 2018). According to this view, to be authentic you should not be a phony. In contrast to Erler's, Rousseau's, and my account, you may be authentic by accident in the case that you are a self-deluded liar who just happens to tell the truth about yourself. Enhancement technologies can undermine authenticity as truthful self-presentation if they are not sufficiently disclosed. Using enhancement to gain an advantage in sports or professional life without being open about it would be phony and inauthentic (Kadlac, 2018). Of course, this would depend on current common expectations. If enhancement became the norm in a certain setting, an explicit disclosure of one's use of enhancement would not be required for truthful self-presentation.

The true self can furthermore find expression in one's actions, emotions, and body beyond settings of other-directed self-presentation. In this sense, to be authentic can mean to express who you are in completely private circumstances by enacting, feeling, and embodying the true self. What this kind of self-expression entails depends on the conception of the true self. It could mean to act, feel, and look in accordance with wholehearted, rationally endorsed, or independently formed decisions, or it could mean to freely express one's natural inclinations (Schechtman, 2004).

Meyers offers an account focusing on enactment for authenticity (Meyers, 2000, 2005) that links authenticity to autonomy competency. The authentic self arises from a set of autonomy skills, including introspection, imagination, memory, communication, reasoning, interpretation, and volition that enable self-discovery and self-creation. Insofar as enhancement technologies may foster those skills, they can contribute to enacting and constituting an authentic self.

The President's Council on Bioethics has raised concerns about the authenticity of enhanced emotions (The President's Council on Bioethics, 2003). They argue that enhancement technologies could detach our emotions from reality. Enhancement technologies could make us happy or confident even if we have no reason to be either (Dees, 2007). However, in most situations, more than one emotional reaction would be appropriate (Erler, 2011). Thus, simply changing an emotional reaction through enhancement would not necessarily mean it is inappropriate. Enhanced emotions could still be responsive to reality. Moreover, when we look at which emotions people describe as feeling authentic, there seems to be no link between an artificially induced emotion and a feeling of authenticity (Kraemer, 2011). The increased control over your emotions through enhancement can however allow you to ignore emotions that might be considered authentic. Particularly in the philosophy of Rousseau and the Romantics, deep emotions are considered as revealing the true self and should be followed, not suppressed or changed (Ferrara, 1993; Rousseau, 1997).

The true self can also be embodied insofar as it can be expressed through bodily appearance. An involuntary mismatch between one's body and one's self-conception can cause great distress and a feeling of alienation, as in the case of transgender people (Mason-Schrock, 1996). Cosmetic surgery, sex-reassignment surgery, and even healthy limb amputations have been described as a way of getting in touch with the true self (Elliott, 2011). Enhancement technologies can help people to express who they take themselves to be through their bodies. In turn, if someone is mistaken about who they are, enhancement equally facilitates the expression of an inauthentic self.

9.4 The value of authenticity

The discussion so far has revealed a highly multidimensional concept of authenticity, entailing conditions of coherence, endorsement, and independence that guide the creation and change of the true self as well as norms about how the true self should correspond to and be expressed in other dimensions of the self (self-conception, self-presentation, and one's actions, body, and emotions). Enhancement technologies can influence those dimensions individually, sometimes increasing authenticity with respect to one aspect while threatening another. This leads to the question as to which dimension/s of authenticity we should pursue and try to protect from threats through enhancement technologies as well as what the value of authenticity is.

Authenticity is typically considered as instrumentally rather than intrinsically valuable. Several candidates have been suggested for the instrumental value of authenticity, such as increasing well-being, autonomy, or the moral good. Authenticity can contribute to well-being in many cases because feeling authentic is generally considered a positive mental state in comparison to inauthenticity or alienation (Kraemer, 2013). However, being authentic can entail giving up comfort, pleasure, or easy routes to happiness. Unless we assume the true self is fundamentally good,[5] being authentic would not necessarily entail being morally good. A paradigmatic example would be Gaugin who abandoned his family to become an artist in pursuit of authenticity. An authentic life is furthermore claimed to be fulfilled and meaningful (Strohminger et al., 2017; Taylor, 2003), but how authenticity contributes to a fulfilled and meaningful life often remains vague (see Schlegel et al., 2022 for a valuable recent exploration of this topic). For accounts that define authenticity as instrumental for or constitutive of autonomy, its value is linked to the value of autonomy.

Arguments for the value of authenticity in the ethics of human enhancement regularly rely on 1) the common appeal of authenticity as an ideal, 2) empirical studies investigating how people understand and value authenticity (Sutton, 2020), 3) showing how authenticity contributes to well-being, autonomy, or other pragmatic advantages (Erler, 2011; Leuenberger, 2021; Pugh, 2020), or 4) linking the specific account of authenticity to broader philosophical arguments for the value of authenticity, such as Taylor's work on authenticity as an ethical ideal (Taylor, 2003), John Stuart Mill's defense of individuality (Mill, 1989), or Sartre's notion of bad faith (Sartre, 1956).

These approaches commonly lead to one of two problems. The first problem occurs when data or arguments that are grounded on one account of authenticity are used to argue for the value of a different account (Bublitz & Repantis, 2021). For instance, a psychological study showing that people think in terms of a true self and attribute it with meaning only speaks to the view on authenticity investigated in that study. The second problem arises from applying arguments for the value of authenticity grounded on a broad understanding of authenticity to more specific accounts. The issue does not arise from the validity of the argument but from the aims of the debate on enhancement and authenticity. Mill's views on the value of individuality, for instance, can be applied to accounts that understand authenticity as a matter of endorsement or of independence as well as to different ways to express the true self. This kind of value argument tends not to distinguish between the different accounts and could be applied to different ones equally. Similarly, arguments in favor of the value of authenticity by virtue of its contribution to well-being or autonomy often apply to multiple dimensions of authenticity equally well. Because individual accounts of authenticity can give different recommendations for or against the use of enhancement technologies, it is relevant to be able to decide between them. To show whether we should use enhancement technologies based on authenticity claims requires an argument for why we should value one dimension of authenticity over another, for instance, why we should value experimental self-creation over a coherent self.

The debate on authenticity in the ethics of human enhancement would profit from a more extended discussion on which accounts of authenticity are morally valuable and why, as well as in which circumstances they have prudential value and contribute to well-being. A comparative analysis, which would contrast and weigh the value of different accounts of authenticity and discuss their appeal to people in different circumstances and with different conceptions of the good life would be beneficial. Once we understand the different accounts of authenticity and why or in which cases they are valuable, we are in a better position to weigh the multifaceted impact of human enhancement on authenticity and thereby assess the desirability and the ethics of human enhancement in a broader sense.

A reason why this has proven difficult so far is that bioethicists generally try not to make specific claims about what counts as a good, flourishing life. Instead, they want to rely on broad claims to leave room for diverse views. But the impact of enhancement technologies on authenticity is so multifaceted and dependent on the specific interpretation of the concept of authenticity and the good life that it is hard to tackle through broad, non-committal claims. This does not mean that we should stop discussing authenticity in the context of human enhancement. People still care about authenticity and worry whether they should use or avoid enhancement technologies to achieve it. If we consider authenticity as a multidimensional concept, an argument that enhancement technologies are threatening or supporting authenticity across the board is almost impossible. Bioethics can however clarify how enhancement technologies impact specific dimensions of authenticity, uncover which conceptions of the self and the good life are at the heart of the individual dimensions of authenticity, and give reasons for why we should pursue them.

Acknowledgments

I would like to thank Jonathan Pugh, Przemysław Zawadzki, Neil Levy, Thomas Douglas, and Gabriel DeMarco for valuable comments on earlier versions of this chapter. This work was funded by the Swiss National Science Foundation.

Notes

1 However, studies have shown that the idea of a true, unchanging self is a common belief (Strohminger et al., 2017), although the authors argue that it is rather a useful fiction than a scientific concept.

2 They argue that their account of authenticity is diachronic because authenticity must appeal to diachronic values, but the notion of coherence is synchronic – a coherence of a person's characteristics at a specific time.
3 I would like to thank Jonathan Pugh for raising this point.
4 A similar idea of authenticity as combining self-knowledge and self-presentation can be found in *Rameau's Nephew* by Diderot and the idea of authenticity reconstructed through this novel by Williams (Diderot, 2016; Williams, 2002). Rameau's nephew is also honest to himself and to others (he may occasionally be lying and flattering others, but he is also honest about that) but in contrast to Rousseau, he is a figure who constantly changes who he is. There is no coherence or permanence in his personality, but he is always truthful in representing who he momentarily is. Based on two very different ideas of the true self, Diderot and Rousseau introduce the same conditions for authentic self-expression.
5 Empirical studies have shown that people seem to consider the true self as fundamentally good (Strohminger et al., 2017). This would however imply a radically subjectivist and unverifiable true self.

References

Ahlin, J. (2018). The impossibility of reliably determining the authenticity of desires: Implications for informed consent. *Medicine, Health Care and Philosophy, 21*(1), 43–50.
Almodóvar, P. (1999). *All About My Mother*. Sony Pictures Classics.
Baylis, F. (2013). 'I am who I am': On the perceived threats to personal identity from deep brain stimulation. *Neuroethics, 6*(3), 513–526.
Bolt, L. L. E. (2007). True to oneself? Broad and narrow ideas on authenticity in the enhancement debate. *Theoretical Medicine and Bioethics, 28*(4), 285–300.
Bublitz, J. C., & Repantis, D. (2021). Memory, authenticity, and optogenethics. *AJOB Neuroscience, 12*(1), 30–32.
Caspi, A., & Roberts, B. W. (2001). Personality development across the life course: The argument for change and continuity. *Psychological Inquiry, 12*(2), 49–66.
Dees, R. H. (2007). Better brains, better selves? The ethics of neuroenhancements. *Kennedy Institute of Ethics Journal, 17*(4), 371–395.
DeGrazia, D. (2000). Prozac, enhancement, and self-creation. *The Hastings Center Report, 30*(2), 34–40.
DeGrazia, D. (2005). *Human Identity and Bioethics*. New York: Cambridge University Press.
Diderot, D. (2016). *Rameau's Nephew: Le Neveu de Rameau* (2nd ed.). Cambridge: Open Book Publishers.
Elliott, C. (2004). *Better than Well: American Medicine Meets the American Dream*. New York: W.W. Norton.
Elliott, C. (2011). Enhancement technologies and the modern self. *Journal of Medicine and Philosophy, 36*(4), 364–374.
Erler, A. (2011). Does memory modification threaten authenticity? *Neuroethics, 4*(3), 234–249.
Ferrara, A. (1993). *Modernity and Authenticity: A Study in the Social and Ethical Thought of Jean-Jacques Rousseau*. Albany: State University of New York Press.
Frankfurt, H. (1987). Identification and wholeheartedness. In F. D. Schoeman (Ed.), *Responsibility, Character, and the Emotions: New Essays in Moral Psychology*. Cambridge University Press.
Gordon, E. C. (2022). Cognitive enhancement and authenticity: Moving beyond the impasse. *Medicine, Health Care and Philosophy, 25*, 281–288.
Heidegger, M. (1996). *Being and Time: A Translation of Sein und Zeit*. Albany: State University of New York Press.
Iftode, C. (2019). Assessing enhancement technologies: Authenticity as a social virtue and experiment. *The New Bioethics, 25*(1), 24–38.
Iftode, C., Zorilă, A., Vică, C., & Mihailov, E. (2022). Experimental and relational authenticity: How neurotechnologies impact narrative identities. *Phenomenology and the Cognitive Sciences*, 1–18.
Juth, N. (2011). Enhancement, autonomy and authenticity. In J. Savulescu, R. Meulen, & G. Kahane (Eds.), *Enhancing Human Capacities*. Oxford: Blackwell.
Kadlac, A. (2018). The challenge of authenticity: Enhancement and accurate self-presentation. *Journal of Applied Philosophy, 35*(4), 790–808.
Kraemer, F. (2011). Authenticity anyone? The enhancement of emotions via neuro-psychopharmacology. *Neuroethics, 4*(1), 51–64.
Kraemer, F. (2013). Me, myself and my brain implant: Deep brain stimulation raises questions of personal authenticity and alienation. *Neuroethics, 6*(3), 483–497.
Leuenberger, M. (2020). In defense of narrative authenticity. *Cambridge Quarterly of Healthcare Ethics, 29*(4), 656–667.
Leuenberger, M. (2021). What is the point of being your true self? A genealogy of essentialist authenticity. *Philosophy, 96*(3), 409–431.
Leuenberger, M. (2022). Memory modification and authenticity: A narrative approach. *Neuroethics, 15*(1), 10.

Levy, N. (2007). Rethinking neuroethics in the light of the extended mind thesis. *The American Journal of Bioethics*, 7(9), 3–11.
Levy, N. (2011). Enhancing authenticity. *Journal of Applied Philosophy*, 28(3), 308–318.
Levy, N. (2018). Choices without choosers: Toward a neuropsychologically plausible existentialism. In G. Caruso & O. Flanagan (Eds.), *Neuroexistentialism: Meaning, Morals, and Purpose in the Age of Neuroscience* (pp. 111–126). Oxford University Press.
Lindemann, H. (2001). *Damaged Identities, Narrative Repair*. Ithaca: Cornell University Press.
Mackenzie, C., & Walker, M. (2015). Neurotechnologies, personal identity, and the ethics of authenticity. In J. Clausen & N. Levy (Eds.), *Handbook of Neuroethics* (pp. 373–392). Dodrecht: Springer.
Mason-Schrock, D. (1996). Transsexuals' narrative construction of the "true self". *Social Psychology Quarterly*, 59(3), 176–192.
Mele, A. R. (2001). *Autonomous Agents: From Self-control to Autonomy*. Oxford: Oxford University Press.
Meyers, D. T. (2000). Authenticity for real people. In *The Proceedings of the Twentieth World Congress of Philosophy*. (pp. 195–202). Charlottesville: Philosophy Documentation Centre.
Meyers, D. T. (2005). Decentralizing autonomy: Five faces of selfhood. In J. Anderson & J. Christman (Eds.), *Autonomy and the Challenges to Liberalism: New Essays* (pp. 27–55). Cambridge: Cambridge University Press.
Mihailov, E., Zorila, A., & Iftode, C. (2021). Taking relational authenticity seriously: Neurotechnologies, narrative identity, and co-authorship of the self. *AJOB Neuroscience*, 12(1), 35–37.
Mill, J. S. (1989). *'On Liberty' and Other Writings*. Cambridge: Cambridge University Press.
Parens, E. (2005). Authenticity and ambivalence: Toward understanding the enhancement debate. *The Hastings Center Report*, 35(3), 34–41.
Pugh, J. (2020). *Autonomy, Rationality, and Contemporary Bioethics*. Oxford: Oxford University Press.
Pugh, J., Maslen, H., & Savulescu, J. (2017). Deep brain stimulation, authenticity and value. *Cambridge Quarterly of Healthcare Ethics*, 26(4), 640–657.
Rousseau, J.-J. (1992). *Discourse on the Origins of Inequality (Second Discourse): Polemics; and, Political Economy*. Hanover, London: University Press of New England.
Rousseau, J.-J. (1997). *Julie, or, The New Héloïse: Letters of Two Lovers Who Live in a Small Town at the Foot of the Alps*. Hanover, London: University Press of New England.
Rousseau, J.-J. (2009). *Emile, or, On Education: Includes, Emile and Sophie, or, The Solitaries*. Hanover, London: University Press of New England.
Sartre, J.-P. (1956). *Being and Nothingness: An Essay on Phenomenological Ontology* (H. E. Barnes, Trans.). New York: Philosophical Library.
Schechtman, M. (2004). Self-expression and self-control. *Ratio*, 17(4), 409–427.
Schlegel, R. J., Holte, P. N., Maffly-Kipp, J., Guthrie, D., & Hicks, J. A. (2022). Authenticity as a pathway to coherence, purpose, and significance. In K. Tobia (Ed.), *Experimental Philosophy of Identity and the Self* (1st ed., pp. 169–181). London: Bloomsbury Academic.
Strohminger, N., Newman, G., & Knobe, J. (2017). The true self: A psychological concept distinct from the self. *Perspectives on Psychological Science*, 12(4), 551–560.
Sutton, A. (2020). Living the good life: A meta-analysis of authenticity, well-being and engagement. *Personality and Individual Differences*, 153, 109645.
Taylor, C. (2003). *The Ethics of Authenticity* (11th print ed.). Cambridge: Harvard University Press.
The President's Council on Bioethics. (2003). *Beyond Therapy: Biotechnology and the Pursuit of Happiness*. New York: Regan Books.
Williams, B. (2002). *Truth & Truthfulness: An Essay in Genealogy*. Princeton: Princeton University Press.

PART III
Physical enhancement

10
THE ETHICS OF GENETIC ENHANCEMENT
Key Concepts and Future Prospects

Jonny Anomaly and Tess Johnson

10.1 Introduction

Human enhancement occurs when we improve an existing capacity, or create a new capacity, so that we can perform a task better or our lives as a whole go better. Depending on how we define the term, enhancement can be intentional or accidental.[1] It can be environmental, biochemical, physical, technological, or genetic. And enhancement can be performed on ourselves or on our children in order to make our own life, our children's lives, or even other people's lives go better. After all, the traits our children have profoundly effect how they interact with other people.

In many ways, the story of human progress has been a story of technologies that enhance our ability to survive and flourish. The advent of controlled fire allowed us to keep warm at night and to cook our food, which increased the absorption of nutrients. The invention of tools to build houses and the deliberate breeding of crops for food gave us more security. And the development of written language and mathematics allowed us to think more complex thoughts, control risks associated with climate, and develop the kinds of science and technology that modern humans rely on. These are all examples of altering our environment in ways that affect our bodies and minds. Cultural innovations change the way we think and how we live, and in many cases, cultures and genes have co-evolved to alter our capacities.

Perhaps more importantly, different cultures are evolutionary processes that select different traits by sifting out bodies and brains that are poorly adapted to those cultures (Henrich 2015). Cultures that reward patience and planning, for example, tend to get more of those traits to the extent that patient and intelligent people have more surviving offspring, or perhaps in some cases, more reproductive opportunities (Clark 2009, Kuijpers et al. 2022).

Modern debates over enhancement usually focus on *intentionally* altering ourselves through medicine, surgery, or genetic engineering. Humans have long used medicine to influence their health, and we have selected mates in ways that predictably affect the traits of our offspring. But the scientific revolution that began with the European Renaissance and culminated in modern genetics has enabled us to understand how heredity works and to use this understanding to transform humanity. We will focus on genetic enhancement because of its ability to dramatically alter our capacities and its potential effects across generations.

Genetic enhancement can come from selecting between alternative mates with the intention of influencing the traits of offspring, using a sperm or egg donor, or using in vitro fertilization (IVF) and preimplantation genetic testing (PGT) to select against diseases or in favor of desired traits. Another form of genetic enhancement involves gene editing using bacteria-derived enzymes (especially the CRISPR system), which is likely to become much more powerful, precise, and affordable in the current century (Jinek et al. 2012).

In the following sections, we explore some moral principles and economic concepts from the literature that can be useful in assessing ethical concerns with genetic enhancement. The principles and concepts include positional goods, treatment *vs* enhancement, consent and parental choice, eugenics, network effects, collectivism, and disability.

10.2 Positional goods and inequalities

Attempting to enhance ourselves or our children does not imply that we will be successful. Cosmetic surgery, for example, can fail to make you more attractive. And even when it succeeds, it doesn't guarantee that you will be happy. Moreover, even if cosmetic surgery succeeds at increasing your attractiveness, if everyone in your social circle gets a similar surgery, there may be no overall improvement in human welfare to the extent that beauty is a positional good. Positional goods, then, may be able to tell us how beneficial an enhancement is for an overall population, and therefore perhaps how morally desirable it is to pursue that enhancement.

A **positional good** is one whose value depends on how many other people have it, and how much of it they have. For example, height is a positional good in the sense that not everyone can be tall, and taller men (up to some threshold) are often considered more attractive to women than shorter men. Height may be a possible genetic enhancement that some parents would pursue for their children. An **all-purpose good** is one whose value does not depend on how it is distributed in a population. For example, a healthy heart is good for us regardless of whether other people's hearts work well. A healthy heart is an all-purpose good because no matter what specific goals we have, all of them depend on crucial parts of our body, including our heart, functioning well. Immunity to an infectious disease is another example, and "genetic immunization" as a form of genetic enhancement might be one way parents pursue this all-purpose good in the future.

Positional goods raise interesting ethical problems for enhancement because if one person spends money to increase a positionally valued trait in themselves or their children, this tends to make other people worse off. If only some people can afford to increase the height of their children, for example, this might be considered *unfair* to those who can't afford to enhance. Those whose parents can most afford the height enhancement will be those who receive the added advantage of out-competing those with poorer parents who cannot afford it. And if each of us selects embryos for taller kids so that all of us spend resources on increasing the height of our children, the enhancement is collectively self-defeating – no one's position changes much in terms of their relative height.

Such scenarios are often described as a **prisoner's dilemma** or **public goods problem** in economics, or as a **collective action problem** in political science. These terms refer to cases in which it is rational for each of us to act in a way that makes all of us worse off. Such problems are difficult to solve without two things. The first is an ethical appraisal that looks at the collective, social, or group-level effects of enhancement. The second is the application of enforceable rules, such as laws or social norms, that prohibit collectively self-defeating or harmful behavior. When considering regulating access to enhancement, it is always worth asking whether there is a self-equilibrating process that might avoid collective harms even in the absence of regulations. For example, if especially tall people have health problems, parents are unlikely to want very tall children. We should also bear in mind that the cure can be worse than the disease: laws intended to solve collective action problems might drive the emergence of black markets that lead to worse consequences overall than if individuals were left free to pursue the enhancement.

When demand for a good is strong and black markets emerge to supply the good (in this case, genetic enhancement), goods are often more expensive and less reliable than they would be on an open market. Such restrictions can have some benefits, such as lowering the demand for certain kinds of enhancements by raising the price of accessing them. But restrictions can also produce new problems. For example, if we worry about inequalities that might emerge from unregulated access to expensive enhancements, banning such enhancements would likely ensure that only the wealthiest people who can pay a high black-market price (at home or abroad) could access them (Anomaly 2020). And this means inequalities would increase.

Whether such inequalities would be *unjust* depends on background moral assumptions about which there is reasonable disagreement. For example, some scholars (Daar 2017) advocate ameliorating unjust inequalities in access to enhancement technologies with state subsidies for those who can't afford them. Deciding which procedures to subsidize (or penalize) would probably require us to sort out which are likely to produce positive externalities – benefits for other people in a population – and which are likely to have negative externalities. And this will depend in part on the choices other parents are expected to make. Whatever intuitions we have about using enhancement technologies, or regulating their use, the *predictable effects* of policies that influence access to such technologies should probably inform our moral view about the desirability of such policies. To the extent that both proponents and opponents of enhancement are committed to promoting desirable outcomes, they should pay attention to the kinds of incentives that policies create within and between countries for people to enhance their children. Such policies have the power to increase or decrease arms races associated with positional goods, and to make access to enhancement technologies more or less equal.

10.3 Treatment and enhancement

Many people, especially those with strong religious views, are skeptical of genetic *enhancement* even if they endorse the use of genetic technology to treat disease. While there are big differences between attitudes toward enhancement in different countries, surveys suggest that in all countries people tend to be more wary about *enhancement* than they are about *treatment* (Funk et al. 2020). If there is a morally relevant difference between treatment and enhancement, then this might inform how morally desirable pursuing enhancement is.

Take current ethical guidance surrounding uses of gene editing tools in the US. The American Medical Association's Code of Medical Ethics states that "genetic manipulation should be reserved for therapeutic purposes. Efforts to enhance 'desirable' characteristics or to 'improve' complex human traits are contrary to the ethical tradition of medicine" (2016, S7.3.6). There seems to be a strong line drawn between the ethical acceptability of gene editing to treat, and gene editing to enhance, despite the fact that both types of genetic manipulation might improve how well a person's life goes, or their capacity to perform a certain task.

One explanation for this attitude is that people tend to see the human body as the end result of a process in which nature or God has designed us in an optimal way. While there are obvious objections to this view, especially if we look at the world through a Darwinian lens (Powell and Buchanan 2011), there are also perfectly good reasons why some people may be skeptical about radical enhancement – that is, enhancement that significantly changes capacities which we see as core to our humanity (Buchanan 2011, chapter 5; Agar 2013). To the extent that there will always be unanticipated consequences when we try to alter complex traits, some people may oppose enhancement simply because they are risk-averse, especially when we have incomplete information about the overall consequences of editing or selecting specific clusters of genes. Of course, present uncertainty would only merit caution, not a permanent fear of genetic enhancement. Moreover, since treating diseases also involves manipulating complex traits, it's unclear why most people fear enhancement more than treatment.

Nick Bostrom and Toby Ord (2006) developed the "reversal test" to probe our intuitions about enhancement. The point of the test is to distinguish when skepticism about enhancement is an irrational or unjustifiable bias toward the present, and when it might be justified. Before explaining the test, consider an example. Suppose a couple is using IVF and selecting from multiple embryos. Suppose also that the embryos are identical except that one has below-average intellectual capacities ("intelligence" for short), one has average intelligence, and the other has above-average intelligence. If they select the embryo with average intelligence, they are selecting *against* both high and low intelligence. Unless they can provide a reason for doing so, they seem to be exhibiting status quo bias. They might be motivated by a heuristic that leads them to believe average capacities are ideal for living a good human life. Or they might think deviations away from the average tend to be bad for human welfare (which could, of course, be true, given some uncertainty about what large changes will bring). Either way, they need a theory of why they are selecting in one direction or another.

> According to Bostrom and Ord (2006, pp. 664–5):
> When a proposal to change a certain parameter is thought to have bad overall consequences, consider a change to the parameter in the opposite direction. If this is also thought to have bad overall consequences, then the onus is on those who reach these conclusions to explain why our position cannot be improved through changes to this parameter. If they are unable to do so, then we have reason to suspect that they suffer from status quo bias.

The reversal test is supposed to apply to any trait that people might enhance, using genetic, environmental, or other interventions.

Some philosophers have argued that the treatment/enhancement distinction is neither clear nor useful (Resnik 2000). On David Resnik's view, we must first settle on a conception of health and disease relative to which we consider a trait enhanced. That is, in order to establish a moral difference between treating a disease and enhancing a trait, we first need to establish a descriptive difference between health and disease. Suppose we stipulate that a "healthy" person has capacities that are normal for our species, whereas an unhealthy person lacks these capacities. As Resnik argues, if we think what is normal is healthy, and what is abnormal is unhealthy, we also seem committed to the view that having crooked teeth (which is normal for our species) is healthy, while a trait like extremely high intelligence (which is abnormal for our species) is unhealthy – a disease. On this view, lowering the intelligence of Einstein or von Neumann would be framed as treating a disease, and straightening crooked teeth would be an enhancement. But this seems counterintuitive, both descriptively in terms of what each intervention involves, and normatively, if we were to say it is morally better to treat the "disease" of abnormally high intelligence than to straighten someone's crooked teeth. At the very least, this is not what people have in mind when they say that treating a disease is morally benign but enhancement is morally suspicious.

Given the counterintuitive implications of the treatment/enhancement distinction, and the blurry line between the two categories, Resnik thinks we should not place too much weight on how we define health and disease, or how we try to demarcate treatments and enhancements. Instead, he thinks, we should ask whether particular interventions are likely to promote the welfare of the person or respect the autonomy of the person who gets them. On this view, whether we classify an intervention as a treatment or enhancement is not a morally interesting question.

Others disagree. For example, Norm Daniels (2000) argues that although the line between treatment and enhancement isn't always sharp, or morally significant, it is clear enough to use in the context of public policy. For example, he thinks that certain disabilities tend to have an especially deleterious effect on people's prospects and that "fair equality of opportunity" requires that we prioritize eliminating these deprivations more than implementing enhancements when governments design a health care system. Daniels does not oppose enhancement, and he does not think treatments of serious disabilities should always trump enhancements. Instead, Daniels argues that the treatment/enhancement distinction often tracks how scarce medical resources should be allocated in a government healthcare system in which allocation decisions must be made.

10.4 Consent and choice

Let us say, then, that the treatment/enhancement distinction does not provide a knock-down argument against genetic enhancement. In that case, there is at least some room for discussing its ethical acceptability. We might be concerned with two levels of ethical decision-making. First, at the individual level, is it ethically acceptable for parents to undertake genetic enhancement for their future children? Second, is the implementation of policies permitting access to genetic enhancements acceptable in a future society? In this section, we explore some useful concepts for examining individual couples' decisions.

While certain types of genetic enhancement might be performed in people who are already born, many of the modifications we might think of as enhancements must occur when the future person is still an embryo. One relevant consideration is whether the choice to genetically enhance an embryo expresses parental **reproductive autonomy**.

A second consideration concerns the future child's choice. Embryos are not decision-makers – they cannot conceive of their own interests, make decisions, or communicate their decisions to consent to an enhancement. **Informed consent** is usually considered a core principle of medical ethics. Living people can usually give informed consent about whether to enhance themselves. To secure the interests of future people, however, we might rely on proxy consent. Proxy consent occurs when a representative accepts or refuses an intervention on behalf of someone who cannot.

One complication, in this case, is that it is unclear whether the embryo is a person who can be represented through another, or whether rather the parents simply have a decision to make that accords with what would be considered the usual standards of parental responsibility. This second view is more common in the literature and has given rise to principles such as **procreative beneficence**, which holds that "couples should select the child, of the possible children they could have, who is expected to have the best life…based on the relevant, available information" (Savulescu 2001, p. 413). The implications of procreative beneficence in terms of whether parents should genetically enhance their future child in a particular way might then be balanced against their reproductive autonomy.

10.5 Eugenics and collectivism

With this section, we move on to assessing genetic enhancement at the group level. There are three particularly useful moral concepts in evaluating the pursuit of genetic enhancement: eugenics, network effects, and collectivism.

In one way, genetic enhancement might be considered a form of eugenics, with which we have past policy experience. "Eugenics" is often considered a loaded term, but it has been widely employed in the literature on enhancement (Veit et al. 2021). "Classical" or "old" **eugenics** tended to focus on the welfare of populations, and historically some eugenic practices strayed from this goal and were implemented in unacceptable ways that have influenced how we view eugenics today.[2] By contrast, "liberal" eugenics in modern academic discussions of genetic enhancement tends to focus on individuals and their free pursuit of genetic changes that will improve their or their offspring's lives. However, these dividing lines are not always clear, and an exclusive focus on individual autonomy would be odd, since ethics tends to focus on obligations toward other people, including future people. Moreover, individual welfare is often a function of group traits, and the welfare of groups depends on the composition of the individuals who comprise them. While considering the individual benefits of genetic changes is useful, to consider broader effects of genetic changes to an individual or population, we might want to employ another concept that captures the broader social effects of genetic changes to a population.

To take a simple example, some proponents of cognitive enhancement emphasize that if only some people in a population were to enhance themselves or their children, the enhanced would likely develop technological breakthroughs that would benefit everyone, including the unenhanced (Bostrom and Sandberg 2009). Others have argued that apart from improving material welfare, having more intelligent people in a population tends to have positive externalities – or **network effects** – because groups of smarter people tend to produce societies that are less corrupt and more cooperative than societies with a lower average IQ (Anomaly and Jones 2020).

Network effects occur when, as more people adopt a technology, the gains (or losses) to a group of people increase exponentially. Having a few smart or virtuous people in a population, for example, may be good. But the more such people there are in a population, the more gains there will be in terms of cooperation and innovation. Because our reproductive choices influence the welfare of many future people, not just our individual children, a narrow focus on individual obligations toward our children has seemed insufficient to many – both for individual decision-making concerning enhancement and for developing ethically informed policy. Allen Buchanan et al. (2000, p. 210) observe that

> the costs and benefits of having children are externalized in virtually all societies – that is, borne by others besides the parents (or children). The more this happens, the greater claim these others might make to have some say in, or control of, the costs imposed on them.

Ethically informed policy may need to take these costs and benefits into account.

Turning to the parents' individual decision-making, we might build on the concept of procreative beneficence introduced above. Because procreative beneficence doesn't address how our own children might affect the welfare of other children, Thomas Douglas and Katrien Devolder coined a corresponding principle that includes the welfare of future people more broadly. According to **procreative altruism**, "parents have a significant moral reason to select a child whose existence can be expected to contribute more to (or detract less from) the well-being of others than any alternative child they could have" (2013, p. 400). Perhaps, then, parents should only undertake genetic enhancement if it will help (or at least not hinder) others to secure their own well-being. Yet these principles are not incompatible. Enhancements might be available that both benefit the future child and others. These principles illustrate the ways in which proponents of enhancement think we should weigh the welfare of our own children against the ways in which other children will likely be affected by our children.

Ethical policymaking and ethical individual decision-making do not always align. Modern proponents of enhancement tend to reject the more coercive policies advocated by eugenicists of old. It would be going too far to force or require parents to undertake enhancement in order to provide the most benefit to other people or have a child with a particularly high level of well-being. Yet, on an individual level, they still think about **moral obligations** that parents considering enhancement may have toward individuals *and* groups. For example, Chris Gyngell (2012) has discussed some ways in which we might owe future people a range of potential traits that are likely to result in humans surviving population-level catastrophes. Similarly, many philosophers have argued that we should morally enhance our children in ways that make future people flourish and survive existential threats like extreme changes to the climate or pandemic diseases (Powell and Buchanan 2016, Persson and Savulescu 2017, Anomaly 2020, Crutchfield 2021).

The kind of ethical analysis that focuses on enhancements that are collectively beneficial and that might be implemented on a population-wide scale might be termed **collectivism** (Johnson 2021). We might distinguish this approach from one that focuses primarily or purely on individual-level concerns and effects of genetic enhancement, termed **individualism**. Individualism risks not recognizing problems that come from enhancements that confer positional goods or that cause negative externalities. Yet, to avoid going too far in the other direction, a collectivist analysis needs to consider the limits of burdens that can be imposed on individuals as part of fulfilling a moral obligation to benefit (or not harm) others through their pursuit of genetic enhancement.

10.6 Disability

One potential harm that might not be reasonably bearable and may be a consequence of human enhancement concerns the birth of disabled people. There are several different concerns here. They are not specific to human enhancement insofar as this is differentiated from therapeutic uses of gene editing, but they deserve consideration, nonetheless.

The first concern might be raised by those who are born disabled, despite their parents' best efforts (using embryo selection or gene editing) to have them born without that particular disability. Attempts to avoid disability are not always successful, and people born with a disability that makes their life go less well or which decreases their capacity to perform certain tasks may blame their parents for failing to prevent their disability. In other cases, parents may deliberately refrain from genetically enhancing their future child, similarly limiting their capacities. These points have been raised in connection to the choice of whether to genetically select against disability (Purdy 1996). While it may be an expression of parents' reproductive autonomy or their values to have a child with a particular disability – say, if they are active members of deaf communities – this benefit will in many cases be outweighed by the harms of disability for the child.

One common objection to this type of claim is that it rests on the wrong model of disability, a medical/functional model rather than a social one (Shakespeare 2014, Chapter 2). While medical models see disability as similar to illness, social models see the harms of disability as arising not from a physical impairment but from the limitations of the environments in which disabled people live. If these environments were altered, so the argument goes, then disabled people would not experience harm from their disability, and so it is the environments that should be changed rather than the people who are (or might otherwise be) born with impairments. A middle-ground approach adopts a welfarist stance, which neither assumes disabilities are harmful in the way illnesses are, nor that it is only the context surrounding disabilities that is harmful. On this view, each person's welfare is affected differently by a disability, and some disabilities will harm someone, while others may in fact benefit them (say, for a deaf person, by giving them more opportunity to learn and appreciate sign language). In this sense, selection for certain disabilities for certain people may constitute an enhancement. However, given the difficulties of judging this case-by-case and in advance of the child being born, we think it is more often likely to be the case that a disability will not constitute an enhancement.

A final concern surrounding genetic enhancement and disability is the negative externalities of genetic selection against disabilities for those currently living with them. This objection to enhancement has been called the "expressivist objection," and it claims that selecting against disabilities expresses a disvalue of the lives of those living with a disability (Shakespeare 2014, Chapter 6). The potential effects of reducing the number of people living with disabilities are important to consider, but the objection rests on a controversial foundation: that a disability is part of a person's identity, thus that eliminating disabilities expresses disvalue toward those identities. Where disability is a state and not a part of identity, this objection to pursuing enhancement may not apply.

10.7 Conclusion

Human enhancement is an old aspiration. But tools that will enable us to genetically enhance ourselves and our children in dramatic and long-lasting ways are new. These tools create exciting opportunities but also raise profound moral questions that can be clarified by invoking some core concepts from ethics and economics.

Notes

1 According to Allen Buchanan, "A biomedical enhancement is a deliberate intervention, applying biomedical science, which aims to improve an existing capacity that most or all normal human beings typically have, or to create a new capacity, by acting directly on the body or brain" (2011, p. 23). This is a useful general account. But whether we want to define enhancements as merely *attempts* to improve existing capacities or as *successful attempts* at improvements will probably depend on the context of debate. We might also want to distinguish between improvements in performing a task that are incidental to the main goal of the enhancement, and those that are fully intended. For instance, the same change to a gene that can confer resistance to HIV (which me might term a "genetic immunization" enhancement) can also improve memory function (Joy et al. 2019). For alternative accounts of "enhancement," see Eric Juengst and Daniel Moseley (2023).
2 According to Allen Buchanan et al. (2000, p. 43), "Eugenics is mostly remembered for the outrages committed in its name. Terrible as they were, however, these wrongs do not, in themselves, tell us about the validity of eugenic moral thinking…For the history of eugenics to be instructive in ensuring social justice in a society with greater knowledge about genes, and perhaps some ability to alter them, the key question is whether eugenics was wrong in its very inception. Our review finds that much of the bad reputation of eugenics is traceable to attributes that, at least in theory, might be avoidable in a future eugenic program."

Bibliography

Agar, Nicholas. 2013. *Humanity's End: Why We Should Reject Radical Enhancement*. Cambridge, MA: MIT Press.
American Medical Association. 2016. Code of Medical Ethics Opinion 7.3.6, Research in Gene Therapy & Genetic Engineering. In *AMA Code of Medical Ethics*. < https://www.ama-assn.org/delivering-care/ethics/research-gene-therapy-genetic-engineering>, accessed 20 May, 2022.
Anomaly, Jonathan. 2020. *Creating Future People: The Ethics of Genetic Enhancement*. London: Routledge Press.
Anomaly, Jonathan and Garett Jones. 2020. Cognitive Enhancement and Network Effects. *Philosophia* 48: 1753–1768.
Bostrom, Nick and Anders Sandberg. 2009. Cognitive Enhancement: Methods, Ethics, Regulatory Challenges. *Science and Engineering Ethics* 15(3): 311–341.
Bostrom, Nick and Toby Ord. 2006. The Reversal Test: Eliminating Status Quo Bias in Ethics. *Ethics* 116: 656–679.
Buchanan, Allen. 2011. *Beyond Humanity*. Oxford: Oxford University Press.
Buchanan, Allen. 2009. Moral Status and Human Enhancement. *Philosophy & Public Affairs* 37(4): 346–381.
Buchanan, Allen, Dan Brock, Norm Daniels, and Dan Wikler. 2000. *From Chance to Choice: Genetics and Justice*. Cambridge: Cambridge University Press.
Clark, Gregory. 2009. *A Farwell to Alms: A Brief Economic History of the World*. Princeton, NJ: Princeton University Press.
Crew, Fae et al. 1939. Social Biology and Population Improvement. *Nature* 144: 521–522.
Crutchfield, Parker. 2021. *Moral Enhancement and the Public Good*. London: Routledge.
Daar, Judith. 2017. *The New Eugenics: Selective Breeding in an Era of Reproductive Technologies*. New Haven, CT: Yale University Press.
Daniels, Norm. 2000. Normal Functioning and the Treatment / Enhancement Distinction. *Cambridge Quarterly of Healthcare Ethics* 9(3): 309–322.
Darwin, Charles. 1874. *The Descent of Man and Selection in Relation to Sex*. 2nd ed. London, UK: John Murray Publishing.
Douglas, Thomas and Katrien Devolder. 2013. Procreative Altruism. *Journal of Medicine and Philosophy* 38: 400–419.
Funk, Cary et al. 2020. Biotechnology Research Viewed with Caution Globally, But Most Support Gene Editing of Babies to Treat Disease. Pew Research Center. https://www.pewresearch.org/science/2020/12/10/biotechnology-research-viewed-with-caution-globally-but-most-support-gene-editing-for-babies-to-treat-disease/, accessed 15 April, 2022.
Gyngell, Chris. 2012. Enhancing the Species: Genetic Engineering Technologies and Human Persistence. *Philosophy and Technology* 25(4): 495–512.
Gyngell, Chris and Thomas Douglas. 2015. Stocking the Genetic Supermarket. *Bioethics* 29(4): 241–250.

He, Jiankui. 2018. About Lulu and Nana: Twin Girls Born Healthy After Gene Surgery as Single-Cell Embryos. *Youtube* https://www.youtube.com/watch?v=th0vnOmFltc&app=desktop, accessed 20 May, 2022.

Henrich, Joseph. 2015. *The Secret of our Success*. Princeton, NJ: Princeton University Press.

Jinek, Martin, Krzysztof Chylinski, Ines Fonfara, Michael Hauer, Jennifer Doudna, and Emmanuelle Charpentier. 2012. A Programmable Dual-RNA Guided DNA Endonuclease in Adaptive Bacterial Immunity. *Science* **337**(6096): 816–821.

Johnson, Tess. 2021. Enhancing the Collectivist Critique: Accounts of the Human Enhancement Debate. *Medicine, Health Care, and Philosophy* 24: 721–730.

Joy, Mary et al. 2019. CCR5 is a Therapeutic Target for Recovery after Stroke and Traumatic Brain Injury. *Cell* 176: 1143–1157.

Juengst, Eric and Dan Moseley. 2023. Human Enhancement. *The Stanford Encyclopedia of Philosophy*. https://plato.stanford.edu/entries/enhancement/.

Kujipers, Yunus et al. 2022. Evolutionary Trajectory of Complex Traits in European Populations of Modern Humans. *Frontiers in Genetics* 13, article 833190. https://www.frontiersin.org/articles/10.3389/fgene.2022.833190/full.

Persson, Ingmar and Julian Savulescu. 2017. Moral Hard-Wiring and Moral Enhancement. *Bioethics* 31(4): 286–295.

Powell, Russell and Allen Buchanan. 2011. Breaking Evolution's Chains: The Prospect of Deliberate Genetic Modification. *Journal of Medicine and Philosophy* 36: 6–27.

Powell, Russell and Allen Buchanan. 2016. The Evolution of Moral Enhancement. In *The Ethics of Human Enhancement: Understanding the Debate*. Steven Clarke and Julian Savulescu (editors). Oxford: Oxford University Press.

Purdy, Laura. 1996. Loving Future People. In *Reproducing Persons: Issues in Feminist Bioethics*. Ithaca, NY: Cornell University Press.

Resnik, David. 2000. The Moral Significance of the Therapy-Enhancement Distinction. *Cambridge Quarterly of Healthcare Ethics* 9: 365–367.

Savulescu, Julian. 2001. Procreative Beneficence: Why We Should Select the Best Children. *Bioethics* 15: 413–426.

Shakespeare, Tom. 2014. *Disability Rights and Wrongs Revisited*. New York, NY: Routledge.

Veit, Walter et al. 2021. Can 'Eugenics' Be Defended? *Monash Bioethics Review* 39: 60–67.

11
GERMLINE GENE EDITING WITH CRISPR

A risk-analysis response to liberal eugenics

Siddharta B. Chiong OP and Nicanor Austriaco OP

11.1 Introduction

In 1910, American geneticist Charles Davenport founded the Eugenics Record Office (ERO), based at the Cold Spring Harbor Laboratory on Long Island, New York.[1] According to one of its documents, the goal of eugenics was "to improve the natural, physical, mental, and temperamental qualities of the human family."[2] Despite this lofty ideal, however, the eugenics movement of the early 20th century is remembered and universally condemned for its unjust social practices including the forcible sterilization of tens of thousands of Americans who were deemed to be "feeble-minded." Even the US Supreme Court fell under the trance of eugenics. In their 1927 case, *Buck v Bell*, the justices voted 8 to 1 to uphold a state's right to forcibly sterilize a person considered unfit to procreate. It was one of their most infamous decisions.

Fast-forward a century. In 2004, bioethicist Nicholas Agar published a book defending a liberal eugenics that would allow parents to enhance the traits of their children through the use of artificial reproductive technologies and genome editing.[3] Since the publication of his provocative proposal, scientists have discovered a bacterial-based gene editing system, known as CRISPR, that can be used to alter the DNA sequence of any organism, including humans. In principle, it could be used to allow parents to design their children thus fulfilling the aspirations of liberal eugenicists. Should CRISPR be deployed to facilitate liberal eugenics?

In this chapter, we begin by describing the CRISPR genome editing system which has revolutionized molecular biology in the past decade. We then examine the argument put forward by Agar in defense of a liberal eugenics that would give parents access to CRISPR so that they could design their offspring according to their own unique account of the good life. In response, we propose that a liberal society that seeks not to harm anyone should reject germline genome editing with CRISPR because we can never perform the appropriate benefit-risk analysis that would prevent parents from harming their enhanced offspring with germline gene editing. We conclude by interrogating three possible counter-proposals that posit either that animal studies should be sufficient to justify human germline gene editing, that our societal acceptance of IVF which was developed without a benefit-risk assessment would justify the same for germline gene editing, or that society would be able to move forward once rogue scientists do the necessary unethical but inevitable experiments on enhanced future persons.

11.2 Germline genome editing with CRISPR

CRISPR, an acronym for "clustered regularly interspaced short palindromic repeats," is a family of DNA sequences that are found in the genomes of single-celled bacteria.[4] In nature, these DNA sequences are derived from the genomes of bacterial viruses called bacteriophages that had previously infected the bacterial cell. This preserved copy of viral DNA enables the bacteria to detect and defend themselves from future bacteriophage attacks using a molecule called Cas9, an acronym for "CRISPR-associated protein 9."

How does this antiviral defense system work? The CRISPR system activates Cas9 by arming it with an RNA guide sequence that matches one of the CRISPR DNA sequences. This allows the Cas9 protein to surveil the bacterial cell for invading viral DNA molecules that match the CRISPR sequence. Once Cas9 identifies a perfect or near-perfect sequence match, it cuts the viral DNA at a precise point specified by the guide RNA. This destroys the foreign viral DNA preventing the attacking bacteriophage from replicating and destroying its bacterial host.

The CRISPR technological breakthrough that now allows us to edit any genome precisely – recognized by the Nobel Prize in Chemistry in 2020 – occurred when molecular biologists discovered that the CRISPR-Cas9 molecular machine is programmable: anyone can target Cas9 to any predetermined DNA sequence in any genome in any living cell by injecting the Cas9 molecular machine into that cell along with a predetermined guide RNA molecule. This predetermined guide RNA would give Cas9 the novel capacity to interrogate and cut any host DNA sequences that matched the guide RNA. Repairing this cut in different ways would allow scientists to alter the function of the associated gene or genes.

For example, in one study, a team of scientists from the University of Pennsylvania used a viral system to deliver Cas9 and a guide RNA corresponding to the OTC gene to mice liver cells.[5] These mice had a single mutation in their OTC gene which gave them a blood disorder called hemophilia B because they lacked an essential blood clotting factor specified by the OTC gene. The team discovered that the bacterial Cas9 molecular editing machine was able to cut the DNA sequence of the mutant OTC gene in such a way that it could be repaired and restored to its normal, species-typical sequence. After the gene editing experiment, the mice were able to produce enough clotting factor to ameliorate the blood disease. This strategy allows molecular biologists to genetically engineer any target gene in any cell because they would have the power to specify the final DNA sequence of that gene in that cell.

In the past decade, CRISPR has been used to edit the genomes of a diverse range of plant and animal species. It has also been used to genetically engineer human cells. Most significantly, therapeutic interventions are being developed to target human diseases that are caused by mutations in single genes. Two mechanistic strategies are possible. First, CRISPR could be used to genetically engineer the non-reproductive or somatic cells of a patient to correct an inherited mutation. This is called somatic cell gene therapy. As one example, CRISPR is being used to cure hereditary blood disorders by genetically correcting the malfunctioning gene in blood stem cells, which are then reintroduced into the patient after correction.[6] CRISPR is also being used to remedy diseases of the retina that lead to blindness and diseases of the cochlea that lead to deafness by genetically editing malfunctioning cells in the eyes and in the inner ears of patients.[7] In contrast, CRISPR could be used to genetically alter the reproductive cells or gametes of patients to produce human offspring whose genomes have been edited so that they do not inherit a diseased gene from their parents. This is called germline gene therapy. There are still no examples of this therapeutic approach since modifying the human germline is still considered controversial.

Though still undiscovered at the time of Agar's book proposing a liberal eugenics, CRISPR technology has emerged as the preeminent molecular tool for parents who want to enhance the traits of their children using genome editing. In principle, a couple could now use the CRISPR molecular machine to edit the genomes of their sperm or their egg or their embryo to conceive a child with a set of desired characteristics.[8] Though the use of the technology would be the same, this would not be germline gene therapy but germline gene enhancement. Should CRISPR-Cas9 be deployed to facilitate a liberal eugenics?

11.3 The liberal eugenics argument for germline gene enhancement

The liberal eugenics argument for germline gene enhancement is relatively straightforward. According to Nicholas Agar, a liberal society is a society "founded on the insight that there are many different, often incompatible ideas about the good life."[9] Thus, in his view, parents in a liberal society should be allowed "to introduce into their embryos combinations of genes that correspond to their particular conception of good life."[10] No one, including the government, should be able to limit parental choice because "living well in a liberal society involves acknowledging that right of others to make choices that do not appeal to us."[11] Instead, in Agar's account of liberal eugenics,

> the state [...] would foster the development of a wide range of technologies of enhancement ensuring that prospective parents were fully informed about what kinds of people these technologies would make. Parents' particular conceptions of the good life would guide them in their selection of enhancements for their children.[12]

Despite their advocacy for a radical expansion of parental procreative liberties, it is important to acknowledge that liberal eugenicists do not think that parents are radically free to shape their offspring in any way that they desire. Agar explains:

> But pluralism about human flourishing is not a relativism that gives a moral pass mark to absolutely any use of enhancement technologies. While there is no uniquely best way to use enhancement technologies, some uses of them are just plain wrong.[13]

In his view, enhancement technologies are just plain wrong when they harm future persons:

> There are, broadly speaking, two ways in which genetic engineers' shaping of children can cause harm. Some uses of enhancement technologies cause suffering. [...] Another way for the shaping of children to harm them is by infringing on their freedom to choose a life plan and to successfully pursue it.[14]

For the liberal eugenics movement, any human enhancements that harm future persons or that "replace one individual with another who either suffers to a greater extent, or is less free in respect of the course his life takes"[15] have to be rejected as being incompatible with a liberal account of human flourishing that emphasizes autonomy, personal choice, and protection from harm caused by others. Parents cannot be allowed to create enhanced offspring who experience physical or emotional suffering or who are unable to live a life that they may want to choose as they mature. First do no harm. *Primum non nocere.*

11.4 A risk-analysis response to liberal eugenics

A foundational ethical principle in contemporary medicine is that all novel drugs, biologics, and interventions have to be tested for their safety and efficacy before they can be used with patients. Otherwise, we would not know if these novel agents would cause harm. In practice, this entails a benefit-risk assessment that assesses the expected benefits of a potential medical intervention and compares them to possible risks. For a new medical intervention to be approved by a regulatory agency, the assessed benefits must outweigh the potential risks.

In Catholic bioethics, respect for the dignity of persons calls physicians and researchers to acknowledge that human subjects and patients "have a natural law obligation to care for and conserve their health in a manner proportionate to the specific circumstances."[16] As such, subjects and patients can only undertake risk if there is a proportionate benefit for their health and well-being that outweighs that risk. They can only make this judgment if a benefit-risk assessment for their drug or procedure has been completed.

In secular bioethics, the United States National Commission for the Protection of Human Subjects of Biomedical and Behavioral Research articulated the principle of beneficence in the *Belmont Report* that requires investigators to assess the anticipated benefits and the potential risks of novel procedures that impact a patient. The Commission explained: "Two general rules have been formulated as complementary expressions of beneficent actions in this sense: (1) do not harm and (2) maximize possible benefits and minimize possible harms."[17] Clearly, the moral consensus in our liberal, pluralistic society is that the benefits of a novel medical intervention must outweigh its risks to justify its use in the clinic. This requirement ensures that we are not unduly harming others.

In practice, the US Food and Drug Administration (FDA) defines a benefit-risk assessment as "making a judgment as to whether the expected benefits (with their uncertainties) of the drug outweigh the potential risks (with their uncertainties and approaches to manage risks) associated with its expected use."[18] Several conceptual frameworks are currently in use throughout the globe to determine the benefit-risk assessment.[19] The FDA's benefit-risk framework for human drug review examines the evidence and uncertainties associated with four dimensions of a potential new drug's profile.[20] These include an analysis of the condition that it intends to treat, the current treatment options for that condition, the benefits attributed to the drug, and the risks attributed to the drug along with an account of how that risk will be managed.

Key considerations for benefits include the strengths and limitations of the clinical trial and their potential implications for assessing drug efficacy; clinical relevance of the clinical study endpoints; and demonstrated results and their clinical significance. In contrast, key considerations for risks also include serious adverse events or safety signals and their clinical significance and effectiveness of strategies to manage risks. The FDA notes that it is flexible if the therapeutic context warrants it:

> Aspects of the therapeutic context affect FDA's tolerance for uncertainty and the tradeoffs about a product's benefits and risks. For example, in the case of accelerated approval, FDA may accept an effect on a surrogate endpoint that is reasonably likely to predict benefit, rather than requiring a validated surrogate or direct measure of clinical outcomes, if the drug is expected to provide a meaningful advantage over available therapies in the treatment of a serious or life-threatening condition.[21]

For the FDA, assessing benefits and risks is linked to empirically verifiable endpoints involving clinical trials with volunteers who have experienced either a novel medical intervention or a placebo control.

In light of the ethical consensus for a mandated benefit-risk assessment for novel medical interventions, we argue that human germline gene editing can never be justified because we could never undertake this benefit-risk assessment that we would need to complete to make sure that we would not harm enhanced future persons. Why? Because there is no foreseeable way of properly assessing the benefits and risks of germline gene editing without first creating germline gene-edited persons whom we could observe over the course of their lifetimes. However, creating these germline gene-edited persons would in itself be unethical. We would be creating them as experimental subjects, risking their lives and well-being with untested novel technology. On their own terms, therefore, liberal eugenicists – who advocate a do-no-harm principle as their only constraining ethical principle for parental choice – should reject germline gene editing because we will never be able to guarantee that we would not harm germline gene-edited future persons. First do no harm. *Primum non nocere.*

11.5 Responding to possible counter-arguments

Three possible objections can be deployed against our argument that prohibits human germline gene editing because we are unable to do the proper benefit-risk assessment for this technological innovation that would allow us to know that we would not harm future enhanced persons.

First, an interlocutor could propose that experiments with mice, fish, and non-human primates would give us enough of an experimental basis for human germline gene editing. Many of the fundamental discoveries regarding human biology were first made with animal models.

In response, it is true that animal studies are important for drug development and translational medicine. However, they are not enough. Numerous authors have highlighted the failure of many animal studies to reasonably predict the outcome of a human clinical trial.[22] Humans are neither mice nor monkeys. They are complex biological systems that have uniquely evolved within a particular environmental niche. Thus, we should not expect human genes to behave in exactly the same way as their counterparts in other animal models. One recent study has already revealed that using CRISPR-Cas9 to edit the gene, POU5F1, either in mouse or in human embryos had different outcomes because mouse and human developmental biology differ.[23] This suggests that we would not really know all of the effects of modifying a gene in a future enhanced person without actually creating that individual to observe his biology. Moreover, since genetic modifications may have effects later in life, especially during puberty, to really understand the benefits and risks of a gene modification, we would have to observe that enhanced person as he matures into adulthood. Animal studies in themselves would not suffice. Human clinical trials are a must.

Second, an advocate for germline gene editing could appeal to our societal experience of *in vitro* fertilization (IVF). In the 1970s and 1980s, children were conceived *in vitro* without knowing whether or not the technology would have harmed them or not. As Nicholas Agar himself acknowledges, proponents of the new reproductive technologies defend the development of IVF by pointing out that Louise Brown, the first IVF baby, appears to be living a typically healthy human life today.[24] If IVF was developed and adopted without the prerequisite benefit-risk assessment, it could be argued, then, that germline gene editing should likewise be tested as well.

In response, we note that IVF, which is an attempt to recapitulate a natural process in the laboratory, is significantly less risky than modifying a human individual's genome using technology co-opted from a bacterial antiviral system. The former brings sperm and egg together in a Petri dish. The latter involves manipulating molecules that drive the biology of the organism in unprecedented and unpredictable ways. With heightened risk comes the heightened need for a benefit-risk assessment. More importantly, however, a past evil act that was spared potentially grave and tragic consequences does not justify or legitimize a current or future evil action. For example, a past instance of drinking and driving that did not lead to the death of an innocent bystander does not justify my drinking and driving today. Performing experiments with the first IVF babies without knowing whether or not they would be harmed was unjust whether or not Louise Brown was born apparently healthy. Imagine an alternative history where the first IVF children were born disabled or sick or dying. Would we not have been outraged by the hubris of the scientists who pioneered that technology? Would we not have called out to prohibit the future creation of any more such damaged babies? We would have rightfully done so. In the same way, we should work to prevent a possible future where disabled, sick, or dying enhanced babies are created because scientists wanted to dry-run human germline gene editing. First do no harm. *Primum non nocere.*

Third, an advocate could argue that human germline gene editing is inevitable. We simply have to wait until rogue scientists complete the unethical and illicit human experiments that would allow us to know the benefits and risks of this novel technology. We would then be able to use germline gene editing ethically. This certainly is Agar's view. He believes "that underground experimentation is likely to help us to traverse the ethically impossible passage to safe enhancement technologies whether we like it or not. Traversing this passage changes our moral situation."[25] He continues:

> [I]t is a reasonable bet that the biotechnologists of some future century will develop techniques capable of safely enhancing human attributes. Once this point is reached we will

be able to implement a liberal eugenics, granting prospective parents a limited prerogative to use enhancement technologies to choose their children's characteristics.[26]

In response, especially in light of the grave injustices of the Nazi medical experiments, there is already much support for the view that society must not seek to profit from past unethical scientific practices.[27] Agar himself acknowledges that we should not benefit from the medical war crimes of the Nazi period regardless of their scientific merits.[28] But if this is the case, then liberal eugenicists should seek to distance themselves from any rogue germline gene editing experiments that cast aside the do-no-harm principle. Risking the lives and well-being of enhanced future persons with unethical and illicit gene editing experiments should also be a medical crime.[29] Consequently, we should be clear that a liberal society should never seek to use nor attempt to benefit from any data generated from these illicit clinical trials for germline gene editing. Anything less would be liberal hypocrisy. It would give tacit approval and possible encouragement to those rogue scientists who are always seeking recognition for their work, licit or illicit. If we believe that harming another is evil, then we should ensure that any scientific misconduct that risks harming others is condemned and punished as a crime, regardless of any possible scientific merit. First do no harm. *Primum non nocere*.

11.6 Implications for clinical research involving novel therapies

Finally, we need to address the implications of the argument made in this paper that CRISPR cannot be used ethically to modify the genomes of future human beings because the prerequisite benefit-risk analysis has not and cannot be done. Can this argument not be deployed to argue that all research in humans is unethical? There are numerous, novel medical interventions, including mRNA vaccines and CAR-T cell therapies, just to name two, which at some point must be tested in human subjects for the first time without the prerequisite benefit-risk analysis. Indeed, clinical trials are often undertaken precisely to establish the risks and benefits of a novel intervention. Absent the prerequisite benefit-risk analysis, are these novel medical interventions not also ruled out in the same way that CRISPR is ruled out for germline gene editing of future generations?

Not at all. The individuals who volunteered for the clinical trials required to authorize the use of the COVID-19 mRNA vaccines and the CAR-T cell therapies were able to give informed consent after evaluating the potential risks and benefits of the novel medical intervention. A cancer patient with stage 4 melanoma who is facing certain death could decide that the potential benefits of a CAR-T clinical trial would always outweigh the certain risk of death. A healthy volunteer who is told of the potential risks and benefits of the COVID-19 mRNA candidate vaccine could also decide that the potential benefits outweigh the potential risks. The difference between these medical interventions that involve current human beings and the use of CRISPR to modify the genomes of future human beings is that the subjects of the former could give consent while those of the latter could not.

11.7 Conclusion

Liberal eugenicists have worked hard to re-invent a "new" eugenics to distance themselves from the "old" eugenics pioneered by Charles Davenport and his Eugenics Records Office. They do so by emphasizing their liberal credentials. However, with germline gene editing, they are faced with the horns of a dilemma. On the one hand, they can turn a blind eye to unethical experiments that may or may not develop their preferred technological strategy, by completing a benefit-risk analysis. However, in doing so, they would be undermining the very liberal values they espouse, making these values arbitrary rights that can be applied to some and denied to others. They would be doing eugenics the "old" way. On the other hand, liberal eugenicists could condemn and forever rule out germline gene editing. In doing this, they would be acting in a way consistent with their foundational liberal beliefs. However, as a consequence, they would be undercutting the technological developments that are necessary for a liberal eugenics to proceed. Which horn will they choose? We will see. Hopefully, they will remember: First do no harm. *Primum non nocere.*

Notes

1. This introductory paragraph is indebted to Phillipa Levine, *Eugenics: A Very Short Introduction* (Oxford: Oxford University Press, 2017) and Edwin Black, *War Against the Weak: Eugenics and America's Campaign to Create a Master Race* (Washington, DC: Dialog Press, 2003).
2. Cited in Karen Norrgard, "Human Testing, the Eugenics Movement, and IRBs," *Nature Education* 1.1 (2008): 170.
3. Nicholas Agar, *Liberal Eugenics: In Defence of Human Enhancement* (Oxford: Blackwell Publishing, 2004). For a sense of the ongoing debate surrounding liberal eugenics and genetic enhancement, see the following books and essays: Jürgen Habermas, *The Future of Human Nature* (Oxford: Blackwell, 2003); Bernard G. Prusak, "Rethinking 'Liberal Eugenics': Reflections and Questions on Habermas on Bioethics," *The Hastings Center Report* 35.6 (2005): 31–42; Dov Fox, "The Illiberality of 'Liberal Eugenics'," *Ratio* 20.1 (2007): 1–25; "Regulating Eugenics," *Harvard Law Review* 121.6 (2008): 1578–1599; Daniel C. Henrich, "Human Nature and Autonomy: Jürgen Habermas' Critique of Liberal Eugenics," *Ethical Perspectives* 18.2 (2011): 249–268; Robert Sparrow, "Liberalism and Eugenics," *Australasian Journal of Philosophy* 89.3 (2011): 499–501; Jonathan Anomaly, "Defending Eugenics: From Cryptic Choice to Conscious Selection," *Monash Bioethical Review* 35 (2018): 24–35; Giulia Cavaliere, "Looking into the Shadow: The Eugenics Argument in Debates on Reproductive Technologies and Practices," *Monash Bioethical Review* 36 (2018): 1–22; Robert A. Wilson, "Eugenics Undefended," *Monash Bioethics Review* 37 (2019): 68–75; and Veit et al., "Can 'Eugenics' be Defended?" *Monash Bioethics Review*. Published online on May 25, 2021.
4. The narrative of this section is indebted to the following reviews: Janik et al., "Various Aspects of a Gene Editing System-CRISPR-Cas9," *International Journal of Molecular Sciences* 21.24 (2020): 9604; Addison V. Wright, James K. Nuñez, and Jennifer A. Doudna, "Biology and Applications of CRISPR Systems: Harnessing Nature's Toolbox for Genome Engineering," *Cell* 164.1–2 (2016): 29–44; and Eric S. Lander, "The Heroes of CRISPR," *Cell* 164.1–2 (2016): 18–28.
5. Wang et al., "CRISPR/Cas9-mediated in vivo Gene Targeting Corrects Hemostasis in Newborn and Adult Factor IX–knockout Mice," *Blood* 133.26 (2019): 2745–2752.
6. For a recent review, see Chen et al., "Genome Editing using CRISPR/Cas9 to Treat Hereditary Hematological Disorders," *Gene Therapy*. Published online ahead of print on March 9, 2021.
7. For a recent review, see Crane et al., "Gene Therapy to the Retina and the Cochlea," *Frontiers in Neuroscience* 15 (2021): 652215.
8. A. Cecile J.W. Janssens, "Designing Babies through Gene Editing: Science or Science Fiction?" *Genetics in Medicine* 18.12 (2016): 1186–1187. Also see the essay on the controversial use of CRISPR to genetically edit two Chinese babies: Henry T. Greely, "CRISPR'd Babies: Human Germline Genome Editing in the 'He Jiankui Affair'," *Journal of Law and Biosciences* 6.1 (2019): 111–183.
9. Agar, *Liberal Eugenics*, 5.
10. Ibid., 6.
11. Ibid., 5.
12. Ibid.
13. Ibid., 101.
14. Ibid., 101–102.
15. Ibid., 103.
16. The National Catholic Bioethics Center and the Catholic Medical Association, "A Catholic Guide to Ethical Clinical Research," *The Linacre Quarterly* 75.3 (2008): 181–224; p. 186.
17. National Commission for the Protection of Human Subjects of Biomedical and Behavioral Research, *The Belmont Report: Ethical Principles and Guidelines for the Protection of Human Subjects of Research*, April 18, 1979. Available at www.hhs.gov/ohrp/regulations-and-policy/belmont-report/read-the-belmont-report/index.html.
18. US Food and Drug Administration, "Benefit-Risk Assessment Throughout the Drug Lifecycle: FDA Discussion Document," May 3, 2019. Available at https://healthpolicy.duke.edu/sites/default/files/atoms/files/discussion_guide_b-r_assessment_may16_0.pdf.
19. For a review, see Juhaeri Juhaeri, "Benefit-risk Evaluation: The Past, Present, and Future," *Therapeutic Advances in Drug Safety* 10 (2019): 1–10.
20. FDA, "Benefit-Risk Assessment," Table 1.

21 Ibid., 5.
22 For details and discussion, see the following: Niall Shanks, Ray Greek, and Jean Greek, "Are Animal Models Predictive for Humans?" *Philosophy, Ethics, and Humanities in Medicine* 4.2 (2009), https://doi.org/10.1186/1747-5341-4-2; Ray Greek and Lawrence A. Hansen, "Questions Regarding the Predictive Value of One Evolved Complex Adaptive System for a Second: Exemplified by the SOD1 Mouse," *Progress in Biophysics and Molecular Biology* 113.2 (2013): 231–253; Joseph P. Garner, "The Significance of Meaning: Why Do Over 90% of Behavioral Neuroscience Results Fail to Translate to Humans, and What Can We Do to Fix It?" *ILAR Journal* 55.3 (2014): 438–456; Jessica A. Bolker, "Animal Models in Translational Research: Rosetta Stone or Stumbling Block?" *BioEssays* 39.12 (2017). DOI: 10.1002/bies.201700089; and Garner et al., "Introducing Therioepistemology: The Study of How Knowledge is Gained from Animal Research," *Lab Animal* 46 (2017): 103–113.
23 Stamatiadis et al., "Comparative Analysis of Mouse and Human Preimplantation Development following POU5F1 CRISPR/Cas9 Targeting Reveals Interspecies Differences," *Human Reproduction* 36.5 (2021): 1242–1252.
24 Agar, *Liberal Eugenics*, 165.
25 Ibid., 174.
26 Ibid., 175.
27 For discussion, see the following: Kristine Moe, "Should the Nazi Research Data Be Cited?" *The Hastings Center Report* 14.6 (1984): 5–7; Stephen G. Post, "The Echo of Nuremberg: Nazi Data and Ethics," *Journal of Medical Ethics* 17.1 (1991): 42–44; and David Novak, "Is the Use of Data from Nazi Medical Experiments Justifiable or Not?" *Ethics, Medicine and Public Health* 12 (2020): 100431.
28 Agar, *Liberal Eugenics*, 174–175. Agar wants to distinguish the Nazi scientists from the rogue scientists who will perform germline gene editing by suggesting that the attitude of the latter, like scientists in the past who had performed pioneering vaccination and organ transplantation experiments without knowing their benefits and risks, "will want the best for the clones and genetically modified humans they create." Apparently, in his view, this attitude of beneficence somehow mitigates the injustice of their actions. This argument is fallacious. Human traffickers who buy children from impoverished families are still committing a grave injustice whether or not they believe that their actions would lead to better lives for the children they are trafficking.
29 Chinese scientist, He Jiankui, who helped create the world's first gene-edited babies in experiments that were widely condemned around the world was sentenced to three years in prison for his scientific misconduct. He committed a crime. For details, see Julia Hollingsworth and Isaac Yee, "Chinese Scientist Who Edited Genes of Twin Babies is Jailed for 3 Years," *CNN.com*, December 30, 2019. Available at https://edition.cnn.com/2019/12/30/china/gene-scientist-china-intl-hnk/index.html.

12
FRAMING LONGEVITY SCIENCE AND AN "AGING ENHANCEMENT"

Colin Farrelly

12.1 Introduction

Advances in the biomedical sciences, like the potential development of an applied gerontological intervention (or "aging enhancement"), warrant serious ethical reflection and debate to help ensure scientific innovations are pursued in socially responsible ways. Is it morally permissible, indeed even morally obligatory, to aspire to alter human aging by retarding the biological processes that make human bodies and minds susceptible to chronic disease, frailty, and disability in late life? The ethical analyses likely to be developed to answer this question will be influenced by how the details of longevity science and an aging enhancement are "framed." As the research of Daniel Kahneman and Amos Tversky first demonstrated,[1] human decision-making is profoundly influenced by how an issue is framed. To frame an issue "is to select some aspects of a perceived reality and make them more salient in a communicating text, in such a way as to promote a particular problem definition, causal interpretation, moral evaluation, and/or treatment recommendation for the item described."[2]

This chapter will examine some of the ethical issues surrounding the "framing" of life extension and, more specifically, an aging enhancement. That is, an intervention that would slow the average rate of biological aging in humans. Over the past number of years the prospect of altering the way humans age has been framed by bioethicists in many different ways in debates concerning the ethics of life extension. Consider, for example, the different interests, concerns, and moral sentiments invoked when the prospect of intervening in human aging is framed by leading with one of the following questions:

(1) Is extending life *natural*?
(2) How long *should* humans live?
(3) Can we justify trying to extend the lives of those who *have more* already?
(4) Should we aspire to *prevent* disease (e.g. cancer, heart disease, and stroke), frailty, and disability at all stages of the human lifespan?

For the sake of brevity, I will refer to these questions, respectively, as the "Is extending life *natural*?" question, the "How long is *enough* life?" question, the "What about *equality*?" question, and the "Why promote *public health*?" question. The first three of these questions are framed in such a way as to buttress support for the "aging status quo" by suggesting that something of significant moral value is compromised or threatened by altering the rate of biological aging, and little (if anything) of significance could be expected to be gained by slowing the rate of senescence. This contrasts with question (4), the "Why promote public health?" question, which is framed to make vivid the actual harms of the "aging status quo," as well as the benefits of slowing the aging process. When it comes to ethical debates concerning an aging enhancement, I believe it is much more important to ask the right questions than it is to try to provide answers to the wrong questions.

This chapter makes the case for the conjecture that, of the four questions posited above, the "why promote public health?" question is the proper way to frame ethical debates concerning an aging enhancement if one wishes to advance an informed and balanced ethical analysis of the moral imperative to retard human aging. By contrast, when the valuation of an aging intervention is framed in terms of "What is natural?" or "How long is enough?" or "What about equality?," the moral analyses elicited are prone to *moral myopia* (shortsightedness). Drumwright and Murphy describe moral myopia as:

> a distortion of moral vision, ranging from shortsightedness to near blindness, which affects an individual's perception of an ethical dilemma. Moral myopia hinders moral issues from coming clearly into focus, particularly those that are not proximate, and it can be so severe that it may render a person effectively morally blind. If moral issues are not seen at all or are somehow distorted, it is highly unlikely that sound ethical decision making will occur.[3]

In Sections 12.2, 12.3, and 12.4 of this chapter, I critique the first three framing questions, which I argue elicit moral analyses that are prone to moral myopia. In each of these sections, I lay the foundations for the public health framing of biogerontology, which is emphasized in Section 12.4 of the chapter. Public health is "the science and art of preventing disease, prolonging life and promoting health through the organized efforts and informed choices of society, organizations, public and private, communities and individuals."[4] An aging enhancement would be an integral part of public health in the 21st century given the realities of the health vulnerabilities facing today's aging populations.

12.2 What is aging? And what is "natural"?

The 17th-century philosopher Thomas Hobbes famously described life in the state of nature – that is, life before the benefits of social cooperation and government had been established – as "nasty, brutish and short." Hobbes was certainly correct in his assertion that life, for most humans historically, had been short. But his understanding of why that was the case was limited because he focused primarily on the predicaments caused by conflict (e.g. competition for resources, suspicion, etc.) vs the early mortality caused by infectious diseases. "Prehistoric human remains have never revealed individuals older than about 50 years of age, and humans had a life expectancy at birth of 30 years or less for more than 99.9% of the time that we have inhabited this planet."[5] Such a low life expectancy at birth was primarily the result of the world's *extrinsic* risk factors, such as infectious disease, starvation, poverty, violence, and conflict, etc., all of which caused high levels of early and mid-life mortality.

While Hobbes himself lived an exceptionally long life for the 17th century (91 years), he was a rare exception. In modern England between 1580–1720, it is estimated that "a quarter to a third of children died before the age of fifteen, and for every one thousand babies born alive, between 123 and 154 did not live beyond their first birthdays."[6] The 17th century was typical of most of human history in that it was a century dominated by infectious diseases that caused early-life mortality, diseases like smallpox, tuberculous, dysentery, typhoid fever, and cholera. By contrast, the 21st century is unique in human history as it is the first century ever where, at least to date, most disease and death has occurred from the chronic diseases of late life. The World Health Organization notes that significant progress has been made in the past number of decades in reducing early-life mortality:

> Substantial global progress has been made in reducing child deaths since 1990. The total number of under-5 deaths worldwide has declined from 12.6 million in 1990 to 5.2 million in 2019. Since 1990, the global under-5 mortality rate has dropped by 59%, from 93 deaths per 1,000 live births in 1990 to 38 in 2019. This is equivalent to 1 in 11 children dying before reaching age 5 in 1990, compared to 1 in 27 in 2019.[7]

Even with the ongoing challenges of mitigating the spread of infectious diseases like malaria, HIV/AIDS and (more recently) COVID-19, most humans in the world today will live long enough to develop the chronic diseases of late life that are responsible for most deaths in the world. The populations of the world today are aging. This global phenomenon is one of the most significant, but also neglected, societal developments of the 21st century. Declining early and mid-life mortality means that growing numbers of humans are surviving into late life (age > 70) where they become vulnerable to the multi-morbidities of cancer, heart disease, stroke, dementia, etc.

Life expectancy at birth for a baby born in the world is currently age 73[8] and expected to rise to age 81 by the end of the century.[9] Cardiovascular diseases are the leading cause of death in the world, responsible for an estimated 17.9 million deaths (31% of all deaths) each year.[10] And cancer is the second leading cause of death, killing an estimated 10 million people each year.[11] Chronic diseases are complex diseases, meaning they are influenced by many factors (genes, environment, lifestyle, etc.), but the most significant risk factor for chronic diseases is *age*.

Contemplating the first framing question of an aging enhancement posited in the introduction – is extending life *natural*? – our deliberations about the decision to support or eschew an aging intervention are primed by a number of problematic presuppositions. When the "aging status quo" is defended by critics of longevity science on the grounds that altering aging is "unnatural," what critics typically object to is aspiring for immortality. Such critics often contend that immortality is the true motivation or the logical "endpoint" behind the suggestion that aging must be modulated. In the President's Council of Bioethics report *Beyond Therapy: Biotechnology and the Pursuit of Happiness*,[12] for example, this framing of aging modulation as "pursuing immortality" is captured in the following passage:

> The scientific quest to slow the aging process is not explicitly aimed at conquering death. But in taking the aging of the body as itself a kind of disorder to be corrected, it treats man's mortal condition as a target for medicine, as if death were indeed rather like one of the specific (fatal) diseases. There is no obvious end-point to the quest for ageless bodies: after all, why should any lifespan, however long, be long enough? In principle, the quest for any age-retardation suggests no inherent stopping point, and therefore, in the extreme case, it is difficult to distinguish it from a quest for endless life. It seeks to overcome the ephemeral nature of the human body, and to replace it with permanent facility and endless youth.[13]

Writing in *The New Atlantis*, Leon Kass, who was the chairman of the President's Council of Bioethics, warned of succumbing to the seductive promises of biotechnology, the promises of "a perfect, better-than-human future, in which we shall all be as gods, ageless and blissful."[14] While debates about immortality raise fascinating philosophical and theological questions, immortality is not what biogerontology studies nor aspires to deliver by modulating the aging process. To frame such science by equating it with the pursuit of immortality is, at best, an intellectual distraction and, at worst, disingenuous. Death is certainly inevitable for human beings, creatures that are, by definition, *mortal*. So in one obvious sense "life extension is unnatural" is true if one takes "life extension" to mean "immortality" (i.e. "infinite life extension is unnatural"). But modulating aging should not be equated with immortality. The authors of the *Beyond Therapy* report employ a "sleight of hand" by suggesting that desiring to alter aging means one is really trying to "overcome the ephemeral nature of the human body, and to replace it with permanent facility and endless youth."

Death is inevitable, but it is deeply problematic to suggest that attempts to prevent specific causes of death (e.g. cancer, starvation, or automobile accidents) – which would have the effect of "extending life" – are objectionable because they are in some sense "unnatural." Firstly, there is the problem with defining what is "natural." If by "natural" one means "the way things typically were for humans in our evolutionary past (e.g. 85,000 years ago)," then it is "unnatural" to prevent the early-life mortalities caused by infectious disease, poverty, violence, and war. Hobbes was describing the "natural state" of human life when he described it as "nasty, brutish and short." But just because it was the way things were historically does not mean it provides some moral benchmark by which we should critically assess public health measures that could further reduce mortality and morbidity risks. Humans have been motivated to advance science and technology precisely *because* the world's hostile environment is not conducive to our survival and flourishing.

A further problem with the "altering aging is unnatural" sentiment is that it is actually the aging of the human species (or any species) that is "unnatural." In 1953 the Noble laureate Peter Medawar described senescence as something "revealed and made manifest by the most unnatural experiment of prolonging human life by sheltering it from the hazards of its natural existence."[15] "Humans, and the animals we choose to protect, are the only species in which large numbers experience ageing."[16]

In Michael Sandel's short book titled *The Case Against Perfection: Ethics in the Age of Genetic Engineering*, he argues that a quest to perfect our biology "threatens to banish our appreciation of life as a gift, and to leave us with nothing to affirm or behold outside of our own will."[17] When targeted against the aspiration to retard biological aging, the charge that "perfectionism" threatens life as a gift can be abated by responding: "Does the development of a COVID-19 vaccine threaten our appreciation of life as a gift?" or "Does chemotherapy or surgery to unblock a coronary artery threaten our appreciation of life as a gift?" We are motivated to try to prevent and treat disease precisely *because life is a gift*. Likewise, an applied gerontological intervention is also compatible with the sentiment that life is a gift as it is a form of *preventative medicine*.

A defender of the "extending life is unnatural?" position might respond to my criticisms by claiming that it is not only the desire for immortality that is morally objectionable but the attempt to extend life beyond a certain age. Daniel Callahan, for example, has advocated for setting age limits on access to medical care in his book *Setting Limits: Medical Costs in an Aging Society*.[18] According to Callahan:

> The average person in good health in the developed countries of the world (and living in a reasonably safe environment), *already* lives long enough to accomplish most reasonable ends… Neither the human species as a whole, nor most individuals, need more than the present average life expectancy in the developed countries (the mid-seventies to low-eighties) for a perfectly satisfactory life. This idea of a steady-state life expectancy at its present level would establish, happily, a finite and attainable goal: "Enough, already."[19]

It is one thing for a person of advanced age to decide for herself that she has lived enough life and that she voluntarily decides to forfeit medical interventions that could delay the onset of disease, frailty, disability, and death. But it is something else for a bioethicist to proclaim that society should decide, on behalf of the people most at risk of chronic diseases, that they should be satisfied with the health they had up to a certain age and thus now accept the fate of what senescence brings them. Such an attitude is simple ageism. Robert Butler, the first director of the NIH's National

Institutes of Aging, coined the term "ageism" in 1969,[20] which means a systematic stereotyping of, and discrimination against, people because they are old.

Callahan's position is subject to charges of ageism as it rejects the equality of older persons and their entitlement to the benefits of medicine when such benefits include the extension of healthy life (as would be realized by slowing the aging process). I now turn to the second framing of an aging intervention – the "how long is *enough*?" question. The sentiment that there is an age at which humans have "lived long enough" is a key part of Callahan's justification for setting age limits on medical care, so it is an important frame to consider and critically assess.

12.3 How long is too long?

In the previous section, I argued that the wrong societal discussion to have regarding an aging intervention is "what is natural?" or "do we want to be immortal?" Such questions do raise intriguing philosophical and theological questions, but they are not the questions that should be at the forefront of a discussion about the ethics of an aging enhancement. This is so because such questions marginalize the central rationale for wanting to modulate biological aging in the first place – that is, to prevent disease, frailty, and disability – by distracting our deliberations with questions about what is "natural" and if immortality itself is desirable. Rather than tackling the alleged (e.g. metaphysical) "puzzles" posed by longevity science, ethical debates concerning an aging enhancement should focus instead on the pressing *problems* posed by biological and global aging (e.g. the rapid rise in chronic disease, frailty, and disability). This helps guard against myopic ethical analyses that eschew the harms of the aging "status quo."

The second problematic framing of longevity science is raising the question "How long *should* humans live?" Like the "what is natural?" question, the "How long is enough life?" question derails an ethical analysis of longevity science by asking the wrong question. What makes the "How long is enough life?" question the wrong question to ask is that it adopts a myopic lens of the actual moral landscape facing the world's aging populations in the 21st century. To be more specific, I will identify two general framing problems with the "How long is enough life?" question.

Firstly, there is an *ambiguity* inherent in the question, as it leaves open the issue of whether the question is actually concerned with trying to limit the human *healthspan* or the amount of time humans can survive by delaying death via managing multi-morbidity, frailty, and disability. In other words, the question risks conflating the issues of the *quality* and *quantity* of life, and it is critical to disentangle those two issues when evaluating an aging enhancement. Secondly, the framing of the question is misguided because it presumes that the empirically valid, morally defensible, and proportionate response to the potential societal concerns of life extension (e.g. overpopulation, climate change, etc.) is to forfeit public health measures.

With respect to the first concern about the ambiguity of the "how long is enough life?" question, consider the different sentiments we are likely to have when the details of what might be entailed in such a question are made more concrete and specific. Contrast, for example, the following two questions (Q1 and Q2):

> Q1: "How long should older persons survive in long-term care facilities managing multi-morbidity and frailty in the final stage of life?"
> Q2: "How long should humans remain healthy, happy, and independent?"

For the first question, many people might share the (not unreasonable) sentiment that it would be desirable to have a limit on how long human survival should persist in such a vulnerable state. Such a predicament is very costly, not only in terms of the medical resources needed to prolong the survival of people in such circumstances, but there is also the emotional burden placed on families (including the patient) of surviving extended periods of time in such a dependent state.

In the scenario described in Q1 we might feel that Callahan's statement of "enough, already" has traction, but it only does so when applied to the predicament of suffering prolonged periods of suffering and infirmity at the end of life. Whatever force "enough, already" has, it is derived from the sentiment that humans should not aspire to extend the period of time humans survive managing disease, frailty, and disability when doing so has seriously compromised their *quality of life*. This is why many countries have implemented, or are at least considering implementing, medical assistance in dying. But this stance is not incompatible with the position that we should support an aging enhancement to increase the human healthspan.

When we turn to Q2 – "How long should humans remain healthy, happy, and productive?" – very different sentiments are likely to be invoked vs those invoked when contemplating Q1. Is health the kind of good that people can have too much of? Would we consider limiting the number of years of a healthy person who enjoys a quality life? When framed in this way we see that the question "how long is enough?" is an ill-formed question. When framed as "how long should humans remain healthy, happy, and productive?" we are likely to respond – "as long as possible!" The death of a healthy, independent, and happy person, say from an automobile accident, would be considered a "premature" death and tragedy, regardless of their chronological age.

Sometimes the "how long is enough?" question is raised to oppose increasing life extension technologies because it is believed life extension would exacerbate other pressing societal problems, like population size and/or climate change. I am willing to concede the point that increasing the human healthspan raises legitimate *concerns* like population size and climate change, concerns that all societies should take seriously (regardless of new life-extending technologies). In *Beyond Humanity*, Allen Buchanan makes a useful distinction between a *concern* about biomedical enhancement and *an objection*. The former is merely a "con," a reason against it. But an *objection* to an enhancement is a much stronger claim. An objection is an "all-things-considered" judgment that an enhancement is undesirable because the cons outweigh any pros. As Buchanan (2011) notes, "all objections are concerns, but not all concerns are objections."[21] Population density and climate change are certainly concerns worth addressing seriously, but they do not constitute objections to pursuing an aging enhancement.

Suppose the critic of longevity science frames their opposition to altering human aging in one of the following two ways:

> Claim #1 (C1): "The world already faces the problem of overpopulation, so when it comes to the prospect of a new biomedical enhancement that will extend the period of time humans live, we must pause and ask: "How long is enough?"
>
> Claim #2 (C2): "The world already faces the problem of climate change caused by our emission of greenhouse gases, so when it comes to the prospect of a new biomedical enhancement that will extend the period of time humans live, we must pause and ask: "How long is enough?"

These two claims are framed in such a way as to highlight only a potential "con" of altering human aging, but the implication often is that this is *sufficient* for establishing that this concern constitutes an *objection* to altering aging. But both claims are myopic for what they assume (i.e. forfeiting public health measures is the best way to tackle population density and climate change) and what they omit (i.e. the other societal benefits altering aging is likely to confer beyond simply "more life"). Sustainable population sizes and regard for climate change are morally laudable aspirations, but it is a mistake to see the forfeiture of public health measures that prevent disease, frailty, and disability – and yield sizable economic dividends associated with these reductions in health challenges – as the empirically valid, morally sound, and proportionate response to such ends.

In those regions of the world where population density is a serious problem (most of the developed world is well below replacement fertility levels), aspiring to *curb high fertility rates* would be a sensible public policy response versus suggesting that preventative or therapeutic medical interventions should be forfeited. The provision of birth control, further economic development, the education of women, changing attitudes about the gender roles of men and women, etc. – all of these types of policies and cultural changes could address potential concerns about population density in a manner consistent with public health. A society can promote a public health priority of healthy aging *and* a multitude of policies designed to address population density concerns.

A similar response can be made to C2. The error of its implied reasoning is to see forfeiting preventative medicine as a sensible way to redress the problem of climate change. But consider, for example, that the World Health Organization estimates that, under a base case socioeconomic scenario, there will be approximately 250,000 additional deaths due to climate change per year between 2030 and 2050.[22] These are certainly worrying numbers and action should be taken to try to prevent these additional deaths. However, the annual death toll from chronic disease in late life *today* (rather than in 20–30 years) number *millions* of annual deaths every year. Just as one should not endorse forfeiting smoking cessation, peace, or the wearing of seat belts as a way to tackle climate change, one should not propose forfeiting the public health measure of age retardation for such an aim. Instead, one should advocate for empirically valid, morally justified, and proportionate responses to this problem (e.g. promoting the development and widespread use of energy technologies that will help prevent climate change and/or the societal adaptations needed to minimize its harms).

And finally, C1 and C2 are myopic in their framing because they ignore the non-health benefits of age retardation, especially in lower- and middle-income countries. In developing countries that do not have the wealth to fund the pensions and healthcare programs of richer countries, the imperative to promote healthy aging is even more stark. In "The Brasilia Declaration on Ageing" (July 1996), global aging is described as a *development* issue:

> Ageing is a development issue. Healthy, older persons are a resource for their families, their communities and the economy. Their usually unpaid and unsung contributions are indispensable for development.
>
> Ageing is universal, affects every individual and family, community and society. The numbers of older persons are growing steadily. There are gender implications: older women are disproportionately represented among the oldest old and the most disadvantaged and they constitute the backbone of caregiving.[23]

As the WHO statement makes clear, the caring (typically unpaid) duties for older parents typically fall to female family members. Keeping older persons healthier for longer, and compressing the period of disease and frailty at the end of life, could help mitigate (rather than exacerbate) these unequal (gendered) caring duties. When framed correctly, a fair and transparent valuation of an aging intervention will draw attention to its contributions to preventative medicine, as well as economic development and equality between the sexes.

12.4 Equality

The third, and perhaps most prevalent, framing perspective employed in bioethics when assessing an aging intervention concerns the potential predicament posed by the *unequal access* to such technology. This concern is raised when the question of life extension is posed, as Pijnenburg and Leget,[24] and Mauron[25] do, by asking the question: "How can we justify trying to extend the lives of those who have more already?"

Like the other framing questions critiqued so far, this question about inequality possesses a number of problematic premises, and as such, it is not a useful frame to employ when deliberating about the pros and cons of pursuing an aging enhancement. In this section, I identify a number of problematic issues with the equality framing perspective which, taken together, warrant rejecting this way of framing longevity science. The problems I identify are five-fold:

(1) It is a mistake to construe the issue as one of global justice where an aging enhancement would only benefit people living in rich countries and not poor countries (since aging is universal).
(2) It is a mistake to characterize the issue as one of "unequal death" vs "unequal health." An aging intervention is important not because it postpones death but because it promotes *health* in later life (a side-effect of which is life extension).
(3) It is a mistake to construe health as a zero-sum game (an assumption that is often implied in the equality objection to life extension).
(4) It is a mistake to think that public health measures must operate in a *sequential* fashion, completely redressing one particular public health problem before investing any effort (e.g. resources and innovation) into tackling another problem.
(5) It is a mistake to object to slowing aging on the assumption that the "aging status quo" is in some sense either "equal," or at least more equal, than a world where an aging intervention exists.

After detailing these deficiencies of the equality objection to an aging enhancement, I do acknowledge there is a legitimate *concern* at stake in its framing, namely that an applied gerontological intervention ought to be fairly diffused, both globally and domestically. But that aspiration is not incompatible with, indeed I believe it can be complementary to, the claim that altering human aging is a pressing moral imperative.

One common faulty premise of the equality framing on an aging intervention is the mistaken understanding that the world is divided between rich countries where people mostly die "old" and poor countries where people mostly die "young." In this simplistic view of the world, an aging intervention is construed as a technological intervention that could only benefit the people who already enjoy the longest lives in the richest countries. Mauron is perhaps the best example of someone making this point, claiming that we must take seriously the "reality of unequal death in today's world, in which differences in longevity highlight the gap between the haves and the have-nots."[26] And Pijnenburg and Leget echo Mauron, citing the difference in life expectancy in African countries south of the Sahara and life expectancy in developed countries. While it is true that countries with lower life expectancies have higher early-life mortality risks, like those posed by malaria and HIV/AIDS, it would be a mistake to think that chronic diseases like cancer, heart disease, and stroke are *only* a problem in the richest countries in the world. Aging is universal, and population aging is a global phenomenon. Most of the deaths in the world from chronic disease in late life in fact occur in countries that are not among the richest but are the most populous (e.g. China) aging countries. All of the world's populations are aging; it is not only the richest countries that face the public health predicament of promoting health in late life.

Lower- and middle-income countries, like the world's richest countries, face growing health burdens from the chronic diseases of late life. In fact, the risks to the poor are even more significant because of the additional vulnerability they face from aging without the security provisions citizens in wealthier countries enjoy, like the provision of government pensions and universal healthcare. As I already noted in Section 12.3, the World Health Organization conceives of aging as a development issue. Healthy older persons are a resource for their families, community, and economy. Extending the human healthspan would improve the economic, as well as health prospects, of the poor in both developing and developed countries.

Secondly, Mauron's framing of the issue as one of "unequal death" is myopic because it reduces the moral stakes at risk in discussing an aging intervention to simply "preventing death." But the stakes involved in an applied gerontological intervention are much more significant than this.

Instead of focusing on the issue of "unequal death," what Mauron should really address is the predicament of "unequal health." An aging intervention is important not because it postpones death but because it promotes *health* in later life (a side-effect of which is life extension). All humans, rich and poor, will inevitably die. So mortality ensures a certain level of equality will, eventually, be achieved. But the focus of a moral analysis of an aging intervention should really be on health inequities (which the aging process exacerbates) and not on death itself.

The third mistake that is common in the equality framing of opposition to an aging intervention is the presumption that health is a *zero-sum game*. In zero-sum games, there is a fixed distributive good that can be dispersed among persons such that giving more of that good to one person means there is less of that good available to other people. If health were a zero-sum game, we might envision a scenario where we have 100 years of health to distribute among two persons. If we distributed 50 years to each person, we could not increase the healthy years of one person (e.g. add an additional 5 years to boost them to 55 years in total) without taking from the number of healthy years of the other person (reducing by 5 years to 45 years). But in the real world health is not a zero-sum game. Promoting the health of people in late life does not mean there is less health available for those at risk of early and mid-life morbidity and mortality. Preventing cancer, stroke, and Alzheimer's disease among people in later life does not mean there is less health available for children who develop malaria or tuberculosis. There is not a fixed pot of health from which health is distributed. The zero-sum predicament does arise for treatments and therapies where there are limited medical resources, a predicament which is exacerbated when the goal of extending life via attempts to treat every single disease and ailment of aging is pursued in earnest without altering biological aging.

Fourthly, the "What about equality?" framing of longevity science is myopic in that it presumes public health measures must operate in a *sequential* fashion, completely redressing one particular public health problem (e.g. early-life mortality) before investing any effort (e.g. resources and innovation) into tackling another problem. But this is not a valid presupposition. If it were, the vast majority of medical interventions in the developed world would be just as objectionable as an aging intervention. For example, when offering chemotherapy to a 70-year-old patient living in the United States, we must ask "What about equality?" when the reality is there are children dying from malaria in the developing world. Before providing speech and physiotherapy to stroke patients, the equality framing requires us to ask "What about equality?" given the existence of early-life disadvantage. But this posits a distorted vision of the moral landscape because it imposes a dichotomized understanding of the duty to aid others. This duty does not apply only to mitigating all early-life disadvantages before any moral concern and action can be taken to mitigate the health risks of late life. We can, and should, do many things at the same time, including intervening in the aging process to increase the human healthspan.

The fifth and final critique I raise against the equality framework of an aging enhancement is, I believe, the most important and compelling one. It is a mistake to object to slowing aging on the presumption that the "aging status quo" is in some sense either "equal," or at least more equal, than a world where an aging intervention exists.

While both chronological and biological aging are universal, the rate of the latter is not equal for everyone. The "aging status quo" is one of *inequality* with respect to the rate of biological aging. For example, when objecting to the inequality that he believes an aging intervention will create, Mauron remarks:

> This is the biting irony of antiageing: the haves will have earlier access to it than the have-nots, just as for any innovative technology. But in addition, the technology will give them more of what they already have more of: disease-free years of life.[27]

But existing health inequalities are not just determined by socioeconomic inequalities. They are also profoundly shaped by the natural determinants (genes) at play with health, especially as they pertain to the rate of senescence. And this is important to emphasize as it reveals the ways the "aging status quo" is rife with inequality that goes beyond the inequality between "the rich" and "the poor."

While all humans chronologically age at the same rate, there is a vast degree of variation in terms of the rate of biological aging (which influences our risks of disease, frailty, and disability). For example, about one in four million children are born with progeria,[28] a rare condition of accelerated aging. Progeria is caused by a genetic mutation in the LMNA gene, and these children suffer extreme premature aging and an average life expectancy of around 13–14 years. By contrast, the vast majority of humans experience a rate of biological aging that limits average life expectancy to around age 85. Jeffrey Fries explains how estimates of the human lifespan are arrived at:

> There are several methods of estimating the human life span. One may use the anthropological formulas, reconstruct an ideal survival curve from the tail of the present curve using the assumption that these individuals have been essentially free of disease, make extrapolations from the rectangularizing survival curve, or use estimates based on observed decline in organ reserve. All suggest an average life span of approximately 85 years, with a distribution which includes 99 percent of individuals between the ages of 70 and 100.[29]

There is reason to think that the health effects of differential rates of biological aging are manifest by mid-life. In a recent study in *Nature Aging*, which followed a cohort of 1,037 infants born in the same year to age 45, it was found that people who are aging more rapidly than same-age peers in mid-life may prematurely need support to sustain independence that is usually reserved for older adults.[30]

But there is a third category of (rare) persons that do not experience the accelerated aging of progeria nor the average rate of aging of most humans but instead have *decelerated* biological aging and are the longest-lived humans – centenarians (age ≥ 100) and supercentenarians (age ≥ 110). Jeanne Louise Calment, from France, died in 1997 at the age of 122, and she was the oldest person whose age has been verified by official documents. Healthy aging in a person with an average lifespan of around 85 years is a complex phenotype, determined by both environment and genes. But in the case of exceptionally long-lived persons like Jeanne Louise Calment, genetics becomes extremely important. Having a centenarian sibling increases one's chances of survival to very old age.[31] Furthermore, the offspring of long-lived parents have a significantly lower prevalence of hypertension (by 23%), diabetes mellitus (by 50%), heart attacks (by 60%), and strokes (no events reported) than several age-matched control groups.[32]

The maximum human lifespan is believed to be around 125 years.[33] The prevalence of supercentenarians (age ≥ 110) and even centenarians (age ≥ 100) is very low. In the United States and other industrialized nations, centenarians occur at a prevalence rate of about one per six thousand. And supercentenarians occur at a rate of about one per seven million.[34] People with exceptional longevity are not the most affluent persons, former Olympic athletes, etc., which suggests that people with exceptional longevity may interact with environmental factors differently than others.[35] These long-lived humans are an important biological puzzle to examine not simply because they live so long, but because they typically experience a delay, and compression, of morbidity.

With centenarians, for example, there are three different categories of centenarians – "delayers," "survivors," and "escapers."[36] The "delayers" are people who make it to 100 years with a delay of the onset of common age-associated illnesses. "Survivors" are people who were diagnosed with an illness prior to age 80 but survived for at least two more decades. And the third category of centenarians are "escapers," people who escaped the most lethal diseases, such as heart disease, non-skin cancer, and stroke.

When the "aging status quo" is framed within the insights of biogerontology we see that species biologically age at different rates (e.g. mice vs the bowhead whale), but so too do members of the same species. Some humans have accelerated aging which reduces life expectancy by 70 years, most humans age at a rate that makes it feasible for most (provided they live in a safe environment with access to the social determinants of health) to survive seven to eight decades of life, and some (rare) individuals with decelerated aging might enjoy a century of disease-free life. So there already exists an "aging inequality," with decades of healthy life separating the "accelerated," "average," and "slowed" aging groups. Fixating only on the potential inequality that could arise if the rich with an average lifespan could extend their life further with an aging intervention misses this more nuanced understanding of the different types of inequalities at play in the social and natural lotteries of life.

Despite my highlighting of the problems I believe are inherent in the equality framing of an aging enhancement, this framing does raise a significant *concern* (versus objection) that ought to be taken seriously. And that concern is how accessible an aging intervention is likely to be, both to the poor in rich countries and to the global poor. The cost and accessibility of such an intervention will depend largely on the kind of technology it is. If such an intervention required genome editing in a world-class medical facility then the obstacles to ensuring the fair diffusion of the technology would be very significant. The encouraging news is that the most likely, at least for the first generation, "anti-aging" intervention is likely to be something that is not cost prohibitive and can be widely diffused. The aging interventions actually being tested are "anti-aging pills," a technology where the costs are mostly associated with research and development vs the actual dispersal of the intervention.

A fertile source for therapies slowing aging is FDA-approved drugs whose safety has been investigated.[37] Repurposed drugs that have been in existence for many decades will be off-patent (which means they can be developed at a fraction of the original costs) and have an extensive track record for safety. One of the top contenders for the first "aging intervention" is metformin. Metformin is an oral antidiabetic drug that has been used since the late 1950s. Because of its low cost and proven safety over many decades, metformin is among one of the top candidates for a likely first generation of applied gerontological interventions. TAME (Targeting Aging with Metformin) is a clinical trial to test the drug metformin as a safe and effective intervention against several age-related diseases.[38] Another drug that targets aging is rapamycin, originally discovered in the soil on Easter Island more than half a century ago.[39] In a 2009 study of mice[40] Harrison et al found that this intervention increased the median and maximal lifespan of both male and female mice. The initial study concludes that rapamycin may extend lifespan by postponing death from cancer, by retarding mechanisms of aging, or both. Since this initial report in 2009, there have been 14 additional studies showing that rapamycin increased the lifespans of male and female mice. "The current mouse data conclusively demonstrate that rapamycin is effective in preventing/reversing a broad range of age-related conditions, including lifespan with minimal adverse effects or toxicity."[41]

The concern about equal access to an aging "pill" is a valid one, but the appropriate response to this concern is not to reject or forfeit such an intervention but rather to argue that it must be equally accessible to all. Like the COVID-19 vaccines, an "anti-aging drug" would be a critical public health intervention that all persons in the world should have access to. Rather than object to an aging enhancement, the more appropriate response would be to recognize how important an aging intervention is to the public health of the world's aging populations and champion both its development and its fair diffusion.

12.5 The public health frame

The prospect of an "aging enhancement" raises both philosophical *puzzles* (e.g. is immortality desirable?) and pressing ethical *problems* (e.g. preventing chronic disease, frailty, and disability, increasing population size and climate change, etc.) depending on how such an intervention is framed. In this chapter, I have detailed the case for advancing an ethical analysis that conceptualizes the development of an applied gerontological intervention as an important technological innovation to help us redress the health challenges posed by global aging. By critically assessing the frames of the "Is life extension natural?" question, the "How long is enough?" question, and the "What about equality?" question, I have already advanced the case for framing an aging enhancement within a public health framework. So to conclude this chapter, I will bring these more disparate points together to make the case more concise and explicit.

Public health is concerned with promoting the health of populations, and this concern with health applies across the whole human lifespan, including the health of persons in late life. The first three life extension/"aging enhancement" frames I have critically assessed could, and indeed sometimes have been, raised against other significant public health advances that have helped promote the health of populations. Anti-vaxxers often oppose vaccines because they are not considered "natural." And those swayed by Malthusian predictions of the ills of overpopulation may believe that "widely available life extension diminishes the total net welfare of the human race."[42] The myopia of such perspectives is dislodged when the framing of population aging and longevity science puts the disease burden of the aging status quo in the *foreground* of the discussions and debates about an aging enhancement.

Unprecedented numbers of humans are surviving into late life. And surviving beyond the seventh decade of life means increased risks of cancer, heart disease, and stroke, Alzheimer's disease and dementia, etc. The COVID-19 pandemic was a vivid illustration of the health vulnerabilities today's aging populations face. To help protect persons from infectious and chronic diseases in late life, public health must prioritize the effort to alter the rate of biological aging so that the average person can enjoy more healthy years of life, and compress the period of time spent with multimorbidity, frailty, and disability. An aging enhancement is likely to be among one of the most important advances in public health in the 21st century. And I believe the public health frame is the appropriate one to invoke if we hope to inspire informed and socially responsible discussion and debate on the ethics of an aging intervention.

Notes

1 Tversky, A., and Kahneman, D. (1981). "The Framing of Decisions and the Psychology of Choice," *Science* 211(4481): 453–8.
2 Entman, Robert M. (1993). "Framing: Toward Clarification of a Fractured Paradigm," *Journal of Communication* 43: 51–58, p. 52.
3 Drumwright, M., and Murphy, P. (2004). "How Advertising Practitioners View Ethics," *Journal of Advertising* 33(2): 7–24, p. 11.
4 Winslow, C. (1920). "The Untilled Fields of Public Health," *Science* 51(1306): 23–33, p. 23.
5 Hayflick, L. (2000). "The Future of Ageing," *Nature* 408: 267–69, 269.
6 Hannah Newton, *The Sick Child in Early Modern England, 1580–1720*. Oxford: Oxford University Press, 2012, p. 2.
7 www.who.int/news-room/fact-sheets/detail/children-reducing-mortality.
8 www.who.int/data/gho/data/indicators/indicator-details/GHO/life-expectancy-at-birth-(years).
9 United Nations, Department of Economic and Social Affairs, Population Division. (2011). *World Population Prospects: The 2010 Revision, Highlights and Advance Tables*. New York: United Nations, p. xviii.
10 www.who.int/health-topics/cardiovascular-diseases#tab=tab_1.
11 Ferlay, J., Ervik, M., Lam, F., Colombet, M., Mery, L., Piñeros, M., et al. (2020). *Global Cancer Observatory: Cancer Today*. Lyon: International Agency for Research on Cancer (https://gco.iarc.fr/today, accessed March 2021).
12 President's Council on Bioethics. (2003). *Beyond Therapy: Biotechnology and the Pursuit of Happiness*. Available at https://bioethicsarchive.georgetown.edu/pcbe/reports/beyondtherapy/index.html.
13 Ibid., p. 162.
14 /www.thenewatlantis.com/publications/ageless-bodies-happy-souls.
15 Medawar, P. (1952). *An Unsolved Problem of Biology*. Lewis: London, p. 13.

16 Hayflick, L. (2000). "The Future of Ageing," *Nature* 408(6809): 267–269, 269.
17 Sandel, M. (2007). *The Case Against Perfection: Ethics in the Age of Genetic Engineering*. Cambridge: Harvard University Press, pp. 99–100.
18 Callaghan, D. (1987). *Setting Limits: Medical Costs in an Aging Society*. Washington, DC: Georgetown University Press.
19 Callahan, D. (1998). *False Hopes: Why America's Quest for Perfect Health is a Recipe for Failure*. New York, NY: Simon and Schuster, p. 82.
20 Butler, R. N. (1969). "Age-ism: Another Form of Bigotry," *The Gerontologist* 9(4): 243–246.
21 Buchanan, A. (2011). *Beyond Humanity*. Oxford: Oxford University Press, p. 71.
22 World Health Organization. (2014). *Quantitative Risk assessment of the Effects of Climate Change on Selected Causes of Death, 2030s and 2050s*. Geneva: World Health Organization, p. 1.
23 WHO Programme on Ageing and Health, Division of Health Promotion, Education and Communication. (1997). "The Brasilia Declaration on Ageing," *Health Promotion International* 12(2): 175–178, p. 177.
24 Pijnenburg, M. A., and Leget, C. (2007). "Who Wants to Live Forever? Three Arguments against Extending the Human Lifespan," *Journal of Medical Ethics* 33(10): 585–587.
25 Mauron, A. (2005). "The Choosy Reaper. From the Myth of Eternal Youth to the Reality of Unequal Death," *EMBO Reports* 6 Spec No(Suppl 1): S67–S71.
26 Ibid., S67.
27 Ibid., S70.
28 www.genome.gov/Genetic-Disorders/Progeria.
29 Fries, J. (2005). "The Compression of Morbidity," *The Milbank Quarterly* 83(4): 801–823, p. 808.
30 Elliott, M. L. et al. (2021). "Disparities in the Pace of Biological Aging among Midlife Adults of the Same Chronological Age have Implications for Future Frailty Risk and Policy," *Nature Aging* (1): 295–308.
31 Perls, T. et al. (1998). "Siblings of Centenarians Live Longer," *The Lancet* 351(9115): 1560.
32 Atzmon, G. et al. (2004). "Clinical Phenotype of Families with Longevity," *Journal of the American Geriatrics Society* 52(2): 274–277.
33 Weon, B. M., and Je, J. H. (2009). "Theoretical Estimation of Maximum Human Lifespan," *Biogerontology* 10(1): 65–71.
34 Boston University's New England Centenarian Study at: www.bumc.bu.edu/centenarian/overview.
35 Rajpathak, S. N., Liu, Y., Ben-David, O., Reddy, S., Atzmon, G., Crandall, J., and Barzilai, N. (2011). "Lifestyle Factors of People with Exceptional Longevity," *Journal of the American Geriatrics Society* 59(8): 1509–1512.
36 Evert, J. et al. (2007). "Morbidity Profiles of Centenarians: Survivors, Delayers, and Escapers," *The Journals of Gerontology: Series A, Biological Sciences and Medical Sciences* 58(3): M232–M237.
37 Snell, T. W., Johnston, R. K., Srinivasan, B., Zhou, H., Gao, M., and Skolnick, J. (2016). "Repurposing FDA-Approved Drugs for Anti-aging Therapies," *Biogerontology* 17(5–6): 907–920.
38 Barzilai, N., Crandall, J. P., Kritchevsky, S. B., and Espeland, M. A. (2016). "Metformin as a Tool to Target Aging," *Cell Metabolism* 23(6): 1060–1065.
39 Vézina, C., Kudelski, A., and Sehgal, S. N. (1975). "Rapamycin (AY-22,989), a New Antifungal Antibiotic. I. Taxonomy of the Producing Streptomycete and Isolation of the Active Principle," *The Journal of Antibiotics* (Tokyo) 28(10): 721–6.
40 Harrison, D. E., Strong, R., Sharp, Z. D., Nelson, J. F., Astle, C. M., Flurkey, K., Nadon, N. L., Wilkinson, J. E., Frenkel, K., Carter, C. S., Pahor, M., Javors, M. A., Fernandez, E., and Miller, R. A. (2009). "Rapamycin Fed Late in Life Extends Lifespan in Genetically Heterogeneous Mice," *Nature* 460(7253): 392–5.
41 Selvarani, R., Mohammed, S., and Richardson, A. (2020). "Effect of Rapamycin on Aging and Age-related Diseases-past and Future," *Geroscience*. Epub ahead of print. https://doi.org/10.1007/s11357-020-00274-1 P. 15 updated?
42 Davis, John. (2005). "Life-extension and the Malthusian Objection," *Journal of Medicine and Philosophy* 30(1): 27–44, p. 28.

13
CHRISTIAN THEOLOGY AND THE ETHICAL AMBIGUITIES OF AGING ATTENUATION

Todd T.W. Daly

13.1 The challenges of an aging society

The quest for longer life is as old as humanity itself and is marked by a bizarre history that chronicles everything from ancient meditative techniques and fountain legends to the search for potable gold and xenotransplantation (monkey gonads). More recent, scientifically-informed techniques known as "biohacking" have only been slightly less eccentric, involving stem cell transplants, hyperbaric oxygen, and cryotherapy chambers, ketogenic diets with Bulletproof coffee, nootropic smart drugs, and pulsed electromagnetic field therapy.[1] Though the efficacy of most of these biohacks remains highly questionable at best, developed countries have experienced a near doubling in life expectancy over the last century, due in large part to improvements in public health and medicine – such as the reduction in infant mortality – economic growth, and ongoing development in the areas of nutrition, behavior, and education.[2] As a result of these improvements, Americans born in 2000 could expect, on average, to live to nearly 80 years, compared to just 47 years in 1900.[3]

However, these gains have led to an increasingly aged society, characterized by significant increases in a host of age-related diseases such as Parkinson's, high blood pressure, dementia, and heart disease. While the defining characteristic of our age seems to be that we are both younger longer and older longer, there are concerns that we are on the precipice of a "mass geriatric society," where an increasing percentage of the US population is expected to live to the age of 85 and beyond, experiencing a prolonged, irrevocable progression of chronic illness, increased fragility, and disability lasting many years.[4] A Rand Corporation study indicated that this particular trajectory for the chronically ill – described as "prolonged dwindling" from dementia, disabling strokes, or generalized frailty, "usually lasting many years" – had already accounted for roughly 40 percent of all deaths in 2003.[5]

These demographic changes continue to place enormous burdens on a US healthcare system that is still learning to respond to these changes at the end of life. The very system that has contributed to these dramatic increases in life expectancy now faces the intolerable burden of its own success as waves of baby boomers are now requiring treatment for the diseases that accompany old age. Alzheimer's disease and dementia are already more expensive to treat than cancer and heart disease, costing Medicare and Medicaid over 200 billion dollars in 2020.[6] Given that the number of individuals with Alzheimer's is expected to rise from 4 million in 2005 to nearly 14 million in 2050, the cost of treating this disease alone is estimated at 584 billion dollars in 2050.[7] Moreover, any success in significantly mitigating any one disease – whether Alzheimer's or the most common forms of cancer – would result in a mere three-year gain in overall life expectancy and do little to assuage the population growth of those 85 years and older, though not all epidemiologists would agree.[8] These findings have led to the recent formation of the Longevity Dividend Initiative Consortium (LDIC), founded by epidemiologists, gerontologists, and economists, among others, devoted to understanding the human aging process itself in order that it might be attenuated.[9] The Longevity Dividend is founded on a growing body of evidence indicating that human aging can be decelerated, enabling us to live longer, healthier lives, allowing older people to remain "useful" – a rather troubling term – to their communities and society as a whole, creating wealth for such individuals and the nations they inhabit.[10]

13.2 Slowing human aging

Indeed, recent laboratory evidence suggests that human aging may be attenuated. Over the last two decades, scientists have extended the healthy lifespans of nematode worms, fruit flies, and mice by slowing the aging process through genetic engineering, caloric restriction, and other techniques. Scientists are now searching for human analogs, and limited human trials have shown age reversal in older adults as measured by DNA methylation.[11] In contrast to transhumanist doctrine which aims at a radical extension of the lifespan, the Consortium envisions a modest deceleration of aging sufficient to delay all age-related diseases by approximately seven years, a delay that would compress the period of morbidity before death and produce benefits more substantial than what might be achieved by eliminating cancer and heart disease.[12] If successful, the deceleration would not only reduce the age-specific risk of death, frailty, and disability by roughly half at every age but would also, it is believed, yield comparable health and longevity benefits for successive generations. Purportedly, according to the LDIC, devoting increased funds to slowing aging as the underlying cause of all age-related diseases makes good sense from a scientific, economic, and public health perspective.

Though anti-aging research has moved from legend to the laboratory, it is far from certain that even a modest deceleration of aging will produce the desired effects as expressed by the Consortium. More generally, there is no widespread agreement on whether the main goal of life extension should be to focus on significantly extending healthy life (adding years to life) or to compress the period of morbidity with the possibility of a marginal gain in longevity (adding life to years). Transhumanists seem uniformly committed to the former, including engineering immortality, and those of the Longevity Consortium to the latter. The more hyperbolic claims of some transhumanists notwithstanding, both scenarios interpret human aging as a target for our best manipulative efforts. While both see aging as a problem, perhaps the more challenging case, ethically speaking, concerns the possibility of the more modest gains envisioned by the LDIC.

13.3 Christian responses to life extension

While religious responses to life extension have been varied, Christians have tended to view aging attenuation with a considerable degree of suspicion, earning the scorn of those who fully embrace the larger project of human enhancement. Indeed, it is not uncommon for transhumanists to label those who express skepticism about engineering longevity as "Bio-Luddites," or as those who desire nothing more than to "abandon human progress for a perpetual present," whether such suspicions are technological, sociological, political, or religious.[13] As recent surveys have shown, many Christians resist life extension by slowing aging on doctrinal grounds, with two of the common reasons being that it is contrary to the will of God who determines the boundaries of human existence and that the promise of the afterlife considerably relativizes concern over the length of earthly life, thereby rendering it less appealing, especially if the afterlife entails eternal youth.[14] Paul's exclamation to the church in Philippi – "to live is Christ, and to die is gain." (Phil. 1:20 RSV) – is often seen as a biblical expression of this relativization. Indeed, a recent study among students at a

Christian university uncovered an inverse relationship between those who hold certain religious beliefs – especially positive views of an afterlife – and the desirability of life extension.[15] Those who reflected a willingness to defer to God's will and a belief in an afterlife were less likely to desire life extension. Moreover, those who scored higher on intrinsic religiosity showed a "significant negative correlation with a desire to use a strong life extension [i.e. extending the current maximum lifespan] intervention."[16] As co-author Loren Martin concluded: "From our data, it is clear that the Christian population is less in favor of life-extending technologies than non-Christians."[17]

Such attitudes appear to echo more formal statements of some Christian organizations. The Ethics and Religious Liberty Commission, for instance, has asserted that Christians should reject the utopian, technologically-fueled dream of transcending aging.[18] Jason Thacker, who serves as the Commission's chair of research in technology ethics, sees the drive for youth as rooted in a utilitarian understanding of human beings that tempts us to see old age as a burden and encourages us to dismiss the elderly for their supposed failure to contribute to society. However, according to a biblical understanding of humanity as created in God's image (Gen. 1:26–27), and thus endowed with dignity, old age is not something to be avoided, but *embraced*. "God casts a rich vision for growing old – one Christians should champion in a world that fears, fights, and attempts to hide aging."[19] For Thacker and the members of the Commission, there is no middle ground and little ambiguity. While the Commission endorses the use of medical technologies to fight the effects of aging as an expression of God's common grace to humankind, it cites an evangelical statement of principles on the promises and perils of artificial intelligence in relation to medicine which emphatically denies that death and disease – insofar as they are the products of the fall (Genesis 3) – can ever be eradicated apart from Jesus Christ, whom, as Christians confess, was raised from the dead.[20]

More substantive, nuanced arguments against aging attenuation have been put forward by Judith and Richard Hays, who observe that the Bible never presents aging as a problem requiring a solution, an attitude consistent with the early church.[21] The problem is not aging as such, but *death*, which will ultimately be conquered by Christ at the eschaton. Hays and Hays also follow other theologians in asserting that Jesus of Nazareth as depicted in Scripture is normative; Jesus is the picture of humanity as God intended it, including aging and growing older.[22] Moreover, Jesus' radical devotion to God in his willingness to suffer death on the cross "stands as a permanent reminder that *fidelity* is more important than *longevity*."[23] The Apostle Paul described such fidelity as knowing Christ and the power of his resurrection so that he might "share his sufferings, becoming like him in his death." (Phil. 3:10 RSV)[24] Though long life is certainly a blessing (Prov. 16:31; 20:29), no one should presume the right to one. Rather than making an idol of longevity by clinging to life at all costs, the way of discipleship eschews adopting a life of self-protection and includes enduring the suffering that inevitably accompanies aging. Thus, when viewing aging and death through the lens of the cross and resurrection, we are liberated from the paralyzing fear of aging and dying and "set free from the frantic energy to forestall death at all costs."[25]

But perhaps the most theologically forceful response against extending the maximum human lifespan has been made by the Episcopal priest and historical theologian Ephraim Radner. In *A Time to Keep*, Radner argues that the greatest, history-defining event of the modern era, "the Great Transition," is the near doubling of life expectancy over the last two centuries.[26] "The Great Transition" has considerably muted our sense of finitude and our "numbered" days, and has thus dramatically reshaped our thinking about fundamental realities like begetting children, maturation, gender roles, the meaning of work, and our understanding of embodiment.[27] If pre-Transition lifespan unveiled a *creature* – a being with limits whose life belongs to God – the post-Transition lifespan has allowed us to presume that death remains remote. Though we can be thankful for longer life resulting from modernity having stretched its limbs, our current "death-marginalizing life expectancy" obscures the unchanging reality that we remain fundamentally limited creatures who depend on God for our existence.[28] But rather than denying death altogether, Radner asserts that we have drained it of meaning, and struggle to imagine that "our mortality serves as an instrumental grace in our common life."[29] This biblical conjunction of divine purpose with mortal limitations is modernity's enemy, says Radner. But Christians can only see mortality itself as a "vessel of grace" when they remember the bigger, true story of human existence which includes bodily resurrection, reminding us that we all must appear before the judgment seat of Christ to give an account of things we have done on earth as embodied creatures (2 Cor. 5:10).[30] After all, humans were created as mortal, finite beings. The death that has come as a result of the fall (Genesis 3) is not biological, but *spiritual*. Radner argues that Christians need to remember these fundamental realities in order to recover a proper sense of the shape of finite, embodied life, where its generative, filial purposes and ineluctable transitions are given their appropriate weight.

In light of these deeper theological realities, Radner can only see life extension via aging deceleration as a deeply-flawed project of modernity, as another form of masking our creatureliness in ways that only strengthen our false presumptions that every technological breakthrough renders death still more remote, distorting our notions of family, generativity, community and the overall shape of life. "Nothing is gained theologically by extending our lifespan… There's no greater, deeper understanding of who we are as human beings. Tacking on another 15 years will obscure further the reality of who we are as creatures."[31] Thus, even this modest increase in lifespan, an increase that might be considered ethically ambiguous, appears no less problematic than aiming at earthly immortality when situated within the transcendent frame which includes bodily resurrection and divine judgment. It is interesting to observe that, unlike the Christians who rejected life extension in light of the promised afterlife, Radner, who confesses bodily resurrection, is far more concerned with how this transcendent reality impacts the character of earthly life. More generally, he argues that wisdom is derived from honoring the contour of life within its current limits, with all of the stages and weaknesses particular to each stage. For Radner, life extension confuses more life with abundant life.

Given these various positions against life extension, it might appear that they have earned the label of "Luddite," given especially the strong objection to adding even a few more years of life. This becomes even more understandable when those leveling such charges of Ludditism are typically working from a thoroughly naturalistic metanarrative that denies any transcendent reality to which human beings are accountable. If there is no afterlife, it makes sense to extend this earthly life as long as possible.[32] And yet, there are other, earlier Christian voices who not only embraced life extension but saw slowing aging as the foremost goal of a new scientific methodology built on overcoming the effects of the fall (Genesis 3) and reinvesting humanity with the power it possessed in the Garden of Eden.

13.4 Francis Bacon, slowing aging, and the Baconian project

Somewhat surprisingly, there are distinctly theological strands to the origin of the modern quest to slow human aging, which can be traced back to Francis Bacon (1561–1626), and his call for a new scientific methodology, one devoted to the cultivation of *useful* rather than theoretical, or contemplative, knowledge.[33] Indeed, Bacon's work might be considered the fountainhead of contemporary attempts to forestall aging as part of a larger biomedical project of improving the human condition. That contemporary science is often described as "Baconian" to the degree that it seeks to eliminate suffering and expand choice bears witness to his influence.[34] Bacon sought to reorient medicine toward the goal of conquering aging itself through a new methodology devoted to the development and cultivation of practical rationality, a program constituting "a restitution and reinvesting (in great part) of man to the sovereignty and power… which he had in his first state of creation."[35] In distancing himself from the Puritan theology to which he was attracted, Bacon emphasized the role of human effort in overcoming the effects of the fall.

Bacon's most pressing critique was leveled against the Aristotelian approach to science and its deductive approach, particularly its excessive concern with formal and final causality by which the true essence of things might be discerned. Better to leave the investigations of these causes to metaphysics and the holy book of Scripture. More important was the study of material and efficient causes in the "book of nature," for this more focused knowledge would enable humanity to reorder nature, insofar as it was possible, to its prelapsarian state. It is worth noting that Bacon's critique of Aristotelian science was theological in nature, informed by the Reformation's more circumscribed interpretation of Scripture, the nature of salvation, and God's relationship to creation. Moreover, Bacon's ultimate aim of cultivating practical knowledge was no less theological; it must be for "the benefit and relief of the state and society of man," namely, "an enlargement of his power over nature" possessed by Adam before the fall (Gen. 3).[36] Bacon believed this amplification of power had been assigned to man by God himself. If properly and humbly pursued, such knowledge would also lead to a greater exaltation of God's glory. Indeed, "all knowledge is to be limited by religion, and to be referred to use and action," meaning Christian charity.[37] Without such charity, asserted Bacon, it would be impossible to properly advance scientific knowledge.[38]

Bacon's religious vision for the renewal of all things as set forth in *The Great Instauration* was breathtakingly expansive. By *interrogating* nature rather than merely reading it, useful knowledge could be developed to help humanity storm the gates of Eden. Bacon believed that cultivating natural knowledge would enable humanity to make significant inroads against the conditions of fallen, embodied existence marked by diseases, maladies, and all too brief lifespans, including "a discovery of all operations and possibilities of operations from immortality (if it were possible) to the meanest mechanical practice."[39] Of the various aspects of this prelapsarian existence, no feature warranted more attention than greatly extending life by slowing aging. Bacon speculated that aging might be treated by continually addressing the body's own repair functions, enabling it to endure much longer, if not indefinitely. "Whatever can be repaired gradually without destroying the original whole is, like the vestal fire, potentially eternal."[40] Just as a youthful body not only repairs itself entirely but actually increases in both quantity and quality, asserted Bacon, "the matter whereby they [parts of the body] are repaired would be eternal, if the manner of repairing them did not fail."[41]

Though Bacon interpreted aging as a punishment from God, he also believed that aging could be modulated to extend lifespans to those of the biblical patriarchs, spanning centuries (Genesis 5–11). He sharply criticized physicians who too easily declared diseases incurable, and held them culpable for failing to uncover the various mechanisms of aging, the processes which could be modulated to extend the human lifespan. "But the lengthening of the thread of life itself, and the postponement for a time of that death which gradually steals on by natural dissolution and the decay of age," asserted Bacon, "is a subject which no physician has handled in proportion to its dignity."[42] If, as Bacon saw things, humanity's attempt to regain Methuselah-like lifespans through the cultivation of natural knowledge did not run afoul of God's sovereignty, neither was there any perceived conflict between a longer earthly life and the promised eternal life. Indeed, Bacon warned Christians against gazing too intently into the mysterious glories of heaven, lest long life be too lightly esteemed. Though Christians "ever aspire and pant after that land of promise," we should also consider long life as "a mark of God's favour if in our pilgrimage through the wilderness of this world, these our shoes and garments (I mean our frail bodies) are as little worn out as possible."[43]

Bacon contributed little by way of knowledge into human aging, but his urgent call for the inquiry into its causes with the view of bringing it under discrete human control as man's God-given vocation lent considerable prestige to the idea of prolonging life through a more inductive science, given the highly complex and intransigent nature of human aging. Even though his speculation concerning earthly immortality stretches the tension between this life and the next to the breaking point, for Bacon the difficulties of earthly life and the promise of a better life to come presented no real theological impediment to his program of life extension. Moreover, he utterly rejected pursuing longevity for longevity's sake. Long life was inextricably tied to a Christian vocation of bringing an end to sickness and suffering through the cultivation of instrumental knowledge, even as we move inexorably toward our heavenly home.

Bacon drew inspiration for his program of slowing aging from the story of the fall in Genesis 3, construing it as a way to regain at least a portion of life in Eden. In this regard, prelapsarian Adam stood as a figure of hope of what might be recovered through the cultivation of instrumental knowledge while also providing a theological safeguard against imposing any template on nature rooted in "vain imagination."[44] He saw no real conflict between the potential of earthly immortality, "if it were possible," and eternal life. It might be asked whether Bacon's vision is sufficiently Christian, insofar as his references to Jesus Christ – the last Adam (1 Cor. 15:45) – are missing from his account of slowing aging. How might the Incarnation impact a Christian understanding of life extension? Perhaps less than one might think. In turning to Karl Barth's Christological understanding of the human creature, we find a more theologically robust framework, allowing for, in principle, a near-indefinite length of life.

13.5 Karl Barth's (1886–1968) Christocentric anthropology

For Barth, permissible forms of intervention or "enhancement" are ultimately determined not by our own values and desires, but by the reality of human personhood as revealed in the Incarnation of Jesus Christ who took on our full human nature, without ceasing to be divine. Jesus is the "Archimedean point" from which true knowledge of humanity might be established, though there are no simple, straight lines to be drawn from his human nature to ours.[45] For Barth, to be human is to be "determined by God for life *with* God."[46] Barth's theological anthropology rests on the fact that God has determined and created humans to be God's covenant partner; to be God's covenant partner is to *be* human. But if this is the case, notes Barth, then it would seem that our finite, creaturely nature as revealed in Jesus Christ would contradict our divine determination as covenant partners of the eternal God.

Though Barth dismisses any "abstract" longing for an extension of life beyond one's allotted span, he considers whether this covenant relationship with God doesn't actually *demand* that life endures. "What but an unlimited, permanent duration can be adequate for the fulfillment of this determination?"[47] But he is clear that God's Word as a summons to both God and our fellow creatures is the "real reason why duration must be demanded," and why God's allotment of a specific span of life is seen as a problem. In short, this summons as both a "gift and task from the eternal God is the cause of the discontent."[48] Indeed, by following God and serving our fellow creatures, life "may and will and must endure. It has an urge for perfection; it is impatient will all limitations; it storms all barriers."[49] Here, as in Bacon's thought, the tension between our divinely-determined allotted span and our divine determination as God's covenant partners which would seem to demand that earthly continue, life is on full display. And yet, in spite of the strong case he has just made for unlimited life, Barth insists that our natural, bounded lifespan is also a sign of our divine determination on account of the Incarnate Word, Jesus Christ, who took on human nature "in His time."[50] Hence, "the existence of the man Jesus in time is our assurance that time as the form of human existence is willed and created by God and given to man."[51] Not only was Jesus' embodied limitedness necessary for him to die on the cross, but his finitude also means that human mortality is proper to our existence and should not be regarded as intrinsically negative or evil. On the contrary: we should welcome our allotment with gratitude and joy.[52]

In light of this Christological anthropology, Barth acknowledges that "we are right to ask for duration and perfection in our life" while also warning against concluding "that we ourselves can and must achieve this duration and perfection by a power immanent in our life as such."[53] At the same time however, the tension between these two divine determinations for the human creature – for an unlimited duration of fellowship with God as covenantal co-partners on the one hand and the divine allotment of finitude on the other – would seem to allow for the use of technology to radically extend human life so long as immortality itself is not proposed. As Gerald McKenny asserts,

Not only does Barth have no direct objection to such proposals; his conception of the normative significance of human nature [as determined by Jesus Christ] seems to have nothing at all to say about them, unless it is simply to issue a warning not to cross the line into actual immortality and thus eliminate one boundary of our lives.[54]

Though Barth does briefly consider the dangers of an unbounded life in vitiating our responsibility for "the perfection which fellowship with God demands," extending life by an extra 10 to 15 years would hardly seem to threaten this responsibility, much less require a rejection of either aspect of God's divine determination for human life as revealed by the real man Jesus.[55] Indeed, might not anti-aging technology be enlisted in the service of pursuing the perfection demanded of Christians as participants and co-partners in God's gracious covenant?

Though, as McKenney asserts, Barth might have no direct objection to life extension, Barth is nevertheless aware of the reality of sin as determined by the real man Jesus, whose soul was in perfect submission to God, and whose body was perfectly ruled by his soul.[56] Sin, says Barth, manifests itself as sloth (*Trägheit*), a disruption in the proper order of body and soul, and anxiety (*Sorge*) is understood as a disruption of our right relationship to our temporality. In our sloth we are unable to rest in the givenness of our own being but rather fret over our limited existence, wishing things were rather different.[57] Moreover, "we try to arrest the foot which brings us constantly nearer to this frontier."[58] In our anxiety (*Sorge*) too, we make the allotted duration of our life unbearable, which then fuels frenetic, ceaseless activity, and often includes our quests for longer life.[59] From Barth's Christocentric perspective, it seems very possible to consider contemporary attempts to slow aging as products of sloth and anxiety, or care. Nevertheless, the question remains as to whether *all* such attempts to slow aging fall prey to these temptations. It should be noted too that Barth's Christology may prove useful to any larger consideration of human enhancement from a Christian perspective insofar as Jesus Christ presents us with the picture of humanity as determined by God. Though great care is required in drawing out the implications Jesus' humanity has for our humanity – Jesus' maleness for instance in no way denigrates femaleness – the Incarnation bespeaks a divine validation of human creatures *as* human.

13.6 Conclusion

This brief, selective survey has shown that the Christian faith can accommodate various positions on slowing human aging, ranging from wholesale rejection to enthusiastic endorsement.[60] To be sure, determining which, if any of these positions on life extension is "correct" is well beyond the scope of this chapter. Nevertheless, those who argue against slowing aging on a popular level typically do so by referencing God's sovereignty in determining the boundaries of human existence or the promise of heaven. More sophisticated objections ascribe theological normativity to the aging process and thus the organic shape of life itself, arguing that mortality is a gift of God that is to be graciously received. In Radner, for instance, we found a penetrating analysis of how life extension threatens to distort the God-given trajectory of earthly life, including how family relationships, the meaning of maturity, gender roles, the meaning of work, and the meaning of the body may become distorted. Ultimately, however, his objections are grounded in the transcendent reality of the judgment seat of Christ. On the other hand, Bacon and Barth respectively promoted and in principle allowed for, life extension, recognizing the theological tension between our unlimited desires and our limited bodies, whether referencing the first Adam (Bacon) or the second (Barth).

These competing arguments underscore the deeply ambivalent nature of aging and slowing it from within a Christian framework. Certainly, while the claims of those who reject life extension warrant careful consideration, it is difficult to see how a moderate extension in healthy life, say 10 to 15 years, would so radically reshape the nature of finite life so as to warrant its complete dismissal. It would seem that the tension between the goodness of embodied finitude and the possibility of significantly longer life as reflected invite deeper moral questions along the lines of those asked by both Radner and Barth, questions concerning the purpose of the body and how life extension might alter the shape of a well-lived life. Gerald McKenny says it well: "As we deliberate over these technologies, do the reasons that support them express the meaning and value of the biological life-span as a natural sign of divine grace?"[61] We might also inquire how Christians discern if engaging in life extension is the product of care and anxiety (Barth), or how generativity – begetting and rearing children – might train us in virtue.[62] Other questions come to mind, such as considering how living under the assumption of a longer lifespan impacts the cultivation of certain virtues, like patience, forbearance, forgiveness, justice, courage, and fortitude. And what of the theological virtues of faith, hope, and love? Moreover, there is ample room to consider how a theology of contentment that respects the "givenness" of existence might considerably delimit the project of life extension, though these are complex questions, especially within a Christian narrative that recognizes both the goodness and fallenness of the created order.[63] Finally, Christians might also ask how the promise of longer life impacts the life of discipleship, where, in the words of Dietrich Bonhoeffer, one learns to die for the right things.

Notes

1 Biohacking can be defined as "Changing our biological selves, including neurology, biochemistry, physiology, and other physicalities through science and technology for enhancement purposes." See Calvin Mercer and Tracy J. Trothen, *Religion and the Technological Future: An Introduction to Biohacking, Artificial Intelligence, and Transhumanism* (Cham, Switzerland: Palgrave Macmillan, 2021), 230. Dave Asprey, founder of Bulletproof Coffee, has had stem cells extracted from his own bone marrow and fat and reinserted near his spinal cord in an attempt to slow cellular aging.
2 James C. Riley, *Rising Life Expectancy: A Global History* (New York: Cambridge University Press, 2001), x. Riley identifies six major areas of improvement in public health and medicine (listed above) that have contributed to the reduction of mortality, pointing out that the recipe of these elements varies across regions of the world, with the relative contribution of any single element impossible to quantify.
3 Centers for Disease Control/National Center for Health Statistics, Table 22, "Life Expectancy at Birth, at 65 Year of Age, and at 75 Years of Age, by Race and Sex: United States, Selected Years 1900–2007," www.cdc.gov/nchs/data/hus/2010/022.pdf. However, life expectancy is expected to drop as a result of COVID-19, with a disproportionate impact on Black and Latino populations. Theresa Andrasfay and Noreen Goldman, "Reductions in 2020 U.S. Life Expectancy Due to COVID-19 and the Disproportionate Impact on the Black and Latino Populations," *Proceedings of the National Academy of Sciences of the United States of America* 118, no. 5 (February 2, 2021): e2014746118.
4 President's Council on Bioethics, *Taking Care: Ethical Caregiving in Our Aging Society* (Washington, DC: The President's Council on Bioethics, 2005), 9.
5 President's Council, *Taking Care*, 13. See Joanne Lynn and David M. Adamson, *Living Well at the End of Life: Adapting Health Care to Serious Chronic Illness in Old Age* (Santa Monica: RAND Health, 2003); J.R. Lunney, J. Lynn, and C. Hogan, "Profiles of Older Medicare Decedents," *Journal of the American Geriatric Society* 50, no. 6 (2002): 1108–1112.
6 Alzheimer's Association, Alzheimer's Impact Movement: Fact Sheet 2020. https://act.alz.org/site/DocServer/2012_Costs_Fact_Sheet_version_2.pdf?docID=7161, Accessed April 24, 2021.
7 Alzheimer's Association, Alzheimer's Impact Movement: Fact Sheet 2020. Biogen's anti-amyloid agent for the treatment of Alzheimer disease, aducanumab (Aduhelm) is a case in point. Though the drug received FDA approval in 2021, its annual cost was set at $56,000, despite ongoing questions of its efficacy. See Grace A. Lin, Melanie D. Whittington, Patricia G. Synnott, Avery McKenna, Jon Campbell, Steven D. Pearson, and David M. Rind, "Aducanumab for Alzheimer's Disease: Effectiveness and Value; Evidence Report," *Institute for Clinical Economic Review* (June 30, 2021), https://icer.org/assessment/alzheimers-disease-2021/. Accessed September 14, 2021.
8 S. Jay Olshansky, Bruce A. Carnes, and Christine Cassel, "In Search of Methuselah: Estimating the Upper Limits to Human Longevity," *Science* 250, no. 4981 (November 2, 1990): 634–640.
9 S. Jay Olshansky, Perry D. Miller, and R.A. Butler, "In Search of the Longevity Dividend," *The Scientist* 20, no. 3 (2006): 28–36.
10 D. Bloom and D. Canning, "The Health and Wealth of Nations," *Science* 287 (2000): 1207–1209. See also S. Jay Olshansky, John Beard, and Axel Börsch-Supan, "The Longevity Dividend: Health as an Investment,"

57–60, in John Beard, Simon Biggs, David Bloom, Linda Fried, Paul Hogan, Alexandre Kalache, and S. Jay Olshansky, "Global Population Ageing: Peril or Promise?" (working paper no. 89, Program on the Global Demography of Aging, Harvard Initiative for Global Health, World Economic Forum, 2012). www.hsph.harvard.edu/pga/working.htm. Downloaded on April 24, 2021.

11 For a summary of these findings, see Todd T.W. Daly, *Chasing Methuselah: Theology, the Body, and Slowing Human Aging* (Eugene, OR: Cascade, 2021), 46–69. It should also be noted however that there are no theories of aging that earn wide support across the scientific community, much less agreement on how aging should be measured.

12 Olshansky et al., "In Search of the Longevity Dividend," 31, 32.

13 Simon Young, *Designer Evolution: A Transhumanist Manifesto* (Amherst, NY: Prometheus Books, 2006), 41.

14 M. Underwood, H.P. Bartlett, B. Partridge, J. Lucke, and W.D. Hall, "Community Perceptions on the Significant Extension of Life: An Exploratory Study among Urban Adults in Brisbane, Australia," *Social Science and Medicine* 68 (2009): 496–503. However, another study demonstrated that some older adults, who deferred to God's will while facing difficult prognoses, were more likely to engage in life-sustaining treatment than those who did not defer to God's will. See L. Winter, M.P. Dennis, and B. Parker, "Preferences for Life-Prolonging Medical Treatments and Deference to the Will of God," *Journal of Religious Health* 48 (2009): 418–430.

15 Scott Ballinger, Theresa Clement Tisdale, David L. Sellen, and Loren A. Martin, "Slowing Down Time: An Exploration of Personal Life Extension Desirability as it Relates to Religiosity and Specific Religious Beliefs," *Journal of Religion and Health* 56 (2017): 171–187.

16 Ballinger et al., "Slowing Down Time," 182. "Strong" life extension was defined as increasing life-expectancy *beyond* the current limit of 122 years.

17 Loren Martin, quoted in Liuan Huska, "Engineering Abundant Life," *Christianity Today* (March 2019): 50.

18 Jason Thacker, "Our World Wants to Transcend Aging. Christians Should Embrace It," *The Gospel Coalition* (November 7, 2019). www.thegospelcoalition.org/article/transcend-aging-christians-embrace/.

19 Thacker, "Our World Wants to Transcend Aging."

20 The Ethics & Religious Liberty Commission of the Southern Baptist Convention, "Artificial Intelligence: An Evangelical Statement of Principles," Article 4. April 11, 2019. https://erlc.com/resource-library/statements/artificial-intelligence-an-evangelical-statement-of-principles/. One wonders how the ERLC might respond to the claim that aging attenuation might itself be an instance of "common grace" to humankind. While attempting to engineer earthly immortality would be problematic from this Christian perspective, it is not entirely clear how they move the conclusion that death can never be technologically eradicated to the claim that aging cannot be slowed down.

21 Richard B. Hays and Judith C. Hays, "The Christian Practice of Growing Old: The Witness of Scripture," in *Growing Old in Christ*, ed. Stanley Hauerwas, Carole Bailey Stoneking, Keith G. Meador, and David Cloutier (Grand Rapids: W.B. Eerdmans, 2003), 3, 11, 14.

22 Jesus, who lived into his 30s, cannot be said to have grown old by either contemporary or ancient standards. Though the *average* life expectancy during this time was approximately 35 years of age, those who lived this long could not unreasonably expect to see one's seventh or even eighth decade.

23 Hays and Hays, "Christian Practice of Growing Old," 11, emphasis added.

24 Indeed, elsewhere Paul points out that he was always carrying in his body the dying (*nekrosis*) of Jesus so that Jesus' life might also be visible in the body (2 Cor. 4:10).

25 Hays and Hays, "Christian Practice of Growing Old," 16.

26 Ephraim Radner, *A Time to Keep: Theology, Mortality, and the Shape of a Human Life* (Waco: Baylor University Press, 2016), 23–24. The life expectancy of the population on average has increased from 33 years in 1800 in Europe to almost 80 years in 2000.

27 Radner, *A Time to Keep*, 23–24. "What I will call the Great Transition (or the Transition) refers specifically to the rapid increase in life-expectancy of the population on average, from around thirty-three years in 1800 in Europe to almost eighty in the year 2000."

28 Radner, *Time to Keep*, 34.

29 Ephraim Radner, "Whistling Past the Grave," *First Things* (November 2016). www.firstthings.com/article/2016/11/whistling-past-the-grave. Accessed April 16, 2021.

30 Radner, "Whistling Past the Grave."

31 Ephraim Radner, quoted in Liuan Huska, "Engineering Abundant Life," *Christianity Today* (March 2019): 50.

32 It is worth noting, however, that this vision is overwhelmingly promulgated by well-off males living in parts of the world where daily survival is not a concern.

33 Though Bacon was not a theologian by trade, his understanding of slowing aging may nevertheless be described as theological in the broadest possible sense insofar as he draws on themes in Scripture in an

attempt to say something about God and the nature of the world. Considering the degree to which this might diminish Bacon's theological observations is beyond the scope of this chapter.

34 See for instance Gerald P. McKenny, *To Relieve the Human Condition: Bioethics, Technology, and the Body* (Albany: State University of New York Press, 1997).
35 Bacon, *Valerius Terminus* 1, *The Works of Francis Bacon* [hereafter *WFB*] 3:222. Bacon's stance towards reordering nature prefigures contemporary co-creator theology which stresses a divinely ordained, creative exercising of technological power over creation to mitigate human suffering.
36 Bacon, *Valerius Terminus* 1, *WFB*, 3:221–22; Bacon, *Novum Organum* 2.52, *WFB*, 4:247.
37 Bacon, *Valerius Terminus* 1, *WFB*, 3:218.
38 Bacon, *Novum Organum* 1.81, *WFB*, 4:79.
39 Bacon, *Valerius Terminus* 1, *WFB*, 3:222.
40 Bacon, *History of Life and Death*, *WFB*, 5:218.
41 Bacon, *History of Life and Death*, *WFB*, 5:218.
42 Bacon, *Augmentis Scientiarum* 4.2, *WFB*, 4:383.
43 Bacon, *History of Life and Death*, *WFB*, 5:215.
44 Bacon, "The Plan of the Work," *WFB*, 4:32. "God forbid," declared Bacon, "that we should give out a dream of our own imagination for a pattern of the world."
45 Barth, *Church Dogmatics* [hereafter *CD*] 1/2: 117; Barth, *CD* 3/2: 54.
46 Barth, *CD* 3/2: 203, italics added.
47 Barth, *CD* 3/2: 556–57.
48 Barth, *CD* 3/2: 559.
49 Barth, *CD* 3/2: 557.
50 Barth, *CD* 3/2: 439.
51 Barth, *CD* 3/2: 552.
52 Barth, *CD* 3/2: 555.
53 Barth, *CD* 3/2: 566.
54 Gerald P. McKenny, "Biotechnology and the Normative Significance of Human Nature: A Contribution from Theological Anthropology," *Studies in Christian Ethics* 26 (2013): 35.
55 Barth, *CD* 3/2: 561.
56 Barth was no dualist. Though he could distinguish between the body and soul, he also referred to Jesus' humanity – and therefore ours – as an embodied soul and an ensouled body.
57 This understanding of sloth (or acedia) comes from Joseph Pieper, *Leisure: The Basis of Culture*, trans. Alexander Dru (San Francisco: Ignatius, 2009), 43–45.
58 Barth, *CD* 4/2: 468.
59 Barth, *CD* 4/2: 463.
60 An extreme instance of the latter can be found in The Christian Transhumanist Affirmation, Article 1, 3. www.christiantranshumanism.org/affirmation. Christian transhumanists believe that God is actively involved in transforming and renewing creation through the expression of God-given impulses to reach our full potential as God's image-bearers, employing science and technology in following Christ and the way of love.
61 McKenny, "Biotechnology," 35.
62 See for instance Gilbert Meilaender, *Should We Live Forever?: The Ethical Ambiguities of Aging* (Grand Rapids: W.B. Eerdmans, 2013), 71.
63 The author is grateful for this observation from an anonymous reviewer.

References

Alzheimer's Association. "Alzheimer's Impact Movement: Fact Sheet 2020." March 2020. https://act.alz.org/site/DocServer/2012_Costs_Fact_Sheet_version_2.pdf?docID=7161.

Andrasfay, Theresa, and Noreen Goldman. "Reductions in 2020 U.S. Life Expectancy Due to COVID-19 and the Disproportionate Impact on the Black and Latino Populations." *Proceedings of the National Academy of Sciences of the United States of America* 118, no. 5 (February 2, 2021). https://doi.org/10.1073/pnas.2014746118

Bacon, Francis. *The Works of Francis Bacon: Baron of Verulam, Viscount St. Alban, and Lord High Chancellor of England*. 14 vols. Edited by James Spedding, et al. London: Longman, 1857–1874.

Ballinger, Scott, Theresa Clement Tisdale, David L. Sellen, and Loren A. Martin. "Slowing Down Time: An Exploration of Personal Life Extension Desirability as it Relates to Religiosity and Specific Religious Beliefs." *Journal of Religion and Health* 56 (2017): 171–187.

Barth, Karl. *Church Dogmatics*. 4 vols, 14 parts. Edited by G. W. Bromiley and T. F. Torrance. Edinburgh: T & T Clark, 1956–1977.

Bloom, D., and D. Canning. "The Health and Wealth of Nations." *Science* 287 (2000): 1207–1209.

Center for Disease Control/National Center for Health Statistics. Table 22. "Life Expectancy at Birth, at 65 Year of Age, and at 75 Years of Age, by Race and Sex: United States, Selected Years 1900–2007." https://www.cdc.gov/nchs/data/hus/2010/022.pdf.

The Christian Transhumanist Association. "The Christian Transhumanist Affirmation." https://www.christiantranshumanism.org/affirmation.

Daly, Todd T. W. *Chasing Methuselah: Theology, the Body, and Slowing Human Aging*. Eugene, OR: Cascade, 2021.

The Ethics & Religious Liberty Commission of the Southern Baptist Convention. "Artificial Intelligence: An Evangelical Statement of Principles." April 11, 2019. https://erlc.com/resource-library/statements/artificial-intelligence-an-evangelical-statement-of-principles/.

Hays, Richard B., and Judith C. Hays. "The Christian Practice of Growing Old: The Witness of Scripture." In *Growing Old in Christ*, edited by Stanley Hauerwas, Carole Bailey Stoneking, Keith G. Meador, and David Cloutier, 3–18. Grand Rapids: W. B. Eerdmans, 2003.

Huska, Liuan. "Engineering Abundant Life." *Christianity Today* (March 2019): 48–53.

Lin, Grace A., Melanie D. Whittington, Patricia G. Synnott, Avery McKenna, Jon Campbell, Steven D. Pearson, and David M. Rind, "Aducanumab for Alzheimer's Disease: Effectiveness and Value; Evidence Report." *Institute for Clinical Economic Review* June 30, 2021. https://icer.org/assessment/alzheimers-disease-2021/.

Lunney, J. R., J. Lynn, and C. Hogan. "Profiles of Older Medicare Decedents." *Journal of the American Geriatric Society* 50, no. 6 (2002): 1108–1112.

Lynn, Joanne, and David M. Adamson. *Living Well at the End of Life: Adapting Health Care to Serious Chronic Illness in Old Age*. Santa Monica: RAND Health, 2003.

McKenny, Gerald P. "Biotechnology and the Normative Significance of Human Nature: A Contribution from Theological Anthropology." *Studies in Christian Ethics* 26 (2013): 18–36.

McKenny, Gerald P. *To Relieve the Human Condition: Bioethics, Technology, and the Body*. Albany: State University of New York Press, 1997.

Meilaender, Gilbert. *Should We Live Forever? The Ethical Ambiguities of Aging*. Grand Rapids: W. B. Eerdmans, 2013.

Mercer, Calvin, and Tracy J. Trothen. *Religion and the Technological Future: An Introduction to Biohacking, Artificial Intelligence, and Transhumanism*. Cham, Switzerland: Palgrave Macmillan, 2021,

Olshansky, S. Jay, John Beard, and Axel Börsch-Supan. "The Longevity Dividend: Health As an Investment." In *Global Population Ageing: Peril or Promise?*, edited by John Beard, Simon Biggs, David Bloom, Linda Fried, Paul Hogan, Alexandre Kalache, and S. Jay Olshansky, 57–60. Working paper no. 89, Program on the Global Demography of Aging, Harvard Initiative for Global Health, World Economic Forum, 2012. http://www.hsph.harvard.edu/pga/working.htm.

Olshansky, S. Jay, Perry D. Miller, and R. A. Butler. "In Search of the Longevity Dividend." *The Scientist* 20, no. 3 (2006): 28–36.

Olshansky, S. Jay, Bruce A. Carnes, and Christine Cassel. "In Search of Methuselah: Estimating the Upper Limits to Human Longevity." *Science* 250, no. 4981 (November 2, 1990): 634–640.

Pieper, Joseph. *Leisure: The Basis of Culture*. Translated by Alexander Dru. San Francisco: Ignatius, 2009.

President's Council on Bioethics. *Taking Care: Ethical Caregiving in Our Aging Society*. Washington, DC: The President's Council on Bioethics, 2005.

Radner, Ephraim. *A Time to Keep: Theology, Mortality, and the Shape of a Human Life*. Waco: Baylor University Press, 2016.

Radner, Ephraim. "Whistling Past the Grave." *First Things* (November 2016). https://www.firstthings.com/article/2016/11/whistling-past-the-grave.

Riley, James C. *Rising Life Expectancy: A Global History*. New York: Cambridge University Press, 2001.

Thacker, Jason. "Our World Wants to Transcend Aging. Christians Should Embrace It." *The Gospel Coalition* (November 7, 2019). https://www.thegospelcoalition.org/article/transcend-aging-christians-embrace/.

Underwood, M., H. P. Bartlett, B. Partridge, J. Lucke, and W. D. Hall. "Community Perceptions on the Significant Extension of Life: An Exploratory Study among Urban Adults in Brisbane, Australia." *Social Science and Medicine* 68 (2009): 496–503.

Winter, L., M. P. Dennis, and B. Parker. "Preferences for Life-Prolonging Medical Treatments and Deference to the Will of God." *Journal of Religious Health* 48 (2009): 418–430.

Young, Simon. *Designer Evolution: A Transhumanist Manifesto*. Amherst, NY: Prometheus Books, 2006.

PART IV

Cognitive enhancement

14
AI AS IA

The use and abuse of artificial intelligence (AI) for human enhancement through intellectual augmentation (IA)

Alexandre Erler and Vincent C. Müller

14.1 Introduction

14.1.1 *Human enhancement and intellectual augmentation*

It is now widely agreed that we live in the age of artificial intelligence (AI). This paper will discuss the potential and the risks of using AI to achieve human enhancement and what we shall call intellectual augmentation (IA). Let us begin with some clarifications on how we propose to understand those key concepts. Broadly in line with previous work of ours (Erler and Müller, 2022), we shall define human enhancement as encompassing technological interventions that either:

a) Improve aspects of someone's functioning beyond what is considered "normal," or
b) Give that person new capabilities that "normal," non-enhanced humans do not possess.

Our proposed definition is compatible with the so-called therapy-enhancement distinction, insofar as it denies that "pure" therapies (i.e. interventions that restore or maintain health without meeting either condition 1 or 2) count as enhancements, even though they do improve human functioning in some way. That said, we also believe that the therapy-enhancement distinction should not be understood as entailing a strict dichotomy between these two types of interventions. The existence of a hybrid category of "therapeutic enhancements" should also be acknowledged (Wolbring et al., 2013; Erler and Müller, 2022), and we shall see that it includes some applications of AI for human enhancement. Such hybrid interventions either restore or preserve normal functioning in a manner that matches either condition 1 or 2 above. Consider, for instance, the vaccines against COVID-19, which are meant to protect our health by endowing us with a capacity – an immunity to infection against that virus – that is not part of the "normal" human condition.

A distinction is often drawn between enhancements in the full sense and mere useful "tools" (Lin et al., 2013; Erler and Müller, 2022). The former, but not the latter, are assumed to help produce desired outcomes by truly altering a person's physical or cognitive functioning. It might thus be said that a tool like a calculator, while helping us reach the correct result when performing a complex multiplication, nevertheless does not do so by improving our mathematical abilities or general cognitive functioning. Rather, the calculator relieves us of the need to engage in mathematical reasoning by performing that task for us. (That said, we will consider a possible challenge to this view when discussing the extended mind thesis in Section 14.3.4) As we will see, one might suspect that nearest-term applications of AI aimed at improving human decision-making beyond the "normal" will not count as true enhancements, as they will fail to meet the requirement of altered functioning. To take this possibility into account, we propose to recognize a broader category of improvements in decision-making and mental performance that includes enhancements: what we term "intellectual augmentation." Forms of IA that meet the altered functioning requirement also count as enhancements in our view, whereas those that do not are "simply" IA.

Applications of AI for enhancement can either have *broad* or *narrow* effects: they might for instance improve broad human capacities like memory or general intelligence, or they might target narrower aspects of cognitive functioning – say, clinical judgment. Finally, our proposed understanding of IA can be described as "liberal" insofar as the interventions it includes can produce their desired effects either *directly* or *indirectly*. For example, a brain-computer interface (BCI) that directly boosted a person's ability to focus by applying some form of brain stimulation, and a different BCI that indirectly improved that capacity by simply alerting the subject to when she got distracted, will both count as IA ("attention augmentation") on our approach.

14.1.2 Defining AI

The term "artificial intelligence" (AI) is now used in two main meanings:

(a) AI is a research program to create computer-based agents that can show complex behavior, capable of reaching goals (McCarthy et al., 1955), and
(b) AI is a set of methods employed in the AI research program for perception, modeling, planning, and action: machine learning (supervised, reinforced, unsupervised), search, logic programming, probabilistic reasoning, expert systems, optimization, control engineering in robotics, neuromorphic engineering, etc. Many of these methods are also employed outside the AI research programme (Russell, 2019, Russell and Norvig, 2020, Görz et al., 2020, Pearl and Mackenzie, 2018).

The original research program (a) from the "Dartmouth Conference" in 1956 onwards was closely connected to the idea that computational models can be developed for the cognitive science of natural intelligence and then implemented on different hardware, i.e. on computing machines. This program ran into various problems in the "AI Winter" ca. 1975–1995, and the word "AI" got a bad reputation; it thus branched into several technical programs that used their own names (pattern recognition, data mining, decision support system, data analytics, cognitive systems, etc.). After 2000, AI saw a resurgence, with faster hardware, more data, and an emphasis on neural network machine-learning systems. From ca. 2010, "AI" became a buzzword that resonated in circles outside computer science; now everyone wants to be associated with AI. As a result, the meaning of "AI" is currently broadening toward (b). It is this second, broader sense of AI that we will be relying on in our discussion. We shall consider various systems and devices, both present and foreseen, capable of complex information processing and targeted at the pursuit of certain human goals (or the maximization of expected utility).

Some view the ultimate endpoint of the AI research program as the attainment of machine "superintelligence." Superintelligence is typically explained on the basis of *general human intelligence*, where "super" intelligence is just *more of the same:*

> We can tentatively define a superintelligence as any intellect that greatly exceeds the cognitive performance of humans in virtually all domains of interest … Note that the definition is noncommittal about how the superintelligence is implemented. It is also noncommittal regarding qualia; whether a superintelligence would have subjective con-

scious experience might matter greatly for some questions (in particular for some moral questions), but our primary focus here is on the causal antecedents and consequences of superintelligence, not on the metaphysics of mind.
(Bostrom, 2014).

Besides superintelligence strictly understood, which entails a form of artificial general intelligence (AGI), Bostrom also envisages the possibility of "domain-specific" superintelligences (*ibid.*) – AI systems that vastly surpass human performance in specific cognitive domains yet cannot be applied outside of that narrow scope. Deep Blue, the chess-playing supercomputer that beat Gary Kasparov in 1997, and AlphaZero, the software developed by Google to achieve superhuman performance at the games of Go, chess, and shogi, are contemporary examples of domain-specific or narrow superintelligence (although Deep Blue is even narrower than AlphaZero). While we will mostly eschew highly speculative scenarios involving the rise of full-fledged superintelligence, which does not appear to be a likely near-term development, we will occasionally consider the prospect of narrower forms of it, as we will see in the next section, outlining the main possible applications of AI for IA.

14.2 AI technologies of relevance to the prospect of IA

14.2.1 AI advisors/"outsourcing"

The first relevant application is the use of "AI advisors," or what some have called AI outsourcing (Danaher, 2018), to improve human decision-making. AI advisors can be viewed as the logical next step from familiar tools like GPS or the internet. Their existing instantiations include, among others:

a) Well-known virtual assistants like Apple's Siri or Amazon's Alexa, which can help users decide, in line with their personal preferences, which product to buy, which restaurant to go to in an unfamiliar area, etc.
b) Clinical decision support systems, designed to assist healthcare professionals with clinical decision-making and increase the probability of reaching an accurate diagnosis (Sutton et al., 2020)
c) "Robo-advisors," which provide automated, algorithm-based assistance with financial planning, often at a lower cost than traditional human advisors (Frankenfield, 2021).

The kinds of decision-making ability that existing AI assistants or advisors aim to improve tend to be quite narrow, which of course does not refute their importance. Yet as such systems become more sophisticated with further technological development, their range of application might widen. The capacity for *moral* decision-making has received special attention in the academic literature. Some authors have thus proposed to create an AI system that would constantly monitor an agent's physiology, mental states, and environment, and on that basis, make her aware of potential biases in her decision-making or suggest the best course of action in a given situation (Savulescu and Maslen, 2015). To provide such assistance, the moral AI advisor would rely on the agent's own stated values, the implications of which it would draw using its superhuman capacity for information processing (*ibid.*; Giubilini and Savulescu, 2018). Other authors advocate for an alternative approach, involving a moral AI that acted like a Socratic interlocutor, spurring the user to think more carefully and thoroughly (Lara and Deckers, 2020).

The concept of a moral AI advisor does not intrinsically entail the monitoring of the advisee's brain states, yet the proposals just outlined all involve such monitoring, which would likely require the sort of technology discussed in the next section. Furthermore, while some aspects of these proposals do not presuppose the development of superintelligent AI systems (e.g. alerting the user that her level of tiredness might impair her moral reasoning), others do seem to do so. For instance, Giubilini and Savulescu describe their proposed moral AI advisor as "an expert more informed and more capable of information processing than any other human moral expert we trust" (2018, p. 177). While such a system need not represent a form of AGI, it would nevertheless demonstrate superhuman performance with regard specifically to moral reasoning.

Such a development would arguably have momentous practical implications. At the very least, if technology advances to the point where creating superintelligent *moral* AI advisors becomes possible, then we may expect the same to be true of other superintelligent AI advisors that can assist with other aspects of human decision-making: those not belonging to morality strictly understood, but rather to what philosophers would call *prudence*. As evidenced by the popularity of self-help books, coaching, and financial advisors, people do not simply seek to become more moral but also professionally, financially, and socially successful, happier, fitter, and healthier. It is not clear that any of these pursuits call for more complex reasoning capabilities than those required for the provision of sound moral advice.

Should we then anticipate that people will consult different AI advisors targeted at different goals, as they might currently take advice from "experts" in various domains, and then balance input from different sources (perhaps asking their moral AI advisor to help with such balancing)? This will partly depend on whether such stable co-existence of (relatively narrow) superintelligent AI systems is at all possible. Some might conjecture that their development would soon be followed by the arrival of AGI, raising, in turn, the prospect of an "intelligence explosion" (Good, 1965) with radically transformative consequences for the world – what is often labeled the "singularity" (Kurzweil, 2005). Since it is hard to foresee what such an outcome would look like, we will not discuss it further in what follows, yet it is worth noting that its possibility cannot be ruled out.

Even a scenario including only domain-specific superintelligent AIs could cause significant social disruption, threatening the relevance of many human occupations (including, to some extent, professional ethicists!). One response to this challenge might be to try and foster greater integration between humans and AI, using for instance a technology like brain-computer interfaces (BCIs).

14.2.2 *Brain-computer interfaces*

BCIs are designed to establish a direct connection between a person's brain and a computer. *Invasive* BCIs do so using implanted electrodes that require surgery. *Non-invasive* variants, by contrast, capture brain activity using techniques like electroencephalography (EEG), functional Magneto-Resonance Imaging (fMRI), or magnetoencephalography (MEG). While invasive BCIs allow for higher resolution readings, they also tend to be riskier, as we will see later (Ramadan et al., 2015). BCIs are basically used to record and interpret brain activity. In the case of "bi-directional" BCIs, which at the time of writing are still at the research and development stage, they can additionally be used to modulate brain activity via electric stimulation (Hughes et al., 2020).

BCIs are relevant to our discussion through their association with AI, for instance since AI algorithms are used to interpret the brain data they collect. They are primarily designed for therapeutic purposes, and their potential in that regard seems very broad. As demonstrated by various studies, they thus offer promise to people with paralysis, allowing them for instance to control tablet devices (Nuyujukian et al., 2018), wheelchairs, speech synthesizers (Cinel et al., 2019), and robotic or prosthetic limbs (Vilela and Hochberg, 2020), as well as powered exoskeletons (He et al., 2018), using their thoughts. Other potential beneficiaries of BCI technology include patients with residuals of stroke, traumatic brain injury, spinal cord injury, and memory disorders (DARPA, 2018; Klein, 2020).

Uses of BCIs for IA are already a reality, however. Some of the uses just described arguably constitute therapeutic enhancements. While the ultimate purpose behind the BCIs used by paralyzed patients may be therapeutic in nature (restoration of the "normal" ability to use a computer), it is nevertheless achieved via the conferral of a "supernormal" capacity – control of an external device via thought. Existing applications of BCIs for *pure* IA include the use of EEG-based brain-monitoring BCIs to improve capacities like attention and emotional regulation. In the educational context, some thus expect that monitoring the level of attention and engagement of students can help adjust the learning process, and ultimately optimize these different factors (Williamson, 2019). One company called BrainCo thus designed an EEG headband aimed at providing precisely such data to teachers. The company claims the data can then be used to design focus-training games that will enhance users' capacity for sustained attention (BrainCo, 2020) – although the validity of such claims has been questioned. The headband has already been trialed in some Chinese schools, causing controversy (Jing and Soo, 2019).

Looking into the future, there is a broad interest, among various sectors, in using BCIs to monitor the brain activity of employees, for the ultimate purpose of improving performance and productivity. It has thus been suggested that such systems could be designed to automatically adjust environmental conditions such as room temperature, to maximize a worker's efficiency (Valeriani et al., 2019). Another major context in which BCIs are likely to be used for IA is the military. Both the US and Chinese military are reportedly considering the potential of BCIs to enable the direct transfer of thoughts from brain to brain, and thus the ability to communicate silently, as well as allowing for faster communication and decision-making among soldiers and military commanders (Kania, 2019). Other relevant applications include the direct control of semiautonomous systems and drone swarms via thought, and more ambitiously, disruption of pain and regulation of emotions like fear among warfighters – although the latter two applications would require BCI systems featuring some form of brain stimulation (Binnendijk et al., 2020).

On an even more futuristic note, entrepreneurs like Elon Musk have made the headlines by proclaiming their ambition to develop BCIs that would enhance human cognition to the point of ultimately yielding "superhuman intelligence" (Lewis and Stix, 2019). Musk's reasoning is the standard one we have outlined already: continuous progress in AI ultimately threatens to render humans obsolete unless they choose to radically augment themselves by merging with AI. The details of how this process of radical augmentation is to take place are, however, much less clear, at least for now.

Having laid out some of the main foreseeable applications of AI for IA, we now turn to a (necessarily brief) overview of their potential ethical ramifications.

14.3 Philosophical and ethical issues pertaining to the use of AI for IA

14.3.1 Devices not performing as expected

Some have argued that the most relevant present-day concern about consumer EEG headsets is that companies selling them tend to misrepresent their enhancing effects (McCall and Wexler, 2020). To some extent, this concern also applies to future AI advisors: the quality of the advice provided by such a system could in principle fail to meet the standards promised by its manufacturer. This could happen either because of inadequate design, over-hyping of existing technical capabilities, or because the company selling the device had purposefully programmed it to nudge users toward courses of action that were favorable to its own interests, or those of its business partners, even when these were not fully in line with a user's ethical commitments (Bauer and Dubljevic, 2020). Moreover, besides such purposeful distortions of results, biases could also be inadvertently introduced into the underlying algorithms – we consider this latter issue in Section 14.3.5.

In addition to users exercising critical judgment, supplemented with feedback from acquaintances and reviews from other users as well as experts in the relevant domain, forms of quality control that would help mitigate those concerns might include a (presumably optional) certification process, analogous to that applicable to the human equivalents of AI advisors. We are already seeing this idea being implemented in some areas, such as the financial sector in Norway (Iversen, 2020). While moral AI advisors might present unique challenges in this context, the existence in today's world of standardized tests of critical thinking ability (Hitchcock, 2018), and university and high school courses in ethics, suggests that these challenges need not be intractable. Perhaps the "pool of moral experts" whom Giubilini and Savulescu suggest could be consulted when programming such devices (2018, p. 177) could also help design an appropriate certification procedure. Finally, ensuring *transparency* in the functioning of those devices would be key to quality control: they should be designed so as to always provide the user with a detailed justification for any particular recommendation they might offer. Nevertheless, this goal might present challenges related to the design of AI systems (O'Neill et al., forthcoming).

Concerns about efficacy might be especially salient with regard to BCIs, particularly in contexts like those outlined above, in which people might face coercive pressures to use them. Taking for instance the EEG headsets currently used in certain places to monitor the attention levels of students and workers, the reliability with which such devices can measure brain activity has been questioned (McCall and Wexler, 2020). They might conceivably have positive effects on attention even if their measurements are not accurate, simply because of the users' awareness that they are being monitored, combined with the expectations of others. Yet this would still not mean that they were truly efficacious. Furthermore, some worry that even when BCIs can reliably measure attention levels, they might still not – at least for now – allow us to determine whether a user is actually focused on their work or study, as opposed to, say, on their mobile phone (Gonfalonieri, 2020). Since it would clearly be problematic if rewards and punishments were to be meted out, e.g. by employers, based on misleading brain readings, promoting or even enforcing adequate quality standards might be especially important in such contexts.

14.3.2 Safety, coercion, and responsibility

Concerns about safety are mostly relevant to BCIs. First, invasive BCIs present health risks such as scarring, hemorrhaging, infection, and brain damage (Ramadan et al., 2015). Bi-directional BCIs involving electrical brain stimulation might also raise safety concerns, although this would depend on their *modus operandi*. The existing scientific literature suggests that less invasive forms of stimulation such as transcranial direct current stimulation (tDCS) have a good safety profile among both healthy and neuropsychiatric subjects, although uncertainties remain regarding long-term use and increased exposure (Nikolin et al., 2018). Secondly, the malfunction of a BCI, or its hijacking by a malicious third party, could result in harm to the user or to other people.

Addressing the first issue will likely require enforcing standards of good practice for pure enhancement uses of invasive BCIs similar to those already governing their therapeutic applications. These would include appropriate licensing requirements for those performing the needed surgical procedures, as well as a certification process for the implanted devices. Dealing with the second issue requires establishing regulations to promote adequate security standards in the design process, and to hold BCI manufacturers liable when malfunctioning devices have harmful consequences in cases where it is clear that the user herself bears no responsibility for what happened. Admittedly, this still leaves us with cases of a trickier kind: for instance, even if we could determine, based on a BCI recording, that the harmful command had its ultimate source in the brain of the user, would that automatically mean that we could hold that person fully responsible? Could such a command ever be triggered by an "automatic" thought over which they would exert only limited or no control (Burwell et al., 2017)? This, in turn, raises the question of whether such concerns can be alleviated simply via proper BCI design, or whether more will be needed (e.g. new legal provisions).

The issue of safety arguably becomes trickier when it is coupled with coercive pressures to use the relevant devices. The military context might be especially relevant in this regard, given the expectation that members of the armed forces should obey orders from their superiors (Tennison and Moreno, 2012; Ienca et al., 2018; Erler and Müller, forthcoming). Coercive pressures to use invasive BCIs seem less relevant to the civilian sector, at least for the foreseeable future.

What about the coercion issue when divorced from safety concerns? In a professional context, it might especially apply to non-invasive BCIs. An employer might for instance mandate that her employees wear EEG headsets to monitor, and ultimately enhance, their focus at work. This might strike some as intrinsically problematic. However, unlike coercion to use invasive BCIs, which could be viewed as infringing on people's right to bodily integrity, it seems less obvious that coercion to use non-invasive devices must be problematic *per se*. Indeed, one might argue that it is no different from existing and widely accepted forms of coercion aimed at enhancing work performance, such as mandatory employee training programs (Erler, 2020).

That being said, one might plausibly adduce *distinct* considerations in support of the view that there is something uniquely problematic about coercion to use (non-invasive) BCIs: say, that it presents a threat to the users' privacy or cognitive liberty. We will consider these separately, in the next section.

14.3.3 *Privacy and cognitive liberty*

To some extent, the issue of privacy in this context is simply an extension of existing concerns raised by current practices, such as the use of the internet, AI assistants, various "smart" systems, and wearables (Müller, 2020). Yet even though future AI advisors may not raise any fundamentally new concerns in this regard when they do not involve the collection of *brain* data, they are still likely to further intensify existing ones. Tech companies like Apple and Amazon are thus known to be using human contractors to listen to users' recorded conversations with their digital assistants Siri and Alexa (Gartenberg, 2019). Given that many people already feel uneasy about such practices, they will likely have even greater objections if they were applied to the interactions about highly personal matters they might have with their moral or health AI advisor. The risk of data theft would be another concern. This highlights the need for sound policies on data privacy and protection, as well as the promotion of informed consent among users. The latter goal, of course, is a particularly challenging one in an ever-more complex digital world: recent surveys thus find that more than 90% of internet users agree to terms of service they have not read (Guynn, 2020).

A relevant question is whether the sheer collection of brain data, via devices like BCIs, makes a fundamental difference to the privacy issue. What would matter is to extract some meaning from this data, e.g. *decoding* the cognitive content, e.g. down to specific thoughts or attitudes. Such extraction will often be probabilistic and depend on other data sources, including previously observed behavior. However, given the special status usually attributed to the privacy of thought, people could reasonably feel reluctant to use such devices for IA if they knew they were *capable* of decoding content, even if they had been assured that no such intrusive data collection and decoding would occur. To this, we should add the risk that BCIs might get hacked by malicious actors. While having one's private thoughts exposed is already a possibility today, the development of true brain-reading technology would still represent the fall of the last bastion of mental privacy, calling for careful regulation.

Experts diverge about the likelihood that such a development might occur in the foreseeable future (compare for instance Ienca et al., 2018, with Wexler, 2019, and Gilbert et al., 2019). For now, however, we can already ask whether requiring employees or students to consistently use a device that monitored their attention levels would be an infringement on their right to mental privacy. It is not clear to us that the answer must be positive, insofar as attention levels are not typically considered mental states of the kind deserving strict protection from scrutiny in such contexts:

it is, for instance, not improper for a teacher to observe her students' behavior in class and call out those who appear to be distracted.

Perhaps a stronger reason to object to such monitoring is its potential negative *psychological* impact on users, who might feel that they are operating under oppressive surveillance, or being treated in a patronizing manner. Furthermore, inappropriate lessons could also be drawn from the data collected – an issue we address in Section 14.3.5. Finally, even if it is not assumed to disrespect mental privacy, it may be that attention monitoring for IA still violates another right, or as some would say in this context, "neuro-right" (Yuste et al., 2017): namely cognitive liberty, or freedom from unwanted interference with one's neural processes (Bublitz, 2013). Whether or not it does so will depend on the specific scope of that right. For instance, should we think that people have a right to occasionally allow their minds to wander at work, say as a natural way of alleviating boredom? If so, pressures toward attention augmentation could infringe on that right. Seeking to foster constant laser-like focus among students and employees could also prove counterproductive, insofar as mind-wandering appears to be conducive to creative thinking (Fox and Beaty, 2019). However, this is a consequentialist objection to the practice, rather than a rights-based one.

Other violations of cognitive liberty might involve hackers taking control of the relevant AI devices. Such "brain hacking" (Ienca and Haselager, 2016) could be done for the purpose of stealing sensitive brain data but also to seize control of an external device receiving commands from a BCI, or of the input to the user's brain, in the case of bi-directional BCIs. While the first of these three possibilities would again threaten mental privacy, the third one would conflict with cognitive liberty and "mental integrity" (Ienca and Andorno, 2017; Lavazza, 2018). Both civilians and military personnel could be the targets of such attacks, highlighting the importance of striving to incorporate adequate protections into the design of such devices.

14.3.4 Authenticity and mental atrophy

Concerns about "authenticity" are recurrent in discussions of the ethics of enhancement, generally (The President's Council on Bioethics (US), 2003; Erler, 2014). We have already discussed the possibility that some AI advisors or BCIs might not deliver on their promises. Yet even assuming that such devices would allow for better decisions and improved performance, some might still object that they would offer a mere simulacrum of what they ought to be providing. This charge might particularly apply to forms of IA that did not count as full-fledged enhancements. For instance, one might contend that even if a moral AI advisor did provide us with sound ethical advice, it would nevertheless fail to authentically enhance our capacity for moral reasoning, since it would be delivering the end result of such reasoning "on a plate," circumventing the need to effortfully work things out for ourselves. In fact, one might fear that regularly outsourcing moral and prudential reasoning to AI advisors would cause our own capacity to engage in such reasoning to atrophy due to insufficient practice. IA would then entail a form of regression (Danaher, 2018), which is a version of the general "autopilot problem."

Several replies can be given to this argument. First, one might deny that relying on an AI advisor rather than exercising our own judgment, even on important matters, must be problematic. After all, life calls on us to make a large number of decisions, not all of which we may value *intrinsically*. Suppose for instance that Theodore wants to successfully invest his savings for retirement, without relishing the prospect of learning all the tricks of the art of investing. It is not plausible to think that he would deserve criticism for delegating most of his investment decisions to a trusted financial advisor, human or artificial. Theodore could rationally decide to devote his time and energy to other pursuits he considered more rewarding, and accept the resulting underdevelopment of his investment skills.

This reply does go some way toward answering the concern about authenticity and mental atrophy, yet it does not seem equally persuasive in relation to *all* forms of AI outsourcing. The moral domain stands out again here. Someone who systematically deferred to a moral AI advisor when making weighty ethical choices, and could not justify such a choice by themselves, but only repeat the rationale provided by the device, would arguably have failed to develop an important aspect of themselves as a human person.

To avoid such problem cases, one might instead try and respond to the authenticity concern by invoking the extended mind thesis (EMT): namely the claim that external artifacts can become part of an individual's mind or cognitive system if the right conditions are met. As stated by one of the EMT's original proponents, Andy Clark, such conditions include: 1) that the resource in question be reliably available and typically invoked; 2) that any information retrieved from it be more or less automatically endorsed; and 3) that the relevant information be easily accessible as and when required (Clark, 2010). Suppose now that Theodore's moral AI advisor is consistently available to him (via his smartphone or otherwise) wherever he goes and regularly gives him advice which he always accepts without hesitation. Based on the EMT, one might then contend that when the AI advisor engages in ethical reasoning, Theodore does so authentically too, since the device has become an extension of his mind. Clearly, the main vulnerability of this reply is that it stands or falls with the EMT, which is a controversial view (see Coin and Dubljevic, 2021).

Perhaps a stronger response to the concern is that while *some* uses of AI advisors for IA might indeed problematically supersede significant human activities like ethical reasoning, many need not do so. For instance, the "Socratic" moral advisor proposed by Lara and Deckers arguably would not, since it would be designed to prod the user into working out sounder ethical opinions by themselves, rather than delivering "ready-made" advice. The same applies to devices that would simply alert users to ethically risky physiological states, or help them track their progress toward their philanthropic goals. Finally, even devices that did recommend specific solutions to ethical dilemmas need not be blindly obeyed. Users could thus choose to override their advice based on their own reasoning, or only decide to follow it after having carefully considered the justification provided by the device. This could arguably enrich a person's moral thinking, rather than substitute for it. Overall, it seems that the considerations of autonomy are the same for human and IA advisory systems.

14.3.5 Fairness

If applications of AI for IA deliver on their promise, they risk exacerbating the existing "digital divide" (Ragnedda and Muschert, 2013), both at a local and global level. Those who cannot afford the relevant devices, or who are not able to access them via their school or employer, might unfairly find themselves at a disadvantage compared to those who can, in various important life domains from career to health. How to tackle this issue can be viewed as one aspect of the larger, momentous challenge of promoting equitable access to beneficial technologies, a challenge to which there is no simple solution. Beyond inequality of access, differential benefits might also result from differences in digital literacy, including "BCI literacy" (Cinel et al., 2019). While training programs designed to boost people's proficiency at using the relevant devices can help overcome those differences to some extent, other solutions might be required in cases where such differences are not grounded in unequal learning opportunities – but rather, say, in individual differences in the brain activity to be captured by BCI devices.

If used judiciously, the use of BCIs to monitor and augment attention at school and work could have benefits for users beyond any enhancing impact on performance. For instance, it could make it easier to identify students with conditions like attention deficit hyperactivity disorder (ADHD) or gifted students who find their classes insufficiently challenging, and to compare the degree of student engagement achieved by different teaching styles. Constructive adjustments could then be made. Nevertheless, we might also want to warn against inappropriate action being taken in response to the information thus collected. Students with ADHD, or those who get bored by a course that is insufficiently engaging or too easy for them, should not get unfairly penalized for their low attention scores.

Similar remarks apply to workplace applications. McCall and Wexler note that "some individuals may have a higher performance level than others even when in a distracted state" (2020, p. 14). It is plausible to think that professional rewards should be tied to a worker's absolute performance level, rather than to their overall level of attention and wakefulness at work. That said, it also seems that a company could reasonably use the relevant data to try and optimize employee performance, by appropriately adjusting working conditions. This could include making space for naps: a 2016 report by the RAND Corporation thus estimated that the United States lost an equivalent of around 1.23 million working days each year from sleep-deprived workers (Hafner et al., 2016).

An additional fairness-related concern is the issue of algorithmic bias. Even without any intention on the part of their designers, AI advisors could exhibit biases in their recommendations that unfairly disadvantaged certain social groups, whether as a result of the procedure used to issue those recommendations, or of the data on which they would be relying. A health AI advisor, for instance, might not provide equally reliable input to users from ethnic minorities, if the data used to train its algorithms did not feature enough members of those underrepresented groups (Kaushal et al., 2020). This is therefore an issue to be monitored, as part of the broader phenomenon of AI bias. Potential solutions include ensuring that the relevant algorithms are trained on data sets derived from diverse populations. While much more research remains to be done on this topic, it is worth noting that the presence of bias in an AI system does not automatically imply the preferability of relying solely on human decision-making, since biases among people can be even greater (Ledford, 2019).

14.4 Conclusion

This overview of the paths toward mustering the power of AI for IA, including human enhancement, suggests that they hold real promise, while also raising several ethical concerns. Some of these concerns apply across the board, while others differ based on the type of AI application being considered, such as whether it constitutes enhancement or "sheer" IA. The former concerns include the risk that the relevant devices might not perform as expected, threats to data privacy, and issues of equitable access and AI bias. As for the latter concerns, forms of IA that are not full-fledged enhancements seem more vulnerable to objections relating to inauthenticity and mental atrophy. Those that do count as enhancements, by contrast, might be more likely to present threats to cognitive liberty, insofar as they truly involve altering a person's cognitive functioning and elicit safety concerns, as such alterations of functioning might necessitate more invasive interventions. This last point, however, might depend on the position one takes on the extended mind thesis.

As new narrow forms of superintelligent AI get developed, the resulting risk of human obsolescence, both in the professional domain and in activities often considered significant aspects of existence, such as moral deliberation, will likely increase the rationale for pursuing a genuine fusion between humans and machines of the kind advocated by some transhumanists, rather than continuing to treat AI as a useful tool. That said, given the sizable technical challenges to such a prospect, more mundane applications of AI for IA, and their associated ethical conundrums, will remain with us for some time.

References

Bauer, W. A. & Dubljevic, V. 2020. AI Assistants and the Paradox of Internal Automaticity. *Neuroethics*, 13, 303–310.
Binnendijk, A., Marler, T. & Bartels, E. M. 2020. *Brain-Computer Interfaces: U.S. Military Applications and Implications, An Initial Assessment*. Santa Monica, CA: RAND Corporation.
Bostrom, N. 2014. *Superintelligence: Paths, Dangers, Strategies*, Oxford: Oxford University Press.

Brainco. 2020. *Learn To Focus...Now!* [Online]. Available: https://www.brainco.tech/learn-to-focus/ [Accessed 20/04/2021].
Bublitz, J. C. 2013. My Mind Is Mine!? Cognitive Liberty as a Legal Concept. *In*: Hildt, E. & Franke, A. G. (eds.) *Cognitive Enhancement: An Interdisciplinary Perspective*. Dordrecht; New York: Springer, 233–264.
Burwell, S., Sample, M. & Racine, E. 2017. Ethical Aspects of Brain Computer Interfaces: A Scoping Review. *BMC Med Ethics*, 18, 60.
Cinel, C., Valeriani, D. & Poli, R. 2019. Neurotechnologies for Human Cognitive Augmentation: Current State of the Art and Future Prospects. *Front Hum Neurosci*, 13, 13.
Clark, A. 2010. Memento's Revenge: The Extended Mind, Extended. *In*: Menary, R. (ed.) *The Extended Mind*. Cambridge, MA: MIT Press.
Coin, A. & Dubljevic, V. 2021. The Authenticity of Machine-Augmented Human Intelligence: Therapy, Enhancement, and the Extended Mind. *Neuroethics*, 14, 283–290.
Danaher, J. 2018. Toward an Ethics of AI Assistants: An Initial Framework. *Philosophy & Technology*, 31, 629–653.
Darpa. 2018. *Progress in Quest to Develop a Human Memory Prosthesis* [Online]. Available: https://www.darpa.mil/news-events/2018-03-28 [Accessed 04/08/2019].
Erler, A. 2014. Authenticity. *In*: Jennings, B. (ed.) *Bioethics, 4th Edition*. Farmington Hills, MI: Macmillan Reference USA.
Erler, A. 2020. Neuroenhancement, Coercion, and Neo-Luddism. *In*: Vincent, N. A. (ed.) *Neuro-Interventions and the Law*. Oxford: Oxford University Press.
Erler, A. & Müller, V. C. 2022. The Ethics of Biomedical Military Research: Therapy, Prevention, Enhancement, and Risk. *In*: Messelken, D. & Winkler, D. (eds.) *Health Care in Contexts of Risk, Uncertainty, and Hybridity*. Cham, Switzerland: Springer, 235–252.
Fox, K. C. R. & Beaty, R. E. 2019. Mind-Wandering As Creative Thinking: Neural, Psychological, and Theoretical Considerations. *Current Opinion in Behavioral Sciences*, 27, 123–130.
Frankenfield, J. 2021. Robo-Advisor. *Investopedia* [Online]. Available: https://www.investopedia.com/terms/r/roboadvisor-roboadviser.asp [Accessed 31/03/21].
Gartenberg, C. 2019. Apple's Hired Contractors Are Listening to Your Recorded Siri Conversations, Too. *The Verge* [Online]. Available: https://www.theverge.com/2019/7/26/8932064/apple-siri-private-conversation-recording-explanation-alexa-google-assistant [Accessed 06/05/2021].
Gilbert, F., Pham, C., Viana, J. & Gillam, W. 2019. Increasing Brain-Computer Interface Media Depictions: Pressing Ethical Concerns. *Brain-Computer Interfaces*, 6, 49–70.
Giubilini, A. & Savulescu, J. 2018. The Artificial Moral Advisor. The "Ideal Observer" Meets Artificial Intelligence. *Philosophy & Technology*, 31, 169–188.
Gonfalonieri, A. 2020. What Brain-Computer Interfaces Could Mean for the Future of Work. *Harvard Business Review* [Online]. Available: https://hbr.org/2020/10/what-brain-computer-interfaces-could-mean-for-the-future-of-work [Accessed 10/04/2021].
Good, I. J. 1965. Speculations Concerning the First Ultraintelligent Machine. *In*: Alt, F. L. & Rubinoff, M. (eds.) *Advances in Computers*. New York & London: Academic Press.
Görz, G., Schmid, U. & Braun, T. 2020. *Handbuch der Künstlichen Intelligenz*. Berlin: De Gruyter.
Guynn, J. 2020. What You Need to Know Before Clicking 'I Agree' On That Terms of Service Agreement or Privacy Policy. *USA Today* [Online]. Available: https://www.usatoday.com/story/tech/2020/01/28/not-reading-the-small-print-is-privacy-policy-fail/4565274002/ [Accessed 14/05/21].
Hafner, M., Stepanek, M., Taylor, J., Troxel, W. M. & Van Stolk, C. 2016. *Why Sleep Matters – The Economic Costs of Insufficient Sleep: A Cross-Country Comparative Analysis*. Santa Monica, CA: RAND Corporation.
He, Y., Eguren, D., Azorin, J. M., Grossman, R. G., Luu, T. P. & Contreras-Vidal, J. L. 2018. Brain-Machine Interfaces for Controlling Lower-Limb Powered Robotic Systems. *Journal of Neural Engineering*, 15, 021004.
Hitchcock, D. 2018. Critical Thinking. *In*: Zalta, E. N. (ed.) *The Stanford Encyclopedia of Philosophy (Fall 2020 Edition)*. https://plato.stanford.edu/archives/fall2020/entries/critical-thinking/ (accessed 23/04/2021)
Hughes, C., Herrera, A., Gaunt, R. & Collinger, J. 2020. Bidirectional Brain-Computer Interfaces. *In*: Ramsey, N. F. & Millán, J. D. R. (eds.) *Handbook of Clinical Neurology*. Amsterdam: Elseview.
Ienca, M. & Haselager, P. 2016. Hacking the Brain: Brain-Computer Interfacing Technology and the Ethics of Neurosecurity. *Ethics and Information Technology*, 18, 117–129.
Ienca, M. & Andorno, R. 2017. Towards New Human Rights in the Age of Neuroscience and Neurotechnology. *Life Sciences, Society and Policy*, 13, 5.
Ienca, M., Haselager, P. & Emanuel, E. J. 2018a. Brain Leaks and Consumer Neurotechnology. *Nature Biotechnology*, 36, 805–810.
Ienca, M., Jotterand, F. & Elger, B. S. 2018b. From Healthcare to Warfare and Reverse: How Should We Regulate Dual-Use Neurotechnology? *Neuron*, 97, 269–274.

Iversen, H. 2020. Conversational AI and the Future of Financial Advice. *Finextra* [Online]. Available from: https://www.finextra.com/blogposting/18391/conversational-ai-and-the-future-of-financial-advice [Accessed January 29 2021].

Jing, M. & Soo, Z. 2019. Brainwave-Tracking Start-Up BrainCo in Controversy over Tests on Chinese Schoolchildren. *South China Morning Post* [Online]. Available: https://www.scmp.com/tech/start-ups/article/3005448/brainwave-tracking-start-china-schoolchildren-controversy-working [Accessed 10/04/2021].

Kania, E. B. 2019. Minds at War. *PRISM*, 8, 82–101.

Kaushal, A., Altman, R. & Langlotz, C. 2020. Health Care AI Systems Are Biased. *Sci Am* [Online]. Available: https://www.scientificamerican.com/article/health-care-ai-systems-are-biased/ [Accessed 28/05/2021].

Klein, E. 2020. Ethics and the Emergence of Brain-Computer Interface Medicine. *In*: Ramsey, N. F. & Millán, J. D. R. (eds.) *Handbook of Clinical Neurology*. Amsterdam: Elsevier, 329–339.

Kurzweil, R. 2005. *The Singularity Is Near: When Humans Transcend Biology*. New York: Viking.

Lara, F. & Deckers, J. 2020. Artificial Intelligence as a Socratic Assistant for Moral Enhancement. *Neuroethics*, 13, 275–287.

Lavazza, A. 2018. Freedom of Thought and Mental Integrity: The Moral Requirements for Any Neural Prosthesis. *Front Neurosci*, 12, 82.

Ledford, H. 2019. Millions Affected by Racial Bias in Healh-Care Algorithm. *Nature*, 574, 608–609.

Lewis, T. & Stix, G. 2019. Elon Musk's Secretive Brain Tech Company Debuts a Sophisticated Neural Implant. *Sci Am* [Online]. Available: https://www.scientificamerican.com/article/elon-musks-secretive-brain-tech-company-debuts-a-sophisticated-neural-implant1/ [Accessed 21/04/2021].

Lin, P., Mehlman, M. & Abney, K. 2013. *Enhanced Warfighters: Risk, Ethics, and Policy*. The Greenwall Foundation.

Mccall, I. C. & Wexler, A. 2020. Peering Into the Mind? The Ethics of Consumer Neuromonitoring Devices. *In*: Bard, I. & Hildt, E. (eds.) *Ethical Dimensions of Commercial and DIY Neurotechnologies*. Cambridge, MA: Elsevier.

Mccarthy, J., Minsky, M., Rochester, N. & Shannon, C. E. 1955. *A Proposal for the Dartmouth Summer Research Project on Artificial Intelligence* [Online]. Available: http://www-formal.stanford.edu/jmc/history/dartmouth/dartmouth.html [Accessed 28/05/2021].

Müller, V. C. 2020. Ethics of Artificial Intelligence and Robotics. *In*: Zalta, E. N. (ed.) *The Stanford Encyclopedia of Philosophy (Winter 2020 Edition)*. https://plato.stanford.edu/archives/win2020/entries/ethics-ai/ (accessed 06/05/2021).

Nikolin, S., Huggins, C., Martin, D., Alonzo, A. & Loo, C. K. 2018. Safety of Repeated Sessions of Transcranial Direct Current Stimulation: A Systematic Review. *Brain Stimul*, 11, 278–288.

Nuyujukian, P., Albites Sanabria, J., Saab, J., Pandarinath, C., Jarosiewicz, B., Blabe, C. H., Franco, B., Mernoff, S. T., Eskandar, E. N., Simeral, J. D., Hochberg, L. R., Shenoy, K. V. & Henderson, J. M. 2018. Cortical Control of a Tablet Computer by People with Paralysis. *PLoS One*, 13, e0204566.

O'Neill, E., Klincewicz, M. & Kemmer, M. Forthcoming. Ethical Issues With Artificial Ethics Assistants. *In*: Véliz, C. (ed.) *Oxford Handbook of Digital Ethics*. Oxford: Oxford University Press.

Pearl, J. & Mackenzie, D. 2018. *The Book of Why: The New Science of Cause and Effect*. New York: Basic Books.

Ragnedda, M. & Muschert, G. W. 2013. *The Digital Divide: The Internet and Social Inequality in International Perspective*. Abingdon, Oxon; New York, NY: Routledge, Taylor & Francis Group.

Ramadan, R. A., Refat, S., Elshahed, M. A. & Ali, R. A. 2015. Basics of Brain Computer Interface. *In*: Hassanien, A. E. & Azar, A. T. (eds.) *Brain-Computer Interfaces: Current Trends and Applications*. Cham: Springer.

Russell, S. 2019. *Human Compatible: Artificial Intelligence and the Problem of Control*. New York: Viking.

Russell, S. & Norvig, P. 2020. *Artificial Intelligence: A Modern Approach*. Upper Saddle River: Prentice Hall.

Savulescu, J. & Maslen, H. 2015. Moral Enhancement and Artificial Intelligence: Moral AI? *In*: Romportl, J., Zackova, E., Kelemen, J. (eds.) *Beyond Artificial Intelligence*. Cham: Springer.

Sutton, R. T., Pincock, D., Baumgart, D. C., Sadowski, D. C., Fedorak, R. N. & Kroeker, K. I. 2020. An Overview of Clinical Decision Support Systems: Benefits, Risks, and Strategies for Success. *NPJ Digit Med*, 3, 17.

Tennison, M. N. & Moreno, J. D. 2012. Neuroscience, Ethics, and National Security: The State of the Art. *PLoS Biol*, 10, e1001289.

The President's Council On Bioethics (U.S.). 2003. *Beyond Therapy: Biotechnology and the Pursuit of Happiness*. New York: ReganBooks.

Valeriani, D., Cinel, C. & Poli, R. 2019. Brain-Computer Interfaces for Human Augmentation. *Brain Sciences*, 9, 22. DOI: 10.3390/brainsci9020022

Vilela, M. & Hochberg, L. R. 2020. Applications of Brain-Computer Interfaces to the Control of Robotic and Prosthetic Arms. *In*: Ramsey, N. F. & Millán, J. D. R. (eds.) *Handbook of Clinical Neurology*. Amsterdam: Elseview.

Wexler, A. 2019. Separating Neuroethics from Neurohype. *Nature Biotechnology*, 37, 988–990.

Williamson, B. 2019. Brain Data: Scanning, Scraping and Sculpting the Plastic Learning Brain Through Neurotechnology. *Postdigital Science and Education*, 1, 65–86.

Wolbring, G., Diep, L., Yumakulov, S., Ball, N., Leopatra, V. & Yergens, D. 2013. Emerging Therapeutic Enhancement Enabling Health Technologies and Their Discourses: What Is Discussed within the Health Domain? *Healthcare (Basel)*, 1, 20–52.

Yuste, R., Goering, S., Arcas, B. A. Y., Bi, G., Carmena, J. M., Carter, A., Fins, J. J., Friesen, P., Gallant, J., Huggins, J. E., Illes, J., Kellmeyer, P., Klein, E., Marblestone, A., Mitchell, C., Parens, E., Pham, M., Rubel, A., Sadato, N., Sullivan, L. S., Teicher, M., Wasserman, D., Wexler, A., Whittaker, M. & Wolpaw, J. 2017. Four Ethical Priorities for Neurotechnologies and AI. *Nature*, 551, 159–163.

15
CLEARING THE BOTTLENECK OF EMPIRICAL DATA IN THE ETHICS OF COGNITIVE ENHANCEMENT

Cynthia Forlini

15.1 Introduction

Stakeholder and community engagement is a mainstay of modern ethics scholarship. In the form of *empirical ethics*, it denotes when "empirical social scientific analysis is integrated with ethical analysis in order to draw normative conclusions" (Ives et al. 2018, p. 1). These analyses can capture attitudes, perspectives, reactions, acceptability, and willingness of stakeholders, interest groups, communities with a particular experience, and the public toward ethically contentious issues with social and regulatory implications. In turn, these insights are expected to guide appropriate policy and practice that reflect the values of those who are involved or affected by a particular practice or innovation. The multiple critiques of this approach are beyond the scope of this chapter (Hurst 2010). Instead, the goal is to examine how existing data on the attitudes, values, and preferences of stakeholders and the public have influenced the ethics debate on human enhancement, one of the most ethically contentious topics of the past few decades. Cognitive enhancement (CE) is used as a case study to show how stakeholder engagement and the data collected through empirical ethics have both advanced our understanding of the ethics of human enhancement but also contributed novel ethical blind spots to the debate. The case study is not an exhaustive review of all existing empirical evidence on the ethics of CE. Rather, I present studies that are illustrative of trends in the wealth of international published data. I propose that, currently, empirical data on the ethics of CE are contributing to a bottleneck in scholarship and policy.

15.2 Ethical controversy over CE of healthy individuals

For the past two decades, the ethics of CE have been a point of intrigue in academic and public discourses alike (Forlini and Racine 2009b, Partridge et al. 2011, Voarino, Dubljevic, and Racine 2016). Cognitive enhancement is traditionally defined as the "Amplification or extension of core capacities of the mind through improvement or augmentation of internal or external information processing systems" (Sandberg and Bostrom 2006, p. 201). These processing systems usually refer to attention, memory, and alertness but can also comprise motivation and emotional capacities (Erler and Forlini 2020). This definition accommodates a range of interventions that can be behavioral such as sleep, nutrition, and education, or technological, such as pharmacology, supplements, and brain stimulation (Dresler et al. 2019). However, it is mainly the technological interventions that are at the center of ethical controversy as to whether they are coercive, fair, safe, and align with an individual's authentic self (Erler and Forlini 2020). Some technologies like prescription stimulants are contentious because enhancement practices derive from the diversion of highly regulated medical substances (Dunn and Forlini 2020). Others, such as non-invasive brain stimulation (e.g. transcranial direct current stimulation, tDCS) are new technologies that have bypassed safety and efficacy trials to become available direct-to-consumer (Wexler and Reiner 2019). Regardless of technology, there is currently no academic or public consensus on any of the ethical issues in the CE debate.

The ethics of CE are wedged between two prescriptive normative frameworks (Forlini and Hall 2016). On the one hand are arguments in favor of the potential benefits for individuals and society such as promoting autonomy (Schaefer, Kahane, and Savulescu 2014) and increasing equality of opportunity (Ray 2016). This stance is bolstered by statements describing the inevitability of CE such that it: "should be viewed in the same general category as education, good health habits, and information technology – ways that our uniquely innovative species tries to improve itself" (Greely et al. 2008, p. 702). On the other hand, are objections to CE based on its negative impact on human nature and unfairness in competitive environments (President's Council on Bioethics 2003). Given the polarization of ethical positions, empirical data on the perspectives of stakeholders (e.g. students and professionals) and the public hold great promise in helping to determine how CE might fit with existing values and practices.

15.3 Empirical uncertainty about the safety, efficacy, and prevalence of CE

Debates on the ethics of CE have consistently taken place against a backdrop of empirical uncertainty on a few fronts. Efficacy and prevalence were positioned as proxies for the demand and acceptability of this ethically contentious practice. The expectation was that either of these elements could be a rate-limiting step for debating the ethics of CE (Forlini and Racine 2013). For example, if putative enhancers generate a consistent and significant effect, it could be argued that individuals ought to have a choice to engage in or abstain from use. If harmful, CE technologies could be regulated differently or banned to protect the well-being of individuals and communities. Similarly, a significant proportion of individuals or groups using a substance or device for a CE could be interpreted as a sign of social acceptability, which would provide the impetus to characterize an ethical practice. To date, none of the available data on efficacy and prevalence supports any of these contingencies. More robust and detailed evidence of the efficacy and prevalence of CE continues to be the source of perennial calls for further research (Farah et al. 2014).

There is no resounding evidence to support the use of putative CE technologies. Popular pharmacological enhancers such as methylphenidate and modafinil have been shown to have weak (Repantis et al. 2010) and moderate (Battleday and Brem 2016) effects on cognition, respectively. Non-invasive brain stimulation (e.g. tDCS, and transcranial magnetic stimulation) produces only small effects on working memory (Begemann et al. 2020). Each of these interventions used for CE is associated with side effects of varying severity (e.g. disturbances in sleep, appetite, cardiac rhythm, and mental health) (Dresler et al. 2019). However, reports of serious adverse effects from these interventions are generally rare and it is unclear what proportion would be attributable specifically to enhancement uses (Tull et al. 2020). From an ethical perspective, this evidence translates into empirical uncertainty because the potential effects are *promising enough* for those seeking CE to try an intervention while the potential adverse effects are *not serious enough* to discourage use or restrict personal choice (Dunn and Forlini 2020).

Global data on the prevalence of CE does not provide support for claims of widespread use or demand. According to a recent systematic review, international prevalence rates for CE range from 2–33% of samples (Sharif et al. 2021). Most of the studies included in this review hail from North America and Europe, with fewer studies representing Australasia, South America, and Africa. These prevalence rates provide many valuable insights such as confirming CE technologies *are* used in some academic and professional contexts, detecting predisposing factors (e.g. gender, location, academic discipline, profession), identifying diverse motives for use, and indicating instances of polysubstance/technology use for enhancement (Dunn and Forlini 2020). Additionally, Maier et al.'s (Maier, Ferris, and Winstock 2018) analysis of data from the Global Drug Survey showed a 180% increase in the use of prescription and illegal stimulants between the surveys in 2015 (4.9%) and 2017 (13.7%). However, these data still only represent a snapshot of CE and cannot support claims of widespread use (i.e. CE happens *everywhere*) or demand (i.e. individuals, groups, and communities *want* to engage in CE). These data translate into empirical uncertainty because there is still no consensus among academics in a decades-long debate as to whether the current range of prevalence rates is "high" (Farah 2011) or "low" (Lucke et al. 2018). On balance, it appears that the empirical uncertainty about the safety, efficacy, and prevalence of CE has driven the status quo of CE practices and allowed them to continue unchecked from an ethical perspective.

15.4 Highlighting the successes of stakeholder engagement on the ethics of cognitive enhancement

There are three areas where data on the attitudes, perspectives, and preferences of stakeholders have helped to characterize the ethics debate on CE. These successes show that the ethics of CE can be independent of data on safety, efficacy, and prevalence. Overall, empirical research shows that the ethics of CE are highly complex by providing evidence of conditions, context, and contention relating to ethical acceptability.

15.4.1 Delimiting the boundaries of ethical acceptability of CE

Stakeholder data revealed a few context-specific aspects of CE practices that established ethical tipping points for acceptability regardless of the means, technological or otherwise. First, the cognitive target of CE is ethically salient. Targets of CE are divided into two categories: (1) fundamental traits related to the authentic identity and selfhood of an individual such as mood, memory, and emotions; and (2) performance traits such as concentration, attention, focus, and alertness. Young healthy individuals are less willing to use an enhancer to modify fundamental traits out of concern for the impact that it might have on their self-identity (Bergstrom and Lynoe 2008, Riis, Simmons, and Goodwin 2008, Sabini and Monterosso 2005). However, CE of fundamental traits could be acceptable *only* if used to enable expression of one's "true self" (Riis, Simmons, and Goodwin 2008). This ethical tipping point relating to the authenticity of a performance is recurrent throughout empirical ethics data on CE.

Second, data shows that the level of enhancement impacts ethical acceptability. Stakeholders accept enhancements that act as a "normalizer"(Sabini and Monterosso 2005), "enhance to the norm" (Cabrera, Fitz, and Reiner 2015), "restore" cognitive function to prior levels (Banjo, Nadler, and Reiner 2010), help "lower performing individuals" (Sattler et al. 2013), or are used when "performance is low and an extra boost is needed to avoid failure" (Bard et al. 2018). These terms denote the acceptability of interventions that confer abilities aligned with what is considered usual for a particular individual or cohort to which they belong (e.g. age, gender, academic level). Arguably, this stance implies disapproval of interventions that amplify the cognition of individuals who are not experiencing any personal or comparative deficit in function.

Third, stakeholder data on acceptability differentiates between the type of person engaging in CE. In general, support for CE in the public for any motive is low (Bergstrom and Lynoe 2008, Sattler et al. 2013, Schelle et al. 2014). However, some studies have shown that stakeholders who might not personally choose to engage in CE do not automatically disapprove of others who do (Dinh, Humphries, and Chatterjee 2020, Forlini and Racine 2009a). Furthermore, a recent study showed that respondents believe CE was more appropriate for employees than students (Dinh,

Humphries, and Chatterjee 2020). The ethical tipping points that have become evident through empirical ethics studies on the acceptability of CE indicate support for a limited set of cognitive capacities, motives, and groups.

15.4.2 Identifying specific issues of ethical contention about CE

Stakeholder engagement has shown that general (un)acceptability of CE is underpinned by contention about a host of ethical issues. Schelle et al. (2014) reviewed 40 empirical ethics studies on attitudes toward the ethics of CE. The authors found that medical safety, coercion, and fairness are the most recurrent and ethically contentious topics across a range of stakeholders (e.g. students, professionals, and the general public). Indeed, these three topics continue to be discussed in subsequent empirical research. Faber et al. (2016) CE showed that concerns about fairness outweighed those relating to enhanced performances being hollow and undeserving of reward (i.e. authenticity). The much-feared coercion in commercial, high-stakes, and competitive environments as the main driver of CE was recently reframed as more likely to be a potential social pressure rather than direct coercion (Petersen and Petersen 2019). This conclusion reaffirms previous findings that social pressure may constrain the personal choice and values of individuals with respect to CE (Forlini and Racine 2009a). Knowing which issues are most ethically contentious has the potential to focus research on areas that require clarification through additional empirical or theoretical scholarship and identify solutions for modifying areas of policy and practice to align with the core values of stakeholders.

Prioritizing an ethical issue related to CE for further research or practical action poses a significant challenge because stakeholder data shows that the issues of safety, coercion, and fairness are inextricably linked (Forlini and Racine 2012a). Available evidence about safety will impact whether individuals feel they are making an informed choice about CE use (Forlini and Racine 2009a). Stakeholders firmly believe that using CE is a matter of personal choice (Forlini and Racine 2009a, Petersen and Petersen 2019), they recognized the potential for that choice to be influenced by the perception that a significant proportion of peers are using CE (Forlini and Racine 2009a, Sattler et al. 2013). Widespread use in social circles, and belief in efficacy, can also lead to individuals feeling disadvantaged if not using CE (Forlini and Racine 2009a). This disadvantage is expressed both in terms of access to putative modes of CE and experiencing the potential gains in performance (Aikins 2019, Faber, Savulescu, and Douglas 2016, Forlini and Racine 2012a). It could be argued that this cascade of issues is contingent on determining the safety and efficacy of enhancers. However, issues of personal choice, cheating, and fairness of opportunity have persisted despite an unclear safety profile. A truly efficacious CE could incite mandates for higher levels of cognitive performance that would bring about direct coercion and widen disparities in access to opportunities. Getting ahead of those unethical outcomes requires consensus on whether there is room for them in our society and institutions. Thus far, empirical research on the ethics of CE has been unable to produce that consensus.

15.4.3 Demonstrating ambivalence on some ethical issues regarding cognitive enhancement

The third success of empirical data is helping to demonstrate that stakeholder perspectives on the ethics of CE are founded on ambivalence. The term *substantial ambivalence* denotes the "coexistence of conflicting perspectives" (Forlini and Racine 2012a, p. 39). It means that stakeholders are not categorical in their perspectives on the ethics of CE. This ambivalence manifests in a few ways.

First, the ethics of CE are difficult to align with analogies to existing modes of performance enhancement (e.g. substances such as caffeine and performance-enhancing steroids) and regulation (e.g. food and nutritional, direct-to-consumer, prescription, banned). Studies have shown both convergences and divergences with respect to the ethics of CE with caffeine (i.e. a freely available substance that can enhance some cognitive capacities) and sports doping (i.e. a banned substance that acts on physical not cognitive attributes) (Forlini and Racine 2012b, Partridge et al. 2013, Heyes and Boardley 2019). Franke et al. (2012) reported that a small majority of students found no *moral* difference between prescription stimulants for CE and caffeine use but would be deterred from using a prescription stimulant for fear of side effects and legal ramifications. Research using analogies and metaphors has also pointed to the malleability of attitudes toward CE based on the analogies or metaphors that are presented. In one study, interviewees appealed to analogies to justify CE based on its benefits rather than acknowledging any of the harmful or unethical features (Heyes and Boardley 2019). Conrad et al. embedded analogies into their vignette-based survey and showed that CE was rated more acceptable when described as "fuel" for an individual rather than "steroids," the latter having a negative and unethical connotation (Conrad, Humphries, and Chatterjee 2019). Using the "contrastive vignette technique," which used different analogies to detect incremental changes in ethical acceptability, Fitz et al. (2014) found that the general public is "biopolitically moderate," adhering to neither conservative nor liberal stances consistently. None of these results indicate indecision about CE on the part of stakeholders but rather acknowledge the common features in various analogical contexts. Using analogies in empirical research on the ethics of CE demonstrated that existing modes of CE do not align neatly with familiar substances in terms of effect or regulation, and they can influence whether an instance of CE is deemed ethically acceptable or not (Forlini and Hall 2016).

Second, unlike the ethical tipping points that exist for the overall acceptability of CE, stakeholders have expressed substantial ambivalence on contentious issues in the ethics of CE irrespective of context. Empirical studies of the perspectives of healthcare professionals showed a lack of consensus (interpreted as substantial ambivalence) on the safety and appropriateness of using and prescribing a controlled substance for CE (Banjo, Nadler, and Reiner 2010, Hotze et al. 2011, Ram et al. 2020). Stakeholders are still balancing their beliefs about the moral agency with which individuals engage or abstain from CE. Available data supports that CE *should* be a personal choice but there are instances where that personal choice could be constrained by social pressures or expectations (Forlini and Racine 2009a, Petersen and Petersen 2019). In terms of fairness, Fitz et al. found that "the public endorses meritocratic principles yet values effort" (Fitz et al. 2014, p. 183). Whether an "enhanced" effort is genuine is yet another topic of substantial ambivalence (Forlini and Racine 2012a). On the one hand, an individual who used CE still exerts an effort to perform given that no existing mode confers knowledge or skills. On the other hand, individuals using CE are believed to be taking shortcuts and potentially discounting opportunities to learn and develop skills. Most studies reported here have tethered analogies or ethical issues to specific modes of CE, which suggests that ambivalence does not emerge from a lack of context in empirical studies. Bard et al. (2018) explain that overall ambivalence about the ethics of CE reflects concurrent collectivist and individualist values among stakeholders that are not easily reconciled into normative positions to guide practice and policy.

15.5 Highlighting the novel blind spots of stakeholder engagement on the ethics of cognitive enhancement

Stakeholder engagement has created a few significant blind spots in the ethics of CE that might have been foreseen and prevented as the empirical evidence base on this topic evolved. One blind spot pertains to inclusive research methodologies. The others derive from assumptions that were made early in the ethics debate but rarely revisited alongside emerging empirical data about the acceptability of CE and evidence of ethical contention.

15.5.1 Limited representation of diverse communities among samples in empirical research

Representation is a major problem in CE ethics scholarship, especially in empirical studies. The range of social, racial, professional, economic, and geographical contexts represented is narrow. There are prevalence studies from Africa, Asia, Europe, North America, Oceania, and South America, which confirm that CE happens in many parts of the world (Maier, Ferris, and Winstock 2018, Sharif et al. 2021). However, existing prevalence data remain piecemeal across the globe leaving the *extent* to which CE needs to be a global concern currently unanswerable. From an empirical ethics perspective, the type of stakeholders recruited for studies is repetitive. A review of literature on the social context of CE, "found that research efforts have chiefly targeted college students, yet there is a lack of knowledge concerning other social groups likely to use these pharmaceuticals nonmedically, such as persons with high strain employment" (Robitaille and Collin 2016, p. 357). A minority of studies have sought to take the temperature of health professionals focusing on the gatekeepers of some of the medications and devices (i.e. physicians) (Forlini and Racine 2012a, Ram et al. 2020, Banjo, Nadler, and Reiner 2010, Hotze et al. 2011). Research into this narrow scope of context has yielded an abundance of data, but there are still unexamined applications of CE. For example, some uses like memorizing phone numbers of sports statistics (Glannon 2008) would not produce any collective or individual gain. The absence of contexts outside competition and professional practice suggests a potentially misleading assumption that non-competitive contexts are and will remain ethically uncontroversial.

Much of the empirical research on the ethics of CE is based on studies that recruited convenience samples through schools, universities, professional societies, and advertising in public venues. The recent shift to using tools like Amazon Mechanical Turk was expected to provide access to a variety of respondents that more accurately reflect the diversity of populations (Paolacci, Chandler, and Ipeirotis 2010). However, despite using this tool, the sample of Dinh et al.'s (2020) survey of public opinion on CE was still approximately 75% white, which led the authors to call for further studies that actively include culturally and linguistically diverse groups. In a direct response to this survey, Ray (2020) critiqued that Dinh et al.'s "research tells us what mostly White people think of CE," which perpetuates the underrepresentation of people of color in scientific research (Ray 2020, p. 238). Ray proposes that ethical perspectives on CE may change dramatically if more people of color were included in study samples. Namely, fairness could be discussed differently with respect to using CE to increase equality of opportunity or widen competitive advantage for groups with privilege. In Aikins' (2019) interview study, a few respondents evoked differences in perceived rates of CE use among different racial groups (i.e. more prevalent among white students) with one dubbing the use of stimulants for CE as "the white version of cheating" (p. 121). Respondents also noted that the differences in CE use are part of broader issues related to access to healthcare and wealth. These results are good indications that there is still more to learn about the social-economic-cultural-racial context influencing CE practices (Forlini and Hall 2016). Engaging in this learning will require more than inclusive recruitment practices. Methods, research questions, and empirical tools must be tailored to the context and issues of diverse populations recruited for future studies. Reproducible results are a hallmark of rigorous research. However, uncritically recreating existing studies risks using tools and asking questions that are not fit for purpose in addition to wasting time and resources. The current body of empirical studies on the ethics of CE can be used as a springboard for conducting research with diverse groups and in different contexts, but not a template.

15.5.2 Few viable options for regulation of enhancement

There is no overarching regulation about the intentions, actions, and consequences relating to enhancing (or at least attempting to) any aspect of cognition. Regulation of CE practices currently relies entirely on the regulation of the modes (substance or device) used, which to date are medical and consumer. The focus on technology is reflected in empirical studies that compare CE with doping in sports (a well-regulated and unethical practice) and caffeine (an accepted substance that is freely accessible). In doing so, these studies present only two viable outcomes of regulation: permitting or prohibiting. Neither model has emerged as a clear preference from stakeholder engagement. Some data shows recognition that CE is an unethical behavior in competitive environments, but it is differentiated from sports doping because of the visible physical effects that steroids produce (Forlini and Racine 2012; Bell, Partridge et al. 2013). Even though students in Franke et al.'s (2012) study found no moral difference between cognitive enhancement and caffeine, there was uncertainty about the most appropriate policy framework (permissive or restrictive) for CE. This ambivalence is harder to decipher than the substantial ambivalence described above. It is unclear whether stakeholders are indifferent, undecided, or conflicted about appropriate regulation. Another possibility is that the regulatory options presented in studies to date are far too blunt to capture the complexity of CE practices and ethical issues. Alternatives for regulating CE based on justice (i.e. taxation) (Dubljevic 2012), autonomy, and informed consent (Dubljevic 2013, Jwa 2019) are present in the literature but have not been investigated empirically. Furthermore, there is an unresolved question as to whether CE ought to be regulated on a case-by-case basis per technology (Dubljevic 2013) or on a practice level via a more general analytic framework (Jwa 2019). The kind of regulation of CE, if any, that will resonate with stakeholders will depend on adding more representative research to the literature and recognizing that it may be impossible to regulate uniformly across all modes, environments, contexts, regions, and groups where CE occurs.

Empirical evidence from studies with university students indicates that CE might not require additional regulation at all. In one study, low prevalence, and ethical concern about CE among students showed that policy was not a priority (Forlini et al. 2015). Another study reported that the illegality of using controlled substances for CE was not a major issue for students (Petersen and Petersen 2019). This finding suggests that regulation would not be an effective deterrent for CE practices that are currently taking place despite substances such as prescription stimulants only being available from a doctor. However, Petersen and Petersen (2019) propose that gray zones in regulation related to CE could be detrimental to the autonomy of individuals. Without clear and consistent regulation, individuals exercise their autonomy with respect to the benefit they perceive CE will confer, which is sometimes a function of how much disadvantage they are experiencing. While regulation may be bypassed or disregarded, its presence communicates some shared social values for individuals to incorporate into their consideration of CE. Arriving at those shared values is the next major challenge in CE research.

15.5.3 Lack of consensus on who is responsible for regulation

Empirical data on the ethics of CE provides few clues about which group, professional, institution, or governing body ought to take responsibility for regulating CE. Medical associations and academic institutions are frontrunners for regulating CE given that they already have long-standing policies about professional standards and academic integrity, respectively, which could scaffold positions on CE. Neither of these entities has been vocal about debating or actioning regulation. Medical associations could revise prescription practices to reduce the diversion of medications or new prescriptions for individuals expressly seeking CE. Generally, health professionals are uncomfortable with prescribing cognitive enhancers (Banjo, Nadler, and Reiner 2010, Bergstrom and Lynoe 2008, Hotze et al. 2011, Ram et al. 2020). Yet only two associations have specific policies about CE that attempt to establish common values and practices for their members. The American Academy of Neurology issued guidance for neurologists on responding to requests from patients for CE that says, "prescription of medications for neuroenhancement is 1) not ethically obligatory, 2) not ethically prohibited, and therefore, 3) is ethically permissible" (Larriviere et al. 2009, p. 1408). This guidance relies entirely on a practitioner's professional autonomy and judgment. This approach allows for prescription practices that are flexible practice yet ambiguous such that they accommodate "doctor shopping" (Aikins 2019). Conversely, the American Medical Association discourages physicians from prescribing medications for CE based on safety concerns for otherwise healthy individuals (American Medical Association 2016). Who can prescribe the types of substances used for CE and their availability differs between countries, therefore, these existing position statements have little traction outside the USA. Furthermore, regulation stemming from medicine would not cover access and oversight of consumer substances and devices used for CE. There is a further objection to the expectation that the medical profession alone ought to curb the non-medical use of prescription medication (Rosenfield et al. 2011). The argument is that academic institutions ought to be shouldering the responsibility of regulating CE given that it is mostly happening on campus and in pursuit of academic goals, not medical ones.

Though the focus of much of the empirical ethics research on CE has been conducted in a higher education setting, academic institutions have been relatively silent on the issue. Duke University (USA) is the only academic institution known to have a policy explicitly prohibiting the non-medical use of prescription stimulants (Aikins, Zhang, and McCabe 2017). This inaction could be explained by the perspectives of university policymakers. There is emerging evidence that university policymakers see CE as a health problem, not an academic integrity issue (Dunn et al. 2021). Indeed, in Dunn et al.'s study, university policymakers proposed addressing CE on campus mainly by promoting the benefits of a healthy lifestyle. This stance and the general absence of CE policies in universities push CE back into the health space. Consequently, the ethics of CE in competitive environments are repositioned as being contingent on safety and efficacy (Mihailov and Savulescu 2018). It also skirts issues of coercion and fairness, two of the most contentious issues in the ethics of CE, which is incomprehensible given their alignment with the purpose of academic integrity policies. Detecting CE and enforcing policies in academic environments would be no small feats, but it is now being recognized that "authorities, such as police officers and university teachers, are not very motivated to reduce or prevent students' use of cognitive enhancers, and doctors are, according to students, easily persuaded to prescribe PCEs" (Petersen and Petersen 2019, p. 362). The indifference of authorities and the disregard of some CE users for the regulation of common CE substances in the student context (i.e. the most extensively studied manifestation of CE) sets a poor precedent for professional, non-competitive, and social contexts of CE. To date, these contexts are less frequently considered and studied. They risk being ignored based on inaction in the health and academic spaces.

15.6 Asking a fundamental question about cognitive enhancement to clear the bottleneck of empirical data

The evidence base on the ethics of CE has grown steadily over the past two decades with the expectation that more data will unlock perspectives that will guide policy and practice. Despite the abundance of data, there have been very few real-world outcomes as evidenced by the novel blind spots discussed in this chapter. Even the successes of stakeholder engagement reveal what appears to be intractable ethical contention on a range of issues. These conclusions are supported by myriad studies that consistently report contention and ambivalence. Recurrent results are confirmatory of a phenomenon or trend in stakeholder perspectives. However, studies using the *same* methods, reporting the *same* results, and calling for the *same* future research may be hindering progress in the debate about the ethics of CE by creating a bottleneck in data (Forlini 2020). Save for Schelle et al.'s (2014) review, few efforts have been made to distill the findings of existing data into normative recommendations. This chapter is the first step in taking stock of not only the data that speaks to the ethics of CE but also applying those lessons to the general CE debate.

There are a few options for addressing the bottleneck in data. Recurrent data can be interpreted as having reached saturation (Hennink and Kaiser 2019). It is possible that we have learned all we can with the available methods and the research questions used to examine stakeholder perspectives. However, declaring saturation would mean leaving significant loose ends in terms of representation and determining actionable policy. Another option is to reorient stakeholder engagement and empirical ethics toward new research questions (Racine, Sattler, and Boehlen 2021). Racine et al. (2021) propose that the next frontier of stakeholder engagement ought to address human social and psychological behavior. Their interest is in examining the role of CE in human flourishing (e.g. stigmatization, burnout, mental well-being, and work motivation). These avenues are certainly promising as they would engage with some of the sociological contexts that were noted to be missing from the CE literature (Robitaille and Collin 2016). However, it is unclear to what extent more data would be an effective solution to an existing bottleneck in data. There is a serious risk of contributing to the recurrent results that created this impasse in the first place (Forlini 2020).

Part of the problem is that much of the data on the ethics of CE in the bottleneck was collected in an anticipatory fashion based on what ethical issues *might* arise rather than the major problems that individuals and institutions are grappling with. Wexler and Specker Sullivan (2021) identify this speculation as a major fault in the emergence and development of neuroethics scholarship. They argue that neuroethics inquiry must be integrated into real-world practices, inclusive of diverse perspectives, and focused on implementation (Wexler and Specker Sullivan 2021). With respect to the modes, motivations, and ethics of CE, we are no longer in a "discovery" phase. There is ample data about prevalence and attitudes in the literature and the media, so it is plausible to expect knowledge of CE practices to be sufficiently widespread among institutions and communities. Therefore, moving into an "implementation phase" requires calls for research on the ethics of CE to come directly from institutions and communities that are actively considering the practice.

The next phase in research on the ethics of CE requires academics, institutions, and communities alike to answer a fundamental question: is cognitive enhancement currently ethically problematic? This question is responsible for the narrow end of the bottleneck. Conceptually, CE has been described as a bubble (Lucke et al. 2011) and a myth (Zohny 2015) but also a public health problem (Arria and DuPont 2010). Collectively, empirical data on the ethics of CE have not succeeded in definitively answering this question. Petersen and Petersen's (2019) study stands out as the only one that does not designate social pressure related to CE as morally problematic. The answer to whether CE should *still* be considered an ethical problem can only be determined through honest conversations in workplaces, academic institutions, competitions, and communities. The current picture of low prevalence, mild efficacy, few adverse effects, and relative policy inaction (Erler and Forlini 2020) would suggest that CE is perhaps not the emerging or urgent ethical problem it was expected to be. Details of future technological, medical, or social innovations may well change this conclusion as their ethical implications are re-evaluated (Rogers, Draper, and Carter 2021). In the meantime, those researching the ethics of CE ought to consider how to proceed sustainably by re-examining existing scholarship, prioritizing areas of inquiry, and adding novel high-quality data specifically and sparingly.

References

Aikins, R., X. Zhang, and S. E. McCabe. 2017. "Academic doping: Institutional policies regarding nonmedical use of prescription stimulants in U.S. higher education." *Journal of Academic Ethics* 15:229–243.
Aikins, Ross. 2019. "'The White version of cheating?' Ethical and social equity concerns of cognitive enhancing drug users in higher education." *Journal of Academic Ethics* 17 (2):111–130. doi: 10.1007/s10805-018-9320-7.
American Medical Association. 2016. AMA Confronts the Rise of Nootropics. Chicago.
Arria, A. M., and R. L. DuPont. 2010. "Nonmedical prescription stimulant use among college students: Why we need to do something and what we need to do." *Journal of Addictive Diseases* 29 (4):417–426. doi: 10.1080/10550887.2010.509273.

Banjo, O. C., R. Nadler, and P. B. Reiner. 2010. "Physician attitudes towards pharmacological cognitive enhancement: Safety concerns are paramount." *PLoS One* 5 (12):e14322. doi: 10.1371/journal.pone.0014322.
Bard, I., G. Gaskell, A. Allansdottir, R. V. da Cunha, P. Eduard, J. Hampel, E. Hildt, C. Hofmaier, N. Kronberger, S. Laursen, A. Meijknecht, S. Nordal, A. Quintanilha, G. Revuelta, N. Saladie, J. Sandor, J. B. Santos, S. Seyringer, I. Singh, H. Somsen, W. Toonders, H. Torgersen, V. Torre, M. Varju, and H. Zwart. 2018. "Bottom up ethics – Neuroenhancement in education and employment." *Neuroethics* 11 (3):309–322. doi: 10.1007/s12152-018-9366-7.
Battleday, R. M., and A. K. Brem. 2016. "Modafinil for cognitive neuroenhancement in healthy non-sleep-deprived subjects: A systematic review." *European Neuropsychopharmacology* 26 (2):391. doi: 10.1016/j.euroneuro.2015.12.023.
Begemann, M. J., B. A. Brand, B. Curcic-Blake, A. Aleman, and I. E. Sommer. 2020. "Efficacy of non-invasive brain stimulation on cognitive functioning in brain disorders: A meta-analysis." *Psychological Medicine* 50 (15):2465–2486. doi: 10.1017/S0033291720003670.
Bergstrom, L. S., and N. Lynoe. 2008. "Enhancing concentration, mood and memory in healthy individuals: An empirical study of attitudes among general practitioners and the general population." *Scandinavian Journal of Public Health* 36 (5):532–537.
Cabrera, L., N. S. Fitz, and P. B. Reiner. 2015. "Empirical support for the moral salience of the therapy-enhancement distinction in the debate over cognitive, affective and social enhancement." *Neuroethics* 8:243–256.
Conrad, E. C., S. Humphries, and A. Chatterjee. 2019. "Attitudes toward cognitive enhancement: The role of metaphor and context." *AJOB Neuroscience* 10 (1):35–47. doi: 10.1080/21507740.2019.1595771.
Dinh, C. T., S. Humphries, and A. Chatterjee. 2020. "Public opinion on cognitive enhancement varies across different situations." *AJOB Neuroscience* 11 (4):224–237. doi: 10.1080/21507740.2020.1811797.
Dresler, M., A. Sandberg, C. Bublitz, K. Ohla, C. Trenado, A. Mroczko-Wasowicz, S. Kuhn, and D. Repantis. 2019. "Hacking the brain: Dimensions of cognitive enhancement." *ACS Chemical Neuroscience* 10 (3):1137–1148. doi: 10.1021/acschemneuro.8b00571.
Dubljevic, V. 2013. "Prohibition or coffee shops: Regulation of amphetamine and methylphenidate for enhancement use by healthy adults." *American Journal of Bioethics* 13 (7):23–33. doi: 10.1080/15265161.2013.794875.
Dubljevic, V. 2012. "Principles of justice as the basis for public policy on psychopharmacological cognitive enhancement." *Law, Innovation and Technology* 4 (1):67–83. doi: 10.5235/175799612800650617.
Dunn, M., P. Dawson, M. Bearman, and J. Tai. 2021. "'I'd struggle to see it as cheating': The policy and regulatory environments of study drug use at universities." *Higher Education Research & Development* 40 (2):234–246. doi: 10.1080/07294360.2020.1738351.
Dunn, M., and C. Forlini. 2020. "The non-medical uses of prescription stimulants in the Australian context." In *Human Enhancement Drugs*, edited by Katinka van de Ven, Kyle J.D. Mulrooney and Jim McVeigh, 156–169. London: Routledge.
Erler, A., and C. Forlini. 2020. "Neuroenhancement." In: *Routledge Encyclopedia of Philosophy*, Taylor and Francis, viewed 31 March 2023, <https://www.rep.routledge.com/articles/thematic/neuroenhancement/v-1>. doi:10.4324/9780415249126-L162-1
Faber, N. S., J. Savulescu, and T. Douglas. 2016. "Why is cognitive enhancement deemed unacceptable? The role of fairness, deservingness, and hollow achievements." *Frontiers in Psychology* 7 (232). doi: 10.3389/fpsyg.2016.00232.
Farah, M. J. 2011. "Overcorrecting the neuroenhancement discussion." *Addiction* 106 (6):1190; author reply 1190-1. doi: 10.1111/j.1360-0443.2011.03394.x.
Farah, M. J., M. E. Smith, I. Ilieva, and R. H. Hamilton. 2014. "Cognitive enhancement." *Wiley Interdisciplinary Reviews: Cognitive Science* 5 (1):95–103. doi: 10.1002/wcs.1250.
Fitz, N. S., R. Nadler, P. Manogaran, E. W. J. Chong, and P. B. Reiner. 2014. "Public attitudes toward cognitive enhancement." *Neuroethics* 7 (2):173–188. doi: 10.1007/s12152-013-9190-z.
Forlini, C., and W. Hall. 2016. "The is and ought of the ethics of neuroenhancement: Mind the gap." *Frontiers in Psychology* 6:1998. doi: 10.3389/fpsyg.2015.01998.
Forlini, C., and E. Racine. 2009a. "Autonomy and coercion in academic 'cognitive enhancement' using methylphenidate: Perspectives of a pragmatic study of key stakeholders." *Neuroethics* 2 (3):163–177.
Forlini, C., and E. Racine. 2009b. "Disagreements with implications: Diverging discourses on the ethics of non-medical use of methylphenidate for performance enhancement." *BMC Med Ethics* 10:9.
Forlini, C., and E. Racine. 2013. "Does the cognitive enhancement debate call for a renewal of the deliberative role of bioethics?" In *Cognitive Enhancement: An Interdisciplinary Perspective*, edited by E. Hildt and A. Franke, 173–186. Dordrecht: Springer.
Forlini, C., and E. Racine. 2012a. "Added value(s) to the cognitive enhancement debate: Are we sidestepping values in academic discourse and professional policies?" *AJOB Empir Bioeth* 3 (1):33–47.

Forlini, C., and E. Racine. 2012b. "Stakeholder perspectives and reactions to 'academic' cognitive enhancement: Unsuspected meaning of ambivalence and analogies." *Public Understanding of Science* 21 (5):606–625.

Forlini, C., J. Schildmann, P. Roser, R. Beranek, and J. Vollmann. 2015. "Knowledge, experiences and views of German university students toward neuroenhancement: An empirical-ethical analysis." *Neuroethics* 8:93–92.

Forlini, C. 2020. "Empirical data is failing to break the ethics stalemate in the cognitive enhancement debate." *AJOB Neurosci* 11 (4):240–242. doi: 10.1080/21507740.2020.1830883.

Franke, A. G., K. Lieb and E. Hildt (2012). "What users think about the differences between caffeine and illicit/prescription stimulants for cognitive enhancement." *PLoS One* 7(6): e40047

Glannon, W. 2008. "Psychopharmacological enhancement." *Neuroethics* 1:45–54.

Greely, H., B. Sahakian, J. Harris, R. C. Kessler, M. Gazzaniga, P. Campbell, and M. J. Farah. 2008. "Towards responsible use of cognitive-enhancing drugs by the healthy." *Nature* 456 (7224):702–705.

Hennink, M., and B. Kaiser. 2019. "Saturation in qualitative research." In *SAGE Research Methods Foundations*, edited by P. Atkinson, S. Delamont, A. Cernat, J. W. Sakshaug and R. A. Williams. London: SAGE Publications Ltd. Available at: <https://doi.org/10.4135/9781526421036822322> [Accessed 31 Mar 2023].

Heyes, A. R., and I. D. Boardley. 2019. "Psychosocial factors facilitating use of cognitive enhancing drugs in education: A qualitative investigation of moral disengagement and associated processes." *Drugs* 26 (4):329–338. doi: 10.1080/09687637.2019.1586831.

Hotze, T., K. Shaw, E. Anderson, and M. Wynia. 2011. "'Doctor, would you prescribe a pill to help me…?' A national survey of physicians on using medicine for human enhancement." *AJOB* 11 (1):3–13.

Hurst, S. 2010. "What 'empirical turn in bioethics'?" *Bioethics* 24 (8):439–444. doi: 10.1111/j.1467-8519.2009.01720.x.

Ives, J., M. Dunn, B. Molewijk, J. Schildmann, K. Baeroe, L. Frith, R. Huxtable, E. Landeweer, M. Mertz, V. Provoost, A. Rid, S. Salloch, M. Sheehan, D. Strech, M. de Vries, and G. Widdershoven. 2018. "Standards of practice in empirical bioethics research: Towards a consensus." *BMC Medical Ethics* 19 (1):68. doi: 10.1186/s12910-018-0304-3.

Jwa, A. S. 2019. "Regulating the use of cognitive enhancement: An analytic framework." *Neuroethics* 12 (3):293–309. doi: 10.1007/s12152-019-09408-5.

Larriviere, D., M. A. Williams, M. Rizzo, and R. J. Bonnie. 2009. "Responding to requests from adult patients for neuroenhancements. Guidance of the Ethics, Law and Humanities Committee." *Neurology* 73 (17):1406–1412.

Lucke, J. C., S. Bell, B. J. Partridge, and W. D. Hall. 2011. "Deflating the neuroenhancement bubble." *AJOB Neuroscience* 2 (4):38–43.

Lucke, J., C. Jensen, M. Dunn, G. Chan, C. Forlini, S. Kaye, B. Partridge, M. Farrell, E. Racine, and W. Hall. 2018. "Non-medical prescription stimulant use to improve academic performance among Australian university students: Prevalence and correlates of use." *BMC Public Health* 18 (1):1270. doi: 10.1186/s12889-018-6212-0.

Maier, L. J., J. A. Ferris, and A. R. Winstock. 2018. "Pharmacological cognitive enhancement among non-ADHD individuals-A cross-sectional study in 15 countries." *International Journal of Drug Policy* 58:104–112. doi: 10.1016/j.drugpo.2018.05.009.

Mihailov, E., and J. Savulescu. 2018. "Social policy and cognitive enhancement: Lessons from chess." *Neuroethics* 11 (2):115–127. doi: 10.1007/s12152-018-9354-y.

Paolacci, G., J. Chandler, and P. G. Ipeirotis. 2010. "Running experiments on Amazon Mechanical Turk." *Judgment and Decision Making* 5 (5):411–419.

Partridge, B., S. Bell, J. Lucke, and W. Hall. 2013. "Australian university students' attitudes towards the use of prescription stimulants as cognitive enhancers: Perceived patterns of use, efficacy and safety." *Drug and Alcohol Review* 32 (3):295–302. doi:10.1111/dar.12005.

Partridge, B., S. Bell, J. Lucke, S. Yeates, and W. Hall. 2011. "Smart drugs 'As common as coffee': Media hype about neuroenhancement." *PLoS One* 6 (11):e28416. doi: 10.1371/journal.pone.0028416. PONE-D-11–11295 [pii].

Petersen, M., and T. Petersen. 2019. "Why prohibit study drugs?" *Drugs* 26 (4):356–364. doi: 10.1080/09687637.2019.1573878.

President's Council on Bioethics. 2003. *Beyond Therapy*. Washington, DC: President's Council on Bioethics/Harper Collins.

Racine, E., S. Sattler, and W. Boehlen. 2021. "Cognitive enhancement: Unanswered questions about human psychology and social behavior." *Science and Engineering Ethics* 27 (2):19. doi: 10.1007/s11948-021-00294-w.

Ram, S., B. Russell, C. Kirkpatrick, K. Stewart, S. Scahill, M. Henning, L. Curley, and S. Hussainy. 2020. "Professionals' attitudes towards the use of cognitive enhancers in academic settings." *PLoS One* 15 (11):e0241968. doi: 10.1371/journal.pone.0241968.

Ray, K. S.. 2016. "Not just 'study drugs' for the rich: Stimulants as moral tools for creating opportunities for socially disadvantaged students." *AJOB* 16 (6):29–38. doi: 10.1080/15265161.2016.1170231.

Ray, K. S.. 2020. "When people of color are left out of research, science and the public loses." *AJOB Neuroscience* 11 (4):238–240. doi: 10.1080/21507740.2020.1830885.

Repantis, D., P. Schlattmann, O. Laisney, and I. Heuser. 2010. "Modafinil and methylphenidate for neuroenhancement in healthy individuals: A systematic review." *Pharmacological Research* 62 (3):187–206.

Riis, J., J. P. Simmons, and G. P. Goodwin. 2008. "Preferences for enhancement pharmaceuticals: The reluctance to enhance fundamental traits." *Journal of Consumer Research* 35:495–508.

Robitaille, C. and J. Collin. 2016. "Prescription psychostimulant use among young adults: A narrative review of qualitative studies." *Substance Use & Misuse* 51 (3):357–369. doi: 10.3109/10826084.2015.1110170.

Rogers, W. A., H. Draper, and S. M. Carter. 2021. "Evaluation of artificial intelligence clinical applications: Detailed case analyses show value of healthcare ethics approach in identifying patient care issues." *Bioethics* 35 (7):623–633. doi: 10.1111/bioe.12885.

Rosenfield, D., P. C. Hebert, M. B. Stanbrook, K. Flegel, and N. E. Macdonald. 2011. "Time to address stimulant abuse on our campuses." *CMAJ* 183 (12):1345. doi: 10.1503/cmaj.111149.

Sabini, J., and J. Monterosso. 2005. "Judgments of the fairness of using performance enhancing drugs." *Ethics & Behavior* 15 (1):81–94.

Sandberg, A., and N. Bostrom. 2006. "Converging cognitive enhancements." *Annals of the New York Academy of Sciences* 1093:201–227.

Sattler, S., C. Forlini, E. Racine, and C. Sauer. 2013. "Impact of contextual factors and substance characteristics on perspectives toward cognitive enhancement." *PLoS One* 8 (8):e71452. doi: 10.1371/journal.pone.0071452.

Schaefer, G. O., G. Kahane, and J. Savulescu. 2014. "Autonomy and enhancement." *Neuroethics* 7 (2):123–136. doi: 10.1007/s12152-013-9189-5.

Schelle, K. J., N. Faulmuller, L. Caviola, and M. Hewstone. 2014. "Attitudes toward pharmacological cognitive enhancement-a review." *Frontiers in Systems Neuroscience* 8:53. doi: 10.3389/fnsys.2014.00053.

Sharif, S., A. Guirguis, S. Fergus, and F. Schifano. 2021. "The use and impact of cognitive enhancers among university students: A systematic review." *Brain Sciences* 11 (3):355.

Tull, J., C. Montgomery, L. J. Maier, and H. R. Sumnall. 2020. "Estimated prevalence, effects and potential risks of substances used for cognitive enhancement." In *Human Enhancement Drugs*, edited by Katinka ven de Ven, Kyle J. D. Mulrooney and Jim McVeigh, 112–127. London: Routledge.

Voarino, N., V. Dubljevic, and E. Racine. 2016. "tDCS for memory enhancement: Analysis of the speculative aspects of ethical issues." *Frontiers in Human Neuroscience* 10:678. doi: 10.3389/fnhum.2016.00678.

Wexler, A., and P. B. Reiner. 2019. "Oversight of direct-to-consumer neurotechnologies." *Science* 363 (6424):234–235. doi: 10.1126/science.aav0223.

Wexler, A., and L. Specker Sullivan. 2021. "Translational neuroethics: A vision for a more integrated, inclusive, and impactful field." *AJOB Neurosci*:1–12. doi: 10.1080/21507740.2021.2001078.

Zohny, H. 2015. "The myth of cognitive enhancement." *Neuroethics* 8 (3):257–269.

16
NOT EXTENDED, BUT ENHANCED

Internal improvements to cognition and the maintenance of cognitive agency

Nada Gligorov

16.1 Introduction

Cognitive enhancement refers to the medical and technological means of improving cognition. Some of the most familiar cognitive enhancers are pharmacological, including methylphenidate and dextroamphetamine, both of which have medical uses for the treatment of attention deficit and hyperactivity disorder (ADHD), but have also shown, modest and often variable, efficacy in improving cognition in typically functioning individuals, i.e., individuals not diagnosed with any psychiatric, neurological, or medical conditions known to cause cognitive impairment (Elliott et al., 1997; Izquierdo et al., 2008; Mehta et al., 2000). Additional means of cognitive enhancement have been considered in terms of their potential to improve human cognition, including genetic modification (Persson & Savulescu, 2008) or the use of brain technology, such as deep brain stimulation (DBS).

There are a variety of ethical issues related to the use of purported cognitive enhancers, including questions related to their safety and efficacy as well as their just allocation (Farah et al., 2004). A more recent debate related to cognitive enhancers is concerning their impact on cognitive character and the acquisition of knowledge (Carter & Pritchard, 2019; Gordon & Dunn, 2021; Wang, 2021). This current debate centers on the question of whether the use of cognitive enhancers threatens the maintenance of cognitive character in a way that would compromise the epistemological justification of beliefs. In order to respond to this objection, Carter and Pritchard (2019) propose that the extended mind hypothesis, an argument originally proposed by Clark and Chalmers (1998), can be used to argue that at least some types of cognitive enhancers can become properly incorporated into our cognition and therefore would not undermine cognitive character. The extended mind hypothesis is the argument that cognition extends past the biological boundaries of the human organism to incorporate external tools, e.g., notepads and smartphones, into human cognitive processes.

In this chapter, I argue mostly in agreement with Carter and Pritchard (2019) that the use of cognitive enhancers need not undermine cognitive character. However, I will demonstrate that at least some cognitive enhancers cannot be likened to external tools, i.e., they are not akin to notepads or smartphones. I will then argue that in order to expand the argument that cognitive enhancers do not undermine the epistemological integrity of knowledge to most cognitive enhancers, we need to show that the argument for cognitive integration does not require the extended mind hypothesis. In this chapter, I demonstrate that the use of cognitive enhancers that cause changes to cognition within the boundaries of the human organism can be properly incorporated into cognition and do not violate cognitive character or undermine knowledge acquisition.

16.2 Varieties of cognitive enhancers

Carter and Pritchard (2019) introduce Google Glass, among others, as a potential cognitive enhancer. Smart glasses, like smartphones, make stores of information easily available to an individual using this wearable technology. This technology is not inner to the human body, as it is not within the confines of the skull; instead, it is part of the environment that becomes incorporated into an individual's cognitive processes. Google Glass, for example, can utilize facial recognition technology to identify any individual one walks past on the street and immediately make all the publicly available information about that individual accessible to the Google Glass user. This information can then be used to modify behavior, e.g., either to start a conversation or to cross the street. But many purported cognitive enhancers, including pharmacological enhancers, are not akin to Google Glass because they do not modify the knower's environment; rather, they directly modify the individual's endogenous cognitive abilities.

Before I describe some of those cognitive enhancers and the data that supports their efficacy, I wish to note that biomedical enhancement has been used to designate improvements in typically functioning individuals. This can be contrasted with the use of medicine for the restoration of typical function in people with cognitive deficits due to psychiatric, neurological, or medical disease. This designation of certain medical or technological means as enhancers has often been made utilizing a distinction between uses of medicine for the treatment of disease, i.e., restoration of typical function, and its uses for enhancement, i.e., improvements of function for typically functioning individuals. The treatment and enhancement distinction has been controversial. Some of those who challenge the distinction point out that normality, often used to designate typical functioning, is a normative term that cannot be defined using purely biological means (Daniels, 2000), and others argue that all medicine is aimed at enhancing human functioning (Synofzik, 2009). Despite this controversy, I will maintain the usual use of cognitive enhancers to designate the medical or technological means of improving cognition in typically functioning individuals. In what follows, I will describe the array of potential cognitive enhancers that modulate cognitive capacities by relying on different mechanisms and that vary in their level of invasiveness. Some require the taking of medication that alters cognition by modulating the biological underpinning of cognitive faculties, such as memory, attention, or learning. Other potential enhancers are more invasive and might require the use of a wire lead inserted into a particular area of the brain in order to provide deep brain stimulation (DBS) to alter aspects of neurological function. I will primarily present evidence for the claim that these medical interventions have an effect on the cognitive functioning of individuals without diagnosed neurological or psychiatric conditions, i.e., that they have the potential for being used as cognitive enhancers.

Many purported cognitive enhancers have established medical uses for the treatment of neurological or psychiatric conditions. Some of those enhancers are pharmacological. For example, two often-studied enhancers are methylphenidate and dextroamphetamine. Both of these drugs are approved by the Food and Drug Administration (FDA) for the treatment of ADHD, but there have been a number of studies testing the effectiveness of these agents in improving aspects of cognition in normal individuals. Elliot et al. (1997) studied the effects of methylphenidate in 28 healthy volunteers. The participants were given a battery of tests, including tests for spatial working memory, planning, verbal fluency, and attention. The use of methylphenidate was shown to improve spatial working memory on some tasks, although the improvements were only seen when the task was novel. In repeated performances of this task, the stimulant seemed to be detrimental, and individuals who did not take the drug performed better on the task of spatial working memory. The drug had no effect on verbal fluency or attention (Elliot et al., 1997). An additional study by Mehta et al. (2000) showed methylphenidate to produce improvements in working memory. Those were most prominent for individuals who started with a lower baseline of working memory prior to the administration of the drug. Izquierdo et al. (2008), investigated the effects of methylphenidate on memory decline using two types of memory tasks: one was focused on the retention of incidental information, such as details of a recently viewed movie, and the other was a formal memory test where participants were asked to learn and recall new information. The study investigated memory in human volunteers aged 16–82. Younger individuals between the ages of 16 and 30 did not experience significant memory loss even seven days after the initial event. However, individuals older than 41 demonstrated a significant decline in recall on both memory tests. Methylphenidate was shown to mitigate that loss in older participants. In particular, methylphenidate was studied in individuals older than 35 and was shown effective in mitigating memory loss on the formal memory task in that group.

A further class of drugs with the potential for use as cognitive enhancers is acetylcholinesterase inhibitors, including donepezil, galantamine, and rivastigmine. Out of these three the one most studied for its enhancing properties in normal individuals is donepezil, which is FDA-approved for the treatment of Alzheimer's disease (AD). Yesavage et al. (2002) performed a randomized, double-blind study of 18 licensed pilots ranging from 30 to 70 years of age to determine the effects of donepezil on the long-term retention of skills required for aviation after training in a flight simulator. The study showed that pilots treated with donepezil retained their ability to perform the set of complex flight-related tasks even a month after training while pilots treated with a placebo experienced deterioration in performance (Yesavage et al., 2002).

A yet another potential neuroenhancer is modafinil, which has been FDA-approved for the treatment of narcolepsy but has been prescribed off-label for a variety of sleep disorders, including sleep apnea. Two studies on normal healthy adults showed that modafinil could be successfully used to abate the negative effects of sleep deprivation. In a study by Grady et al. (2010), healthy patients underwent a protocol in which the period of sleep-wakefulness was significantly different from their usual. The participants remained awake for longer and slept fewer hours. The study was a randomized double-blind, placebo-controlled study. The participants who received modafinil for the duration of the experiment were better able to remain awake and alert. Modafinil was particularly efficacious in improving cognitive psychomotor speed and attention. Furthermore, a study of sleep-deprived physicians showed that modafinil was successful in diminishing the cognitive deterioration associated with sleep deprivation (Sugden et al., 2012).

In addition to these pharmacological means of cognitive improvement, Persson and Savulescu (2008) explore the potential of genetic modification as a mode of cognitive enhancement. For example, they suggested that genetic memory enhancement, currently demonstrated only in animal models, might have translational application and result in human genetic modification to improve memory formation and retention.

Recently, there has been research on the underlying circuitry of learning and memory that has enabled researchers to identify potential areas of the brain (the fornix or nucleus basalis of Meynert) that if targeted by deep brain stimulation (DBS) could have potential therapeutic benefits in improving memory. The data from animal models demonstrates that the use of DBS can induce neuroanatomical, neurophysiological, and neurochemical changes within the memory circuits (Lozano et al., 2019). These changes in turn have sometimes resulted in improvements in memory and amelioration of memory loss in rodent models (Aldehri et al., 2018).

There have been clinical studies investigating the effectiveness of DBS in delaying and restoring cognitive decline in patients with AD. The use of DBS for patients with Parkinson's has been associated with cognitive decline, although it is not clear whether that decline was due to DBS or because patients treated with DBS no longer take dopaminergic drugs used for the treatment of Parkinson's, which can support certain aspects of cognitive functions. However, there have also been small and early studies of DBS for the treatment of AD. In these studies, some patients experienced changes at the neurological level, such as an increase in the size of the hippocampus, but evidence of improvements at the clinical level is still lacking (Aldehri et al., 2018).

16.3 The extended mind hypothesis

The use of cognitive enhancers has been controversial. For example, Kass (2003), Sandel (2004), and Harris (2011) have argued that cognitive enhancement removes the obstacles required for cognitive achievement in a way that renders the acquisition of knowledge trivial. Carter and Pritchard (2019) call this the axiological objection. Based on the axiological objection, cognitive enhancers diminish cognitive achievement by improving our biological ability to remember or by supplementing memory through the use of smart technology and thereby removing the difficulty inherent in mastering any given subject.

The basis for the argument in defense of cognitive enhancers has emerged from a strain of epistemology that identifies cognitive agency as a way of justifying true beliefs. Based on this view, an individual has cognitive agency only when the acquisition of true belief can be properly credited to that knower. To clarify the notion of cognitive agency one can liken it to moral agency. In order for an individual to be credited with a good deed, they should be primarily or mostly responsible for it. For example, if I attempt to buy a lottery ticket but inadvertently donate to charity, most would argue that I should not be credited with a good deed. Similarly, if I come by a true belief without properly utilizing any of my cognitive abilities to acquire it, I should not be credited with knowledge.

An example of this view is proposed by Pritchard (2010), who argues that knowledge is a product of a reliable cognitive process appropriately integrated into an individual's cognitive character. A reliable cognitive process is one that regularly leads to true beliefs, such as perception, memory, or problem-solving. Furthermore, a cognitive process is appropriately integrated into the person's cognitive character when the beliefs it generates can be credited to that individual's agency, i.e., when the individual is responsible for obtaining that belief. The notion of cognitive character is akin to the notion of psychological or moral character, where an individual develops a stable cognitive character as they might develop a stable moral character.

The emphasis on cognitive agency aims to avoid attributing knowledge to individuals who for internal or external reasons cannot take responsibility for their beliefs. An individual might acquire a true belief due to environmental luck, which is when features of their environment are favorable to acquiring justified true belief even if the individual is not gaining them by utilizing their cognitive abilities. For example, this could be because every time you look at a broken clock unbeknownst to you a stealth helper has adjusted the clock to reflect the correct time in your part of the world. Or it could be due to factors internal to the agent that obviate the need for the agent to apply their cognitive abilities; for example, an individual who is unaware that they have a brain implant that automatically generates accurate belief about external temperature. In both those cases, the individual, according to Pritchard (2010), has true beliefs, but they do not have knowledge because the belief-forming process does not exploit the individual's cognitive agency.

According to both Pritchard (2010) and Carter and Pritchard (2019), this view of knowledge does not exclude the possibility that at least some types of enhancers could become incorporated into an individual's character. To argue that cognitive enhancers can become incorporated into cognitive character, they rely on the extended mind hypothesis, which is the view that some external tools, such as notebooks, smartphones, or Google Glass, when properly incorporated into our cognition, can be said to become part of cognition. If that is the case, then cognitive enhancers can become incorporated into an individual's cognitive process and therefore become part of their cognitive character.

The extended mind hypothesis was originally proposed by Clark and Chalmers (1998), who argue for a thesis called active externalism, which is the view that the environment plays a role in cognitive processes. This view is not merely that elements of the environment may provide data for cognitive processes. Instead, it is the view that parts of the environment become incorporated into our cognition – the mind becomes extended to include parts of the environment. To support this claim, Clark and Chalmers (1998) describe the example of Otto, who because of his waning memory compensates for this loss by writing down in a notebook information he can no longer remember. When he needs to, Otto utilizes his notebook to gain access to facts that aid him in making decisions regarding what to do next, such as how to get to the grocery store. Clark and Chalmers argue that Otto's notebook becomes part of his cognition.

Based on the criteria proposed by Clark (2008, p. 79), an environmental resource can become incorporated into an individual's cognition if it fulfills the following criteria:

1. "That the resource be reliably available and typically invoked."
2. "That any information thus retrieved be more-or-less automatically endorsed. It should not usually be subject to critical scrutiny. […] It should be deemed about as trustworthy as something retrieved clearly from biological memory."
3. "That information contained in the resource should be easily accessible as and when required."
4. "That the information in the notebook has been consciously endorsed."

Otto's notebook fits all criteria. Otto carries his notebook with him and has reliable access to it, i.e., he can look up information without much difficulty. And he uses it in his daily life whenever he needs to reach the grocery store or purchase the right items when in the store. Otto endorses the information in the notebook and does not, for the most part, question the veracity of the information contained within it. Hence, Otto's notebook has become a reliable part of Otto's cognitive process as it has assumed the functional role of Otto's biological memory. This particular thesis of cognitive integration is used to argue for the view that tools external to the person's biological organism can become incorporated into their cognitive function. This argument can then be used to argue that certain types of cognitive enhancers can become incorporated into an individual's cognitive character, rebuffing the view that the use of enhancers in some way undermines cognitive agency. But it can also be used to expand the boundaries of cognitive enhancers to include things like smartphones or smart glasses.

16.4 Internal enhancement

In Section 16.2, I described a variety of potential cognitive enhancers, including pharmacological enhancers, genetic enhancers, DBS, and Google Glass. The axiological objection, in particular as endorsed by Kass (2003), is an objection to the use of medicine for human improvement and would apply to the use of any cognitive enhancers and not just to enhancers that modulate our environment. The extended mind hypothesis provides a direct defense only for the type of cognitive enhancers that would extend our cognition beyond the anatomical confines of the skull. The active externalism thesis leaves some cognitive enhancers open to the attack from the axiological objection. For example, pharmacological enhancements and genetic enhancers aim to improve cognitions by changing our biology not by changing any aspect of our environment. These enhancers would not fit into the framework of the extended mind hypothesis as they are changes internal to the organism.

Clark and Chalmers (1998) take it for granted that something akin to DBS, i.e., a brain implant, is part of Otto's cognition because it is within the skull. They use this example to identify a prejudice in favor of internalist views of cognition. They argue that most of us would not hesitate to accept that a brain implant would become part of Otto's cognition, but some of us would object to the claim that Otto's notebook would be incorporated into his cognition. So, perhaps, those using the extended mind hypothesis in order to reject the axiological objection take it for granted that internal modification to cognition, i.e., modifications made within the boundaries of the biological human organism need not be defended against the axiological objection. But some of the proponents of this objection, such as Kass (2003), would not distinguish between enhancers based on the internalist/externalist distinction; instead, they would distinguish the permissible use of medicine and technology based on the treatment and enhancement distinction. This would mean that Otto using DBS to improve his memory because of the advancing of AD would be justified, but the use of DBS to improve cognition, if Otto were healthy and his memory were intact, would not be permissible.

One could put this in terms of preserving cognitive character in the following way: neurological disease changes an individual's cognitive character, e.g., by affecting their memory, and the use of medicine is permissible in such cases because it contributes to the restoration of the original cognitive character. The use of medicine and technology to change cognitive character, however, is not permissible. And this is true whether such changes are internal or external to the individual.

Thus, in order to argue against the axiological objection, one needs to show how cognitive integration can be used to justify cognitive improvements *tout court*. This means that one needs to show that the use of cognitive enhancers would not affect cognitive agency even when enhancement causes internal changes to cognition. Luckily, this argument could be made by relying on Pritchard's view of cognitive agency.

Pritchard (2010) defines cognitive agency thusly:

> S knows that p iff S's true belief that p is the product of a reliable belief-forming process which is appropriately integrated within S's cognitive character such that her cognitive success is to a significant degree creditable to her cognitive agency.
> *(Pritchard, 2010, 224).*[1]

To assess, which of the cognitive enhancers fit Pritchard's criteria and can be used without violating cognitive character, let's imagine a detective who is contemplating the use of cognitive enhancers in order to resolve a backlog of cold cases.

Let us begin by imagining that the detective decides to use modafinil first. Modafinil has been shown to be effective in diminishing the deleterious effects of fatigue on cognition. Hence, the use of modafinil would not improve the detective's cognition in any particular way; it would merely maintain the detective's usual cognitive function even if she decides to work through the night in order to solve a case. The detective would be able to rely on her usual mode of solving cases: she would rely on the usual belief-forming processes and would be able to provide an explanation for her endorsement of certain beliefs related to the case. Modafinil would enable her to maintain her cognitive character for longer. Thus, the use of modafinil would not violate cognitive integration. Modafinil would also not introduce external influences that would violate the detective's cognitive agency because none of the environmental facts within which the detective is working would be altered. She would not be given the medication surreptitiously, as she is choosing to take it herself, so the maintenance of her cognitive character despite sleep deprivation could be credited entirely to her agency.

The other two potential pharmacological cognitive enhancers that the detective could use are the stimulants dextroamphetamine and methylphenidate. The effects of dextroamphetamine include improvements in spatial working memory, planning, verbal fluency, attention, and long-term memory. The use of these stimulants for cognitive enhancement would similarly not violate cognitive character or cognitive agency because they do not alter the repertoire of cognitive processes that would be brought to bear in order to solve a case or to accomplish a particular task. If spatial working memory is required in order for the detective to survey a scene of the crime and to derive clues from it, the use of stimulants would merely improve this ability in a way that might increase the likelihood that the detective would identify a clue that helps resolve the murder.

This, on its own, would not violate any cognitive habits the detective has. She would still rely on the same belief-forming processes and would still be able to justify why a particular item in the scene of the crime would count as a clue and how that clue, e.g., a piece of ripped fabric, would help identify an individual with a torn jacket as the murderer. Again, as is the case with modafinil, the changes directly caused by the cognitive enhancer would be internal to the detective's biological organism and would not be due to changes in the environment.

In addition, the data about the benefits of stimulants on cognition does not indicate an outsized improvement in cognitive ability. Much of the studies on stimulants were placebo-controlled, which means that the improvement in performance was compared to a control group that had not received stimulants. Although the differences in performance between the two groups were statistically significant, they did not show prodigious improvements in performance. The benefits that each individual might experience from the use of stimulants can vary, but most would not experience an extreme increase in performance that would violate cognitive character. For example, if we imagine that the detective has bad episodic memory and with the help of medication becomes able to remember everything that ever happened to her, an increase in performance might cause a change in cognitive character. For one, the detective might be suspicious of this sudden endowment, and not lend automatic endorsement to beliefs formed based on her episodic memories. In addition, being able to remember everything might affect the detective's usual way of obtaining knowledge, she might stop relying on memory aids, e.g., taking notes. In addition, she might adopt a different cognitive style where more of her problem-solving would become reliant on her episodic memory. But the use of dextroamphetamine and methylphenidate regrettably does not result in such large improvement. But even if they did, this would not be a determinative argument that the use of stimulants changes cognitive character in a way that is different from the likely changes that might occur naturally over time. For example, as the detective becomes more experienced in solving cases, her cognitive character – e.g., the way she approaches cases and what types of clues she identifies – might adapt and change over time.

Beyond pharmacological enhancers, the detective will run out of options for currently available cognitive enhancers. But I will consider whether some proposed, but not yet available, enhancers would violate cognitive integration. Persson and Savulescu (2008) cite genetic modification to improve memory. Assuming that these changes would occur by modifying the genome either at the embryonic stage or early in childhood, these changes would be present at the early stages of the development of cognitive character. They would be part of a genetically modified individual's cognitive development and would be at least partially determinative of the individual's cognitive character from the outset of their life. One could, of course, object to genetic modification for reasons unrelated to the epistemic integrity of beliefs, including concerns related to the risks associated with genome modification and the opposition to the modification of the human genome especially when it might cause heritable changes. Such objections, however, are outside of the scope of this chapter.

I will now turn to improvements in cognitive function that requires direct modification of neurological function, such as DBS. DBS requires the insertion of a wire lead with electrodes into a specific area of the brain, the lead is connected to a neurostimulator that is implanted near the patient's collarbone. It is this neurostimulator that sends electrical signals to the implanted lead. When used to treat Parkinson's disease, the neurostimulator has to be adjusted by medical professionals in order to obtain optimal stimulation for symptom relief. The patient can, however, turn the stimulator on or off. Thus, the actual neurostimulator could be characterized as being external to the individual both because it is not contained within the skull and because the locus of control is external. In addition, there is some evidence that, at least phenomenologically, the externality of the stimulation affects the individual using DBS as they report feeling as though they are remotely controlled (Agid et al., 2006) and that they do not feel quite like themselves (Agid et al., 2006).

These facts about DBS could support a disanalogy between Otto with the notebook, who has control over this cognitive aid, and Otto with a stimulator, who does not directly control his stimulator.

This then complicates the question of whether DBS should fall under the category of an internal cognitive modulator or whether it should be considered also as an external tool that becomes incorporated into an individual's cognition. If we draw the line between internal and external influences based on the modification of biological function, the stimulator works by disrupting the endogenous electrical signals that result in neurological symptoms, so in that regard, it could be characterized as modifying the biological function of the brain internally just like pharmacological treatments. On the other hand, one could argue that because the lead has to be inserted into the brain to modify the signal, DBS does not modify the endogenous neurological function in the same way pharmacological interventions do. DBS could be characterized as changing the input to certain areas of the brain, which perhaps makes it more akin to a pair of glasses that modify vision by changing the refraction of the light rather than changing how the light is processed within the visual system. Based on this view, DBS could probably be more aptly characterized as an element of the environment being inserted into the skull instead of being characterized as an internal cognitive resource. Hence, depending on which view one takes, DBS could be characterized as either an internal or an external modification to cognitive function.

Given that I have adopted the criterion of cognitive integration to determine whether cognitive character would undermine cognitive agency, I can then just assess to what extent DBS is likely to threaten the maintenance of cognitive character. Given that at least some individuals who utilize DBS for the treatment of Parkinson's have reported psychological changes that indicate that the use of DBS is not seamlessly incorporated into an individual's psychology, there might be reason to think that perhaps DBS used to improve cognition might affect cognitive character. If the individual, for example, feels like they are being externally controlled, this might undermine their inclination to automatically endorse beliefs formed after the activation of the device. But making this judgment would be too rash given the current paucity of empirical evidence about the non-therapeutic effects of DBS, especially as it might pertain to its uses to improve cognitive function. Only some patients who have utilized DBS for the treatment of Parkinson's have reported feelings of diminished control, and there is no evidence that speaks to whether this feeling actually interferes with cognitive integration. After all feelings of alienation might not have any corollary effects on how individuals justify beliefs. In order to determine whether DBS could undermine cognitive integration, more empirical work would be needed. There are no *a priori* reasons, however, to assume that such integration could not happen for many patients if DBS ever becomes available as a memory enhancer.

16.5 Conclusion

The extended mind hypothesis, as utilized by Clark and Pritchard (2019), is aimed at defending the use of cognitive enhancers against the axiological objection. The reliance on the extended mind hypothesis, however, limits the scope of the argument for enhancers to only those interventions that are external to the human organism. I argued that it is important to broaden the defense to include cognitive enhancers that effect primarily internal changes in the organism. In particular, I argued that at least some proponents of the axiological objection also endorse the treatment and enhancement distinction and utilize it to adjudicate the use of medicine and technology along those lines, whereby the use of enhancers to restore normal function is deemed permissible but their use to improve normal function is not. To defend the use of enhancers more broadly, I argued that we should provide a defense of cognitive enhancement that does not rely solely on the extended mind hypothesis. In this chapter, I considered a number of different enhancers, including those that change cognition by changing the knower's environment, but I focused on pharmacological enhancers that affect cognitive change within the boundaries of the human body and leave the environment intact. I argued that a defense of cognitive enhancers that relies on the extended mind hypothesis leaves open to attack the use of enhancers that are, arguably, the most likely to become available for current use, e.g., methylphenidate and dextroamphetamine. I proposed instead that the criteria of cognitive integration proposed by Pritchard (2010) can be used to defend most cognitive enhancers that do not undermine cognitive agency regardless of whether they promote internal or external changes to the organism.

Note

1 Pritchard distinguishes between weak and strong versions of the cognitive agency thesis. The one cited in this chapter is the weak version of the definition, which is the one he thinks can accommodate the extended mind thesis. The distinction between the two definitions is regarding the degree to which knowledge can be credited to an individual's agency. The weak version requires that it be significantly creditable, and the strong is that it be primarily or mostly creditable to the individual's cognitive agency. The distinction does not have particular bearing on my argument, so I will just adopt the weak version of it, as this is the version Pritchard seems to favor.

References

Agid, Y., Schüpbach, M., Gargiulo, M., Mallet, L., Houeto, J. L., Behar, C., Maltête, D., Mesnage, V., Welter, M. L. (2006). Neurosurgery in Parkinson's disease: The doctor is happy the patient less so? *Journal of Neural Transmission, 70,* 400–414.

Aldehri, M., Temel, Y., Alnaami, I., Jahanshahi, A., & Hescham, S. (2018). Deep brain stimulation for Alzheimer's disease: An update. *Surgical Neurology International, 9,* 58. https://doi.org/10.4103/sni.sni_342_17

Carter, J. A., & Pritchard, D. (2019). The epistemology of cognitive enhancement. *The Journal of Medicine and Philosophy: A Forum for Bioethics and Philosophy of Medicine, 44*(2), 220–242. https://doi.org/10.1093/jmp/jhy040

Clark, A. (2008). *Supersizing the Mind: Embodiment, Action, and Cognitive Extension.* https://doi.org/10.1093/acprof:oso/9780195333213.001.0001

Clark, A., & Chalmers, D. (1998). The extended mind. *Analysis, 58*(1), 7–19.

Daniels, N. (2000). Normal functioning and the treatment-enhancement distinction. *Cambridge Quarterly of Healthcare Ethics, 9*(3), 309–322. https://doi.org/10.1017/S0963180100903037

Elliott, R., Sahakian, B. J., Matthews, K., Bannerjea, A., Rimmer, J., & Robbins, T. W. (1997). Effects of methylphenidate on spatial working memory and planning in healthy young adults. *Psychopharmacology, 131*(2), 196–206. https://doi.org/10.1007/s002130050284

Farah, M. J., Illes, J., Cook-Deegan, R., Gardner, H., Kandel, E., King, P., Parens, E., Sahakian, B., & Wolpe, P. R. (2004). Neurocognitive enhancement: What can we do and what should we do? *Nature Reviews Neuroscience, 5*(5), 421–425. https://doi.org/10.1038/nrn1390

Gordon, E. C., & Dunn, L. (2021). Pharmacological cognitive enhancement and cheapened achievement: A new dilemma. *Neuroethics, 14*(3), 409–421. https://doi.org/10.1007/s12152-021-09477-5

Grady, S., Aeschbach, D., Wright, K. P., & Czeisler, C. A. (2010). Effect of modafinil on impairments in neurobehavioral performance and learning associated with extended wakefulness and circadian misalignment. *Neuropsychopharmacology: Official Publication of the American College of Neuropsychopharmacology, 35*(9), 1910–1920. https://doi.org/10.1038/npp.2010.63

Harris, J. (2011). Moral enhancement and freedom. *Bioethics, 25*(2), 102–111. https://doi.org/10.1111/j.1467-8519.2010.01854.x

Izquierdo, I., Bevilaqua, L. R., Rossato, J. I., Lima, R. H., Medina, J. H., & Cammarota, M. (2008). Age-dependent and age-independent human memory persistence is enhanced by delayed posttraining methylphenidate administration. *Proceedings of the National Academy of Sciences, 105*(49), 19504–19507. https://doi.org/10.1073/pnas.0810650105

Kass, L. R. (2003). *Beyond therapy: Biotechnology and the pursuit of human improvement.* Washington, DC: The President's Council on Bioethics.

Lozano, A. M., Lipsman, N., Bergman, H., Brown, P., Chabardes, S., Chang, J. W., Matthews, K., McIntyre, C. C., Schlaepfer, T. E., Schulder, M., Temel, Y., Volkmann, J., & Krauss, J. K. (2019). Deep brain stimulation: Current challenges and future directions. *Nature Reviews Neurology, 15*(3), 148–160. https://doi.org/10.1038/s41582-018-0128-2

Mehta, M. A., Owen, A. M., Sahakian, B. J., Mavaddat, N., Pickard, J. D., & Robbins, T. W. (2000). Methylphenidate enhances working memory by modulating discrete frontal and parietal lobe regions in the human brain. *The Journal of Neuroscience: The Official Journal of the Society for Neuroscience, 20*(6), RC65.

Persson, I., & Savulescu, J. (2008). The perils of cognitive enhancement and the urgent imperative to enhance the moral character of humanity. *Journal of Applied Philosophy, 25*(3), 162–177. https://doi.org/10.1111/j.1468-5930.2008.00410.x

Pritchard, D. (2010). Cognitive ability and the extended cognition thesis. *Synthese, 175*(S1), 133–151. https://doi.org/10.1007/s11229-010-9738-y

Sandel, M. J. (2004, April 1). The case against perfection. *The Atlantic.* https://www.theatlantic.com/magazine/archive/2004/04/the-case-against-perfection/302927/

Sugden, C., Housden, C. R., Aggarwal, R., Sahakian, B. J., & Darzi, A. (2012). Effect of pharmacological enhancement on the cognitive and clinical psychomotor performance of sleep-deprived doctors: A randomized controlled trial. *Annals of Surgery, 255*(2), 222–227. https://doi.org/10.1097/SLA.0b013e3182306c99

Synofzik, M. (2009). Ethically justified, clinically applicable criteria for physician decision-making in psychopharmacological enhancement. *Neuroethics, 2*(2), 89–102. https://doi.org/10.1007/s12152-008-9029-1

Wang, J. (2021). Cognitive enhancement and the value of cognitive achievement. *Journal of Applied Philosophy, 38*(1), 121–135. https://doi.org/10.1111/japp.12460

Yesavage, J. A., Mumenthaler, M. S., Taylor, J. L., Friedman, L., O'Hara, R., Sheikh, J., Tinklenberg, J., & Whitehouse, P. J. (2002). Donepezil and flight simulator performance: Effects on retention of complex skills. *Neurology, 59*(1), 123–125. https://doi.org/10.1212/wnl.59.1.123

17
IS ENHANCEMENT WITH BRAIN–COMPUTER INTERFACES ETHICAL? EVIDENCE IN FAVOR OF SYMBIOTIC AUGMENTATION

Tomislav Furlanis and Frederic Gilbert

17.1 Introduction

The terminology of brain–computer interface (BCI) was first tossed into the academic literature in the early 1970s by Vidal and was presented as a promising clinical solution for a range of therapeutic applications (Vidal 1973). It took 20 years before the term BCI started to be used in news media as a topic of discussion describing the advancements of the technology (Gilbert, Pham et al. 2019). Since appearing for the first time in news media (1993), there has been increasing attention devoted to BCI. A characteristic of BCI portrayals in news media is that the technology has been depicted with great enthusiastic positivity up to 76.91% of the time; importantly, 26.64% of all publications contain claims about futuristic BCI-enabled enhancement (Gilbert, Pham et al. 2019). When looking closely at the futuristic depictions of BCI-enabled enhancement, we observe a common narrative, namely, the hypothesis of mergence (Pham and Gilbert 2019).

In recent years, the idea that humans might merge with intelligent machines has received much media attention, mostly because it is echoing some billionaire entrepreneurs' agendas, such as Musk, Johnson, and Itskov who launched their respective new BCI companies (e.g. Neuralink, Kernel, 2045 Initiative), as well as military-funded agencies (e.g. the Defense Advanced Research Projects Agency). Millions of dollars are currently being invested into the development of BCIs that aim to connect humans with machines in prior unparalleled ways.

Among the reasons to race for merging the human brain with a computer, in particular the efforts of private companies such as Neuralink and Kernel, is the conception that artificial intelligence can be said to represent an existential danger to humanity. Central to BCI augmentative and enhancement claims is the hypothesis, pushed in particular by Musk, that "human beings [need to] merge with software and keep pace with advancements in artificial intelligence" (Statt 2017). Musk has previously spoken of his belief that "mankind's failure to advance artificial intelligence could allow the robot to take over" (*The Daily Telegraph* 2017).[1] Accordingly, the hypothesis of mergence suggests that because AI is a plausible existential threat (e.g. it will become more intelligent than humans in the future and control us), we should already plan (and work on) to resolve the issue of super-intelligent AI. Ultimately, the aim for Musk and other entrepreneurs is to "achieve a symbiosis with artificial intelligence" (Lopatto 2019).

To our knowledge, few researchers have looked at the concept of symbiosis as a characteristic of enhancement (Nagao 2019; Karnouskos 2021), and little importance has been given to the concept of "human–AI symbiosis" from the humanistic perspective. A recent study by Soekadar et al. (2021)

highlights the importance of hybridity as a conceptual tool to un/blur the various boundaries where humans intertwine with machines; medical BCI is an example.

Hybridity is a promising concept to explore. However, in this chapter,[2] we wish to examine the lines of current AI-related research on symbiotic cooperation and capacity augmentation (Hassani et al. 2020, Zhou et al. 2021, Dominijani et al. 2021) rather than looking at the philosophical categories of hybridism, including human cyborgization (Barfield and Williams 2017), morphological freedom (Sandberg 2013), or digitalized minds (Sorgner 2021). It is especially important to explore the concept of capacity augmentation via AI-related components, given that BCI devices predominantly lie in the goal-oriented autonomy by which these devices are functionally used as autonomous systems, which may not require any kind of human intervention or supervision in their operations (thus, closed-loop). This includes both sensory monitoring (i.e. recognizing various bodily states), medical evaluation (based on some algorithmic, data-representation, model), and administration of treatment (through actuators, which are usually electrodes).

As such, we aim to provide the first step toward an ethical conceptualization of the human–AI symbiotic relationship that is directly informed by the current state of AI and medical BCI research. Consequently, this relates the topic of symbiosis with some of the vital ethical concerns relating to the design, development, and use of autonomous BCI technologies. These include the problem of scientific and clinical validity in BCI testing, the risk of neurodiscrimination in using BCI devices, harms to one's neuroprivacy, accountability in the medical decision-making process, the impacts on the subject's agency and self-experience which BCI devices produce, and the question of governance over the distribution of these devices (Ienca 2021; Ienca and Ignatiadis 2020, Kellmeyer 2019). Notwithstanding the importance of these ethical concerns, in this chapter we aim to initiate the discussion on human–AI symbiosis through the notion of acceptance.

The motivation for acceptance lies in the user-related phenomenon that some human subjects, even with the device functioning under medically approved parameters, might experience the need to reject the device post-implementation due to the perceived changes in one's self-experience. This begs the question of whether the ethical understanding of the relationship which occurs between the BCI and the human subject can be solely evaluated through functional terms, rather than an existential narrative. The purpose of this narrative is to prepare the user for the initiation of the symbiotic relationship, by providing a transparent functional understanding of the symbiotic link and ameliorating possible post-operational identity breaches by fostering an understanding of the self as a symbiont.

17.2 On symbiosis

The etymology of the notion of symbiosis roots in the Greek concept of συμβίωσις, which means "living together." Traditionally, the notion of symbiosis has been used to describe biological organisms existing in a mutually beneficial relationship. Incorporating technological elements in a biological organism to induce symbiosis is novel. The question follows, what is human–AI symbiosis? To define it, we have to take a look at the original concept elaborated by Licklider, in 1960, who was the first to envision that,

in not too many years, human brains and computing machines will be coupled together very tightly, and that the resulting partnership will think as no human brain has ever thought and process data in a way not approached by the information-handling machines we know today....

To think in interaction with a computer in the same way that you think with a colleague whose competence supplements your own will require much tighter coupling between man and machine than is suggested by the example and than is possible today.

(Licklider 1960)

Based on this initial conceptualization, we can posit three necessary conditions for a symbiotic relationship, the third one resulting from the first two.

First, the relationship that humans form with AI systems as symbiotic is dissimilar from the relationship humans form with their tools, which lack autonomy. Instead, it is similar to a relationship we form with another intelligent and interactive agent in a collaborative relationship – in the words of Licklider, "a colleague whose competence supplements" our own.

Second, the beneficiary interaction between the human and the machine is so tightly coupled that it allows humans to transcend their ordinary range of possible actions. Moreover, it does the same for the machine – it allows the computational device to process data in a manner that is unobtainable outside of the symbiotic cooperation with the human. Importantly, the "tight coupling" or "tight symbiotic coupling" does not only produce augmented cooperation between the two agents. The tight symbiotic coupling is a new kind of agency. In terms of Licklider, within the symbiotic partnership, it is not the agents who think (and act): it is the partnership.

Third, the tight symbiotic coupling connecting the human and the machine agent impacts the human's sense of self. When the tight symbiotic coupling is established, it can impact one's identity in such accord that it changes the answer to the question "Who am I"? (De Grazia 2005). This third point reflects the words of Licklider who envisioned the human-machine symbiosis not only a functional cooperative relationship but a relationship that is more similar to "two dissimilar organisms living together."

Consequently, tight symbiotic coupling necessarily impacts the subject's orientation toward human existence, self-understanding, and the meaning and value of human life as we know it. In doing so, it begets the question: "What does it mean to be human with a BCI"? As such, it is important to have in mind that a valid conceptualization of the symbiotic relationship cannot remain solely within a functionalistic framework of goal-oriented systems, within the notion of "partnership."

Naturally, if we aim to provide cognitive, physical, or moral augmentations with symbiotic machines, we have to be concerned with the safety and efficiency conditions,[3] such as operability and reliability, the quality of interaction, joint-processing, and goal achievement capacities of symbiotic partnerships. But this is not enough, as symbiotic relationships do not only bring about beneficial changes in the way we act in the world. They also affect the way we "live" in the world and the understanding of what we are in the world, and in doing so prompt concrete ethical concerns.

Let us take a closer look.

17.3 Human–AI symbiosis: The functional understanding

The human–AI symbiotic relationship is comprised of minimally two agents, one human and the other artificial. In a symbiotic relationship, humans and machines share the same goals and augment each other's capacities to accomplish these goals. This makes the relationship comparable with hybrid systems of distributed agency, for instance, the multi-agent systems in which artificial agents[4] act jointly with human agents to achieve specific goals.

The crucial condition of distributed systems lies in the collective, system-like, representation of joint actions. A single individual agent reasons and acts not as an "I" but rather as a "we" (Pacherie 2013). In other words, when an individual agent plans to act out on a goal shared with other agents in the group, the content of the intent is always in terms of "we are doing this" or "I intend that we do something." Consequently, this allows group planning and joint-action execution – in totality the group acts as a single agent with a unified purpose. As such, the group can be evaluated as a single system, of which the members are its parts. However, the subject, the bearer, of such collective intentions is always the individual agent and not some emergent collective mind which subsumes, gobbles up, individual agency.

Consequently, this demand makes interactions the vital breaking point for the system's constitution. If the interaction is not finely tuned to accommodate the needs of the collective planning and action, the distribution of agency within the system may not be constituted as it is precisely in recognizing individual agents' attitudes that the complex (shared) intentions can be formed and acted out in a joint manner (Schweikard 2017). What symbiotic systems share with distributed systems is then the transparency of intention and joint-action execution – as is already present in concepts of human–robot symbiotic systems (Veloso et al. 2015, Wang et al. 2019).

However, the difference between distributed and symbiotic systems lies in the kind of interactive relation between the agents in the system. In the symbiotic system, this interaction is so tightly coupled that human and machine agency, for lack of a better term, intertwine and in doing so form a system of augmented properties that exceeds not only the range of individual agent capacities but also their sum. In other words, within the tight symbiotic coupling, individual agents form a system of emergent properties (i.e. new agential capacities).

But with what to relate this tight-coupling relation? The contemporary understanding of human–AI extended systems is that these systems are constituted by humans as autonomous agents and "extenders" which include systems, tools, artifacts, or processes that extend the (cognitive and physical) operations of the autonomous agent above and beyond her capacities' range (Hernández-Orallo and Vold 2019).

Crucially, extenders cannot function without the human agent on whose autonomy their service is based, as[5] they operate only when they are "connected to" and utilized by a human agent. In other words, *the autonomy of the extended system is always human autonomy*, although the system's capacity for agency is not reducible solely to human agency. Like a well-fitting haptic glove, a custom-tailored exoskeleton, augmented reality lenses, or writing assistants, extenders operate optimally when they are finely tuned toward the action preferences, the mental and physical characteristics of each user. When such deep integration is achieved, the practice becomes consciously transparent as when one seamlessly experiences using one's capacities, only now with newfound possibilities.

Similarly, in symbiotic systems, humans also form a closely coupled relationship with the machine. The difference is that in symbiotic systems, the link does not connect one autonomous and another non-autonomous entity. Instead, it connects two agents. One way to understand this distinction is to see that the tight symbiotic coupling is not a case of "acting through" the extender as it happens when one extends through the novel capacities of the artificial system. Nor is it a case of "acting with" another agent as is the case in systems of distributed agency. Rather, the interweaving of intentions and actions is so tightly related that one "acts within" the symbiotic space for decision and action. In other words, one acts as a symbiont. This means to say that in the symbiotic system, one cannot but act symbiotically. When one agent acts, so does the other – their capacities are intertwined in such a tightly coupled manner that the source of agency is now the symbiotic system.[6]

17.4 Effective augmentation: What can the symbiotic relationship accomplish?

The effectiveness (of augmentation) that the symbiotic system accomplishes depends on two conditions: the autonomous capacities of agents within the tight symbiotic coupling and the quality of the tight symbiotic coupling itself.

The first condition relates to the kind of capacities the two agents are capable of manifesting within the tight symbiotic coupling. Dependent on the goal the agents aim to achieve, the kind of capacities utilized will differ. This entails that symbiotic systems formed from human–robot, human-exoskeleton, or human–BCI agents will differ in the kind of goals they can accomplish, the kind of agency required to accomplish that goal, and the kind of interaction best suited for the accomplishment of that goal. For instance, if we aim to augment cognitive operations through tight symbiotic coupling, the human–BCI seems like a solid choice. If we wish to augment physical operations, an exoskeleton seems like a preferred choice. And if we wish to provide moral augmentation, both human–robot and human–BCI systems could be utilized – dependent on the moral situation we aim to resolve.

Consequently, the kind of symbiotic partnerships humans form with machines depends on the kind of machine agent the human links with (in a symbiotic manner). And the choice of the machine (i.e. what kind of a machine will humans link with) depends on the kind of goal the symbiotic relation aims to accomplish. For instance, if we aim to accomplish some complex physical task, we might symbiotically link with robots as we already do with guard or search dogs in complex rescue operations. And if we wish to augment our cognition or moral decision-making, we might use symbiotic BCI implants and some form of interactive assistant.

Importantly, for the symbiotic systems to be optimally effective, both the human and artificial agents have to use their autonomous capacities to their fullest, as it is precisely through the use of their capacities that they augment each other's actions.[7] And to synergize the use of their capacities they have to be capable of interacting in a tightly coupled, finely tuned manner.[8] As such, when we aim to evaluate the effectiveness of the tight symbiotic coupling we are primarily concerned with the interactions which are manifested by actions, decisions, choices, intentions, etc.

How do we best approach the conceptualization of the tight symbiotic coupling relation? We propose basing our understanding on its impact on human personal identity; that is, the strong and the weak version of the tight symbiotic coupling. Again, the inspiration for such an understanding is derived from the biological example:

> Symbiosis is an evolved interaction or close living relationship between organisms from different species, usually with benefits to one or both of the individuals involved…Symbioses may be "obligate," in which case the relationship between the two species is so interdependent that each of the organisms is unable to survive without the other, or "facultative," in which the two species engage in a symbiotic partnership through choice, and can survive individually.
>
> (BD Editors 2019)

In the weak version of symbiotic interaction, the formation of the symbiotic system does not influence the sense of one's own identity. Instead, the human experiences symbiotic cooperation occurring on the level of the shared goal, that is on the level of sharing one's intentions and actions – similar to a distributed system. This, again, might be the case in human–robot symbiotic partnerships.

In the strong version of the symbiotic relation,[9] the sense of symbiosis one accomplishes with the machine occurs not only at the level of a shared goal, as in tightly coupled cooperation, but also at the level of personal identity.

Here, the practice of human autonomy stands intertwined with the machine's agency in such accord that accomplishing basic (bodily or mental) actions cannot be done without the cooperation of the device (as in some BCI cases; Gilbert, Cook, et al. 2019; Gilbert et al. 2018). When this happens, the human subject can experience the device becoming a part of them, a part of their bodies and their personal selves. Thus, the manner of interaction in which one interacts with the symbiotic entity is similar to the experience one has when interacting with oneself, with one's thoughts or bodily states and actions.

Moreover, since the machine supplements and augments us with novel capacities, finely tuned for our needs, the human subject can experience the sense of being related to an entity that is closer, more knowledgeable, or more active in us than we ordinarily perceive ourselves to be. Here, the symbiotic link does not only produce an experience of symbiotic cooperation which for instance could be accomplished in human–robot symbiosis (Wang et al. 2019). It produces an experience of a symbiotic identity, as testified in some BCI cases: "We were calibrated together." "We became one." (Kenneally 2021). Let us take a closer look.

17.5 Symbiotic identity: Machine and me (within me)

What could it mean, that "the device became me" (Gilbert, Cook, et al. 2019), as one human person testified to have experienced after interacting with the BCI device? If we take the experience at its base value, it seems clear that the human subject transparently distinguishes the device as a separate entity from herself. But at the same time, she also acknowledges that this separate device has become a part of herself, of her own personal identity.

So, if I ask myself "What am I?," the answer remains the same as before the tight symbiotic coupling – I remain myself, I am me. It seems that no breach, no crisis of identity occurs. However, I am also aware that I am not alone within myself. The machine (in this case the interactive device) is also a part of me. So, when I relate to myself, I do so as a symbiont (or compound) – within me, there is a clear distinction but no division of identity.

How do we explain such a judgment? First, it seems obvious to state that the reason behind the judgment of distinction (i.e. there is an interactive device implanted in my brain) lies in the knowledge one has of the device's implementation. That is, one has consciously decided to undergo the procedure, retains the memory of the device's implementation, and interacts with the device post-procedure. The reason for the judgment of unification, on the other hand, seems more confounding and requires further investigation because not all implanted individuals will experience it (Gilbert et al. 2019; Kenneally 2021; Gilbert 2013).

A good starting point to understand this process might include looking at the sense of body ownership which designates the experience of bodily self-ascription, that is the experience that I am the sole and unique owner and controller of my body. The sense of bodily ownership is usually understood to be achieved by an integrative process that unifies multimodal bodily information derived from internal bodily senses (somatic proprioception, interoception, touch) within the perceptual field of the first-person perspective (DeVignemont 2011; Tsakiris 2017). Thus, if we aim to delineate the experience of BCI-induced identity changes more finely, then interoception[10] might be the most promising candidate for further investigation, as BCI implants interact directly and solely with the brain's physiological states.

Importantly, judgments of bodily ownership derived from the bodily sense of interoception are understood as information sources that can "provide information only about the self" (Bermudez 2011) or more specifically give rise to judgments that are immune to error through misidentification (IEM) (Evans 1982). This entails that when I rely on the sense of interoception to experience my body, I cannot be mistaken that it is "I" who am this body.

The intuition is that when the BCI device is operating in a non-disruptive manner and becomes finely calibrated with our brain's physiological states when we determine the bodily self-ascription as it relates to the implanted device; the "awareness of the internal states of our bodily organs" (i.e. interoception; Bermudez 2011) is not disturbed. Consequently, I cannot be mistaken that the "I" now also includes the device since the sense of interoception provides information only about my own body in a self-specific manner, and the experiences grounded in this bodily sense are presented to me in such a way that no additional process of self-identification is present or required, and no misidentification of my body is possible. If this is true, then calibrating the device so as not to disturb the brain's physiological state (and sense of interoception) might prevent a possible identity crisis.[11] As Tsakiris points out, human subjects need "an accurate sense of her own interoceptive body in order to be able to correctly attribute mental and bodily states to oneself…and understand the causes of those states, while maintaining the distinction between self and other" (Palmer and Tsakiris 2018).

17.6 Accepting the tight symbiotic coupling as a transformative experience

Crucially, with the possibility of impacting the sense of one's identity in such a fundamental manner (i.e. interoceptionally), the strong version of the tight symbiotic coupling becomes heavily dependent on the condition of acceptance – the human willingness to accept the changes in one's identity occurring after the initiation of the symbiotic relationship. Without acceptance, the formation of tight symbiotic coupling does not seem to be possible. Moreover, without acceptance, a concrete identity crisis may occur as was shown in cases where the implanted individuals requested a removal of the device ("I want it out of my head") despite the device fulfilling its functional effectiveness (i.e. executing its role properly) (Gilbert et al. 2019; Kenneally 2021; Gilbert 2013).

Consequently, some form of preparation for the relationship ought to be employed. This could include the need for a clear elucidation of the symbiotic relation, proper education of the capacities of AI systems, the level and scope of accountability for the human agent, and, if necessary, motivational encouragement (Miletic and Gilbert 2020).

However, the problem with the strong type of symbiotic link, as is arguably the case in BCI implementations, is that they may be a source of transformative experiences for the user. As Paul describes, there are two kinds of transformative experiences, epistemically and personally transformative experiences. Experiencing an "epistemically transformative experience" gives one "new abilities to imagine, recognize, and cognitively model possible future experiences of that kind" (Paul 2015, 761).

A personally transformative experience, on the other hand, "changes you in some deep and personally fundamental way, for example, by changing your core personal preferences or by changing the way you understand your desires and the kind of person you take yourself to be" (Paul 2015, 761), which is "revising how you experience yourself" (Paul 2014, 16), "your point of view," and "what it is like for you to be you" (Paul 2014, 16).

The problem with transformative experiences (and transformative choices) lies in the inability of the transformee to know what kind of transformation is she embarking on, into what she will transform into. In other terms, even with acceptance, and having a device fully meeting its functional endpoint, the transformative effects of enhancing and augmenting one cognitive capacity might impair one self-understanding, and as such might induce harm experienced as a burden, which would be an ethical indication for BCI removal (Gilbert and Tubig 2018).

The question arises as to how to control and welcome the new range of experiences, the new traits and preferences resulting from the transformative experience. Alternatively, should the implantee avoid the transformation and remain positioned within the range of her current (known) preferences and experiences? Unfortunately, the answer seems impossible to determine rationally if the decision is based on the evaluation of possible outcomes in accordance with specific values that the transformee currently holds.

As Paul shows with the case of deaf children receiving a hearing implant, the choice of becoming a biological parent, or even the fictitious example of becoming a vampire, you simply cannot make an informed and rational decision by "assigning subjective values to these outcomes and then modeling your preferences on this basis" (Paul 2014). In other words, since you cannot know what the experiences of this new state of being will be, you cannot make decisions based on evaluating these states as being rationally preferable or not (from your current perspective).

However, as Paul argues, there is a possibility to make a rational choice for the transformative experience. Again, you cannot make a rational choice based on the knowledge of "what it will be like" to be transformed or "what you will become" after the transformation. Rather, you can make the decision "in order to discover who you'll become" (Paul 2014, 119). So the choice is between retaining your current identity and current preferences or choosing to discover your new identity and your new preferences. Similarly, when you reject the transformative experience, you can do so rationally because you "reject this kind of revelation – you don't want to discover the new preferences and new identity" (Paul 2014, 120).

If we apply this solution to our symbiotic case, for one to endorse the symbiotic relationship (in the strong sense) one should prefer to discover the new symbiotic life, the new kind of being one will become. The question is then, why decide "for" rather than "against" this discovery? What can motivate us to "plunge into the unknown of a new self?" What reasons can motivate us to actively choose to alter one's self-understanding as we become part of the symbiotic relationship? We propose that lacking a specific and detailed description of the experience they will go through human subjects might be helped with the provision of an ethical narrative.

As Frank (2014) describes, "narrative ethics seeks not to formulate its own preferred solutions, but rather to help people tell stories that imagine the best possible ways to act." One of the goals of the narrative ethics approach is to support "making sense" of the new situation "in terms of the stories in which they imagine their lives, or else resistance is predictable" (Frank 2014, 16). In doing so, ethical narratives aim to "prevent situations from turning into cases" to "teach people how to recognize the best versions of themselves in whatever circumstances they find themselves" (Frank 2014, 16).

Here then, what we can provide is an endorsed narrative that places the human subject as the protagonist of her life's story as she embarks on the transformative experience of the symbiotic relationship. Predominantly, this narrative should mitigate identity crisis. To do so, it should be capable of portraying the nature of the tight coupling in a psychologically beneficial and ethically acceptable manner. If such an endorsed narrative is found, it could motivate the user to enter into the symbiotic relationship and facilitate easier integration of the changes in one's identity after the procedure. Moreover, if precise conditions are derived, they could be used to guide the design of the artificial agents' interaction and personality traits (El Bolock 2020; Koay et al 2020), which would support the symbiotic narrative post-procedure.

The question is then what kind of narrative could correspond to the existential demands of the symbiotic link, the demands that the symbiotic relationship puts on one's personal identity? Precisely, what kind of a narrative allows a safe transition from a self-understanding of a single individual to that of two co-joined individuals? As a start, we propose the narrative of the symbiotic companion.

17.7 The symbiotic companion: Machines being "with" humans

The word companion, in English, comes from the Latin word *companio* and is composed of com, which means "with," and *panis* which means "bread." Thus, a companion is someone with whom you share your daily bread, one's means of sustenance, life itself. Being a companion to someone entails having a meaningful, authentic (Crowell 2020) relationship, a deep personal bond with that particular someone which cannot be reduced solely to the notion of partnership. It necessarily includes an affective dimension, personal meaning, satisfaction, and intimacy. As the great French existentialist, Gabriel Marcel wrote, this deep relation of being "with" another person "corresponds neither to a relationship of inherence or immanence nor to a relationship of exteriority. It is of the essence of genuine *coesse*…of genuine intimacy" (Marcel 1956, 39).

When two persons are so closely related, Marcel explains, the sense of one's self is never lost or diminished but a change in the understanding of myself, in the manner I live out my existence, does occur. In becoming so closely related to another human being, I do not suffer any division in my understanding of myself. I am still myself, fully and completely, before and after the relationship establishes itself. But at the same time, the experience I have of myself, my innermost understanding of myself now stands enriched, added upon, by "a specific kind of interior accretion or accretion from within" (Marcel 1956, 38).[12]

Most interestingly, perhaps, the nature of this close relationship evades conscious understanding and remains a mystery to me, even though I now understand myself through this relationship. So, when I introspect, I am always "I," but at the same time "I" am also "with you." That is, I understand that you have become part of me but not at the expense of my personal self, as when I introspect myself I remain whole. But I cannot explain how is this possible since the phenomenon is a mystery to me.[13]

According to Marcel, the reason for this phenomenon being a mystery lies in my inability to extricate myself from this close relationship "with" the other person:

> I…cannot place myself outside it or before it; I am engaged in this encounter, I depend upon it, I am inside it in a certain sense, it envelops me and it comprehends me even if it is not comprehended by me.
>
> *(Marcel 1956, 22)*

So, when two persons become so closely connected the usually clear border between our identities diffuses:

> between him and me there arises a relationship which, in a sense, surpasses my awareness of him; he is not only before me, he is also within me-or, rather, these categories are transcended, they have no longer any meaning.
>
> *(Marcel 1956, 38)*

Strikingly, it seems that Marcel's descriptions fit adequately, if not precisely, with the symbiotic experiences of BCI patients. It seems then, that the human ability to form this kind of deep, meaningful, identity-affecting relations is not limited solely to other humans but also machines.

If this is true, then to create a machine that is "with" humans we have to determine the conditions which constitute the "with" relation. For Marcel this is predominantly the availability (*disponibilité*) condition:

> The person who is at my disposal is the one who is capable of being with me with the whole of himself when I am in need; while the one who is not at my disposal seems merely to offer me a temporary loan raised on his resources. For the one I am a presence; for the other I am an object.
>
> *(Marcel 1956, 40)*

Are there any examples of artificial interactive agents accomplishing a relation of being "with" another human? Arguably, the BCI device is already, albeit in a severely limited interactional manner, fully disposed toward the human being in times of their (medical) need.

However, if we aim to investigate interaction examples of humans and artificial agents being "with" one another, we might have to venture into the digital realm. Here, in the past decade, humans have already been forming relations with computationally generated characters, the non-playable game characters or NPCs (who serve as adventure companions to the story protagonist)[14] in a vast number of cases with tangible and life-affecting impacts.

Deducing the character traits of NPC companions which could be utilized as conditions for the design of symbiotic companions interaction goes beyond the scope of this work. Still, some fundamental traits might include the possibility to affect mutual decision choices and character traits (fine-tuning) and the possibility to explore and test out one's preferences and (moral) values in an empowering, supporting, and life-like, company (autonomy and pluralism of choice).[15]

Notwithstanding the precise traits, symbiotic companions that support humans in establishing meaningful and affective relations with companion characters remain a plentiful and promising resource for further investigation.

17.8 Conclusion

Medical research into human–BCI technologies progresses steadily, and BCI patients who have experienced the interaction with an intelligent device implanted in their brains testify various subjective feelings about the smart system. In some cases, the connection they achieve with the implemented interactive device goes beyond mere interaction and cooperation. It impacts the sense of their own identity (Gilbert Cook et al. 2019).

In some of the human–BCI cases, human subjects have experienced becoming "one" with the machine but not at the expense of their self-integrity – an experience that draws striking similarities with the symbiotic concept, resulting in an augmentative version of oneself with novel capabilities. These observations require further examination of the notion of human–AI symbiosis with regard to possible degrees of enhancement.

In this chapter, we have seen that potential augmentative capacity via BCI can be incorporated into the sense of bodily self-ownership while being experienced as genuine interactions with an intelligent agent by the implanted subject. We observed that the use of the device creates a transformative experience for the user, which shifts the subject's self-understanding from the sense of a single individual to that of two co-joined individuals.

The main motivator for developing a framework through which we can understand the augmentative dimensions of human–AI symbiosis is to establish a tunable tool that can present us with the opportunity for users and AI systems to co-adapt to each other in order to truly maximize task performance (Verhoeven et al. 2015). Crucially, such a tool would also diminish potential rejection or non-acceptance of the system into one self-understanding and decrease the risk of postoperative harms and vulnerabilities.

Notes

1 The idea of AI outpacing human capacities is not new. In 2005, Hugo de Garis, a famous transhumanist and an AI researcher, hypothesized that the future development of AI technology will bring about a global catastrophe by splitting humanity into three distinct groups based on their orientation towards the existence of super intelligent artificial intelligence. As de Garis explains in a reiterated 2008 piece:
"The first group is the "Cosmists" (based on the word Cosmos) who are in favor of building artilects. The second group is the "Terrans" (based on the word Terra, the earth) who are opposed to building artilects, and the third group is the "Cyborgs," who want to become artilects themselves by adding artilectual components to their own human brains" (de Garis 2008).
2 This book chapter incorporates elements of an unpublished doctoral thesis defended by Tomislav Furlanis, née Miletić, deposed at University of Rijeka, Faculty of Humanities and Social Sciences. www.ffri.uniri.hr/files/vijesti/2020-2021/Doktorski_rad-T_Miletic.pdf.
3 For the sake of our argument, we will assume that potential BCIs uses for symbiotic endpoints are technically and medically safe. Obviously, we are aware there are intrinsic safety concerns with any implantable devices, but discussing these aspects is not the aim of this chapter. We have discussed these issues elsewhere (Gilbert 2015). Accordingly, we will focus on effectiveness in this chapter.
4 As Russel and Norvig explain: "Of course, all computer programs do something, but computer agents are expected to do more: operate autonomously, perceive their environment, persist over a prolonged time period, adapt to change, and create and pursue goals… A rational agent is one that acts so as to achieve the best outcome or when there is uncertainty, the best-expected outcome" (Russell and Norvig 2021, 21-22).
5 For instance, Rita, an author, is using Grammarly to assist her in writing a manuscript. Now, Grammarly cannot write anything autonomously for her. For the text to exist, she must write it down. But, once she has written her sentences down, the Grammarly assistant provides many corrections and improvements to the written text. As such, her text is truly the product of augmented Rita, augmented by extension of Grammarly. However, if Grammarly was capable of autonomous writing and could complete entire sentences on her behalf (or even paragraphs), then she would stand augmented by collaboration rather than "mere" extension.
6 This also entails that when we delineate the symbiotic system's autonomy (i.e. symbiotic autonomy), we are actually looking top-down, or more precisely from the inside-out, from the system's point of view and

7. A symbiotic human–AI system "should provide the opportunity for a significant adaptation of the augmentation means to individual characteristics. The compounding effect of fundamental human cognitive powers suggests further that systems designed for maximum effectiveness would require that these powers be developed as fully as possible – by training, special mental tricks, improved language, new methodology" (Engelbart 1962).
8. Interestingly, this also entails humans learning how to "fine-tune" their interaction, and broadly their capacities, towards the symbiotic machine (similarly to that famous sci-fi example of "Human Mentats" from the Dune Universe). This is not a radical notion, as humans are already tuning-up into a world of internet and mobile technologies, learning how to code and use intelligent AI systems. Moreover, as recent research shows, developed AI-businesses, such machine-tuned skills and machine-oriented interaction, are already in demand (Daugherty and Wilson 2018).
9. The third point relates to the tightly coupled interaction between humans and the AI in the symbiotic system. Here we propose there is a fundamental distinction of "durability" from which to interpret the "tight coupling" as it exists in symbiotic relationships. The distinction of durability seems like a straightforward candidate on which to base the initial ethical analysis of BCI symbiotic relations. Is the implant removable? If so, we are dealing with the weak version of symbiosis. Is it non-removable, or removable at a high-risk for the health of the user? Then we are dealing with the strong version of symbiosis.
10. Interoception designates the experience of the body's physiological condition which originates from within the body's internal organs and is counted to be a "fundamental component of our sense of personal identity and overall well-being" since it shapes "a wide range of subjective experiences, and fundamental aspects of body experience, such as body ownership and self-awareness" (Badoud and Tsakiris 2017).
11. As Makin et al. 2017 warn: "The realization of this vision could be restricted by the ability of the human brain to successfully and safely control augmentation technology. Poor neurocognitive design could lead to side effects as a result of limitations in the brain's capacity to operate the body and senses (maladaptive plasticity), which could lead to serious and long-lasting effects" (Makin, De Vignemont, and Faisal 2017).
12. This description shares a remarkable similarity with one BCI experience, where the user experienced that the interaction with the device produced positive and integrative effects on her own personality: "with the device, I found myself" (Gilbert, Cook et al. 2019).
13. Again, similarly to cases of BCI implementations where users cannot explain how they share such a close connection with their device.
14. More recently, digital companions are also becoming integrated with developed interactive capacities that resemble personality characteristics of NPC companions (Replika.ai).
15. For instance, one such famous example includes the Cortana character from the HALO series, where popularity was so big that Microsoft based their digital assistant on the game character. And no wonder, as the sense of being "with" the main protagonist of the story in this concrete story narrative is of literal symbiotic and heroic proportions. Similar kinds of experiences are also available in many other role-playing gaming narratives.

Reference list

Badoud, D., & Tsakiris, M. (2017). From the body's viscera to the body's image: Is there a link between interoception and body image concerns?. *Neuroscience & Biobehavioral Reviews*, 77, 237–246.
Barfield, W., & Williams, A. (2017). Cyborgs and enhancement technology. *Philosophies*, 2(1), 4. https://doi.org/10.3390/philosophies2010004
BD Editors. (2019, April 8). Symbiosis. Biology Dictionary. https://biologydictionary.net/symbiosis/
Bermúdez, J. (2011). Bodily awareness and self-consciousness. In Shaun Gallagher (ed.), *The Oxford Handbook of the Self* (pp. 157–180). Oxford, UK: Oxford University Press.
Crowell, S. (2020). Existentialism. In Edward N. Zalta & Uri Nodelman (Eds.) *The Stanford Encyclopedia of Philosophy*. https://plato.stanford.edu/archives/win2022/entries/existentialism/
Daugherty, P. R., & Wilson, H. J. (2018). *Human+ machine: Reimagining work in the age of AI*. Boston, Massachusetts: Harvard Business Press.
de Garis, H. (2008, June). The artilect war: Cosmists vs. Terrans. A bitter controversy concerning whether humanity should build godlike massively intelligent machines. In *Proceedings of the 2008 Conference on*

Artificial General Intelligence 2008: Proceedings of the First AGI Conference (pp. 437–447), Memphis, TN, USA: University of Memphis.

DeGrazia, D. (2005). Enhancement technologies and human identity. *The Journal of Medicine and Philosophy*, 30(3), 261–283.

Dominijanni, G., Shokur, S., Salvietti, G., et al. (2021). The neural resource allocation problem when enhancing human bodies with extra robotic limbs. *Nature Machine Intelligence*, 3, 850–860. https://doi.org/10.1038/s42256-021-00398-9

El Bolock, A. (2020). What is character computing?. In A. E. Bolock, J. Salah, S. Abdennadher, & Y. Abdelrahman (eds.) *Character Computing* (pp. 1–16). Cham: Springer.

Engelbart, D. C. (1962). *Augmenting Human Intellect: A Conceptual Framework*. Menlo Park, CA.: Stanford Research Institute, Reprinted by permission of SRI International.

Evans, Garreth. (1982). *Varieties of Reference*. Oxford: Oxford University Press.

Frank, A. W. (2014). Narrative ethics as dialogical story-telling. *Hastings Center Report*, 44(s1), S16–S20.

Gilbert, F. (2013). Deep brain stimulation for treatment resistant depression: Postoperative feeling of self-estrangement, suicide attempt and impulsive-aggressive behaviours. *Neuroethics*, 6(3), 473–481. https://doi.org/10.1007/s12152-013-9178-8

Gilbert, F. (2015). A threat to autonomy? The intrusion of predictive brain implants. *AJOB Neuroscience*, 6(4), 4–11. https://doi.org/10.1080/21507740.2015.1076087

Gilbert, F., & Tubig, P. (2018). Cognitive enhancement with brain implants: The burden of abnormality. *Journal of Cognitive Enhancement*, 2, 364–368. https://doi.org/10.1007/s41465-018-0105-0

Gilbert, F., Cook, M., O'Brien, T., & Illes, J. (2019). Embodiment and estrangement: Results from a first-in-human "intelligent brain computer interface" trial. *Science and Engineering Ethics*, 25(1), 83–96. https://doi.org/10.1007/s11948-017-0001-5

Gilbert, F., O'Brien, T., & Cook, M. (2018). The effects of closed-loop brain implants on autonomy and deliberation: What are the risks of being kept in the loop? *Cambridge Quarterly of Healthcare Ethics (Neuroethics Now)*, 27(2), 316–325.

Gilbert, F., Pham, C., Viana, J. N. M., & Gillam, W. (2019). Increasing brain-computer interfaces media depictions: Pressing ethical concerns. *Brain-Computer Interfaces*, 6(3), 49–70. https://doi.org/10.1080/2326263X.2019.1655837

Hassani, H., Silva, E. S., Unger, S., TajMazinani, M., & Mac Feely, S. (2020). Artificial Intelligence (AI) or Intelligence Augmentation (IA): What is the future? *AI 2020*, 1, 143–155. https://doi.org/10.3390/ai1020008

Hernández-Orallo, J., & Vold, K. (2019). Ai extenders: The ethical and societal implications of humans cognitively extended by Ai. In *Proceedings of the 2019 AAAI/ACM Conference on AI, Ethics, and Society* (pp. 507–513), Honolulu HI USA.

Ienca, M. (2021). *Common Human Rights Challenges Raised by Different Applications of Neurotechnologies in the Biomedical Dields*. Report commissioned by the Committee on Bioethics (DH-BIO) of the Council of Europe. Council of Europe.

Ienca, M., & Ignatiadis, K. (2020). Artificial intelligence in clinical neuroscience: Methodological and ethical challenges. *AJOB Neuroscience*, 11(2), 77–87.

Karnouskos, S. (2021). Symbiosis with artificial intelligence via the prism of law, robots, and society. *Artificial Intelligence and Law*. https://doi.org/10.1007/s10506-021-09289-1

Kellmeyer, P. (2019). Artificial intelligence in basic and clinical neuroscience: Opportunities and ethical challenges. *Neuroforum*, 25(4), 241–250.

Kenneally, C. (2021). Do brain implants change your identity?. *The New Yorker*, April & May 3, 2021 Issue.

Koay, K. L., Syrdal, D. S., Dautenhahn, K., & Walters, M. L. (2020). A narrative approach to human-robot interaction prototyping for companion robots. *Paladyn, Journal of Behavioral Robotics*, 11(1), 66–85.

Licklider, J. C. (1960). Man-computer symbiosis. *IRE Transactions on Human Factors in Electronics*, 1(1), 4–11.

Lopatto, E. (2019). Elon Musk unveils Neuralink's plans for brain-reading 'threads' and a robot to insert them. *The Verge*, https://www.theverge.com/2019/7/16/20697123/elon-musk-neuralink-brain-reading-thread-robot, Last retrieved July 07 2021.

Makin, T. R., De Vignemont, F., & Aldo Faisal, A. (2017). Neurocognitive barriers to the embodiment of technology. *Nature Biomedical Engineering*. https://doi.org/10.1038/s41551-016-0014

Marcel, G. (1956). *The Philosophy of Existentialism*, (trans. Manya Harari). New York: Citadel Press Inc.

Miletić, T., & Gilbert, F. (2020). Does Ai brain implant compromise agency? Examining potential harms of brain-computer interfaces. In Steven S. Gouveia (ed.) *The Age of Artificial Intelligence: An Exploration* (pp. 253–272). Delaware: Vernon Press.

Nagao, K. (2019). Symbiosis between humans and artificial intelligence. In *Artificial Intelligence Accelerates Human Learning*. Singapore: Springer. https://doi.org/10.1007/978-981-13-6175-3_6

Pacherie, E. (2013). Intentional joint agency: Shared intention lite. *Synthese*, 190(10), 1817–1839.

Palmer, C. E., & Tsakiris, M. (2018). Going at the heart of social cognition: Is there a role for interoception in self-other distinction?. *Current Opinion in Psychology*, 24, 21–26.

Paul, L. A. (2014). *Transformative Experience*. Oxford: OUP.

Paul, L. A. (2015). *Précis of Transformative Experience*. https://doi.org/10.1111/phpr.12249

Pham, C., & Gilbert, F. (2019). Unbacked futures: Ethical issues raised by news media futuristic depiction of Brain-Computer Interfaces. *Bioethica Forum*, 12(1/2), 15–28.

Russell, S., & Norvig, P. (2021). *Artificial Intelligence: A Modern Approach*, 4th Edition, Harlow, UK: Pearson Education.

Sandberg, A. (2013). Morphological freedom-why we not just want it, but need it. In Max More and Natasha Vita-More (eds.) *The Transhumanist Reader* (pp. 56–64), West Sussex, UK: Wiley-Blackwell

Schweikard, D. P. (2017). Cooperation and social obligations. In N. J. Enfield, & P. Kockelman (Eds.) *Distributed Agency* (pp. 233–242), Oxford, UK: Oxford University Press.

Soekadar, S., Chandler, J., Ienca, M., & Bublitz, C. (2021). On the verge of the hybrid mind. *Morals & Machines*, 1(1), 30–43.

Sorgner, S. L. (2021). *We Have Always been Cyborgs: Digital Data, Gene Technologies and an Ethics of Transhumanism*. Bristol, UK: Policy Press.

Statt, N. (2017). Elon Musk launches Neuralink, a venture to merge the human brain with AI. *The Verge*. https://www.theverge.com/2017/3/27/15077864/elon-musk-neuralink-brain-computer-interface-ai-cyborgs, Last retrieved June 29 2018.

The Daily Telegraph. (2017). Chips in human brains 'to prevent a robot takeover'. *The Daily Telegraph*, 29 March.

Tsakiris, M. (2017). The multisensory basis of the self: From body to identity to others. *Quarterly Journal of Experimental Psychology*, 70(4), 597–609. https://doi.org/10.1080/17470218.2016.1181768.

Veloso, M., Biswas, J., Coltin, B., & Rosenthal, S. (2015, June). Cobots: Robust symbiotic autonomous mobile service robots. In Twenty-Fourth International Joint *Conference on Artificial Intelligence*, Buenos Aires, Argentina.

Verhoeven, T., et al. (2015). Towards a symbiotic brain–computer interface: Exploring the application–decoder interaction. *Journal of Neural Engineering*, 12, 066027.

Vidal, J. J. (1973). Toward direct brain-computer communication. *Annual Review of Biophysics and Bioengineering*, 2(1), 157–180.

Vignemont, F. De (2011). A self for the body. *Metaphilosophy*. https://doi.org/10.1111/j.1467-9973.2011.01688.x

Wang, L., Gao, R., Váncza, J., Krüger, J., Wang, X. V., Makris, S., & Chryssolouris, G. (2019). Symbiotic human-robot collaborative assembly. *CIRP Annals*, 68(2), 701–726.

Zhou, L., Paul, S., Demirkan, H., Yuan, L., Spohrer, J., Zhou, M., & Basu, J. (2021). Intelligence augmentation: Towards building human-machine symbiotic relationship. *AIS Transactions on Human-Computer Interaction*, 13(2), 243–264. https://doi.org/10.17705/1thci.00149

18
ANTICIPATING THE FUTURE OF NEUROTECHNOLOGICAL ENHANCEMENT

Nathan Higgins, Cynthia Forlini, Isobel Butorac, John Gardner, and Adrian Carter

18.1 Introduction

Neuroscience promises to deliver a range of technological innovations that will enable individuals to enhance their behavior and cognition in ways that would not otherwise be possible (Yuste et al., 2017). These technologies include psychoactive drugs, brain imaging devices, invasive and non-invasive brain stimulation technologies (e.g., DBS, tDCS), and other monitoring devices to decode brain activity or control external prosthetics. The ability to enhance human capacities has long been a concern of social conservatives who worry about how these powerful technologies may undermine societal values, such as privacy and fairness, and fundamental aspects of what it means to be human. These concerns have been portrayed in numerous science fiction films and novels, from *Frankenstein* to *Minority Report* and *Eternal Sunshine of the Spotless Mind*. Contrary to the alarmist attitudes driving these dystopian imaginations, others have welcomed technological neuroinnovation as the path to meeting the grand challenges facing humanity, such as climate change, environmental degradation, and artificial intelligence (AI) (Persson & Savulescu, 2008). The extent to which we should be concerned with these competing accounts of the future depends on what new abilities emerging neurotechnologies allow. Despite decades of research on the brain, an understanding of precisely how neural activity results in human thought and experience remains elusive. It is therefore difficult to predict whether neurotechnological innovation will realize the future scenarios that worry or excite forecasters.

In this chapter, we examine the challenges and potential pitfalls of speculating about the future of neurotechnology. We briefly review the history of psychopharmacological enhancement to understand how claims about the prevalence and effectiveness of drugs to enhance cognition can be exaggerated. We then examine current applications of more nascent neurotechnological innovations, such as direct-to-consumer brain imaging and stimulating devices, and surgically implantable brain–computer interfaces. We conclude by offering some recommendations for how the ethical impacts of neurotechnological enhancement can be anticipated in a way that is realistic and critical of the underlying science.

18.2 The impact of an unreflective anticipatory ethics

Anticipatory ethics aims to identify and prevent harmful consequences before they emerge. Ethicists have rightly been critical of scientists who have failed to draw attention to obvious abuses of their research, such as atomic energy and reproductive technologies. Failing to identify these abuses can raise unfounded worries that may unjustifiably impede research. On the other hand, overly optimistic and uncritical promises can shift research funding priorities into areas of little need, wasting limited resources on low-impact technologies, and distracting attention away from approaches that are generally more effective.

It can be difficult to regulate or unwind practices once they have been established in society. Anticipatory ethics encourages researchers and developers to engage in a design process that considers ways in which harms can be minimized or prevented. Harms are often realized only after a technology has been disseminated, by which time addressing or mitigating these harms can be expensive or impossible. It is imperative that ethical harms be vigilantly anticipated in the development of novel products with an eye toward who these harms might affect. Recognition of this need is evident in practices such as ethically aligned design and value-sensitive design, which seek to identify potential harms by engaging with end-users throughout the process of development. The need to proactively anticipate the impact of technological innovation has been codified in several government initiatives, such as the European Union Horizons 2020 Responsible Research and Innovation and UK Foresight programs.

Exaggerated claims about technology can lead to unrealistic expectations about safety and effectiveness. Unreflective speculation can feed into the portrayal of neurotechnologies as miracle cures and magic bullets. This is particularly relevant when media reports describe neurotechnologies in a way that is uncritical of the science and the intended applications of the technology (Racine & Forlini, 2010; Gilbert & Goddard, 2014). In recent years, media reporting on neurotechnologies has risen dramatically, with the number of articles sharply increasing between 2010 and 2016 and doubling between 2016 and 2017 (Gilbert et al., 2019). Many of these articles are positively biased, with over a quarter introducing the possibility of devices equipping humans with greatly enhanced capacities (Gilbert et al., 2019). If potential device users have unrealistic expectations about the ability of neurotechnologies to monitor or change thoughts and behaviors, they may be disposed to engage with these technologies in ways that cause harm. Research has shown that patients with overinflated expectations have poorer health outcomes and significant disappointment when their expectations are not met. For example, patients undergoing neurosurgery for intractable neurological conditions may experience poorer clinical outcomes when their understanding of the effectiveness of the technology is overinflated (Bell et al., 2010) or when they are not aware of or have not fully appreciated adverse effects (Thomson et al., 2021).

Much of the debate over neurotechnologies for enhancement has focused on preserving user autonomy (Schelle et al., 2014; Schaefer et al., 2014), but there has been more recent concern over the employment of neurotechnologies in inherently coercive environments (Bruhl et al., 2019; Butorac & Carter, 2021). Neurotechnologies may be used by third parties, such as governments, employers, educators, and commercial entities, to improve productivity, reduce costs, or drive prosocial behavior. These concerns are compounded by the increasing role of commercial interests in neurotechnological innovation. Companies such as Facebook, Amazon, and Google are increasingly investing in neurotechnological innovation that occurs outside traditional institutional oversight. Brain-monitoring systems have already been introduced in the commercial sector as part of wellness programs, and several transport companies have mandated the use of wearable brain devices to monitor driver performance (Burr et al., 2020).

It is not unusual for scientific claims about safety and efficacy in the literature to be promoted uncritically in news media to general audiences (Partridge et al., 2011). This has led to the creation of overinflated cognitive enhancement bubbles that are difficult to deflate (Lucke et al., 2011). As we will see next, unwarranted speculation can also drive up the use of emerging technologies, such as pharmaceuticals for cognitive enhancement.

18.3 Lessons from the history of psychopharmacological enhancement

Much of the contemporary debate about the ethics of neurotechnological enhancement stems from debates about the repurposing of therapeutic pharmaceuticals for the enhancement of cognitive functions such as concentration, alertness, and memory (Erler & Forlini, 2020). Notable examples include the use of stimulants like amphetamines and methylphenidate, which are typically used to treat attention deficit hyperactivity disorder, and the wakefulness-promoting agent modafinil used for sleep-cycle regulation (Dresler et al., 2018). These types of substances have a history of dual use among military pilots (Mehlman, 2015) and, more recently, by students in higher education as means of academic performance enhancement (Sharif et al., 2021). The confluence of historic examples, current prevalence, and expectations of the benefit of cognitive enhancement has created the perfect context for a contentious and complex debate that remains unresolved (Forlini & Hall, 2016). Insights from the ethics of cognitive enhancement over the past two decades could usefully inform future efforts at neurotechnological enhancement. However, as we will show, concerns about the societal impacts of cognitive enhancement have relied on overly optimistic assumptions about the current and future effectiveness of nootropic ("smart") drugs and overinflated estimates of their likely prevalence.

18.3.1 Efficacy of pharmaceuticals for cognitive enhancement

Empirical data that would normally inform the ethical analysis of a new practice has remained elusive on the topic of cognitive enhancement. There is no resounding scientific support for the use of repurposed or investigational psychopharmacological drugs by healthy individuals for cognitive enhancement (Dresler et al., 2018). Evidence of enhancement effects produced by methylphenidate is weak (Repantis et al., 2010). Modafinil used for cognitive enhancement has been shown to be moderately effective and is reportedly a popular option because there are few or no side effects (Battleday & Brem, 2015). However, one study found that, outside the lab, students using prescription medication for cognitive enhancement did not experience improvement in their grades (Arria et al., 2018). Bell et al. (2012) likened the persistence of pharmacological cognitive enhancement in the absence of solid safety and efficacy data to early uses of cocaine and amphetamines. In these historic examples, the adverse effects of psychoactive substances, notably addiction, were only recognized once they had become widespread. The authors cautioned that reliance on anecdotal evidence of the safety and efficacy of cognitive enhancers data can fuel "uncritical enthusiasm that encourages their widespread use" (Bell et al., 2012, p. 27). Some authors have proposed that empirical uncertainty (i.e. inconsistent evidence as opposed to a lack of evidence) has given rise to several assumptions sustaining a "myth" that cognitive enhancement is effective and in demand (Zohny, 2015). The use of psychopharmacological substances in medicine and research offered a veil of safety, legitimacy, and efficacy for cognitive enhancement that was not warranted.

18.3.2 Prevalence of pharmacological enhancement

There is also great uncertainty about the prevalence of pharmacological enhancement. It would be easy to attribute the perpetuation of the "myth" that cognitive enhancement is in high demand to the undiscerning public, student experimentation, and hype-loving media reports. However, ethicists have also leveraged empirical uncertainty about the efficacy and prevalence to create a "cognitive enhancement bubble" that amplifies the urgency of the ethics debate. Racine and Forlini (2010) showed how determining the exact prevalence of cognitive enhancement is methodologically fraught. Different study methodologies, data analyses, definitions of cognitive enhancement, and measures of lifetime or past-year use produce highly variable estimates. This variability is reflected in the results of a recent systematic review of international cognitive enhancement prevalence rates among students using prescription stimulants that ranged from 2% to 33% (Sharif et al., 2021). A cross-sectional study of results from the Global Drug Survey, an anonymous web survey on substance use conducted annually in 15 countries with participants aged 16–65, found a 180% increase in the use of prescription and illegal stimulants for "cognitive enhancement" between 2015 (4.9%) and 2017 (13.7%) (Maier et al., 2018). While this evidence suggests that cognitive enhancement exists globally to varying degrees, it does not support claims that it is widespread nor that it is in high demand (Forlini, 2020).

18.3.3 Public attitudes toward pharmacological enhancement

A survey of public opinion on cognitive enhancement by Dinh et al. (2020) found that the acceptability of cognitive enhancement is highly dependent on context. Acceptability was lowest in vignettes describing competitive environments (e.g., academic institutions) and creating a potential disadvantage (e.g. exclusive access to enhancers). These findings reiterate a decade's worth of studies reporting substantive ambivalence in public and professional perspectives on the ethics of cognitive enhancement where both sides of ethical issues relating to personal choice, unfairness, safety, and authenticity are equally appreciated (Forlini, 2020). The mismatch between what the prevalence of a practice was expected to indicate (i.e. confirming that cognitive enhancement is embedded in social practices and values) and the results of empirical ethics studies (i.e. context-dependent acceptability and ambivalence) should caution us against drawing ethical conclusions based on prevalence and unsubstantiated claims of efficacy.

18.4 The future of neurotechnological enhancement

There is a wide range of neurotechnologies that may be used to enhance cognition. Broadly, neurotechnology includes "devices and procedures that are used to access, monitor, investigate, manipulate and emulate the structure and function of neural systems" (Giordano, 2012; c.f. Garden et al. 2019). We briefly review these technologies and evaluate whether current concerns are proportionate to the state of the science or whether we may be witnessing an enhancement bubble like that seen for pharmacological enhancement.

18.4.1 Deep brain stimulation

Deep brain stimulation (DBS) is an invasive brain stimulation procedure involving the implantation of electrodes in specific regions of the brain that modulate local neural activity. DBS has been hugely successful in the treatment of motor diseases such as Parkinson's disease, essential tremor, and dystonia (Larson, 2014) and has more recently been used to treat psychiatric indications such as treatment-resistant depression (Dandekar et al., 2018), obsessive-compulsive disorder (Naesstrom et al., 2016), and anorexia nervosa (Whiting, Oh, & Whiting, 2018). Speculation that DBS may be used for cognitive enhancement can be traced back to the late 2000s, when studies were first conducted on the effects of DBS in neurological diseases characterized by impairment of memory and learning, such as Alzheimer's disease and epilepsy (Williams & Eskander, 2006; Hamani et al., 2008). Positive findings from these studies were optimistically disseminated by major media outlets such as *The Telegraph*, *BBC News*, and *The Independent* (Gilbert & Ovadia, 2011), as well as *Nature*, which published a news article entitled "Brain electrodes can improve learning" (Abbott, 2008). However, reviews suggest poor replicability of memory-increasing effects of DBS in neurological patients due to high variation in neuroanatomy and imprecise electrode placement (Mankin & Fried, 2020; Suthana & Fried, 2014). Small case studies of experimental technologies such as DBS are also particularly susceptible to publication bias (Schlaepfer & Fins, 2010).

There are significant barriers to the widespread use of DBS for cognitive enhancement. DBS remains an extremely invasive procedure. The initial surgery has a high risk of infection (1–2%), seizures (1–2%), and intracerebral hemorrhage (3–4%) (Kleiner-Fisman et al., 2006). Post-implantation, there are additional risks associated with lead adjustment, battery replacement, hardware malfunction, and lead breakage. The use of DBS to treat neurological conditions such as Parkinson's disease can induce significant changes in behavior and cognition, including increased motivation, arousal, and energy (Pham et al., 2015; Thomson et al., 2019). In some instances, these changes can lead to severe impulsivity, behavioral addictions, and mania, causing some patients to lose thousands of dollars and experience breakdowns in their relationships with carers, family, and friends (Agid et al., 2006).

DBS has now been used to treat over 200,000 patients worldwide, but it remains an extremely expensive procedure. Device and surgical implantation costs can be as much as USD $50,000, and ongoing maintenance, battery replacement, and stimulation adjustments can cost upto $10,000 every three years. There are also limited clinical teams and hospital resources available to provide these treatments. The invasiveness of the procedure, cost, and risk of long-term health consequences has resulted in DBS remaining a last-resort therapy for patients suffering from intractable neurological illnesses (Bell et al., 2009). The use of these limited resources to serve a wealthy few would put considerable pressure on already stretched health systems and ultimately limit access to the technology by those who require it to treat intractable neurodegenerative disorders. Even if safety improvements are sufficient to justify use in healthy individuals, there remains the challenge of developing an affordable, self-managed DBS device with everyday applications outside tightly controlled lab-based settings.

18.4.2 *Neurosurgical brain–computer interfaces*

A brain–computer interface (BCI) is a device that reads neural activity and translates it into artificial output intended to replace, restore, enhance, supplement, or improve natural brain function (Wolpaw & Wolpaw, 2012). Examples include prosthetic limbs for patients with amputations and whole-body systems for locomotion for patients suffering from paralysis due to trauma of the spinal cord (Lebedev & Nicholelis, 2017). BCIs have also been used to enable communication in patients with amyotrophic lateral sclerosis (ALS), traumatic head injury, and locked-in syndrome. Cortical monitoring of locked-in patients' attentional direction can be used to register responses to "yes" or "no" style questions, as well as allow them to write entire paragraphs by selecting letters and sentences displayed on a screen (Chaudhary et al., 2016).

In contrast to speculation around the use of DBS for cognitive enhancement, the anticipated applications of BCIs have been far more sensational. BCIs for sensory enhancement, such as cochlear and retinal implants, have historically been used only in the treatment of deafness and blindness, with the sensory acuity being vastly inferior to that provided by healthy ears and eyes. More recent research has attempted to equip sensory prosthetics with some degree of "intelligence" (Jebari, 2013). This has created excitement about "hi-fi" cochlear implants for listening to music (Clark, 2008) or bionic eyes that apply filters and image processing to provide a tailored virtual reality (Caspi et al., 2009). It has been speculated that so-called "telepathic" BCIs may one day enable user-to-user collaboration and decision-making by recording neural activity from multiple individuals simultaneously. Some have considered their potential use in military situations, with BCIs enabling communication on the battlefield without the use of vocalized speech (Trimper et al., 2014; Cinel et al., 2019; Moreno, 2011).

Even more sensational commentaries have claimed that BCIs may one day co-adapt with users, forming a "symbiotic" relationship between brains and hardware like smartphones. Elon's Musk has described his Neuralink cortical implant as a "Fitbit in your skull" that will one day enable "complete symbiosis with artificial intelligence." This is despite the company's lead neurosurgeon stressing that the system is "only intended for patients with serious medical diseases," such as complete paralysis due to an upper spinal cord injury (Vance, 2019). Using the Neuralink BCI as an example, enhancing cognition or facilitating brain-to-brain communication would require recording cortical neural activity via a technique called electrocorticography (ECoG) and transmitting this neural data to a device that delivers finely-tuned stimulation to regions of the user's brain or to a computer that integrates the neural data of multiple brains. Four years of work and hundreds of millions of dollars of investment into Musk's Neuralink device have failed to yield any evidence of cognitive enhancement, knowledge transfer, or "symbiosis." The device has not yet delivered on the more modest promise of an efficacious restoration of movement in paralysis (Regalado, 2020).

The extensive optimistic media coverage of Neuralink highlights a tendency for neurotechnology developers and journalists to emphasize the secondary effects of research before the primary therapeutic goals of research have been realized (Schlaepfer & Fins, 2010). One review of BCIs in the mainstream media found that 75% of articles were portrayed positively, of which 25% were overly positive, making regular use of utopian tropes such as "super brains" and "thought control" (Gilbert et al., 2019). Gilbert et al.'s findings suggest some journalists are too quick to embrace the notion of a transparent mind that can be read by a BCI, which "reduces our utmost secretive thoughts to a mere package of exportable and importable qualia." In reality, invasive closed-loop BCIs that decode and respond to an individual's unique brain signals are largely being explored in the therapeutic realm. Closed-loop DBS has been used to provide personalized treatment for Parkinson's (Fleming et al., 2020), depression, and obsessive-compulsive disorder (Figee & Mayberg, 2021) and in the prediction and prevention of focal seizures in epilepsy. One recent proof-of-concept study in epileptic patients with memory impairment found that direct stimulation of hippocampal CA1 neurons using a novel model of memory encoding produced significant improvements across subjects in short- and long-term retention of visual information (Hampson et al., 2018). However, closed-loop (i.e., read-write) prosthetics for the enhancement of memory (Deadwyler et al., 2017; Hampson et al., 2013) and brain-to-brain communication (Pais-Vieira et al., 2013) have yet to be tested in humans. The reality is that many of the challenges to the expansion of DBS to healthy subjects also apply to neurosurgical BCIs: the technology will need to become more accessible, sophisticated, and generalizable before commercial applications become a realistic prospect, would be largely restricted to a wealthy few, and would significantly impact the health care for the majority accessing treatment for established conditions.

18.4.3 Self-monitoring brain–computer interfaces

BCIs are also being explored in the realm of neurofeedback, allowing users to regulate their mental states by reacting to a live reading of their brain activity. There is some evidence to suggest that neurofeedback in a research setting may be used to induce positive emotional states (Zotev et al., 2014), improve memory function (Escolano et al., 2014), and visuospatial skills (Zoefel, Huster, & Hermann, 2011) by conscious self-regulation in response to real-time electroencephalogram (EEG) or fMRI data displayed on a screen. Direct-to-consumer (DTC) neurofeedback devices could be useful as wearable memory aids integrated into a user's lifestyle (Dresler et al., 2018). However, there is a paucity of evidence to support the benefits of DTC neurofeedback prostheses (Wexler & Thibault, 2019). Even in a research setting, scientists cannot reliably decode mental states, such as beliefs, thoughts, and interests, using EEGs. Extrapolating from a measured neural response requires detailed contextual information, such as the content and timing of stimuli presented to subjects (Wexler, 2019). High spatial resolution neuroimaging technologies such as fMRI are also unlikely to become available in a DTC capacity in the near future, and the consumer-grade EEGs are vastly inferior to those used in the clinic (Ratti et al., 2017).

18.4.4 Non-invasive brain stimulation

Transcranial magnetic stimulation (TMS) is a non-invasive neurostimulation technique that involves inducing a magnetic field in the brain tissue beneath the scalp to modulate cortical excitability. TMS is a relatively expensive procedure, requiring a large magnetic coil to be held over the appropriate region of the brain by a trained operator. The coil induces a magnetic field in the underlying brain tissue to modulate cortical excitability. TMS is a well-established clinical treatment for depression (Mutz et al., 2018) and migraine headaches (Lan et al., 2017), and has recently been FDA approved for the treatment of obsessive-compulsive disorder (Carmi et al., 2019) and smoking cessation (Chang et al., 2018). In combination with certain behavioral interventions and imaging techniques (e.g., fMRI, EEG), TMS has also been found to be effective in treating cognitive deficits in conditions such as schizophrenia and autism (Sathappan et al., 2019; Beynel et al., 2019). It has also been explored as a cognitive enhancer. A number of small studies have reported cognitive-enhancing effects ranging from memory consolidation, name and spatial recall, and verbal fluency, and improved performance in more complex cognitive tasks, such as mental rotation, analogic reasoning, and matchstick puzzles (see review by Luber & Lisanby, 2014). But these small-sample studies exhibit high variability in effect sizes, and there have been some seemingly contradictory results. It is likely that effect sizes will increase with improved temporal resolution or when complemented by high-acuity imaging techniques accounting for anatomical and physiological differences in human brains. Nevertheless, the high cost and requirements of technical expertise suggest that TMS is unlikely to provide a widely used and accessible form of cognitive enhancement in healthy adults.

Transcranial electrical stimulation (tES) is a more portable and affordable form of non-invasive brain stimulation, involving the attachment of low-current electrodes to the surface of the scalp that delivers either a direct (transcranial direct-current stimulation or tDCS) or alternating (transcranial alternating-current stimulation) current to a region of the cortex. tDCS has also been used clinically in the treatment of various psychiatric disorders such as depression and addiction (Luigjes et al., 2019), but it remains an understudied technique relative to TMS and needs larger trials delivering longer treatment courses. Despite this, there is much enthusiasm about the potential applications of tES for cognitive enhancement. Research on the modulation of cognition of healthy patients using tDCS is rapidly evolving, with some promising findings reported in small-sample studies (see review by Coffman et al., 2014).

Over the past ten years, tDCS has been pursued as a more practical avenue for cognitive enhancement in healthy adults. A number of neurotechnology companies have developed affordable direct-to-consumer tDCS devices marketed specifically for cognitive enhancement (Ienca et al., 2018). For example, the Go Flow tDCS sports cap is marketed for the improvement of control, coordination, and sporting skills by "enhancing the rate at which the brain adapts to the demands of any sporting pursuit" (Foc.us, 2016). The Focus V3 headband on the other hand offers multiple modes, such as "Ripple" for increasing working memory, "Gamer" for "focus and vigilance," and "eDream" designed to "let you try and induce lucid dreaming in your sleep" (Foc.us, 2019). None of the available direct-to-consumer tDCS devices – which sell for around $100 to $200 USD – has been FDA approved, as companies can sell their products without regulatory approval, provided they only make claims about the device's capacity to promote "wellness."

Owing to the nascency of tDCS technology, and the fragmentary nature of regulatory oversight of commercial neurotechnologies, there is very little empirical data on whether direct-to-consumer tDCS devices promote cognitive enhancement (Steenbergen et al., 2016). Current clinical tDCS devices suffer from a lack of spatial specificity to target specific functional networks, with identical electrode placements having a diffuse effect on basic cognitive functions (e.g., attention) required by most tasks. Focal stimulation methods are likely to improve, but the evidence to support the enhancement of specific functions such as "vigilance" in a direct-to-consumer context is weak (Coffman et al., 2014). While therapeutic TMS is still preferred over tDCS in a clinical context, one study of direct-to-consumer tDCS users found that those who used their device to treat depression were more likely than non-treaters (i.e., enhancers) to report tDCS as being effective (Wexler, 2018) – a finding that is consistent with clinical studies that found the benefits of tDCS to be larger in depression than for cognitive enhancement (Horvath et al., 2015).

The exact prevalence of tDCS used for cognitive enhancement is unclear (Schleim & Quednow, 2018). Jwa (2015) found that nearly three-quarters of tDCS were being used at home for cognitive enhancement, with a significant minority using tDCS as a method of self-treatment for neurological and psychiatric conditions. However, Wexler (2018) found that despite a significant spike in media attention in 2014 and 2015 the number of DTC tDCS devices sold up until 2016 "is a relatively low, five-digit figure," suggesting that concerns about the widespread use by ethicists may reflect another neuroenhancement bubble. Wexler's study, which involved collecting data from seven of the ten companies selling tDCS devices in the US showed that, far from being widespread, tDCS use for cognitive enhancement was restricted to a rather narrow "white, healthy, educated, liberal forty-something male living in the USA."

18.5 Recommendations for responsible anticipatory ethics

What are the lessons then for ethicists and commentators considering the potential impacts of emerging technologies? When ethicists worry about neuroenhancing technologies posing a threat to privacy and autonomy, it suggests to the public that these technologies can achieve these things. Worrying about futuristic outcomes that are unlikely to be realized is a form of ethical scaremongering that can needlessly impede innovation (Carter et al., 2009). Outram (2012) observes that an improper account of findings from lab-based research and the social sciences restricts the narrative framework and conceptualization of "cognitive enhancement," reifying it as an entity despite the lack of evidence.

18.5.1 Speculation in anticipatory ethics

Ethicists must express realistic concerns about the potential harms of emerging technologies. Critics of speculative ethics have argued that "rather than credulity, we should employ skepticism; rather than taking a paper's conclusions for granted, we should interrogate them; rather than detaching from the science, we should engage with it" (Wexler, 2019). Focusing on speculative ethical concerns, they argue, can distract from more proximal and pragmatic issues involving the responsible research and innovation of emerging neurotechnologies in clinical contexts. For example, there remains a dearth of ethical scholarship on whether researchers have a duty to provide post-trial access to neurosurgical implants at the end of clinical trials, despite calls for ethical guidance from clinical researchers (Lázaro-Muñoz et al., 2018; Sierra-Mercado et al., 2019). Even for ethical issues that have received ample attention, it is possible to exaggerate their consequences such that the developmental process is unnecessarily hindered. While current regulatory oversight of direct-to-consumer neurotechnologies is fragmentary and inconsistent (Wexler & Thibault, 2019), concrete policy changes that are based on speculation about future device capabilities (e.g., the ability to "read thoughts") might needlessly impede innovation in this area. Wexler & Specker Sullivan (2021) argue that ethics scholarship that engages in "speculative futurology" "not only ignores the actual shortcomings of existent technologies but may also alienate technologists and scientists who are optimistic about the future value of their work."

On the other hand, the scope of potential harms posed by neurotechnologies has left some ethicists dissatisfied with the sentiment that "the technology is not there yet." It is precisely the *absence* of proactive and anticipatory ethics, they argue, that explains the emergence of big data and facial recognition technologies that are too entrenched to be modifiable through ethically aligned design and governance (Ienca et al., 2018), as captured by the Collingridge dilemma. Speculating about temporally remote scenarios may usefully inform ethical reflection rather than weaken it (Roache, 2008). It has been argued that the raison d'etre of ethics is to anticipate "what an enhanced ability to peer into and modulate the brain may mean for individuals, communities, and societies" (Wexler & Specker Sullivan, 2021). That neurotechnology could fundamentally change how we think about the privacy of mental life, individual agency, and individuals as entities bound by their bodies is reason to embrace attitudes toward policy change that underscore a duty to prepare the ethical and regulatory terrain now. This stance has motivated efforts to recognize specific "neurorights," such as fundamental rights to privacy, autonomy, and freedom of thought. In response to these concerns, the Chilean government has recently introduced two laws in order to protect citizens' privacy and mental integrity (Ienca & Andorno, 2017).

How do we determine what is a reasonable or appropriate form of anticipatory ethics? Traditional approaches to the governance of innovative technologies have focused on impacts only once they are recognized as unacceptable or harmful to society or the environment (Stilgoe, 2013). Inherent to anticipatory ethics is the view that retrospective accounts of responsibility are limited, and that lessons learned from past innovations are not reliable guides to the future. Succumbing to moral luck by appealing to unpredictability and an inability to "reasonably foresee" the future will not do, either. What anticipatory ethics needs is a range of inputs, from scientists, research funders, innovators, and others, to ensure that the right concerns are being expressed about the right issues. Anticipatory ethics would not be "anticipatory" if it concerned itself exclusively with the present harms or with the "products" of science and innovation. But deliberating over every theoretically feasible demonstration or application of a technology, or exploring every hypothetical trajectory of product development, could leave unresolved real harms affecting real people. Dwelling too long on the anticipated benefits and harms of a neurotechnology might allow the status quo to persist, which in some cases would indicate a tacit acceptance of uses of neurotechnology that fall between regulatory cracks (Forlini et al., 2013). We next explore ways in which anticipatory ethics must adhere to empirical evidence, seek the perspectives of key stakeholders, and embrace multiple empirical methodologies.

18.5.2 Adherence to scientific data

Ethical scholarship has traditionally emphasized the importance of a commitment to the factual aspects of ethical cases (Beauchamp & Childress, 2019). Reporting on novel technologies with great scientific complexity necessitates an approach to anticipatory ethics that is "grounded." This requires the expertise of professionals working in the relevant discipline, as well as those experts well-positioned to be skeptical about the kinds of scientific claims being made. But complexity can also reside in the present or anticipated social impacts of technologies, such as uncertainty about the prevalence of use, how it might be used and by whom. An assumption that often goes unrecognized in ethics is that evidence of increasing or high prevalence necessarily calls for proactive ethics discussion. While this may be an assumption worth holding, a critical analysis of the science needs to be supplemented by an "explicit statement of underlying assumptions (e.g., about efficacy, prevalence) as well as the importance (or value) assigned to them" (Racine et al., 2014). Rather than allow assumptions about prevalence to solely direct the gaze of the ethical lens, an appreciation of the temporal dimensions of the future (e.g., present day, five years from now, fifty years from now) should be used to identify the issues that are worthy of attention. Issues appearing in the present-day window, such as misleading claims from companies about the safety and efficacy of their products, should be more deserving of attention than those potentially arising in the near future (e.g., neurotechnologies to improve productivity in the workplace) or distant future (e.g., telepathic neurotechnologies) (Wexler, 2019).

18.5.3 Diverse stakeholder perspectives

In considering the social impacts of innovative technologies, ethicists should be careful to solicit contributions from stakeholder groups with a diversity of perspectives and cultural backgrounds. This allows for the examination of key social or contextual issues that may be neglected by ethical debates that are largely undertaken within privileged academic silos in advanced economies (e.g., social determinants of health, vulnerable or underserved populations). Care needs to be taken in considering what is an appropriate ethics question and when, lest we continue to replicate patterns in scientific conduct and discourse that have failed to proportionately benefit, or have disadvantaged, historically marginalized, and oppressed communities (Brown et al., 2020). Wexler & Specker Sullivan (2021) have advanced a model of "translational neuroethics" – defined as a "grounded and diverse approach to identifying neuroethical research questions, as well as a greater focus on feasibility and impact" – that seeks to bring together practitioners well-placed to comment on the science (e.g., neuroscientists, neurologists, engineers) and people who may be disadvantaged by certain technological innovations. Many in society may not have access to the latest technological advances, raising important questions about how or whether these products can be distributed in a way that does not exacerbate existing social inequalities (Matshabane, 2021), particularly as most of the disability and morbidity associated with neurological, psychiatric, and substance-use disorders occurs in people who live in low- and middle-income countries (Vos et al., 2015).

18.5.4 Empirical methodologies

There is a tendency for media reports to collapse sometimes contradictory phenomena into a single framework of understanding (i.e., "cognitive enhancement") – a tendency that must be resisted by a critical and pragmatic anticipatory ethics (Outram, 2012). Distinguishing between disagreements about the science or technology of a novel device and disagreements about its prevalence or potential uses in the future is essential to anticipatory ethics. Social science methodologies, such as surveys and semi-structured interviews, can also help address empirical questions (e.g., prevalence, use, and harm) that are critical to understanding the impact of neurotechnological enhancement on society. Importantly, just as anticipatory ethics must be critical of empirical data about safety and efficacy, so too must we be critical of findings from the social sciences. For example, surveys investigating the prevalence of pharmaceuticals used for cognitive enhancement may conflate recreational use and dependence with use for the purpose of enhancement (Racine et al., 2014; Lucke et al., 2011). Finally, although the history of innovations in technology should not be solely relied upon to structure governance frameworks to effectively regulate present and future innovations, an examination of historical antecedents may help understand how this technology may be used and viewed within society and to anticipate future misuses of emerging technologies (Bell et al., 2012).

18.6 Conclusion

Anticipating the future impact of complex and emerging technologies, particularly those that interface with the brain, is fundamental to responsible innovation, developing technologies that meet all community needs, and minimizing harm. However, as we show, doing so requires a degree of responsibility on behalf of ethicists, commentators, and journalists. Unreflective anticipatory ethics can in itself cause harm to society. Responsible anticipatory ethics requires that we also anticipate the potential harms and misuses, and address this in our analysis, research, and communication.

References

Abbott, A. (2008). Brain electrodes can improve learning. *Nature News, January, 29*.

Agid, Y., Schüpbach, M., Gargiulo, M., Mallet, L., Houeto, J. L., Behar, C., Maltete, D., Mesnage, M. L. & Welter, M. L. (2006). Neurosurgery in Parkinson's disease: The doctor is happy, the patient less so?. *Parkinson's Disease and Related Disorders, 70*, 409–414. https://doi.org/10.1007/978-3-211-45295-0_61

Arria, A. M., Geisner, I. M., Cimini, M. D., Kilmer, J. R., Caldeira, K. M., Barrall, A. L., ... Larimer, M. E. (2018). Perceived academic benefit is associated with nonmedical prescription stimulant use among college students. *Addictive Behaviors, 76*, 27–33.

Battleday, R. M., & Brem, A. K. (2015). Modafinil for cognitive neuroenhancement in healthy non-sleep-deprived subjects: A systematic review. *European Neuropsychopharmacology, 25*(11), 1865–1881.

Beauchamp, T. L., & Childress, J. F. (1994). *Principles of biomedical ethics*. Edicoes Loyola.

Bell, E., Mathieu, G., & Racine, E. (2009). Preparing the ethical future of deep brain stimulation. *Surgical Neurology, 72*(6), 577–586.

Bell, E., Maxwell, B., McAndrews, M. P., Sadikot, A., & Racine, E. (2010). Hope and patients' expectations in deep brain stimulation: Healthcare providers' perspectives and approaches. *The Journal of Clinical Ethics, 21*(2), 112–124.

Bell, S. K., Lucke, J. C., & Hall, W. D. (2012). Lessons for enhancement from the history of cocaine and amphetamine use. *AJOB Neuroscience, 3*(2), 24–29.

Beynel, L., Appelbaum, L. G., Luber, B., Crowell, C. A., Hilbig, S. A., Lim, W., Nguyen, D., Chrapliwy, N., Davis, S. W., Cabeza, R., Lisanby, S. H., & Deng, Z.-D. (2019). Effects of Online Repetitive Transcranial Magnetic Stimulation (rTMS) on Cognitive Processing: A Meta-Analysis and Recommendations for Future Studies. *Neuroscience and Biobehavioral Reviews, 107*, 47–58.

Brown, T., Rommelfanger, K., & Sullivan, L. S. (2020). The social impact of brain machine interfaces: Bias and (big) neural data. *The Neuroethics Blog*. http://www.theneuroethicsblog.com/2020/08/the-social-impact-of-brainmachine.

Brühl, A. B., d'Angelo, C., & Sahakian, B. J. (2019). Neuroethical issues in cognitive enhancement: Modafinil as the example of a workplace drug?. *Brain and Neuroscience Advances, 3*, 2398212818816018.

Burr, C., Morley, J., Taddeo, M., & Floridi, L. (2020). Digital psychiatry: Risks and opportunities for public health and wellbeing. *IEEE Transactions on Technology and Society, 1*(1), 21–33.

Butorac, I., & Carter, A. (2021). The coercive potential of digital mental health. *The American Journal of Bioethics, 21*(7), 28–30.

Carmi, L., Tendler, A., Bystritsky, A., Hollander, E., Blumberger, D. M., Daskalakis, J., ... Zohar, J. (2019). Efficacy and safety of deep transcranial magnetic stimulation for obsessive-compulsive disorder: A prospective multicenter randomized double-blind placebo-controlled trial. *American Journal of Psychiatry, 176*(11), 931–938.

Carter, A., Bartlett, P., & Hall, W. (2009). Scare-mongering and the anticipatory ethics of experimental technologies. *American Journal of Bioethics, 9*(5), 47–48.

Caspi, A., Dorn, J. D., McClure, K. H., Humayun, M. S., Greenberg, R. J., and McMahon, M. J. 2009. Feasibility study of a retinal prosthesis spatial vision with a 16-electrode implant. *Archives of Ophthalmology* 127(4): 398–401.

Chang, D., Zhang, J., Peng, W., Shen, Z., Gao, X., Du, Y., ... Wang, Z. (2018). Smoking cessation with 20 Hz repetitive transcranial magnetic stimulation (rTMS) applied to two brain regions: A pilot study. *Frontiers in Human Neuroscience, 12*, 344.

Chaudhary, U., Birbaumer, N., & Ramos-Murguialday, A. (2016). Brain–computer interfaces for communication and rehabilitation. *Nature Reviews Neurology, 12*(9), 513–525.

Cinel, C., Valeriani, D., & Poli, R. (2019). Neurotechnologies for Human Cognitive Augmentation: Current State of the Art and Future Prospects. *Frontiers in Human Neuroscience, 13*, 13.

Clark, G.M. 2008. Personal reflections on the multichannel cochlear implant and a view of the future. *Journal of Rehabilitation Research & Development* 45(5): 651–694.

Coffman, B. A., Clark, V. P., & Parasuraman, R. (2014). Battery powered thought: Enhancement of attention, learning, and memory in healthy adults using transcranial direct current stimulation. *Neuroimage, 85*, 895–908.

Dandekar, M. P., Fenoy, A. J., Carvalho, A. F., Soares, J. C., & Quevedo, J. (2018). Deep brain stimulation for treatment-resistant depression: An integrative review of preclinical and clinical findings and translational implications. *Molecular Psychiatry, 23*(5), 1094–1112.

Deadwyler, S. A., Hampson, R. E., Song, D., Opris, I., Gerhardt, G. A., Marmarelis, V. Z., & Berger, T. W. (2017). A cognitive prosthesis for memory facilitation by closed-loop functional ensemble stimulation of hippocampal neurons in primate brain. *Experimental Neurology, 287*, 452–460.

Dinh, C. T., Humphries, S., & Chatterjee, A. (2020). Public opinion on cognitive enhancement varies across different situations. *AJOB Neuroscience, 11*(4), 224–237.

Dresler, M., Sandberg, A., Bublitz, C., Ohla, K., Trenado, C., Mroczko-Wasowicz, A., ... Repantis, D. (2018). Hacking the brain: Dimensions of cognitive enhancement. *ACS Chemical Neuroscience, 10*(3), 1137–1148.

Erler, A., Forlini, C. (2020). Neuroenhancement. In *The Routledge Encyclopedia of Philosophy*. Taylor and Francis. Retrieved 28 Mar, from https://www.rep.routledge.com/articles/thematic/neuroenhancement/v-1.

Escolano, C., Navarro-Gil, M., Garcia-Campayo, J., Congedo, M., De Ridder, D., & Minguez, J. (2014). A controlled study on the cognitive effect of alpha neurofeedback training in patients with major depressive disorder. *Frontiers in Behavioral Neuroscience, 8*, 296.

Figee, M., & Mayberg, H. (2021). The future of personalized brain stimulation. *Nature Medicine, 27*(2), 196–197.

Fleming, J. E., Dunn, E., & Lowery, M. M. (2020). Simulation of closed-loop deep brain stimulation control schemes for suppression of pathological beta oscillations in Parkinson's disease. *Frontiers in Neuroscience, 14*, 166.

Foc.us. (2016). Go flow sports: User manual & warranty. Retrieved: https://foc.us/manuals/GoFlowSports_A4_20160928.3.pdf

Foc.us. (2019). Foc.us V3 headband: User manual & warranty. Retrieved: https://foc.us/manuals/v3-instructions-0.pdf

Forlini, C. (2020). Empirical data is failing to break the ethics stalemate in the cognitive enhancement debate. *AJOB Neuroscience, 11*(4), 240–242.

Forlini, C., & Hall, W. (2016). The is and ought of the ethics of neuroenhancement: Mind the gap. *Frontiers in Psychology, 6*, 1998.

Forlini, C., Hall, W., Maxwell, B., Outram, S. M., Reiner, P. B., Repantis, D., ... Racine, E. (2013), 'Navigating the enhancement landscape. Ethical issues in research on cognitive enhancers for healthy individuals', *EMBO Reports, 14*(2), 123–128.

Functional Neuromodulation. (2021). Functional neuromodulation announces breakthrough device designation from the U.S. FDA for deep brain stimulation for Alzheimer's disease. Retrieved: https://www.prnewswire.com/news-releases/functional-neuromodulation-announces-breakthrough-device-designation-from-the-us-fda-for-deep-brain-stimulation-for-alzheimers-disease-301201439.html

Garden, H., Winickoff, D., Frahm, N. M., & Pfotenhauer, S. (2019). *Responsible Innovation in Neurotechnology Enterprises* (OECD Science, Technology and Industry Working Papers No. 2019/05; OECD Science, Technology and Industry Working Papers, Vol. 2019/05). https://doi.org/10.1787/9685e4fd-en

Gilbert, F., & Goddard, E. (2014). Thinking ahead too much: Speculative ethics and implantable brain devices. *AJOB Neuroscience, 5*(1), 49–51.

Gilbert, F., & Ovadia, D. (2011). Deep brain stimulation in the media: Over-optimistic portrayals call for a new strategy involving journalists and scientists in ethical debates. *Frontiers in Integrative Neuroscience, 5*, 16.

Gilbert, F., Pham, C., Viaña, J., & Gillam, W. (2019). Increasing brain-computer interface media depictions: Pressing ethical concerns. *Brain-Computer Interfaces, 6*(3), 49–70.

Giordano, J. (2012). Neurotechnology as demiurgical force: Avoiding Icarus' Folly. In J. Giordano, *Advances in Neurotechnology: Ethical, Legal, and Social Issues* (Vol. 20121457, pp. 1–14). CRC Press. https://doi.org/10.1201/b11861-2

Hamani, C., McAndrews, M. P., Cohn, M., Oh, M., Zumsteg, D., Shapiro, C. M., Wennberg, R. A., & Lozano, A. M. (2008). Memory enhancement induced by hypothalamic/fornix deep brain stimulation. *Annals of Neurology, 63*(1), 119–123. https://doi.org/10.1002/ana.21295

Hampson, R. E., Song, D., Opris, I., Santos, L. M., Shin, D. C., Gerhardt, G. A., ... Deadwyler, S. A. (2013). Facilitation of memory encoding in primate hippocampus by a neuroprosthesis that promotes task-specific neural firing. *Journal of Neural Engineering, 10*(6), 066013.

Hampson, R. E., Song, D., Robinson, B. S., Fetterhoff, D., Dakos, A. S., Roeder, B. M., ... Deadwyler, S. A. (2018). Developing a hippocampal neural prosthetic to facilitate human memory encoding and recall. *Journal of Neural Engineering, 15*(3), 036014.

Horvath, J. C., Forte, J. D., & Carter, O. (2015). Quantitative review finds no evidence of cognitive effects in healthy populations from single-session Transcranial Direct Current Stimulation (tDCS). *Brain Stimulation, 8*(3), 535–550. https://doi.org/10.1016/j.brs.2015.01.400

Ienca, M., & Andorno, R. (2017). Towards new human rights in the age of neuroscience and neurotechnology. *Life Sciences, Society and Policy, 13*(1), 5. https://doi.org/10.1186/s40504-017-0050-1

Ienca, M., Haselager, P., & Emanuel, E. J. (2018). Brain leaks and consumer neurotechnology. *Nature Biotechnology, 36*(9), 805–810.

Jebari, K. (2013). Brain Machine Interface and Human Enhancement – An Ethical Review. *Neuroethics, 6*(3), 617–625. https://doi.org/10.1007/s12152-012-9176-2

Jwa, A. (2015). Early adopters of the magical thinking cap: A study on do-it-yourself (DIY) transcranial direct current stimulation (tDCS) user community. *Journal of Law and the Biosciences, 2*(2), 292–335.

Kleiner-Fisman, G., Herzog, J., Fisman, D. N., Tamma, F., Lyons, K. E., Pahwa, R., Lang, A. E., & Deuschl, G. (2006). Subthalamic nucleus deep brain stimulation: Summary and meta-analysis of outcomes. *Movement Disorders: Official Journal of the Movement Disorder Society, 21*(Suppl 14), S290–S304. https://doi.org/10.1002/mds.20962

Lan, L., Zhang, X., Li, X., Rong, X., & Peng, Y. (2017). The efficacy of transcranial magnetic stimulation on migraine: A meta-analysis of randomized controlled trails. *The Journal of Headache and Pain, 18*(1), 1–7.

Larson, P. S. (2014). Deep brain stimulation for movement disorders. *Neurotherapeutics*, 11, 465–474.

Lázaro-Muñoz, G., Yoshor, D., Beauchamp, M. S., Goodman, W. K., & McGuire, A. L. (2018). Continued access to investigational brain implants. *Nature Reviews Neuroscience, 19*(6), 317–318. https://doi.org/10.1038/s41583-018-0004-5

Lebedev, M. A., & Nicolelis, M. A. (2017). Brain-machine interfaces: From basic science to neuroprostheses and neurorehabilitation. *Physiological Reviews, 97*(2), 767–837.

Luber, B., & Lisanby, S. H. (2014). Enhancement of human cognitive performance using transcranial magnetic stimulation (TMS). *Neuroimage, 85*, 961–970.

Lucke, J. C., Bell, S., Partridge, B., & Hall, W. D. (2011). Deflating the neuroenhancement bubble. *AJOB Neuroscience, 2*(4), 38–43.

Luigjes, J., Segrave, R., de Joode, N., Figee, M., & Denys, D. (2019). Efficacy of Invasive and Non-Invasive Brain Modulation Interventions for Addiction. *Neuropsychology Review, 29*(1), 116–138. https://doi.org/10.1007/s11065-018-9393-5

Maier, L. J., Ferris, J. A., & Winstock, A. R. (2018). Pharmacological cognitive enhancement among non-ADHD individuals—A cross-sectional study in 15 countries. *International Journal of Drug Policy, 58*, 104–112.

Mankin, E. A., & Fried, I. (2020). Modulation of human memory by deep brain stimulation of the entorhinal-hippocampal circuitry. *Neuron, 106*(2), 218–235.

Matshabane, O. P. (2021). Promoting diversity and inclusion in neuroscience and neuroethics. *EBioMedicine, 67*, 103359. https://doi.org/10.1016/j.ebiom.2021.103359.

Mehlman, M. J. (2015). Captain America and Iron Man: Biological, genetic, and psychological enhancement and the warrior ethos. In Lucas, G. (Ed.), *Routledge Handbook of Military Ethics* (pp. 432–446). Abingdon: Routledge.

Moreno, J. D. (2011) *Mind Wars: Brain Science and the Military in the 21st Century*. New York City: Bellevue Literary Press.

Mutz, J., Edgcumbe, D. R., Brunoni, A. R., & Fu, C. H. (2018). Efficacy and acceptability of non-invasive brain stimulation for the treatment of adult unipolar and bipolar depression: A systematic review and meta-analysis of randomised sham-controlled trials. *Neuroscience & Biobehavioral Reviews, 92*, 291–303.

Naesström, M., Blomstedt, P., & Bodlund, O. (2016). A systematic review of psychiatric indications for deep brain stimulation, with focus on major depressive and obsessive-compulsive disorder. *Nordic Journal of Psychiatry, 70*(7), 483–491.

Outram, S. M. (2012). Ethical Considerations in the Framing of the Cognitive Enhancement Debate. *Neuroethics, 5*(2), 173–184. https://doi.org/10.1007/s12152-011-9131-7

Pais-Vieira, M., Lebedev, M., Kunicki, C., Wang, J., & Nicolelis, M. A. (2013). A brain-to-brain interface for real-time sharing of sensorimotor information. *Scientific Reports, 3*(1), 1–10.

Partridge, B. J., Bell, S. K., Lucke, J. C., Yeates, S., & Hall, W. D. (2011). Smart drugs "as common as coffee": Media hype about neuroenhancement. *PloS One, 6*(11), e28416.

Persson, I., & Savulescu, J. (2008). The perils of cognitive enhancement and the urgent imperative to enhance the moral character of humanity. *Journal of Applied Philosophy, 25*(3), 162–177.

Pham, U., Solbakk, A. K., Skogseid, I. M., Toft, M., Pripp, A. H., Konglund, A. E., Andersson, S., Haraldsen, I. R., Aarsland, D., Dietrichs, E., & Malt, U. F. (2015). Personality changes after deep brain stimulation in Parkinson's disease. *Parkinson's Disease, 2015*, 490507. https://doi.org/10.1155/2015/490507.

Racine, E., & Forlini, C. (2010). Cognitive enhancement, lifestyle choice or misuse of prescription drugs?. *Neuroethics, 3*(1), 1–4.

Racine, E., Rubio, T. M., Chandler, J., Forlini, C., & Lucke, J. (2014). The value and pitfalls of speculation about science and technology in bioethics: The case of cognitive enhancement. *Medicine, Health Care and Philosophy, 17*(3), 325–337.

Ratti, E., Waninger, S., Berka, C., Ruffini, G., & Verma, A. (2017). Comparison of medical and consumer wireless EEG systems for use in clinical trials. *Frontiers in Human Neuroscience, 11*, 398.

Regalado, A. (2020). Elon Musk's Neuralink is neuroscience theater. *MIT Technology Review*. Retrieved from: https://www.technologyreview.com/2020/08/30/1007786/elon-musks-neuralink-demo-update-neuroscience-theater/

Repantis, D., Schlattmann, P., Laisney, O., & Heuser, I. (2010). Modafinil and methylphenidate for neuroenhancement in healthy individuals: A systematic review. *Pharmacological Research, 62*(3), 187–206.

Roache, R. (2008). Ethics, Speculation, and Values. *NanoEthics*, 2(3), 317–327. https://doi.org/10.1007/s11569-008-0050-y

Sathappan, A. V., Luber, B. M., & Lisanby, S. H. (2019). The dynamic duo: Combining noninvasive brain stimulation with cognitive interventions. *Progress in Neuro-Psychopharmacology and Biological Psychiatry*, 89, 347–360.

Schaefer, G. O., Kahane, G., & Savulescu, J. (2014). Autonomy and enhancement. *Neuroethics*, 7(2), 123–136.

Schelle, K. J., Faulmuller, N., Caviola, L., & Hewstone, M. (2014). Attitudes toward pharmacological cognitive enhancement-a review. *Frontiers in Systems Neuroscience*, 8, 53.

Schlaepfer, T. E., & Fins, J. J. (2010). Deep brain stimulation and the neuroethics of responsible publishing: When one is not enough. *JAMA*, 303(8), 775–776.

Schleim, S., & Quednow, B. B. (2018). How Realistic Are the Scientific Assumptions of the Neuroenhancement Debate? Assessing the Pharmacological Optimism and Neuroenhancement Prevalence Hypotheses. *Frontiers in Pharmacology*, 9, 3. https://doi.org/10.3389/fphar.2018.00003

Sharif, S., Guirguis, A., Fergus, S., & Schifano, F. (2021). The use and impact of cognitive enhancers among university students: A systematic review. *Brain Sciences*, 11(3), 355.

Sierra-Mercado, D., Zuk, P., Beauchamp, M. S., Sheth, S. A., Yoshor, D., Goodman, W. K., McGuire, A. L., & Lázaro-Muñoz, G. (2019). Device Removal Following Brain Implant Research. *Neuron*, 103(5), 759–761. https://doi.org/10.1016/j.neuron.2019.08.024.

Steenbergen, L., Sellaro, R., Hommel, B., Lindenberger, U., Kühn, S., & Colzato, L. S. (2016). "Unfocus" on foc. us: Commercial tDCS headset impairs working memory. *Experimental Brain Research*, 234(3), 637–643.

Stilgoe, J., Owen, R., & Macnaghten, P. (2013). Developing a framework for responsible innovation. *Research Policy*, 42(9), 1568–1580. https://doi.org/10.1016/j.respol.2013.05.008.

Suthana, N., & Fried, I. (2014). Deep brain stimulation for enhancement of learning and memory. *Neuroimage*, 85, 996–1002.

Thomson, C. J., Segrave, R. A., Fitzgerald, P. B., Richardson, K. E., Racine, E., & Carter, A. (2021). "Nothing to Lose, Absolutely Everything to Gain": Patient and Caregiver Expectations and Subjective Outcomes of Deep Brain Stimulation for Treatment-Resistant Depression. *Frontiers in Human Neuroscience*, 15, 565. https://doi.org/10.3389/fnhum.2021.755276

Thomson, C. J., Segrave, R. A., & Carter, A. (2021). Changes in Personality Associated with Deep Brain Stimulation: A Qualitative Evaluation of Clinician Perspectives. *Neuroethics*, 14(S1), 109–124. https://doi.org/10.1007/s12152-019-09419-2.

Trimper, J. B., Root Wolpe, P., & Rommelfanger, K. S. (2014). When "I" becomes "We": Ethical implications of emerging brain-to-brain interfacing technologies. *Frontiers in Neuroengineering*, 7, 4.

Vance, A. (2019). Elon Musk's neuralink says it's ready for brain surgery. *Bloomberg Businessweek*.

Vos, T., Barber, R. M., Bell, B., Bertozzi-Villa, A., Biryukov, S., Bolliger, I., ... Brugha, T. S. (2015). Global, regional, and national incidence, prevalence, and years lived with disability for 301 acute and chronic diseases and injuries in 188 countries, 1990–2013: A systematic analysis for the Global Burden of Disease Study 2013. *The Lancet*, 386(9995), 743–800.

Wexler, A. (2019). Separating neuroethics from neurohype. *Nature Biotechnology*, 37(9), 988–990.

Wexler, A., & Specker Sullivan, L. (2021). Translational neuroethics: A vision for a more integrated, inclusive, and impactful field. *AJOB Neuroscience*, 1–12. https://doi.org/10.1080/21507740.2021.2001078

Wexler, A., & Thibault, R. (2019). Mind-reading or misleading? Assessing direct-to-consumer electroencephalography (EEG) devices marketed for wellness and their ethical and regulatory implications. *Journal of Cognitive Enhancement*, 3(1), 131–137.

Whiting, A. C., Oh, M. Y., & Whiting, D. M. (2018). Deep brain stimulation for appetite disorders: A review. *Neurosurgical Focus*, 45(2), E9.

Williams, Z. M., & Eskandar, E. N. (2006). Selective enhancement of associative learning by microstimulation of the anterior caudate. *Nature Neuroscience*, 9(4), 562–568.

Wolpaw, J. R., & Winter Wolpaw, E. (2012). Brain–Computer Interfaces: Something New under the Sun. In J. Wolpaw & E. W. Wolpaw (Eds.), *Brain–Computer Interfaces: Principles and Practice* (p. 0). Oxford University Press. https://doi.org/10.1093/acprof:oso/9780195388855.003.0001

Yuste, R., Goering, S., Arcas, B. A. Y., Bi, G., Carmena, J. M., Carter, A., ... Wolpaw, J. (2017). Four ethical priorities for neurotechnologies and AI. *Nature*, 551(7679), 159–163. https://doi.org/10.1038/551159a

Zoefel, B., Huster, R. J., & Herrmann, C. S. (2011). Neurofeedback training of the upper alpha frequency band in EEG improves cognitive performance. *Neuroimage*, 54(2), 1427–1431.

Zohny, H. (2015). The myth of cognitive enhancement. *Neuroethics*, 8(3), 257–269.

Zotev, V., Phillips, R., Yuan, H., Misaki, M., & Bodurka, J. (2014). Self-regulation of human brain activity using simultaneous real-time fMRI and EEG neurofeedback. *NeuroImage*, 85, 985–995.

PART V

Mood enhancement and moral bioenhancement

19
MORAL ENHANCEMENT THROUGH NEUROSURGERY? – FEASIBILITY AND ETHICAL JUSTIFIABILITY

Sabine Müller

19.1 Introduction

International bioethics has been discussing technological "moral enhancement" for several years now. First, some bioethicists promoted several pharmaceuticals (e.g., SSRIs and Oxytocin) as "moral enhancers." After being questioned again, some bioethicists introduced the idea of performing moral enhancement by neurosurgery into the debate. In this article, I will first address the question of whether or not moral enhancement is possible by neurosurgical methods that are currently available or at least seem conceptually feasible and, if so, to what extent. This does not rule out the prospect of moral enhancement through neurosurgery using conceptual analysis or a theoretical derivation from a fundamental physical principle (such as the derivation of the impossibility of a perpetual motion machine from the law of conservation of energy).

The foundation for my examination of the prospect of neurosurgical moral enhancement is current empirical research. In other words, based on this research, I will anticipate and evaluate developments that can realistically be expected, but I will not speculate about just conceptually possible scenarios.

The moral improvement of humanity is one of the great goals of the Enlightenment and humanism. Their strategies are education, science, and self-awareness. The term "moral enhancement," on the other hand, does not refer to moral betterment in the sense of humanism but to the endeavor to improve (moral) behavior through direct brain intervention. In the utilitarian tradition, the behavior – rather than the moral attitude or moral competence – is what counts.

Some influential bioethicists advocate using genetic techniques for moral enhancement. Halley S. Faust (2008) suggests preimplantation diagnosis for selecting embryos with a haplotype that would predispose individuals to have a higher level of morality than the average. Ingmar Persson and Julian Savulescu (2010) promote the genetic enhancement of humanity with the goal of creating a new species that is more altruistic and justice-oriented than the human species with reference to the great evils of modernity, such as the threat of nuclear weapons, biological weapons, terrorism, climate change, and other environmental problems.

Bioethicists have proposed biomedical interventions for individual enhancement in addition to programs for the moral enhancement of the human population. Thomas Douglas (2008) advocates the use of biomedical means to improve one's morality. He argues that moral enhancement is a counter-example to the notion that biomedical enhancement is always morally impermissible. David DeGrazia (2014) calls for publicly funded research to develop moral enhancement methods to lessen moral defects like antisocial personality disorder, sadism, moral cynicism, defective empathy, significant prejudice, weakness of will, the impulsive propensity to violence, and even the inability to grasp subtle, complicated details that are of undeniable moral relevance. Walter Glannon (2014) advocates pharmacological moral enhancement for psychopathic offenders and nascent psychopaths. David DeGrazia (2014) and Ingmar Persson and Julian Savulescu (2010) advocate serotonin reuptake inhibitors (SSRIs); the latter also enthusiastically recommend the hormone oxytocin. James Hughes (2015) suggests a whole range of substances and measures to optimize virtues: oxytocin, testosterone, modafinil, methylphenidate, ecstasy, gene therapy, and electrical stimulation of the brain. Elvio Baccarini and Luca Malatesti (2017) argue for the compulsory treatment of psychopaths with unspecified but presupposed safe and reliable biotechnologies.

All these proposals are based on the (over-)interpretation of particular empirical studies and not on a comprehensive, critical evaluation of the relevant empirical material. Such an evaluation cannot support enthusiasm. For example, SSRIs are inappropriate for moral enhancement because they may increase the risk of violent acts if serotonin levels are too high, a fact that has already been acknowledged in court cases ("Prozac defense") (Wiseman, 2014). Stimulants (amphetamines, Ritalin) are not recommendable because of their great potential for abuse and addiction, and their risk of severe adverse effects (Morton & Stockton, 2000; Steiner & Van Waes, 2013; Heinz & Müller, 2017; Liu, Feng & Zhang, 2019; Shellenberg et al., 2020; Koren & Korn, 2021). Even oxytocin is unsuitable because its effects are weak, inconsistent, and context- and person-specific (Bartz et al., 2011).

Meanwhile, some bioethicists have raised the idea of performing neurosurgical interventions on psychopaths in order to improve their moral behavior (Merkel et al., 2007; DeGrazia, 2014; Jotterand, 2014; Hughes, 2015; critical comments: Hübner & White, 2016; Dubljević & Racine, 2017). Also, some neurosurgeons, neurologists and sexologists discuss deep brain stimulation (DBS) and cortical stimulation for treating psychopaths or sex offenders (De Ridder et al., 2009; Hoeprich, 2011; Fumagalli & Priori, 2012; Canavero, 2014; Fuß et al., 2015). These suggestions are substantiated by successful neurosurgical treatments of hyper-aggressiveness in severely intellectually and developmentally disabled persons as well as by the psychosurgery of the 1970s.

The initially transhumanist debate about moral enhancement has thus shifted from grandiose, humanity-saving goals to crime control. The recent debate is no longer focused on improving the whole of humanity or saving mankind from nuclear war and environmental catastrophes but on the prevention of criminal acts and the control of criminal individuals.

19.2 Is moral enhancement possible through neurosurgery?

19.2.1 Model of moral intelligence

Developing a universally accepted definition of moral enhancement is probably a futile endeavor since there are irreconcilable differences between the understandings of moral action held by utilitarians, deontologists, and virtue ethicists. In fact, the protagonists of moral enhancement refer to different moral theories (Dubljević & Racine, 2017).

For developing effective methods of moral enhancement, a realistic model of the moral agent is needed. Only then it can be more precisely determined which functions of the person should be acted upon to improve her moral character or behavior. For example, David DeGrazia (2014) propagates SSRIs as moral enhancers because they may reduce the tendency to attack others. However, the study he is referring to (Crocket et al., 2010) showed that under SSRI use, the willingness to reject unfair offers decreases (Wiseman, 2014). Thus, a particular intervention may strengthen one component of moral behavior (e.g., harm avoidance) at the cost of weakening another (e.g., justice pursuit). The same is valid for oxytocin. While it enhances prosocial behavior within one's own group, it increases aggression toward strangers. Thus, it is more of a "nepotism enhancer" than a morality enhancer (Bartz et al., 2011; Dubljević & Racine, 2017). Therefore, the euphoric claims of certain pharmaceuticals as moral enhancers turn out to be too undifferentiated to be true upon a more thorough examination.

I apply Carmen Tanner and Markus Christen's (2013) model of moral intelligence to properly analyze whether specific interventions are appropriate for moral enhancement, and if so, for what kind of enhancement and at what cost. The first reason for using this model is that it provides a suitable theoretical framework based on empirical moral psychology to differentiate different components of individuals' moral abilities. The second reason is that despite the universalistic approach, the model takes into account that moral concepts vary between individuals and change historically. Therefore, it adopts a broad definition of "morality" as a set of norms, principles, values, and virtues that are governed by an orientation toward the good, reflect a respect and concern for oneself and for other entities, and are embedded in a justification structure.

This model is a skill-based conception of moral behavior, analogous to the concept of emotional intelligence that describes the ability to deal with emotions. The framework describes the sequential logic of moral behavior along with the associated underlying psychological processes, and the way in which implicit and explicit knowledge of morality and its justifications are included (Christen & Müller, 2015).

Tanner and Christen's model of moral intelligence integrates the findings of (moral) psychological research into a unified model. As such, it enters an area with a rather long tradition. What distinguishes this model from other approaches is the central role of moral commitment, i.e., the capacity to uphold the demands of morality throughout this entire process and to align one's cognitions, decisions, and actions with one's moral ends. Moral commitment can be understood as the bridge between the moral compass and the other competencies of moral intelligence and expresses the will to apply the contents of the moral compass (Christen & Müller, 2015).

According to Tanner and Christen's model, moral intelligence is the capability to process moral information and to manage self-regulation in any way that desirable moral ends can be attained. Moral intelligence is thus based on the integration of five basic components:

1. The *moral compass* refers to some pre-established or newly formulated moral standards and norms, which direct the agent's reactions. The moral compass helps to define which goals and ends may be desirable.
2. The *moral commitment* is the ability to selectively focus on moral goals and strive for desirable ends. Moral commitment requires self-monitoring, self-reflective, and self-influencing capabilities. It carries with it the urge to comply with the moral goals.
3. *Moral sensitivity* refers to the key issue that individuals must first recognize that they may be facing a moral problem.
4. *Moral problem-solving:* Once a moral problem and the involved key parties have been identified, the next challenge consists of finding viable ways of coping with it. Moral decision-making is about finding out what ought to be done while dealing with competing pressures, and generating and evaluating different options with moral and other consequences.
5. *Moral assertiveness* (or *moral resoluteness*) is the competence that enables people to overcome external obstacles, face dangers and threats to themselves, and have stamina when pursuing moral actions. Moral assertiveness refers to the ability to act consistently and persistently upon moral standards, despite pressures.

Each component can be restricted or disturbed, which can lead to different forms of moral misconduct.[1]

The model of moral intelligence allows for determining which components can be influenced by a given intervention and in what way.

19.2.2 Moral dysfunctions caused by brain disfunctions

It is necessary to understand how to go from moral psychological constructs to the localization of underlying functions in the brain before one can intervene in the brain to enhance certain components of moral intelligence.

The necessary intermediate step is to identify neural networks underlying certain basic functions (e.g., empathy) that must be accessed for specific moral operations (e.g., considering the interests of those affected by an intended action). However, the components of moral intelligence cannot be assigned to clearly defined and distinguishable neural modules. Presumably, different moral psychological constructs are each associated with the activation of multiple neural networks (some the same, some different). Lesion studies and neuroimaging studies can provide information about which brain areas and neuronal networks must be functional for moral thinking and acting (Christen & Müller, 2015). Furthermore, neuro-plasticity has to be considered, particularly in regard to behavioral changes following brain lesions.

Manuela Fumagalli and Alberto Priori (2012) postulate a brain network for moral behavior, a "moral brain," involving primarily the frontal and temporal cortices, as well as some subcortical structures. From a retrospective analysis of brain lesions resulting in patients committing crimes for the first time, R. Ryan Darby and his coauthors identified a network whose damage appears to have contributed significantly to criminal behavior (Darby et al., 2018). This network contains brain regions that have been associated with morality, value-based decision-making, and Theory of Mind but not empathy or cognitive control. Darby's study shows, on the one hand, that there is no brain region that was damaged in all cases studied, and on the other hand, that all lesions were functionally linked to the identified network. However, the authors also emphasize that most people with brain lesions do not become criminals and that many other factors take part in the occurrence of criminal behavior, including pre-injury personality and social environment (Darby et al., 2018).

For most "moral dysfunctions," it is largely unknown whether they have an organic cause. Undoubtedly, social circumstances and life history also have an enormous influence on moral misconduct and criminal behavior.

How unclear and dependent on interpretation the association between neurological dysfunctions and moral dysfunction is becomes particularly clear in the example of psychopathy. On the one hand, psychopathy can be a consequence of brain diseases or lesions such as frontotemporal dementia or frontal brain syndrome ("acquired psychopathy"). On the other hand, psychopathy may arise in adaptation to an unpredictable, violent environment in childhood and adolescence ("developmental psychopathy"). Whereas a causal link between neurological and moral dysfunction is plausible for acquired psychopathy, this is questionable for developmental psychopathy. It is true that some neuroimaging studies show that the amygdalae of psychopaths are underactivated in response to stimuli that normally elicit fear. This is interpreted under the disease paradigm of psychopathy as a dysfunction of the amygdalae (Blair & James, 2013). However, Marga Reimer (2008) convincingly argued in terms of evolutionary theory that the norm deviations typical of psychopaths (fearlessness, lack of compassion, and resistance to attempts at "moral" social reinforcing) are not dysfunctions at all, but competitive advantages. Psychopathy is a disadvantage only in the few societies in which amoral behavior is severely punished in most cases. In most societies, it is to the contrary, where psychopathic behavior often pays off in material as well as in reproductive success (Harris, Skilling & Rice, 2001; Troisi, 2005; Reimer, 2008). Even in constitutional states, by no means are all psychopaths in prison but many are successful and mighty. The proportion of psychopaths among managers, the "snakes in suits" (Babiak & Hare, 2006), is above average (Babiak, Neumann & Hare, 2010).

According to the view of developmental psychopathy under the prevailing disease paradigm, pharmacological and neurosurgical interventions to correct psychopathy would be considered "therapy." According to the evolutionary model, on the other hand, it is also conceivable to influence developmental psychopathy with drugs or neurosurgery. But under this model, which does not view psychopathy as a disorder, its treatment would not be classified as therapy but as moral enhancement. Nevertheless, whether such a treatment would benefit the psychopath himself and not only society, as it is assumed under the disease paradigm of psychopathy, is questionable.

Although biomedical moral enhancement is propagated for humanity in general, most proponents suggest it specifically for psychopaths and sex offenders. Therefore, I will now discuss what specific neurosurgical treatment approaches for psychopaths and sex offenders are being proposed. These proposals are primarily concerned with three goals: (1) reduction of aggressiveness, (2) reduction of sex drive, (3) reduction of psychopathy or sociopathy.

19.2.3 Neurosurgical interventions for reducing aggressiveness

Moral enhancement could be achieved by reducing aggression. Surgical removal of the amygdalae reduces anxiety, anger, and aggression in monkeys (Faria, 2013). In some cases, hyper-aggressive behavior decreased after the resection of brain tumors (Nakaji et al., 2003), and often hyper-aggressiveness improves after the resection of epileptogenic brain tissue (Foong & Flugel, 2007; Faria, 2013). Based on these findings, over a thousand patients with and without epilepsy have been treated for aggressive behavior with stereotactic amygdalotomy (Langevin, 2012; Mpakopoulou et al., 2008).

After psychosurgery was largely abandoned in the late 1970s due to its frequent misuse and many complications, a renaissance of psychiatric neurosurgery has been taking place since 1999 (Müller, 2017). Nowadays, ablative neurosurgical procedures and DBS are used in psychiatric neurosurgery. The ablative neurosurgical procedures currently in use include radiofrequency thermocoagulation, Gamma Knife or CyberKnife radiosurgery, and magnetic resonance-guided focused ultrasound (MRgFUS) (Müller et al., 2022). Ablative neurosurgical procedures are mainly used for performing capsulotomies, cingulotomies, amygdalotomies, nucleus accumbens lesioning, subcaudate tractotomies, and limbic leucotomies (Wang & Li, 2015). From a clinical perspective, evidence indicates that each of these approaches has a different profile of advantages and disadvantages, therefore no treatment can be deemed absolutely superior to another (Müller et al., 2022).

A review summarized seven papers with 38 patients in total who underwent different ablative microsurgery or radiosurgery interventions for reducing therapy-refractory aggressiveness (Wang & Li, 2015). Improvement was reported in 74% of patients. Further cases have been reported recently (Zhang et al., 2017; García-Muñoz et al., 2019; Torres et al., 2021; Martínez-Álvarez & Torres-Diaz, 2022).

DBS (particularly in the hypothalamus) has been used to treat patients with therapy-refractory aggressiveness and mostly severe intellectual and developmental disability (Hernando et al., 2008; Maley et al., 2010; Franzini et al., 2013; Torres et al., 2013; Harat et al., 2015; Torres et al., 2020; Blasco García de Andoain et al., 2021; Benedetti-Isaac et al., 2021; Contreras Lopez et al., 2021; Escobar Vidarte et al., 2022). In the majority of patients, the aggressive and disruptive behavior was significantly reduced.

The benefits and risks of such interventions are difficult to assess. Some patients with auto- or hetero-aggression can obviously benefit from it, since fixations, isolation, sedatives, or neuroleptics can be (largely) dispensed after successful treatment. On the other hand, the risks of surgical complications, inflammation, stimulation-related adverse effects, and hardware problems have to be considered (Müller et al., 2022). However, as reported at neurosurgery conferences, the cases that are published in English are only the tip of the iceberg. Therefore, a comprehensive evaluation of neurosurgical treatments to reduce hyper-aggressiveness in terms of their effectiveness, risks, and side effects is currently not feasible.

In the future, closed-loop implants that permanently measure and automatically regulate neuronal activity in specific areas will probably be available. Such systems are already in development for the control of epilepsy; similar models could be developed for the control of aggressive outbursts or sexual arousal (Gilbert, 2015). Neurosurgeon and radiosurgeon Antonio De Salles, who has operated on many patients for psychiatric indications, describes such a treatment method in his novel "Why fly over the cuckoo's nest?". A young scientist suffering from uncontrollable violent outbursts after provocation and in forensic placement for manslaughter is treated with advanced closed-loop DBS in the mamillothalamic tract. This allows emerging aggressive impulses to be detected by the brain implant and automatically downregulated before the man is even aware of them (De Salles, 2011). The procedure described in detail in the novel is technically already feasible today.

19.2.4 Neurosurgical interventions for reducing sex drive

Another possibility of moral enhancement is to reduce or control pathological sexuality and hypersexuality.

Sexual urges can be reduced by (unilateral) hypothalamotomy. Between 1962 and 1979, 74 sexually deviant men[2] and one woman, who had become hypersexual following a brain tumor resection, were treated with hypothalamotomy in the Federal Republic of Germany (Schmidt & Schorsch, 1981; Timmermann & Müller, 2003). In most cases, a reduction of sexual desire and/or the disappearance of pedophilia and/or homosexuality was achieved, as well as a consolidation of social relationships and the professional situation (Roeder, Orthner & Müller, 1972; Dieckmann, Schneider-Jonietz & Schneider, 1988; Timmermann & Müller, 2003). However, the effects and side effects of the interventions are difficult to assess due to insufficient documentation and methodological weaknesses (Schmidt & Schorsch, 1981).

In the USA, the first deep brain stimulation experiment with the aim of conversion to heterosexuality was carried out on a 24-year-old homosexual man (Moan & Heath, 1972). Electrodes were implanted in eight different brain areas (presumably bilaterally). Afterwards, it was tested in which areas electrical stimulation led to pleasurable sensations. This was only the case in the septal region. As a result, this region was stimulated while he was shown heterosexual pornography to recondition his sexual preference toward women. In the next step, his septum was stimulated just before he was brought together with a prostitute. According to the experimenters, the treatment was successful even after the stimulation electrodes were removed, because the man reported only two homosexual contacts for money and an ongoing affair with a married woman after this treatment (Moan & Heath, 1972).

Male homosexuality was classified as a disease by the WHO in the *International Classification of Diseases* (ICD) until 1992, and so its neurosurgical treatment had been considered a therapy. Since its elimination from diagnostic manuals, conversion therapies are no longer considered therapies. Thus, if religious men who consider their homosexuality a sin had successful neurosurgical treatment for it, one would have to speak of moral enhancement (in terms of their own understanding of morality). This is different with pedophilia, which is further classified as a disorder.

Although neurosurgical interventions to alter sexuality have been historically discredited, DBS for the control of sexual deviance is discussed again (De Ridder et al., 2009; Fumagalli & Priori, 2012; Fuß et al., 2015).

Dirk De Ridder et al. (2009) suggested treating pedophilia by electric stimulation of the following brain areas: nucleus accumbens, anterior cingulum, amygdalae, orbitofrontal cortex, and dorsolateral prefrontal cortex (DLPFC). They recommended deactivating the nucleus accumbens during the presentation of pedophilic stimuli by high-frequency DBS to uncouple the stimulus and the reward. Thus, unlike Moan and Heath, they aim to achieve sexual reorientation not by reinforcing the desired sexual orientation but by suppressing the undesired sexual orientation.

In contrast, based on experience with stereotactic lesions, Johannes Fuß et al. (2015) proposed DBS of the ventromedial hypothalamus for reducing sexual urges.

A sophisticated closed-loop procedure is again described in fiction. In "Die Auswilderung von Pädo 1" ("The wilding of Pedo 1"), Sabine Bruno (2017) tells how a convicted pedophile receives a closed-loop DBS system that constantly measures the activity of his septum (as a measure of his sexual arousal). In addition, he must constantly wear Google Glasses with automatic person classification. Only when a child is in his visual field, his septal activity, and thus his sexual arousal, automatically is downregulated, while in the presence of adults sexual arousal is permitted. With this trick, his sexuality is not suppressed completely but only his sexual urge toward children.

The control and selective, possibly situation-specific, suppression of the sexual drive are presumably already possible with today's technical means.

19.2.5 Neurosurgical interventions for reducing psychopathy or sociopathy

A more ambitious variant of neurosurgical moral enhancement would be the reduction of psychopathy, antisocial personality disorder, or dissocial personality disorder.[3]

Indeed, Dirk De Ridder and his coauthors proposed the "moral reconditioning" of individuals with antisocial personality disorder (De Ridder et al., 2009). To do this, they suggested a variety of treatments: (1) high-frequency electrical stimulation of the left DLPFC to suppress hyperactivity; (2) low-frequency stimulation of the right DLPFC to strengthen resistance to temptation and suppress impulsive responses; (3) high-frequency DBS of the nucleus accumbens during the presentation of immoral stimuli to uncouple stimulus and reward. On the one hand, impulse control is to be improved by strengthening the rational control instance, while on the other hand, behavioristic reconditioning is to be performed by making immoral stimuli unattractive.

Mark R. Hoeprich proposed using DBS to rehabilitate psychopathic offenders at the annual meeting of the *Michigan Association of Neurological Surgeons*. He emphasized the economic, medical, and social feasibility of his suggestion (Hoeprich, 2011).

Sergio Canavero has proposed trying noninvasive cortical stimulation (TMS or tDCS) of the right DLPFC on psychopaths, as it is thought to improve compliance with social norms enforced by punishment. In the future, closed-loop cortical stimulation systems could also be used to automatically eliminate inappropriate aggression. While Canavero's first proposal targets a trait typical of psychopaths, his second proposal aims to reduce aggression, although this does not necessarily need to be associated with psychopathy (Canavero, 2014).

Manuela Fumagalli and Alberto Priori have proposed the use of DBS to treat antisocial behavior or violence (Fumagalli & Priori, 2012). Thereby, they refer to DBS experiments with patients with disruptive behavior and intellectual and developmental disability. However, this analogy is invalid because the etiology of antisocial behavior is quite different from that of the behavior of these patients.

Unlike the proposals for reducing aggressiveness or the sex drive, the proposals for the therapy of psychopathy or sociopathy are not scientifically convincing, since they are not supported by any empirical studies. Either they reproduce the suggestions for reducing aggressiveness, or they suggest that self-control can be improved by strengthening rational control. But this misses the core of psychopathy or sociopathy, namely the lack of moral motivation, the lack of empathy, and extreme selfishness. For "snakes in suits" (Babiak & Hare, 2006), proposals to reduce uncontrollable aggression are completely inappropriate because they normally are able to control their aggression.

19.2.6 Interim conclusion

All of the neurosurgical interventions proposed to date are intended to improve the ability to behave in a morally correct manner despite external or internal resistances or temptations. This is to be achieved in two fundamentally different ways: (1) temptations are to be reduced by attenuating aggressive or sexual impulses, or "immoral stimuli," or by automatically suppressing them in a situation-specific manner (interventions in the limbic system, particularly in the amygdalae or in the hypothalamus). (2) The self-control (resistance to temptation and suppression of impulsive responses) is to be improved (by interventions in the DLPFC).

These two paths can be compared with two paths to alcohol abstinence for alcohol addicts: in the first path, the craving for alcohol is suppressed with medication; one then needs little self-control to resist alcohol. In the second path, the craving for alcohol remains, but one learns techniques to resist the craving (Ray et al., 2019; Burnette et al., 2022).

Although both methods can lead to the same result, only the second way (increasing self-control) can be said to improve steadfastness.

The question of whether moral enhancement is possible through neurosurgery can be answered as follows according to the current state of knowledge and discussion: it is theoretically conceivable that neurosurgical interventions can increase self-control and thus possibly also moral assertiveness (the fifth component in the model of Tanner and Christen), but this is so far speculative due to a lack of empirical evidence. Realistically, however, reducing aggression or sex drive may make moral assertiveness less demanding, making aggressive and sexually deviant behavior less likely. The latter, however, would not be *moral enhancement* (except in the utilitarian sense) but only behavioral enhancement because the person's moral abilities and attitudes would not have improved.

For all other components of moral intelligence, none of the neurosurgical procedures proposed so far are even theoretically suitable because they require higher cognitive functions and are strongly dependent on an individual's experiences and education. Thus, none of the proposals to date aims to the improvement of the moral compass, moral commitment, moral sensitivity, or moral problem-solving.

19.3 Is moral enhancement through neurosurgery ethically justifiable?

Several bioethicists have simply presupposed that neurosurgical moral enhancement is possible without analyzing whether it is feasible at all, and then directly philosophized about whether it should be done (e.g., Merkel et al., 2007; DeGrazia, 2014; Jotterand, 2014; Hughes, 2015). But an "ought" presupposes a "can." If neurosurgical moral enhancement should be practically impossible, the question of its ethical legitimacy becomes superfluous – unless one pursues speculative rather than anticipatory ethics.

19.3.1 Medico-ethical issues of moral enhancement through neurosurgery

Whether and to what extent neurosurgical interventions for moral enhancement are ethically justifiable depends, among other things, on whether the person concerned is of age, capable of giving consent, and living in freedom (i.e., not in custody, forensic placement, or preventive detention). Furthermore, it depends on whether the intervention is chosen by the patient, forced upon him or her, or even carried out forcibly against his or her will.

While compulsory treatment for behavior control is fundamentally ethically problematic and justifiable only under special circumstances, it does not apply to voluntary interventions aiming at improving the behavior.

A person may have reasonable and rational reasons to undergo neurosurgery to make certain socially or morally problematic behaviors less likely in the future (see also Gilbert, Vranic, & Hurst, 2013). Examples that can be considered include the notorious adulterer who desperately wants to be faithful, the hot-tempered father who repeatedly beats his children even though he does not want to, or the pedophile who morally condemns his sexual preference and fears committing crimes.

If a person capable of giving consent and living in freedom decides to undergo a brain intervention in order to prevent a certain morally problematic behavior in the future, the following aspects play a role in the ethical evaluation: (1) the informed consent of the person after complete and truthful information about the chances and risks and the experimental character of the intervention as well as possible conflicts of interest, (2) voluntariness, (3) an acceptable benefit-risk balance of the intervention.

Whether offering a neurosurgical procedure for moral enhancement to persons capable of giving consent who are in custody, forensic placement or preventive detention is ethically justifiable depends on the following aspects: (1) the adequacy of informed consent, (2) the voluntary nature of the decision, (3) the expected health benefits, (4) the effectiveness of the procedure, and (5) its risks and side effects.

A health benefit can only be expected for the person concerned if that person herself suffers from the characteristic to be changed by the intervention. An example is a pedophile who condemns his sexual preference and suffers from his fantasies.

A controversial issue is whether a criminal sentenced to a long, possibly indefinite prison term, preventive detention, or forensic placement can make a free decision to undergo brain surgery for moral enhancement, or whether this is a case of blackmail that precludes a free decision. According to Reinhard Merkel and his coauthors, if the deprivation of liberty is legal, there can be no question of blackmail, just as there can be no question of blackmail if there is pressure from natural circumstances such as a life-threatening illness (Merkel et al., 2007, pp. 380–382). This must be offset by the fact that for the prisoner the legality of the deprivation of liberty plays no role and that other persons allow him only to choose between two evils. From the prisoner's subjective point of view, this is blackmail. The criterion of voluntariness, which is a prerequisite for informed consent, cannot be met here. Unlike the decision in favor of risky and stressful therapy in the case of a life-threatening illness, no health benefit can be expected for the prisoner. The only benefit would be release. Psychopaths in particular, because they do not suffer from their psychopathy and have no intrinsic desire not to be psychopathic, would at most agree to neurosurgical psychopathy treatment in order to be released (Hübner & White, 2016).

19.3.2 Meta-ethical discussion about neurosurgical moral enhancement

On a meta-ethical level, the question arises as to whether behavior that is only technically induced to conform to morality is moral behavior at all. John Harris, a proponent of cognitive enhancement, argues that neurotechnical moral enhancement would restrict freedom and thus make moral action impossible (Harris, 2011). This argument is fundamentally true, since only free action, not automatic behavior, can be moral.

On the other hand, the methods of neurosurgical moral enhancement proposed so far cannot deprive the person of all freedom and do not turn that person into an externally determined automaton. The suggestions aim at making moral assertiveness less demanding by reducing aggressiveness or sex drive so that morally appropriate behavior becomes easier and more likely. More far-reaching, but empirically unsupported proposals additionally aim to improve moral assertiveness, for example, by improving impulse control. If the latter were successful, the person's freedom of will and capacity for autonomy would be increased, as he or she would be better able to pursue higher-order goals rather than being driven by impulses and urges.

Moreover, a self-chosen restriction of freedom should be evaluated morally differently than an externally enforced restriction.[4] Thus, Thomas Douglas' argument is correct that even if a self-chosen technical manipulation of one's own emotional disposition in a more moral direction were to restrict freedom, this would be acceptable because this restriction would be freely chosen (Douglas, 2008).

However, the question arises whether a self-chosen restriction of one's freedom in favor of more moral behavior in the future is acceptable in principle, or whether there are exceptions. For example, David DeGrazia (2014) suggests that while moral enhancement does not pose a systematic threat to freedom – except in extreme cases, such as when a brain–computer interface reliably causes the person to change his or her intention to act immorally as soon as that intention occurs. In theory, this argument is undoubtedly true, but in practice, it is not. This is because closed-loop systems can detect aggressive or sexual impulses, and, if necessary, automatically down-regulate them. But no brain implant can read out intentions and determine whether they are immoral. That is precisely the problem. A justified aggression in self-defense or in defense of an attacked person would be downregulated as an unjustified aggression. Likewise, sexuality would be fundamentally reduced – unless, as described by Sabine Bruno, a closed-loop system recognizes and prescribes with what kind of person sexuality is permitted or prohibited.

The freedom to engage in morally wrong behavior remains with all the interventions discussed here. It is true that for certain forms of morally wrong behavior (e.g., rape) the incentives are reduced (e.g., by suppressing the sex drive) so that hardly any self-control is required to resist temptation. However, violence can still be used instrumentally. Sexual violence can be exercised even when sexual arousal is suppressed, e.g., to exert power, to achieve sadistic gratification, or to humiliate war opponents. Since the freedom to engage in amoral behavior remains, these interventions also offer no guarantee that moral misconduct will not occur in the future. For this very reason, the objection that neurosurgical moral enhancement restricts freedom to such an extent that moral action is no longer possible is incorrect.

Whether neurosurgical interventions that can effectively control aggressiveness or sexual urges are to be considered the therapy of disease, techniques of social control or moral enhancement depend primarily on the concept of disease. Additionally, in individual cases, it depends on whether a disease in a strictly medical sense is present. If, for example, a brain tumor resection leads to a decrease in psychopathy, one can rightly speak of therapy. If, on the other hand, a "snake in a suit" (Babiak & Hare, 2006) were transformed into a non-psychopath by psychiatric neurosurgery, one would not have achieved therapy but moral enhancement.

However, the methods available and proposed so far are all unsuitable for this purpose, as they do not address the moral motivation that is deficient in psychopaths. The same is true for persons with a disturbed moral compass, a lack of moral sensitivity, or deficient moral judgment. The conviction of having to kill non-believers, contempt for weaker people, unlimited egoism, or indifference toward other living beings cannot be operated out of brains, nor can they be suppressed by electrical stimulation. To remedy such deficiencies of moral intelligence, methods such as good education, Socratic dialogue, criticism of ideology, promotion of logical thinking and argumentation, and empathy training are more promising.

From a consequentialist, especially a utilitarian, perspective, effective moral enhancement would be welcome, even if it were to restrict freedom. DeGrazia (2014), for example, argues that we should not overstate the value of freedom because ultimately it is the end product, i.e., moral behavior that matters, regardless of how free it is.

This utilitarian view contradicts humanistic ethics, for which the inner freedom of the individual is a high, non-negotiable value. According to humanistic ethics, moral enhancement would only be acceptable if it not only increased the individual's freedom of action (e.g., thanks to release from prison) but also his or her freedom of will or capacity for self-determination. The latter would be increased if impulse control and thus moral steadfastness were improved but not if merely aggressive or sexual impulses were reduced or automatically downregulated.

Acknowledgments

This work has been partly funded by the Federal Ministry for Research and Education of Germany (01GP1621A). This chapter is based on a publication in the German journal *Ethik in der Medizin* (Sabine Müller, 2018, 30, pp. 39–56, doi: 10.1007/s00481-018-0476-x). This has been kindly approved by Springer Nature. For this book, the text has been translated, updated, and partly extended, also due to the helpful comments of two anonymous reviewers.

Notes

1 Examples for restricted or disturbed components of the moral intelligence: (1) persons who kill people in the name of their religion; (2) psychopaths; (3) persons with a severe empathy lack; (4) persons with a poor capacity for judgement; (5) persons who do not want to commit violence but who do strike or commit sexual assault in situations where they feel challenged or sexually provoked.
2 Some of these men would not have been liable to prosecution under today's German law, because nowadays neither consensual sexual acts with minors over the age of 14 nor such acts between men are punishable. However, the majority of these men would also have been considered criminals under today's German law because they had committed sexual assault, rape, and/or child sexual abuse.
3 Antisocial personality disorder (ASPD) and psychopathy are largely overlapping concepts. Psychopathy, conceptualized by the Hare Psychopathy Checklist Revised (PCL-R), contains much more interpersonal and affective symptoms than ASPD but is not a diagnosis in ICD-10 or DSM-5. The DSM focused on behavior in the definition of ASPD, which was intended to be an equivalent of psychopathy. The equivalent of ASPD in ICD-10, dissocial personality disorder (DPD), refers less to behavioral and more to affective symptoms than ASPD. The population of persons diagnosed with psychopathy is a subset of the population of persons diagnosed with ASPD or DPD. Exceptions are typically fraudulent personalities (or so-called "white collar offenders") who are psychopaths but do not meet the criteria of dissocial or antisocial personality disorder (Münch, Walter, & Müller, 2020).
4 The concept of "cognitive liberty" or "right to mental self-determination" is advocated among others by Wrye Sententia (2004) and by Jan C. Bublitz and Reinhard Merkel (2014). This concept aims at protecting a person's right to determine his or her own state of mind and be free from external control over the state of mind.

References

Babiak, P., & Hare, R. D. (2006). *Snakes in suits: When psychopaths go to work*. New York: HarperCollins.
Babiak, P., Neumann, C. S., & Hare, R. D. (2010). Corporate psychopathy: Talking the walk. *Behavioral Sciences & the Law, 28*, 174–193.
Baccarini, E., & Malatesti, L. (2017). Moral bioenhancement of psychopaths. *Journal of Medical Ethics, 43*(10), 697–701.
Bartz, J. A., Zaki, J., Bolger, N., & Ochsner, K. N. (2011). Social effects of oxytocin in humans: Context and person matter. *Trends in Cognitive Sciences, 15*(7), 301–309.
Benedetti-Isaac, J. C., Camargo, L., Gargiulo, P., & López, N. (2021). Deep brain stimulation in the posteromedial hypothalamic nuclei in refractory aggressiveness: Post-surgical results of 19 cases. *International Journal of Neuropsychopharmacology, 24*(12), 977–978.
Blair, R., & James, R. (2013). Psychopathy: Cognitive and neural dysfunction. *Dialogues in Clinical Neuroscience, 15*, 181–190.
Blasco García de Andoain, G., Navas García, M., González Aduna, Ó., Bocos Portillo, A., Ezquiaga Terrazas, E., Ayuso-Mateos, J. L., Pastor, J., Vega-Zelaya, L., & Torres, C. V. (2021). Posteromedial hypothalamic deep brain stimulation for refractory aggressiveness in a patient with Weaver syndrome: Clinical, technical report and operative video. *Operative Neurosurgery, 21*(3), 165–171.
Bruno, S. (2017). Die Auswilderung von Pädo 1 [The wilding of Pedo 1]. *Am Erker, 73*, 8–11.
Bublitz, J. C., & Merkel, R. (2014). Crime against minds: On mental manipulations, harms and a human right to mental self-determination. *Criminal Law and Philosophy, 8*, 61.
Burnette, E. M., Nieto, S. J., Grodin, E. N., Meredith, L. R., Hurley, B., Miotto, K., Gillis, A. J., & Ray, L. A. (2022). Novel agents for the pharmacological treatment of alcohol use disorder. *Drugs, 82*(3), 251–274.
Canavero, S. (2014). Criminal minds: Neuromodulation of the psychopathic brain. *Frontiers in Human Neuroscience, 8*, 124.
Christen, M., & Müller, S. (2015). Effects of brain lesions on moral agency: Ethical dilemmas in investigating moral behavior. In G. Lee, J. Illes, & F. Ohl (Eds.), *Ethical issues in behavioral neuroscience* (pp. 159–188). Heidelberg et al.: Springer.
Contreras Lopez, W. O., Navarro, P. A., Gouveia, F. V., Fonoff, E. T., Lebrun, I., Auada, A. V. V., Lopes Alho, E. J., & Martinez, R. C. R. (2021). Directional deep brain stimulation of the posteromedial hypothalamus for

refractory intermittent explosive disorder: A case series using a novel neurostimulation device and intraoperative microdialysis. *World Neurosurgery, 155*, e19–e33.

Crockett, M. J., Clark, L., Hauser, M., & Robbins, T. (2010). Serotonin selectively influences moral judgment and behavior through effects on harm aversion. *Proceedings of the National Academy of Sciences of the United States of America, 107*, 17433–17438.

Darby, R. R., Horn, A., Cushman, F., & Fox, M. D. (2018). Lesion network localization of criminal behavior. *Proceedings of the National Academy of Sciences of the United States of America, 115*(3), 601–606.

DeGrazia, D. (2014). Moral enhancement, freedom, and what we (should) value in moral behavior. *Journal of Medical Ethics, 40*, 361–368.

De Ridder, D., Langguth, B., Plazier, M., & Menovsky, T. (2009). Moral dysfunction and potential treatments. In J. Verplaetse, J. De Schrijver, S. Vanneste, & J. Braeckman (Eds.), *The moral brain* (pp. 155–183). Luxemburg and Berlin: Springer Science + Business Media.

De Salles, A. (2011). *Why fly over the cuckoo's nest? Psychosurgery in my brain please!* ISBN 9781460961292.

Dieckmann, G., Schneider-Jonietz, B., & Schneider, H. (1988). Psychiatric and neuropsychological findings after stereotactic hypothalamotomy, in cases of extreme sexual aggressivity. *Acta Neurochirurgica. Supplementum, 44*, 163–166.

Douglas, T. (2008). Moral enhancement. *Journal of Applied Philosophy, 25*(3), 228–245.

Dubljević, V., & Racine, E. (2017). Moral enhancement meets normative and empirical reality: Assessing the practical feasibility of moral enhancement neurotechnologies. *Bioethics, 31*(5), 338–348.

Escobar Vidarte, O. A., Griswold, D. P., Orozco Mera, J., Arango Uribe, G. J., & Salcedo, J. C. (2022). Deep brain stimulation for severe and intractable aggressive behavior. *Stereotactic and Functional Neurosurgery, 100*(4), 1–4.

Faria, M. A. (2013). Violence, mental illness, and the brain – A brief history of psychosurgery. Part 1–3. *Surgical Neurology International, 4*, 49, 75, 91.

Faust, H. S. (2008). Should we select for genetic moral enhancement? A thought experiment using the MoralKinder (MK+) haplotype. *Theoretical Medicine and Bioethics, 29*, 397–416.

Foong, J., & Flugel, D. (2007). Psychiatric outcome of surgery for temporal lobe epilepsy and presurgical considerations. *Epilepsy Research, 75*, 84–96.

Franzini, A., Broggi, G., Cordella, R., Dones, I., & Messina, G. (2013). Deep-brain stimulation for aggressive and disruptive behavior. *World Neurosurgery, 80*(3/4), S29.e11–S29.e14.

Fuß, J., Auer, M. K., Biedermann, S. V., Briken, P., & Hacke, W. (2015). Deep brain stimulation to reduce sexual drive. *Journal of Psychiatry & Neuroscience, 40*(6), 429–431.

Fumagalli, M., & Priori, A. (2012). Functional and clinical neuroanatomy of morality. *Brain, 135*, 2006–2021.

García-Muñoz, L., Picazo-Picazo, O., Carrillo-Ruíz, J. D., Favila-Bojórquez, J., Corona-García, F., Meza-Bautista, M. Á., & Jiménez-Ponce, F. (2019). Effect of unilateral amygdalotomy and hypothalamotomy in patients with refractory aggressiveness. *Gaceta medica de Mexico, 155*(Suppl 1), S49–S55.

Gilbert, F. (2015). A threat to autonomy? The intrusion of predictive brain implants. *American Journal of Bioethics Neuroscience, 6*(4), 4–11.

Gilbert, F., Vranic, A., & Hurst, S. (2013). Involuntary & voluntary invasive brain surgery: Ethical issues related to acquired aggressiveness. *Neuroethics, 6*, 115–128.

Glannon, W. (2014). Intervening in the psychopath's brain. *Theorical Medicine and Bioethics, 35*, 43–57.

Harat, M., Rudaś, M., Zieliński, P., Birska, J., & Sokal, P. (2015). Deep brain stimulation in pathological aggression. *Stereotactic and Functional Neurosurgery, 93*, 310–315.

Harris, J. (2011). Moral enhancement and freedom. *Bioethics, 25*(2), 102–111.

Harris, G., Skilling, T. A., & Rice, M. E. (2001). The construct of psychopathy. In M. Tonry, & N. Morris (Eds.), *Crime and justice: An annual review of research, 28* (pp. 197–264). Chicago: University of Chicago Press.

Heinz, A., & Müller, S. (2017). Exaggerating the benefits and downplaying the risks in the bioethical debate on cognitive neuroenhancement. In: R. ter Meulen, A. D. Mohamed, & W. Hall (Eds.), *Rethinking cognitive enhancement. A critical reappraisal of the neuroscience and ethics of cognitive enhancement* (pp. 69–86). Oxford: Oxford University Press.

Hernando, V., Pastor, J., Pedrosa, M., Pena, E., & Sola, R. G. (2008). Low-frequency bilateral hypothalamic stimulation for treatment of drug-resistant aggressiveness in a young man with mental retardation. *Stereotactic and Functional Neurosurgery, 86*, 219–223.

Hoeprich, M. (2011). An analysis of the proposal of deep brain stimulation for the treatment of the intermittent explosive behavior. Presentation for Michigan Association of Neurological Surgeons. 11.06.2011.

Hübner, D., & White, L. (2016). Neurosurgery for psychopaths? An ethical analysis. *American Journal of Bioethics Neuroscience, 7*(3), 140–149.

Hughes, J. J. (2015). Moral enhancement requires multiple virtues. Toward a posthuman model of character development. *Cambridge Quarterly of Healthcare Ethics, 24*(1), 86–95.

Jiménez, F., Soto, J. E., Velasco, F., Andrade, P., Bustamante, J. J., Gómez, P., Ramírez, Y., & Carrillo-Ruiz, J. D. (2012). Bilateral cingulotomy and anterior capsulotomy applied to patients with aggressiveness. *Stereotactic and Functional Neurosurgery, 90*(3), 151–160.

Jotterand, F. (2014). Psychopathy, neurotechnologies, and neuroethics. *Theorical Medicine and Bioethics, 35*(1), 1–6.

Koren, G., & Korn, L. (2021). The use of methylphenidate for cognitive enhancement in young healthy adults: The clinical and ethical debates. *Journal of Clinical Psychopharmacology, 41*(2), 100–102.

Langevin, J. P. (2012). The amygdala as a target for behavior surgery. *Surgical Neurology International, 3*(Suppl 1), S40–S46.

Liu, H., Feng, W., & Zhang, D. (2019). Association of ADHD medications with the risk of cardiovascular diseases: A meta-analysis. *European Child & Adolescent Psychiatry, 28*(10), 1283–1293.

Maley, J. H., Alvernia, J. E., Valle, E. P., & Richardson, D. (2010). Deep brain stimulation of the orbitofrontal projections for the treatment of intermittent explosive disorder. *Neurosurgical Focus, 29*(2), E11.

Martínez-Álvarez, R., & Torres-Diaz, C. (2022). Surgery of autism: Is it possible? *Progress in Brain Research, 272*(1), 73–84.

Merkel, R., Boer, G., Fegert, J., Galert, T., Hartmann, D., Nuttin, B., & Rosahl, S. (2007). *Intervening in the brain: Changing psyche and society.* Berlin: Springer.

Moan, C. E., & Heath, R. G. (1972). Septal stimulation for the initiation of heterosexual behavior in a homosexual male. *Journal of Behavior Therapy and Experimental Psychiatry, 3*, 23–30.

Morton, W. A., & Stockton, G. G. (2000). Methylphenidate abuse and psychiatric side effects. *Primary Care Companion to the Journal of Clinical Psychiatry, 2*(5), 159–164.

Mpakopoulou, M., Gatos, H., Brotis, A., Paterakis, K. N., & Fountas, K. N. (2008). Stereotactic amygdalotomy in the management of severe aggressive behavioral disorders. *Neurosurgical Focus, 25*(1), E6.

Müller, S. (2017). Ethical challenges of modern psychiatric neurosurgery. In J. Illes (Ed.), *Neuroethics. Anticipating the future* (pp. 235–263). Oxford: Oxford Press.

Müller, S., van Oosterhout, A., Bervoets, C., Christen, M., Martínez-Álvarez, R., & Bittlinger, M. (2022). Concerns about psychiatric neurosurgery and how they can be overcome: Recommendations for responsible research. *Neuroethics, 15*(6), 1–26.

Münch, R., Walter, H., & Müller, S. (2020). Should behavior harmful to others be a sufficient criterion of mental disorders? Conceptual problems of the diagnoses of Antisocial Personality Disorder and Pedophilic Disorder. *Frontiers in Psychiatry, 11*, 558655.

Nakaji, P., Meltzer, H. S., Singel, S. A., & Alksne, J. F. (2003). Improvement of aggressive and antisocial behavior after resection of temporal lobe tumors. *Pediatrics, 112*, e430–e433.

Persson, I., & Savulescu, J. (2010). Moral transhumanism. *The Journal of Medicine and Philosophy, 35*, 656–669.

Ray, L. A., Bujarski, S., Grodin, E., Hartwell, E., Green, R., Venegas, A., Lim, A. C., Gillis, A., & Miotto, K. (2019). State-of-the-art behavioral and pharmacological treatments for alcohol use disorder. *The American Journal of Drug and Alcohol Abuse, 45*(2), 124–140.

Reimer, M. (2008). Psychopathy without (the language of) disorder. *Neuroethics, 1*, 185–198.

Roeder, F., Orthner, H., & Müller, D. (1972). The stereotactic treatment of pedophilic homosexuality and other sexual deviations. In E. Hitchcock, L. Laitinen, & K. Vaernet (Eds.), *Psychosurgery* (pp. 87–111). Springfield: Charles C Thomas.

Schmidt, G., & Schorsch, E. (1981). Psychosurgery of sexually deviant patients: Review and analysis of new empirical findings. *Archives of Sexual Behavior, 10*, 301–323.

Sententia, W. (2004). Neuroethical considerations: Cognitive liberty and converging technologies for improving human cognition. *Annals of the New York Academy of Sciences, 1013*(1), 221–228.

Shellenberg, T. P., Stoops, W. W., Lile, J. A., & Rush, C. R. (2020). An update on the clinical pharmacology of methylphenidate: Therapeutic efficacy, abuse potential and future considerations. *Expert Review of Clinical Pharmacology, 13*(8), 825–833.

Steiner, H., & Van Waes, V. (2013). Addiction-related gene regulation: Risks of exposure to cognitive enhancers vs. other psychostimulants. *Progress in Neurobiology, 100*, 60–80.

Tanner, C., & Christen, M. (2013). Moral intelligence – A framework for understanding moral competences. In M. Christen, J. Fischer, M. Huppenbauer, C. Tanner, & C. van Schaik (Eds.), *Empirically informed ethics* (pp. 119–136). Berlin: Springer.

Timmermann, H.-D., & Müller, D. (2003). *Stereotaktische Hirnoperationen bei sexuell Devianten [Stereotactic brain surgery in sexually deviant patients].* Norderstedt: Books on Demand.

Torres, C. V., Sola, R. G., Pastor, J., Pedrosa, M., Navas, M., García-Navarrete, E., Ezquiaga, E., & García-Camba, E. (2013). Long-term results of posteromedial hypothalamic deep brain stimulation for patients with resistant aggressiveness. *Journal of Neurosurgery, 119*(2), 277–287.

Torres, C. V., Blasco, G., Navas García, M., Ezquiaga, E., Pastor, J., Vega-Zelaya, L., Pulido Rivas, P., Pérez Rodrigo, S., & Manzanares, R. (2020). Deep brain stimulation for aggressiveness: Long-term follow-up and tractography study of the stimulated brain areas. *Journal of Neurosurgery*, 1–10. Epub ahead of print.

Torres, C. V., Martínez, N., Ríos-Lago, M., Lara, M., Alvarez-Linera, J., Cabanyes, J., Dorado, M. L., Cabrera, W., Rey, G., & Martínez-Alvarez, R. (2021). Surgery and radiosurgery in autism: A retrospective study in 10 patients. *Stereotactic and Functional Neurosurgery*, *99*(6), 474–483.

Troisi, A. (2005). The concept of alternative strategies and its relevance to psychiatry and clinical psychology. *Neuroscience and Biobehavioral Reviews*, *29*, 159–168.

Wang, W., & Li, P. (2015). Surgical management for aggressive behavior. In B. Sun, & A. De Salles (Eds.), *Neurosurgical treatments for psychiatric disorders* (pp. 203–209). Dordrecht et al.: Springer.

Wiseman, H. (2014). SSRI as moral enhancement interventions: A practical dead end. *American Journal of Bioethics Neuroscience*, *5*(3), 21–30.

Zhang, S., Zhou, P., Jiang, S., Li, P., & Wang, W. (2017). Bilateral anterior capsulotomy and amygdalotomy for mental retardation with psychiatric symptoms and aggression: A case report. *Medicine*, *96*(1), e5840.

20
TRANSHUMANISM AND MORAL ENHANCEMENT

Johann S. Ach and Birgit Beck

20.1 The world's most dangerous idea?

The assumption that the human body and mind can or even must be transformed and ameliorated is part and parcel of the credo of transhumanist thinking. Nick Bostrom, a leading transhumanist, takes this to be one of the essential components of transhumanism. According to Bostrom, the transhumanist movement is characterized by promoting "an interdisciplinary approach to understanding and evaluating the opportunities for enhancing the human condition and the human organism opened up by the advancement of technology" (Bostrom, 2005).

The idea of such a new body and accordingly mind which is less decrepit than the current human condition, free from disease and unnecessary suffering, equipped with physical, emotional, and intellectual properties which enable humans to lead a self-determined life and cope with the manifold material and social risks with which they are confronted, is certainly no transhumanist invention. In fact, not even the assumption that there is a moral duty to enhance human nature is of genuine transhumanist origin. This idea has already been brought forward by John Stuart Mill in his essay *On nature* from 1874, in which he stated that "the duty of man is the same in respect to his own nature as in respect to the nature of all other things, namely not to follow but to amend it" (Mill, 1874, 54).

In an article from 2004, Francis Fukuyama called transhumanism "the world's most dangerous idea" and warned against "dismiss[ing] transhumanists as some sort of odd cult, nothing more than science fiction taken too seriously" (Fukuyama, 2004).[1] According to Fukuyama, the core idea of transhumanism is in no way obscure or "outlandish," but "implicit in much of the research agenda of contemporary biomedicine" (ibid.). In retrospect, Fukuyama's warning has gained topicality, for example, from the recent scandal about the birth of genetically modified twins which has shocked the scientific community worldwide (Beck, 2020). After all, the greatest threat of transhumanism, according to Fukuyama, lies in leading to a "posthuman future" in which several (bio-)technologies will inevitably be used to alter human "essence" or "nature" (Fukuyama, 2002; cf. also Habermas, 2003).

In contrast, one could argue that it would be a much more dangerous idea to leave human nature unaltered, at least when it comes to our moral capacities. In a series of articles (Persson and Savulescu, 2008, 2010, 2011, 2013, 2014a, 2014b, 2015, 2017, 2019a, 2019b) and in a monograph (Persson and Savulescu, 2012), Julian Savulescu and Ingmar Persson made a case for the urgency of "moral bioenhancement" by pharmaceutical or biotechnical means with the aim of preventing "ultimate harm" (Persson and Savulescu, 2015, 49), i.e., "to make worthwhile life on this planet forever impossible" (ibid.), which, they assume, is likely to occur due to humanity's moral state of underdevelopment in relation to ever-growing and accelerating technological progress.

In the following, we will first introduce a differentiation between transhumanism and posthumanism which can be found in the literature and present two rival concepts of "human nature" to which proponents and critics of transhumanism usually refer in order to illustrate that the (dangerous) idea of overcoming "human nature" turns out to be a paper tiger. In contrast, the project of enhancing human properties and capacities by (bio-)technical means is debatable and there has been a controversial discussion about human enhancement going on for years (Harris, 2007; Savulescu and Bostrom, 2009; Savulescu, ter Meulen, and Kahane, 2011; Clarke et al., 2016). The focal point of our discussion will be on the latest strand of the enhancement debate, namely moral (bio-)enhancement and moral enhancement by means of artificial intelligence. However, we conclude, depending on the underlying moral theory, moral enhancement by (bio-)technical means may turn out to be a paper tiger as well.

20.2 Transhumanism and posthumanism

Transhumanism and posthumanism share a number of similarities. The advocates of both trans- and posthumanism "on the one hand, place themselves in the technologically enlarged tradition of renaissance humanism, and, on the other hand, take a critical distance towards this tradition" (Loh, 2018, 10).[2] Both trans- and posthumanism "take a humanist idea of the human being as a starting point for their philosophical and scientific considerations" (ibid., 11). The ultimate goal of both trans- and posthumanism is the creation of a kind of "posthuman being." However, there are conceptual differences between the respective aims and means favored by trans- and posthumanist theories.[3]

The aim of *transhumanism*, according to Loh, is to

> develop, optimize, modify and enhance the human being. The transhumanist method is technological transformation of the human being into a posthuman being. […] Human evolution is regarded as generally uncompleted. In transhumanist thinking, technology plays the part of a medium and means for optimizing the human being.
>
> *(Loh, 2020, 277)*

Technological *posthumanism*, in contrast, primarily aims at "creating an artificial alterity, which will replace the human species […] and thus overcome 'the human being'" (ibid.). The ultimate goal of technological posthumanism is not creating better humans who eventually reach a "posthuman" status by way of improving their capacities, but "the creation of a mechanical 'superspecies'. […] Therefore, technology is rather seen as aim than as medium and means" (ibid.).

Not all advocates of transhumanism adopt this conceptual differentiation. Particularly, the lines between transhumanism and technological posthumanism are often blurred. One could argue that it would be wise for transhumanists to distance themselves from some posthumanist ideas which appear quite adventurous, to say the least. However, transhumanist thought as introduced by the transhumanist organization *Humanity+* also implies at least in part "science fiction taken too seriously" (Fukuyama, 2004), for example cryonics or mind uploading (Transhumanist FAQ). The latter poses intricate philosophical problems about (self-)consciousness, the mind–body problem, and synchronic as well as diachronic personal identity (Agar, 2016), which are for the most part ignored by advocates of transhumanism and technological posthumanism.

According to the *Transhumanist Declaration* which was originally composed by a group of authors around Bostrom in 1998 for the former *World Transhumanist Association* and adopted by *Humanity+* in 2009, transhumanists regard themselves as pioneers of a better, more just, and more humane world for (future generations of) humans and all sentient beings through the reasonable application of technological achievements (Transhumanist Declaration). They basically accord with the narrative of transhumanism as the intellectual heir to classical humanism, adopt a broadly construed liberal stance, emphatically advocate a naive faith in technology, and aim at improving and eventually overcoming human nature:

> Transhumanism can be viewed as an extension of humanism, from which it is partially derived. Humanists believe that humans matter, that individuals matter. We might not be perfect, but we can make things better by promoting rational thinking, freedom, tolerance, democracy, and concern for our fellow human beings. Transhumanists agree with this but also emphasize what we have the potential to become. Just as we use rational means to improve the human condition and the external world, we can also use such means to improve ourselves, the human organism. In doing so, we are not limited to traditional humanistic methods, such as education and cultural development. We can also use technological means that will eventually enable us to move beyond what some would think of as "human."
>
> *(Transhumanist FAQ)*

The crucial point in this self-assessment is, of course, the notion of "human" referred to in the last sentence. Concerning this matter, proponents and critics of transhumanism often implicitly refer to different concepts, as we will elucidate in the following paragraph.

20.3 Human nature

As already indicated, transhumanists support the view that human evolution should be actively taken over with the aid of technological means[4] according to their normative outlook on human nature – and as if there was an external standpoint from which evolution could be assessed. The ultimate goal is to free humanity from the limitations of the "human meat machine" (Robinett, 2003, 167), which includes, for example, attaining improved health, extraordinary physical capacities, longevity – if not immortality – and intellectual brilliance. However, transhumanism allegedly also aims for improving human nature by focusing on becoming more *humane*, rather than just staying *human*:

> One might say that if "human" is what we are, then "humane" is what we, as humans, wish we were. Human nature is not a bad place to start that journey, but we can't fulfill that potential if we reject any progress past the starting point.
>
> *(Transhumanist FAQ)*

This plea not only includes an idea of moral improvement, with which we will be concerned in the following paragraph, but it also presumes that there is actually something it is like to be "human" and "humane," respectively. However, it is, firstly, not clear how these two notions interrelate. Secondly, advocates and critics of transhumanism usually differ in their assumptions about relevant "human" and "humane" making features. While transhumanists usually take a *biological* understanding of human nature as a starting point for fantasies about transformation and improvement, critics of transhumanism typically argue on the basis of an *essentialist* notion of human nature.[5]

The alteration of biological nature (what makes us "human") *per se* is not very interesting from a normative point of view. If one does not take evolution to be a teleological process, current human nature is just a contingent, intermediary state, a random outcome of evolution. For example, the average lifespan of a human organism is just a biological datum among others and varies in relation to surrounding conditions. However, biological nature in itself being normatively neutral does not preclude that altering the biological features of humans may have normatively relevant consequences. For example, if "normal" and "superintelligent" persons were to exist simultaneously one day – on earth or elsewhere – it appears dubious if successful communicative relations between them would still be possible (Siep, 2005, 168). A radically extended lifespan would probably pose various problems of (intergenerational) justice (Harris, 2007, ch. 4; Mordacci, 2011).

Accordingly, what critics of transhumanism usually warn against is not the alteration of biological nature in itself, but as a basis for an essentialist understanding of human nature (what makes us "humane"). However, the assumptions about exactly which essential features make for such a metaphysical human nature differ. Erik Parens (2005) has differentiated two normative "frameworks" in which concepts of human nature in a metaphysical sense are enrooted.

From the perspective of the so-called *gratitude framework*, on the one hand, human nature consists in a pre-given, essential "true self" which can and must be identified and nurtured – both on an individual level and on a collective level of human existence – and must not be interfered with. The transhumanist aim of improving or even overcoming (biological) human properties and capacities by technological means obviously contradicts this assumption. Since human nature is a precious gift, we must be true to it and value its giftedness (Sandel, 2007, 2009), instead of trying to interfere with nature and "playing God" (Coady, 2009; Weckert, 2016). However, there is no unanimous conception of relevant features of human nature in this sense. Therefore, Fukuyama (2002) has proposed a "Factor X" which he takes to comprise all relevant features which in their totality form the essential core of a human person, a suggestion that is clearly more an indication of a problem than a convincing answer to the question raised.

From the perspective of the so-called *creativity framework*, on the other hand, the nature of human beings – somewhat paradoxically – consists in having no (pre-given) nature or essence. On the contrary, human nature is precisely characterized by its openness and malleability. We ourselves – again both on an individual level and on a collective level of human existence – have to create ourselves like we want to be, in the first place, according to our (shared) anthropological, normative, and evaluative standards. From this viewpoint, both the transhumanist idea of *overcoming* human nature by actively creating and shaping it and its essentialist critique lose ground.

Even if (bio-)technology should someday turn out to be a suitable means to alter human nature, this would not be a great novelty, since humans have always tried to shape the (biological) conditions of their lives according to prevailing standards, albeit predominantly with the aid of traditional cultural means like physical training, medicine, education or attempts of virtuous self-improvement. Transhumanism could indeed turn out as just a kind of "humanism with different means."

In the end, the whole debate about transhumanism may be regarded as much ado about nothing – or at least little: if one understands human nature in terms of our current biological condition, the idea of overcoming this nature is of little normative interest (except for the above-mentioned possible consequences). If, on the contrary, one conceives of human nature in metaphysical terms, the question arises, whether transhumanism is not just the idea of a radical, technologically shifted realization of this very nature.

To be sure, suggestions about a (re-)moralization of human nature (Jonas, 1979; Habermas, 2003; President's Council on Bioethics, 2003; Sandel, 2007, 2009) do not appear very promising. However, that does not render discussion about transhumanism and human enhancement futile from the perspective of philosophical anthropology. Anthropological arguments, functioning as a condensed experience of recent conditions of human existence, make sense in that they provide normative orientation about the status quo and desirable visions of the future of humanity (Heßler and Liggieri, 2020). In other words, they contribute to our reflective self-understanding. However, they do not provide grounds for a moral critique of trans- or posthumanist projects.

The aspiration or threat (depending on the viewpoint) of overcoming human nature, therefore, turns out to be not so much a dangerous idea, but rather a paper tiger. In any case, there is no danger of a "dangerous" violation of normative boundaries. However, the aforementioned danger of *not* improving human nature concerning our moral capacities still has to be addressed. We will take up this issue in the following section.

20.4 Moral bioenhancement

20.4.1 What actually is moral enhancement?

After a predominant occupation with cognitive and mood enhancement (Beck and Stroop, 2015), the latest strand of the debate about human enhancement which was initiated by Thomas Douglas' paper "Moral Enhancement" (2008)[6] centers on the improvement of human morality. Some leading bioethicists (who are not necessarily tuning in to a transhumanist agenda) promote a biotechnical manipulation of our biological condition to save the world from "ultimate harm" (Persson and Savulescu, 2015, 49). The plea for this kind of moral improvement did not find unanimous approval. Even staunch advocates of human enhancement like John Harris (2007, 2009) have raised concerns over this suggestion (Harris, 2011, 2012, 2013a, 2013b, 2014a, 2014b). The debate has shown that there is persistent disagreement concerning the *meaning, prospect of success*, and *ethical evaluation* of moral bioenhancement.

Apart from notorious conceptual problems concerning the definition of enhancement (Agar, 2014) the primary controversial subject is an adequate concept of morality. There is dissent about which *morally relevant properties and capacities* should be improved and which *means* are suitable for this endeavor. Depending on underlying (meta-)ethical premises, suggestions for moral bioenhancement comprise the improvement of ethical *judgment* or moral *conduct* (or both) by influencing moral *motives*, morally relevant *emotions*, rational *deliberation*, moral *virtues*, or a combination of these features. Moreover, the debate has revealed the need for further conceptual clarification regarding the notions of *liberty, autonomy, authenticity* as well as a *moral and legal responsibility*. Besides genuine ethical issues, the debate raises questions concerning the *philosophy of mind*[7] and *political philosophy* (Sparrow, 2014; de Araujo, 2014).

Moreover, practical problems of implementation have been addressed. These concern both the *acceptance of the aims* and the *efficiency* as well as the *ethical evaluation of means* of moral bioenhancement. Although there are indeed massive global moral problems, not least due to technological progress, it appears dubious if possibly obligatory moral bioenhancement and accompanying constraints on liberal rights – albeit for noble purposes – can provide an adequate solution (Rakić, 2014a; Persson and Savulescu, 2014b) or if it is even necessary for moral progress (Powell and Buchanan, 2016); all the more so because *structural* societal and global moral problems cannot be explained, much less solved, by adjustment of *individual* moral deficits (de Melo-Martin and Salles, 2015).[8] At the present state of knowledge about the efficiency of available means for moral bioenhancement, it appears beside the point to believe that complex moral problems could be tackled by experimental application of pharmaceuticals (Shook, 2012) or other biomedical technologies (Specker et al., 2014, 13 f.). Although at first glance it appears almost tautological that moral enhancement is desirable, this estimation hinges on several conceptual and empirical preconditions (Beck, 2015, 2016).

20.4.2 The concept of enhancement

One fundamental problem that the discussion on moral bioenhancement has inherited from the general enhancement debate consists of heterogeneous definitions of the term enhancement. Advocates and critics use different notions of enhancement in order to back up their respective arguments (Ach, 2016). The (standard) *medical approach* which differentiates enhancement from therapeutic interventions (Juengst, 1998) has been criticized for the vagueness of underlying normative concepts of health, disease, naturalness, and normality (Rehmann-Sutter, Eilers, and Grüber, 2014, 13 f.). In the case of moral bioenhancement, a differentiation between therapy and enhancement appears complicated as well, since one has to determine what counts as ordinary, average, species-typical moral capacity, and which capacities, in turn, exceed a "normal" limit (Specker et al., 2014, 13). To this effect, it has to be kept in mind that any such determination is inevitably normative and, accordingly, in need of justification (Raus et al., 2014, 266 f.). Contrary to "normal" moral capacities, also deviant moral capacities have to be defined and determined as pathological, in order to meaningfully apply the notion of therapy. This could, in turn, raise the danger of prematurely medicalizing morally undesired behavior (ibid., 267).

From the perspective of the so-called *welfarist approach*, enhancement includes therapeutic interventions, provided that they effect a subjectively and/or objectively evaluated improvement. Human enhancement comprises "[a]ny change in the biology or psychology of a person which increases the chances of leading a good life in the relevant set of circumstances" (Savulescu, Sandberg, and Kahane, 2011, 7).[9] Accordingly, which interventions count as enhancement depends not least on the underlying theory of the good life. Since there is no conceptual consensus on this matter, the definition does not lead to a distinct notion of enhancement. Moreover, it can only be determined ex post if an intervention is actually conducive to leading a good life. Thus, the intervention cannot be classified as enhancement unless it has actually proven to be beneficial.[10] To this effect, Zohny (2019, 267) notes that an intervention

> can account for moral enhancement only when it tends to be beneficial to the interests of the person undergoing that moral enhancement. If a moral improvement leaves a person with better moral motives but simultaneously reduces how well their life goes overall, then according to a welfarist account of enhancement they have not been enhanced in any sense.

Finally, if everything that actually contributes to leading a good life counts as enhancement, the definition obviously loses any discriminatory power. Such an estimation leaves no room for ethical critique.[11]

20.4.3 Moral enhancement and the notion of morality

While one obstacle to agreement on the meaning and prospects of moral bioenhancement stems from the heterogeneous definitions of enhancement, another problem arises due to controversy regarding the right notion of morality. Inmaculada de Melo-Martin and Arleen Salles assert that "[w]hether one believes that moral bioenhancement is a possible solution to the problems that befall humanity depends in great part on how one conceives of morality" (de Melo-Martin and Salles, 2015, 224). There are competing assumptions regarding which properties and capacities are morally relevant and suitable target points for moral bioenhancement. While Persson and Savulescu suggest moral improvement by means of reinforcing pro-social feelings and attitudes like empathy, fairness, and altruism (cf. also Jebari, 2014), Harris, on the other hand, considers only rational capacities as morally relevant. Therefore, he is convinced that only cognitive enhancement comes into consideration as moral enhancement:

> Rather than tinkering with chemicals or molecules that influence attitudes and emotions, I would recommend that the most effective and ethical moral enhancer so far available is learning to subject emotional reactions to the scrutiny of reason. [...] I take moral enhancement to involve enhancing our ability to think ethically (cognitive enhancement).
>
> *(Harris, 2014b, 373)*

Sarah Chan and John Harris suggest that enhancing empathy and pro-social attitudes could possibly even entail immoral and anti-social behavior (Chan and Harris, 2011, 131). Harris (2011, 105) argues that a reasonable degree of negative reactive attitudes is often appropriate and considers it dangerous to impair the capacity to react adequately to injustice and violence. Wasserman (2014) even argues that individual moral flaws frequently entail benefits for the common good, because "all complex societies have a division of labour in which some roles call for characteristics that most of us would regard as moral defects" (ibid., 374).

Harris emphasizes another point that concerns the relational structure and social dimension of morality, due to which it appears unpromising to address "complex philosophical, ethical, legal, and social questions" (Harris, 2014a, 253) by means of neuroscientific or evolutionary psychological findings.[12] Studies on neural mechanisms, chemical transmitters, and pro-social motives, according to Harris, add nothing to the understanding of morality. Morality, or so one could argue referring to Hilary Putnam (1975), "just ain't in the head." Accordingly, one can infer that influencing morality via the modification of individual brain chemistry is at least a questionable endeavor (Wiseman, 2016). This critique also (partly) concerns Douglas' definition of moral enhancement which he takes to be compatible with every reasonable moral theory and which focuses on a person's moral motives: "A person morally enhances herself if she alters herself in a way that may reasonably be expected to result in her having morally better future motives, taken in sum, than she would otherwise have had" (Douglas, 2008, 229). According to Douglas, motives are "psychological – mental or neural – states or processes that will, given the absence of opposing motives, cause a person to act" (ibid.). Moral enhancement, Douglas explains, alters a whole set of motives of the person and can be accomplished both by traditional means like education[13] and by biotechnical means. However, the assumption that altering motives – particularly by sidestepping cognitive capacities – accounts for moral enhancement has been questioned: "[O]nly by presuming that increasing moral motivation guarantees some enhancement to moral conduct [...] can enhancement of motives be taken as a reliable way to enhance morality" (Shook, 2012, 5).

As already mentioned, there is disagreement about the question of whether improvement of moral *judgment* or moral *conduct* should be the target of moral enhancement. David DeGrazia (2014, 362 f.) suggests a threefold classification of moral enhancement: "motivational improvement," "improved insight," and "behavioral improvement." According to DeGrazia, the third option, the improvement of moral behavior, would be "highly desirable in the interest of making the world a better place and securing better lives for human beings and other sentient beings" (ibid., 363; original emphasis removed). In contrast, Harris (2012, 2013a, 172) concentrates primarily on moral *judgment* instead of moral conduct. These rival assumptions refer to different levels of argumentation: a *theoretical* and a *practical* level. Improvement of rational judgment could be seen as merely ameliorating the capacity for ethical reflection and argumentation, without necessarily entailing improvement of moral personality or action (Raus et al., 2014, 269). Accordingly, such an improvement could be seen as an *ethical* enhancement rather than a *moral* enhancement (Shook, 2012, 8).

In sum, controversial (and narrow)[14] concepts of morality which are referred to in the debate impede a consistent understanding of moral enhancement. To this effect, Raus et al. (2014, 263) assert that it is "far from clear what precisely constitutes moral enhancement."

20.4.4 Moral enhancement and freedom

One last obstacle to moral bioenhancement that we want to address is a noted objection regarding a possible restriction of freedom which has been repeatedly brought forward by John Harris (2011, 2013, 2014b; cf. also Kaebnick, 2016, 228 ff.; Rakić, 2017). There has been controversy concerning the question of which kind of freedom is at stake: *freedom of the will*, *personal autonomy*, or *political liberty*. In the meantime, the debate has mainly shifted toward the latter two notions.

In reaction to Harris' paper "Moral Enhancement and Freedom" (Harris, 2011), in which he argues that moral bioenhancement should be refused because it undermines freedom of will, Savulescu and Persson introduced the thought experiment of the "God Machine"[15] (Savulescu and

Persson, 2012) in order to clarify their line of argument. The God Machine eliminates any immoral motivation without the person being aware of this intervention and thus makes voluntary immoral action impossible. Savulescu and Persson argue that this does not amount to a loss of desirable freedom and emphasize the positive consequences of such an intervention. In contrast, Harris (2014a, 253) does not regard the God Machine as a helpful thought experiment, but rather "a rhetorical device that seeks to persuade us that, seen in this light, things are not so bad. But they are!" Contrary to Savulescu and Persson's claim, he holds on to the primacy of freedom and argues that free choice is a necessary condition for responsible moral action. In order to clarify his position, Harris explains in a reply to DeGrazia (2014) that he is not concerned with the respective merits of a libertarian or compatibilist theory of freedom of the will. For him, debating these topics is "just smoke and mirrors" (Harris, 2014b, 372). Instead, he is concerned with a "common or garden freedom" (ibid.) and admits by the way that "some version of compatibilism is probably right" (ibid.).

However, from a compatibilist perspective, it is suggested that freedom can be understood in terms of *personal autonomy*. Referring to Frankfurt (1971), autonomy can, in a nutshell, be conceived of as a state of absence of insurmountable internal compulsion with which the person cannot positively identify (DeGrazia, 2014, 366).[16] As for the example of the God Machine, even if the person *actually* does not have the possibility to act immorally, this does not necessarily impair her autonomy, as long as the resulting moral action corresponds with her moral beliefs and dispositions – in short: with her moral personality. The philosophical problem underlying this understanding of autonomy obviously consists in providing a plausible account of *authenticity*, one of the conditions for personal autonomy (Bublitz and Merkel, 2009). However, disagreement remains on whether "[m]oral compulsion undermines free will" (Simkulet, 2012, 18) and whether the "freedom to fall" (Harris, 2011, 110) is a necessary condition for personal autonomy, which Persson and Savulescu (2012), Douglas (2013, 165 f.) and DeGrazia (2014, 366) explicitly deny.

Of more practical relevance than discussions about metaphysical conditions of freedom of the will and autonomy is Persson and Savulescu's suggestion of mandatory moral bioenhancement (Persson and Savulescu, 2008, 174, 2012, 2019b).[17] Due to the precarious global situation, they advocate constraints of liberal rights for the greater public good. Thus, the debate raises questions from the realm of political philosophy and law. Robert Sparrow (2014) notes that moral bioenhancement which, in Persson and Savulescu's version, he deems perfectionist and elitist (ibid., 23) is not compatible with egalitarian and liberal principles of democracy. He assumes that only comprehensive and compulsory moral bioenhancement would actually be effective (ibid., 21). However, even in this case, probably not all members of society would reach the same level of moral capacities (ibid., 23). Given such a situation, there is the danger that the morally "best" enhanced members of society could – along the lines of an ideal Platonic state – disproportionately gain participatory rights and political power (ibid., 24). If, however, the project of moral bioenhancement turns out to be utopian – which Sparrow assumes – there is the danger that pseudo-scientific evidence in combination with wishful thinking could lend political power to persons who only *pretend* to be morally better than the rest of society and, in the worst case, deliberately abuse their status as seemingly morally "enhanced" for gaining and retaining political power (ibid., 26). Finally, Sparrow assumes that the debate on moral bioenhancement could already have a detrimental impact on the wider public, in that dubious sociobiological and gene-deterministic opinions about morality get reinforced, while trust in the effect of education and social reform gets undermined (ibid., 26 f.).

In their reply to Sparrow's concerns, Persson and Savulescu (2014a) object to all these criticisms and insinuate that Sparrow "displays a fetish about egalitarianism and labors under a prescientific understanding of the relationship between the brain and moral behavior" (ibid., 39). From this heated dispute, it becomes obvious that, besides personal autonomy, political liberty is the relevant notion of freedom for further debate on moral (bio-)enhancement. Vojin Rakić (2014b) argues that the "solution to Sparrow's concerns" consists of *voluntary* moral enhancement. However, which reason should someone have to enhance themselves morally, unless assuming that being a morally virtuous person is a necessary condition of (or at least conducive to) leading a good life (Rakić, 2018)? And even under this assumption, is there a way to prevent possible risks and side effects of pharmaceutical and/or biotechnical moral enhancement? Fortunately, there is. Presumably, the easiest and most up-to-date way to convince people of trying to improve their moral capacities is to provide them with some fancy, smart digital tool.

20.4.5 Moral enhancement by means of artificial intelligence

In reaction to manifold critique of moral bioenhancement, Alberto Giubilini and Julian Savulescu have proposed a less invasive option for moral enhancement which, according to their estimation, "takes conservatives' objections to human bioenhancement seriously" (Giubilini and Savulescu, 2018, 169). They term this option *Artificial Moral Advisor* (AMA). The AMA is "a form of moral artificial intelligence that could be used to improve human moral decision-making" (ibid.). Why should there be a need for such a moral assistant? The underlying assumption is

> a simple truth about humans: we are often incapable of making choices consistent with our own moral goals[.] […] [E]motive and intuitive judgments often replace information collection, reflection, and calculation […]. In short, we are suboptimal information processors, moral judges, and moral agents.
>
> *(ibid., 170)*

The authors give an example of a situation in which an AMA could be useful:

> You might be committed to social justice, or to alleviating animal suffering. So you might want to buy authentically fair trade products, or genuinely free range eggs. But when you are at the supermarket shelf, you do not have the time and the mental resources to gather and process all the information you would need in order to choose consistently with your principles. You might buy products based on the images or colors on the packaging, but again your choice would often fall short of your own moral standard
>
> *(ibid.).*

In such a situation, the AMA could give advice regarding the morally appropriate choice. The advantage of an AMA compared to a human moral agent is that it "is disinterested, dispassionate, and consistent in its judgments" (ibid., 169). The advantage of an AMA compared to means of (compulsory) moral bioenhancement is that it can be utilized voluntarily, it is non-invasive (i.e., it functions without chemically or biotechnically tinkering with our emotions and affects),[18] and it "would take into account the human agent's own principles and values" (ibid.).

How does the AMA work? The AMA functions on the basis of software which

> is a type of artificial intelligence capable of gathering information from the environment, processing it according to certain operational criteria we provide – for example, moral criteria such as moral values, goals, and principles – and of advising on the morally best thing to do.
>
> *(ibid., 172)*

It can be tailored to the individual user's subjective moral standards.

> The AMA could ask the agent a set of questions about what the agent considers morally appropriate in different circumstances, memorize and elaborate these answers, and work

out a set of moral rules that are appropriate for that agent, which could be used to provide personalized moral advice in the future.

(ibid., 174 f.)

The AMA should be a tool that fits the liberal requirements of critics of moral bioenhancement and at the same time solves the problem of giving a unanimous account of morality, in that it "leaves the question of what counts as 'moral' to the human agent, according to his or her own values" (ibid., 175). Of course, there should be some reasonable constraints regarding the moral rules with which the AMA's self-learning algorithm is trained. To avoid misuse, such constraints should be implemented by default on the basis of suggestions from "a pool of moral experts being consulted when programming the AMA" (ibid., 177). Such a default programming should ensure that "different moral agents would then be able to use the AMA to pursue their different moral goals, thus promoting a pluralism of ethical views within reasonable moral boundaries" (ibid.).

Interestingly, at first sight, the AMA appears to provide a kind of *cognitive* moral enhancement, the kind of enhancement advocated by Harris and, as shown above, vigorously disputed by advocates of moral bioenhancement. However, on closer examination, the AMA cannot provide cognitive enhancement, strictly speaking, because it does not *improve* its users' cognitive capacities but rather *spares* its users from rational ethical reflection. Whether this function suffices to speak of moral enhancement, probably depends on particular conceptual presuppositions.

Contrary to the authors' invocation of reasonable moral pluralism, it appears that the AMA can only be considered a suitable tool for moral enhancement from a particular ethical perspective. It may be a perfect tool for utilitarians and other consequentialists. After all, by performing "information collection, reflection, and calculation" (ibid., 170) for its users, it influences their choices and actions and, accordingly, the subsequent consequences of these actions. If consequences of actions are all that matters for moral evaluation, as is the case from the perspective of utilitarian and generally consequentialist ethical theory, better outcomes – according to users' respective standards within the boundaries of default programming by moral "experts" – may account for moral enhancement of users' actions (*nota bene*: not of users themselves).

However, from a Kantian perspective, for example, it might appear odd for the moral subject to "outsource" the moral effort to an a-rational machine. Presumably, this would mean missing the very point of what it means to be an autonomous moral subject. In this respect, the claim that the AMA "would respect and indeed enhance individuals' moral autonomy" (ibid., 185) is at least in need of further clarification. One could even assume that using an AMA implies "*self-incurred immaturity*" which Kant famously introduced in "An Answer to the Question: 'What is Enlightenment?'" (Kant, 2009, 1). With just slight variations, the following quote from Kant represents cutting-edge ethics of technology:

> It is so convenient to be immature! If I have [an app] to have understanding in place of me, [an AMA] to have a conscience for me, a [digital health device] to judge my diet for me, and so on, I need not make any efforts at all. I need not think, so long as I can pay [with my personal data]; others will soon enough take the tiresome job over for me.
>
> *(ibid.)*

Likewise, from the perspective of virtue ethics, for example, it appears dubious whether a person who relies on digital advice instead of performing their acquired reflective moral know-how could be considered virtuous at all.

Apart from these considerations, it appears safe to say that the AMA is most probably not the predestined tool for avoiding "ultimate harm" (nor for making people morally better). Whether and in what sense it is a suitable means for moral enhancement remains open for discussion. Nevertheless, the AMA is an interesting practical example for discussion about the plausibility of "moral machines" in the context of philosophy and ethics of technology (Wallach and Allen, 2009). At least, this is an honorable function for a paper tiger.

20.5 Conclusion

As matters stand, neither transhumanism nor moral bioenhancement nor assistive technologies like the AMA appear to be terribly dangerous ideas. Nor are they very likely to provide "a possible solution to the problems that befall humanity" (de Melo-Martin and Salles, 2015, 224). It goes without saying that it would be highly desirable to boost humanity's rational and moral capacities in order to avoid ultimate harm, or at the very least, to use a current example, to enable human beings to engage their rational faculties to such an extent as to avoid repeatedly and negligently causing zoonoses and resulting pandemics. It is doubtful, to say the least, that moral enhancement really is the solution to problems of this kind.

Notes

1 Transhumanists actually appear to take pleasure in this characterization as, for example, indicated by the title of Stefan Lorenz Sorgner's book *Transhumanismus: "Die gefährlichste Idee der Welt"!?* (Sorgner, 2016).
2 All citations from the German originals have been translated by the authors.
3 Janina Loh (2018) differentiates between *transhumanism, technological posthumanism*, and *critical posthumanism*. She takes a critical stance towards transhumanism and technological posthumanism and classifies her own philosophical position as critical posthumanism. According to Loh, critical posthumanism "is not primarily concerned with 'the human being,' but questions traditional, mostly humanist dichotomies, like woman/man, nature/culture or subject/object, which have significantly contributed to our contemporary understanding of humanity and our world view" (Loh, 2020, 277). Critical posthumanism aims at "overcoming 'the human being' by breaking with conventional categories and their accompanying reasoning. This way, it reaches a philosophical position beyond ('post') a specific and recent substantial understanding of humanity" (ibid.).
4 "Transhumanism is a class of philosophies of life that seek the continuation and acceleration of the evolution of intelligent life beyond its currently human form and human limitations by means of science and technology" (Max More, quoted in Transhumanist FAQ).
5 Besides the question of whether existing or reasonably imaginable (bio-)technologies are suitable means to improve human nature (Dubljević and Racine, 2017), it is necessary to clarify the said concepts in the first place.
6 The debate on moral enhancement has been initiated and advanced by Thomas Douglas (cf. Douglas, 2013, 2014, 2015). Since his introduction of the topic, "there has been a shift from moral enhancement as a thought experiment to moral enhancement as practical advice" (Agar, 2019: 55).
7 For example, the debate is preoccupied with "cerebrocentric" positions in philosophy of mind, as a matter of course (cf., e.g., Earp, Douglas, and Savulescu, 2017), while persistently ignoring current accounts of situated cognition.
8 Cf. also Powell and Buchanan (2016: 254 ff.); Wasserman (2014: 375): "[W]e tend to exaggerate the role of individual moral defects in causing grave harms and underestimate the role of defective institutions." For the inevitability of moral failure of individuals under the conditions of (global) structural injustice and a proposal for coping with this circumstance by adopting an ethos of cosmopolitan responsibility, cf. Heilinger (2020).
9 The authors differentiate *human* enhancement which aims at improving a person's well-being in terms of the good life from *functional* enhancement which only refers to improving single capacities without necessarily affecting the person's overall well-being.
10 However, some authors apply the term enhancement to such an extent that it comprises only successful interventions, while others include attempts of improvement into the definition (Raus et al., 2014, 267 f.).
11 For a defence of the welfarist approach cf. Zohny (2014).
12 Cf. Crockett (2014) for a neuroscientific perspective; for a substantial critique of the alleged "moral brain," cf. Wiseman (2016).
13 DeGrazia (2014, 362) adds "explicit moral instruction, mentoring, socialization, carefully designed public policies, consciousness-raising groups, literature and other media that encourage moral ref[l]ection, and individual efforts at improvement."

14 Fabrice Jotterand (2011, 2014) points out that morality depends on *both* emotional *and* cognitive capacities and that one-sided approaches miss the point of moral improvement.
15 The God Machine is conceptualized along the lines of a famous thought experiment by Harry Frankfurt (1969).
16 Of course, Frankfurt's hierarchical internalist account has been substantially criticized, cf., e.g., Mackenzie and Stoljar (2000); Christman (2009).
17 Cf. also Savulescu's statement in Harris and Savulescu (2015, 11): "But if the intervention is very effective and safe, and uncontroversially good, we should do it compulsorily."
18 This appears to be why the authors think the AMA could smooth out bioconservative critique: The AMA "would shift the burden of proof back onto bioconservatives: they would have to show why this particular form of technological moral enhancement would be impermissible. Until then, we can say that another advantage of our proposal is that it takes some of the conservatives' objections to human bioenhancement seriously, because our artificial moral enhancement does not involve 'playing god' with human nature" (ibid., 179).

References

Ach, J. S. (2016) Gibt es eine Pflicht zur Verbesserung des Menschen? In K. P. Liessmann (Ed.). *Neue Menschen. Bilden, optimieren, perfektionieren.* Wien: Zsolnay, pp. 116–144.

Agar, N. (2014) A Question about Defining Moral Bioenhancement. *Journal of Medical Ethics* 40(6): pp. 369–370.

Agar, N. (2016) Enhancement, Mind-Uploading, and Personal Identity. In S. Clarke, J. Savulescu, C. Coady, A. Giubilini, and S. Sanyal (Eds.). *The Ethics of Human Enhancement. Understanding the Debate.* Oxford: Oxford University Press, pp. 184–197.

Agar, N. (2019) Commentary: The Implementation Ethics of Moral Enhancement. *Cambridge Quarterly of Healthcare Ethics* 28(1): pp. 55–61.

Beck, B. (2015) Conceptual and Practical Problems of Moral Enhancement. *Bioethics* 29(4): pp. 233–240.

Beck, B. (2016) Moralisches Enhancement – Philosophy Fiction oder Conditio sine qua non für die Zukunft der Menschheit? In R. Schütz, E. Hildt, and J. Hampel (Eds.). *Neuroenhancement. Interdisziplinäre Perspektiven auf eine Kontroverse.* Bielefeld: transcript, pp. 109–125.

Beck, B. (2020) The ART of Authenticity. In M. C. Kühler and V. L. Mitrović (Eds.). *Theories of the Self and Autonomy in Medical Ethics.* Cham: Springer, pp. 85–98.

Beck, B. and Stroop, B. (2015) A Biomedical Shortcut to (Fraudulent) Happiness? An Analysis of the Notions of Well-Being and Authenticity Underlying Objections to Mood Enhancement. In J. H. Søraker, J.-W. van der Rijt, J. de Boer, P.-H. Wong, and P. Brey (Eds.). *Well-Being in Contemporary Society.* Cham: Springer, pp. 115–134.

Bostrom, N. (2005) *Transhumanist Values.* https://nickbostrom.com/ethics/values.html (accessed: 17.04.2021).

Bublitz, J. C. and Merkel, R. (2009) Autonomy and Authenticity of Enhanced Personality Traits. *Bioethics* 23(6): pp. 360–374.

Chan, S. and Harris, J. (2011) Moral Enhancement and Pro-social Behaviour. *Journal of Medical Ethics* 37(3): pp. 130–131.

Christman, J. (2009) *The Politics of Persons. Individual Autonomy and Socio-historical Selves.* Cambridge: Cambridge University Press.

Clarke, S., Savulescu, J., Coady, C., Giubilini, A., and Sanyal, S. (Eds.). (2016) *The Ethics of Human Enhancement. Understanding the Debate.* Oxford: Oxford University Press.

Coady, C. A. J. (2009) Playing God. In J. Savulescu and N. Bostrom (Eds.). *Human Enhancement.* New York: Oxford University Press, pp. 155–180.

Crockett, M. J. (2014) Moral Bioenhancement: A Neuroscientific Perspective. *Journal of Medical Ethics* 40(6): pp. 370–371.

De Araujo, M. (2014) Moral Enhancement and Political Realism. *Journal of Evolution and Technology* 24(2): pp. 29–43.

DeGrazia, D. (2014) Moral Enhancement, Freedom, and What We (should) Value in Moral Behaviour. *Journal of Medical Ethics* 40(6): pp. 361–368.

De Melo-Martin, I. and Salles, A. (2015) Moral Bioenhancement: Much Ado About Nothing? *Bioethics* 29(4): pp. 223–232.

Douglas, T. (2008) Moral Enhancement. *Journal of Applied Philosophy* 25(3): pp. 228–245.

Douglas, T. (2013) Moral Enhancement Via Direct Emotion Stimulation: A Reply to John Harris. *Bioethics* 27(3): pp. 160–168.

Douglas, T. (2014) Enhancing Moral Conformity and Enhancing Moral Worth. *Neuroethics* 7(1): pp. 75–91.

Douglas, T. (2015) The Morality of Moral Neuroenhancement. In J. Clausen and N. Levy (Eds.). *Handbook of Neuroethics*. Dordrecht: Springer, pp. 1227–1249.

Dubljević, V. and Racine, E. (2017) Moral Enhancement Meets Normative and Empirical Reality: Assessing the Practical Feasibility of Moral Enhancement Neurotechnologies. *Bioethics* 31(5): pp. 338–348.

Earp, B. D., Douglas, T., and Savulescu, J. (2017) Moral Neuroenhancement. In L. S. M. Johnson and K. S. Rommelfanger (Eds.). *The Routledge Handbook of Neuroethics*. New York: Routledge, pp. 166–184.

Frankfurt, H. (1969) Alternate Possibilities and Moral Responsibility. *The Journal of Philosophy* 66(23): pp. 829–839.

Frankfurt, H. (1971) Freedom of the Will and the Concept of a Person. *The Journal of Philosophy* 68(1): pp. 5–20.

Fukuyama, F. (2002) *Our Posthuman Future. Consequences of the Biotechnology Revolution*. New York: Farrar, Straus and Giroux.

Fukuyama, F. (2004) *Transhumanism – The World's Most Dangerous Idea*. https://www.au.dk/fukuyama/boger/essay/ (accessed: 17.04.2021).

Giubilini, A. and Savulescu, J. (2018) The Artificial Moral Advisor. The "Ideal Observer" Meets Artificial Intelligence. *Philosophy & Technology* 31(2): pp. 169–188.

Habermas, J. (2003) *The Future of Human Nature*. Cambridge: Polity Press.

Harris, J. (2007) *Enhancing Evolution. The Ethical Case for Making Better People*. Princeton: Princeton University Press.

Harris, J. (2009) Enhancements Are a Moral Obligation. In J. Savulescu and N. Bostrom (Eds.). *Human Enhancement*. New York: Oxford University Press, pp. 131–154.

Harris, J. (2011) Moral Enhancement and Freedom. *Bioethics* 25(2): pp. 102–111.

Harris, J. (2012) What It's Like to Be Good. *Cambridge Quarterly of Healthcare Ethics* 21(3): pp. 293–305.

Harris, J. (2013a) 'Ethics is for Bad Guys!' Putting the 'Moral' into Moral Enhancement. *Bioethics* 27(3): pp. 169–173.

Harris, J. (2013b) Moral Progress and Moral Enhancement. *Bioethics* 27(5): pp. 285–290.

Harris, J. (2014a) ."..How Narrow the Straight!" The God Machine and the Spirit of Liberty. *Cambridge Quarterly of Healthcare Ethics* 23(3): pp. 247–260.

Harris, J. (2014b) Taking Liberties with Free Fall. *Journal of Medical Ethics* 40(6): pp. 371–374.

Harris, J. and Savulescu, J. (2015) A Debate About Moral Enhancement. *Cambridge Quarterly of Healthcare Ethics* 24(1): pp. 8–22.

Heilinger, J.-C. (2020) *Cosmopolitan Responsibility. Global Injustice, Relational Equality, and Individual Agency*. Berlin: de Gruyter.

Heßler, M. and Liggieri, K. (Eds.). (2020) *Technikanthropologie. Handbuch für Wissenschaft und Studium*. Baden-Baden: Nomos.

Jebari, K. (2014) What to Enhance: Behaviour, Emotion or Disposition? *Neuroethics* 7(3): pp. 253–261.

Jonas, H. (1979) *Das Prinzip Verantwortung. Versuch einer Ethik für die technologische Zivilisation*. Frankfurt am Main: Insel Verlag.

Jotterand, F. (2011) "Virtue Engineering" and Moral Agency: Will Post-Humans Still Need the Virtues? *AJOB Neuroscience* 2(4): pp. 3–9.

Jotterand, F. (2014) Questioning the Moral Enhancement Project. *American Journal of Bioethics* 14(4): pp. 1–3.

Juengst, E. T. (1998) What Does Enhancement Mean? In E. Parens (Ed.). *Enhancing Human Traits. Ethical and Social Implications*. Washington, DC: Georgetown University Press, pp. 29–47.

Kaebnick, G. E. (2016) Moral Enhancement, Enhancement, and Sentiment. In S. Clarke, Savulescu, J., C. Coady, A. Giubilini, and S. Sanyal (Eds.). *The Ethics of Human Enhancement. Understanding the Debate*. Oxford: Oxford University Press, pp. 225–238.

Kant, I. (2009) *An Answer to the Question: 'What is Enlightenment?'*, translated by H. B. Nisbet. London: Penguin Books.

Loh, J. (2018) *Trans- und Posthumanismus zur Einführung*. Hamburg: Junius.

Loh, J. (2020) Transhumanismus und technologischer Posthumanismus. In M. Heßler and K. Liggieri (Eds.). *Technikanthropologie. Handbuch für Wissenschaft und Studium*. Baden-Baden: Nomos, pp. 277–282.

Mackenzie, C. and Stoljar, N. (2000) *Relational Autonomy. Feminist Perspectives on Autonomy, Agency, and the Social Self*. New York: Oxford University Press.

Mill, J. S. (1874) *Three Essays On Religion – Nature, The Utility of Religion And Theism*, 3rd ed. London: Longmans Green Reader And Dyer.

Mordacci, R. (2011) Intergenerational Justice and Lifespan Extension. In J. Savulescu, R. ter Meulen, and G. Kahane (Eds.). *Enhancing Human Capacities*. Oxford: Wiley-Blackwell, pp. 410–420.

Parens, E. (2005) Authenticity and Ambivalence. Towards Understanding the Enhancement Debate. *Hastings Center Report* 35(3): pp. 34–41.

Persson, I. and Savulescu, J. (2008) The Perils of Cognitive Enhancement and the Urgent Imperative to Enhance the Moral Character of Humanity. *Journal of Applied Philosophy* 25(3): pp. 162–177.

Persson, I. and Savulescu, J. (2010) Moral Transhumanism. *Journal of Medicine and Philosophy* 35(6): pp. 656–659.

Persson, I. and Savulescu, J. (2011) Unfit for the Future? Human Nature, Scientific Progress, and the Need for Moral Enhancement. In J. Savulescu, R. ter Meulen, and G. Kahane (Eds.). *Enhancing Human Capacities.* Oxford: Wiley-Blackwell, pp. 486–500.

Persson, I. and Savulescu, J. (2012) *Unfit for the Future. The Need for Moral Enhancement.* Oxford: Oxford University Press.

Persson, I. and Savulescu, J. (2013) Getting Moral Enhancement Right: The Desirability of Moral Bioenhancement. *Bioethics* 27(3): pp. 124–131.

Persson, I. and Savulescu, J. (2014a) Against Fetishism About Egalitarianism and in Defense of Cautious Moral Bioenhancement. *American Journal of Bioethics* 14(4): pp. 39–42.

Persson, I. and Savulescu, J. (2014b) Should Moral Bioenhancement be Compulsory? Reply to Vojin Rakic. *Journal of Medical Ethics* 40(4): pp. 251–252.

Persson, I. and Savulescu, J. (2015) The Art of Misunderstanding Moral Bioenhancement. *Cambridge Quarterly of Healthcare Ethics* 24(1): pp. 48–57.

Persson, I. and Savulescu, J. (2017) Moral Hard-Wiring and Moral Enhancement. *Bioethics* 31(4): pp. 286–295.

Persson, I. and Savulescu, J. (2019a) The Evolution of Moral Progress and Biomedical Moral Enhancement. *Bioethics* 33(7): pp. 814–819.

Persson, I. and Savulescu, J. (2019b) The Duty to be Morally Enhanced. *Topoi* 38(1): pp. 7–14.

Powell, R. and Buchanan, A. (2016) The Evolution of Moral Enhancement. In S. Clarke, J. Savulescu, C. Coady, A. Giubilini, and S. Sanyal (Eds.). *The Ethics of Human Enhancement. Understanding the Debate.* Oxford: Oxford University Press, pp. 239–260.

President's Council on Bioethics (2003) *Beyond Therapy. Biotechnology and the Pursuit of Happiness.* New York: Dana Press.

Putnam, H. (1975) The Meaning of "Meaning". *Minnesota Studies in the Philosophy of Science* 7: pp. 131–193.

Rakić, V. (2014a) Voluntary Moral Enhancement and the Survival-at-any-cost Bias. *Journal of Medical Ethics* 40(4): pp. 246–250.

Rakić, V. (2014b) Voluntary Moral Bioenhancement Is a Solution to Sparrow's Concerns. *American Journal of Bioethics* 14(4): pp. 37–38.

Rakić, V. (2017) The Issues of Freedom and Happiness in Moral Bioenhancement: Continuing the Debate With a Reply to Harris Wiseman. *Bioethical Inquiry* 14(4): pp. 469–474.

Rakić, V. (2018) Incentivized Goodness. *Medicine, Health Care and Philosophy* 21(3): pp. 303–309.

Raus, K., Focquaert, F., Schermer, M., Specker, J., and Sterckx, S. (2014) On Defining Moral Enhancement: A Clarificatory Taxonomy. *Neuroethics* 7: pp. 263–273.

Rehmann-Sutter, C., Eilers, M., and Grüber, K. (2014) Refocusing the Enhancement Debate. In M. Eilers, K. Grüber, and C. Rehmann-Sutter (Eds.). *The Human Enhancement Debate and Disablility. New Bodies for a Better Life.* Basingstoke: Palgrave Macmillan, pp. 1–20.

Robinett, W. (2003) The Consequences of Fully Understanding the Brain. In M. C. Roco and W. S. Bainbridge (Eds.). *Converging Technologies for Improving Human Performance. Nanotechnology, Biotechnology, Information Technology and Cognitive Science.* Dordrecht: Springer, pp. 166–170.

Sandel, M. J. (2007) *The Case Against Perfection. Ethics in the Age of Genetic Engineering.* Cambridge, MA: Belknap Press of Harvard University Press.

Sandel, M. J. (2009) The Case Against Perfection. What's Wrong with Designer Children, Bionic Athletes, and Genetic Engineering. In J. Savulescu and N. Bostrom (Eds.). *Human Enhancement.* New York: Oxford University Press, pp. 71–89.

Savulescu, J. and Bostrom, N. (Eds.). (2009) *Human Enhancement.* New York: Oxford University Press.

Savulescu, J. and Persson, I. (2012) Moral Enhancement, Freedom, and the God Machine. *Monist* 95(3): pp. 399–421.

Savulescu, J., ter Meulen, R., and Kahane, G. (Eds.). (2011) *Enhancing Human Capacities.* Oxford: Wiley-Blackwell.

Shook, J. R. (2012) Neuroethics and the Possible Types of Moral Enhancement. *AJOB Neuroscience* 3(4): pp. 3–14.

Siep, L. (2005) Normative Aspekte des menschlichen Körpers. In K. Bayertz (Ed.). *Die menschliche Natur. Welchen und wie viel Wert hat sie?* Paderborn: mentis, pp. 157–173.

Simkulet, W. (2012) On Moral Enhancement. *AJOB Neuroscience* 3(4): pp. 17–18.

Sorgner, S. L. (2016) *Transhumanismus: „Die gefährlichste Idee der Welt"!?* Freiburg im Breisgau: Herder.

Sparrow, R. (2014) Egalitarianism and Moral Bioenhancement. *American Journal of Bioethics* 14(4): pp. 20–28.

Specker, J., Focquaert, F., Raus, K., Sterckx, S., and Schermer, M. (2014) The Ethical Desirability of Moral Bioenhancement: A Review of Reasons. *BMC Medical Ethics* 15: pp. 67. doi: 10.1186/1472-6939-15-67.

Transhumanist Declaration. https://humanityplus.org/transhumanism/transhumanist-declaration/ (accessed: 01.05.2021).

Transhumanist FAQ. https://humanityplus.org/transhumanism/transhumanist-faq/ (accessed: 01.05.2021).

Wallach, W. and Allen, C. (2009) *Moral Machines. Teaching Robots Right from Wrong*. New York: Oxford University Press.

Wasserman, D. (2014) When Bad People Do Good Things: Will Moral Enhancement Make the World a Better Place? *Journal of Medical Ethics* 40(6): pp. 374–375.

Weckert, J. (2016) Playing God: What is the Problem? In S. Clarke, J. Savulescu, C. Coady, A. Giubilini, and S. Sanyal (Eds.). *The Ethics of Human Enhancement. Understanding the Debate*. Oxford: Oxford University Press, pp. 87–99.

Wiseman, H. (2016) *The Myth of the Moral Brain. The Limits of Moral Enhancement*. Cambridge, MA: MIT Press.

Zohny, H. (2014) A Defence of the Welfarist Account of Enhancement. *Performance Enhancement & Health* 3(3–4): pp. 123–129.

Zohny, H. (2019) Moral Enhancement and the Good Life. *Medicine, Health Care and Philosophy* 22(2): pp. 267–274.

21
PROTECTING FUTURE GENERATIONS BY ENHANCING CURRENT GENERATIONS

Parker Crutchfield

21.1 Introduction

Almost all adults currently living will be dead by 2100, and the vast majority of them well before then. They will enjoy pleasures and suffer pains, be thankful and regretful, get sick, recover, then get sick and die, maybe in a hospital, maybe alone. They will get cancer and the coronavirus and have heart attacks and strokes. Much of the time between now and 2100 will be a time in which currently living adults don't exist at all. But if they do exist, much of that time will be spent suffering, not only in the physical sense but also in the more important existential sense. They will watch their children and parents and spouses and siblings die; they will struggle for resources such as adequate food and water and shelter. The die for much of this suffering has already been cast, either through genetic and social inheritance or through individual habitual behaviors. Some of this suffering will result not from individual behaviors like smoking or drinking or eating unhealthy foods or risk-taking but from behaviors that individually are nominally risky or harmful but collectively devastating. Eating meat may clog the arteries and lead to congestive heart failure, but collectively eating meat degrades the land and contributes to global warming. Consuming fossil fuels may harm an individual's lungs or other organ systems, but collectively it warms the planet. Not getting vaccinated may expose the individual to the risk of disease, but collectively it makes it more likely that infectious diseases will run rampant. Voting for poor leaders and policies may have no discernible impact on the outcome or one's well-being, but when lots of people so vote policies and customs are implemented which may harm the individual or expose them to risk.

However, plausibly most living adults will not suffer or die from the consequences of this sort of collective behavior, though many will suffer and die from things like congestive heart failure and flu. Today's adults will suffer and die from the things that ordinarily kill humans. Also plausible: today's children and the immediately descendant generations will disproportionately suffer and die from collective action. As compared to today's adults, today's children and subsequent generations will be more likely to suffer and die from the consequences of climate change, among other threats. Perhaps the food supply will be more limited and they will die of hunger, or perhaps they will be displaced and be forced to migrate to overpopulated areas. Or perhaps they will die in a natural disaster, which may become both more frequent and severe. Or they may die from the consequences of the political destabilization that results from climate change.

These paths to future generations' suffering and death will result from the collective actions and omissions of current and immediately past generations. And it's not that these paths are currently merely potential – they are already before us and are likely to only get more catastrophic, as a result of the collection of current and immediately past individuals' actions and omissions. Members of future generations will suffer and die at the hands of current generations to a greater degree than other generations suffered and died at the hands of those before them.

Given that this suffering and death will result from previous and current generations' collective action, what, if anything, is owed to future generations? And if something is owed to them, who owes it and what does it require of them? The present purpose is to offer an answer to these questions, albeit an answer that is incomplete and unconventional. My answer is, roughly, that we (currently living adults) have a moral duty to protect the well-being of future generations and can only do so by undergoing widespread enhancement of our cognitive and moral capacities. Everything that follows serves to support this claim.

The article proceeds this way: I first argue that we have a duty to protect future generations. The only way to satisfy this duty, however, is to behave in ways that are far beyond our capacity. We can't do what needs to be done to satisfy our duty to protect future generations. In particular, most people lack the self-discipline to establish and sustain the behaviors that are necessary for successful collective action. Drawing on the commonly but not universally held notion that "ought" implies "can," I then argue that we must either abandon our duty to protect or improve our skills in self-discipline. Since, as I claim, abandoning the duty to protect is much worse than enhancing our discipline, we ought to enhance our discipline so that we are able to meet our moral duty to future generations.

21.2 Duties to future generations

Examples of the duties to future generations abound. Suppose a bomb-maker, as his last act, plants a small bomb under a playground for toddlers at a city park, and sets it to go off in ten years. When it goes off, it will kill or maim anyone on the playground, which will be almost entirely toddlers who, at the time of planting, are not yet alive. Obviously, it is wrong for him to do this. There are number of reasons it might be wrong. One is that it violates a duty he, like everyone else, has toward other people – the duty to not harm others. That is, it is wrong for him to plant the bomb because it violates the duty to non-maleficence. We must all refrain from harming others, no matter their relation to us in time and space, unless the harm is justifiable, such as in self-defense. And since his act will harm others, even though they are not yet alive, it is wrong at the time of planting.

If this is why the bomb-maker's act is wrong, then it is plausible to say something similar about climate change. By continuing to eat meat, consume fossil fuels, and otherwise act in ways that change the climate, we are harming future generations. They, after all, will be harmed by these actions. Routinely eating meat and driving a gas guzzler is like helping to craft and set the bomb under the playground. Thus, if we have a duty to not harm future generations, then our current actions violate that duty. It's a plausible first step in explaining why it's wrong to ruin the environment for the next generations.

There are a few problems with this approach, however; one related to whether we have a duty to not harm future generations and others related to whether insignificant individual contributions to collective actions violate it, if we have it. The problems are familiar. First, there is at least one good reason to think that we don't have a duty to not harm future generations, and that's the non-identity problem (Boonin, 2014; Kavka, 1982; Parfit, 1986). Suppose that we pursue a policy of depleting all available resources in a way that is most convenient for us, but that this depletion will cause future generations to suffer (Parfit, 1986). Plausibly, the pursuit of this policy also affects decisions about reproduction such that if a different policy were pursued different children would be born. Thus, the people who are alive to suffer the consequences of our pursuit of resource depletion are not the same people who would be alive if we were to pursue conservation instead. This means that the people who do suffer the consequences of depletion would not have existed in other circumstances. Given that it is better to live and suffer than to not live at all, the people who suffer the consequences of depletion are better off than they otherwise would be, since otherwise they just wouldn't exist. And since they are better off than they otherwise would be, it's difficult to see how the depletion of resources harms them, because it doesn't make them worse off.

A second problem is that it's not clear how to reconcile the fact that any harms that future generations might experience result only from very many individuals and their actions, each one of which is insignificant and has no bearing on the outcome, but collectively cause it (Sinnott-Armstrong, 2005). One act, one person, doesn't affect the outcome. And if they don't affect the outcome, plausibly they have not harmed future generations by pursuing resource depletion.

There are large bodies of literature addressing these problems and that include some potential solutions. Here it suffices to note that the problems are significant enough to warrant looking elsewhere to account for our duties to future generations. The problems may not undermine the idea that we have a duty to non-maleficence to future generations, but they do make it a little less plausible.

There are other duties we might have toward future generations. Furthermore, these other duties might be able to avoid the above problems that face the alleged duty to not harm members of future generations, though this point is not one I offer a vigorous defense of. The duty to non-maleficence holds for all people – everyone has a duty to not harm others unless of course the harm is justified by other circumstances. Whether one has a duty to not harm another person is independent of the relation between the duty-bound and the right-holder. I have a duty to not harm my children and my neighbors, but I also have a duty to not harm perfect strangers, wherever and whoever they may be. But it is quite intuitive that we have some obligations by virtue of a relation we have to another person. Everyone everywhere has a duty to not harm my children. But I have additional obligations toward them that no one else has. For example, I must protect them from various risks and threats.

My duty to protect my children requires that I, for example, keep the bleach and knives inaccessible. It requires that up until a certain age I hold their hand while they cross the street. It requires that I ensure that their car seats are properly installed. It requires that I anchor tall, heavy furniture. And it requires that I do the very many other things to protect them from a wide range of risks and threats. Others do not have these duties. My neighbors have no such obligations toward my children, though they do have them toward their own. A faraway stranger has no obligation to make sure that my children safely cross the street, but they do have an obligation to not harm my children.

There are a couple of features of this duty to protect that distinguish it from the duty to not harm. The first is that the duty is violated even if there is no bad outcome. Such is not the case for the duty to non-maleficence. If I aim and shoot an arrow at a person from a distance, but miss without them any wiser to my attempt, I have not violated the duty to not harm. They are just as well off as they were before I took the shot. If they know of my attempt, then it is reasonable to think that this knowledge makes them worse off. But absent this knowledge, their life is no worse off than it was. It doesn't mean that what I did wasn't wrong, but my wrong act did not violate the duty to non-maleficence.

Note at this point that if one claims that I did violate the duty to non-maleficence, then it must be true that harm is not a matter of making a person worse off than they otherwise would have been. Some people think it is true that harm is not a matter of being worse off than they otherwise would have been, that harm is non-comparative (Harman, 2009; L. Meyer, 2003). But even on these accounts of harm, a necessary condition for a person to be harmed, and therefore for the duty to not harm to have been violated, is that the victim's well-being is somehow affected by the act. But if shooting and missing, unbeknownst to my target, violates the duty to not harm, then harming another person is not necessarily a matter of the victim's well-being. On such an account one person could harm another without affecting their well-being or, even less plausibly, harm the person but promote the person's well-being. It is far better to say that in shooting and missing I did not violate my duty to not harm my target.

The violation of the duty to non-maleficence requires that a person actually be harmed; the violation is tied in part to the outcome of the act. But there is no such tie that binds the violation of the duty to protect. Suppose I am with my child and we are crossing a busy street. As children often are, also suppose my child is disposed to dart off. When we are crossing the busy street together, I neglect to hold his hand and he darts off. Oncoming traffic swerves and misses and we both reach the other side of the street. Of course, I did not violate my duty to not harm him. After all, his well-being is unchanged. But I did violate my duty to protect him. The same would be true if I left the knives and bleach and the bow and arrow easily accessible, say, next to his bed. He may never touch them and even if he does his well-being may not be affected. But I still violate my duty to protect him.

The above examples also work to illuminate a second feature that distinguishes the duty to protect from the duty to non-maleficence. Presuming that there is a morally relevant difference between acts and omissions, the duty to non-maleficence primarily proscribes acts rather than omissions. Typically, for one person to harm another the former must *do* something such that the latter's well-being is affected. But the duty to protect proscribes both acts as well as omissions. Indeed, the duty to protect may even primarily proscribe omissions. When crossing the street or storing dangerous objects, I violate my duty to protect because of what I fail to do. The duty to protect requires that I shield my children from some things. The primary way in which I violate the duty is by failing to put up the shield.

So, we have these two characteristic features of the duty to protect: it can be violated in the absence of a bad outcome; and it proscribes (maybe even primarily) omissions as well as acts. These are not features of the duty to non-maleficence. A third difference is that everyone everywhere has a duty to not harm, and everyone everywhere holds the corresponding right against everyone else. But the duty to protect and the corresponding right only arise in the context of particular relationships. My claim is that the relation that gives rise to the duty to protect holds between members of current generations and members of future generations.

A fourth difference is that a person can have a duty to protect, even when there is no identifiable holder of the right to be protected. A ship's captain has a duty to protect her passengers. Satisfying this duty requires various preparations prior to any passenger embarking, such as ensuring that there are sufficient lifeboats and provisions and that the ship is in good working order. If she fails to make these preparations, she violates her duty to protect. She violates it regardless of whether anyone else is on board, and even whether anyone has purchased passage. Her duty is to future passengers, who may not be identifiable. There are thus some clear instances in which the duty to protect holds to future, unidentifiable individuals.

21.3 Duty to protect

There are multiple accounts of what grounds special obligations such as the duty to protect. Some think that special obligations arise out of the duty-bound self-assuming them, such as when people voluntarily participate in particular relationships (Brake, 2010). A far less common account is the vulnerability model, which Robert Goodin (1985) develops in detail. According to the vulnerability model, one person has a duty to protect another when the latter's interests and their satisfaction are vulnerable to the former's actions. A child's interests are vulnerable to the actions of their caregivers. An elderly parent's interests are vulnerable to the action of their adult children. Adult children thus have a duty to protect their elderly parents (and, arguably, the adult child never voluntarily assumes that relation). Passengers on a ship are vulnerable to the actions of the captain, so the captain has a duty to protect her passengers.

Goodin bases the vulnerability model on common sense morality; most of us recognize obligations that hold between specific individuals. Such recognition is common enough that it represents a strong objection to theories that imply there are no such obligations, such as agent-neutral utilitarianism. Apart from common sense morality, however, Goodin's argument for why we should prefer the vulnerability model to other models is that the vulnerability model can explain both the *scope* as well as the *content* of the duty to protect and other special obligations, which, according to him, other models cannot do. That is, the vulnerability model is supposed to explain who holds the obligations and to whom, and it can explain what the obligations require of the people who hold them.

Specifically, when a person has a duty to protect another person – when the person's interests are vulnerable to their actions – they must protect that person's interests. But they must only protect those interests to the extent that (a) the other person's interests are vulnerable to them and (b) as with all obligations, the extent to which one is able to do so. One implication of this account is that as vulnerability varies, so does one's duty. If you are the only person near a child drowning in a shallow pond (Singer, 1972), their interests are highly vulnerable to you, which engages a strong duty to protect those interests. But if you are far away, and there are many others in a better position to save the child, then their duty to protect is stronger than yours. Thus, the content of the duty to protect on the vulnerability model can vary by, among other factors, time and distance, as these impact vulnerability between two individuals. Children are highly vulnerable to their caregivers, and so a strong duty to protect holds between them. Elderly parents are highly vulnerable, especially emotionally, to their adult children, and so a duty to protect holds between them. The same goes for a ship's passengers and its captain.

Another implication is that one can involuntarily be obligated to protect another person's interests, as in the example of a child drowning in a shallow pond. Because engaging the duty to protect merely requires a vulnerability relation, and the vulnerability relation can be engaged whether one wants to be in such a relation, having the duty to protect another person is not necessarily a matter of one volunteering or assuming that role. This feature of the vulnerability model of the duty to protect counts in its favor, for it can easily explain why we think someone has a duty to protect another even when that role was not invited. For examples, it can account for the adult child's duty to protect their vulnerable elderly parents and for the parent's duty to protect their unplanned or unwanted children. Importantly, the vulnerability model also implies that we have a duty to protect members of future generations, even though many people currently living would not assume that role for themselves. The same may not be true for the duty to non-maleficence, for the reasons outlined above.

Whether currently living people have a duty to protect members of future generations depends on whether their interests are vulnerable to our actions (scope). What the potential duty to protect requires of us depends, in part, on the extent to which their interests are vulnerable to our actions (content).

On the one hand, it is clear that future generations will suffer because of what we do or fail to do now. Their interests and well-being will be compromised because of current generations' actions and omissions. Thus, they are clearly vulnerable to us. Since vulnerability triggers a duty to protect, current generations have a duty to protect future generations. Indeed, that current generations have a duty to protect future generations on the grounds that the latter are vulnerable to the former has some appealing features. One is that it can account for the intergenerational duty even when one doesn't invite or volunteer for it, whereas more prominent theories of how special obligations arise cannot. Another is that it doesn't necessarily get caught up in the problems that, for example, the duty to non-maleficence has.

The duty to protect may evade the non-identity problem. The duty to protect can be violated even when there is no harm, such as when the protector merely exposes the protectee to unacceptable risk. Thus, there is no need to compare future generations' well-being to how it otherwise might have been. Failing to protect someone to whom you owe protection is wrong, regardless of whether they are harmed. Thus, the duty to protect represents a way in which one can be wronged without being harmed, which is one way the non-identity problem may be avoided (Boonin, 2014).

A third feature is that it can account for how a moral duty to future generations wanes for subsequent generations. The duty to protect varies with the strength of the vulnerability relation, which varies according to, among other things, time and distance. The next generation is more vulnerable to current generations than generations hundreds of years in the future. Thus, our duty to protect the next generation is stronger than the duty to protect the generation that follows, and so on. That we owe more to the next generation than the one after that seems right, but other accounts of special obligations have a more difficult time with that intuition. For example, it is a challenge for the voluntarist to explain how the duty to protect can vary according to time and distance, or how the current generations' moral obligations toward generations in the distant future are weaker than the obligations toward the next generation.

So, on the one hand, it seems plausible that we have a duty to protect future generations and that we violate that duty by continuing the behavior that will lead to their suffering and failing to do the things that are necessary to protect them from that suffering. On the other hand, for a person to have a duty to protect another person, the latter must be vulnerable to the former. A future person is not significantly vulnerable to a person currently living. One person makes very little difference. If I were to suddenly vanish and my contributions to global warming end, there would be no discernible difference in the outcome. Future generations would still suffer from the actions and omissions of the current generations. The same is true of any particular person – an individual makes very little difference. Thus, it is hard to see how any individual has a duty to protect a future individual, on the vulnerability model.

However, future individuals are highly vulnerable to the *collection* of current individuals. Setting aside issues related to the distribution of duties across collections of individuals, the *collection* of currently living individuals has a duty to protect future generations. And whether the *collection* succeeds or fails in satisfying this duty is dependent on individual members' actions and omissions (Bowles & Gintis, 2011; Fehr & Fischbacher, 2004; Fehr & Gächter, 2000). The welfare and interests of future generations are highly vulnerable to the actions of the collection, and whether the collection satisfies its duty to protect more significantly depends on the individuals' actions and omissions. In pursuing collective action, one person who fails to cooperate can sink the whole enterprise (Bowles & Gintis, 2011), which means that in collective cooperation to secure a good (i.e., the satisfaction of the duty to protect) one person can make a difference as to whether the collection succeeds. The welfare of future individuals may not be highly sensitive to the behavior of currently living people, but the success of collective action is highly sensitive to individual behavior. Thus, future individuals' welfare and interests are indirectly vulnerable to currently living individuals, because currently living individuals can make a significant difference to the success of the collection. An individual may not have a duty to protect future generations, but an individual is critical to the success of the satisfaction of the collective's duty. Or, *we* have a duty to protect future generations, but *I* don't. Rather, *I* can make a difference as to whether the collection satisfies this duty because if I defect from cooperation, satisfying the duty is less likely.

And this is where, finally, moral enhancement takes the stage. I, and almost all other members of the collection (which has the duty to protect future individuals), am generally incapable of doing the things necessary for the collection to be successful. That is, I, and almost everyone else, am incapable of not defecting. Most people, in order to cooperate in the way necessary for the satisfaction of the collective duty to protect, need a boost, an enhancement.

21.4 Discipline and enhancement

Cooperation, or failing to defect, requires quite a lot of an individual. The person must be motivated to cooperate. The motivation itself may require the judgment that one ought not to do things that undermine future individuals' welfare and interests. This motivation and judgment are the typical targets for moral enhancement (Douglas, 2008; Harris, 2011; Jebari, 2014; Ingmar

Persson & Savulescu, 2013; Wiseman, 2016). But often ignored is a different capacity necessary for successful collective action: the discipline sufficient for *sustained* cooperation. One public defection can encourage others to defect, which amplifies throughout the collection, undermining the goal (Bowles & Gintis, 2011). Defection signals to others that success is unlikely, causing them to withhold their own contributions. Defection indicates that one's own sacrifices are likely to be wasted, causing others to withhold further contributions. Thus, for success to be possible, public defection must be eliminated, which means that public cooperation must be sustained. Not only must an individual be able to cooperate once (which requires things like the judgment that they ought to cooperate and the motivation to act on that judgment), but they must also be able to sustain that cooperation. This in turn requires extraordinary self-discipline. Few of us have the capacity to maintain the discipline required for sustained cooperation.

Consider just a few of the things that would count as a defection – public behaviors that generally contribute to global warming. Buying or eating meat, driving rather than biking or walking, buying or otherwise consuming anything made of plastic, using heat or air conditioning, and leaving your house lights on are all publicly observable behaviors that indicate to others that one is defecting from cooperation. In order to cooperate and the collection of currently living individuals to satisfy their duty to protect future generations, one needs to refrain from these behaviors and many more. Others observing one perform these behaviors undermines cooperation, as it encourages them to defect themselves.

Very few people in those areas most undermining the collective duty to protect (i.e., US, China, and Europe) have the discipline to refrain from doing these things. Most of the behaviors are well integrated into the normal routines of daily living. For the very few people who consistently refrain from these behaviors, it is important that they not slip up, and relapse into eating beef and pork, or driving, or leaving the lights on, or flying to a conference. If they do, it tells others that the goal of satisfying the collective duty to protect is less likely achieved, causing them to continue their own damaging behaviors.

Supposing that such people have the appropriate psychological arrangement of judgment and motivation; people generally don't have the self-discipline to change their behaviors so significantly or to consistently maintain that change. Regardless of the source of this lack of discipline, it is beyond most individuals' capacity to consistently refrain from these behaviors. Since consistently maintaining this discipline is necessary for the collection of currently living individuals to satisfy its duty to protect future generations, satisfying this duty to protect is not currently possible. There are other reasons to think that satisfying this duty to protect is not possible, such as the notion that cooperation in achieving the collective goal can't be sustained when one's contributions are primarily in private. Anything other than public and accurate demonstrations of cooperation is likely to undermine satisfying the duty to protect.

To be clear: I am claiming that even if a person's moral psychological state is otherwise appropriately arranged – they have the proper moral judgments, emotions, and motivations – without the discipline needed to avoid defection, the collective duty to protect will go unsatisfied. The moral enhancement literature has rightly focused on these other states, along with cognition. But all of the improved capacities that arise from such enhancements won't do anything to help future generations if they aren't coupled with the discipline to sustain and maintain the behaviors necessary for successful collective action.

Most people accept that what one is obligated to do is dependent on what one can do. Often this idea is expressed as though *ought implies can*. But the relation between "ought" and "can" may not be the implication. I have argued elsewhere that if *ought implies can* means anything that is useful, it must mean that "ought" implies (or makes probable, etc.) "deliberately can" (Scheall & Crutchfield, 2020). But "deliberately can" just means "knows enough to." Thus, *ought implies can* really means *ought implies knows enough to*. Knowledge in this case encompasses both propositional knowledge ("knows that") and skills ("knows how"). Currently living individuals lack the knowledge and skills for the collection of such people to satisfy the duty to protect. We are widely ignorant not only of what we need to do but also of how to go about behavior change and sustenance.

Given that we are not currently capable of satisfying the duty to protect, due to our ignorance and subsequent lack of discipline, if being incapable of satisfying a duty releases one from that duty, it is plausible that we don't have a duty to protect future generations. The same is true of the duty to non-maleficence. The following three claims cannot all be true: (a) we have a duty to protect future generations; (b) we are currently incapable of satisfying the duty to protect future generations; (c) *ought implies can*.

Others may wish to challenge (c). I find it plausible, however. Denying (a) is extremely costly, not only for future generations. It is costly because we intuitively owe something to future generations, and accounting for this obligation by appealing to the duty to protect seems right. It doesn't seem like it is permissible to use resources however we want, future generations be damned. Some degree of conservation *seems* obligatory, and the vulnerability model of the duty to protect is a plausible way of accounting for this obligation. However, so long as we have any obligation to future generations, and satisfying this obligation requires successful collective action, then the problem of insufficient self-discipline remains. That is, even if our duty to future generations is the duty to non-maleficence, this duty can be satisfied only if current generations have the appropriate self-discipline, which is in need of improvement.

Thus, if supporting a plausible obligation to future generations is important, the only other option is to deny (b). To deny (b) is to claim that we are currently capable of satisfying the duty to protect. But as I claimed above, the necessary behaviors are beyond our current capacities, in particular our self-discipline. To deny (b) then, what we are capable of must change. If it is going to be true that we *can* satisfy the duty to protect, then what we *can* do must be other than what it currently is. Our capacities must change if we are to satisfy any duty to protect future generations. To rescue our obligation to future generations, we must make (b) false. Until then, we are the captain of the ship who thinks that they don't need to check the lifeboats yet again.

One might believe that we can satisfy the duty to protect as we are – our capacity for discipline is adequate as it is. This claim could take two forms. One is that no intervention in our self-discipline is necessary. This needs significant defense, however. One would need to demonstrate that potential defectors (i.e., everyone) won't publicly defect; that our self-discipline to consistently maintain the behaviors necessary to protect future generations is already sufficient. It is plainly false that this is the case. As mentioned above, even the most disciplined occasionally slip up. Indeed, a common dieting recommendation is to incorporate "cheat days," days in which one can let down one's discipline. Such advice is an implicit recognition that most of us can't maintain self-discipline.

The second way one might resist the claim that we can satisfy our duty to protect only through enhancement is to claim that intervention upon our self-discipline is necessary. It just doesn't need to be a biomedical enhancement. Other interventions might work. This is a common strategy in the debate about the appropriateness of enhancement. It presumes that effective non-biomedical interventions are available. For example, we don't need moral bioenhancement to improve a person's moral psychology, because inducing the targeted states and behaviors can be accomplished with education.

I don't think in the case of moral psychology that education is sufficient; but leave that aside. In the case of enhancing self-discipline, education is insufficient. It is insufficient because (a) it's not something that is incorporated into contemporary curricula and (b) more informal methods of education are far too limited. I've spent the entirety of my education in public schools, some large and some small, and not once in any educational setting has anyone attempted, or even mentioned, ways of improving my skills in self-discipline. And I don't know of anyone who is any different. Getting through school and being a high achiever in education indeed requires some self-discipline. But no one teaches that skill – you either have it or you don't. And if you don't, it's on you to get it. The importance of the absence of developing skills in self-discipline from modern education is that we are already so far behind in the implementation of non-biomedical interventions upon self-discipline that they'll never catch up to the need. We've been shaping moral psychology with education for thousands of years and we still get it wrong. If we start on self-discipline now, and that's all we do, it will be too late. And even if it's not too late, just as there are failures in any educational subject some people will fail the curriculum in self-discipline then go out into the world and defect, dooming the ability to satisfy the duty to protect. More informal methods of education in self-discipline, such as the continued widespread dissemination of books, apps, fads, and lifehacks, will fare even worse.

Our capacity for self-discipline isn't presently enough to satisfy the duty to protect future generations. Education, the most common alternative to biomedical enhancements, isn't sufficient to enhance these capacities. If we are to satisfy our duty to protect, our self-discipline must improve. Non-biomedical means of improving it are insufficient.

Alternatively, we may satisfy our duty to protect by enhancing our self-discipline in other ways. Buchanan and Powell (2018) argue that by intervening in the broader socio-political environment it is possible to implement non-biomedical moral enhancement. For example, by preventing the conditions that give rise to immoral behavior, such as the pandemic, we can enhance moral capacities. But such a strategy is also insufficient to improve our capacity for self-discipline. One lesson from the COVID-19 pandemic is that it takes a lot of self-discipline from everyone to prevent a pandemic. The same is true for intervening in other socio-political factors. So, this strategy relies on the very skills that need enhancing, undermining its effectiveness.

Many arguments for moral enhancement recommend the improvement of some direct moral capacity, such as the capacity to make moral judgments and be motivated to act morally. Other arguments focus instead on the improvement of more general capacities, such as cognitive capacities (Agar, 2013; Ingmar Persson & Savulescu, 2013) or the hormonal and emotional foundation of moral action (Persson & Savulescu, 2014). For example, making someone smarter may cause her to make better moral judgments, or providing someone with a substance that increases empathy may make her more cooperative with members outside of her own social group.

The present argument assumes that one's broad moral capacities are up to the task of cooperation and that people understand that they ought to do the things necessary to protect future generations and then be motivated to do them. For most people, these are not true, and the extent to which people are incapable of making such judgments and being so motivated is the extent to which the argument for the necessity of moral enhancement is strengthened. But even if a person has these capacities, for them to not encourage others' defection, the person must have the self-discipline to develop and sustain these behaviors and never publicly deviate from their performance.

Behavioral change is difficult. Most attempts at it fail. Weight loss and substance abuse are notoriously resistant to change. People often succeed at changing their behaviors related to diet, exercise, sleep, and substances, but it usually takes more than one attempt to succeed, and many continue to fail to change their behavior. The behavioral change required for satisfying the duty to protect future generations would require most people to upend their normal patterns of living and re-organize everything related to their work, home, travel, education, and eating behaviors. It requires significantly more discipline than that required for someone to maintain a low-carb diet or exercise an additional two times per week. My claim is that most peoples' well of discipline is not deep enough to make and sustain these necessary behavioral changes.

21.5 Conclusion

It is beyond most currently living individuals' capacity to contribute to the satisfaction of the duty to protect future generations. Rather than excuse everyone from the obligation, it is better to change what these individuals can do. What they need to do is beyond their reach. Thus, an intervention is required. Standard interventions upon a person's attempts at behavioral change, such as education and cognitive behavioral therapy, are either obviously insufficient or inefficiently administered. Something stronger is needed. We aren't going to do it on our own.

One option is for the state to punish these behaviors such that they are extinguished. However, this intervention would be so invasive that one might wonder whether what is gained (i.e., satisfying the duty to protect) is worth the price (surrendering a great deal of liberty).

Another option is to biologically intervene in a person's self-discipline, presuming such an intervention is possible. Because the lack of self-discipline is normal, it is not pathological. Since it's not pathological, it is inaccurate to say that an intervention upon the capacity is a treatment. It would be a bioenhancement. Moreover, since it would significantly enhance our capacity to satisfy our special obligations, our duty to protect, it is a moral bioenhancement. There are no obvious candidate substances for use as such an enhancement, however. Bowles and Gintis (2011) suggest that a sense of shame is important to sustaining an individual's sustained contribution to a collective goal. Shame may also be effective in inducing behavioral change – it's certainly one that is commonly used (e.g., in changing behaviors related to smoking tobacco). Thus, a substance that increases shame may be a plausible starting point for the development of an appropriate moral bioenhancement. But shame itself is quite unpleasant. And it's possible that the lives of large groups of ashamed currently living individuals would be worse than the lives of future individuals whom we fail to protect.

I and others have written that moral bioenhancements don't require the enhanced to sacrifice much of moral value. Although state coercion at the level needed to sufficiently punish the problematic behaviors and widespread shame would arguably be too high a price, moral bioenhancements, even if compulsory or administered secretly, generally don't come with nearly as a high cost. We don't have to sacrifice liberty, autonomy, equality, or utility to be better able to satisfy our moral obligations (Crutchfield, 2021). But if we don't enhance our ability to make and sustain significant behavioral changes, we will be sacrificing the well-being of future individuals. Protecting future generations, in the absence of enhancement, is so far out of our reach that we are excused from it, freeing ourselves to eat meat, guzzle gas, blast the air conditioning, and fly to conferences with no moral qualms.

References

Agar, N. (2013). Why is it possible to enhance moral status and why doing so is wrong? *Journal of Medical Ethics*, *39*(2), 67–74. https://doi.org/10.1136/medethics-2012-100597

Boonin, D. (2014). *The Non-Identity Problem and the Ethics of Future People*. Oxford University Press.

Bowles, S., & Gintis, H. (2011). A Cooperative Species: Human Reciprocity and Its Evolution. Princeton University Press. Retrieved from https://books.google.com/books?id=dezaI9XMp0UC

Brake, E. (2010). Willing parents: A voluntarist account of parental role obligations. In D. Archard & D. Benatar (Eds.), *Procreation and Parenthood: The Ethics of Bearing and Rearing Children*. Oxford University Press.

Buchanan, A., & Powell, R. (2018). *The Evolution of Moral Progress: A Biocultural Theory*. Oxford University Press.

Crutchfield, P. (2021). *Moral Enhancement and the Public Good*. Routledge.

Douglas, T. (2008). Moral enhancement. *Journal of Applied Philosophy*, *25*(3), 228–245. https://doi.org/10.1111/j.1468-5930.2008.00412.x

Fehr, E., & Fischbacher, U. (2004). Third-party punishment and social norms. *Evolution and Human Behavior*, *25*(2), 63–87. https://doi.org/10.1016/S1090-5138(04)00005-4

Fehr, E., & Gächter, S. (2000). Cooperation and punishment in public goods experiments. *American Economic Review*, *90*(4), 980–994. https://doi.org/10.1257/aer.90.4.980

Goodin, R. (1985). *Protecting the Vulnerable: A Reanalysis of Our Social Responsibilities*. Chicago: Chicago University Press

Harman, E. (2009). Harming as causing harm. In M. A. Roberts & D. T. Wasserman (Eds.), *Harming Future Persons*. Springer Verlag.

Harris, J. (2011). Moral enhancement and freedom. *Bioethics*, *25*(2), 102–111. https://doi.org/10.1111/j.1467-8519.2010.01854.x

Jebari, K. (2014). What to enhance: Behaviour, emotion or disposition? *Neuroethics*, 7(3), 253–261. https://doi.org/10.1007/s12152-014-9204-5

Kavka, G. S. (1982). The paradox of future individuals. *Philosophy and Public Affairs*, 11(2), 93–112.

Meyer, L. (2003). Past and future. In L. H. Meyer, S. L. Paulson, & T. W. Pogge (Eds.), *Rights, Culture and the Law: Themes From the Legal and Political Philosophy of Joseph Raz*. Oxford University Press.

Parfit, D. (1986). *Reasons and Persons*. OUP Oxford. Retrieved from https://books.google.com/books?id=i5wQaJI3668C.

Persson, I., & Savulescu, J. (2014). *Unfit for the Future: The Need for Moral Enhancement*. Oxford University Press. Retrieved from http://books.google.com/books?id=EGHengEACAAJ

Persson, Ingmar, & Savulescu, J. (2013). Getting moral enhancement right: The desirability of moral bioenhancement. *Bioethics*, 27(3), 124–131. https://doi.org/10.1111/j.1467-8519.2011.01907.x

Scheall, S., & Crutchfield, P. (2020). The priority of the epistemic. *Episteme*, 1–12. https://doi.org/DOI: 10.1017/epi.2019.56

Singer, P. (1972). Famine, affluence, and morality. *Philosophy & Public Affairs*, 1(3), 229–243.

Sinnott-Armstrong, W. (2005). It's not my fault: Global warming and individual moral obligations. *Advances in the Economics of Environmental Resources*, 5, 285–307. https://doi.org/10.1016/S1569-3740(05)05013-3

Wiseman, H. (2016). *The Myth of the Moral Brain: The Limits of Moral Enhancement*. MIT Press. Retrieved from https://books.google.com/books?id=_TuQCwAAQBAJ

22
WHAT KINDS OF MORAL BIOENHANCEMENT ARE DESIRABLE? WHAT KINDS ARE POSSIBLE?

Harris Wiseman

22.1 Introduction

Moral bioenhancement (MBE, hereon) is a highly fluid term that admits many varieties and kinds. In essence, it would include the use of any technology or pharmacology on human biology in order to produce some morally-relevant effect. The targets of enhancement are generally taken to be human drives, capacities, and powers of any sort, and the ideal would be to diminish the morally problematic things persons do and to facilitate the morally good things persons do. Expressed in this broad way, MBE can be presented as a desirable mode of human enhancement worth pursuing.

Before continuing, it is worth noting the diversity of MBE discourse. In surveying the discourse, taken as a whole, it is clear that one of the problems that has dogged discussion has been an unwillingness to set out a common ground with common distinctions and definitions of MBE, leading to many commentators simply talking past one another. The reader should keep in mind that there are many types of MBE proposed, from voluntary to compulsory, with differing targets (emotions, drives, intelligence, dispositions, and more), with some definitions of MBE aspiring to affect a wide-scope of moral values, where others aim to deal with individual moral virtues and vices in a piecemeal fashion. Some view the purview of MBE as covering treatment for moral sickness, some see it as pure enhancement, and some reject the distinction altogether. In terms of plausibility and realism, MBE discourse spans the whole range of extremes, from wildly impossible future-fantastical speculation all the way to gritty, present-day realism.

Thus, confusingly, MBE is an umbrella term that contains a multitude within it. The reader should be sensitive to the presence of different modes and voices being considered here, and should keep clear in the mind that each type of MBE can be combined in different ways, with each permutation raising idiosyncratic ethical issues. What cannot be issued is some blanket assessment such as "MBE, as a whole, is bad," or "MBE per se is good." The discourse is just too varied to allow that kind of assessment.

For making some judgments however, this chapter will pose a distinction between two broad types of MBE; that is, between "realistic" MBE (which would be of an indirect, weak, and diffuse sort, and which arguably already exists) and "salvatory" MBE (which presents MBE as offering some direct and substantive potential for making concrete alterations to human moral functioning).

This chapter will outline the core claims regarding why aspects of MBE might be desirable, and the counterclaims, that aspects of MBE are something to be avoided. The chapter then reflects on the feasibility of MBE and concludes that while some limited aspects of salvatory MBE might be desirable in principle, none of it is feasible in practice. However, some highly constrained forms of realistic MBE are both possible and desirable, under certain very tight conditions, albeit at the cost of reining back one's hopes about what MBE can ever realistically achieve. Whether what remains of MBE, after one's hopes have been so reined back, constitutes anything to get excited about or even really counts as MBE is another question. However, the core insight this chapter seeks to make clear is the following: to understand what moral functioning is, and how it operates in real life, is to understand that it is just not the sort of thing that can be substantively enhanced by manipulating human biology.[1]

22.2 The case for MBE

22.2.1 "Wouldn't it be nice if …"

No matter how optimistic one's view of the human person, there is never any way of seriously holding that people could not do better, morally speaking. The number of extremely serious moral problems around the globe is sobering, from human trafficking, concentration camps, organized crime, torture, bloodshed, bigotry, hatred, corruption, and a seemingly endless list of appalling activities causing suffering still blight the world, even now, internationally and at home. The case for the desirability of MBE begins there. If one could find some way of getting people to be a little more compassionate, cooperative, and a little less hateful and destructive, then why would anyone be opposed to that?

Echoing this sort of perspective, David DeGrazia presents a list of generally agreeable moral goods and evils that, as he suggests, "any reasonable view of morality" (DeGrazia 2013, 228) should agree make worthy targets for MBE. DeGrazia's "moral anatomy" includes promoting powers such as moral imagination, compassion, cooperative qualities; and cutting away conditions such as narcissistic and antisocial personality disorders, sadistic pleasures, moral cynicism, defective empathy, xenophobia, and a general unwillingness to confront problematic aspects of the status quo (ibid.). It is hard to take issue with DeGrazia's list, though the question "how?" presents itself – the issue of how one would go about achieving such improvements through biological means is not really confronted. DeGrazia himself acknowledges that attempting to manipulate such sophisticated moral powers through biological means would be like using "an axe to mend a watch" (ibid.), though other contributors are more optimistic (e.g., Tom Douglas 2013, Conan 2020).

In effect, this first strand of MBE discourse can be thought of as expressing a wish list, mapping out a terrain of contemporary moral failings and virtues that it would be desirable to target. This, in itself, is valuable. As a wholly "in principle" argument, this portion of MBE discourse simply poses a way of opening the door for moral discussion. What is being asserted is little more than the following: should it be *possible*, *effective*, and *safe*, then MBE is something that might be worth considering, given the nature of human moral failings, given the serious moral problems blighting the world.

22.2.2 "Enhance or die"

Beyond this, MBE discourse takes a more sinister turn. It is one thing to state that moral functioning could benefit from some improvement. However, discussion turns quickly to the proposition that human nature is profoundly defective, or at least, not at all fit for purpose (supposing human survival, lived with a basic level of wellbeing, is the purpose), and needs to be transformed by biomedical means, with the utmost urgency, using compulsion, for the sake of human survival. The idea in this "ultimate harm" strand of the discourse is that humans are not sufficiently evolved to responsibly handle the technology they have developed, and that human intellect far outstrips its moral capacities (Persson and Savulescu 2008, 2012; Savulescu 2009, 2013; Crutchfield 2019). Natural evolution, so the argument goes, has not fitted human creatures to function in a fast-paced, globally interconnected world rife with value- and resource-conflicts.[2] If moral evolution is just too slow a process to be left to its own devices (Araujo Fabiano, 2018), then some technological shove is needed to get humans up to the point of being responsible enough to handle the pollution-generating and world-annihilating technologies we have devised. MBE is presented as the solution.

The claim here is, in essence, that humanity is about to self-destruct, and must, quite literally, enhance or die. On this basis, advocates suggest that the entire human race be compelled to undergo MBE (were it to be safe and effective), before the living conditions on the planet become so dire that no worthwhile standard of life remains.

Some aspects of the argument do have merit. It is hard to deny that human intellect far outstrips human wisdom, or that humanity is in a very precarious ecological and technological situation. Humans have been bright enough to devise how to split the atom, create plastics and engineer chemical weapons, but do not always use our faculties and material inventions as beneficently as we might. However, by the admission of those advancing ultimate harm arguments, no such MBE exists to prevent such a disaster, and nothing that would even remotely fit the bill is anywhere on the cards. On the one hand, MBE is presented as being of the utmost urgency, of world-salvatory significance. On the other hand, advocates recognize that nothing able to do the job is even on the horizon. As Persson and Savulescu themselves state:

> A moral enhancement of the magnitude required to ensure that this [ultimate harm] will not happen is not scientifically possible at present and is not likely to be possible in the near future.
>
> *(Persson and Savulescu 2008, 174)*

So, why advance the argument in the first place? In effect, the ultimate harm rationale is built on hot air. As with DeGrazia's list of moral goods to be enhanced, the ultimate harm argument is just an "in principle" statement that: *if* it were possible to create a safe and effective means of enhancing humanity, then everyone in the entire world should be forced to undergo such enhancement. The argument is a purely theoretical cost/benefit analysis weighing some abstract notion of compulsory global enhancement against the prospect of no worthwhile standard of life existing on planet Earth. The judgment here is as Araujo Fabiano puts it: "if it helps us prevent nuclear war, then it's worth it" (2018). Yet, without stipulating what exactly this world-saving "it" consists in (particularly when recognizing that no such MBE is on the cards), then it is hard to make any real sense of the argument.

22.2.3 "Free to enhance"

Another rationale for MBE is libertarian. If one wanted to enhance oneself morally, on what grounds would a government have the right to prevent this? A chief advocate of this "virtue engineering" position (the term which predates MBE) is James Hughes (2004, 2006, 2012a, 2012b). For Hughes, the drive to moral improvement, just as with any human power, is part of a larger human need to self-improve, to extend and develop human capacities. This argument is part of the expanded posthuman worldview, which sees human enhancement as having started out tens of thousands of years ago, with the invention of tools to augment human powers, a trend which has continued uninterruptedly since then.

For Hughes, the enhancement of moral functioning is all part of this larger drive to self-improve, and he notes a series of long-standing spiritual "technologies" that humans have employed throughout the ages for moral and religious purposes, from fasting to meditation and prayer, and use of hallucinogenic drugs. In short: moral enhancement is something humans have always sought to do, and modern technologies are just the most recent tools one has to hand for achieving these primeval goals.

Hughes' libertarian account presents MBE as a democratically grounded activity, a free choice to select and improve the moral values one considers to be worthwhile, so long as these fit within the bounds of a broadly pluralistic, liberal-democratic political framework. A desirable MBE would be, for Hughes, entirely elective and wholly self-directed.

Hughes' rationale for a desirable MBE has two key facets:

First, a desirable MBE must be dynamic, flexible, and contextually-responsive (i.e., there is a high burden MBE must meet before counting as something desirable at all). Hughes uses happiness as an analogy: what matters in happiness, as with moral living, is the manner in which it authentically responds to its context. Anything providing a mindless, drug-induced, completely static mental state would neither be happiness, nor a moral life, worthy of the name. In short: any sort of technological sledgehammer which merely overrides human functioning, that does not contribute to the wise and mindful application of virtue, is not a desirable moral bioenhancement.

Second, Hughes emphasizes the political embeddedness of MBE. This is a key insight. While all MBE enthusiasts recognize that some constraints must be placed on MBE, Hughes shows that worthwhile MBE has a broader social context, beyond the intervention itself, namely, the political atmosphere in which MBE is deployed. Hughes stipulates that MBE must be a *democratic* option in a democratically pluralistic political milieu. If MBE were going to present any danger, it would be in a totalitarian context, an oppressive, morally-narrow political regime with a very constrained view of what counts as right and wrong, being ready to demand of its citizens absolute adherence to some inflexible moral standard.

In making clear that enhancement interventions cannot be severed from socio-political context, Hughes has made a very important point. What makes an intervention worthy is *not just the technology in itself*, but the very social milieu in which that technology is put to use. Political context is an absolutely crucial aspect of the desirability of any given MBE proposal, as it is with many new technologies. Because virtually all new technologies offer capacities to be used for good or evil, the larger social framework constitutes an important limiting (or enabling) factor in directing how new technologies are allowed to be used.

Taken together then, Hughes is saying the following: in thinking through the significance of a piece of moral biotechnology, one needs to consider both political context and the dynamic qualities of the intervention. If a moral bioenhancement is given as a free choice, fits within the wide pluralism of liberal-democratic values, and contributes to the moral intelligence of a person, then a government should not impede its use. This is a completely unique take on MBE, and it is unfortunate that MBE discourse has followed the "enhance or die" stream rather than the much more intelligent starting point that Hughes set forth when he initiated the entire discourse.

22.2.4 "Evil is a disease to be treated"

The discussion now turns from the salvatory rationales for MBE to realistic MBE. One of the classic distinctions in the broader enhancement discourse is, of course, the treatment/enhancement distinction. Applied as an MBE concern, one is invited to think about whether certain extreme behaviors (some of which might be called: *evil*) might actually constitute a biological sickness and thereby constitute apt objects for treatment. The idea that extreme moral aberration can be understood in biological terms, and thus be physiologically treated, has a disturbing psychiatric history. Indeed, if any aspect of MBE discourse has some real-world foundation, it is to be found in the extreme sledgehammer approaches that have been used for dealing with pathological behavior, primarily of aggressive and sexual forms.

One reaches controversial territory here. Should extreme immoral behavior be thought of as a literal sickness to be treated as one would treat any other physical or mental disorder? The "mad or bad?" debate has a broad psychiatric import. As with many such ethical debates, difficulties emerge in defining the gray areas between categories of acceptable social deviance, moral corruption, and genuine physiological sickness.

Addiction is a case where this element of ambiguity exists. Addictions of various kinds (illicit drugs, alcohol, gambling) are often simultaneously regarded as moral failings (failures of the will, something to be morally judged for); also, as socially damaging (bringing concerns of state intervention and the judiciary); but also, as being medically diagnosable as a neurological sickness. According to the National Institutes of Health:

> Addiction is defined as a chronic, relapsing disorder characterized by compulsive drug seeking and use despite adverse consequences. It is considered a brain disorder, because it involves functional changes to brain circuits involved in reward, stress, and self-control.
> *(NIH website 2019)*

Thus, there is a blurring and overlap between moral and medical categories which are not always easy to reconcile, and yet often hard to draw any clear, sharp lines between.

In practice, the boundaries between moral behavior and physiological or mental sickness do get blurred – pathological behavior and addiction are perfect cases in point. These are instances that show that, sometimes, medicine and morality cannot be neatly separated from one another. In such cases, one might be said to be getting a *de facto* MBE just through the act of receiving treatment. Put simply: moral values and medical definitions of disease sometimes overlap.

In actual medical practice, there is a range of definitions of what counts as a disease – these definitions vary broadly (Juengst 1998). One is used to thinking of disease as some sort of objective biological malfunction. However, while a disease can be characterized in such terms (e.g., a ruptured kidney), various diseases are also defined in statistical terms (e.g., one patient is significantly shorter, on average, than the rest of a comparative demographic at that time, so that person's diminutive stature is treated as a medical issue and the patient is given HGH).

More pertinently, sometimes diseases are defined purely in terms of social valuations and mores (e.g., menopause and mid-life hormonal changes, which are completely natural bodily processes of aging, but socially undesirable states, are then constructed as subjects of medical treatment for which hormone replacement therapy is provided). In this case, a completely natural bodily process gets treated as a disease and given a treatment (using a treatment which, ironically, makes the body sick in the objective sense – HRT does palpable harm to the body over the long term). This is purely because of a social devaluation of the aging process.

As such, the idea that medical diseases are always an objective, value-neutral, scientifically-defined category is not borne out in actual practice. There is nothing too controversial, then, in remarking that moral valuations and medical diagnoses sometimes do overlap in a range of questionable ways. Indeed, if the line between enhancement and treatment is often hard to pin down (as most commentators suggest, Daniels 2000), then medicalization – the gradual expansion of the range of medical diagnoses – becomes an important frame for thinking about MBE.

An example of how certain social mores are turned into mental health disorders will help illustrate this point. When released in 2011, the DSM-V (Diagnostic and Statistical Manual of Mental Disorders) was met with some international consternation for its blatant medicalization of a range of normal (if frowned upon) social behaviors. It was alleged that the DSM-V took a range of ordinary behaviors, which it then presented as newly "discovered" mental health conditions, which it had created simply by adding the word "disorder" as a suffix to the valuation involved. Thus, smoking became "tobacco use disorder," gambling became "gambling disorder," drug abuse became "severe substance abuse disorder," and so on (DSM-V 2011 and 2013[3]). The British Psychological Society issued a letter of rebuke, stating that the DSM-V is:

> clearly based largely on social norms, with "symptoms" that all rely on subjective judgments ... not value-free, but rather [reflecting] current normative social expectations ... Clients and the general public are negatively affected by the continued and continuous

medicalization of their natural and normal responses to their experiences … which do not reflect illnesses so much as normal individual variation.

(Allan 2011)

In this case, part of what is happening is the attribution of a medical diagnosis to a moral valuation. Therewith, a moral judgment has become a medical fact. A particular behavior is no longer a moral problem, it is a mental health disease (and this has profound implications for questions of personal responsibility and agency – if it is decided that vice is a mental health illness, then one does not bear as much, or any, moral culpability for such problems). Such a moral-medical fact is something to be treated through biomedical and pharmaceutical means. In this sense, a problematic and greedy kind of MBE is not only real but currently still in the process of expanding its remit. What begins with the gray line between extreme pathology and evil behavior, has increasingly become about diagnosing every little inconvenience and frowned upon behavior a person might show. As the discourse surrounding medicalization suggests (Braslow and Messac 2018), this is a trend that is only accelerating as time goes on.

22.3 The case against MBE

22.3.1 MBE is not desirable

It is better to discuss the potential desirability of salvatory MBE before discussing its feasibility. This is because there is such a paucity of credible proposals for how a such MBE might be brought to bear. This is highly problematic for the discourse. Ultimately, MBE positions itself in the bioethics domain and treats itself as a serious facet of medical ethics. What concrete possibilities for MBE are presented by MBE enthusiasts? Omega-3 fish oil tablets, MDMA, magic mushrooms, lithium, SSRIs, transcranial magnetic stimulation, beta-blockers, bioengineered oxytocin receptors, tubing to deliver glucose directly to the brain, positive eugenics for people with MAOH gene variants, and (perhaps unsurprisingly from the same group that brought the "enhance or die" argument) isolation and segregation of people with that said genetic variant.[4]

It is difficult to know how to respond to a discourse that says MBE is desirable, even to the point of being morally compulsory, but then presents a list of vitamin supplements, brain surgery, illicit drugs, psychopharmacological treatments for depression, bipolar disorder, and anxiety, as well as brain tubing, and Nazi-level eugenic proposals.

For reasons of scope, it is impossible to dissect here all the empirical work these proposals are built upon (see Wiseman 2016 for an extended account of why such empirical work provides an extremely weak foundation for making salvatory MBE claims). It is to be noted that the scientists actually carrying out these studies are the first to recognize the limitations of their studies, and are themselves the first to point these limitations out. However, because of the paucity of concrete MBE options, enthusiasts in the MBE domain have elected to completely disregard the limitations of the empirical studies made explicit by the scientists who carried them out. This speaks to the extreme desperation of the enthusiasts, and the complete lack of feasibility, from the outset, of salvatory MBE hopes.

It is true that there have been a range of counter-arguments presented in the discourse about why MBE would not be a desirable prospect. For example, there is the argument that one's moral freedom is a power more valuable than any possible benefits that might come from MBE, per John Harris (the "freedom to fall" argument, Harris 2011). There is also the case to be made that moral perfectionism is intrinsically problematic, particularly regarding the authoritarian strain that imposes ideas of moral perfection in ways that are repressive and very morally problematic. Ironically, moral ideologues can be the most morally dubious, even evil, characters of all (for example, the Islamic State, the Taliban, or the Spanish Inquisition). Persons, institutions, and countries on a moral crusade usually operate under an "I am right, you are wrong, that's all there is to it"-type mentality that justifies any kind of violence in the name of its moral crusade.

There is also the case to be made that MBE could stultify moral progress by "locking in" current moral values rather than allowing human moral sensibility to naturally develop in response to societal changes and needs. Thus, MBE could then actually impede moral progress. It has been argued that MBE could pose a threat to the diversity of moral values (Jotterand 2014), locking in and narrowing one's moral vision. As John Mackie once quipped: "if human genetic engineering had been available in Victorian times, people might have designed their children to be patriotic and pious" (in Miah 2008, 1).

One might also say that there is something dehumanizing about MBE. Thinking of moral issues as biological defects and regarding persons as mechanical devices whose moral errancy is nothing more than a technical problem serves to reduce the human person to the level of machines (Wiseman 2018). The immoral person is treated as a mechanical object needing to be fixed by technicians who have the right schematic know-how. Such mechanistic bioreduction of morality would increasingly remove any sense of personal agency or responsibility in moral activity, and this could be psychologically and socially disastrous.

Moreover, there is the case to be made that MBE is grossly insulting to the individuals and groups who have striven (and still strive) to make social progress against moral failings in societies around the world. Population-level moral changes are very hard-won and very costly. Yet, instead of offering some profitable intellectual analysis of real-world problems, or instead of offering some concrete potential solutions, MBE misdirects attention toward some Sugarcandy Mountain of implausible techno-fantasies and magic bullet fixes for entrenched social problems.[5] This does an insulting disservice to the costliness of genuine moral change (Wiseman 2018). Moreover, there is something highly individualistic about MBE discourse – it treats moral problems as purely personal issues when most of the world's most pressing problems need extremely subtle and complicated collaborative action not readily captured in individual pharmacological terms.

MBE enthusiasm, in a word, grossly misrepresents the real multi-level cooperative action that is still urgently needed for the benefit of the environment and human world. In the face of such urgent real-world problems, misdirecting attention into techno-fantasies, like suggesting that public servants should be legally compelled to take Omega-3 fish oil supplements and lithium to make them less racist (Conan 2020), is simply beyond the pale. These sorts of claims show just how out of touch with reality many of the MBE enthusiasts are. Yet, that is the general standard of much MBE enthusiasm, and Conan's claim is not even the most ridiculous to be found in the discourse.[6]

Lastly, in all seriousness, there is a case to be made for saying that salvatory MBE is undesirable because, actually, a bit of immorality is sometimes an ingredient in what makes life worth living. Put differently, extreme saintly behavior is not always good for one's wellbeing, not always indicative of a life well lived. Salvatory MBE can speak to a sinister moral perfectionism, a crushing kind of excessively moralistic meanness that can suck all the joy out of life and which can be the bane of everything enjoyable, healthy, and interesting in the human character. Frankly, such MBE is to be avoided at all costs.

22.3.2 Ought implies can

As a thought experiment, MBE discourse is certainly interesting. Such discourse helps one plumb the idea of what really matters in moral living. However, MBE considers itself to be a serious branch of bioethics – *practical* ethics, concerned with issues raised by emerging technologies. MBE papers are overwhelmingly published in bioethical and medical ethics journals. Yet, if there is nothing concrete in salvatory MBE, if there is no substance to any of the MBE proposals, no concrete measures that raise some genuine ethical concern in the real world, then MBE is of no bioethical concern, it is nothing more than fantastical speculation.

As far as criticism of salvatory MBE goes, a more interesting case is formed by focusing on its lack of feasibility. MBE is not feasible in at least three senses:

a) There is no clear mapping of morality and biology, so biology is just the wrong means of approaching moral functioning to begin with.
b) There is no moral good outside of a context, and MBE could not possibly respond to a sufficient range of contexts in an adequately dynamic way.
c) The logistics of MBE are completely impractical, necessitating the creation of either lifelong drug users across the whole population, and/or subjecting every man, woman and child to brain surgery, or regular brain stimulation.

In the final sections, it will be argued that these practical realities suggest that there is very little to fear, or hope, in salvatory MBE. There can be no MBE so strong as to take away human freedom. There can be no MBE so strong as to lock in a certain set of values. There can be no MBE that prevents people from setting off nuclear bombs or ruining the environment. Such hopes and fears are all far outside the scope of what a realistic MBE might plausibly achieve.

22.3.3 Context

Context poses a range of problems for MBE intervention. Simply put: what is morally good in one context can be morally problematic in another. Mercy is a clear example of how context in part constitutes what makes for moral goods, the manner in which some moral goods stand in a necessary relation to others. Mercy, if shown in the right circumstances, shows excellence of character. However, when a parole board, for example, is considering the case of a sadistic, predatory sex offender, questions of mercy become more problematic. Mercy is not good in and of itself, and it does not have some unique definition or singular expression through which it can be wisely deployed. Depending on context, mercy takes different meanings and different forms, and sometimes needs to be withheld.

Moreover, different moral traits are sometimes in conflict. In the case of the parole board, one finds a range of conflicting moral pressures: mercy and the demands of justice are often in tension, as are the balance of compassion for the victims and the duty of care for the community at large. MBE enthusiasts would like to enhance all of these traits, mercy, compassion, and care. But, if these moral goods are stood in tension, with one or other moral good needing to be withheld with respect to another, then the idea of improving moral living by enhancing moral goods starts to come apart. So many of the problems of moral living involve moral conflicts between the genuine moral claims of different parties. Where moral values stand in tension, one cannot make any easy appeal to enhancement – which value is one to enhance, and in which conflict, at which time and in which place?

Context generates more and more problems for MBE. Justice, to illustrate, is not a unitary concept. Justice, in the context of international relations, is completely different to justice in the household, which is completely different to justice in the courtroom, which is completely different to distributive justice, and so on. Depending on one's situation, completely different senses of justice are called for. More significantly, there is constant disagreement as to what exactly constitutes a just outcome to a situation. Even if one person's definition of justice could be enhanced, how one would respond to a group who had a different idea of what justice demands, that made alternative moral claims?

A large measure of enhancement, then, could be in the eye of the beholder. *Which* justice is one to enhance? And whose definition of that form of justice is the one to privilege? Is one to have a new drug for each kind of justice? How many drugs would one need to take in order to become a roundly just person? Taking the point further, how many additional drugs would one need to become a compassionate person, with all the competing kinds of compassion demanded by all the possible range of daily circumstances? How many additional drugs are needed to make one less morally cynical, more morally imaginative? Would one need a new drug for every moral trait and moral failing? And for every context? Quickly, the discussion becomes farcical.

Context throws up more and more problems. As Aristotle noted, in addition to having a right time and place, all goods also have their right intensity. There is a "too much" and a "too little" regarding the concrete expressions of moral traits, depending on their situation, beyond which they cease to be virtuous at all. Generosity, for example, stands between too extremes. Too much generosity can do more harm than good to both giver and receiver, and being too stingy makes life worse for everyone. But at what point has generosity gone too far or falls too short? The question is pointless to ask in the abstract. It is context that often defines the too much and too little of a given trait. So, what sense is there in saying that MBE can be used to just amplify a given trait? Advocating for an a-contextual sledgehammer involves an unsophisticated account of real-world moral functioning, and promises to do as much harm as good.

All these remarks constitute comprehensive arguments against the feasibility of salvatory MBE, and it is little wonder that MBE enthusiasts flatly refuse to even acknowledge the problem of context in their arguments. How would it be possible to conceive of some situational bioenhancement that would have the ability to discern, in context, and in real time, the intensity, duration, object, and appropriateness of a given moral expression for a given situation, to weigh competing moral theories, definitions of moral goods, take into account opposing cultural valuations, and tensions between moral goods, and then enhance just the appropriate trait, by just the right amount, and for just that moment? This way of thinking cannot be taken seriously at all.

Yet, without these dynamic, context-based considerations, all one is left with is just the sort of mindless, blanket approach to enhancement that Hughes was so suspicious of, above. It is nothing other than the same sledgehammer approach used in psychiatric and punitive care. Not only would something so crude and undiscerning fail to meet the burden of a worthwhile MBE, but such an intervention might also do more moral harm than good by fostering a certain trait in situations completely inappropriate to it. So far from being an enhancement, such a one-size-fits-all approach would actually serve to reduce one's morally responsive capacities. One would be less dynamically able to respond to one's situation. Thus, so far from being an enhancement, such sledgehammer interventions would be morally disabling.

22.3.4 Biologizing morality

Morality, one might say, is given through both biological and cultural evolution. The cultural shaping of a given group's morality means that moral goods can in no way be reduced to biological markers. Every sophisticated moral good (and what moral good is not sophisticated?) is profoundly interwoven with various socio-cultural norms and conventions. It is true, of course, that moral functioning is biologically mediated, but it is culturally and conceptually mediated too. The profound bio-cultural interweaving of moral goods means that sophisticated moral functioning cannot be articulated in biological terms alone. This cultural and conceptual overlay is an irrevocable part of what makes a given sophisticated moral expression recognizable as the moral good that it is.

As such, *there is no direct link between biological processes and the concrete expression of a moral good*. This is a crucial point. There is just too much variation in what counts as empathy, generosity, compassion, and so on, to directly map these expressions onto some imagined biological source – as if to say: here is the gene for empathy, here is the neuronal pathway for compassion (whose version of empathy? Whose version of compassion? In what time and in what place?). Concrete expressions of moral goods do not map onto biology in this way at all – there is just too much conceptual mediation between biological source and concrete expression.

What about the more basic drives which cause moral problems? If MBE cannot directly produce sophisticated moral goods, as fully formed, then perhaps it could target the more basic biological rudiments of moral functioning? Perhaps MBE could take as its targets the drives, emotions, powers, and capacities which undergird these moral expressions. Perhaps by changing the biological underpinnings of certain behaviors, there might be some indirect trickle effect on moral functioning? Perhaps MBE could work in that sort of indirect manner?

Such hopes are not well founded. The basic rudiments of our moral powers are morally ambiguous, they can be applied for good as much as for harm. Until such drives and powers take shape as concrete expressions, they are neither good, nor bad, nor neutral in themselves. Put differently: the same drives, capacities, and powers that can be used to do harm can also be used to do good. Depending on how they are brought to bear, the same drives and capacities can be used for good or ill.

Aggression makes for a paradigm example of a drive that, taken in itself, is neither morally evil, nor morally good, nor necessarily moral at all. In and of itself, aggression has no moral content. There are circumstances in which aggression is morally harmful (e.g., attacking someone for no reason), there are times where it is morally neutral (e.g., aggression used in sports to push oneself harder, to excel), and there are times when aggression can be used for positively moral goals (e.g., in defense of one's loved ones against physical harm). The question resolves itself into one of formation (i.e., how one forms and utilizes one's drives) and, again, the context in which that drive is expressed.[7]

Much the same is true of all human drives. In and of themselves, they are neither good, bad, nor neutral. One might say that there is no such thing as a "moral emotion" or "moral drive," per se. Every capacity and drive that moral functioning depends upon is part of an overall biological architecture that has myriad possible uses. One cannot just find the errant cog or mechanism that causes a moral problem, isolate it and fix it. Rather all human powers are part of an integrated biological system, and to sever one part of the system is to sever an entire range of powers, for good and ill.

The same points hold whether one is talking about drives, like aggression, sexual impulses, or morally-related capacities, as for imagination or moral reasoning. *Shaping determines everything*, and precisely the same ambiguity exists with one's capacities. The power to reason in a morally benevolent way is the power to reason in a malevolent way. The power to imagine the good is the power to imagine harm.

The point quickly becomes clear. Every single trait, power, capacity, and drive can be brought to bear for good or ill. All biological operations are tied into a system: serotonin decreases explosive aggression but increases premeditated aggression (Carrillo et al. 2009). Oxytocin increases in-group bonding, then increases out-group aggression in return (De Dreu et al. 2010). To enhance a person's willpower could be to enhance their determination to do harm. What is given with one hand is taken with the other.

With these points, taken together with the problems raised by context, the case against the feasibility of salvatory MBE is overwhelming. Such MBE has nothing substantive to work on, it has no biological target, there is nothing for it to enhance that might not do just as much harm as good. The whole thing is a mirage. Once one understands the co-dependence of one's faculties for good and evil, the entire salvatory MBE discourse collapses.[8]

22.4 Conclusion: What is left for MBE?

22.4.1 Has MBE run its course?

A survey of MBE discourse over the past five years indicates that the domain has completely stalled. Many of the same arguments and debates are still being raised over and over again in exactly the same form. A strong case could be made for saying that MBE discourse has hit a dead-end, has run its course, and either needs to be fundamentally reconstituted or needs to have a line drawn under it, at least for the foreseeable future. It has, after all, no concrete basis whatsoever. There are neither practical nor theoretical advances at present nor in sight to suggest that MBE might have any kind of realistic purchase worth talking about. In light of the contextual problems raised above, one sees why. As a salvatory prospect, MBE offers nothing to get worried about, nor anything to get excited about. Inasmuch as bioethics is concerned with thinking through the ramifications of emerging technologies, salvatory MBE discourse has no bioethical or medical foundation and has nowhere to go. Without some technological advances to raise some further issues, or to drive some new discussion, one might well argue that there is no sense in pursuing the salvatory MBE debate any further.

Indeed, regarding enhancement and bioethics, there is an abundance of much more pressing issues in the public space needing to be discussed. One needs only to consider nanotechnology, human-computer interfaces, bionic limbs, automated drones, soldier enhancements, quantum computing, artificial intelligence, news-bots, the loss of privacy, the incredibly fast-paced datafication consuming all human existence, bio-surveillance, predictive neuroscience, and the greedy, profit-driven medicalization of the public domain. When one considers how significant these all-too-real contemporary issues are, salvatory MBE shows itself to be fantastical, baseless, and wholly trivial in comparison.

22.4.2 Realistic MBE

Beyond salvatory MBE, there remains the prospect of the realistic forms of MBE, some of which do in fact exist today. As has been suggested, some of these prospects are disturbing, and some of them are promising. More than anything, presenting a case for a realistic MBE means substantially reining back one's expectations about what biological intervention can achieve in altering moral behavior.

What is left over in MBE is but three forms:

a) A sledgehammer approach (e.g., chemical castration, and sedation of the pathologically violent)
b) The ongoing medicalization of social deviance (i.e., taking social/moral values and turning them into medical facts)
c) A much looser and weaker kind of MBE that would operate in a bio-psycho-social manner, usually in a psychotherapeutic context

It is this last suggestion that contains all the worthwhile prospects of realistic MBE (proposals along these lines have been presented by Wiseman 2016, Specker and Schermer 2017, Cole-Turner 2020). An example of such therapy would be the use of opioid inhibitors in the course of addiction treatment. Again, addiction is one of those gray area issues that seem to sit on an unclear line between moral failing, social problem, and biological sickness. Looking at addiction is very helpful in clarifying what is worthwhile in realistic MBE, and how any pharmaceutical or technological approaches would need to work in a non-reductive, open-ended, and multi-level manner.

The main pharmaceutical tool for treating addiction is the use of opioid inhibitors. Such drugs, like nalmefene or vivitrol, function by making it impossible for persons to feel the effects of alcohol and narcotics. Such pharmacological interventions are currently used (in the UK and USA) as part of a battery of approaches taken in treating persons who have addictions (in and out of prison, see Johnson 2016). As such, addiction treatments regard the problem as being, at once, a social, personal, as well as a medical problem. All three dimensions of the problem need to be tackled, and all three are currently managed as part of the overall protocol.

What is characteristic of this bio-psycho-social approach is a deep realism about the nature of the problems at hand. In line with the remarks above, one needs to avoid the idea that opioid inhibitors will ever be able to function as some kind of magic bullet against addiction. Where the inhibitor drugs are used on their own, the moment the treatment is curtailed, the addict recommences using (ibid). The reality is that reliance on opioid-blockers creates no genuine transformation in the person, it does not deal with the underlying causes of a given person's addiction. Of course, such treatments might be necessary in cases of an extreme medical emergency (e.g., impending liver failure caused by substance abuse), but outside a prison setting, these drugs are left as an elective, voluntary treatment on the part of the addict. Moreover, because of the underlying problems involved in addiction, merely blocking the use of a particular substance generally results in the user acting out their problem through some other self-destructive means. Therefore, drugs on their own do not suffice – there must be a personal and social element to the treatment too.

Equally, the same problems arise with taking any one treatment level in isolation. Person-centered therapy, used on its own, has also tended to yield poor results. The mentality in treating addiction has to be that sophisticated, multi-causal problems need sophisticated, multi-causal solutions.

Treating addiction in this manner represents a medically responsible, and humane, way of bringing biological factors to bear as a single prong in tackling a very difficult problem with significant moral dimensions and issues regarding personal and social responsibility.

With this kind of mindset, one has a prospect for fostering moral development in the context of a therapeutic or socially grounded setting in a patient-directed, openly consenting manner. Note that the MBE in this instance is geared toward questions of moral and personal *development*. So far from thinking that an enhancement can solve any problems, the process of moral growth is conceived as a long and difficult one, even with biological assistance, and certainly not something to be achieved overnight.

Reconstructing MBE discourse in this way has numerous benefits. It is actually grounded in the real world, it is scientifically literate and compassionate, but it comes at a cost – it does not have the glitz of a discourse getting excited over brain tubes and so-called God machines. Yet, for the price of actually being able to do some genuine good in the world regarding those in need, the wild hopes presented in the salvatory MBE literature have to be dispensed with completely. Realistic MBE necessitates a severe reining in of one's expectations about what biological interventions can really hope to achieve in working to foster genuine moral development. MBE, if it is possible at all, must be constrained to some loose, generalized effects which only serve a person's pre-existing intention to work on their moral issues. MBE would then be little more than a broad-scope device for assisting a person, in some limited way, as part of a hard-won, multi-level, moral developmental struggle. Within these much more constrained, but concretely plausible bounds, one might say that there is scope for a desirable and feasible moral bioenhancement.

Notes

1 It should be noted that this chapter is concerned with biological manipulation, *bio*enhancement. Other prospects for moral/behavioral manipulation that do not involve the targeting of biological substrates shall be excluded from this chapter, e.g., nudge techniques.
2 The reader is invited to consider whether moral evolution is identical to moral progress.
3 The DSM-V remains the dominant psychiatric mental health diagnostic manual in use in the USA today.
4 List gathered from Hughes 2006, Savulescu 2009, Bostrom (in Hughes 2006), Tachibana 2017, Araujo Fabiano 2018, Cole-Turner 2020, Sadeghi-Tari 2019, and Conan 2020. Savulescu encourages: increased surveillance, increased encroachment into privacy, and restraining or segregating those "at greatest risk to the community" (Savulescu 2009). In particular, Conan's paper "Frequently overlooked realistic moral bioenhancement interventions" (2020), indicates just how lacking in substance the domain is. As argued below, there are very good reasons why such "realistic" interventions are so frequently overlooked.

5 Sugarcandy Mountain: "that happy country where we poor animals shall rest forever from our labours!" (Orwell 1945). Yet, in the face of current real-world problems, effort – collaborative effort – is exactly what needs to be emphasized.
6 See Wiseman 2018 for an exhaustive list of the more absurd claims made in the MBE.
7 What of pathological aggression? These issues return us to the medical/psychiatric domain, see realistic MBE, Section 1D above, and below.
8 As if more needed to be said, there exists a range of logistical difficulties that MBE would face if it is to be brought to bear. Enthusiasts seem to conceive of MBE as something one can just go to the doctor, take a tablet, or have some brain stimulation, and the whole thing is done. Practical realities concerning side-effects, drug interactions, allergies, reactions, resistance, dosage, long-term physiological damage, and a whole range of other dynamic factors are just completely excluded from the debate. The medical interventions presented above are not to be taken lightly. As any medical professional would seek to make crystal clear: advising otherwise healthy persons to undergo surgical procedures or take pharmacotherapeutic drug regimens would be so medically irresponsible as, in some cases, to constitute criminal negligence. MBE enthusiasts rarely show cognizance of these factors.

References

Allan, C. 2011. British Psychological Society Response. http://apps.bps.org.uk/_publicationfiles/consultation-responses/DSM-5%202011%20-%20BPS%20response.pdf.
Araujo Fabiano, Joao Lourenco. 2018. Probing the Risks of Moral Enhancement. Doctoral Thesis, https://ethos.bl.uk/OrderDetails.do?uin=uk.bl.ethos.770491.
Braslow, J. T., and L. Messac. 2018, November 15. Medicalization and Demedicalization – A Gravely Disabled Homeless Man with Psychiatric Illness. *The New England Journal of Medicine* 379 (20): 1885–1888. doi: 10.1056/NEJMp1811623. PMID: 30428298.
Carrillo, M., L. Ricci, G. Coppersmith, and R. Melloni Jr. 2009. The Effect of Increased Serotonergic Neurotransmission on Aggression: A Critical Meta-Analytic Review of Preclinical Studies. *Psychopharmacology* 205 (3): 349–368.
Cole-Turner, Ronald. 2020. Loving Better (People)? Moral Bioenhancement and Christian Moral Transformation. In Scott Midson, ed., *Love, Technology and Theology*. LONDON, UK: T & T Clark, BLOOMSBURY.
Conan, Gregory Mark. 2020. Frequently Overlooked Realistic Moral Bioenhancement Interventions. *Journal of Medical Ethics* 46: 43–47.
Crutchfield, Parker. 2019. Compulsory Moral Bioenhancement Should Be Covert. *Bioethics* 33 (1): 112–121. doi: 10.1111/bioe.12496. Epub 2018 Aug 29. PMID: 30157295.
Daniels, N. 2000. Normal Functioning and the Treatment-Enhancement Distinction. *Cambridge Quarterly of Healthcare Ethics* 9 (3): 309–322.
De Dreu, C., L. Greer, M. Handgraaf, S. Shalvi, G. Van Kleef, M. Baas, F. Ten Velden, E. Van Dijk, and S. Feith. 2010. The Neuropeptide Oxytocin Regulates Parochial Altruism in Intergroup Conflict Among Humans. *Science* 328 (5984): 1408–1411.
DeGrazia, D. 2013. Moral Enhancement, Freedom, and What We (Should) Value in Moral Behavior. *Journal of Medical Ethics* 25 (3): 228–245.
American Psychiatric Association (2013) *Diagnostic and Statistical Manual of Mental Disorders (DSM–5)* (5th ed. 2013). Washington, D.C.: American Psychiatric Publishing. https://www.psychiatry.org/psychiatrists/practice/dsm.
Douglas, T. 2013. Moral Enhancement Via Direct Emotion Modulation: A Reply to John Harris. *Bioethics* 27 (3): 160–168.
Harris, J. 2011. Moral Enhancement and Freedom. *Bioethics* 25 (2): 102–111.
Hughes, J. 2004. *Citizen Cyborg: Why Democratic Societies Must Respond to the Redesigned Human of the Future*. Cambridge: Westview Press.
Hughes, J. 2006. Virtue Engineering. http://ieet.org/.
Hughes, J. 2012a. Morality in a Pill? http://ieet.org/index.php/IEET/more/hughe20121009.
Hughes, J. 2012b. The Benefits and Risks of Virtue Engineering. http://bioethics.as.nyu.edu/object/bioethics.events.20120330.conference.
Johnson, C. K. 2016. *Prisons Fight Opioids With $1000 Injection: Does it Work?* Associated Press. https://www.cbsnews.com/news/prisons-fight-opioids-with-1000-vivitrol-injections-does-it-work/
Jotterand, F. 2014. Questioning the Moral Enhancement Project. *American Journal of Bioethics* 14 (4): 1–3.
Juengst, E. 1998. What Does Enhancement Mean? In E. Parens, ed., *Enhancing Human Traits: Ethical and Social Implications*, 29–47. Washington: Georgetown University Press.

Miah, Andy. 2008. Engineering Greater Resilience or Radical Transhuman Enhancement? *Studies in Ethics, Law, and Technology* 2 (1): 1–18.
National Institutes of Health Information on Drug Addiction. https://www.drugabuse.gov/publications/drugs-brains-behavior-science-addiction/drug-misuse-addiction (last accessed 27th March 2021).
Orwell, George. 1945. *Animal Farm.* London: Secker and Warburg.
Persson, I., and J. Savulescu. 2008. The Perils of Cognitive Enhancement and the Urgent Imperative to Enhance the Moral Character of Humanity. *Journal of Applied Philosophy* 25 (3): 162–177.
Persson, I., and J. Savulescu. 2012. *Unfit for the Future: The Need for Moral Enhancement.* Oxford: Oxford University Press.
Sadeghi-Tari, Daniel. 2019. Socio-Affective Moral Enhancement a Cognitive Neuroscientific Perspective. https://his.diva-portal.org/smash/get/diva2:1338472/FULLTEXT02.pdf
Savulescu, J. 2009. Unfit for Life: Genetically Enhance Humanity or Face Extinction. http://humanityplus.org/2009/11/genetically-enhance-humanity-or-face-extinction/.
Savulescu, J. 2013. Pills That Improve Morality. http://tedxtalks.ted.com/video/.
The-need-for-moral-enhancement. https://www.oxfordmartin.ox.ac.uk/videos/the-need-for-moral-enhancement-te-dx-barcelona/. ACCESSED 30TH MARCH 2023
Specker, Jona, and Maartje Schermer. 2017. Imagining Moral Bioenhancement Practices. Drawing Inspiration from Moral Education, Public Health Ethics, and Forensic Psychiatry. Cambridge Quarterly of Healthcare Ethics 26 (3): 415–426.
Tachibana, Koji. 2017. Neurofeedback-Based Moral Enhancement and Traditional Moral Education *Journal of Philosophical Studies* 33: 19–42.
Wiseman, H. 2016. *The Myth of the Moral Brain – The Limits of Moral Enhancement.* Cambridge, MA: The MIT Press.
Wiseman, H. 2018. The Sins of Moral Enhancement Discourse. In M. Hauskeller, and L. Coyne, ed., *Moral Enhancement: Critical Perspectives. Proceedings of the Royal Institute of Philosophy.* Cambridge: Cambridge University Press.

PART VI

Human enhancement and medicine

23
THE MEANING OF ENHANCEMENT IN THE POST-COVID-19 WORLD

Ruth Chadwick

You are not going to get a new species flourishing unless it has a food supply. In a sense that is what we are becoming. We are the food. [...] We're not exactly a desirable animal to let loose in unlimited numbers on the planet.

(James Lovelock, 2020)

23.1 Introduction: COVID-19 and human enhancement

The quotation above from Lovelock is sobering: for a species used to thinking of itself as the superior one on planet Earth, to be described as virus food and as "not exactly a desirable animal" is hardly appealing. It is relatively easy to see how the experience of the COVID-19 pandemic could be leveraged to support an argument for human enhancement, in terms of what it has shown us about both physical vulnerabilities and our strategic, moral, and cognitive abilities to deal with them. Mo Gawdat, for example, has pointed to the ways in which humans have been "stupid" in relation to the virus – for example, in taking risks, overlooking evidence, and panicking (Gawdat, 2021). First, however, it is interesting to explore what if anything, it might *mean* to enhance humans.

Why has enhancement been prioritized as a concept, rather than, for example, "amelioration" or "advancement"? Marilyn Strathern has talked, although in a different context from the one addressed here, of a culture of enhancement, which she identifies as a late twentieth-century culture (Strathern, 1995, 24–5), although Bostrom and Sandberg wrote much later, in 2009, in relation to cognitive enhancement that "society needs a culture of enhancement" (Bostrom and Sandberg, 2009, 333). She writes: "The very term enhancement implies we are bound to want it, and this is where things begin to get out of hand" (Strathern, 1995, 24). This is a point that needs to be taken seriously in thinking about how we are to understand the concept. Strathern is surely right in saying both that it seems to imply desirability and that this is potentially also undesirable from another point of view.

Another observation that Strathern makes about the culture of enhancement is that it is "devoted to making everything explicit" and speaks of the problem that "persons become obliged to demonstrate they have been enhanced" (ibid., 25, 24). The consequence of targeted interventions is the requirement for measurement of success.

In line with the suggestion that the term itself implies that it will be wanted, it has been said that a simple definition of enhancement links it with improvement. Thus, Sparrow writes, "At the most basic level, to enhance something is to make it better" (Sparrow, 2019). I have argued elsewhere, however, that trying to link the central meaning of "enhancement" with "improvement" is a mistake: it makes it true by definition, but it has to be an open question whether or not we should want to pursue any given enhancement project. Returning to the point above, about the choice of term, it would be quite possible to have debates about human improvement rather than enhancement, along with self-improvement. The rhetorical force, however, of enhancement is quite different from that of improvement. The latter conjures up images of (possibly unexciting) worthiness in relation to human beings, although we may be attracted, in advertising, by the "new and improved" version of a domestic appliance. One reason for choosing "enhancement" rather than "improvement," then, is that it "sexes up" the debate, which suggests, then, that to try to say that enhancement just means improvement is potentially misleading.

The concept of enhancement is also different from that of amelioration. The meaning of amelioration is essentially connected with making things better, improving things, but typically by making things less bad or unsatisfactory. For some authors, however, even those who argue that the basic meaning of enhancement is making things better, the improvement has to go beyond amelioration: enhancement should not be understood as making things better simply by making them less bad. Thus, Sparrow continues:

> An intervention might only count as an enhancement if it increased a welfare-promoting character-trait [...]beyond what is species typical for human beings of the relevant reference class.
>
> *(Sparrow, 2019)*

There are different elements in this quotation: the criterion of promoting welfare (where outcome is important), and the point about the reference class. Perhaps another aspect of the attractiveness of enhancement as the concept of choice is that it fits with narratives of superhumans. At a time of multiple threats to human existence, including not only climate change and pandemics already mentioned but also global instability and multiple physical and mental health concerns, however, there is arguably a place for re-emphasizing amelioration.

Possible reasons for enhancing humans include the idea that it is an aspect of human nature to seek to improve itself; the view that there is a duty to pursue human enhancement; and a broadly consequentialist argument, based on purported essential or current features of the human predicament, that it is urgent to try to make things *go better* for human beings. Of these possible reasons, the argument from human nature will not be considered in detail here. The concept of human nature has made multiple appearances in the enhancement debate, for different purposes – to set limits to human enhancement or to argue against it, as well as an argument for enhancement suggesting that enhancement is inevitable. Baylis and Robert, for example, speak of a "biosocial drive to pursue human perfection" as an essential characteristic of humanness (Baylis and Robert, 2004, 25). As Allen Buchanan argued, however, appeals to human nature tend to be unhelpful in the enhancement debate (Buchanan, 2009). There is an ongoing question about how much human nature could be enhanced while still counting as human, but it is beyond the scope of the present discussion to address it. The other two possible reasons mentioned above will be considered in terms of what, if anything, they can reveal about the meaning of enhancement.

23.2 Toward an understanding of the concept of enhancement

There is a considerable and growing literature on the concept of enhancement itself and also on different types of human enhancement. Distinctions may be drawn between bio- and non-bioenhancement, for example. Within bioenhancement, there is a divide between interventions such as genetic modification and pharmaceutical interventions, some of which may be feasible already or in the near future while others are more speculative. Then there are subcategories of enhancement such as physical, cognitive, and moral enhancement. Increasingly debate is about these subtypes, although the question of the definition of the central concept is far from settled. An initial clarification, however, is pertinent. In discussing enhancement, we could focus on enhancement of individuals, with or without their requesting it. For example, an individual might want to be cognitively enhanced to improve their career prospects. This already happens via the intake of cognitive-enhancing drugs (see, e.g., Greely et al., 2008). On the other hand, in the context of the criminal justice system, there might be support for an option of moral enhancement of someone with sociopathic tendencies, which might not be in accord with that individual's personal choice. Macro-level questions in light of episodes such as the COVID-19 pandemic arise, concerning the enhancement of the human species overall. In what follows I shall be concerned with the latter. By that it should not be assumed, of course, that every single human being could or should be subject to an intervention: rather the issue is what it might mean for humans to take control of their future as a species. Why, if at all, should the enhancement of humans be pursued and how are we to understand that? In this chapter I will draw on previous work in trying to tease out some of the issues.

23.2.1 Enhancement and improvement

First, however, let us return to the view that an enhancement is to be understood as improvement and examine the implications of that. Even if an enhancement *is* an improvement, I suggest that it is necessary at a minimum to be clear about the *respect* in which it is an improvement and for whom. To enhance an x may be an improvement in one respect but not in another. I could enhance the color of my eyebrows with an eyebrow pencil, making them darker, for example: that surely does not guarantee that the result is an improvement or that it will be regarded as such by others. I can use a flavor enhancer in cooking to make the flavor more intense: similarly, that does not make it certain that it will be regarded as an improvement by my guests. For this reason, I have previously argued that an enhancement is better understood as adding (or intensifying) something in relation to a particular characteristic, which may or may not be an improvement. It must be possible to say, of an enhancing intervention, that it amounts to gilding the lily.

Interestingly, flavor enhancers are defined as

> compounds that are *added* [my emphasis] to a food in order to supplement or enhance its own natural flavour. The concept of flavour enhancement originated in Asia, where cooks added seaweed to soup stocks in order to provide a richer flavour.
>
> *(Encyclopedia Britannica, 2021)*

Similarly in the context of jewelry, what are known as enhancers "snap into place on an already-finished necklace or bracelet. These hinged components … were first introduced as a way to *add* [my emphasis] removable pendants to strands of pearls" (Halstead, 2021). The words "already finished" here are significant: the enhancement is an add-on rather than a remedial alteration.

I called this understanding of enhancement the additionality view (Chadwick, 2008; see also Chadwick and Schüklenk, 2021). Enhancement in this view could be an addition of something new or an intensification of an existing trait. Where enhancement of humans is at issue, the "addition" must be something that goes beyond what is typical of the species (bearing in mind Sparrow's point about the reference class: in this case. the reference class is the species). For judgment concerning whether or not it is an improvement, considerations include: for whom is it an improvement, and in what way?

A supporter of what I call "the improvement view" might respond that if it is not an improvement, it is not an enhancement. It is difficult to see how asserting it to be true by definition in this way is helpful. It makes perfectly good sense, after all, to speak about enhancing the red color in a painting – making it deeper or more vibrant, without that being an improvement of the painting overall – or even of the color itself. Is a red enhanced to be more vibrant necessarily an improved red? It might shift the balance of color in a way that does not please from an aesthetic point of view.

A further objection to the additionality view, however, might be that enhancement could involve subtracting something rather than intensifying or adding a characteristic. For example, it seems to make sense to speak of enhancing the flavor of a dish by making it less salty (though this might not be to everyone's taste) or of enhancing someone's beauty by removing a blemish. Here we get into the issues of negative and positive, the difference between amelioration and enhancement, and the view that to count as an enhancement intervention must go "beyond therapy."

23.2.2 Therapy and enhancement

An explanation of enhancement has frequently been attempted, in biomedicine at least, via a distinction between enhancement and therapy. This may seem to have some intuitive appeal in that context. It is easy to understand an argument for different priorities in the use of cosmetic surgery for example, which can be employed both to repair significant burn damage and to make someone appear younger or (it is hoped) more beautiful. On closer inspection, however, this appears to be less helpful. Even if it is likely that interventions deemed to count as enhancements may be brought about by using techniques that originally have been developed for therapeutic ends, what counts as therapeutic is itself a subject of considerable controversy.

With regard to the human species the therapy-enhancement distinction itself seems less relevant in any case, except perhaps in relation to preventive enhancements of the immune system, of increased importance following COVID-19 (c.f., Holm, 1994). This is however arguably best understood not in terms of the therapy-enhancement distinction but, via the additionality view, as an addition to or strengthening of the immune system.

It is now pertinent to examine what light some possible arguments for enhancement might shed on the meaning of the term.

23.2.2.1 The duty to enhance: Kant and the duty to perfect humanity

In the formula of humanity, Immanuel Kant argued that humanity is an end in itself. Humanity, whether in one's own person or that of others, is something we should try to perfect, by developing our own talents and furthering the ends of others. To choose not to develop one's talents is to forgo the possibility of furthering humanity toward higher degrees of perfection.

Several commentators have examined the question of whether and if so to what extent Kant's own ethics could support bioenhancement. Questions to be addressed include the respect in which humanity could and should be enhanced; the issue of effort in moving toward perfection; whether moral enhancement in a Kantian approach could include intervening in emotional capacities (Carter, 2017); or whether, if bioenhancement is deemed less worthy than traditional methods, the upshot is that a view which advocates moral perfection has to countenance an outcome of humanity being less moral than it could be (see Chance, 2021).

For present purposes, there are at least two key challenges. The first is that Kant discusses the duty to perfect humanity in the context of duties to oneself, rather than humanity as such.

> A human being has a duty to himself to cultivate (*cultura*) his natural powers (powers of spirit, mind, and body), as means to all sorts of possible ends. – He owes it to himself (as a rational being) not to leave idle and, as it were, rusting away the natural predispositions and capacities that his reason can someday use
>
> *(Kant, 1996, 6:445)*

The second potential difficulty is the distinction between the two aspects of humanity, as empirical and as moral agent.

> When a human being is conscious of a duty to himself, he views himself, as the subject of duty, under two attributes: first as a sensible being, that is, as a human being (a member of one of the animal species), and second as an intelligible being (not merely as a being that has reason, since reason as a theoretical faculty could well be an attribute of a living corporeal being). The senses cannot attain this latter aspect of a human being; it can be cognized only in morally practical relations, where the incomprehensible property of freedom is revealed by the influence of reason on the inner lawgiving will
>
> *(Kant, 1996, 6:419)*

The present focus is on whether anything can be gleaned from a Kantian approach as to what enhancement might mean. He talks of perfection. The duty of striving for perfection does not imply that perfection will ever be reached.

> It is a human being's duty to strive for this perfection, but not to reach it (in this life), and his compliance with this duty can, accordingly, consist only in continual progress. Hence while this duty is indeed narrow and perfect with regard to its object (the idea that one should make it one's end to realize), with regard to the subject it is only a wide and imperfect duty to himself
>
> *(Kant, 1996, 6:446)*

A Kantian duty-based reason for enhancement suggests a reason connected with the intrinsic value of what is to be enhanced, rather than to promote an outcome. Clearly, however, bioenhancement could only affect the empirical being, and the implication of what Kant says is that individuals should aim to make their natural dispositions suitable for use by reason. This could in principle be understood in terms of improvement or additionality. It sits uneasily, however, with the idea of a program of enhancing the species beyond what is species-typical. From the third-party perspective, there is the challenge of avoiding the using of humanity in the person of another as a mere means. Nevertheless, it might be argued that it is at least not *incompatible* with duty that humans as empirical beings be bioenhanced as a condition of the continuance of the exercise of the rational will. If humanity does not survive, in light of current and future threats, such as becoming the food for another species, then that will not be possible. In what way they could and should be bioenhanced is another matter. We need to examine the human predicament more closely.

23.2.3 The human predicament and the need for enhancement

Taking into account the current situation for humanity, the strongest argument for enhancement, and the one most revealing about what that might mean, I suggest, is a consequentialist one. The extent of the need to try to make things go better for humans is becoming more obvious. However, this is hardly a new thought. In *The Object of Morality* (1971) and in a subsequent piece (1993), Geoffrey Warnock asked the question, speaking of human beings, "Why do we need something to make things go better for us?" Warnock's answer lay in certain features of "what one might rather pompously call the human predicament," of which he says that even if we do not take the same view as Hobbes, it "is inherently such that things are liable to go badly" (Warnock, 1971, 17). For Warnock the problem was certain limitations:

> the resources with which to satisfactory our fundamental needs […]are, in fact, limited. Then, our knowledge, our information, and our intellectual powers are limited. I am afraid our capacity to make rational use of such powers […]is also limited […]Additionally, we live in an environment that is in some respects unfriendly on all sorts of scales. […]And then there is […]the phenomenon of "limited sympathies."
>
> *(Warnock, 1993, 255–6)*

It is relevant to our present discussion to explore the extent to which the way in which the human predicament is here described might have changed, including what limitations are essential and enduring, and what are contingent.

What were not made much of by Warnock, although they are arguably relevant to the issues and certainly are in the contemporary bioenhancement debate, were the physical limitations of human biology such as vulnerability to diseases, whether infectious or not, the process of aging and the frailty it brings, and the normal limits to the powers of our senses. He does *mention* biological needs and the fact that the life span is "in any case limited" (Warnock, 1971, 17) and also says that things might be very different if humans were less vulnerable (ibid., 23). but biological limitations are not listed among the "big four": limited resources, intellectual powers, rationality, and sympathies. Yet biological limitations, together with the limitations in resources, give rise to significant challenges and ethical issues given, for example, the potential tendency to inadequate capacity for showing sympathy to the frail, aged, and weak. They have also revealed themselves with a vengeance in the COVID-19 pandemic. Lovelock says:

> After this virus, I suspect quite a hefty change will be discernible. I think people will discover all sorts of things they can do that they didn't do before. Maybe they'll realise it is not such a good idea to get fat; that much of the suffering they get in middle age and later life is caused by just eating too much of the wrong sort of food.
>
> *(Lovelock, 2020)*

A change in behavior rather than bioenhancement is mentioned in this quotation, but the main point for present purposes is that there is a need to pay attention to physical limitations.

The point about the "unfriendly" environment in Warnock is worthy of remark. The fact of climate change at the present time is indeed used as an argument for the need for the bioenhancement of human beings (among other strategies). At the time of the publication of *The Object of Morality,* although environmental concern was by no means absent in public debate (see. e.g., Carson, 1962), it was possible for Warnock to say that

> some human needs, wants and interests are, special and exceptional circumstances apart, just naturally satisfied by the human environment […] there is naturally available in the atmosphere of the planet […] enough air for everybody to breathe.
>
> *(Warnock, 1971, 18)*

There is considerably more alarm, and the "unfriendliness" of the environment is said to be at least partly the result of human behavior. It is not only widely recognized that human behavior needs to change, but it is also further argued by supporters of bioenhancement that we may need to take charge of our biology and not leave it to evolutionary processes:

> The problem is that progress via Darwinian evolution is extremely slow, and the direction unpredictable; all we know is that it will facilitate gene survival. It is probable that, in the interests of human survival and certainly those of human welfare and well-being, we may

simply not be able to wait. For example, we will need to accelerate the development of better resistance to bacteria, disease, viruses, or hostile environments or of the technologies that will eventually be necessary to find, and travel to, habitats alternative to the earth.

(Harris, 2016)

In today's context, then, and perhaps to an even greater degree following the experience of the COVID-19 pandemic, Warnock's observations about the human predicament could be taken as grounds for supporting, in principle, both cognitive and moral enhancement, to make things go better for humanity. In so far as change is possible, this might be taken to imply that the limitations Warnock identifies are not in fact limited – at least not to the same degree – as Warnock suggests. Rather than enhancement, Warnock uses the term "amelioration" of the human condition: he was writing before the development of Strathern's purported late-twentieth-century culture of enhancement. However, although he is not concerned with the possibilities of bioenhancement discussed today, the points he makes in this passage are clearly relevant to those contemporary discussions.

A new feature and possible threat to the human predicament however has arisen since Warnock's time, and that is the development of AI (see Bostrom, 2014). Mo Gawdat writes

For as long as humanity has existed, we have been the smartest beings on the face of planet earth. That has placed us on top of the food chain. We have done whatever we wanted to do, and every other being had to comply. This is about to change […] Humanity is about to be outsmarted, and the consequences could be dire. There is no way to maintain control indefinitely.

(Gawdat, 2021, 157–8)

This could be seen as a development, unforeseen in Warnock's time, of the second limitation in the human predicament, namely human intellectual powers.

If the human predicament is as described, the question arises as to what to do about it: enhancing humans may be one way to make things go better but is it the best option? Clearly, "making things go better" is not the same as "making things better." However, making things better *could* be read as equivalent to making things go better, depending on how we understand "making things better," or it could be understood as a means to making things go better, depending on what the "things" are. And if making humans better is understood to be the optimal way of making things go better *for* humans, there is still a question over whether bioenhancement is the best means to that end and how we understand enhancement within that. What are the criteria for success?

23.3 Making things go better: Criteria of success

The ways in which we might judge things to be going better might be divided into different categories – first, economic, such as greater prosperity as measured, for example, by growth. Growth, however, although looked to by policy makers, has been heavily criticized as a measure of success on the grounds of the biases built into it (see, e.g., Pilling, 2018).

Second, there are health-related criteria as such greater life expectancy, a reduction in the incidence or, or eradication of, particular diseases such as smallpox, malaria, and COVID-19. Third, there are criteria concerned with the reduction of conflict, including fewer wars and disputes, and greater tolerance of difference. Fourth, there are considerations of social justice, including the reduction of social inequalities both intranationally and internationally.

Finally, however, and perhaps most importantly and urgently, playing a significant role in the bioenhancement debate, there are issues about the very survival of the species on Earth. Whereas it might seem attractive to focus on goals such as social justice, some of the arguments for the urgency of bioenhancement are concerned with humanity's future in light of worries about the future of the planet. James Lovelock, the originator of the Gaia hypothesis, has suggested that the biosphere is in the last 1% of its life and that humans are evolving rapidly (but arguably not fast enough) (Lovelock, 2020). If making things go better just means survival, a more far-reaching program of bioenhancing the species may be required such as envisaged in Olaf Stapledon's *Last and First Men* (Stapledon, 1930).

At the time of Warnock's writing, it was still possible to think of making things go better in less radical ways. Warnock's main interest was in the role of morality itself in counteracting the last mentioned limitation, that of limited sympathies. However he does discuss the comparative importance of limited rationality and limited sympathies. Of limited rationality he says:

> Even if they are not positively neurotic or otherwise maladjusted, people are naturally prone to be moved by short-run rather than long-run considerations, and often by the pursuit of more blatant, intense, and obtrusive satisfactions rather than of those cooler ones that on balance would really be better.
>
> *(Warnock, 1971, 21)*

Nevertheless, while rationality may be in shorter supply than sympathy, and limited rationality may have a very significant effect on whether or not things go better, what is important is how it is used and this requires morality. Interestingly Mo Gawdat also sees the answer – to that aspect of the human predicament concerning the future of AI – as being in ethics. Cognitive enhancement is not what is required. On the one hand, (some) humans have shown they have the intellectual powers to develop vaccines very quickly against COVID-19, but on the other, they will not be able to outsmart AI. Humans need to interact with machines in such a way that those machines pick up human values:

> We need to teach the machines the right ethical code [...] The machines we are building, so far, are mainly tasked to maximise money and power.
>
> *(Gawdat, 2021, 302)*

Warnock's view of morality as a device for counteracting limited sympathies could be seen as a type of enhancement via influencing human behavior rather than changing people "from the inside" by bioenhancement techniques. Unfortunately, the phenomena witnessed during the COVID-19 pandemic, such as panic buying, which is not only a response to limited resources but itself a cause of them, suggests that morality still has some way to go before we can consider it effective. So, might bioenhanced morality be the answer? Again, there are questions about what this means. A greater capacity for empathy, which might, at first sight, appear to be a suitable response to limited sympathies, gives rise to the question of how much empathy is desirable. The problem of burnout in cases of too much empathy is already familiar.

23.4 Improvement or additionality

Enhancing the capacity for empathy could be understood either from the improvement view or from the additionality interpretation of the concept. However, there are at least two ways pointed to in the literature in which an enhancement framed as an improvement can have a downside. It has already been mentioned that an improvement in one respect may not be regarded as such in another. The "no gains without compensating losses" argument as discussed by Jonathan Glover, suggests this is always the case:

> On this view, if we bring about a genetically based improvement, such as higher intelligence, we are bound to pay a price somewhere else: perhaps the more intelligent people will have less resistance to disease, or will be less physically agile.

(Glover, 1984, 33)

Glover points out, however, that a "more cautiously empirical version […] says there is a *tendency* [my emphasis] for gains to be accompanied by losses" (Glover, 1984, 34). It is enough for the argument presented here that it may be the case. Speaking in terms of explicit additionalities makes this more transparent, enabling an overall assessment of improvement. Criteria for improvement are still needed, such as maximizing the survival capacity of the species.

The second point to consider is the "obsolescence" argument put forward by Sparrow, who has argued that no matter how much a thing is enhanced, it can always be enhanced further, and so earlier models will become obsolete, which hardly seems to be welfare-promoting:

> on any of these definitions [of enhancement] further enhancement is always possible, which […] means that as long as progress in enhancement technology continues, each and every set of enhancements will eventually be rendered obsolete.
>
> *(Sparrow, 2019)*

If we think of a series of enhancements of empathy however, in successive generations, each one having a greater capacity than the one before, it does not follow that the latest in the line will be the most improved. It is quite possible that empathy could be enhanced to a point where it becomes disabling. On the additionality view of enhancement, this is not a problem (see Chadwick, 2019).

Conclusions

The experience of COVID-19, and current concerns about climate change, have emphasized the drawbacks of the human predicament as described decades ago by Warnock, and also what needs to be added to his depiction. It has demonstrated the need to pay attention to physical vulnerabilities; to recognize limitations to our rationality while at the same time celebrating scientific achievements; and to acknowledge ongoing limitations in sympathies. Also, new challenges are emerging, such as AI. In light of that, there are questions about how to make things go better for human beings, perhaps in terms of their very survival. Warnock argued for the role of morality, but arguably making things go better for humans by enhancing humans themselves – e.g., through bioenhancing, the capacity for empathy to counteract limited sympathies – really is needed. It seems clear, however, that there are several problems with understanding enhancement in terms of improvement. It is necessary to have regard not only for the fact that an intervention may be an improvement in one respect and not in another but that it may not be an improvement overall. In that case. we cannot simply assume, without more, that enhanced moral capacity (or indeed anything else) constitutes an improvement. The additionality view avoids this problem and allows us to be explicit (bearing in mind Strathern's point about explicitness) about what is added, before assessing whether and to what extent the overall result is an improvement.

References

Baylis, Francoise and Robert, Jason Scott (2004) 'The inevitability of genetic enhancement techniques' *Bioethics* 18 (1): 1–26.
Bostrom, N. (2014) *Superintelligence: Paths, Dangers, Strategies* Oxford: Oxford University Press.
Bostrom, N. and Sandberg, A. (2009) 'Cognitive enhancement: Methods, ethics, regulatory challenges' *Science and Engineering Ethics* 15: 311–41.
Buchanan, Allen (2009) 'Human nature and enhancement' *Bioethics* 23 (3): 141–50.
Carson, Rachel (1962) *Silent Spring* Boston, MA: Houghton Mifflin.
Carter, Sarah (2017) 'A Kantian ethics approach to moral bioenhancement' *Bioethics* 31 (9): 683–90.

Chadwick, Ruth (2008) 'Enhancement, therapy and imprpovement' In B. Gordijn and R. Chadwick (eds) *Medical Enhancement and Posthumanity* Dordrecht: Springer.

Chadwick, Ruth (2019) 'Which enhancement? What kind of obsolescence?' *American Journal of Bioethics* 19 (7): 20–22.

Chadwick, Ruth and Schüklenk, Udo (2021) This is Bioethics Hoboken, NJ: Wiley.

Chance, Brian A. (2021) 'Kant and the enhancement debate: Imperfect duties and perfecting ourselves' *Bioethics* 35 (8): 801–11.

Encyclopedia Britannica (2021) www.britannica.com Accessed on 3 October 2021.

Gawdat, Mo (2021) *Scary Smart: The Future of Artificial Intelligence and How You Can Save Our World* London: Bluebird.

Glover, Jonathan (1984) *What Sort of People Should There Be?* Harmondsworth: Penguin.

Greely, Henry et al. (2008) 'Towards responsible use of cognitive-enhancing drugs by the healthy' *Nature* 456: 702–705 https:doi.org.10.1038/456702a.

Halstead (2021) http://www.halsteadbead.com Accessed on 3 October 2021.

Harris, John (2016) 'Germline modification and the burden of human existence' *Cambridge Quarterly of Healthcare Ethics* 25 (1): 6–18.

Holm, Søren (1994) 'Genetic engineering and the North-South divide' In Anthony Dyson and John Harris (eds) *Bioethics and Biotechnology*. London: Routledge.

Kant, I. (1996) *The Metaphysics of Morals* Edited by Mary J Gregor. Cambridge: University Press.

Lovelock, James (2020) Interviewed by Jonathan Watts The Guardian 18 July https://www.theguardian.com/environment/2020/jul/18/james-lovelock-the-biosphere-and-i-are-both-in-the-last-1-per-cent-of-our-lives Accessed on 4 October 2021.

Pilling, David (2018) *The Growth Delusion: The Wealth and Well-Being of Nations* London: Bloomsbury.

Sparrow, Robert (2019) 'Yesterday's child: How gene editing for enhancement will produce obsolescence – And why it matters' *American Journal of Bioethics* 19 (7): 6–15.

Stapledon, Olaf (1930) *Last and First Men* York: Methuen.

Strathern, Marilyn (1995) *The Relation: Inaugural Lecture* Cambridge: Prickly Pear Press.

Warnock, Geoffrey (1971) *The Object of Morality* London: Methuen.

Warnock, Geoffrey (1993) 'The Object of Morality' *Cambridge Quarterly of Healthcare Ethics* 2 (3): 255–8.

24
CLINICAL PRACTICE AND HUMAN ENHANCEMENT
Blurred borders and ethical issues

Mirko D. Garasic and Andrea Lavazza

24.1 Introduction: Enhancement and cure

Enhancement is the improvement of a person's natural capacities by heterogeneous means, for them to acquire more skills and, therefore, access more opportunities. However, enhancement also means change, and this may raise unprecedented problems, different forms of competition or new social inequalities, or even changes in the *human condition* itself.

The enhancement of human performance is the increase in skills (abilities, attributes, or competences) by means of medical or technological methods, so as to improve a person's overall performance (see better, run faster, remember more accurately). Examples include intraocular lenses and doping in sport but also special training programs that resort to technological aids. Clinical practice (i.e., therapy or care) is generally the restoration (or preservation) of a previous (or average) condition in the population. Enhancement concerns an *improvement* with respect to average conditions. But it appears overly difficult to draw a line between the two (e.g., think of the physiological decay of the elderly).

The debate on enhancement schematically puts liberals and conservatives against each other (without these terms implying a moral or political judgment on the two views). On the one hand, liberal views are characterized by an emphasis on individual autonomy, but also imply public support for the disadvantaged if it is needed at the expense of the wealthy or fortunate (in other words, liberals are willing to intervene to change the social order and do not consider the natural order immutable). Conservatives, on the other hand, are mostly convinced that there are values that individuals should not violate, that there is a natural order to be largely respected, although they emphasize individual effort in improving one's position through ingenuity and hard work. They appreciate personal success stories, when one has "fought" on equal terms, without subterfuge or shortcuts. In general, it is not for others, let alone the state or other collective bodies, to act to correct natural or social inequalities. Liberals instead, emphasize the idea of justice, with maximum freedom of choice for the individual, nevertheless deeming it lawful for the public hand to intervene in favor of those in disadvantaged situations.

Enhancement has always existed, whether for our tools, our production process, or our bodies, but the concept of enhancement as a specific medical/technological process and socially and ethically sensitive phenomenon is much more recent. Today, technological advancements are pushing the boundaries of our intervention to new levels, and this might have repercussions on how we might conceptualize illness and cure – hence representing an epochal turning point for clinical practice.

24.2 The boundaries of technology and humanity

Since its inception, human enhancement has been linked to its vicious predecessor of eugenics, (Sandel, 2007) pushing for a widespread use of existing, emerging, and speculative biotechnologies that could help humanity "become better" (though many have rejected this comparison) (Agar, 1999).

The most common argument used by human enhancement supporters – including especially Savulescu (2005, 2006), Harris (1975, 2007), and Bostrom (2003, Bostrom & Roache, 2008) – is mostly straightforward (notwithstanding degrees of difference between their positions): not only should we implement enhancement from a practical point of view, but we also have a moral *duty* to do so because acting otherwise (hence not benefiting our society by "bettering" ourselves as individuals) would be unwise and go against the very essence of human nature. As a species, we are inclined to better ourselves and shape nature to our needs and dreams.

Through these enhancements, according to Nick Bostrom (2005, 2008, 2020) and others, humanity is ready to evolve into a new species and voluntarily and consciously become posthuman.[1] Posthumanists argue that we need to implement our findings in science and technology not only to improve our experience of life and surpass the innate limits of our human condition but – more crucially – because this might be the only way for our species (or rather its posthuman evolution) to have a chance of surviving the many existential threats that we are facing on our planet (Persson & Savulescu, 2012).

Whether there should be limits to human enhancement and what kind of ethical guidelines, if any, are needed is a topic addressed elsewhere in this volume. In the light of what has been highlighted so far, we now want to dwell on what the relationship between clinical practice and enhancement is and what ethical issues arise in their confluence.

To some extent, it can be argued that the increasing possibilities offered by contemporary medicine entail clinical interventions that can hardly be distinguished from forms of physical enhancement, if one stays within a classical paradigm (itself intertwined with normative views) with respect to the distinction between therapy in the strict sense and other types of treatment. Take the case of short stature, beyond dwarfism, as a disease. Until not so many decades ago, the physician could simply take note of a young person's below-average development, in the knowledge that short stature, even if not associated with other organic disorders, would constitute a social disadvantage and might be experienced by the individual as a physical handicap, on a par with mutilation.

Today, however, it is possible to intervene early with the administration of growth hormones as well as bone lengthening surgery. Considering that in the future, interventions may become more targeted and effective, we might ask what the recommended height is for women and men respectively. Given that growth cannot be determined to the centimeter, should the goal be a little below or a little above the average of the reference population? And if individuals destined to remain short in stature are brought above the average height by 5 or more centimeters, will they be considered to have an unfair advantage over other members of the group, given that above-average height is a socially valued and advantageous characteristic?[2] (Liao et al., 2012).

The definition of "therapeutic enhancement" was introduced to indicate "those interventions that are often performed to return an individual's health/performance to their baseline but may also increase health/performance beyond the baseline" (Jensen, 2020). To make another example, it seems that certain advances in bionics (the replacement or enhancement of organs or other body parts by mechanical versions) contribute to changing the classical perspective on the partition between clinical practice and enhancement. Indeed, bionic implants differ from prostheses by mimicking or even surpassing the body part's original function.

An exemplary case is the story of Oscar Pistorius, the South African Paralympic athlete, both of whose legs were amputated at knee height: thanks to special prostheses, he was able to achieve the same performance level as an able-bodied professional athlete. His participation in competitions was denied, at first, because the prostheses he used were not considered to be simply leg replacements but enhancers, capable of giving a demonstrable mechanical advantage. The prostheses thus constituted an unfair advantage over other athletes, just like doping (Pistorius was eventually allowed to participate in the 2008 Olympics and run with the able-bodied).[3]

It is clear, however, that pharmacological doping, apart from the question of safety, is a tool designed to improve performance without the athlete having to make an extra effort and allowing an increase in performance that would in any case be unattainable for the athlete. Prostheses, mobile or permanent, once perceived as "only" an aid to compensate for a handicap, can now provide an improvement that goes beyond the mere restoration of a lost function (Jotterand, 2008).

The Cybathlon, a competition based on everyday activities completed with the help of state-of-the-art assistive systems, is a unique championship devised by ETH Zurich in 2016, where people with disabilities, called "pilots," assisted by sophisticated technologies, compete in many disciplines, defending the colors of their teams belonging to the world's leading research centers in the field.[4] The six disciplines planned for the four-year editions of the event, the next being in 2024, are Brain-Computer Interface Race, Functional Electrical Stimulation Bike Race, Powered Arm Prosthesis Race, Powered Leg Prosthesis Race, Powered Exoskeleton Race, and Powered Wheelchair Race. The aim of the competition is to develop increasingly advanced technological tools to enable disabled individuals to restore the full capabilities of a healthy adult human being.

Due to the hybridization with bionic devices, the idea of biological normality no longer exists in these *sui generis* Olympic Games, the main objective being the functionality and well-being of the individual with the help of technology. This same tendency also manifests itself in other ways, when Paralympic or disabled athletes try to overcome their limits and perform feats that are difficult even for the average normal athlete: this comes as proof of a newfound ability in and of itself.

Medical development means that this does not only happen in the field of sport. In at least three areas, which we will now consider, the possibilities opened up by therapy make it increasingly difficult to draw a clear line between mere clinical practice and enhancement. Since it does not seem to make sense to preemptively limit the possibilities of curing or improving a person's discomfort or impairment, we will describe the ethically sensitive issues at stake and propose some caveats, aimed also at the introduction of rules that are in tune with the shared values of a democratic society, such as freedom, autonomy, well-being, equality, justice, and social responsibility. In this light, the maximization of individual interest is not always the primary criterion for decisions that are meant to draw a distinction between therapy and enhancement.

The paradigms that seem to emerge and unite the three areas we will describe are the *paradigm of availability* from the user's point of view and the *paradigm of possibility of therapy* from the researchers' point of view. On the one hand, once a drug, medical technique, device, or prosthesis is available, one sees no reason why it should not be used since it has been presumptively made for the purpose of human well-being. On the other hand, research in the biomedical sciences puts as the first motivation for each new strand of study the opportunity to find applicable solutions in medicine. This is largely due to a sincere desire to contribute to people's well-being, but it is also the best way to attract the interest of the public as well as funders. In this way, these two paradigms seem to be working to pave the way for enhancement through clinical practice. However, it cannot be forgotten that hubris has also been a motivation in the history of the development of science and technology. Some researchers did not have sincere desires to contribute to people's well-being but were motivated by individual interest or the will to empower their group or country. And even today, there is no shortage of cases where science is driven by morally reprehensible goals.

24.3 Genetic engineering in medicine

Genome editing are "technologies that enable scientists to make changes to DNA, leading to changes in physical traits, like eye color, and disease risk."[5] The newest and most promising technology is CRISPR-Cas9 (Clustered Regularly Interspaced Short Palindromic Repeats-associated protein 9). CRISPR-Cas9 is not the first method made available to perform gene editing, but the low cost, precision, and easy handling of this technique make it a very powerful tool that is going to be used more widely compared to others, creating an even more intense bioethical concern regarding its application.

CRISPR-Cas9 caused much enthusiasm, as it could help treat many illnesses, not only of genetic origins but also viral ones or cancer. We can divide its therapeutic use into two main areas: research and direct application. In research, CRISPR-Cas9 could be used to get a better understanding of human diseases, for example by creating a simulation of the disease in animal models. Later, CRISPR-Cas9 could be used on humans. The most obvious application would be to treat genetic diseases that result from a gene mutation. In this sense, the CRISPR-Cas9 technology could be used to correct the mutation, add a missing DNA-sequence, or remove a problematic sequence. There are more than 6,000 diseases with genetic origin on record, so the use of genome editing to treat them is likely to be revolutionary (Mali et al., 2013; Wright et al., 2016). CRISPR-Cas9 succeeded in fixing the mutation that is responsible for Duchenne muscular dystrophy (Ayanoğlu et al., 2020). CRISPR-Cas9 could also be ground-breaking in AIDS research. Other studies have shown great potential for healing Parkinson's and cataract diseases, but the effects are not limited to physical diseases with obvious genetic roots. Military research also succeeded in identifying genes that are for example linked to PTSD, often affecting soldiers (Greene and Master, 2018).

As mental illnesses are almost impossible to cure (often medication only alleviates symptoms), a genetic treatment, if efficient, could be a revolutionary step forward in the field of psychiatry and mental health. The therapeutic use is not only limited to curative treatment but also has potential preventive effects. For instance, the efficiency of the smallpox vaccine has been genetically increased. The vaccine against hepatitis B was also improved by blocking the replication of the virus (CRISPR-Cas9 was used to modify the genome).

Yet, the technique might be more hazardous than often portrayed as the potential consequences of this genome editing technology are not as clear-cut as one might hope. The first controversial aspect concerns its non-targeted effects: side effects of the genome editing, which studies have proved to be more present than experts first thought. These are unplanned mutations that occur after the use of CRISPR-Cas9. Studies have shown that with one use of CRISPR-Cas9, sequences of up to 9.500 base pairs can be lost while some parts of DNA can end up being inserted in wrong places. In other words, CRISPR-Cas9 appears to be not as precise as scientists thought after its discovery. These non-targeted effects can result in severe genetic diseases. The second aspect to consider is the complex relationship between the genotype and the phenotype. This relationship is not fully understood by scientists yet. In addition, some studies have proved that CRISPR-Cas9 can provoke a reaction of the human immune system by activating interferons of type 1 (Charlesworth et al., 2019; Kim et al., 2018). The consequences and severity of these reactions still need to be fully determined.

Should we "enhance" people through gene editing?

Genetic engineering tools are also suitable for modifications that are not part of clinical practice. Faced with such possibilities, the ethical debate is heated. A controversial argument is that allowing gene editing would reduce diversity. Most people in favor of this practice disagree because everyone is different and not everyone wants the same things, so people would never choose the same characteristics for their children. Agar, for example, says that this is what makes genetic engineering different from Nazi eugenics: it is not based on a single conception of a desirable genome, and it is voluntary and not obligatory (Agar, 2004). Yet, the risk of moving from "you can have a genetically modified baby" to "you must have a genetically modified baby" cannot be easily discarded.

In terms of the genetic modification of embryos, Savulescu believes that not only is it ethically sound to do it but that it would be wrong not to, if that modification could lead to the child having a "better life." (Savulescu, 2005). How could we convincingly decide what constitutes a "better" life? For Savulescu, a better life would be made up of more friends, better academic performance, motivation to succeed and having more impulse control. In his view, the virtues (practical wisdom, fortitude, etc.) behind such achievements help us to lead happier lives and be better human beings. Buchanan also has a list of "virtues" that are valuable no matter what kind of life the child decides to lead (Buchanan, 2011). Those include intelligence, memory, self-discipline, patience, empathy, a sense of humor, optimism, and having a sunny temperament. But who is to say that better academic performance, having more friends, or a sunny temperament is a "better" life? You could have few but meaningful friendships, you could have been awful at school but be amazingly talented with painting or have no talent at all, have the worst memory in the world but be happier with it than someone with a better amnestic ability. For those that reject moral perfectionism,[6] there is not only one formula of a "good life": each individual has their own version of what that means. Each person is unique and modifying their genes would be robbing that person of their identity, their opportunity to be their true unique selves and who they should have been. One could argue that it is quite paternalistic to believe that one knows what a "good life" is for others, even within the parent-child relationship.

This connects with what is seen as one of the biggest advantages of CRISPR-Cas9, namely that it could be used to modify disease-causing genes, removing the faulty script of that person's and their future descendants' genetic code forever – potentially erasing hereditary conditions off the face of the Earth and reducing global suffering. This would undoubtedly be a great advantage, but that is also what makes it so risky. Editing embryos is not only dangerous because it would alter the children that would come out of it but also future generations, thus altering humanity forever. That is why, since the beginning of the debate more than 15 years before the development of CRISPR-Cas9, around 40 countries passed laws against human germline modification, against using genetically altered embryos or gametes to produce a child.

Furthermore, utilizing gene editing to eliminate diseases or undesirable traits could lead to a slippery slope. At first, we might start by correcting the gene that causes Huntington's disease, or the possibility of having cancer. Once that is doable, what is next? How long until parents are editing embryos to remove shortness, shyness, or other qualities they may find undesirable? At the moment, being overweight is not taken to be a disease; is it okay to try to correct it too? Would that generate a discriminative feeling toward overweight people? In addition, we know that while genes have a role, they are triggered by environmental and social aspects, so why not start working on those first? (Lavazza, 2019b).

Indeed, one of the biggest problems concerning enhancement and autonomy is genetic modification for prospective children (Schaefer et al., 2013). Changing genes as a parental decision can undermine the child's autonomy. As the child cannot have a say in the matter, this can be a difficult matter. The values the child might choose or the life they might want might not be the same as what their parents imagined. Parents cannot limit their child's future opportunities through enhancements – let alone, as Habermas warned us, through a designed genetic makeup (Habermas, 2003).

The most infamous example is surely that of He Jiankui, the Chinese scientist that in 2018 openly affirmed to have used CRISPR-Cas9 to modify the CCR5 gene of twin girls while still embryos, justifying his choice with the intention to make them more resistant to HIV. Aside from issues of consent common to all such situations, this example is particularly useful to show how shortsighted a *a priori* choice of this kind can be. A study claims that the very same doubling of the CCR5 gene (the modification needed to immunize against HIV consists in having two copies of it) substantially increases the chances of shortening the lifespan by two years.[7] Other negative effects consist in lowering one's resistance to the West Nile fever. Was it worth it? Probably not. Jiankui was jailed in December 2019 and fined for 3 million yuan, but, after an initial sentence of three years, he came out in April 2022 – making the whole stigma of "bad science" disappear and opening the gates for others to follow.

24.4 Clinical practice and cognitive enhancement

Attempts to maintain or restore cognitive functions, primarily memory, attention, and reasoning ability occupy a large area of biomedical research and clinical practice. The need for intervention in this field is due to congenital disorders of the nervous system, trauma, strokes, tumors, and increasingly common neurodegenerative diseases. With respect to the latter, research and therapy aim to offer forms of prevention that can preserve a person's cognitive function in an optimal or suboptimal condition for as long as possible (Berger et al., 2005).

In this field, even more so than in the field of genetic interventions, the available drugs and tools can be used off-label to improve one's cognitive function and bring it to a level above the population average, realizing true enhancement. Moreover, the line between maintenance and enhancement seems very blurred, especially with some new techniques that have been on the market for a few years, such as the various forms of noninvasive brain stimulation (Polanía et al., 2018).

The crucial and difficult point to deal with here is what is normal (or optimal) in a certain context that is linked to our cognitive capacities, so as to – supposedly – be able to assess whether the intervention can be ethically problematic or not. The specific challenge raised by pharmacological or technical interventions when related to clinical practice is the attempt to strike a balance between our way of seeing and perceiving the world and the implicit altruistic nature of a clinical setting. In other words, what is at stake when seeking constant improvement in performance is the possible jeopardy of our authenticity, autonomy, and identity (Lavazza, 2019).

Here we will not discuss the specific efficacy of each drug or device, whose ability to modify cognitive functions in a relevant and long-term way is still the subject of dedicated research (Tatti et al., 2016; de Boer et al., 2021). From the point of view of conceptual clarification, ethical issues and possible forms of regulation, however, it is already possible to make considerations that may also apply to likely biomedical developments.

Take a very recent study that seems to confirm the effectiveness of transcranial stimulation with alternating current in improving memory. Grover and colleagues were able to enhance the working and long-term memory of elderly people aged 65 to 80 through repetitive neuromodulation (Grover et al., 2022). The greatest effects occurred in individuals starting from a lower baseline. These results, obtained with an inexpensive and easy-to-use tool, are prompting many people who do not have cognitive deficits to turn to devices developed as clinical tools to improve their intellectual or even sport performance (Lavazza, 2020). The very possibility of improving the average cognitive abilities without risk or excessive effort is also prompting the conception of new social scenarios in which enhancement becomes commonly accepted or even required in some specific contexts (Sharif et al., 2021).

In relation to our cognitive capacities and their possible enhancement within clinical settings, one aspect that can be considered is the possible raise of new duties within certain professions (Santoni de Sio et al., 2014). From motivational to cognitive enhancers, the doubt remains: should we hope that airplane pilots or surgeons would undergo a cognitive enhancing treatment if available? Should we enforce it under specific conditions? Or should we ask them to declare the use of altering substances and technologies even if not strictly required by the current legislation? (Garasic & Lavazza, 2016).

The possibility of treating a deficit, whatever its origin, is a legitimate goal, but this might quickly turn into the wish to make some individuals more cognitively efficient for the benefit of society as a whole, as in the cited case of pilots or surgeons. It is easy to see, however, that such a framework can create a short-circuit in the human enhancement debate itself because the clinical provenance of the tools employed and the extreme difficulty of drawing a line between maintenance and enhancement complicate the classical arguments put forward in that discussion (Racine et al., 2021). Thus, between cure (which also consists of increasing cognitive abilities in the lowest end of the spectrum) and enhancement of those who are already healthy there is no discernible difference: the same drugs and tools are used in both cases. This makes the area of interventions on cognition an extraordinarily sensitive field from an ethical standpoint (Lewis, 2021).

As human beings, we are self-aware. We are able to understand that we are an entity with a past, a present and a future that can be full of pleasure but also pain and suffering. We remember what happened to us and so we make projections about what we do want or do not want for the future. Pain, whether physical or mental, is something that we generally try to avoid as much as we can, yet it can also be very helpful and instructive. Should we delete the memory of a traumatic surgery from the mind of a physician so as to increase their willingness to continue with practice under stressful conditions? Maybe by doing that we could increase the chances of keeping her doing her job, but we would also "numb" part of who she is. This might be true also in technical terms: for example, they might have an intuition on how to save a life precisely by recalling a past bad experience or failure.

This involves memory interventions, particularly memory-modulation techniques, which are currently being researched in many laboratories (Glannon, 2019). The aim is to free trauma victims from unpleasant memories, which often give rise to traumatic stress disorder, a syndrome that can prevent those affected from having a fulfilling life. But drugs such as propranolol, which is taken to be able to mitigate the emotional component of negative memories, can also be used to intervene on memory in extra-clinical settings, raising strong questions about the permissibility of cosmetic memory modifications (Pigeon et al., 2022). Such interventions may have relevant consequences on the legal level (witnesses to a crime may erase relevant memories), on the social level (commitments and promises might be removed), and on the strictly anthropological level (one might choose to "edit" one's biography at will) (Lavazza, 2015).

These issues bring attention back to the fact that self-enhancement could be a threat to one's identity. What do we mean by that? DeGrazia explains that there are two kinds of identity: the numeric and the narrative one (Degrazia, 2006). Numeric identity is the continuity of experiential contents or the maintaining of psychological connection over time, where psychological connection is the capacity of reasoning or even just of conscious experience. From a psychological standpoint, the latter are indispensable, even though psychological continuity is not needed from a strictly biological perspective, whereby we exist as long as we remain alive. As for narrative identity, DeGrazia says that it involves self-conception: someone's "most central values, implicit autobiography, and identifications with particular people, activities, and roles" (Degrazia, 2006). This identity is a creation of our own and our environment. There will come a time in our lives when our reasoning and logic will show us the way we want to build ourselves.

Based on the numeric definition of identity, human enhancement would not change us in our whole individuality. Would we still be the same conscious human being whether we have a new bionic arm, receive a vaccine which immunize us from malaria, or after taking a pill to be more efficient and productive? Concerning the narrative identity, if we see these alterations as a product of ourselves, an extension of who we are and a representation of our surroundings, then we need to accept the fact that enhancements are just one of the possibilities of how we are going to change. This way to see enhancers aimed at adding value to our lives can then be taken to be just as another second order desire that will have an impact on our identity.

In this vein, we could then be prone to see cognitive enhancement as a praiseworthy attempt to extend our impact on society by enabling ourselves to outperform and contribute beyond our "normal" capacities. In a way, this may amount to overcoming a limitation, a deficit, and thus be included in the therapeutic process in a broad sense. But this approach might hide more concerns than we might think.

For instance, on the one hand an "enhanced" surgeon may be able to increase the number of surgeries per day by, say, 10%; on the other hand, however, we would have to consider the parallel impacts on society (let us not forget that the argument justifying the use of enhancement is based on the positive impact on society as whole). Such a scenario gives rise to at least three problems that might be called "dysfunctional":

1) The "hyperperformance" of some particularly valuable and cherished surgeons would reduce even more the possibility for the "average surgeon" to perform. Even from a strictly utilitarian perspective, such a calculus might not be as straightforward as initially portrayed (Santoni de Sio et al., 2014).
2) If cognitive enhancers were optional, considering the ubiquitous quantifications of performance in our society, good surgeons unwilling to use cognitive enhancers would either be pushed to use them under peer pressure or be ostracized for not being "as committed" as their enhanced colleagues (with the risk of losing many excellent and valuable professionals).
3) If the use were instead to be compulsory, the problem would be related to the impact on society more broadly. Would people be forced to cognitively enhance themselves so as to be able to be more alert during longer shifts (while being paid the same)? (Garasic & Lavazza, 2016).

Hence, the view of cognitive enhancement as ethically sound is connected to larger social considerations that, as mentioned before, are themselves shaped by cultural and societal inputs. In this sense, the assessment is extremely difficult to standardize.

24.5 Longevity and medical practice

Should we "cure" people from dying? Is it ethical to consider life extension as a clinical achievement? With the increased attention given by multibillionaires such as Jeff Bezos and Larry Page on research focused on longevity, this theme is ever timelier and deserves careful ethical analyses – and the way in which this revolution could impact our way of conceptualizing clinical practice.[8]

The most powerful and controversial argument in relation to life extension is the one put forward, among others, by de Grey (2008). For de Grey, aging is something that we should treat. No more, no less than for AIDS or Alzheimer's, we should use scientific progress to eradicate this "disease." Unlike other posthumanists who are more prone to focus on hyper-longevity "only" as an enhancement, de Grey strategically places the discussion into the field of therapy – leveling aging with other, accepted illnesses. However, his position is rather extreme when he states that accepting death as part of life is just the result of a social stigma that needs to be addressed and changed, as it is deeply irrational.

Despite experimental attempts in line with this view – such as seeking ways to get rid of aging cells from our bodies with a direct increase of lifespan[9] – the cultural and axiological framework is still unconvincing for many scholars. Indirectly responding to Buchanan as well, one should probably point out that embracing lifespan extension might end up resulting in a zero-sum result. In fact, as explained by Di Paola and Garasic, imagining a "feasible" life extension to 500 years would put us in front of two deeply problematic scenarios (2013). First, we would damage the planet and future generations with a drastic increase of the world population. Second, we would likely find ourselves in a situation in which only a few wealthy individuals might have access to a biotechnologically induced longevity, and this would worsen discrimination. The impact would affect future generations as well as the distribution of resources across already existing individuals on the planet. Notably, a single person living 500 years would consume resources such as air, water, and food in the same amount that would have otherwise supported the existence of six or more generations of people.

In relation to issues of intergenerational justice and the implicit value of this constant reshuffling of energy within the human species, a strong voice would be that of Hannah Arendt, who stressed the importance of looking at human civilization through its succession of generations, calling into question the moral legitimacy of prolonging our lives – both from an individual and societal perspective. Arendt refers to the non-biological evolutionary process, a process in which we accumulate and exchange knowledge, by concentrating on the intrinsic and widespread power of natality (Arendt, 1958). Natality represents what is new in this world, the challenge for (mental or physical) institutions to keep on progressing. Death is crucially linked to birth; the last step, death itself, allows humanity to gradually progress toward new perspectives, giving visibility and strength to innovative ways of conceiving the world that are simply beyond the reach of previous generations.

Of course, one could argue that the interests and desires of an individual can (and often do) differ from the ones of humanity as a whole, so each person able to access the right technology and with the economic resources to do so, could rationally choose to extend their life. However, aside from the contributory responsibility dimension of this choice that could find this version of rationality not necessarily applicable to climate change concerns, it is important to consider that our initial enthusiasm for the reaching of life extension might be misplaced.

Hans Jonas is a good reference to question such an optimistic view of life extension. Aside from other concerns more broadly connected to technology, Jonas warned us against forsaking the acceptance of our mortality and finitude as a "blessing" (Jonas, 1992; Lavazza & Garasic, 2020). We should keep in mind that focusing on trying to increase our lifespan would mean a decrease of empathy – something so intrinsic in clinical practice that its loss cannot be seen as either virtuous or ethical.

24.6 Conclusion

As we have seen, in at least three areas of clinical practice the theoretical boundary between therapeutic interventions and forms of enhancement tends to disappear for both technical reasons and from the point of view of social perception as well. This means that certain forms of enhancement may be more easily introduced and accepted as healthcare. This is not without consequences, however, as forms of enhancement that result from therapeutic interventions may also raise ethical concerns. In this chapter, we have considered the use of genetic engineering in medicine, various forms of cognitive interventions, and longevity research.

In all these areas, achieved and reasonably foreseeable advances are to be welcomed insofar as they can help patients or improve the average condition of those who are not currently suffering from any disease, in particular the elderly. On the other hand, interventions that originate in the realm of therapy but which bring about a clear enhancement of some individuals over the rest of the population may create imbalances or negative side effects that should be carefully monitored and, in some cases, regulated.

As for genetic techniques from the CRISPR family, intervening in the germ line could represent a valuable shortcut to prevent and cure many illnesses and diseases. However, the line between therapeutic and enhancement-oriented interventions can become rather thin, with very significant implications. Parental choices for a child to be as "healthy" and "equipped for life" as possible may conflict with the freedom of young people to determine their own lives independently. Also, society may become more unfair and uneven due to specific genetic selections implemented by individual families (e.g., prevalence of males and shortage of females).

In the case of cognitive enhancement, both the *paradigm of availability* and the *paradigm of possibility of therapy* converge: any tool for reducing cognitive deficits or maintaining cognitive performance is a legitimate means of intervening on one's cognition. If the principle of autonomy applies, whereby the individual can decide how to intervene on their own mind/brain, the recommendation is then to consider the social consequences and undesirable effects that would result from the enhancement-use of certain drugs and devices intended to treat cognitive abilities.

Finally, in the case of longevity, the idea of private companies allowing some wealthy individuals to have a lifespan that is three or four times longer than the average population seems to be clearly far removed from the idea of therapy – which instead could be encapsulated in the improvement of the health conditions of elderly patients. The principle of equal opportunity should be what guides public policy and the allocation of research funds, provided that scientists are free to pursue the studies they find most interesting, useful, or promising.

A universalistic principle of therapy (i.e., the possibility for everyone to receive treatment when needed) as opposed to enhancement, which is selective and less inclusive, may ultimately be a good compass to guide ethical analysis and operational decisions at the boundary between clinical practice and individual improvement.

Notes

1 Some clarifications concerning this key term in our work are needed here. First, we are not referring to the version of posthumanism belonging to the political sphere of the discussion. Secondly, to avoid confusion, we will not use the term transhumanism, though Bostrom himself (as mentioned, one the major representatives of the transhumanist movement) uses the two terms interchangeably.
2 In relation to this, it is important to consider Matthew Liao et al.'s suggestion that shortening people could be a way forward to combat climate change (we would consume less resources), underlining how this and other characteristics are context and culture dependent and not as objective as often portrayed.
3 https://en.wikipedia.org/wiki/Oscar_Pistorius.
4 https://cybathlon.ethz.ch/en.
5 NIH and National human genome research institute. "What is genome editing?." *USA government*. www.genome.gov/about-genomics/policy-issues/what-is-Genome-Editing.
6 https://plato.stanford.edu/entries/perfectionism-moral/.
7 www.nature.com/articles/s41591-019-0459-6.
8 www.cnbc.com/2021/09/21/silicon-valleys-quest-to-live-forever-could-benefit-the-rest-of-us.html.
9 www.nature.com/articles/s41574-022-00701-7; https://www.science.org/content/article/suicide-aging-cells-prolongs-life-span-mice.

References

Agar, N 1999, 'Liberal Eugenics' in H Kuhse & P Singer (eds.), *Bioethics: An Anthology*, Blackwell, Oxford.
Agar, N 2004, *Liberal Eugenics: In Defence of Human Enhancement*, Blackwell, Oxford UK.
Arendt, H 1958, *The Human Condition*, University of Chicago Press, Chicago.
Ayanoğlu, FB, Elçin, AE & Elçin, YM 2020, 'Bioethical Issues in Genome Editing by CRISPR-Cas9 Technology', *Turkish Journal of Biology*, vol. 44, no. 2, pp. 110–20.
Berger, TW, Ahuja, A, Courellis, SH, Deadwyler, SA, Erinjippurath, G, Gerhardt, GA, Gholmieh, G, Granacki, JJ, Hampson, R, Hsaio, MC, LaCoss, J, Marmarelis, VZ, Nasiatka, P, Srinivasan, V, Song, D, Tanguay, AR & Wills, J 2005, 'Restoring Lost Cognitive Function', *IEEE Engineering in Medicine and Biology Magazine*, vol. 24, no. 5, pp. 30–44.
Bostrom, N 2003, 'Human Genetic Enhancements: A Transhumanist Perspective', *Journal of Value Inquiry*, vol. 37, no. 4, pp. 493–506.
Bostrom, N 2005, 'Recent Developments in the Ethics, Science, and Politics of Life Extension', *Ageing Horizons*, no. 3, pp. 28–33.
Bostrom, N 2008, 'Why I Want to Be a Posthuman When I Grow Up', in B Gordijn & R Chadwick (eds.), *Medical Enhancement and Posthumanity*, Springer, Dordrecht, pp. 107–37.
Bostrom, N 2020, 'A Letter from Utopia, Version 3.3', available at: http://nickbostrom.com/utopia.

Bostrom, N & Roache, R 2008, 'Ethical Issues in Human Enhancement', in J Ryberg, T Petersen & C Wolf (eds.), *New Waves in Applied Ethics*, Palgrave Macmillan, Basingstoke, pp. 120–52.

Buchanan, A 2011, *Beyond Humanity? The Ethics of Biomedical Enhancement*, University Press Oxford, Oxford.

Charlesworth, CT, Deshpande, PS, Dever, DP, Camarena, J, Lemgart, VT, Cromer, MK, Vakulskas, CA, Collingwood, MA, Zhang, L, Bode, NM, Behlke, MA, Dejene, B, Cieniewicz, B, Romano, R, Lesch, BJ, Gomez-Ospina, N, Mantri, S, Pavel-Dinu, M, Weinberg, KI & Porteus, MH 2019, 'Identification of Preexisting Adaptive Immunity to Cas9 Proteins in Humans', *Nature Medicine*, vol. 25, no. 2, pp. 249–54.

de Boer, NS, Schluter, RS, Daams, JG, van der Werf, YD, Goudriaan, AE & van Holst, RJ 2021, 'The Effect of Non-invasive Brain Stimulation on Executive Functioning in Healthy Controls: A Systematic Review and Meta-analysis', *Neuroscience & Biobehavioral Reviews*, vol. 125, pp. 122–47.

de Grey, A 2008, *Ending Aging: The Rejuvenation Breakthroughs that Could Reverse Human Aging in Our Lifetime*, St. Martin's Press, New York.

Degrazia, D 2006, 'Enhancement Technologies and Human Identity', *Journal of Medicine and Philosophy*, vol. 30, no. 3, pp. 261–83.

Di Paola, M & Garasic, MD 2013, 'The Dark Side of Sustainability: On Avoiding, Engineering, and Shortening Human Lives in the Anthropocene', *Rivista di Studi sulla Sostenibilità*, vol. 3, no. 2, pp. 59–81.

Garasic, MD & Lavazza, A 2016, 'Moral and Social Reasons to Acknowledge the Use of Cognitive Enhancers in Competitive-selective Contexts', *BMC Medical Ethics*, vol. 17, no. 1, pp. 1–12.

Glannon, W 2019, *The Neuroethics of Memory: From Total Recall to Oblivion*, Cambridge University Press, Cambridge.

Greene, MZ & Master, Z 2018, 'Ethical Issues of Using CRISPR Technologies for Research on Military Enhancement', *Journal of Bioethical Inquiry*, vol. 15, no. 3, pp. 327–35.

Grover, S, Wen, W, Viswanathan, V, Gill, CT & Reinhart, RM 2022, 'Long-lasting, Dissociable Improvements in Working Memory and Long-term Memory in Older Adults with Repetitive Neuromodulation', *Nature Neuroscience*, vol. 25, no. 9, pp. 1237–46.

Habermas, J 2003, *The Future of Human Nature: On the Way to a Liberal Eugenics?*, Polity Press, Cambridge.

Harris, J 1975, 'The Survival Lottery', *Philosophy*, vol. 50, no. 191, pp. 81–7.

Harris, J 2007, *Enhancing Evolution: The Ethical Case for Making Better People*, Princeton University Press, Princeton NJ.

Jensen, SR 2020, 'SIENNA D3.4: Ethical Analysis of Human Enhancement Technologies', Zenodo, p. 14 (V1.1). https://doi.org/10.5281/zenodo.4068071.

Jonas, H 1992, 'The Burden and Blessing of Mortality', *Hastings Center Report*, vol. 22, no. 1, pp. 34–40.

Jotterand, F 2008, 'Beyond Therapy and Enhancement: The Alteration of Human Nature', *NanoEthics*, vol. 2, no. 1, pp. 15–23.

Kim, S, Koo, T, Jee, HG, Cho, HY, Lee, G, Lim, D-G, Shin, HS & Kim, J-S 2018, 'CRISPR RNAs Trigger Innate Immune Responses in Human Cells', *Genome Research*, vol. 28, no. 3, pp. 367–73.

Lavazza, A 2015, 'Erasing Traumatic Memories: When Context and Social Interests can Outweigh Personal Autonomy', *Philosophy, Ethics, and Humanities in Medicine*, vol. 10, no. 1, pp. 1–7.

Lavazza, A 2019a, 'Moral Bioenhancement through Memory-editing: A Risk for Identity and Authenticity?', *Topoi*, vol. 38, no. 1, pp. 15–27.

Lavazza, A 2019b, 'Parental Selective Reproduction: Genome-editing and Maternal Behavior as a Potential Concern', *Frontiers in Genetics*, vol. 10, p. 532.

Lavazza, A 2020, 'Transcranial Electrical Stimulation for Human Enhancement and the Risk of Inequality: Prohibition or Compensation?', *Bioethics*, vol. 33, no. 1, pp. 122–31.

Lavazza, A & Garasic, MD 2020, 'Vampires 2.0? The Ethical Quandaries of Young Blood Infusion in the Quest for Eternal Life', *Medicine, Health Care and Philosophy*, vol. 23, pp. 421–32.

Lewis, J 2021, 'Autonomy and the Limits of Cognitive Enhancement', *Bioethics*, vol. 35, no. 1, pp. 15–22.

Liao, M, Sandberg, A & Roache, R 2012, 'Human Engineering and Climate Change', *Ethics, Policy and Environment*, vol. 15, no. 2, pp. 206–21.

Mali, P, Yang, L, Esvelt, KM, Aach, J, Guell, M, DiCarlo, JE, Norville, JE & Churchet, GM 2013, 'RNA-guided Human Genome Engineering via Cas9', *Science*, vol. 339, no. 6121, pp. 823–82.

Persson, I & Savulescu, J 2012, *Unfit for the Future: The Need for Moral Enhancement*, Oxford University Press, Oxford.

Pigeon, S, Lonergan, M, Rotondo, O, Pitman, RK & Brunet, A 2022, 'Impairing Memory Reconsolidation with Propranolol in Healthy and Clinical Samples: A Meta-analysis', *Journal of Psychiatry and Neuroscience*, vol. 47, no. 2, pp. 109–22.

Polanía, R, Nitsche, MA & Ruff, CC 2018, 'Studying and Modifying Brain Function with Non-invasive Brain Stimulation', *Nature Neuroscience*, vol. 21, no. 2, pp. 174–87.

Racine, E, Sattler, S & Boehlen, W 2021, 'Cognitive Enhancement: Unanswered Questions about Human Psychology and Social Behavior', *Science and Engineering Ethics*, vol. 27, no. 2, pp. 1–25.

Sandel, M 2007, *The Case against Perfection*, Harvard University Press, Cambridge MA.
Santoni de Sio, F, Robichaud, P & Vincent, NA 2014, 'Who Should Enhance? Conceptual and Normative Dimensions of Cognitive Enhancement', *Humana.Mente Journal of Philosophical Studies*, vol. 7, no. 26, pp. 179–97.
Savulescu, J 2005, 'New Breeds of Humans: The Moral Obligation to Enhance', *Reproductive BioMedicine Online*, vol. 10, pp. 36–9.
Savulescu, J 2006, 'Genetic Interventions and the Ethics of Enhancement of Human Beings', in B Steinbock (ed.), *The Oxford Handbook on Bioethics*, Oxford University Press, Oxford, pp. 516–35.
Schaefer, GO, Kahane, G & Savulescu, J 2013, 'Autonomy and Enhancement', *Neuroethics*, vol. 7, pp. 123–36.
Sharif, S, Guirguis, A, Fergus, S & Schifano, F 2021, 'The Use and Impact of Cognitive Enhancers among University Students: A Systematic Review', *Brain Sciences*, vol. 11, no. 3, p. 355.
Tatti, E, Rossi, S, Innocenti, I, Rossi, A & Santarnecchi, E 2016, 'Non-invasive Brain Stimulation of the Aging Brain: State of the Art and Future Perspectives', *Ageing Research Reviews*, vol. 29, pp. 66–89.
Wright, AV, Nunez, JK & Doudna, JA 2016, 'Biology and Applications of CRISPR Systems: Harnessing Nature's Toolbox for Genome Engineering', *Cell*, vol. 164, pp. 29–44.

25
CYBORGS AND DESIGNER BABIES
The human body as a technological design space

Michael Bess

25.1 A humane cyborg

"I went deaf," recalls the technology writer Michael Chorost, "on July 7, 2001, at ten-thirty in the morning."[1] Chorost, then 36 years old, had just arrived at the airport in Reno, Nevada, for a consulting job. He already wore two hearing aids because his ears had been severely damaged by the rubella virus before he was born. Outfitted with his first hearing aids at age 3, he had learned how to function normally in the world of the hearing and had eventually gone on to earn a Ph.D. in writing and rhetoric.

Now, as he looked around the Reno airport, preparing to pick up his rental car, he noticed that his hearing was rapidly declining in quality. "Batteries," he thought to himself, and swapped out the tiny batteries in his hearing aids. No improvement. He turned up the volume on the devices to the maximum, but his hearing continued to decline. The familiar sound of cars rushing by faded to a distant whisper. For reasons still unknown to Chorost and his doctors today, the tiny cilia in his cochlea that transmit sound vibrations to the auditory nerve were ceasing to function.

About a month later, Chorost underwent outpatient surgery to install a cochlear implant in his head, just above and behind his left ear. He was joining more than 700,000 other persons who have had the device installed since it was first developed in the late 1950s (with tremendous improvements in cost, size, and performance, especially since the 1980s). Chorost wrote a book in 2005 about his experience with the cochlear implant, provocatively titled *Rebuilt: How Becoming Part Computer Made Me More Human*. In this thoughtful account, he describes not only the many difficulties he encountered in adapting to the new device but also the ways in which it forced him to rethink his place in the Great Chain of Being. He looked up the definition of the word "cyborg," which he had long associated with futuristic sci-fi creations like the Terminator or Robocop, and discovered that the dictionary's take on the word was actually far simpler: "a person whose physiological functioning is aided by or dependent upon a mechanical or electronic device."[2] If that's the definition, he realized, then a cyborg was precisely what he had become.

Chorost's great contribution to the study of cyborgs lies in the way he charts the human impact of living as a part-machine being, describing the countless mundane, ephemeral, and seemingly trivial implications that are actually as subtle as they are profound. What one realizes, after reading Chorost's narrative, is that the essence of being a cyborg does not really lie in the fact itself of incorporating machine elements into one's body. Rather, it lies in the myriad ways that the machine changes Chorost's daily life, his connections with other people, his range of fears and hopes, and his relation to his own body. Here are three examples.

To celebrate my new ear, I go out to buy my first portable CD player. I want to play my familiar old CDs as a way of mapping my new auditory world onto my old one. ... An hour later, I'm home with a patch cable and a new Walkman. As I sit down on the couch to listen, [my cat] Elvis arches his back and rolls belly-up to greet me. It occurs to me that there's no way he can hear the music. If I were wearing headphones, he'd be able to hear whatever little bit of sound leaked out. But I'm plugged directly into the player. Its electrical output goes straight into the processor, which converts it to binary and passes it on to the implant. The implant decides which electrodes to trigger in my cochlea. There are no physical vibrations anywhere. All Elvis is ever going to hear is the hum of the player itself. I'm hearing music that never actually exists as sound.[3]

―――

A normal cochlea uses physical mechanisms to separate out the [sound] frequencies the way a coin sorter rattles coins into piles. A cochlear implant, however, has to do the task with binary logic, digitally taking sound apart and figuring out which electrodes to fire on the array every passing millisecond. The software that manages this process is one of the monumental achievements of bionics. Here is a very small piece of it, written in a language called C.

```
DualLoopAGC () {
Int incre;
If (Env > CslowInt) {
/* attack mode */
Int FastThresh = qMultClip (CslowInt, dBplus8,3);
Int EnvLimit;
If (Env > FastThresh) {
Incr = 0;
} else {
/* incr = 3; */
```

When I first read this code, I was eerily aware that these very instructions were being executed *right now*, over and over, thousands of times per second, in my processor and inside my head. They were what enabled me to hear the paper rustling as I paged through it, my own voice muttering lines here and there. I was reading my own software.[4]

―――

Progress happens not just between one generation of implants and the next, but also between new generations of software loaded into a single person's implant. Such advances are the hope of every person with a cochlear implant: that however well they hear now, new software and faster processors will someday enable them to hear better. The online bulletin boards are full of chatter comparing one algorithm to another and swapping rumors about when the next one will come out. It's sort of like listening to techies talk about the latest version of Windows or Linux. Except these people are cyborgs, and the platforms are their bodies.[5]

These experiences are not congruent with the imagery that science-fiction novels and Hollywood movies conjure up around cyborgs.[6] We have no splashy techno-wizardry here, no flying over buildings. Instead, we encounter in Chorost's world a different order of the alien, a strangeness tucked astonishingly into the intimate and mundane details of everyday life. To recognize, all of a sudden, the isolation that comes from hearing music piped directly from CD player to brain, music unavailable to other biological organisms sitting close by; to read the software code that is currently operating one's own sensorium; to browse eagerly through the various technological upgrades that one will soon be able to install for one's own body – this is what it really means to be a cyborg.

It could mean many other things as well, of course, depending on the specific capabilities that machines gradually come to add to our bodies and minds. But this, at heart, is Chorost's underlying message in *Rebuilt*: the cyborg capabilities are extraordinary in themselves, but their most important impact has to do with how those new modes of sensing, feeling, acting, or communicating affect our identity. And in speaking of identity here, we are not referring to some abstract change of status that comes with incorporating a machine into one's being ("I am now a cybernetic organism"). Rather, it is the much richer, more visceral kind of identity that grows out of the simple concreteness of daily events. To find oneself on the couch, here and now, acutely aware of the experiential gulf that has just emerged between oneself and one's pet cat: we are no longer linked by our common occupancy of a world of sound waves. I have my machine-mediated universe over here, you have your biological universe over there. Our shared familiar space – this room, the life we live together here – has experienced a tear in its fabric. The cat seems a little farther away from me now, even though it has not moved from its place on the couch. Then, after a little while, life goes on as before. I get up to make dinner. But I cannot see myself in quite the same way anymore. My angle of vision has changed.

The identity shift we are describing here possesses a nuanced complexity that our customary moral categories do not easily capture. Think of the concepts we usually adopt for assessing the ethical implications of a new technology: words such as "dehumanization" or "dignity." Has Chorost been dehumanized by his new brain-direct mode of apprehending music? Has his dignity been diminished? A simple "yes" or "no" answer won't do. What has taken place is a multi-leveled set of intricate ongoing trade-offs, with some valued qualities of life lessened, while others have benefited. Chorost is now distanced from his cat and presumably from other hearing beings in a basic way. But he can still listen to the Beatles and Bach, whereas without the machine he would have had to rely on nothing but the memory of that sound. He has to learn how to compensate for the distance the machine has created between him and his animal companion, perhaps by taking the extra time to stroke the cat's soft fur a bit more attentively. Perhaps by fixing its favorite meal a bit more often. He gradually discovers, moreover, that he has to do this sort of thing with his professional and interpersonal relationships as well.

There is something deeply human about this. A man has taken a hit from life, and he has to learn how to adapt, how to recover the richness and challenge of his relationships with others, with nature, with himself. This does not necessarily result in a net impoverishment of his existence – far from it. The heightened attention he now must pay to the quality of his interactions may actually result in a more fulfilling experience of life. The dignity, the humanity, of the situation lies not in the presence or absence of a machine inside his skull but in how he responds to the new configuration of capabilities and weaknesses that the machine has brought into his being. Becoming a cyborg, in other words, is neither an automatic enhancement nor an automatic debasement: it is simply an opportunity, a challenge.

To be sure, some kinds of future bioelectronic interventions may prove to be profoundly dehumanizing. One thinks for example of a brain-reading device that allowed people to listen in on other people's thought processes without their consent. Such a technology would implode the distinction between public and personal mental spaces, grievously undermining the elemental privacy of our subjective personhood, with devastating implications for the coherence and authenticity of our moral lives. But my point here is that our evaluation of such technologies should not focus on broad, highly generalized, and a priori categories. It should concentrate instead on the lived experience of the altered person, and how that person's flourishing has been affected in concrete practice – for better, for worse, or (in most cases) for the complex admixtures of both.

25.2 The autonomy of designer babies

The world's first two children who might be said to qualify as full-fledged "designer babies" came into existence in November 2018, in China.[7] In order to protect their family's privacy, their real names were kept secret: they came to be known to the public as Lulu and Nana. A biophysicist named He Jiankui presided over their creation. With the consent of the two girls' parents (given before Lulu and Nana were conceived), Jiankui used cutting-edge CRISPR technology to edit the girls' genomes, making a single modification that promised to render them less susceptible to the HIV virus. Since the modification also altered the DNA in the girls' sex cells, it would be passed on to any offspring that Lulu or Nana might eventually conceive – and it would be transmitted down the germline of their families through subsequent generations.

Jiankui expected to win international acclaim for this path-breaking scientific feat, but it was not to be. Bioethicists and scientists around the world resoundingly condemned what he had done, arguing that Jiankui had violated a consensus-based moratorium on using CRISPR for germline modifications in humans. They also pointed out that the modification was reckless and unnecessary since plenty of medical and pharmaceutical options were available for treating HIV without resorting to genetic manipulation. The Chinese government, which had initially trumpeted the breakthrough achievement of one of their scientists, swiftly reversed course and hit Jiankui with a variety of ethical and legal charges. He was eventually hauled into a Chinese court, which fined him the equivalent of $430,000 and sentenced him to three years in prison.[8]

The moral debate surrounding designer babies has generated heaps of scholarly and popular literature in recent decades.[9] Let us imagine, for the sake of argument, that a method is found one day to modify children's genomes in a way that is safe and effective, and that society therefore embarks on the project of introducing modifications into new generations of humans. From what we understand today about genetic causation, this will rarely be a direct form of shaping, with clear and predictable results. To the extent that genetic bioenhancement becomes technologically feasible at all, it will be a relatively uncertain enterprise, whose outcomes will be probabilistic in nature: the complex interaction of genetic, epigenetic, and environmental factors in determining phenotypic traits all but guarantees this.[10] Nevertheless, by combining targeted alterations in DNA and gene regulation with carefully-choreographed environmental conditions, parents may someday acquire the ability to increase the *probability* that a certain trait or suite of traits will predominate in a particular child's phenotype.

Such powers are considerably less dramatic and impressive than those sometimes depicted in science-fiction movies and novels. We will not be able to "order up" character traits in our offspring, confidently expecting specific results, as one would do in selecting items from a menu at a restaurant. Having said this, however, it is also important not to underestimate the significance of the shaping capabilities that we might plausibly acquire. These limited probabilistic powers would still add up to a major recalibration of what it means to be a parent, a child, or a sibling. We would be introducing a new element of deliberate design into the dynamics of family life.[11]

25.3 Psychological and moral challenges for parents

Zen teachers sometimes relate a parable about a man who is rowing his boat on a river. Suddenly a canoe comes floating downstream: it has come loose from its moorings, and there is no one in it to steer, so the empty canoe collides with the man's rowboat. The man becomes red-faced with anger and yells at the canoe as it drifts off down the stream; he shakes his fist, berating it for its dangerous behavior.

In the Buddhist context, this story about the absurdity of yelling at an empty canoe is meant to illustrate the concept of "No Self" – the idea that our conception of ourselves as solid, well-defined beings with an unchanging inner core is actually a kind of optical illusion. Buddhist psychology holds that we are constantly changing, moment by moment, and that our identity is far more fluid and tenuous than we tend to believe.[12] According to the Buddhist tradition, therefore, this illusory belief in a solid self leads us to take ourselves far too seriously – a mental habit that is actually as nonsensical as someone yelling at the irresponsible conduct of an empty canoe. When someone offends us with the things they say or do, we often get angry and respond with aggression of our own: but this is based on a fundamental misconception, and if we realize that there is actually no solid person in front of us but only an ever-shifting set of interacting causes and effects, we may be able to respond more compassionately and reasonably to the situation. We won't take it so "personally" and will therefore be able to respond with greater equanimity and empathy. Don't get so angry at what has happened, the Zen teacher is saying: for when you look more carefully, you will see that the canoe actually has no one in it.

Taken out of its Buddhist context, this story highlights a key moral implication of creating designer babies. In today's world, no one has any direct say in the shaping of my genome. My parents happened to fall in love with each other, and as a result, I ended up with a mixture of their genes. At no point has anyone made any direct "shaping" choices here. If I come to dislike certain aspects of my genetic makeup, I can't really blame my parents for these defects because they never really had any conscious choice in the matter. I can certainly blame fate, or luck, or the gods, if I wish, but it would be unreasonable for me to hold any human being responsible. The canoe was empty.

But with the advent of designer babies, this situation fundamentally changes. My parents *did* have a choice in deciding which genes to insert into my genome (and which ones to exclude). The advent of CRISPR and other genetic manipulation technologies suddenly brings my genetic makeup within the range of human agency. If something goes wrong with this process, or if I simply dislike the outcome, I now have someone whom I can reasonably hold responsible for what has transpired. A paddler has been put into the canoe.

This technological and societal shift will put unprecedented moral pressure on parents: suddenly they will have become partially responsible for overseeing the functioning of an extremely complex biological process that powerfully contributes to shaping the identity of their offspring. Where once it was primarily the "nurture" element that they could expect to influence with their child-rearing strategies, now it will be the entire nature/nurture interaction that comes within the purview of their active decision-making. Even though this will still be only a partial and limited form of control, the expanded reach of their shaping powers will confront them with a whole new range of dauntingly important decisions to make. For example: which genome-shaping company should we entrust with this process? How can we know the long-term implications of choosing "gene package A" as opposed to "gene package B"? How will our choices affect not only this current child but the family dynamics among the other siblings?

Some parents may understandably balk at accepting such powers and responsibilities. Whether for religious reasons or simply out of a sense of humility or caution, they may refuse to go down the designer baby road. But this in itself will constitute a momentous moral decision: for in a society in which large numbers of parents have embraced the option of partially shaping their children's genomes, the act itself of refusing such powers will bring morally significant results. One can imagine a child coming home from school one day, weeping with rage: "All the bioenhanced kids have so many awesome genetic traits, and I'm one of the genetic losers in my class! How can you possibly have shown such neglect when you were conceiving me?"

For those parents who do opt to partially shape their children's genomes, one can expect that this process will have a profound impact on parental expectations regarding the future personal character and life trajectory of their offspring. Unavoidably, they will need to sit down and map out some of the character traits that they hope to inculcate within their future child, and this will compel them to explicitly articulate their hopes and dreams for that child's future. Already today, to be sure, many parents tend to harbor such implicit expectations for their children – but the advent of genetic manipulation technologies will leave a new generation of parents no choice but to render those tacit expectations far more concrete, detailed, and openly expressed. It is hard to see how this would not increase pressure on the children, as they develop and mature, to live up to the expectations that their parents will have laid out for them.

And what about that little "design session" itself? Today's parents certainly face challenging child-rearing choices as they make decisions about what kind of school they want for their children, what kinds of friendships and extracurricular activities they wish to encourage, and so on. But genetic manipulation technologies would take such choices to a qualitatively new level. A whole gamut of phenotypic traits would suddenly come within range of partial human agency, ranging from physical attributes like disease resistance to more ethereal qualities such as introversion/extroversion, personal character, and cognitive aptitudes.

Even though manipulating such traits will unavoidably be a tenuous matter of altering propensities and probabilities, such choices cannot help but be momentous ones. What if the parents cannot reach agreement regarding the suite of traits they wish to include or exclude in the genetic intervention? One reasonable solution would be for parents to compromise in crafting the genetic package: *You prefer traits A, B, and C, whereas I definitely want X, Y, and Z. But the genetic counselor tells us that not all these traits are compatible with each other. So let's compromise by going with traits A, C, and Y.* Another solution might be for one parent to have predominant say in shaping the genetic package for the firstborn child, and for the other parent to have priority in choosing the suite of traits for the next child. This procedure would bring a certain kind of fairness into play in an abstract way, of course, but it could lead to disastrous consequences if it resulted in each parent subsequently feeling greater affinity and affection for the child whose trait package they had been primarily responsible for designing.

25.4 Knowing that you were partially designed

Arduous as the design process will be for parents, I suspect it will in some ways pose even more profound psychological challenges for the offspring. At the most immediate level, we might expect to see new kinds of sibling rivalries developing: *You got fantastic math skills, and I got stuck with this stupid literary flair that no one cares about.* Or: *I catch so many more colds than you because Mom and Dad were too cheap to plunk for a decent Immune Pack when I was born.* The tendency to think of enhancement interventions in crudely commodified ways will probably become especially prevalent in the context of sibling relationships. This should not be surprising, because siblings often perceive each other in comparative terms, closely scrutinizing the distribution of advantages and privileges across the members of the household. Under these circumstances, the temptation to reify a certain trait, comparing its relative value to other equally reified traits, will be strong.

At a deeper level, what would it be like to know, as you were growing up, that your parents had partially designed your genome? For myself, I would imagine that my natural response would be to insist on finding out what my "design specs" were. Faced with this knowledge, I would presumably have at least two options. I could choose to conform, deliberately aligning my pursuits, activities, and relationships in accordance with my designated trait profile. Or I could choose to rebel, defiantly opting for pursuits, activities, and relationships that ran counter to my alleged predispositions. Either way, something of a self-fulfilling prophecy will have come into play: my behaviors would be wrenched powerfully one way or the other by my knowledge of the kind of person I was "supposed" to become. Whether I conform or rebel, the knowledge itself shapes me: it constrains my primordial freedom to discover who I wanted to make of myself.

It is possible, of course, that this issue will not end up being such a big deal. For one thing, the actual shaping powers exerted by even the most eagerly interventionist and control-seeking parents will only be very limited and probabilistic in nature. Individuals brought into being in the era of trait selection will still possess powerful grounds for exercising autonomous decisions about their own life plans, undertakings, and behavior patterns. The very nature of genetic causation precludes their character traits from being "preprogrammed" in highly specific and deterministic ways – and many of them will understand this fact and take it into account. At most, they will have to deal with the psychological impact of knowing that certain broad predispositions *may* be at work in nudging their development down certain pathways rather than others. The difference between "shaping as destiny" vs. "shaping as possible limited influence" is a significant one. Perhaps, therefore, the children of that era will learn to shrug off these philosophical concerns, and will simply get on with their lives the way people do today.

But perhaps not. Suppose that I discover, while growing up, that I have a deep, abiding passion for the visual arts, and derive my most significant pleasure and personal meaning in my studio where I create all manner of paintings and sculptures. At the same time, I also know that my parents explicitly targeted precisely this kind of affinity for me when they designed my genome. They could not know for sure that I would become an artist, of course, but I have seen their pride and satisfaction as they observed the flourishing of my artistic career. How would this feel? Would I feel that my artistic pursuits and achievements were truly my own – or would I feel more like an extension of my parents' will?

The philosopher Jürgen Habermas addresses this topic in his book, *The Future of Human Nature*.[13] At the root of all these kinds of questions, he argues, lies the very nature of autonomous volition itself, which is predicated on my possessing a distinct individuality and personal identity, and a fundamental dimension of sovereignty over my own choices.[14] My values, tastes, and preferences dictate my choices, which in turn shape my behaviors. But where do my values, tastes, and preferences themselves come from? In today's world, they take form gradually over the course of my lifetime, through the dynamic interaction of my innate characteristics and my experiences as I grow up. They form an aspect of the continuously evolving, emergent whole that is my personhood. The influence of other people plays a significant part in shaping these elemental aspects of my being, but so do the innate predispositions arising from my unique genetic makeup. These two causal factors, and the ongoing interplay between them, gradually co-construct my identity over time.

A key assumption, in this equation, is that the genetic component of this ongoing formative process lies beyond direct human control. It is not subject to the preferences of other people and constitutes a basic constraining factor that limits the extent to which other people can influence my development and behaviors. (For example: "You may do everything in your power to make me choose a career in the family business, but you will never be able to suppress the free-spirited musician in me.") In this sense, my genetic inheritance is like a kind of internal ballast in the ongoing constitution of my identity over time. It plays a key role in giving substance to my autonomy and helps define the specific constellation of qualities and characteristics that make up what is most deeply "mine" about my selfhood at any given moment. When I say that my values, tastes, and preferences are *my own*, it is to this delicately-balanced causal dance of external and internal factors, nurture and nature, that I am implicitly referring.

However, if my parents have partially designed my genome, this balance is disrupted: Mom and Dad have inserted an element of their own values, tastes, and preferences into the suite of innate causal factors that co-determine who I become over time. Although this is only a very partial shaping – they have not *totally* designed who I am – it nonetheless introduces an additional element of "otherness" into the overall profile of my identity. The balance between what other people contribute to my identity formation, and what comes from within me, has been altered. Indeed, the boundary itself between "internal" and "external" shaping factors has been blurred, because the internal vector, which operates partly through genetic causal processes, has now come under direct external influence from other humans.

When I exercise my volition, henceforth, the set of values, tastes, and preferences that I call my own, and that determine my choices, will therefore contain a higher proportion of elements that come from other people. In Habermas's terminology, these will constitute heteronomous rather than autonomous elements operating in my will. I may *feel* as though I am exercising my own will when I make a certain choice, but a portion of the factors that determine this choice will now be coming from decisions made on my behalf by other people before I was born. These are certainly still "*my*" values, tastes, and preferences – I have no other basis from which to make my choices. But they also bear the partial signature of the purposes my parents had in mind when they selected certain components of my genome. My parents have inserted an additional (limited) element of themselves into an aspect of my selfhood, at a core place where my autonomy resides. My autonomy is partially diminished, therefore, and the very boundary between "mine" and "theirs" will have been slightly but irretrievably blurred.

Another way of saying this is that, once my parents acquire these shaping powers, I become, to a new degree, a partial extension of their will. To be sure, in certain important ways, this is already the case today: my parents have exerted a significant influence on the process by which my identity gradually emerged, over the decades of my growing into adulthood. For better or worse, they helped make me who I am. But someday, if they are *also* able to partially configure my genome before my conception, this element of parental influence will ratchet up a few more notches. Through their newfound ability to intervene intentionally in my development via the causal pathways of both nurture *and* nature, they will be reaching deeper than ever before into the formative processes of my being, into the very platform of my selfhood, from which all my preferences, decisions, behaviors, and experiences originate. From this point forward, whenever I choose to do something, or not to do something, my choice will also reflect, in a more pronounced way, the projected will of Mom and Dad.

25.5 Conclusion

The tender humanity of a cyborg, the intricacies of autonomy in a partially designed human – these are some of the complexities that probably await humankind in the coming century if bioenhancement technologies come into increasingly widespread use. All too often, discussions of bioenhancement tend to focus rather narrowly on the novel powers or augmented capabilities that such modifications will confer. Such functional assessments can take on a clearly positive valence: *Now that I can see in the ultraviolet spectrum, a whole new kind of beauty has opened up for me.* Or, in other cases, they may be trenchantly negative: *My epigenetic boost package was supposed to augment my ability to withstand hot weather, but my friends all got far better results from theirs than I got from mine.*

My underlying argument in this chapter has been that we need to step back from these kinds of narrow, functional appraisals and pose a broader, more demanding set of evaluative questions. Instead of asking, "How well does it work?" or "What new capabilities does this offer me?" – we need to ask more difficult questions such as, "What impacts has this actually had on the overall quality of my life?" If we are to avoid the dehumanizing effects of a shallow, consumerist mentality in adopting such modifications, the core challenge will be to keep ourselves grounded in the more holistic kinds of values that contribute to human flourishing, to a life well lived. These qualities have been the subject of fruitful research by philosophers and positive psychologists in recent years, and a sizable literature now exists on the topic.[15] Scholars in these fields have created impressive lists of the attributes we should be cultivating if we wish to deepen and enrich our lives in truly impactful ways: friendships, mindfulness, authenticity, service, equilibrium, or the ability to take perspective, for example.

And here, too, in this domain of deeper assessments informed by the holistic qualities of human flourishing, the impact of bioenhancements is likely to be a mixed bag. Some of the critical evaluations we make may be negative: *This neurotechnology headset granted me seamless access to the virtual realms, but since I've been using it my marriage has failed.* Or, in other cases, they may turn out to be positive: *The little green pills have allowed me to connect with other people in entirely new ways and opened up a whole world of meaningful relationships.* Whether positive or negative, the evaluations we make will tend to be more accurate and fruitful if they insistently return to the ambiguities and gray areas that reflect our full humanity in all its messy complexity.

★ ★ ★

Notes

1. Michael Chorost, *Rebuilt: How Becoming Part Computer Made Me More Human* (Houghton Mifflin, 2005), 169.
2. Dictionary.com Unabridged (v 1.1). Random House, Inc. http://dictionary.reference.com/browse/cyborg.
3. Chorost, 57, 58.
4. Chorost, 70–71.
5. Chorost, 107–108.
6. Chris Gray, ed., *The Cyborg Handbook* (Routledge, 1995); Edward James and Farah Mendlesohn, eds., *The Cambridge Companion to Science Fiction* (Cambridge U. Press, 2003); Sean Redmond, *Liquid Metal: The Science Fiction Film Reader* (Wallflower, 2004).
7. The scientist's family name is He and first name is Jiankui: since "He" can be confusing in an English sentence, I'll refer to him henceforth as Jiankui. I draw heavily in my discussion here on Walter Isaacson, *The Code Breaker: Jennifer Doudna, Gene Editing, and the Future of the Human Race* (Simon & Schuster, 2021); and Jennifer Doudna and Samuel Sternberg, *A Crack in Creation: Gene Editing and the Unthinkable Power to Control Evolution* (Mariner, 2018).
8. David Cyranoski, "The CRISPR-baby scandal: What's next for human gene-editing," *Nature* 566 (26 February, 2019), 440–442: https://www.nature.com/articles/d41586-019-00673-1.
9. See the bibliography in Michael Bess, *Our Grandchildren Redesigned: Life in the Bioengineered Society of the Near Future* (Beacon, 2015).
10. Erik Parens, Audrey Chapman, and Nancy Press, eds., *Wrestling with Behavioral Genetics: Science, Ethics, and Public Conversation* (Johns Hopkins, 2006); Michael Rutter, *Genes and Behavior: Nature-Nurture Interplay Explained* (Blackwell, 2006).
11. Throughout this chapter, for the sake of brevity, I will use language along the lines of "parents selecting a trait for their offspring." This should be interpreted as a shorthand way of conveying the more cumbersome idea behind human genetic engineering: that parents can introduce targeted alterations into their offspring's genome or epigenome, thereby increasing the probability that subsequent interactions between that particular genomic combination and environmental factors will eventually yield a desired phenotypic outcome.
12. Jack Kornfield, *The Wise Heart: A Guide to the Universal Teachings of Buddhist Psychology* (Bantam, 2009).
13. Jürgen Habermas, *The Future of Human Nature* (Polity, 2003). On Habermas's philosophy see Craig Calhoun, ed., *Habermas and the Public Sphere* (MIT, 1992).
14. Robert Kane, ed., *The Oxford Handbook of Free Will* (Oxford, 2002).
15. Christopher Peterson and Martin Seligman, *Character Strengths and Virtues: A Handbook and Classification* (Oxford, 2004); Jonathan Haidt, *The Happiness Hypothesis: Finding Modern Truth in Ancient Wisdom* (Basic Books, 2006); Mihaly Csikszentmihalyi, *Flow: The Psychology of Optimal Experience* (Harper, 2008); Christopher Peterson, *A Primer in Positive Psychology* (Oxford, 2006); Daniel Kahneman, Ed Diener and Norbert Schwarz, *Well-Being: The Foundations of Hedonic Psychology* (Russell Sage, 2003); Sonja Lyubomirsky, *The How of Happiness: A New Approach to Getting the Life You Want* (Penguin, 2008).

26
PHARMACEUTICAL COGNITIVE ENHANCEMENT

Entanglement with emotion, morality, and context

Kevin Chien-Chang Wu

26.1 Introduction

Cognitive enhancement has aroused heated debates in academia regarding its conceptual, philosophical, ethical, and policy issues in the past two decades (Jotterand & Dubljevic, 2016). Being vague and ambiguous, the definition of cognitive enhancement is related to the position we take on the issue. For example, if we compare health enhancement with disease treatment, then as the definitions of health and disease change, enhancement might become a pursuit of perfection through extraordinary measures. If enhancement means making healthy humans better, then the technology would seem trivial (Wu, 2016) and cognitive enhancement would be nothing but cognitive inflation (Meacham, 2017). For the convenience of discussion, this chapter adopts the second definition for two reasons: (1) to cover different kinds of cognitive functions, such as memory, attention, judgment, and execution, which can be enhanced; and (2) to address cognitive enhancement based on real-life situations, in which the magic pill has yet to be invented.

It is intuitively appealing to ingest pharmaceuticals to make ourselves better at doing things efficiently and correctly. Roughly speaking, there has been a long history of using drugs to enhance cognition such as memory, attention, response speed, decision-making correctness, etc. of healthy people in different cultures. For example, ephedrine was used in China, khat in North America, and coca in South America (Brühl et al., 2019). Around the early 20th century, amphetamine and cocaine were deemed good medicines for treating depression and enhancing cognition in Western countries (Brühl et al., 2019). However, it was later found that these drugs do not have high effectiveness in enhancing cognition (Roberts et al., 2020; Spronk et al., 2013). Furthermore, amphetamine and cocaine have side effects such as addiction and related health and socioeconomic problems. Almost all countries have listed them as scheduled drugs, i.e. ones that need high regulation intensity due to their high abuse and dependence potential. History shows that over-enthusiasm regarding the cognitive enhancement effects of some pharmaceuticals with later disenchantment has been repeating itself (Bell et al., 2012), but the endeavor to search for pharmaceuticals to enhance cognition has continued.

In 1990, United States (US) President George H.W. Bush announced the coming of the decade of the brain (Jones & Mendell, 1999). The proclamation ignited a boom of discourse regarding how to use neuroscience and technology to promote well-being. As part of the broad sense of well-being that includes enhancing one's life (Savulescu et al., 2011), cognitive enhancement became a hot topic. The annual number of articles addressing cognitive enhancement increased in the past

30 years following the proclamation. Since 1990, more than 1,000 papers have been published about cognitive enhancement (Schleim & Quednow, 2018). Among them, many scholars expressed their optimistic expectations or pessimistic concerns about using pharmaceuticals for cognitive enhancement.

Some pharmaceuticals have been reported to have cognitive enhancement effects. Among them are commonly used over-the-counter pharmaceuticals such as caffeine and nicotine, and drugs known for treating disorders such as attention deficit, memory impairment, and even depression (i.e. with collateral effects on cognition). Almost everyone wants to be smart, but how we become smart matters. A main concern is the ethical issues surrounding cognitive enhancement broadly. These issues include utilitarianism (risk, safety, cost, and benefit), Kantianism (freedom, autonomy, and social pressure), virtue theory (authenticity, hyperagency, and self-cultivation), distributive justice (fairness and different theories of justice), and human nature with non-violable intrinsic values. In 2016, under the assumption of the certainty of effective cognitive enhancement technology (including genetic management, food, drugs, brain-computer interfaces, training and education, etc.), Wu argued that there is no absolute ethical reason to oppose cognitive enhancement (Wu, 2016). Furthermore, Confucianism would accept cognitive enhancement as a way to self-cultivation (Wu, 2016). However, as the issue here is the uncertainty of pharmaceutical cognitive enhancement, the technology might not be able to pass muster based on the utilitarian perspective.

In contrast to the initial optimism about cognitive enhancement, many scholars doubt the real situation data, effectiveness, and ethical justification of cognitive enhancement (Ilieva & Farah, 2013). For example, scholars have challenged the validity of epidemiological methods utilized in the reports in which more and more healthy people were using pharmaceuticals for cognitive enhancement (Schleim & Quednow, 2018; Zohny, 2015). Scholars did not believe pharmaceutical cognitive enhancement (PCE) was scientifically proven. They suggested that the data might be incorrect, exaggerated, or even worse, that the reports themselves might induce social imitation and increase social acceptance of PCE (Schleim & Quednow, 2018; Zohny, 2015). For them, only after clarifying the scientific presumptions underlying PCE, could we engage in good ethical, legal, and policy dialogue on its feasibility (Schleim & Quednow, 2018; Zohny, 2015).

On the other hand, based on the precautionary principle that emphasizes avoiding uncertain severe and irreversible harms rather than welcoming foreseeable technological advancement, and as new data reveals that many healthy people (especially university students) utilize pharmaceuticals for cognitive enhancement (lifetime prevalence about 5–55%) (Maier et al., 2018; Roberts et al., 2020; Sharif et al., 2021; Vargo & Petróczi, 2016), there is a need to collect more comprehensive and accurate data to prevent and prepare for the inappropriate use of PCE. To achieve the optimal use of PCE, the first step is to explore the mechanism and effects of drugs, medicines, and pharmaceuticals often used in PCE. Different human physiological systems and tissues have functional connections. Usually, one drug would influence not only cognition but also emotion (including motivation) (Farah, 2015; Vrecko, 2013) and decision-making (including moral decisions) (Pavarini et al., 2018). Different people may have different reactions to pharmaceuticals (Farah, 2015). The recognition and expression of pharmaceutical effects are the product of complex interactions involving interpersonal relationships, society, culture, economy, and the law (Hardon & Sanabria, 2017; Hupli, 2023).

The chapter aims to elucidate the empirical data about the cognitive enhancement effects of select pharmaceuticals. Empirical studies have shown that pharmaceutical cognitive enhancers might also have effects on the emotions that may modify human cognition (including moral cognition) (Zohny, 2015). It is important that we examine the evidence regarding the effects of pharmaceuticals utilized in PCE and consider ways to address the PCE issue that has often neglected the multilevel and multi-dimensional complexity and entanglement of cognition, emotion, and morality.

The second section of the chapter briefs the readers on the cognitive and emotional, and even moral effects of the selected pharmaceutical cognitive enhancers. It indicates that the context of pharmaceutical use also influences the effectiveness and that the category names of pharmaceuticals are oversimplified and sometimes misleading. The third section first elucidates how we could recognize the enhancement effects of pharmaceuticals in multilevel contexts. Using psychedelics as an example, it proposes a potential context-sensitive way of PCE policy-making that considers the entanglement of emotion, morality, and context. In conclusion, the chapter advises the proper arrangement of contexts to construct and facilitate cognitive, emotional, and moral enhancement at the same time.

26.2 The cognitive enhancement and non-negligible emotional effects of selected common pharmaceuticals

There is an abundance of literature and reports that focus on medicines, drugs, pharmaceuticals, and substances with cognitive enhancement effects, which this chapter cannot cover in the limited space. For conducting a brief narrative review, the often-discussed or promising emerging pharmaceuticals, such as psychedelics, were selected as the main focus to briefly introduce the mechanisms and PCE. Mood or emotional effects will be mentioned when deemed non-negligible. The covered pharmaceuticals include nicotine, caffeine, psychostimulants (methylphenidate, d-amphetamine, modafinil), anti-dementia medication (acetylcholinesterase inhibitors), antidepressants (SSRI, SNRI, NDRI), and psychedelics (ketamine, esketamine, and classic psychedelics). Through the review, the readers can see that most of these substances have not only cognitive effects but also emotional and even moral modulation effects.

26.2.1 Nicotine

Tobacco use is one of the leading public health hazards in the world. According to the estimation of the World Health Organization, 6.6 million people died from tobacco use, including 0.6 million due to secondhand smoke, in 2015 (World Health Organization, 2015). As one ingredient in tobacco that has high dependence potential, nicotine is deemed the main culprit for the continued use of tobacco. In addition, the potential cognitive enhancement effects, including "staying focused" and others that will be described below, may be another important reason why some users do not stop smoking (Valentine & Sofuoglu, 2018).

Categorized as a psychomotor stimulant (Bizarro et al., 2004), nicotine binds to nicotine acetylcholine receptors with fast-acting excitatory effects. It facilitates the release of other neurotransmitters, such as acetylcholine, dopamine, serotonin, glutamate, and norepinephrine. Many dopamine receptors located in the brain's ventral tegmental area are related to the mechanisms of reward and addiction. Persistent use of nicotine induces the secretion of dopamine and increases the risk of addiction. Some α, β subunits of nicotine receptors (e.g. α7, α4β2) exist in the brain's prefrontal cortex and hippocampus, which have been reported to be individually associated with the cognitive functions of signal-noise differentiation and memory (Gandelman et al., 2018; Valentine & Sofuoglu, 2018).

Based on the review by Valentine and Sofuoglu, nicotine might enhance attention (alertness and orientation), response time, working memory, fine motor skills, and episodic memory functions (Valentine & Sofuoglu, 2018). However, the dose-response curve is not linear, which means that more nicotine does not always lead to better effects. Literature shows cognitive improvement appeared only in individuals who smoked and had cognitive deficits due to abstinence (Valentine & Sofuoglu, 2018). Other studies revealed that nicotine could shift the users' attention from negative stimuli or alleviate the dysphoria associated with nicotine withdrawal. Both mechanisms might bring about a later positive or relaxed effect (Tattan-Birch & Shahab, 2020; Valentine & Sofuoglu,

2018). Some research also suggests that nicotine has cognitive enhancement effects even in non-smoking persons (Heishman et al., 2010).

To summarize, stronger evidence supports that nicotine could improve the cognitive functions of habitual smokers. It would be better to deem nicotine as a cognitive maintainer rather than a cognitive enhancer. Although studies did suggest nicotine might enhance the cognition and mood of some non-smokers to a mild or moderate extent, there is no linear dose-response relationship in either smokers or non-smokers. Whether nicotine enhances cognition and mood needs further research to tease out nicotine's PCE effectiveness (Gandelman et al., 2018; Waters & Sutton, 2000).

26.2.2 Caffeine

Caffeine is the most popular psychoactive substance in the world (Nehlig, 1999). Similar to nicotine, caffeine has stimulating effects (Bizarro et al., 2004). Compared to nicotine, which has a negative image associated with tobacco use, caffeine has a higher and more acceptable status in society. Caffeine can lead to dependence, insomnia, and other negative impacts in specific populations, such as children, adolescents, pregnant and nursing women, and persons with cardiovascular or mental illnesses (Temple et al., 2017). However, it was removed from the list of banned substances in sports in 2004 (Lorenzo Calvo et al., 2021).

Having a molecular structure similar to adenosine, caffeine is an antagonist to adenosine receptors (A1, A2a). As we work or exercise for a long time, accumulated adenosine will bring about the feeling of tiredness and sleepiness. As caffeine binds to the adenosine receptors, increased release of dopamine will alleviate the feeling of sleepiness and increase activity levels (McLellan et al., 2016; Stahl, 2021, p. 440). Though with individual differences, caffeine might also induce alertness, and vigilance, enhance attention, and shorten reaction time at low to moderate doses (0.5mg–4mg / kg). Less consistent evidence revealed that caffeine might enhance memory and higher-order cognitive functions such as judgment and decision-making. In the working situation with sleep deprivation, people might have enhanced cognition and activity levels when using caffeine repeatedly (McLellan et al., 2016). Consuming caffeine before or during exercise results in enhanced energy, mood, and cognitive functions such as attention (Lorenzo Calvo et al., 2021). Caffeine may also improve simple reaction time, choice reaction time, memory, and fatigue (Lorenzo Calvo et al., 2021). However, there is no stable linear dose-response relationship between caffeine and memory enhancement. The potential influencing factors include the preparation and source of caffeine, differences in sleep and diet, demographic characteristics (sex and age), individual tolerance, and metabolism.

The evidence supports caffeine's limited effect in enhancing cognition. High doses and long-term use of caffeine might cause intoxication and impairment. Caffeine could have mood-enhancing effects, but the mechanisms underlying the cognitive and mood effects need further research and clarification.

26.2.3 Psychostimulants: methylphenidate, D-amphetamine, and modafinil

Psychostimulants, including methylphenidate, D-amphetamine, and modafinil, are the most often used pharmaceutical cognitive enhancers (Ragan et al., 2013). Having impacts on dopamine and norepinephrine, they are used to treat attention deficit hyperactivity disorder (ADHD) and narcolepsy. Due to their potential for abuse, methylphenidate and D-amphetamine are listed as schedule II drugs (i.e., drugs in the second leading group of abuse or dependence potential) by the United Nations (Roberts et al., 2020). Methylphenidate and D-amphetamine bind to dopamine transporters and norepinephrine transporters and block the reuptake of these two neurotransmitters. The increased density of the transmitters in the neuronal synapses generates stimulating effects. But, at high doses, D-amphetamine and its derivatives could cause the direct release of dopamine from neurons and lead to reinforcement and euphoria through actions on the dopaminergic reward system (Stahl, 2021, p469–478). Modafinil has been used to treat narcolepsy, obstructive sleep apnea, and shift-worker disorder. In contrast to methylphenidate and D-amphetamine, modafinil blocks the reuptake of dopamine more moderately and for a longer time. The effect is sufficient for users to maintain wakefulness. Since it does not facilitate the large release of dopamine which impacts the neuronal reward system, the potential of abuse is not as strong as the other two psychostimulants (Stahl, 2021, p442–444).

A recent meta-analysis found that methylphenidate and amphetamine medicines enhance healthy users' inhibitory control, episodic memory, and processing speed accuracy (Roberts et al., 2020). Above all, recall memory enhancement was the most prominent. Methylphenidate's effect on school or work performances were related to recall memory and persistence, but the effect was moderate and short (Roberts et al., 2020). For simple executive function tasks, modafinil might enhance users' attention, learning, and memory. However, the creativity of users might be limited at the same time. For complicated task items, modafinil consistently enhanced attention, executive function, and learning without prominent mood effects (Battleday & Brem, 2015). In another review analysis, modafinil showed moderate enhancement effects on the attention, executive function, memory, and processing speed of healthy users (Kredlow et al., 2019).

In general, no publication bias was found in the review literature and meta-analyses (Kredlow et al., 2019; Roberts et al., 2020). The above-mentioned cognitive enhancement effects found in the research probably do exist. However, it is not certain whether the cognitive enhancement effects could be duplicated in real life (Kredlow et al., 2019). On the other hand, the effects of psychostimulants are not limited to the cognitive domain. Some literature showed that modafinil might enhance the mood of healthy users (Randall et al., 2003). Other evidence showed that these psychostimulants have antidepressant effects (McIntyre et al., 2017). It would be worthwhile to conduct further research to understand the cognitive and emotional effects of psychostimulants.

26.2.4 Pharmaceuticals for delaying the progression of dementia: Acetylcholinesterase inhibitors

Acting on muscarinic acetylcholine receptors, the neurotransmitter acetylcholine is associated with memory capacity. As people age or have dementia, the loss of neurons secreting acetylcholine will lead to impaired memory. Acetylcholinesterase in the brain is in charge of breaking down acetylcholine. By inhibiting the action of acetylcholinesterase and increasing the concentration of acetylcholine in neuronal synapses, some medicines could delay the progression of dementia and maintain memory capacity for a period of time (Stahl, 2021, p505–514). Drugs included in this category are donepezil, rivastigmine, and galantamine (Fond et al., 2015).

In the items of complex aviation tasks, donepezil was found to improve the maintenance of training achievements (Yesavage et al., 2002). Further, it might improve verbal and episodic memory, however, the findings were inconsistent, especially in episodic memory (d'Angelo et al., 2017; Repantis et al., 2010). After 24-hour sleep deprivation, donepezil could contribute to the recovery of the memory of persons with prominent memory impairment. In contrast, some literature showed that acetylcholinesterase inhibitors do not have cognitive enhancement effects (Franke & Lieb, 2013).

Many scholars suggest these anti-dementia drugs do not have consistent and prominent effects on cognitive enhancement. The drugs might have effects for those with ex ante cognitive difficulty, but not for healthy people. One study showed that in young healthy people, donepezil might have mood enhancement effects, such as feelings of power, agility, and happiness (Zaninotto et al., 2009). Although the evidence for the mood effect of anti-dementia drugs was not strong, both the cognitive and emotional effects of this category of pharmaceuticals still warrant further exploration.

26.2.5 Non-psychedelic antidepressants

Psychedelic means "mind manifesting" (Inserra et al., 2021). Having effects of a magical experience and depression alleviation, this category of pharmaceuticals will be addressed in Section 26.2.6. Currently, the most common non-psychedelic antidepressants on the market have effects through modulations of brain serotonin, norepinephrine, or dopamine. Diminished dopamine concentration in neuronal synapses might reduce the degree of people's positive affect, whereas diminished serotonin concentration might contribute to aggravated negative affect. However, a lack of norepinephrine might have both of the aforementioned effects (Stahl, 2021, p279–282; 289–306). Therefore, categories of non-psychedelic antidepressants include selective serotonin reuptake inhibitors (SSRI, such as fluoxetine, sertraline), serotonin-norepinephrine reuptake inhibitors (SNRI, such as venlafaxine, duloxetine), and norepinephrine dopamine reuptake inhibitors (NDRI, such as bupropion). After ingestion of these antidepressants, the concentration of related neurotransmitters in neuronal synapses may increase in a matter of hours. However, mood improvement may take days or weeks. Potential reasons for this may be because (1) these drugs do not act on the core target directly and take time to reach the target; (2) it takes time for the brain to adapt to the effects of antidepressants through the mechanism of neuroplasticity; and (3) it also takes time for persons with depression to adjust the negativity bias (e.g. inclination to remember negative information) in their cognitive styles (Harmer et al., 2017).

Persons with depression often have cognitive impairments in memory, attention, executive function, and processing speed. Research showed that if antidepressants have anticholinergic and antihistaminic effects, the long-term use of these drugs might aggravate cognitive impairments. Fortunately, compared to older generations of antidepressants, recent antidepressants have less anticholinergic effects, and persons with depression might have cognitive improvement after the treatment. One recent systematic review showed that these non-psychedelic antidepressants might have a moderate effect on enhancing divided attention, executive function, immediate memory, processing speed, recent memory, and sustained attention (Prado et al., 2018). The cognitive effects might be related to the positive influence of mood on motivation, self-monitoring, or planning capacity. Another possible explanation is that after negativity bias and fixation improved with mood, the cognitive processing resources of depressed persons are released (Harmer et al., 2017). Some literature did not find a consistent correlation between cognitive and mood improvements (McIntyre et al., 2013). Although these antidepressants might enhance the capacity of some healthy persons to differentiate between positive and negative facial emotions (Harmer et al., 2009), similar to the results of one previous systematic review (Repantis et al., 2009), in general, these antidepressants do not have cognitive enhancement effects in healthy people (Prado et al., 2018).

Non-psychedelic antidepressants have intricate positive impacts on mood and cognition in persons with depression. In general, these antidepressants do not have cognitive enhancement effects in healthy persons. However, these antidepressants might induce mania or hypomania in some otherwise healthy persons (Akiskal et al., 2003). People with induced hypomania might experience or be recognized to have mental function enhancement, which includes lower stress scores, more positive self-instructions, higher levels of exploration, self-efficacy, and physical activity. The perceived mental function enhancement comes at the cost of irritability, poor interpersonal relationships, and excessive risk-taking. As these people experience both mood and cognitive enhancement effects, this phenomenon warrants further systematic research (Delvecchio et al., 2018).

26.2.6 Ketamine and classic psychedelic antidepressants

Current scientific evidence supports that psychedelics could convert consciousness, perception, mood, and self-experience in healthy people (Inserra et al., 2021). Although they have been listed as schedule substances for many years, classic psychedelics (e.g. psilocybin, ayahuasca, LSD) and non-classic psychedelics (e.g. ketamine) may rapidly alleviate depression and suicidal tendencies, with these effects potentially dissipating within days. In 2019, the US Food and Drug Administration (FDA) approved esketamine nasal spray as a supplemental treatment for depression (Inserra et al., 2021; Riggs & Gould, 2021). Other scientific evidence showed that MDMA (3,4-methylenedioxymethamphetamine) is a candidate drug for treating post-traumatic stress disorder (PTSD) (Mitchell et al., 2021).

These psychedelics modulate a variety of neurotransmitters, such as serotonin, glutamate, dopamine, and norepinephrine (Inserra et al., 2021). Take ketamine as an example. It has analgesic effects at a high dose but rapid anti-depressive effects at a low dose. Two hypotheses have been proposed to explain this rapid effect. First, ketamine antagonizes NMDA (N-methyl-D-aspartate) receptors, leads to the increase of glutamate concentration in neuronal synapses, and excites the cerebral cortex. Second, ketamine binds to AMPA (α-amino-3-hydroxy-5-methyl-4-isoxazolepropionic acid) receptors and facilitates the release of brain-derived neurotropic factor (BDNF), which promotes neuronal survival, connectivity, and transmission efficiency. In contrast, classic psychedelics' main anti-depressive effect is deemed to be related to their agonist activity on the serotonin $5-HT_{2A}$ receptor (Inserra et al., 2021).

Most literature shows that ketamine could improve the processing speed, verbal memory, visual memory, working memory, and cognitive flexibility of persons with treatment-resistant major depression, while esketamine does not (Souza-Marques et al., 2021). On the other hand, for healthy persons, ketamine has negative effects on memory encoding and recall (Souza-Marques et al., 2021). Studies have demonstrated that psilocybin has therapeutic effects on treatment-resistant major depression. When combined with nondirective and supportive psychotherapy, it might have anti-depressive effects by disrupting the brain's default mode network of depressed research participants, making their brains more flexible, susceptible, and receptive to the cognitive contents of psychotherapy (Reiff et al., 2020). In addition to the drug, the therapeutic setting is an important determinant of the therapeutic effect (Carhart-Harris et al., 2018). For example, in a double-blind randomized crossover trial of psilocybin on terminal-cancer patients with anxiety or depression, the treatment setting and procedure included a before-dose discussion session in which patients discussed the meaning of life with a study monitor; then, during the psilocybin dose session, a psychotherapist non-directively interacted with the patients to encourage them to trust, let go, and be open. The high-dose (22mg/70kg) group experienced prominent improvements in depression and anxiety even after six months (Griffiths et al., 2016).

People who have the personality traits of absorption, openness, acceptance, and surrender tend to have positive experiences after using classic psychedelics (Aday et al., 2021). In a double-blind trial with a placebo-controlled parallel group, participants developed more spontaneous creative thoughts shortly after using psilocybin at the dose of 0.17mg/kg, but their task-based creativity diminished. Seven days after the use of classic psychedelics, the number of novel ideas increased (Mason et al., 2021). Based on a systematic review, in subjective reports or standard task tests, classic psychedelics tend to enhance sociality, openness, spirituality, and mindfulness (Bălăeţ, 2022; Goldberg et al., 2020). Research also showed that some people adopted psychedelic microdosing, which means using 1/20 of the standard dose or less than the dose used for recreation. They would not experience the "high" but might experience cognitive and emotional enhancement effects including wisdom, energy, creativity, absorption, open attitude, empathy, well-being, trust, reduced mind wandering, and lessened depression and anxiety. Some studies showed that people might still develop changes in time perception, increased neuroticism, and suggestibility (Polito & Stevenson, 2019). Research found that before microdosing, these persons expected the effect to be more than what they actually got after microdosing. However, their expectation had no association with the actual effect (Polito & Stevenson, 2019). Some scholars found that long-term psychedelic microdosing is related to cognitive and emotional enhancement effects, including "cognitive empathy" or emotion recognition, and even the collective intelligence of groups. The effects might be related to the mechanisms of increased neuroplasticity, neurogenesis, or the reduction of neuro-inflammation, which are similar to those of ketamine's actions (Rifkin et al., 2020). But some literature showed that LSD and psilocybin might diminish sustained attention in healthy users (Pokorny et al., 2020). In a trial using standard task tests on 25 healthy participants who previously used LSD (100 μg), the participants were found to have impaired executive function, cognitive flexibility, and working memory, but risk decision-making remained uninfluenced (Pokorny et al., 2020). At low doses of classic psychedelics, impairment was not found in spatial and verbal working memory, semantic memory, and non-autobiographical episodic memory, but it appeared and was aggravated as the dose increased. On the other hand, for autobiographic memory with strong positive or negative valence, classic psychedelics had the effect of enhancing recall and re-experience (Healy, 2021).

To sum up, most literature shows that ketamine and classic psychedelics have anti-depressive effects. For healthy people performing standard cognitive tasks, the drugs tend to have negative effects. However, healthy persons reported the enhancement of specific cognitive and emotional experiences that are difficult to be incorporated into standard tasks. In appropriate contexts, the experiences might enhance pro-sociality at the interpersonal or group levels. Due to the limitations of the current research, no solid general conclusion could be drawn regarding the cognitive enhancement effects of classic psychedelics.

26.3 Pharmaceutical cognitive enhancement policy: The entanglement with emotion, morality, and context

Considering the limitations of the current research, such as double-blindness, control, sample size, tasks for examining cognition, drug administration, contexts, and external validity, it would be inappropriate to assert that any pharmaceutical has a definite cognitive enhancement effect. However, we are certain that there is no magic pill for this purpose. In general, the pharmaceuticals mentioned above could not prominently enhance performance speed and accuracy in standard cognitive tasks; namely, they usually do not produce a genius out of an ordinary person, although some could prominently improve the cognitive functions of persons with mental illnesses. They might have side effects and some moderate cognitive enhancement effects. On the other hand, some drugs might have emotional enhancement effects, which might facilitate the enhancement of some cognitive functions. Findings in the laboratory may not necessarily be applicable to the real world, especially since it is not easy to use standardized tests to examine some of the cognitive enhancement effects of classic psychedelics. So how do we interpret the mixed data and come up with some feasible PCE policies? Do we continue to conduct active research or let the public do their own self-trials (Farah, 2015)? Addressing the entanglement of emotion, morality, and context, this section explores a potential choice for PCE policy-making.

26.3.1 *What could be enhanced through pharmaceutical cognitive enhancement?*

To evaluate whether PCE is feasible, not only do we have to define what enhancement is, as mentioned in the introduction, but we also have to consider the scope of cognition. Currently, cognitive scientists do not have a consensus on what cognition is. For example, there are fierce debates about whether simple multicellular creatures have cognition and whether we have extracorporeally extended cognition or group cognition (Allen, 2017). If we limit the scope of cognition to those who have agency, the variation of cognition is still large. Cognition includes but is not restricted to memory, attention, planning, motivation, social interaction, actuation, reasoning, communication, learning, modeling self or others, creation, quantitation, perception, decision-making, emotional cognition, moral cognition (Adams et al., 2012; Baez et al., 2017; Lerner et al., 2015). Past research often focused on university students' academic performance and mainly utilized standardized tasks to assess whether the users of candidate cognitive enhancers do become smarter as revealed in their task performance. The inclination actually restricts the definition and scope of cognition. This chapter's review found it advisable that we explore cognitive functions beyond the standard task tests, which might include, among others, decision-making, wisdom, and creativity. We should conduct comprehensive examinations of all the variations of cognitive functions before we come to a conclusion regarding the feasibility of PCE.

A semi-structured qualitative interview study found that most of the interviewees thought their performance was not bad, and had feelings of drivenness, interestedness, and enjoyment after they used the study drugs such as Ritalin and Adderall. Although the main purpose was to enhance academic performance, the narratives of the interviewees were full of emotional dynamics. The emotional enhancement appeared not only during the period of pharmaceutical effect but also when they recalled the experience. Many interviewees knew that the study drugs did not have cognitive enhancement effects, however, they tied the emotional enhancement to improvements in their academic performance. They often bundled the cognitive and emotional changes together in their discourse, which indicated that the study drugs made them motivated or interested in their studies (Vrecko, 2013). This chapter's review of the pharmaceuticals in Section 26.2 also found that candidate cognitive enhancers are often candidate emotional enhancers. Even though those drugs are not used for treating depression, they might have positive emotional effects. Therefore, the enhancement of cognitive and emotional functions should be addressed together if a sensible PCE policy is to be established (Farah, 2015; Vrecko, 2013).

The relationship between cognition and emotion, no matter positive or negative, has been well-known in the sciences of the human mind (Angie et al., 2011). Take decision-making as a typical case. Scholars have proposed several theories explaining how emotion exerts an impact on cognition: (1) both integral emotion (related to the task at hand) or incidental emotion (emotion carried over from another situation to the current) have impacts on the results of decision-making; (2) emotion might help shift one's appraisal-tendency framework in responding to certain contexts; and (3) emotion might further influence the content of thought (e.g. certainty, control, responsibility attribution), depth of thought (rumination and deep systematic information processing vs. heuristic processing), goal activation (emotion induced adaption coordination for setting goals to solve problems), interpersonal decision-making (influencing interpersonal decision-making through reciprocal emotional influences), and emotion management by certain measures (Lerner et al., 2015). Scholars have proposed ways to adjust emotion and context for enhancing decision-making, such as time delay, reappraisal, induced counteracting emotion, crowding out emotion, increasing awareness of misattribution, and modifying choice architecture (e.g. nudging) (Lerner et al., 2015; Sunstein, 2015). Thus, from the perspective of PCE, emotional enhancement is not necessarily making people happier all the time. Since people with hypomania sometimes have impaired cognitive function (Delvecchio et al., 2018), a worthy goal is to induce appropriate emotions that enhance cognitive functions at feasible risks and costs. As candidate pharmaceutical cognitive enhancers also could enhance emotions, we ought to thoroughly consider the cognitive and emotional effects of pharmaceuticals at the same time and combine the above psychological and contextual measures to induce appropriate emotions for cognitive enhancement.

As moral reasoning and judgment are parts of decision-making, candidate pharmaceutical cognitive enhancers might have effects on both moral emotion (e.g. anger, empathy, contempt, guilt, shame, gratitude, disgust) (Helion & Pizarro, 2015) and moral cognition (moral sensitivity, moral reasoning, moral judgment) (Baez et al., 2017). Moral emotion and moral cognition have intricate relationships that influence moral decision-making. Early moral cognition theories and research emphasized the role of reason. Based on the classic utilitarian perspective, people should reason the cost and benefit/utility of alternative moral decisions before they make the choice that maximizes balanced benefit/utility (Sen, 1979). But scholars in behavioral economics have argued that in decision-making, people have a dual mental process (i.e., emotional, intuitive and quick vs. calm, rational, and deliberative), through which decisions are the outcome of the antagonism between emotion and cognition (Kahneman, 2011). Although emotion has impacts on cognition, the literature shows that we could develop skills and technologies for emotional regulation and further enhance the quality of moral judgment (Baez et al., 2017; Helion & Pizarro, 2015). Supporters of moral enhancement have argued that we could utilize pharmaceuticals to modulate our moral emotions and enhance our moral cognition (Earp et al., 2018). Opponents have criticized that hollow emotions cannot actually guide us to make correct moral decisions (Jotterand & Levin, 2019). Often, the assumption underlying the polarized debate is that cognition and emotion are separable both in theory and real-life scenarios, but empirical research often shows it is not the case. While cognition and emotion are bundled together, moral decision-making is embedded and modulated in the cognition-emotion tangle. Furthermore, some moral judgments are almost universally accepted across cultures (e.g. we should not kill arbitrarily), and many other moral norms actually reflect the specific socio-cultural context in different localities (Baez et al., 2017). If some candidate pharmaceutical cognitive enhancers could also modulate our emotions, then under certain context arrangements for moral education, it is possible that the candidate might facilitate moral enhancement (Earp et al., 2018; Van Bavel et al., 2015).

Focusing on the utilization of psychedelic antidepressants, the following subsection explores the possibility of a context-sensitive PCE policy that incorporates the themes of cognition, emotion, morality, and context at the same time.

26.3.2 The entanglement of emotion, morality, and context in pharmaceutical cognitive enhancement: Psychedelics as an example

Based on the above review, we have learned: (1) psychotropic pharmaceuticals often have co-existing cognitive, emotional, and even moral effects; (2) the multilevel contexts do influence how we construct, recognize and modify the fluid pharmaceutical effects. Therefore, it is important to adopt a context-sensitive PCE framework or policy that considers the adjustment of contextual factors to facilitate enhancement effects. Currently, the discourse on the effectiveness of psychedelics is the best candidate for showing the features of a context-sensitive PCE framework.

In the 1950s, classic psychedelics were often used by psychologists and psychiatrists, and sometimes in psychotherapy. In the late 1960s, these drugs were linked to deviant behavior, crime, and anticulture, and their users were depicted as indulging in feelings (Gearin & Devenot, 2021). As the political context changed, classic psychedelics became the symbols of immorality. In 1970, the US listed LSD and psilocybin as schedule I drugs (i.e., drugs with the highest potential of abuse or dependence). Research into the clinical use of classic psychedelics halted in the new moral context (Carhart-Harris & Goodwin, 2017). Around the end of the 20th century, the revival of research on classic psychedelics facilitated the accumulation of scientific evidence showing that they have therapeutic effects on depression, psychological stress, or even addiction (Carhart-Harris & Goodwin, 2017) (see Section 26.2.6 for more). In the everchanging medical science context, findings about their pharmacological effects on patients and healthy persons have implications for the enhancement of cognition, emotion, and morality (Langlitz et al., 2021). The discourse regarding classic psychedelics went through the stages of acceptance, condemnation, and conditioned allowance (i.e. the drugs are still on the schedule drugs list) (Gearin & Devenot, 2021).

Anthropological research has shown that pharmaceutical effects have fluidity and are always in the dynamic process of constitution and recognition in multilevel contexts (Hardon & Sanabria, 2017). At the research level, based on the population perspective, before lawfully entering the market, a drug must pass through the stages of therapeutic efficacy assessment in clinical trials. Researchers must set up a trial protocol to test a targeted therapeutic goal, which may unfortunately omit other potentially important effects. At the individual level, the actions of pharmaceuticals actually are not qualities solely belonging to the molecules, but the results of interactions between the molecules and human users, whose physical and/or mental functions are the location of effect manifestation. The actions could be modulated by interpersonal relationships and other contextual variables. For example, a good therapeutic relationship between a physician and their patient may induce beneficial placebo effects. After being ingested, the positive effects of psychedelics may change with the treatment procedure, atmosphere, and environment. In other words, the therapeutic effects are constituted by the molecular chemical structure and characteristics, human body, ritual, space, relationships, and expectations (Reiff et al., 2020). The purposes for constituting drug effects may differ between different entities. Pharmaceutical companies create and construe the effect for profit and the government for public health. When demanded by the market or regulation density, pharmaceutical concentrations and effects are malleable to reinterpretation and recognition. Pharmaceutical companies could release information regarding the link between the pills and specific individual images or lifestyles to conform to moral norms. For example, classic psychedelics have been reconstituted as antidepressants, but not substances for recreation or broadening personal experiences. However, the public can often find alternative ways (e.g. microdosing) to test, constitute, and construe pharmaceutical effects. In clinical encounters, pharmaceutical effects are realized, modified, and re-realized. Via physician-patient interactions, new versions and effects of pharmaceuticals evolve and gain local stability (Hardon & Sanabria, 2017). The trials conducted by individuals or subculture groups also may create partially stable discourses about the therapeutic or enhancement effects of specific pharmaceuticals.

Following the change in the portrayed images of classic psychedelics in politics, society, culture, and law, the ethical acceptability of using classic psychedelics in research and therapy has risen. Recent literature shows that classic psychedelics should be listed as schedule IV drugs (e.g. benzodiazepine, hypnotics) rather than schedule I. (Reiff et al., 2020) This might soften people's concerns about their abuse potential and in turn, speed up the transformation process of their attitudes toward pharmaceutical effects. In the coming decades, more indications for psychedelic treatment may be approved and newer enhancement effects explored.

The brief review in Section 26.2.6 shows that classic psychedelics could exert cognitive, emotional, and even moral enhancement effects. While intermingled and non-separable, the effects are at the same time malleable by contexts including the moral status of drugs. The above pharmaceutical anthropological discourse does not aim to demonstrate that the pharmaceutical effects are fake, but it encourages the appreciation that all pharmaceutical effects, no matter therapeutic or enhancing, count on concurrent mixed multilevel determinants and epistemic efforts. It would be simple-minded to disregard the above contextual multiplicity and construe a drug as having specific effects only in one domain. Accepting the complexity of pharmaceutical discourses while the context unfolds rapidly, we would find that we are still far from making any solid and consistent conclusions about the fluid enhancement effects of candidate cognitive enhancers such as classic psychedelics.

Some literature has argued that in appropriate contexts, psychedelics might induce the mixed cognitive and emotional effects of pro-sociality and altruism, which could meet the expectation of moral bioenhancement (Earp et al., 2018); namely, the composition of pharmaceutical effects is comprised of interpersonal and environmental elements, which warrant concurrent attention and management. In the situation of moral enhancement, moral education is a necessary part of successful moral enhancement technology. This might weaken the view that hollow emotional enhancement contributes nothing to moral content.

As shown above, no prominent enhancement effect could be certified at the population level. On the other hand, it might be feasible for individuals to conduct Number of One randomized controlled trials (using self in different time periods as the control) (Guyatt et al., 1990) to accumulate individualized discourse on PCE. It would be easy to make an ecological fallacy when asserting individual responses solely based on group-averaged data. While scientific data regarding PCE accumulates, governments tend to adopt policies with precautionary overtones that emphasize harm avoidance and restrict research in the areas of enhancement by psychedelics.

Even after less stringent control of laboratory trials, it is still necessary to conduct ethnographic research to supplement real-life data to establish sound policies for the use of psychedelics in enhancement situations. Apart from examining the elements in different biological and social contexts that might have impacts on the pharmaceutical effects, policy-makers have the moral duty to assess how to ethically deliver the effects of psychedelics for enhancing cognition, emotion, and morality.

26.4 Conclusion

This chapter reviews the major candidate pharmaceuticals for cognitive enhancement. It includes pharmaceuticals consumed in daily life (nicotine, caffeine) and therapeutic drugs (psychostimulants, anti-dementia drugs, non-psychedelic antidepressants, and psychedelic antidepressants). Due to issues with internal validity (research design and implementation) and external validity (research vs. real-life situations), we can only conclude that some of the above pharmaceuticals might have cognitive enhancement effects in some cognitive domains. It all depends on how we constitute the effects in a certain context. These pharmaceuticals could have prominent effects in helping those with cognitive deficits to recover or maintain their neurotypical cognitive functions, but their cognitive enhancement effects are often modest and non-linear in healthy persons. The human brain has limited resources and energy; when one cognitive function is enhanced, another might be suppressed (e.g. focus vs. flexibility). Therefore, it is certain that no magic pill with comprehensive enhancement effects exists (Colzato et al., 2021). Considering the potential side effects, some of which might cause severe harm, we should proceed along the path of pharmaceutical cognitive enhancement with caution and thorough assessment.

On the other hand, does the impossibility of creating a magic pill make cognitive enhancement a trivial issue? The deliberated answer would be no. These substances have overlapping physiological mechanisms and entangled enhancement effects on cognition, emotion, and even morality. These so-called cognitive enhancers often have effects outside of the cognitive domain. Under appropriate circumstances, cognition and emotion could have mutual enhancement effects. The above anthropological discourse about pharmaceutical effects illuminates the complicated issue of constituting and recognizing the effects through the stages of laboratory research, market research, clinical encounters, and self-experiment. In practice, pharmaceutical effects continue to reconfigure themselves through the mingled interactions of elements and contexts at different levels, such as body characteristics, imagination, interpersonal interactions, spatial settings, and even cultural and legal norms. Thus, pharmaceuticals never act alone. All the conditions of pharmaceutical use should be integrated to conduct an appropriate assessment and policy-making of PCE.

Taking psychedelics as an adjunct technology, some scholars have argued that psychedelic moral enhancement could be modeled on psychedelic-assisted psychotherapy. Combined with appropriate moral education and processes performed in a trusting relationship, psychedelics might facilitate the development of moral emotion and moral cognition to a level that reaches moral enhancement (Earp, 2018; Gordon, 2022). Incorporating the empirical scientific evidence and keen anthropological observations from above, we can expand the scope of this context-sensitive enhancement framework to cognition, emotion, and morality all at the same time.

Acknowledgement

Kevin Chien-Chang Wu is funded by the research grant (109-2410-H-002-136-MY3) from Taiwan National Science and Technology Council.

References

Adams, S., Arel, I., Bach, J., Coop, R., Furlan, R., Goertzel, B., Hall, J. S., Samsonovich, A., Scheutz, M., & Schlesinger, M. (2012). Mapping the landscape of human-level artificial general intelligence. *AI Magazine, 33*(1), 25–42.

Aday, J. S., Davis, A. K., Mitzkovitz, C. M., Bloesch, E. K., & Davoli, C. C. (2021). Predicting reactions to psychedelic drugs: A systematic review of states and traits related to acute drug effects. *ACS Pharmacology & Translational Science, 4*(2), 424–435.

Akiskal, H. S., Hantouche, E.-G., Allilaire, J.-F., Sechter, D., Bourgeois, M. L., Azorin, J.-M., Chatenêt-Duchêne, L., & Lancrenon, S. (2003). Validating antidepressant-associated hypomania (bipolar III): A systematic comparison with spontaneous hypomania (bipolar II). *Journal of Affective Disorders, 73*(1–2), 65–74.

Allen, C. (2017). On (not) defining cognition. *Synthese, 194*(11), 4233–4249.

Angie, A. D., Connelly, S., Waples, E. P., & Kligyte, V. (2011). The influence of discrete emotions on judgement and decision-making: A meta-analytic review. *Cognition & Emotion, 25*(8), 1393–1422.

Baez, S., García, A. M., & Santamaría-García, H. (2017). Moral cognition and moral emotions. In Agustín Ibáñez, Lucas Sedeño, & Adolfo M. García (Eds.), *Neuroscience and social science: The missing link* (pp. 169–197). Springer.

Bălăeţ, M. (2022). Psychedelic cognition-the unreached frontier of psychedelic science. *Frontiers in Neuroscience, 16*, 832375–832375.

Battleday, R. M., & Brem, A.-K. (2015). Modafinil for cognitive neuroenhancement in healthy non-sleep-deprived subjects: A systematic review. *European Neuropsychopharmacology, 25*(11), 1865–1881.

Bell, S. K., Lucke, J. C., & Hall, W. D. (2012). Lessons for enhancement from the history of cocaine and amphetamine use. *AJOB Neuroscience, 3*(2), 24–29.

Bizarro, L., Patel, S., Murtagh, C., & Stolerman, I. (2004). Differential effects of psychomotor stimulants on attentional performance in rats: Nicotine, amphetamine, caffeine and methylphenidate. *Behavioural Pharmacology, 15*(3), 195–206.

Brühl, A. B., d'Angelo, C., & Sahakian, B. J. (2019). Neuroethical issues in cognitive enhancement: Modafinil as the example of a workplace drug? *Brain and Neuroscience Advances, 3*, 2398212818816018.

Carhart-Harris, R. L., & Goodwin, G. M. (2017). The therapeutic potential of psychedelic drugs: Past, present, and future. *Neuropsychopharmacology, 42*(11), 2105–2113.

Carhart-Harris, R. L., Roseman, L., Haijen, E., Erritzoe, D., Watts, R., Branchi, I., & Kaelen, M. (2018). Psychedelics and the essential importance of context. *Journal of Psychopharmacology, 32*(7), 725–731.

Colzato, L. S., Hommel, B., & Beste, C. (2021). The downsides of cognitive enhancement. *The Neuroscientist, 27*(4), 322–330.

d'Angelo, L. S. C., Savulich, G., & Sahakian, B. J. (2017). Lifestyle use of drugs by healthy people for enhancing cognition, creativity, motivation and pleasure. *British Journal of Pharmacology, 174*(19), 3257–3267.

Delvecchio, G., Pigoni, A., Altamura, A., & Brambilla, P. (2018). Cognitive and neural basis of hypomania: Perspectives for early detection of bipolar disorder. In J. C. Soares, C. Walss-Bass, & P. Brambilla (Eds.), *Bipolar disorder vulnerability* (pp. 195–227). Academic Press.

Earp, B. D. (2018). Psychedelic moral enhancement. *Royal Institute of Philosophy Supplements, 83*, 415–439.

Earp, B. D., Douglas, T., & Savulescu, J. (2018). Moral neuroenhancement. In L. S. M. Johnson & K. S. Rommelfanger (Eds.), *The Routledge handbook of neuroethics* (pp. 166–184). Routledge.

Farah, M. J. (2015). The unknowns of cognitive enhancement. *Science, 350*(6259), 379–380.

Fond, G., Micoulaud-Franchi, J.-A., Brunel, L., Macgregor, A., Miot, S., Lopez, R., Richieri, R., Abbar, M., Lancon, C., & Repantis, D. (2015). Innovative mechanisms of action for pharmaceutical cognitive enhancement: A systematic review. *Psychiatry Research, 229*(1–2), 12–20.

Franke, A. G., & Lieb, K. (2013). Pharmacological neuroenhancement: Substances and epidemiology. In E. Hildt & A. G. Franke (Eds.), *Cognitive enhancement: An interdisciplinary perspective* (pp. 17–27). Springer.

Gandelman, J. A., Newhouse, P., & Taylor, W. D. (2018). Nicotine and networks: Potential for enhancement of mood and cognition in late-life depression. *Neuroscience & Biobehavioral Reviews, 84*, 289–298.

Gearin, A. K., & Devenot, N. (2021). Psychedelic medicalization, public discourse, and the morality of ego dissolution. *International Journal of Cultural Studies, 24*(6), 917–935.

Goldberg, S. B., Shechet, B., Nicholas, C. R., Ng, C. W., Deole, G., Chen, Z., & Raison, C. L. (2020). Post-acute psychological effects of classical serotonergic psychedelics: A systematic review and meta-analysis. *Psychological Medicine, 50*(16), 2655–2666.

Gordon, E. C. (2022). Trust and psychedelic moral enhancement. *Neuroethics, 15*(2), 1–14.

Griffiths, R. R., Johnson, M. W., Carducci, M. A., Umbricht, A., Richards, W. A., Richards, B. D., Cosimano, M. P., & Klinedinst, M. A. (2016). Psilocybin produces substantial and sustained decreases in depression and anxiety in patients with life-threatening cancer: A randomized double-blind trial. *Journal of Psychopharmacology, 30*(12), 1181–1197.

Guyatt, G. H., Keller, J. L., Jaeschke, R., Rosenbloom, D., Adachi, J. D., & Newhouse, M. T. (1990). The n-of-1 randomized controlled trial: Clinical usefulness: Our three-year experience. *Annals of Internal Medicine*, *112*(4), 293–299.

Hardon, A., & Sanabria, E. (2017). Fluid drugs: Revisiting the anthropology of pharmaceuticals. *Annual Review of Anthropology*, *46*(1), 117–132.

Harmer, C. J., Duman, R. S., & Cowen, P. J. (2017). How do antidepressants work? New perspectives for refining future treatment approaches. *The Lancet Psychiatry*, *4*(5), 409–418.

Harmer, C. J., Goodwin, G. M., & Cowen, P. J. (2009). Why do antidepressants take so long to work? A cognitive neuropsychological model of antidepressant drug action. *The British Journal of Psychiatry*, *195*(2), 102–108.

Healy, C. (2021). The acute effects of classic psychedelics on memory in humans. *Psychopharmacology*, *238*(3), 639–653.

Heishman, S. J., Kleykamp, B. A., & Singleton, E. G. (2010). Meta-analysis of the acute effects of nicotine and smoking on human performance. *Psychopharmacology*, *210*(4), 453–469.

Helion, C., & Pizarro, D. A. (2015). Beyond dual-processes: The interplay of reason and emotion in moral judgment. In J. Clausen & N. Levy (Eds.), *Handbook of neuroethics* (pp. 109–125). Springer.

Hupli, A. (2023). Instrumentalising therapeutic and enhancement drugs as pharmacological technologies with politicogenic drug effects. *Drugs: Education, Prevention and Policy*, *30*(1), 60–69.

Ilieva, I., & Farah, M. J. (2013). Cognitive enhancement with amphetamine: History repeats itself. *AJOB Neuroscience*, *4*(1), 24–25.

Inserra, A., De Gregorio, D., & Gobbi, G. (2021). Psychedelics in psychiatry: Neuroplastic, immunomodulatory, and neurotransmitter mechanisms. *Pharmacological Reviews*, *73*(1), 202–277.

Jones, E. G., & Mendell, L. M. (1999). Assessing the decade of the brain. *Science*, *284*(5415), 739–739.

Jotterand, F., & Dubljevic, V. (2016). Introduction. In F. Jotterand & V. Dubljević (Eds.), *Cognitive enhancement: Ethical and policy implications in international perspectives* (pp. 1–11). Oxford University Press.

Jotterand, F., & Levin, S. B. (2019). Moral deficits, moral motivation and the feasibility of moral bioenhancement. *Topoi*, *38*(1), 63–71.

Kahneman, D. (2011). *Thinking fast and slow*. Farrar, Straus and Giroux.

Kredlow, M. A., Keshishian, A., Oppenheimer, S., & Otto, M. W. (2019). The efficacy of modafinil as a cognitive enhancer: A systematic review and meta-analysis. *Journal of Clinical Psychopharmacology*, *39*(5), 455–461.

Langlitz, N., Dyck, E., Scheidegger, M., & Repantis, D. (2021). Moral psychopharmacology needs moral inquiry: The case of psychedelics. *Frontiers in Psychiatry*, *12*, 680064.

Lerner, J. S., Li, Y., Valdesolo, P., & Kassam, K. S. (2015). Emotion and decision making. *Annual Review of Psychology*, *66*(1), 799–823.

Lorenzo Calvo, J., Fei, X., Domínguez, R., & Pareja-Galeano, H. (2021). Caffeine and cognitive functions in sports: A systematic review and meta-analysis. *Nutrients*, *13*(3), 868.

Maier, L. J., Ferris, J. A., & Winstock, A. R. (2018). Pharmacological cognitive enhancement among non-ADHD individuals – A cross-sectional study in 15 countries. *International Journal of Drug Policy*, *58*, 104–112.

Mason, N., Kuypers, K., Reckweg, J., Müller, F., Tse, D., Da Rios, B., Toennes, S., Stiers, P., Feilding, A., & Ramaekers, J. (2021). Spontaneous and deliberate creative cognition during and after psilocybin exposure. *Translational Psychiatry*, *11*(1), 1–13.

McIntyre, R. S., Cha, D. S., Soczynska, J. K., Woldeyohannes, H. O., Gallaugher, L. A., Kudlow, P., Alsuwaidan, M., & Baskaran, A. (2013). Cognitive deficits and functional outcomes in major depressive disorder: Determinants, substrates, and treatment interventions. *Depression and Anxiety*, *30*(6), 515–527.

McIntyre, R. S., Lee, Y., Zhou, A. J., Rosenblat, J. D., Peters, E. M., Lam, R. W., Kennedy, S. H., Rong, C., & Jerrell, J. M. (2017). The efficacy of psychostimulants in major depressive episodes: A systematic review and meta-analysis. *Journal of Clinical Psychopharmacology*, *37*(4), 412–418.

McLellan, T. M., Caldwell, J. A., & Lieberman, H. R. (2016). A review of caffeine's effects on cognitive, physical and occupational performance. *Neuroscience & Biobehavioral Reviews*, *71*, 294–312.

Meacham, D. (2017). Introduction: Critiquing technologies of the mind: Enhancement, alteration, and anthropotechnology. *Phenomenology and the Cognitive Sciences*, *16*(1), 1–16.

Mitchell, J. M., Bogenschutz, M., Lilienstein, A., Harrison, C., Kleiman, S., Parker-Guilbert, K., Ot'alora, G. M., Garas, W., Paleos, C., & Gorman, I. (2021). MDMA-assisted therapy for severe PTSD: A randomized, double-blind, placebo-controlled phase 3 study. *Nature Medicine*, *27*(6), 1025–1033.

Nehlig, A. (1999). Are we dependent upon coffee and caffeine? A review on human and animal data. *Neuroscience & Biobehavioral Reviews*, *23*(4), 563–576.

Pavarini, G., McKeown, A., & Singh, I. (2018). Smarter than thou, holier than thou: The dynamic interplay between cognitive and moral enhancement. *Frontiers in Pharmacology*, *9*, 1189.

Pokorny, T., Duerler, P., Seifritz, E., Vollenweider, F. X., & Preller, K. H. (2020). LSD acutely impairs working memory, executive functions, and cognitive flexibility, but not risk-based decision-making. *Psychological Medicine, 50*(13), 2255–2264.

Polito, V., & Stevenson, R. J. (2019). A systematic study of microdosing psychedelics. *PloS One, 14*(2), e0211023.

Prado, C. E., Watt, S., & Crowe, S. F. (2018). A meta-analysis of the effects of antidepressants on cognitive functioning in depressed and non-depressed samples. *Neuropsychology Review, 28*(1), 32–72.

Ragan, C. I., Bard, I., & Singh, I. (2013). What should we do about student use of cognitive enhancers? An analysis of current evidence. *Neuropharmacology, 64*, 588–595.

Randall, D. C., Shneerson, J. M., Plaha, K. K., & File, S. E. (2003). Modafinil affects mood, but not cognitive function, in healthy young volunteers. *Human Psychopharmacology: Clinical and Experimental, 18*(3), 163–173.

Reiff, C. M., Richman, E. E., Nemeroff, C. B., Carpenter, L. L., Widge, A. S., Rodriguez, C. I., Kalin, N. H., McDonald, W. M., & the Work Group on Biomarkers and Novel Treatments, a Division of the American Psychiatric Association Council of Research. (2020). Psychedelics and psychedelic-assisted psychotherapy. *American Journal of Psychiatry, 177*(5), 391–410.

Repantis, D., Laisney, O., & Heuser, I. (2010). Acetylcholinesterase inhibitors and memantine for neuroenhancement in healthy individuals: A systematic review. *Pharmacological Research, 61*(6), 473–481.

Repantis, D., Schlattmann, P., Laisney, O., & Heuser, I. (2009). Antidepressants for neuroenhancement in healthy individuals: A systematic review. *Poiesis & Praxis, 6*(3), 139–174.

Rifkin, B. D., Maraver, M. J., & Colzato, L. S. (2020). Microdosing psychedelics as cognitive and emotional enhancers. *Psychology of Consciousness: Theory, Research, and Practice, 7*(3), 316.

Riggs, L. M., & Gould, T. D. (2021). Ketamine and the future of rapid-acting antidepressants. *Annual Review of Clinical Psychology, 17*, 207–231.

Roberts, C. A., Jones, A., Sumnall, H., Gage, S. H., & Montgomery, C. (2020). How effective are pharmaceuticals for cognitive enhancement in healthy adults? A series of meta-analyses of cognitive performance during acute administration of modafinil, methylphenidate and D-amphetamine. *European Neuropsychopharmacology, 38*, 40–62.

Savulescu, J., Sandberg, A., & Kahane, G. (2011). Well-being and enhancement. In J. Savulescu, R. ter Meulen, & G. Kahane (Eds.), *Enhancing human capacities* (pp. 1–18). John Weley & Sons.

Schleim, S., & Quednow, B. B. (2018). How realistic are the scientific assumptions of the neuroenhancement debate? Assessing the pharmacological optimism and neuroenhancement prevalence hypotheses. *Frontiers in Pharmacology, 9*, 3.

Sen, A. (1979). Utilitarianism and welfarism. *The Journal of Philosophy, 76*(9), 463–489.

Sharif, S., Guirguis, A., Fergus, S., & Schifano, F. (2021). The use and impact of cognitive enhancers among university students: A systematic review. *Brain Sciences, 11*(3), 355.

Souza-Marques, B., Santos-Lima, C., Araujo-de-Freitas, L., Vieira, F., Jesus-Nunes, A. P., Quarantini, L. C., & Sampaio, A. S. (2021). Neurocognitive effects of ketamine and esketamine for treatment-resistant major depressive disorder: A systematic review. *Harvard Review of Psychiatry, 29*(5), 340–350.

Spronk, D. B., van Wel, J. H., Ramaekers, J. G., & Verkes, R. J. (2013). Characterizing the cognitive effects of cocaine: A comprehensive review. *Neuroscience & Biobehavioral Reviews, 37*(8), 1838–1859.

Stahl, S. M. (2021). *Stahl's essential psychopharmacology: Neuroscientific basis and practical applications*. Cambridge University Press.

Sunstein, C. R. (2015). The ethics of nudging. *Yale Journal on Regulation, 32*, 413.

Tattan-Birch, H., & Shahab, L. (2020). The psychobiology of nicotine vaping: Impact on addiction, cognition, mood, anxiety and appetite. In P. N. Murphy (Ed.), *Psychobiological issues in substance use and misuse* (pp. 265–288). Routledge.

Temple, J. L., Bernard, C., Lipshultz, S. E., Czachor, J. D., Westphal, J. A., & Mestre, M. A. (2017). The safety of ingested caffeine: A comprehensive review. *Frontiers in Psychiatry, 8*, 80.

Valentine, G., & Sofuoglu, M. (2018). Cognitive effects of nicotine: Recent progress. *Current Neuropharmacology, 16*(4), 403–414.

Van Bavel, J. J., FeldmanHall, O., & Mende-Siedlecki, P. (2015). The neuroscience of moral cognition: From dual processes to dynamic systems. *Current Opinion in Psychology, 6*, 167–172.

Vargo, E. J., & Petróczi, A. (2016). "It was me on a good day": Exploring the smart drug use phenomenon in England. *Frontiers in Psychology, 7*, 779.

Vrecko, S. (2013). Just how cognitive is "cognitive enhancement"? On the significance of emotions in university students' experiences with study drugs. *AJOB Neuroscience, 4*(1), 4–12.

Waters, A. J., & Sutton, S. R. (2000). Direct and indirect effects of nicotine/smoking on cognition in humans. *Addictive Behaviors, 25*(1), 29–43.

World Health Organization. (2015). *WHO global report on trends in prevalence of tobacco smoking 2015*. https://apps.who.int/iris/bitstream/handle/10665/156262/9789241564?sequence=1

Wu, K. C.-C. (2016). Cognitive enhancement: A confucian perspective from Taiwan. In F. Jotterand & V. Dubljević (Eds.), *Cognitive enhancement: Ethical and policy implications in international perspectives* (pp. 111–130). Oxford University Press.

Yesavage, J. A., Mumenthaler, M. S., Taylor, J. L., Friedman, L., O'Hara, R., Sheikh, J., Tinklenberg, J., & Whitehouse, P. J. (2002). Donepezil and flight simulator performance: Effects on retention of complex skills. *Neurology, 59*(1), 123–125.

Zaninotto, A. L., Bueno, O. F., Pradella-Hallinan, M., Tufik, S., Rusted, J., Stough, C., & Pompéia, S. (2009). Acute cognitive effects of donepezil in young, healthy volunteers. *Human Psychopharmacology: Clinical and Experimental, 24*(6), 453–464.

Zohny, H. (2015). The myth of cognitive enhancement drugs. *Neuroethics, 8*(3), 257–269.

PART VII

Legal, social, and political implications

27
COGNITIVE ENHANCEMENT FROM A LEGAL PERSPECTIVE

Jennifer A. Chandler and Kai Vogeley

27.1 Introduction

Cognitive enhancement, as a subset of human enhancement, is a topic of considerable ethical interest, where the focus has been primarily on the use of novel biomedical technological methods including drugs, brain stimulation, and genetic interventions. This ignores the many commonplace methods of cognitive enhancement in general use such as education or caffeine. This is understandable and justified since societies have not accrued experience with them, established their advantages and disadvantages, and integrated their use into the culture. Here we take a broad view of cognitive enhancement, as it will help us to identify legal precedents that might have developed for prior – now common – methods of cognitive enhancement.

The ethical literature on cognitive enhancement is well-developed. Among the main themes raised are cognitive liberty, freedom from coercion, safety, authenticity, human nature and dignity, fair competition, unequal access, and societal disruption, among other concerns (see e.g. the Presidential Commission for the Study of Bioethical Issues, 2015). Related ethical literature addresses moral enhancement, or interventions intended to do things like improving sensitivity to moral concerns, moral reasoning, or a person's motivation and self-control so as to be able to act morally (Shook, 2012).

The *law* of cognitive enhancement has attracted less thorough attention than the *ethics* of cognitive enhancement, with a couple of key exceptions (Goold, 2017; Greely, 2004, 2008, 2011). There are good reasons for this. It is hard to engage in concrete discussion of how the law applies or should apply without specifying details regarding the cognitive enhancement method (and its safety, effects, and side effects), the target cognitive function, the reasons for its use, the context of use, and the target population. There is a wide range of existing laws that could conceivably apply depending upon these concrete details, including employment law, child protection law, tort and criminal law, regulation of medical practice, drug and medical device regulation, and consumer protection legislation, among other domains of law.

The purpose of this chapter is to offer a structured framework within which to think through the legal implications of cognitive enhancement. It attempts to organize and summarize the legal issues identified to date regarding cognitive enhancement in the legal literature, supplemented with additional ideas along the way. A couple of caveats should be noted. Doubtless, some legal issues have not been captured. Furthermore, jurisdictions vary in the structure of their legal systems and the content of their laws and regulations. This chapter is written from a common law and developed country perspective, and the issues of primary concern and the legal responses will undoubtedly vary between societies.

The legal issues covered in this chapter are organized into higher-level themes such as freedom, responsibility, access, and ownership as opposed to the usual legal classifications such as criminal law, tort law, and human rights law. The themes, sub-themes, and examples are presented in Table 27.1.

Following our discussion of these themes, we conclude with a brief comment on the topic of calls for the international and domestic recognition of novel "neurorights" (Ienca & Andorno, 2017; Yuste et al., 2021). This is a relatively recent development in the ethico-legal discussion of neuroscience and technology, which raises the question of whether existing laws are adequate to address the kinds of issues posed by advances in the neurosciences. Although time and space foreclose a more complete discussion of these issues here, we expect the discussion in coming years to be interesting and increasingly relevant as these and other technological developments permit us to manipulate brain activity as well as mental experiences (e.g. the expanding use of virtual reality offers another example; Marloth et al., 2020).

Table 27.1 Cognitive Enhancement: Legal Themes and Sub-Themes

Theme	Sub-theme	Examples
Freedom	Obligation to use cognitive enhancement interventions	• Can a person be obliged to use a cognitive enhancement intervention?
	Obligation to NOT use cognitive enhancement interventions	• Can a person be legally obliged to not use a cognitive enhancement intervention?
Responsibilities	Of the cognitively enhanced person	• Is legal responsibility increased when a cognitive enhancement intervention increases a person's capacities?
	Of makers, providers, prescribers of cognitive enhancement interventions	• Are the providers of cognitive enhancement interventions responsible for harms associated with their use?
	Of people toward their dependents	• Do people have an obligation to provide (or NOT to provide) cognitive enhancement interventions to their dependents?
Rights of access	Access to cognitive enhancement interventions	• Are there legally recognizable claims to state provision or funding of cognitive enhancement interventions?
Ownership	Rights to the intellectual products of enhanced minds	• What type or form of cognitive enhancement interventions (if any) would justify re-conceptualizing the "author" or "creator" of original works?
Government regulation	Reasons for government regulation	• When and why should governments regulate cognitive enhancement interventions? • What existing regulations apply to cognitive enhancement interventions?
International legal issues	Law of armed conflict	• What is the impact of enhancement on the legal status of soldiers? • What is the impact on the legal status of medics when they provide enhancement versus therapy?

27.2 Freedom

27.2.1 Can a person be obliged to use a cognitive enhancement intervention?

As a general proposition, the law provides very strong protection against forcible physical interference with the body, at least for people with preserved decision-making capacity. As a result, most instances in which one can imagine a person being *obliged* to undergo a cognitive enhancement intervention would not involve forcible application but would instead be situations in which there are inducements to do so. A person may accept an intervention to avoid an undesired consequence or to secure a desired consequence. This section will discuss (1) whether a person could be held liable for negligence if they did not use a cognitive enhancement intervention, (2) whether employers might require an employee to use an enhancement as a condition of employment, (3) whether a person might be obliged to accept an enhancement as a form of rehabilitation in the criminal context, and (4) whether the availability of enhancement interventions might affect disability discrimination protections under human rights laws.

If cognitive enhancement technologies are effective in improving a person's capacity to avoid harm to others, their use may come to be expected. In the common law of negligence, a duty of care may be imposed by law to avoid harming others. A person under such a duty must satisfy the legal standard of care, which is essentially a reasonableness standard that examines the risk and severity of potential harm as well as the burdensomeness of the precautions that a person could take. Sometimes the reasonable course of action is to refrain from the risky activity (e.g. driving while it is unsafe because of poorly controlled epilepsy), and sometimes it is to continue the activity but reduce risk by taking medications to address that risk (e.g. anti-epileptic drugs). An obligation to either refrain from an activity that poses foreseeable risks or to use a cognitive enhancement intervention to reduce those risks could fit within the structure of negligence law.

For someone whose capacities meet the current standard, it is possible that as others adopt a risk-reducing enhancement, the failure to do so will come to be seen as unreasonable. There are various legal precedents for medical malpractice liability where physicians were slow to adopt new technologies or procedures (Maslen et al., 2015). Of course, there is a difference between the adoption of a tool or technique, even one worn on the body like eyeglasses, and a bodily intervention like drugs that may pose risks to the surgeon. Legal systems are reluctant to require people to submit to interferences with bodily integrity or to face health risks for others' sake (Goold & Maslen, 2014). This may not hold true for all types of cognitive enhancement, however. Enhancements such as education or periods of supervised practice are already legally obligatory.

In addition to establishing a breach of the duty of care, a plaintiff would need to also establish that the breach of duty *caused* the harm. If it was likely to have occurred in any event, then the failure to enhance will not be viewed as the cause. As Goold and Maslen point out, the effects of cognitive enhancement interventions may be rather subtle, making it more challenging to clearly establish that they would have made a difference (Goold & Maslen, 2015).

The foregoing has discussed the possibility of liability for failing to use a cognitive enhancement intervention. It is important to note that liability may also flow from using a cognitive enhancement intervention if it instead degraded the user's capacities in a way that caused foreseeable harm (Drabiak-Syed, 2011; Goold & Maslen, 2014).

A person could feel pressure to use an enhancement in order to secure or retain employment. This is because an employer will need to manage its own legal risks, and may demand a higher standard as a condition of employment. Employers may be vicariously liable for the negligence of employees, and so will likely respond to a sub-par performance that puts others at risk. For example, some vision clinics advertise specifically that they can improve vision so that patients can obtain jobs that demand high visual acuity (Fiser & Hopkins, 2017, p. 77)

Employers sometimes require the use of certain enhancements as a condition of employment. For example, some hospitals and nursing homes require influenza vaccination as a condition of employment (Gruben et al., 2014). Whether or not employment law or human rights laws would constrain the ability of employers to impose these demands would depend on the particular case and legal jurisdiction. Human rights laws typically prohibit discrimination in employment on the basis of certain grounds such as sex, race, religion, or disability. Preference for a person with superior cognitive abilities due to enhancement would not appear to be covered. As Goold suggests, this would most likely be understood as "selecting the person best placed to perform the job. The reason for their being in this position is not relevant" (Goold, 2017). Even though training, education, and experience are not usually understood as cognitive enhancements, it is worth noting that employers routinely demand these as conditions of employment. Rather than requiring cognitive enhancement as a condition of employment, a more subtle form of pressure to enhance would exist if employers preferred those who had been enhanced.

Soldiers are also required to accept enhancement interventions including vaccinations or drugs intended to address cognitive and emotional functions (Parasidis, 2012). Some of these interventions appear to be primarily preventive interventions for soldiers in the field against potential infection and psychiatric disturbance. However, the military is also evidently interested in enhancing fighting efficacy and capacity, and research programs are also considering how to do this through cognitive enhancement technologies (Parasidis, 2012, p. 1129). As Parasidis points out, the position of the soldier differs from that of an employee. The former may face punitive measures for disobeying orders while the employee may face loss of employment for refusing an enhancement intervention. Furthermore, recourse in tort for injuries caused by the intervention may be limited for soldiers (Parasidis, 2012, pp. 1131–1132).

People may be induced to accept cognitive enhancements as forms of rehabilitation within the criminal justice system. For example, interventions to enhance self-control and empathy or to suppress aggressivity might be classified as cognitive enhancements since there is not necessarily a clear disease being targeted (Shaw, 2013, 2018). It seems very unlikely that cognitive interventions would be forcibly applied to prisoners; it is more likely that such interventions would be offered in a quasi-coercive manner (i.e. consent to the intervention would be associated with a preferable legal outcome) because this is already being done routinely. People who consent to pharmacological treatment of addiction or sex-drive-reducing medication may fare better in the legal system because they are judged as posing less risk and as taking responsibility for their actions (Chandler, 2014; Chandler et al., 2019). The legal benefits include an increased chance of diversion from prosecution, preferable sentences, or parole. These interventions are generally understood as therapies rather than enhancements. However, the classification – therapy or enhancement – remains slippery, and depends upon the pathologization of the criminogenic traits. This malleable classification makes it easier for practitioners to reconcile the demands of medical ethics with the quasi-coercive context of criminal justice (Chandler, 2014).

Cognitive enhancement interventions also interact with human rights laws that protect against discrimination on the basis of disability in sectors such as employment, residential accommodation, and the provision of goods and services (Ontario Human Rights Code R.S.O. 1990 c. H.19, n.d.). Under Ontario's Code, it is not discrimination contrary to the Code to refuse to employ a person who is "incapable of performing or fulfilling the essential duties or requirements" (s 17(1)). However, a person cannot be found incapable if it is possible to accommodate the needs of the person with a disability without undue hardship (s.17(2)).

A question arises as to whether a person is expected to use treatments or other supports that could mitigate the impact of an impairment (e.g. eyeglasses that could restore normal visual acuity) and how non-use of those options affects an employer's accommodation obligation (Ontario Human Rights Commission, 2014). The problem with reducing the employer's accommodation obligation when there are mitigating measures available for "self-accommodation" is that it presupposes that such measures are effective, easily accessible, and suitable for everyone. It also puts the primary burden of accommodation on people with disabilities. On the other hand, Hamlet points to the problems that arise if the law ignores mitigating measures in competitive higher educational contexts (Hamlet, 2014). He argues that there is a risk of unfair over-accommodation if a person uses medications that effectively mitigate the impairment related to ADHD and also receives additional accommodations such as more time for tests.

This legal issue is relevant to our discussion of cognitive enhancement since it shows how a particular treatment might operate more as an enhancement rather than a therapy if the disabling impact of an impairment has already been accommodated pursuant to human rights legislation. Lee and Read broaden this critique, arguing generally that the proliferation of enhancement technologies will make natural biological disabilities meaningless, and that legal remedies are not necessary "when super mitigating factors are present" (Lee & Read, 2018). In their view, the law of the future should shift to address whether an employer can require the use of a mitigating factor as a condition of employment and whether it is the unenhanced, "natural" worker who will be the class of workers viewed as disabled and in need of protection from discrimination (Lee & Read, 2018, p. 266)

27.2.2 Can a person be legally obliged to not use a cognitive enhancement intervention?

State restriction of cognitive enhancement interventions is not new. The prohibition or regulation of the so-called recreational use of psychoactive drugs, some of which could be intended by their users as forms of cognitive enhancement, is a long-standing legal topic (Walsh, 2016). Legal academics have evaluated existing constitutional rights to assess whether they extend to the use of cognitive enhancement interventions (Blitz, 2010; Bublitz, 2013). For example, Blitz examines the potential applicability to cognitive enhancement of the right to freedom of thought, as well as whether freedom of thought is a necessary component of other protected rights such as the rights to freedom of speech or religion, or of the general right to liberty.

Ethical discussions of human enhancement often raise concerns about fairness in competition and unequal access. Legal attention to this point has primarily focused on the regulation of performance-enhancing drugs in sports. More recently, legal scholars have identified a range of other sport or game-like contexts where the permissibility of cognitive enhancement interventions is at issue.

Casinos try to eject or at least make it difficult for blackjack players to count cards to increase their chances of winning (Kolber, 2012). A gambler can legally use his or her cognitive faculties to count cards, although some US states criminalize the use of devices to keep track of cards. Kolber asks the intriguing questions of how these laws might apply to cognitive enhancement interventions, and whether they should do so. He speculates that caffeine, glucose, or potential cognitive enhancement drugs would not fall within the criminal ban on devices but that portable neurostimulation devices might. It is not clear whether cognitive enhancement interventions *should* be legally prohibited, and whether such laws are practically enforceable. This legal example illustrates in another context the familiar problems of whether and how to regulate doping: defining cheating in a given context, determining which forms of enhancement are cheating, and finding ways to detect enhancement and enforce prohibitions.

E-sports or competitive online computer gaming is another area that these issues will need to be worked out as "cognitive athletes" openly use performance-enhancing drugs and other enhancement interventions such as neurostimulation are being (Holden et al., 2020; Machado et al., 2021; Maiberg, 2015). In 2021, the International Olympic Committee is presenting an Olympic Virtual Series of e-sports, a move that the IOC says "encourages sports participation and promotes the Olympic values" (Bieler, 2021). Concern for the competitive integrity of e-sports has resulted in the implementation of drug testing in some leagues, but the fragmentation of the industry into various leagues and oversight bodies is currently undermining the adoption of a consistent approach (Holden et al., 2020).

The non-medical use of prescription stimulants for academic cognitive enhancement is also a legal matter since the possession and trafficking of these controlled substances without a prescription is a criminal offense (Aikins et al., 2017; Downie et al., 2010). A recent survey of a sample of American universities reveals that very few universities prohibit the use of cognitive enhancement drugs within their academic integrity policies (Aikins et al., 2017). Duke University is a rare example that identifies the non-medical use of prescription stimulants as a form of cheating (Duke University, n.d.). Many American universities have alcohol and drug use policies that require compliance with state or federal laws, implicitly capturing the diversion of prescription stimulants. Another approach taken by some university student health services is to require students to sign contracts promising not to share their prescribed medications with classmates (Schwarz, 2013). Some have called for more aggressive measures to be taken to combat academic use of cognitive enhancement drugs such as random drug trusting of students (Schieffelin, 2007). This approach raises its own issues with respect to privacy intrusion and possibly also constitutionality (see e.g. Smith, 2015).

27.3 Responsibilities

27.3.1 Is legal responsibility increased when a cognitive enhancement intervention increases a person's capacities?

Several authors have considered the possibility that people who enhance their cognitive capacities may be held to higher standards, and so may be viewed as not just morally blameworthy, but also legally liable where an unenhanced person might not (Goold, 2017; Maslen et al., 2015).

In general, the law adopts a capacity-based view of responsibility. Those who satisfy the threshold of legal capacity – i.e. the basic ability to understand and appreciate the nature and consequences of one's acts – may be held legally responsible. Below that threshold, a person is incapable and is not held responsible. Note, however, that in some limited contexts where fault is not required (i.e. strict liability contexts), incapacity may not be exculpatory.

However, we are interested here in what happens when people enhance their capacities beyond normal. The analysis may be a bit different depending upon the form of legal fault at issue. In the civil law of negligence, a person is at fault for failing to exercise reasonable care to avoid injuring another. Their conduct is judged according to a standard of care applicable equally to all, although certain roles attract a higher standard of care (e.g. a physician is expected to exercise the same degree of skill and judgment as would be exercised by reasonable physicians in the same specialty). The question posed in relation to cognitive enhancement is whether that uniform standard of care should be adjusted upward to acknowledge the greater capacities of an enhanced person. As for crimes like assault, should a person be viewed as more morally blameworthy if they had undergone cognitive enhancements that help them to better control their own behavior?

As far as negligence is concerned, the standard of care is an objective general one that is not adjusted according to the capacities of the actor (Goold, 2017). Furthermore, the usual remedy is compensation which is meant to restore the victim to their prior position; the cognitive capacity and moral blameworthiness of the wrongdoer are not relevant to the quantification of compensatory damages. That being said, it is possible that the psychology of legal decision-makers may be affected. Perhaps decision-makers will view an enhanced person as more morally blameworthy, and this may influence their evaluation of the victim's losses, particularly those that are not easily expressed in money (e.g. pain and suffering).

Turning to intentional wrongdoing in criminal law, capacity is relevant at the stage of sentencing because punishment is supposed to be proportionate to moral blameworthiness, and diminished capacity is often taken to mitigate blame. But again, we are concerned with the possibility of increased moral blame for those with enhanced capacities. If we look at advantaged social background (which presumably includes better access to a range of enhancing opportunities), a complex picture emerges. It appears that privileged social background is sometimes mitigating at sentence perhaps because it is taken to suggest better chances at rehabilitation, while it is also sometimes aggravating perhaps because it suggests the defendant should have done better (Kaye, 2011). One speculative way in which cognitive enhancement might lead to harsher sentencing is by creating a gap in cognitive abilities between an enhanced perpetrator and the unenhanced victim. The particular vulnerability of the victim (e.g. children, the elderly, and people with mental or physical disabilities or illnesses) is already an aggravating factor when it comes to sentencing (Manson, 2001). At present, cognitive enhancement interventions do not create such a difference that an unenhanced person would be viewed as vulnerable by that fact alone.

27.3.2 Are the providers of cognitive enhancement interventions responsible for harms associated with their use?

The designers, manufacturers, and distributors of products may be held liable under legal regimes of "product liability" that vary among jurisdictions. Some impose strict liability (i.e. liability without fault) and others impose liability only if these actors were negligent in the design, manufacture, or communication of risks related to the products (Goold, 2017; Greely, 2011). Note that even if people use products for unintended purposes, there may be legal obligations to warn if a manufacturer becomes aware of the risky misuse or unintended use of its products (Edgell, 2000, p. 76). This last point is relevant given evidence of off-label use of drugs and brain stimulation devices for cognitive enhancement purposes. In addition to common law regimes like product liability law, consumer protection legislation in some jurisdictions may also support consumer remedies where sub-standard services or defective goods for cognitive enhancement are supplied to consumers (Goold, 2017).

Physicians also have legal responsibilities in relation to enhancement interventions. Although it is not a cognitive enhancement, the prevailing standard of care would demand that physicians recommend and provide vaccinations to enhance the immune response. The medical standard of care would not require that non-therapeutic (enhancing) cosmetic surgery or dentistry be offered but would accept that it could be offered by a physician even if it poses some risk to a properly informed consenting patient. In other cases, such as with emerging pharmacological cognitive enhancement, physicians may have other obligations. Off-label prescribing is widespread, and so doesn't furnish an absolute barrier to prescribing stimulants for cognitive enhancement purposes (Gunter, 2015). On the other hand, Downie et al. suggest that prescribing stimulants for the purpose of cognitive enhancement (an off-label use) might violate the medical standard of care, particularly since it is not clear that the benefits outweigh the risks in the absence of medical necessity (Downie et al., 2010).

27.3.3 What obligations are owed to dependents in relation to cognitive enhancements?

Greely observes that parents have "at some level [a] duty to enhance their children" (Greely, 2011, p. 515). A parental duty to ensure the cognitive enhancement of children through education is already legally recognized in many jurisdictions (Harris, 2020). For example, in Ontario, a parent or guardian who refuses or neglects this duty can be convicted of an offense and may be required to pay a fine. Educational neglect is also a basis for engaging state intervention under child protection legislation, although it is not often the sole basis for state intervention. Disputes over whether to medicate children for attention deficit hyperactivity disorder (ADHD) have occasionally been framed in terms of educational and medical neglect by parents (Lenz, 2005). In principle, the law may require parents to ensure some types of cognitive enhancement, particularly education, but this seems unlikely to include enhancement via drugs or other physical interventions in the absence of a medical disorder.

Looking at the issue in the other direction, would legal issues arise if parents were to apply cognitive enhancement interventions to their children? Given the pressures on children and parents to succeed in competitive cultures, there is a possibility that ineffective or potentially harmful cognitive enhancement interventions may be applied to children. The idea of parental enhancement of children is not new. Across many cultures, parents have long made cosmetic modifications to the bodies of their children that they judged to be in their children's best interests for non-medical aesthetic, social or cultural reasons (Ouellette, 2010). As for novel cognitive enhancement interventions, it seems unlikely that the law would become involved in parents' choices for their children unless there was evidence of harm, in which case child protection legislation could be invoked (Goold, 2017).

This does not exhaust the potential legal ramifications of parental enhancement decisions, however. In custody disputes, a parent may use the position of the other on whether to provide an intervention to the child to support an argument that they are the more fit parent. This includes cases involving interventions falling along the spectrum between treatment and enhancement such as the use of Ritalin for ADHD (Chandler, 2013), the use of growth hormone for a child with "idiopathic short stature" (*G.A. v. K.B.*, 2014; *Sheila R v. David R.*, 2011) and circumcision (*Izyuk v Bilousov*, 2011; *M.S. v. R.C.*, 2015). So even if an intervention is not clearly medically required, judgments about whether it is beneficial or not may bear on other types of legal disputes.

27.4 Rights of access

Do people have a legally recognized right of access to cognitive enhancement interventions? A right of access is different from the freedom to enhance, discussed earlier. The first is a positive right entailing a claim that others (e.g. governments) must provide or facilitate access to cognitive enhancements, while the second is a negative right to be left free to do as one wishes.

International human rights instruments have long recognized a right of access to some state-sponsored cognitive enhancement in the form of education. This right was listed in the Universal Declaration of Human Rights (United Nations, 1948) Some countries, such as South Africa, have recognized an explicit right to education within their constitutions (Constitution of the Republic of South Africa, Bill of Rights, 1996), while others have enacted education laws stating that all resident children have a right of access to public education systems (Ontario Education Act R.S.O. 1990 c. E.2, n.d.).

Education is a non-controversial and socially well-entrenched form of cognitive enhancement. Turning to more novel technological forms of cognitive enhancement, it seems unlikely that one could establish a legally enforceable right to government provision of things like cognitive enhancement interventions in the form of drugs or brain stimulation devices, particularly since a positive right to the government provision of even medical therapies is usually limited if it exists at all. There are many competing claims on government resources and most legal systems would likely leave to governments the task of allocating resources among the most pressing governmental objectives.

Things may be different if a cognitive enhancement is viewed as a therapy to address a disability or disorder. Returning to the level of international law, the Convention on the Rights of Persons with Disabilities (CRPD) commits states to support research into assistive technologies and to promote access by persons with disabilities to these technologies (United Nations, 2008). The CRPD also declares that all persons with disabilities have a right to enjoy legal capacity on an equal basis with others and that states agree to "take appropriate measures to provide access by persons with disabilities to the support they may require in exercising their legal capacity" (United Nations, 2008) Cognitive enhancements seem particularly relevant here, given that legal capacity turns primarily on cognitive abilities. This article reflects the recent movement away from substitute decision-making toward supported decision-making. This movement discourages too rapid a move toward declaring a person incapable on the basis of cognitive or communication disabilities and focuses the attention on what can be done to change the context, presentation of information, communication modality, and availability of supporters to assist. The point for our purposes is whether states have an obligation also to provide access to cognitive enhancement interventions that could be of assistance.

At the domestic level, if cognitive enhancement is viewed as a therapy, it might be possible to establish a claim to state provision of that intervention. Taking Canada as an example, the publicly funded healthcare system covers some but not all healthcare services. Claims have been successfully brought in relation to the discriminatory provision of services that are generally available to the whole public, but claims based on a right to currently unfunded services have been less successful. On the other hand, where the state limits the liberty of a person with a mental disorder for their own protection or the protection of others, claims to specialized treatments may fare better (e.g. *Pinet v. Penetanguishene Mental Health Centre*, 2006). This is because the state is supposed to minimize liberty restrictions, and so should provide reasonable access to rehabilitation treatments that will allow a person to regain their freedom.

27.5 Ownership

Cognitive enhancement raises futuristic but interesting legal questions about the ownership of intellectual property created by cognitively enhanced people (Dunagan & Halbert, 2015). As a general proposition, the author or inventor of an original work or invention is the owner of intellectual property (IP) rights in that work. Sometimes the law provides that it is the employer who owns the IP rights in an employee's works or inventions. This is achieved by the operation of a statute unless there is some arrangement to the contrary (Copyright Act of Canada, 1985) or through a clause in the employment contract (Dunagan & Halbert, 2015). Presumably, the creation of employees using cognitive enhancements would fall within existing legal arrangements that determine the ownership of intellectual property.

It seems most unlikely that the developers of cognitive enhancement interventions could claim intellectual property rights in the creation of an enhanced person, at least if we think of cognitive enhancements like drugs or education. The provider of the cognitive enhancement intervention is not sufficiently involved in the later creative step taken by the enhanced person to justify joint authorship (Stobbe, 2016).

What of the admittedly futuristic possibility that a cognitive enhancement device might provide a more direct contribution to creativity? The possibility that our technologies might cross the line between tools and artificial agents capable of the invention of original works has already been considered in relation to intellectual property law (Dunagan & Halbert, 2015; Gervais, 2020). Could such an artificial agent participate with a human user in the co-creation of original works of authorship? The sources of creative inspiration are obscure, but could intelligent devices be used to enhance this process either through brain stimulation or through the presentation of sensory stimuli in virtual environments? There are many problems with these suggestions, including that ownership of IP is dependent upon legal personhood.

It is worthwhile considering these futuristic possibilities, if only for what they tell us about the conceptual and pragmatic choices underlying our current approach to the ownership of original works of authorship and inventions. In a future forecasting exercise entitled "Intellectual Property for the Neurocentric Age," Dunagan and Halbert speculate about the possibility that technologies of the extended mind might affect the underlying logic of intellectual property law. In their view, the idea of the bounded individual creator may in the future give way in the face of the growing understanding of the social and collaborative nature of innovation and the place of the individual within larger networks of creativity (Dunagan & Halbert, 2015).

27.6 Government regulations

Government regulation is a complex endeavor. While it seems like a natural response to try to ward off anticipated problems with novel technology, there are limits and downsides to regulation. Regulatory systems often increase costs and limit the autonomy of regulated parties (either paternalistically for their own benefit or for others' benefit) and so must be justified by their countervailing benefits. Furthermore, regulatory systems create incentives for regulated parties to change their behavior to either exploit opportunities opened up by regulations or to avoid the regulations, sometimes leading to unintended effects. On the other hand, sometimes regulation is beneficial for technological innovation. At times regulation is required before a particular technology will be socially acceptable or regulation will foster technological innovation (Wiener, 2004). Another problem is timing, and regulation may arrive too early when a technology is still under-developed and we still do not understand its impact, or too late when the technology has become entrenched and it is difficult to change or control. Each horn of this so-called Collingridge dilemma poses its own challenges (Collingridge, 1980).

Despite the complexities and downsides, there are sometimes strong arguments for the regulation of technologies, one of which is the need to address health and safety hazards that market forces are ineffective to manage (Braun & Wield, 1994). In the context of novel types of cognitive enhancement interventions like drugs and brain stimulation devices, this is possibly the case. Where there are information asymmetries or people must choose whether to use cognitive enhancements within quasi-coercive contexts it may be difficult for them to make free and informed choices. To the extent that a type of intervention poses real health and safety risks, regulation may be advisable.

Another reason to regulate technologies is to resolve a collective action problem – i.e. where all would benefit from a certain action but there are costs making it unlikely or impossible for any one individual to take that action. For example, people taking a competitive physical or mental aptitude test would all be better off not taking the risks of cognitive enhancement drugs that do nothing more than temporarily improve function. Individuals who take the drugs gain a positional advantage over those that do not, and so each individual alone faces incentives to use the drug due to a prisoner's dilemma. The reasoning may differ if the drugs supported the development of an enduring skill or the acquisition of knowledge, as more would be gained than a mere positional advantage.

Returning specifically to the regulation of cognitive enhancement interventions, it is necessary to be quite specific about the case being considered. There are multiple types of cognitive enhancement intervention, many aspects or contexts of use that could attract regulatory attention, and many forms of regulation that governments could use. In addition, various general regulations already exist and would govern aspects of many types of cognitive enhancement interventions. These include advertising and consumer protection regulation, medical drug and device regulation, and so on.

Drugs and devices intended for medical use are subject to stringent regulation under food and drug laws for safety and efficacy, but many possible types of cognitive enhancements would not fall under this specific regulatory regime (although other laws might apply). An active discussion has emerged looking at the regulation of consumer brain stimulation devices (including those marketed directly to consumers as well as user-constructed devices) (De Ridder et al., 2014; Dubljević, 2015; Fitz & Reiner, 2015; Goold, 2017; Greely, 2011; Jwa, 2015; King et al., 2014; Kuersten & Hamilton, 2014; Wexler, 2015, 2016). There are differences of opinion on the question of whether regulation is warranted, as well as on whether there is in fact a regulatory gap. The discussion also raises concerns about enforceability, particularly in the case of user-constructed devices, as well as a regulatory burden.

27.7 International legal issues

Although it is not the first domain of law that comes to mind when considering the legal issues posed by cognitive enhancement, international law may also be relevant. Indeed, earlier sections of this chapter have mentioned international human rights treaties in relation to state obligations relevant to cognitive enhancement technologies.

Another domain of international law – the law of armed conflict – has been mentioned in relation to cognitive enhancement in the legal literature. McAllister considers the rule that prisoners of war are considered *hors de combat* and entitled to certain legal protections. She speculates that soldiers who are highly technologically enhanced – perhaps implanted with brain chips that allow continued communication with military operations – might be viewed as fused with their weapons and so never truly *hors de combat* (McAllister, 2019). Liivoja raises an implication for the military medical personnel who are supervising cognitive enhancement interventions of soldiers. Military medical personnel are protected by the laws of armed conflict while providing treatment of illness and disease, but may not be so protected while supplying enhancements because this would take them outside the non-combatant medical role (Liivoja, 2018).

27.8 Conclusion

Recently, concerns that existing human rights are inadequate to capture the challenges to human liberty and privacy that are presented by advances in neuroscience and neurotechnology have led to calls for the recognition of novel "neurorights" including rights to cognitive liberty, mental privacy, mental integrity, and psychological continuity (Ienca & Andorno, 2017) or to identity (the ability to control one's physical and mental integrity), agency (freedom of thought and free will), mental privacy, fair access to mental augmentation, and protection from algorithmic bias (Yuste et al., 2021). These provocative ideas have led to interesting ongoing debates along multiple lines. One set of questions is whether existing legal protections already adequately capture or can be re-interpreted to capture the concerns underlying these calls for novel neurorights (see e.g. Herrera-Ferrá, 2021; Ienca, 2021; Ligthart, 2020; López-Silva, 2021). Another explores the consequences and possible meanings of the rather broadly articulated novel neurorights (see e.g. Borbón & Borbón, 2021; Borbón Rodríguez et al., 2020; Munoz, 2019). Others address questions that presume the adoption of neurorights, such as how to protect those who do not want to be protected (Inglese & Lavazza, 2021). The ease with which people can be induced to waive personal privacy rights underscores the relevance of this issue.

This exploration of cognitive enhancement and the law raises a couple of points of relevance to the debate over neurorights. Laws do not address cognitive enhancement under that specific term, nor do they address it as a single unified phenomenon. Despite this, it is clear that cognitive enhancement interventions fall within a host of existing legal and regulatory structures. In order to evaluate whether the existing structures adequately address the issues posed by a cognitive enhancement intervention, it is necessary to specify the details of the intervention, as well as where, why and on whom it will be used. This will enable a closer examination of what specific laws apply.

Also relevant to the discussion of neurorights are prior legal discussions of how the law should respond to technological innovation. Legal scholars have discussed the problems of timing, of when or whether to aspire to technological neutrality, and so forth, in relation to various waves of novel technology (Brownsword et al., 2016; Moses, 2011; Ranchordás & Roznai, 2020). Furthermore, there is general and perennial tension in the law between two poles: rules articulated at a general level and rules that are more precise and specific. General rules cover more cases, allow for flexibility to capture new cases through interpretation, are more "future-proofed," and discourage actors from making small adjustments to fall outside the law. At the same time, general rules are less predictable and certain than precise and specific rules. Finally, the question of enforceability, as well as the unintended side effects of laws and regulations must be considered.

What can be confidently said is that the coming discussions will be interesting and important, as neuroscience and related technological fields that enable the modification of human experiences, information processing, and behavior continue to present individuals and societies with new knowledge and capabilities, creating the need to make decisions about how to balance the challenges and opportunities they present.

Acknowledgments

This project was prepared in the context of the ERANET-Neuron program project "Therapeutic and Enhancement Uses of Neuroscientific Knowledge: A question of individual autonomy?" supported by funding from the Canadian Institutes of Health Research (CIHR) and the German Ministry of Research and Education (BMBF, Germany; grant: 01GP1822).

References

Aikins, R., Zhang, X., & McCabe, S. E. (2017). Academic doping: Institutional policies regarding nonmedical use of prescription stimulants in U.S. higher education. *Journal of Academic Ethics, 15*(3), 229–243. https://doi.org/10.1007/s10805-017-9291-0

Bieler, D. (2021, April 22). IOC announces inaugural slate of Olympic-licensed esports events. *Washington Post*. https://www.washingtonpost.com/video-games/esports/2021/04/22/ioc-olympics-esports/

Blitz, M. J. (2010). Freedom of thought for the extended mind: Cognitive enhancement and the constitution. *Wisconsin Law Review, 2010*(4), 1049–1118.

Borbón, D., & Borbón, L. (2021). A critical perspective on neurorights: Comments regarding ethics and law. *Frontiers in Human Neuroscience, 15*, 703121. https://doi.org/10.3389/fnhum.2021.703121

Borbón Rodríguez, D. A., Borbón Rodríguez, L. F., & Laverde Pinzón, J. (2020). Análisis crítico de los NeuroDerechos Humanos al libre albedrío y al acceso equitativo a tecnologías de mejora. *Ius et Scientia, 6*(2), 135–161. https://doi.org/10.12795/IETSCIENTIA.2020.i02.10

Braun, E., & Wield, D. (1994). Regulation as a means for the social control of technology. *Technology Analysis & Strategic Management, 6*(3), 259–272. https://doi.org/10.1080/09537329408524171

Brownsword, R., Scotford, E., & Yeung, K. (Eds.). (2016). *The Oxford handbook of law, regulation and technology* (Vol. 1). Oxford University Press. https://doi.org/10.1093/oxfordhb/9780199680832.001.0001

Bublitz, J.-C. (2013). My mind is mine!? Cognitive liberty as a legal concept. In *Cognitive enhancement* (pp. 233–264). Dordrecht: Springer. https://doi.org/10.1007/978-94-007-6253-4_19

Chandler, J. A. (2013). Autonomy and the unintended legal consequences of emerging neurotherapies. *Neuroethics, 6*(2), 249–263. https://doi.org/10.1007/s12152-011-9109-5

Chandler, J. A. (2014). Legally-coerced consent to treatment in the criminal justice system. In D. Holmes, A. Perron, & J.-D. Jacob (Eds.), *Power and the psychiatric apparatus: Repression, transformation and assistance* (pp. 199–216). Ashgate Publishing.

Chandler, J. A., Kilty, J., & Holmes, D. (2019). Medicalized metamorphosis: Biological rehabilitation of criminal offenders. *Critical Criminology*. https://doi.org/10.1007/s10612-019-09479-z

Collingridge, D. (1980). *The social control of technology*. Pinter.

Constitution of the Republic of South Africa, Bill of Rights. (1996). https://www.justice.gov.za/legislation/constitution/saconstitution-web-eng.pdf

Copyright Act of Canada, R.S.C. 1985, c.C-42 (1985).

De Ridder, D., Vanneste, S., & Focquaert, F. (2014). Outstanding questions concerning the regulation of cognitive enhancement devices. *Journal of Law and the Biosciences, 1*(3), 316–321. https://doi.org/10.1093/jlb/lsu024

Downie, J., Outram, S., & Campbell, F. (2010). Legal liability associated with methylphenidate hydrochlorde (MPH) use by postsecondary students. *Health Law Journal, 18*, 51–72.

Drabiak-Syed, K. (2011). Sleep deprived physicians considering modafinil: Using a Controlled substance for cognitive enhancement gambles with differential drug responses and violates ethical and legal duties against physician impairment. *DePaul Journal of Health Care Law, 13*(3), 339–366.

Dubljević, V. (2015). Neurostimulation devices for cognitive enhancement: Toward a comprehensive regulatory framework. *Neuroethics, 8*(2), 115–126. https://doi.org/10.1007/s12152-014-9225-0

Duke University. (n.d.). *Policy: Academic dishonesty*. https://studentaffairs.duke.edu/conduct/z-policies/academic-dishonesty

Dunagan, J., & Halbert, D. (2015). Intellectual property for the neurocentric age: Towards a neuropolitics of IP. *Queen Mary Journal of Intellectual Property, 5*(3), 302–326.

Edgell, D. (2000). *Product liability law in Canada*. Butterworths Canada Ltd.

Fiser, H. L., & Hopkins, P. D. (2017). Getting inside the employee's head: Neuroscience, negligent employment liability, and the push and pull for new technology. *Boston University Journal of Science & Technology Law, 23*(1), 44–87.

Fitz, N. S., & Reiner, P. B. (2015). The challenge of crafting policy for do-it-yourself brain stimulation. *Journal of Medical Ethics*, *41*(5), 410–412. https://doi.org/10.1136/medethics-2013-101458

G.A. v. K.B., ONSC 3913 (2014).

Gervais, D. (2020). Is intellectual property law ready for artificial intelligence? *GRUR International*, *69*(2), 117–118. https://doi.org/10.1093/grurint/ikz025

Goold, I. (2017). The legal aspects of cognitive enhancement. In R. ter Meulen, A. Mohammed, & W. Hall (Eds.), *Rethinking cognitive enhancement* (pp. 250–273). Oxford University Press. https://doi.org/10.1093/acprof:oso/9780198727392.003.0016

Goold, I., & Maslen, H. (2014). Must the surgeon take the pill: Negligence duty in the context of cognitive enhancement. *Modern Law Review*, *77*, 60–86.

Goold, I., & Maslen, H. (2015). Obliging surgeons to enhance: Negligence liability for uncorrected fatigue and problems with proving causation. *Medical Law Review*, *23*(3), 427–454. https://doi.org/10.1093/medlaw/fwu028

Greely, H. T. (2004). The social effects of advances in neuroscience: Legal problems, legal perspectives. In J. Illes (Ed.), *Neuroethics* (pp. 245–263). Oxford University Press. https://doi.org/10.1093/acprof:oso/9780198567219.001.0001

Greely, H. T. (2008). Remarks on human biological enhancement. *Kansas Law Review*, *56*(5), 1139–1157.

Greely, H. T. (2011). Of nails and hammers: Human biological enhancement and U.S. policy tools. In J. Savulescu (Ed.), *Enhancing human capacities* (pp. 503–520). Blackwell Publishing. https://books.scholarsportal.info/uri/ebooks/ebooks3/wiley/2015-08-31/1/9781444393552

Gruben, V., Siemieniuk, R. A., & McGeer, A. (2014). Health care workers, mandatory influenza vaccination policies and the law. *Canadian Medical Association Journal*, *186*(14), 1076–1080. https://doi.org/10.1503/cmaj.140035

Gunter, T. (2015). Cosmetic neurocognitive enhancement and health care providers. *Indiana Health Law Review*, *12*, 730–768.

Hamlet, E. (2014). "Over-accommodation" in higher education: An ADA injustice exposed. *Cardozo Public Law, Policy and Ethics Journal*, *12*(2), 491–528.

Harris, J. (2020). Educational neglect and child protection in Ontario. *Canadian Journal of Children's Rights/Revue Canadienne Des Droits Des Enfants*, *7*(1), 228–240. https://doi.org/10.22215/cjcr.v7i1.2575

Herrera-Ferrá, K. (2021). Bioculture and the global regulatory gap in neuroscience, neurotechnology, and neuroethics. In *Developments in neuroethics and bioethics* (Vol. 4, pp. 41–61). Elsevier. https://doi.org/10.1016/bs.dnb.2021.08.001

Holden, J. T., Edelman, M., & Baker, T. A. (2020). A short treatise on esports and the law: How America regulates its next national pastime. *University of Illinois Law Review*, *2020*, 509–581.

Ienca, M. (2021). On neurorights. *Frontiers in Human Neuroscience*, *15*, 701258. https://doi.org/10.3389/fnhum.2021.701258

Ienca, M., & Andorno, R. (2017). Towards new human rights in the age of neuroscience and neurotechnology. *Life Sciences, Society and Policy*, *13*(1), 5. https://doi.org/10.1186/s40504-017-0050-1

Inglese, S., & Lavazza, A. (2021). What should we do with people who cannot or do not want to be protected from neurotechnological threats? *Frontiers in Human Neuroscience*, *15*, 703092. https://doi.org/10.3389/fnhum.2021.703092

Izyuk v Bilousov, 2011 ONSC 6451 ___ (Ontario Superior Court of Justice 2011).

Jwa, A. (2015). Early adopters of the magical thinking cap: A study on do-it-yourself (DIY) transcranial direct current stimulation (tDCS) user community. *Journal of Law and the Biosciences*, *2*(2), 292–335. https://doi.org/10.1093/jlb/lsv017

Kaye, A. (2011). Excuses in exile. *University of Michigan Journal of Law Reform*, *48*, 437–501.

King, M., Gavaghan, C., & McMillan, J. (2014). Medical regulation of cognitive enhancement devices: Some concerns. *Journal of Law and the Biosciences*, *1*(3), 334–339. https://doi.org/10.1093/jlb/lsu020

Kolber, A. J. (2012). Criminalizing cognitive enhancement at the Blackjack table. In L. Nadel & W. P. Sinnott-Armstrong (Eds.), *Memory and law* (pp. 307–324). Oxford University Press. https://doi.org/10.1093/acprof:oso/9780199920754.003.0012

Kuersten, A., & Hamilton, R. H. (2014). The brain, cognitive enhancement devices, and European regulation. *Journal of Law and the Biosciences*, *1*(3), 340–347. https://doi.org/10.1093/jlb/lsu019

Lee, S., & Read, W. (2018). Technology-enhanced employees and the Americans with Disabilities Act. *Journal of High Technology Law*, *18*, 238–269.

Lenz, C. (2005). Prescribing a legislative response: Educators, physicians and psychotropic medication for children. *Journal of Contemporary Health Law and Policy*, *22*(1), 72–106.

Ligthart, S. (2020). Freedom of thought in Europe: Do advances in 'brain-reading' technology call for revision? *Journal of Law and the Biosciences*, *7*(1), lsaa048. https://doi.org/10.1093/jlb/lsaa048

Liivoja, R. (2018). Biomedical enhancement of warfighters and the legal protection of military medical personnel in armed conflict. *Medical Law Review, 26*(3), 421–448. https://doi.org/10.1093/medlaw/fwx046

López-Silva, P. (2021). Sobre la conveniencia de incluir los neuroderechos en la Constitución o en la ley. *Revista Chilena de Derecho y Tecnología, 10*, 25.

Machado, S., Travassos, B., Teixeira, D. S., Rodrigues, F., Cid, L., & Monteiro, D. (2021). Could tDCS be a potential performance-enhancing tool for acute neurocognitive modulation in eSports? A perspective review. *International Journal of Environmental Research and Public Health, 18*(7), 3678. https://doi.org/10.3390/ijerph18073678

Maiberg, E. (2015, July 14). Counter-strike esports pro: "We were all on adderall." https://www.vice.com/en/article/gvy7b3/counter-strike-esports-pro-we-were-all-on-adderall

Manson, A. (2001). *The law of sentencing*. Irwin Law.

Marloth, M., Chandler, J., & Vogeley, K. (2020). Psychiatric interventions in virtual reality: Why we need an ethical framework. *Cambridge Quarterly of Healthcare Ethics, 29*(4), 574–584. https://doi.org/10.1017/S0963180120000328

Maslen, H., Santoni de Sio, F., & Faber, N. (2015). With cognitive enhancement comes great responsibility? In B.-J. Koops, I. Oosterlaken, H. Romijn, T. Swierstra, & J. van den Hoven (Eds.), *Responsible innovation 2* (pp. 121–138). Springer International Publishing. https://doi.org/10.1007/978-3-319-17308-5_7

McAllister, A. (2019). Cybernetic enhancement of soldiers: Conserving hors de combat protections for combatants under the third geneva convention. *Cyber Warfare, 7*, 35.

Moses, L. B. (2011). Sui generis rules. In G. E. Marchant, B. R. Allenby, & J. R. Herkert (Eds.), *The growing gap between emerging technologies and legal-ethical oversight* (Vol. 7, pp. 77–94). Springer Netherlands. https://doi.org/10.1007/978-94-007-1356-7_6

M.S. v. R.C., 2015 BCPC 407 ___ (British Columbia Provincial Court 2015).

Munoz, J. M. (2019). Chile—Right to free will needs definition. *Nature, 574*, 634.

Ontario Education Act R.S.O. 1990 c. E.2.

Ontario Human Rights Code R.S.O. 1990 c. H.19.

Ontario Human Rights Commission. (2014). *Policy on preventing discrimination based on mental health disabilities and addictions*. http://www.ohrc.on.ca/en/policy-preventing-discrimination-based-mental-health-disabilities-and-addictions

Ouellette, A. (2010). Article: Shaping parental authority over children's bodies. *Indiana Law Journal, 85*, 955–1002.

Parasidis, E. (2012). Human enhancement and experimental research in the military. *Connecticut Law Review, 44*(4), 1117–1132.

Pinet v. Penetanguishene Mental Health Centre, [2006] O.J. No. 678 ___ (2006).

Presidential Commission for the Study of Bioethical Issues. (2015). *Gray matters: Topics at the intersection of neuroscience, ethics and society, volume* 2 Presidential Commission for the Study of Bioethical Issues. See e.g. https://www.cell.com/trends/cognitive-sciences/pdf/S1364-6613(15)00178-3.pdf.

Ranchordás, S., & Roznai, Y. (Eds.). (2020). *Time, law, and change: An interdisciplinary study*. Hart.

Schieffelin, N. W. (2007). Maintaining educational and athletic integrity: How will schools combat performance-enhancing drug use. *Suffolk University Law Review, 40*, 959–979.

Schwarz, A. (2013, April 30). Attention-deficit drugs face new campus rules. *New York Times*. https://www.nytimes.com/2013/05/01/us/colleges-tackle-illicit-use-of-adhd-pills.html

Shaw, E. (2013). Cognitive enhancement and criminal behavior. In E. Hildt & A. G. Franke (Eds.), *Cognitive enhancement* (Vol. 1, pp. 265–281). Springer Netherlands. https://doi.org/10.1007/978-94-007-6253-4_20

Shaw, E. (2018). Retributivism and the moral enhancement of criminals through brain interventions. *Royal Institute of Philosophy Supplement, 83*, 251–270. https://doi.org/10.1017/S1358246118000383

Sheila R v. David R., 719 S.E. 2d 682 (Court of Appeals of South Carolina 2011).

Shook, J. R. (2012). Neuroethics and the possible types of moral enhancement. *AJOB Neuroscience, 3*(4), 3–14. https://doi.org/10.1080/21507740.2012.712602

Smith, T. (2015). Worshiping at the altar of progress: Cognitive enhancing drugs in legal education. *University of Dayton Law Review, 40*(2), 225–258.

Stobbe, R. (2016). Canadian Intellectual Property Review (CIPR) 31. *Canadian Intellectual Property Review, 32*, 18.

United Nations. (1948). *Universal declaration of human rights* (UDHR). New York: United Nations General Assembly.

United Nations. (2008). *Convention on the rights of persons with disabilities*. 13 December 2006, A/RES/61/106, Annex I, Entry into force: 3 May 2008

Walsh, C. (2016). Psychedelics and cognitive liberty: Reimagining drug policy through the prism of human rights. *International Journal of Drug Policy, 29*, 80–87. https://doi.org/10.1016/j.drugpo.2015.12.025

Wexler, A. (2015). A pragmatic analysis of the regulation of consumer transcranial direct current stimulation (TDCS) devices in the United States: Table 1. Journal of Law and the Biosciences, lsv039. https://doi.org/10.1093/jlb/lsv039

Wexler, A. (2016). The practices of do-it-yourself brain stimulation: Implications for ethical considerations and regulatory proposals. *Journal of Medical Ethics*, *42*(4), 211–215. https://doi.org/10.1136/medethics-2015-102704

Wiener, J. B. (2004). The regulation of technology, and the technology of regulation. *Technology in Society*, *26*(2–3), 483–500. https://doi.org/10.1016/j.techsoc.2004.01.033

Yuste, R., Genser, J., & Herrmann, S. (2021). It's time for neuro-rights. *Horizons: Journal of International Relations and Sustainable Development*, *18*, 154–164.

28
ENHANCEMENT AND HYPERRESPONSIBILITY

Anna Hartford, Julian Savulescu, and Dan J. Stein

28.1 Introduction

To begin with an important distinction: one can be *causally* responsible for some state of affairs, even a terrible state of affairs, without being morally responsible for it. Say someone starts a wildfire or causes a traffic accident or makes a fatal error at work. In each of these cases, it is possible, depending on the circumstances, that the person is nevertheless blameless for these tragedies. To determine their *moral* responsibility, we must answer a range of other questions. Could they have anticipated these outcomes, for instance? Or could they have taken reasonable precautions to prevent them?

In saying that someone is "morally responsible" for some wrong act, we mean that they are blameworthy for it and that blaming them would be appropriate. This is a normative conception of responsibility, concerning when blameworthiness is genuinely warranted or deserved, rather than a description of our blaming practice. (When we speak of "responsibility" going forward, we mean moral responsibility.)

Where should we draw the boundary of our responsibility for the world and for ourselves within it? In some respects, it seems to be a small realm, and much smaller than the limits of right and wrong action (we are regularly excused from blameworthiness, after all, despite failing to do the right thing). Responsibility is often thought of as fundamentally capacity-sensitive, and in general, our capacities are very limited: we reason pretty badly; we are deeply self-interested; there's only so much we're able to care about; we forget important things; we make very dangerous mistakes; we are, as we so often say, "only human."

Sometimes our capacities are more limited still, and these diminished capacities often seem to underwrite diminished responsibility. This would explain a range of familiar exemptions and excuses: for immaturity, senility, or certain mental impairments (and even, arguably, for psychopathy). On the face of it, responsibility seems to track the loss of, restoration of, and development of certain agential capacities.[1] It is because a child, for instance, has such under-developed capacities with regard to deliberative moral action that we should excuse them from wrongdoing, or perhaps exempt them entirely. But as a child's capacities gradually develop, so too does their corresponding responsibility for what they have done.[2]

There are different ways of thinking about how and why capacities matter in assessments of responsibility. In this chapter, we will consider three prevalent views. In the first place, you could take capacities to matter *in and of themselves*, where the foundation of moral responsibility (and its extent) resides in our individual capacity to respond to normative demands. Call these "capacity-based" views.

Alternatively, you could hold that capacities are intricately related to other features of our agency that are of more fundamental relevance to assessments of responsibility. We will consider two such views. We will call the first sort of view "control-based." According to these views, responsibility is a function of the degree of control an agent has over her actions and their outcomes, and the foreseeability of these consequences. Thus, we can only be held responsible for a wrongdoing or a harmful outcome insofar as it was within our control to avoid it. (Depending on how "control" is construed, these views can be closely related to capacity-based views, but they can also diverge: for instance, some philosophers have argued that fair appraisals of moral responsibility require deliberate and *conscious* control of one's wrongdoing.)[3]

Let us imagine a surgeon who has been forced to work a double shift, despite her growing exhaustion. In this fatigued state, she makes a fatal error during an emergency appendectomy, and a young patient dies a needless death. One may well feel that the doctor is not responsible for this tragedy, or at least that her responsibility is significantly diminished. On control-based views, we could understand her diminished responsibility as such: the doctor had no control over becoming fatigued (it is, after all, a natural process), and she had no control over her extended shift (we stipulated that she was given no other choice); furthermore, as her capacities diminished with her exhaustion, certain errors, including her fatal error, also became increasingly out of her control, and therefore increasingly out of the ambit of her responsibility.

Alternatively, we could look at this case according to a different prevalent view. We will call this sort of view "revelation-based." According to this view, moral responsibility is fundamentally related to what our acts reveal about us as moral agents, and particularly our moral concern for one another, rather than to what we can control.[4] (Although facts about what we can control will often be deeply relevant to assessments of our moral concerns). In turn, we are blameworthy when we act from ill will or insufficient concern, including negligence. So on revelation-based views, the doctor is excused given that, under the circumstances, it is clear that her wrongdoing did not arise from any objectionable attitudes on her part, or lack of concern for the child in her care.

Note, however, that we can sometimes be responsible *for* our incapacitations. If, instead of being blamelessly fatigued, the doctor in our story made a fatal error because she was drunk, the fact that she had diminished capacities hardly seems to be excusing. As Nicole Vincent writes: "What determines whether someone is responsible for their actions (or for the outcomes of those actions) is not just what capacities they actually had, *but also whether they are responsible for the lack of those capacities.*"[5]

Again, we can understand the culpability of the drunken doctor via the views of responsibility just introduced. On capacity and control-based views, since the doctor was in control of getting drunk (and therefore of diminishing her capacities) the errors that arose from her subsequent incapacitation can be traced back to her earlier controlled decisions, and are therefore reined into the ambit of her moral responsibility. While on revelation-based views, on the other hand, the fact that the doctor chose to drink while knowing she might be operating plainly seems to evince insufficient concern, and indeed callous indifference, for the patients in her care.

For the most part, debates on moral responsibility have focused on diminished capacity, and attendant diminished responsibility. But if responsibility is tied to our capacities – and not only those we possess but also our relationship to those that we lack – then the prospect of *enhanced* capacities seems to pose immediate questions with regard to responsibility. The enhancement debate, therefore, opens up new, and potentially complicating terrain in which to explore debates about responsibility. This chapter concerns the intersection of these debates. It is only possible to overview some of the interesting questions and complexities that emerge at this intersection, and our aim is not to argue for a particular position with regard to enhancement and responsibility, but rather to explore some of this generative terrain. In particular, we will consider the implications of enhancement for the demandingness and the fairness of certain responsibility assessments.

The outline we follow will be: in Section 28.2, we will consider the sorts of capacities that are most relevant to ascriptions of responsibility; with qualifications, we will distinguish between "core moral capacities" and "auxiliary moral capacities" (but we also point to the impossibility of bright-line distinctions here). We will then briefly consider the debate concerning which capacities are amenable to enhancement, and to what extent. In Section 28.3, we turn to engage specifically with questions of responsibility for enhancement. We consider this question at two removes: (1) our responsibility to undertake any safe and effective enhancements that become available (and our culpability for harmful outcomes that arise from our failures to do so); and (2) the ambit of our responsibility *once enhanced*. Some philosophers have argued that we can be "hyperresponsible" once we possess certain enhanced capacities. We will investigate how hyperresponsibility with regard to core moral capacities generates unique divisions between revelation-based views, and control and capacity-based views.

28.2 Capacities and enhancements

The area of greatest concern at the intersection of debates on enhancement and responsibility concerns *what we owe to others* (rather than what advantages we can achieve for ourselves).[6] Of particular interest, with regard to questions of responsibility and blameworthiness, are those capacities that might allow us to better avoid bad outcomes, such as serious harm and wrongdoing. On the face of it, the relevant capacities concern at least the three following aspects: (1) to know what we should do; (2) to want to do it; and (3) to be able to do so.

These aspects can come apart. You can want to do what is right, but be utterly mistaken about what that is. You can apprehend what you are required to do but feel no motivation to comply whatsoever. And you can both know what to do, and want to do it, but fail because you were unable to do so (our exhausted doctor – who wished only to carefully and correctly perform the appendectomy – was in this sorry position).

At other times, however, the boundaries between these aspects can become less clear. Let us return to the drunken doctor. Imagine that the doctor truly does not perceive her action as morally wrong: she knows, of course, that it is against the "rules," but she rationalizes that in her case (as opposed to in general) a few drinks does not hamper her functioning. The doctor, therefore, sees no reason why she should abstain. Imagine further that, at a subconscious level, the doctor reasons in this flawed way precisely because she lacks sufficient concern for the well-being of her patients.

Now in this case it is very hard to clearly distinguish the doctor's failures of reasoning from her failures of moral concern. Though, superficially, her mistake is in "not knowing" what she ought to do (in believing that she is justified when she is not), at a deeper level her mistake emerges from the fact that she lacks adequate moral concern for those affected. In many cases – including those of callous self-interested reasoning, bias, and prejudice – this sort of interplay of moral judgment and moral concern might be at work.

Or imagine a father who knows he should be patient and kind with his children. But he is notoriously foul-tempered and is often so overwhelmed by frustration that he finds himself flying into rages. Once again, it is not straightforward to distinguish between his motivation and his ability to comply with his preferred course of action.

Despite the difficulty of any stable, bright-line distinctions here, and despite the substantive philosophical disagreement about which abilities constitute our moral agency, in this chapter we are going to distinguish between what we call "core moral capacities" and "auxiliary moral capacities," both of which are central to our status and functioning as moral agents. (Despite qualifications, we are drawing this distinction because unique divisions emerge with regard to the enhancement of core moral capacities and assessments of responsibility).

Ingmar Persson and Julian Savulescu, who have undertaken pioneering work on the question of specifically *moral* enhancement, put forward that in order for something to count as moral enhancement, it must enhance your moral *motivation*, your disposition to (*decide* and) *try* to do what you think you ought morally to do, rather than your capacity to *implement or put into effect* such tryings, to succeed if you try. Moreover, it must enhance your disposition to try to do *for its own sake* what you think you ought morally to do.[7]

We understand "core moral capacities" as loosely aligning with this narrower interpretation, focused on motivational capacities. We might imagine a particularly compassionate person or a person who felt deeply compelled by what they took to be their moral duty, as having highly developed capacities of this sort.

In contrast, "auxiliary moral capacities" include those which allow us to better ascertain what we ought to do (including certain cognitive capacities), as well as those that better enable us to comply. Concerning the former category: in a manner intricately intertwined with our status as moral agents (and yet in some respects distinct from our moral motivations), there is our capacity for reasoning, and moral reasoning, itself. This includes, among other things, our ability to deliberate clearly and without bias, to take account of relevant considerations, and to grant them the appropriate weight.

Finally, there are those abilities that allow us to better comply with morality's demands. This is potentially a very wide category, depending on the circumstances.[8] Nevertheless, there will be certain auxiliary capacities that are far more closely associated with our likelihood of avoiding harmful outcomes. The exhaustion of our doctor, for instance, is the sort of incapacitation that would significantly increase the odds of disaster. Likewise, terrible outcomes often arise (sometimes on a spectacular scale) from simple "human error," like our forgetfulness, our inattentiveness to important considerations, or the tendency of our minds to wander even while undertaking dangerous activities.[9]

Again, there are no bright-line distinctions here, and in describing these aspects of moral agency as "capacities" we have not intended to beg any questions about the underlying nature of these capacities, nor how feasible it is that they could be manipulated or enhanced. These matters are, of course, areas of considerable philosophical and empirical dispute.

In appraising the wide range of extant and potential enhancement interventions, a variety of philosophical disputes have arisen. Among these disputes are, prominently: (1) where "treatment" ends and "enhancement" begins; (2) whether there is a difference in kind between "conventional" forms of enhancement (such as educational instruction, nutritional supplementation, and psychotherapy) and "unconventional" forms (such as pharmaceuticals, neurotechnologies, and genetic screening); and (3) how realistic the prospects of some forms of enhancement actually are, and therefore whether aspects of the debate have become pointlessly speculative.

For the purposes of our conversation on responsibility, and in the interests of entering into this conversation in good time, we need not engage with the first two debates. In crucial respects, and in ways we will soon elaborate on, we can treat as similar, in principle, all those interventions that would reliably, safely, and effectively contribute to the avoidance of serious harm and wrongdoing. This can include both treatment and enhancement, as well as conventional and unconventional interventions.

The third debate, however, on the viability of certain forms of enhancement, has pertinence to our discussion insofar as the limits and extents of our powers to intervene in our moral capacities are concerned. One way in which to think of moral enhancements is to describe those interventions we undertake for moral ends.[10] Understood in this way moral enhancement, including moral bioenhancement, is already prevalent. Should the frustrated father we introduced earlier decide to take a mood enhancer *precisely because* he was trying to avoid future violent rages directed toward his children, we might construe this decision as a moral enhancement; this could be true regardless of whether he was using the drug as a treatment or as an enhancement. This conception of moral enhancement will, for the most part, be sufficient for the purposes of our discussion.

It is worth noting, however, that the area of most contestation with regard to the potential for enhancement concerns the *bioenhancement* of what we have been referring to as core moral capacities, such as empathy, altruism, and moral concern and motivation.[11] (Less controversial is the notion that we can "work on our characters," or otherwise improve our moral natures, by non-pharmacological, non-neuroscientific, or non-genetic means.) Some have argued that our core moral capacities are ultimately "biologically based and, therefore, that they are amenable to modification by biomedical means, pharmaceutical, neurological or genetic," and even suggest that the extent of such modification might enable us to morally transform the world.[12] Among the wide range of pharmacological interventions that have been considered with regard to these capacities are SSRIs, oxytocin, MDMA, and psilocybin.[13] Others have raised doubts about approaching moral functioning primarily through a biological lens, and accused such approaches of providing an "impoverished account of the reality of moral functioning and its various influences."[14] We will return to specific examples in the sections which follow. By and large, we will try to remain in less empirically fraught waters. However, because the category generates unique dilemmas and disputes with regard to our question of responsibility, and since much of the debate on moral enhancement has focused on the prospects of moral bioenhancement in particular, we will briefly consider the implications, with regard to responsibility, of successful bioenhancement of what we are calling core moral capacities.

28.3 Enhancement and responsibility

28.3.1 *The responsibility to undergo enhancement interventions*

Generally, the obligation to avoid perpetuating harm is accepted far more readily than the obligation to provide assistance or to intervene (or, indeed, to create a morally utopian world). We commonly take ourselves to have an ordinary duty to avoid harm to others, where feasible, and (in turn) auxiliary duties to better enable ourselves to do so. These duties can concern both what we are obligated to refrain from and what we are obligated to do.[15]

The prospect of new forms of enhancement increases the remit of our auxiliary duties (potentially drastically), and it is in this sense that new forms of enhancement generate complexities for theories of responsibility. Can the emergence of new enhancement interventions increase the realm of our blameworthiness? Can it turn what would have been an excusable error into a culpable error, and potentially even a legally culpable error? How far and how wide can our responsibility for wrongdoings and harmful outcomes extend, as the methods available to us to better avoid them continue to develop and expand?

These questions have become important in various spheres, including with regard to bioenhancement. Philosophers and legal scholars have begun to deliberate about the new realms of culpability and negligence that new bioenhancement technologies potentially generate.[16] Much of this debate has focused on avoiding harmful outcomes through cognitive enhancement (and therefore through what we have been calling auxiliary moral capacities), but in many respects, the key points are relevant to any available intervention, including those regarding core moral capacities, which would better enable us to avoid serious harm and wrongdoing.[17]

Earlier we deemed the exhausted doctor blameless for the death of the patient in her care. After all, there was nothing she could have done to avoid the outcome. But if we imagine that she had ready access to a drug that would reliably reduce the likelihood of resultant harm from her fatigue – methylphenidate and modafinil, for instance, which have been reported to increase wakefulness, attention, concentration, and memory when taken by healthy subjects – would she, therefore, have a responsibility to take it?[18] Would she be made culpable for failing to do so?

There are many quick answers to these questions. Where we imagine that the doctor had better alternatives – where she could have taken a nap, or passed over to a colleague, or where a cup of coffee would have done the trick – it is easy to deny that she had any obligation to further enhance.[19] Similarly, where the proposed intervention is unreliable or ineffective, it would seem to immediately undermine any prospective obligation (the auxiliary obligation is, after all, ultimately derived from the ordinary obligation to avoid bad outcomes and can only be generated when it can reliably achieve this aim). Finally, where the intervention is unsafe or has severe side effects, it would at least seriously complicate or undermine any strong obligations on her part.[20]

To avoid the conversation ending before it begins, it is, therefore, necessary to restrict claims to those occasions where the relevant intervention would genuinely be effective, reliable, and safe. Although the research on these drugs is presently under-developed, it is not fantastical to assume that they (or similar interventions) could come to meet these requirements.[21]

One factor that seems relevant here is that of ease and difficulty. Difficulty is an important consideration in assessments of moral responsibility, and it is often treated as blame-mitigating and in some cases even exculpating. A recent philosophical debate has sought to better understand the relevance of difficulty to degrees of responsibility.[22] This debate has also been explored with regard to questions of enhancement: quite straightforwardly, the extent of our capacities is related to the ease or difficulty of meeting certain normative requirements. Insofar as developments in enhancement reduce difficulty, they can also increase our degree of responsibility. As Naomi Kloosterboer and Jan Willem Wieland write: "when it becomes easier to counter or circumvent one's incapacities and biases, one is less and less excused for harming others due to one's incapacities or biases."[23]

It is interesting to revisit this case from the perspective of the paradigms of responsibility introduced at the outset of this chapter. In the initial case, we saw why the exhausted surgeon would plausibly be excused on capacity, control, and revelation-based accounts of responsibility. However, if we stipulate the availability of a safe, reliable, and effective enhancer that would have significantly reduced the likelihood of the fatal outcome, the surgeon seems to be placed in a very different moral position. Insofar as the doctor was initially excused on the basis of her limited capacities, or her lack of control regarding the diminishment of her capacities, these bases no longer seem to apply: now she is inculpated in her incapacitation, given that she had the option of an enhancer, and the fatal outcome seems to attach to her in a far more meaningful sense than in the initial case. The option of an enhancer also seems to change what is revealed, with regard to assessments of sufficient moral concern, by the fatal error: if she cared adequately, someone might contend, she would have taken all available precautions to avoid the tragic outcome. In this sense, the *mere availability* of an enhancer seems to increase culpability, and compound assessments of moral responsibility and blameworthiness, for certain bad outcomes.

So far, the literature on these expanding responsibilities has largely concerned professionals in high-stakes positions: pilots or doctors, with lives on the line.[24] Under such circumstances, where we already take such individuals to have a demanding set of duties related to their professional roles, it can seem that (while burdensome) the stakes involved might potentially generate requirements that we would not impose more generally. Along these lines, various philosophers have argued that (if we grant the stipulations above) our doctor ought to take the pill, and could be deemed blameworthy for failing to do so. In defense of this requirement, philosophers have pointed to a range of other developments in harm reduction that generated new obligations, and which we now take to be uncontroversial: the availability of antiseptic procedures, for instance, generated the obligation for doctors to use them.[25] This can even be true of available pharmacological interventions if they will reliably reduce the likelihood of harm to others: for instance, if the surgeon caused a death in theater because she had stopped taking her diabetes medication (for no good reason) and subsequently fainted while performing an operation, we might consider her culpable for her failure to medicate herself appropriately.[26]

But while the arguments in favor of these responsibilities are most compelling under these limited conditions, concerning high-responsibility professions, it is difficult to see, without *ad hoc* stipulations, why the principles which inform the obligations under these circumstances do not quickly overspill these limits, and start to apply to all of us. It is not only doctors and pilots and judges, after all, who can cause great harm to others. We are all hazardously loose in the world: we are sometimes implicated in terrible outcomes, and even in the most ordinary of lives we subject other people to our prejudices, cruelties, vindictiveness, negligence, indifference, and selfishness in ways that sometimes constitute legitimate wrongs. Like the frustrated father we discussed earlier, we can all be guilty of bad moods, outbursts, and viciousness that we take out on the people close to us, especially where we lack the emotional resources to respond appropriately. Where a mood enhancer would contribute to the development of these resources, should we be obliged to take it?[27]

Many of us are also causally implicated in massive collective harms: from the perpetuation of child labor in sweatshops to the displacement of people from their lands, to the destruction of environments for extant and future people (among many others). As Judith Lichtenberg memorably put it: "Not harming people turns out to be difficult and to require our undivided attention."[28] What's more, given the information saturation of our present era – an epistemic enhancement, or sorts – it has never been easier to find out about the ways in which our seemingly innocuous actions are implicated in these massive harms. Were we not able to find out (were the effects of carbon on the atmosphere still unknown, for instance; or were the upsurge in breathless patients arriving at hospitals around the world still a medical mystery) we might be blameless for our participation in these harms. But the fact that we *can* find out seems to have immediate relevance with regard to our culpability. As Daniel Dennett writes (almost enviously) about our information-scarce ancestors: "They were thus *capable* of living lives of virtue… Of a virtue that *depended on* unavoidable ignorance."[29]

Initially, attaching responsibility to capacity seems to generate a modest and fair requirement (and even a forgiving one, when we concentrate on diminished capacities). But as the options to enhance these capacities grow, as the realm of what we *could have done* to avoid these harms and bad outcomes extends and extends, the initially modest requirement has the potential to become increasingly burdensome.[30] In what other respects – borne from our expanding abilities to recognize and mitigate harmful outcomes – might we be made incapable of living lives of virtue? And in what other respects might we be deemed culpable, and even legally culpable, for declining to take available measures which would better protect others from our failures and fallibilities, whether cognitive, emotional, moral, or otherwise? Considerations with regard to enhancement, therefore, seem to generate new challenges about demandingness and overdemandingness with regard to the limits of culpability and responsibility.

23.3.2 Responsibility once enhanced, and the prospects of "hyperresponsibility"

In this final section, we would like to consider the implications of responsibility for those who *possess* enhanced capacities. Some philosophers have suggested that highly developed or enhanced capacities generate "hyperresponsibility" and that individuals with relevant enhanced capacities are liable to be *more* blameworthy for wrongdoing than ordinary agents in the same way that people with diminished capacities are *less* blameworthy.

To close this chapter, we will briefly consider the implications of hyperresponsibility with regard to both auxiliary and core moral capacities. To reiterate: we take core moral capacities to refer to moral motivation and concern itself, while auxiliary moral capacities refer to those abilities which allow us to better ascertain and comply with what we ought to do. In particular, we will consider how highly developed *core* moral capacities generate divisions between capacity, control, and revelation-based views of responsibility, especially when it comes to interpretations of fair appraisals of blameworthiness.

To begin exploring hyperresponsibility and auxiliary capacities, let us introduce a case. Imagine Bruce is driving down the freeway when a rogue car comes hurtling into his lane. To spare himself Bruce has only two options: he could swerve onto the shoulder where a hitchhiker is standing, who he would surely kill, or he could swerve into the adjacent lane which is obstructed by a reclining flat-bed truck. Almost any other driver would immediately die on impact with the truck, but Bruce is a famed stunt driver, and he perceives immediately that he'd be able to ramp the back of the truck and land safely on the empty road ahead of it. He really is not in the mood for this maneuver though (fed up with such antics after a day on set), and so he kills the hitchhiker instead.

It seems quite patent that Bruce's exceptional capacities in this situation deeply affect the sense in which he is blameworthy for the death of the hitchhiker. Because of his unusual abilities, Bruce was uniquely able to avoid hitting the hitchhiker; he was in control of the fatal outcome in a way that could never be true of an ordinary driver. In turn, various factors about choice, intention, and volition enter the moral scene, transforming what would have been a tragic accident into something closer to murder.

Extrapolating from this case, we can see that there are various methods via which the enhancement of auxiliary capacities can potentially compound blameworthiness, and lay the groundwork for "hyperresponsibility" depending on how far these auxiliary capacities extend. In capacity-based views, the greater realm of capacity *itself* generates the greater realm of corresponding responsibility. In control-based views, the implications of enhanced capacities for what thereby comes to be within our agential control similarly expands the realm of what we can justly be held accountable for. While in revelation-based views, enhanced auxiliary capacities will often have implications for what our failures reveal about our moral concerns and moral motivations (i.e. given his abilities, Bruce's action reveals a profoundly different quality of will to a person who was unable to avoid hitting the hitchhiker).

Let us now consider the driver of the rogue car that was hurtling into Bruce's lane. Imagine that this driver did not have highly developed auxiliary capacities relevant to the case. Instead, after a long journey the driver's mind was wandering leading him to gradually veer from his path; when he realized his mistake he drastically overcorrected his steering, leading to his fateful swerve toward Bruce. Inattention, wandering minds, blameless tiredness, errant reactions under fright or pressure: these are the "all too human" mistakes that often lead to catastrophic outcomes, but where we nevertheless often feel conflicted about questions of responsibility and blameworthiness (how unlucky, in some respects, to have been the driver who inadvertently caused all this harm).

Part of our conflict in such cases emerges from the fact that it is hard to imagine how we could avoid being all too human when we *are* all too human; what should this driver have done to avoid an unanticipated, unwitting, and deeply unwanted error arising from ordinary inadequacies in his auxiliary capacities? Bioenhancement presents itself as one possible answer to this question. If we could all easily take a (safe and effective) pill before undertaking a long drive that would significantly improve our alertness, concentration, and reaction time – and therefore drastically reduce the incidence of road fatalities caused by human error – appeal to human error among those who had chosen *not* to take the pill would be less compelling, and might lead us to feel less conflicted about attributing responsibility for harmful outcomes. As we have seen, the *mere option* of enhancement (even if we do not take it) therefore has implications for our responsibility, potentially generating the concerns regarding demandingness and overdemandingness that we raised in the previous section.

It is a complicated question, however, how we should appraise (1) an agent who (knowingly and needlessly) failed to enhance, and therefore failed to have adequate capacities, and in turn caused some harmful outcome; and (2) an agent who did enhance, and therefore *did* have adequate capacities, but caused some harmful outcome despite this. Are these agents equivalent, since they both ultimately had control (one because avoiding the bad outcome was within their extant capacities, the other because it could have been)? Or are these agents profoundly different, depending on how we interpret their respective attitudes and moral concerns within their conduct?

Finally, let us turn to the question of *core* moral capacities and the sort of concerns that might be generated with regard to hyperresponsibility. We can look at two kinds of scenarios. One scenario concerns the natural variation in core moral capacities, and the other scenario concerns the bioenhancement of these capacities. As we will see, different issues arise with regard to each scenario: in particular, the "natural scenario" potentially generates concerns with regard to the fairness of hyperresponsibility in proportion to highly developed core moral capacities.

To begin with the natural scenario: irrespective of bioenhancement, there is patently a wide range of core moral capacities already possessed by different individuals; it is a fact of life that some people possess far more moral motivation and moral concern than others. It is also not implausible that (in the normal course of things) these capacities are only within our control to a certain extent, and indeed that they might be susceptible to a "vicious cycle" of sorts: where people with diminished core moral capacities, for that very reason, lack the motivation to develop greater core moral capacities. The lower end of this range has been explored extensively in the debate concerning moral responsibility and psychopathy. In our discussion, however, it is the *higher* end of this range that is of the most interest: what is the implication, as far as responsibility is concerned, for those individuals who naturally possess very *highly* developed core moral capacities?

Imagine two soldiers involved in drone warfare in a foreign land: their missions enacted through keystrokes and cursors and featuring small pixilated targets. Each soldier is ordered to deploy a bomb that they know will generate civilian casualties. Let us grant, for the sake of argument, that these soldiers are wrong to obey the order.

Imagine that the first soldier, easily lulled by the psychological distance established by drone warfare, feels no qualms whatsoever in complying. Imagine further that this ease is ultimately generated through his under-developed core moral capacities: he lacks the ability to register the real consequences of what he is about to do, and he has succeeded in abstracting away any of the real lives involved in his decision. Without any worries, he obeys the order.

On the other hand, imagine that the second soldier, far more developed in terms of his core moral capacities, feels a profound moral concern about the lives he realizes he is about to end. He believes that the order is wrong and he is wrong to obey; nevertheless, fearful of repercussions, this soldier also complies and is left feeling deeply burdened and morally injured in the aftermath.

Understood only in accordance with their relevant capacities, it is the second soldier who is most blameworthy here, and the first soldier who is most excused.[31] From capacity and control-based perspectives, this makes sense: after all, on the basis of his moral insight the second soldier had a far greater capacity to do what morality required, and therefore far more control over his wrongdoing. For such views, this is what fairness in our ascriptions of responsibility demands and the sense in which someone is genuinely *deserving* of blame can only arise when they possess the relevant capacities to respond appropriately. But in other respects, particularly from revelation-based perspectives, this is a troubling determination. Revelation-based views would have a very different understanding of the blameworthiness of the respective soldiers: after all, the first soldier's conduct seems much more representative of his moral personality, and his lack of moral concern, than the second soldier's conduct, and (on such views) this is essential to appraising their respective blameworthiness, irrespective of questions of capacity and control.

In exploring the relevance of ease and difficulty as a foundation for responsibility Kloosterboer and Wieland explicitly exclude cases where "things are difficult because one is insufficiently concerned or because one has certain vices."[32] This is an important stipulation because difficulty seems to have a profoundly different relevance under these circumstances. While, with regard to auxiliary moral capacities (i.e. we lack the physical ability, the time, the intellectual capacity, the concentration span, et cetera, to do what morality seems to demand), the difficulty we face seems to *diminish* blameworthiness, it seems to have quite the opposite effect with regard to our core moral capacities. When meeting a normative demand is difficult for us because we lack the moral concern or motivation to comply, this difficulty does not seem mitigating in any straightforward sense. Questions of ease and difficulty, and the exculpatory nature of difficulty, therefore seem to have a different relevance for responsibility when they concern auxiliary moral capacities than when they concern core moral capacities.

In discussing "hyperresponsibility" for core moral capacities it is also interesting to consider moral standards higher than those we typically hold ourselves to: for the sake of this exploration, we will draw on the debate about what we owe to distant strangers. (For the time being, we are still in the realm of the "natural scenario," rather than the "bioenhanced scenario" which we will soon go on to consider.)

Famously, while we generally take ourselves to have extensive obligations to someone in mortal danger right in front of us (the child drowning in the pond, say), we hold no similar obligations to the many people dying preventable deaths far away. Peter Singer and Peter Unger, among many others, have argued that this is a moral optical illusion of sorts, emerging from our limited moral psychologies and that in fact the two sorts of cases are morally equivalent in crucial respects.[33] Let us grant, for the sake of argument, that they are correct in this appraisal.[34]

While many of us grasp the reasoning at play in these arguments, very few of us are motivated to comply with their conclusions. What's more, we seem quite incapable of complying: we are limited, after all, in the extent of our moral motivation, insight, and compassion; there is only so much we are able to care for strangers, and only so much we can be asked to do on their behalf. Some rare individuals, however, are exceptions. In her book *Strangers Drowning*, the journalist Larissa MacFarquhar profiles a series of "extreme altruists." In one chapter she considers Aaron:

> After he read Singer's article, everything Aaron bought, even the smallest, cheapest thing, felt to him like food or medicine snatched from someone dying. Nobody would buy a soda if there was a starving child standing next to the vending machine, he thought; well, for him now there is always a starving child standing next to the vending machine.[35]

Aaron plausibly possesses more developed core moral capacities than ordinary individuals. Should this imply that where the rest of us are excused for doing little to nothing about distant suffering, Aaron should not be? Does this mean that should Aaron cease the extremity of his commitment, and start behaving more like an "ordinary" person, he would be uniquely blameworthy for his failure? And what's more: would the source of his unique blameworthiness be *precisely because* of how much this suffering and injustice weighed on him, whereas those of us who have been so much less moved by these realities would be excused *precisely because* of how easy it has been for us to forget and do nothing? If the guiding intuition in attaching responsibility to capacities is because we ought to be *fair* in our ascriptions of blameworthiness, then we seem to have simultaneously arrived at an unfair place: a place where, insofar as you do not have control over these aspects of yourself, you are excused in proportion to how callous and uncaring you are, and condemned in proportion with how empathetic and concerned you are.[36]

These are complicated cases, that arise especially with regard to highly developed core moral capacities, and they shine a different sort of light onto the central views of responsibility we have been considering. While some adherents of capacity and control-based views might be comfortable with the implications of hyperresponsibility for the likes of Aaron, there are others who might feel that these cases generate unique concerns. That is to say: some people who feel that it is only fair and right to exempt in accordance with (diminished) capacities at the lower end of the spectrum, might nevertheless feel that there is something amiss with blaming in accordance with (highly developed) capacities at the higher end of the spectrum, especially when it comes to core moral capacities.

Matters are quite different when we turn to the second scenario under consideration: the bioenhanced scenario. As we indicated earlier, the question of whether core moral capacities are amenable to bioenhancement is a central debate within the literature. One important question is therefore what the bioenhancement of core moral capacities would imply for responsibility and hyperresponsibility.

Imagine that some future treatment could make the first soldier more like the second soldier, or ordinary people more like Aaron: a moral bioenhancer that could powerfully increase our moral concern for others, and our moral motivation to do right by them. As we saw earlier, on capacity-based views, it is not only the capacities we actually have that are significant to evaluations of responsibility but also whether we are responsible for the capacities we lack. Relatedly, in control-based views, it is not only the control we actually have but also whether we are responsible for the control we lack.

In a scenario in which a (safe, reliable, and effective) bioenhancer was readily available that would make soldier one as morally astute as soldier two, or an ordinary individual as morally concerned as Aaron, the excuse of incapacity with regard to their moral failures and wrongdoings would no longer be available to these agents in the same way, irrespective of whether they chose to take the enhancer or not. In this respect, the mere availability of effective bioenhancement for core moral capacities might level the playing field between the likes of the first soldier and the second soldier, and the likes of Aaron and the rest of us, even on control and capacity-based views.

It is patent that we often have obligations to take available measures to reduce the likelihood of harm to others. The question of where these obligations end is another matter. Some have argued that there is not necessarily a boundary here: where we can improve ourselves through enhancement, and reduce the likelihood of harm to others, or other forms of moral catastrophe, we have a duty to do so.[37] If we choose not to, we are choosing to have lesser capacities, and lesser control, and we are responsible for our diminished state and the harms that arise from it. From this perspective, if we were to spurn the treatment that would make us as morally compelled and motivated as Aaron, we would not be dissimilar to a drunk driver, who knowingly diminishes their capacities at the potential expense of others.

23.4 Conclusion

The objective of this chapter has not been to defend any particular position, but instead to explore some of the generative terrain at the intersection of enhancement debates and debates about moral responsibility.

In general, theories of responsibility endeavor to describe a realm of responsibility for ourselves, our acts, and their outcomes that is not overwhelming or overdemanding, and that is compatible with concerns about fairness and desert in our assessments of blameworthiness. But while theories of responsibility have often been interrogated and stress-tested with regard to how well they cope with *diminished capacities*, much less has been written about how various theories cope with highly developed capacities, or the prospect of enhanced capacities.

As we have seen, enhancement can generate unique concerns with regard to both the demandingness and the fairness of certain responsibility assessments. To begin with demandingness: initially the obligation to take available precautions to avoid harm to others seems like a modest requirement. Likewise, the stipulation that assessments of responsibility ought to be capacity-sensitive seems to generate reasonable boundaries for the extent of our blameworthiness for harmful outcomes. These conditions seem to place limits on what can be expected of us and protect the requirements of responsibility from becoming overwhelming or overdemanding.

But the availability of enhancement interventions unsettles both of these conditions. As what we *could have done* to avoid bad outcomes extends and extends, the modest requirement of our negative duties to avoid bad outcomes can themselves become overwhelming and overdemanding. Likewise, as the initially restrictive stipulation about "capacity-sensitivity" becomes ever more capacious, the sense in which this stipulation limits the extent of our culpability for outcomes is undermined.

With regard to fairness: the plausibility of capacity-sensitivity with regard to moral responsibility gets most of its strength from concerns about fairness. In some respects, it seems straightforwardly unfair to require someone to do something they were incapable of doing (and to blame them for failing). Tying responsibility to an agent's actual capacities, therefore, seems to generate a realm of responsibility that will always be warranted in an individual case, since it will always concern the relevant abilities of the respective agent. Guided by these (in many respects generous and forgiving) impulses, some philosophers have felt compelled to excuse even the "worst" agents (such as psychopaths) on the basis of their diminished capacities. But once again, viewed from the vantage of highly developed capacities this picture seems to change drastically, especially in the "natural scenario" where agents have less control over the extent of their abilities. When we have to excuse one agent precisely because they lack moral concern while condemning another agent precisely because they possess moral concern in abundance, we might honor one sense of fairness, but we do so at the expense of another. As we saw, the "bioenhanced scenario" changes the dynamics here, since the option of an effective moral enhancer would potentially render agents responsible for their diminished core moral capacities; they would therefore become responsible *for* their lack of concern, in a way which capacity and control-based views could not generate in the "natural scenario."

So we see that focusing on highly developed capacities, and on the prospect of enhanced capacities, potentially generates new dilemmas for our understanding of responsibility. These dilemmas warrant more exploration. In the first instance, they shed new light on certain long-standing debates concerning the foundations of responsibility, and reveal aspects of the dispute which are obscured in the more familiar conversations concerning diminished responsibility. In the second instance, the effectiveness and availability of enhancement interventions are likely to increase in the coming years and make the practical and legal ramifications of these questions far more pressing. Finally, and on a more general level, it is becoming urgent to theoretically explore the limits of responsibility, and the bases for these limits, *even as* certain of our abilities continue to expand. What will the "good enough" person look like, as we continue to know and understand more and more about the potentially harmful ramifications of our actions over time and space? At the time of writing the most patent example seems to be that of the COVID-19 pandemic (at the time of reading it may well be another). But it seems clear the world over that we are already straining to comprehend the appropriate limits of our responsibilities toward one another, as our capacities to understand the risks and harms involved in our actions, as well as our capacities to potentially avoid them, has extended ever further.

Notes

1 Vincent, N.A. 2013.
2 Cf. Von Hirsch, A. 2001.
3 Notably Levy, N. 2014.
4 Contemporary versions of this position are generally traced back to Strawson, P. F. 1962.
5 Vincent, N.A. 2008 (our emphasis).
6 In this respect, the goods associated with one's enhancement accrue to others, rather than only to oneself, and therefore certain concerns about fairness and desert associated with these goods are less manifest (or at least more complicated) than they are in other aspects of the enhancement debate (i.e. cognitive and performance enhancement) which concern personal gain rather than moral gain. Cf. Douglas, T. 2019; Faber, N. S., Savulescu, J. & Douglas, D. 2016.
7 Persson, I. & Savulescu, J. 2019, p. 7; their emphases. (See also Persson, I. & Savulescu, J. 2012).
8 David Wasserman, for instance, considers whether you might sometimes need to *lack empathy* in order to do what you ought. He quotes a neurosurgeon who suggests that: "You can't have too much empathy

for the person that you're operating on, because you wouldn't be able to conduct that operation." More broadly Wasserman argues that "complex societies have a division of labour in which some roles call for characteristics that most of us would regard as moral defects." (Wasserman, D. 2014) (See also Bloom, P. 2016).

9 Kloosterboer, N. & Wieland, J.W. 2017, p. 428.
10 Cf. Spence, S.A. 2008.
11 Cf. Macpherson et al. 2019, p. 996-7 for an overview.
12 The quotation is from Persson, I. & Savulescu, J. 2019, p. 8. The recent theoretical debate on moral enhancement commenced with Thomas Douglas's (2008) argument that we may be able to biomedically decrease countermoral emotions. Persson and Savulescu have argued extensively that moral enhancement is imperative, especially given the extent of the harm (even annihilating harm) certain technological advances have enabled. Many others have responded in turn, notably John Harris (including Harris, J. 2016).
13 Macpherson et al. citing Crockett et al. 2010, Tennison 2012, Terbeck et al. 2013, Schmid et al. 2014, Crockett et al. 2015. See also DeGrazia 2014 and Earp et al. 2017 for a wider range of non-pharmacological examples.
14 Wiseman, H. 2016.
15 See Kloosterboer, N. and Wieland, J.W. 2017 and also Smith, H. 2014.
16 We engage here, in particular, with Vincent, N.A. 2013; Santoni de Sio et al. 2014a; Santoni de Sio et al. 2014b; Goold, I. & Maslen, H. 2014; and Kloosterboer, N. & Wieland, J.W. 2017. This debate is ongoing in certain professions too, cf. Goold, I. & Maslen, H. 2014. Also see Chandler, J.A. 2013.
17 Santoni de Sio et al. 2014a Consider it a template that could be applied, *mutatis mutandis*, to other forms of enhancement.
18 This example is used by Goold, I. & Maslen, H. 2014 as well as Kloosterboer, N. & Wieland, J.W. 2017. (Cf. Repantis et al. 2010 and Wong et al. 1998).
19 Santoni de Sio et al. 2014a, p. 193.
20 Goold and Maslen have provided a detailed legal analysis (in the UK context) arguing against a legal obligation to enhance in such a case. Their argument crucially depends on doubts about safety as well as "added uncertainty about how predictably efficacious these drugs are." Goold, I. & Maslen, H. 2014.
21 Indeed, reports of the use of these drugs for enhancement are already widespread amongst students and professionals (cf. McCabe et al. 2005 and Weyandt et al. 2013) and some hospitals include discussion of modafinil use in their internal recommendations and reports (Cf. Santoni de Sio et al. 2014(b)). The United States Airforce has also long approved the use of modafinil for pilots involved in certain aviation operations (cf. Caldwell, J.A. and Caldwell, J.L. 2005 cited in Goold, I. & Maslen, H. 2014).
22 Cf. Nelkin, D.K. 2016.
23 Kloosterboer, N. & Wieland, J.W. 2017, p. 423.
24 Cf. Vincent, N.A. 2013; Santoni de Sio et al. 2014(a); Santoni de Sio et al. 2014(b); Goold, I. & Maslen, H. 2014; and Kloosterboer, N. & Wieland, J.W. 2017.
25 Santoni de Sio et al. 2014(b).
26 Santoni de Sio et al. 2014(b) points to legal precedents on this issue, involving traffic accidents.
27 Cf. Liao & Roache who consider how mood enhancers may exacerbate our responsibility for failing to have certain emotional reactions: "One way in which the capacity to regulate emotions pharmacologically may affect our responsibility for our emotions is in limiting our excuses for failing to have the appropriate ones. Even if we have a duty to have certain emotions, we are excused from fulfilling it if our best efforts are unavailing. Alternatively, our duty may be only to make our best efforts. The availability of a pill may limit our excuses by making our efforts more likely to succeed." (Liao, S. & Roache, R. 2011).
28 Lichtenberg, J. 2010, p. 558.
29 Dennett, D. 1986, p. 144.
30 Cf. Nagel, S.K. 2010.
31 Certain versions of control-based views, particularly those which endorse an akrasia-requirement such as Levy's (2009), would also deem the first soldier blameless insofar as he was not in conscious control of his wrongdoing (since he believed he was acting permissibly).
32 Kloosterboer, N. & Wieland, J.W. 2017, p. 423
33 Key texts here include Peter Singer's 1972 essay *Famine, Affluence & Morality* (and many subsequent works) and Peter Unger's 1996 book *Living High and Letting Die*.
34 In drawing on this example we are not meaning to take a position on the debate regarding these obligations, but merely using the example as a means of exploring the more capacious and demanding realms that hyperresponsibility could potentially generate.
35 MacFarquhar, L. 2016, p. 44.

36 In response to such concerns Vincent distinguishes between "capacity responsibility" and "virtue responsibility." (Vincent, N. 2013, p. 328; see also Vincent, N. 2009). She indicates, however, that this is an important question that warrants further debate. (cf. Vincent, N. 2013, p. 328).

37 Persson, I. & Savulescu, J. 2012 & 2019.

References

Bloom, P. 2016. *Against Empathy: The Case for Rational Compassion*, Ecco.

Caldwell, J. A., & Caldwell, J. L. 2005. "Fatigue in Military Aviation: An Overview of US Military-Approved Pharmacological Countermeasures," *Aviation, Space, and Environmental Medicine*, 76, 7, pp. 39–51.

Chandler, J. A. 2013. "Autonomy and the Unintended Legal Consequences of Emerging Neurotherapies," *Neuroethics*, 6, 2, pp. 249–263.

Crockett, M. J., Clark, L., Hauser, M. D., & Robbins, T. W. 2010. "Serotonin Selectively Influences Moral Judgment and Behavior Through Effects on Harm Aversion," *Proceedings of the National Academy of Sciences*, 107, 40, 17, pp. 433–438.

Crockett, M. J., Siegel, J. Z., Kurth-Nelson, Z., Ousdal, O. T., ... Dolan, R. J. 2015. "Dissociable Effects of Serotonin and Dopamine on the Valuation of Harm in Moral Decision Making," *Current Biology*, 25, 14, pp. 1852–1859.

DeGrazia, D. 2014. "Moral Enhancement, Freedom, and What We (Should) Value in Moral Behavior," *Journal of Medical Ethics*, 40, pp. 361–368.

Dennett, D. 1986. "Information, Technology, and the Virtues of Ignorance," *Daedalus*, 115, 3, pp. 135–153.

Douglas, T. 2008. "Moral Enhancement," *Journal of Applied Philosophy*, 25, 3, pp. 228–245.

Douglas, T. 2019. "Enhancement and Desert," *Politics, Philosophy & Economics*, 18, 1, pp. 3–22.

Earp, B. D., Douglas, T., & Savulescu, J. 2017. "Moral Neuroenhancement," in Johnson, L. S. M., & Rommelfanger, K. S. (Eds.) *The Routledge Handbook of Neuroethics*, Routledge.

Faber, N. S., Savulescu, J., & Douglas, D. 2016. "Why is Cognitive Enhancement Deemed Unacceptable? The Role of Fairness, Deservingness, and Hollow Achievements," *Frontiers in Psychology*, 7, pp. 232.

Goold, I., & Maslen, H. 2014. "Must the Surgeon Take the Pill? Negligence Duty in the Context of Cognitive Enhancement," *The Modern Law Review*, 77, 1, pp. 60–86.

Harris, J. 2016. *How to be Good: The Possibility of Moral Enhancement*, OUP.

Kloosterboer, N., & Wieland, J. W. 2017. "Enhancing Responsibility," *Journal of Social Philosophy*, 48, 4, pp. 421–439.

Liao, S. M., & Roache, R. 2011. "After Prozac," in Savulescu, J., ter Meulen, R., & Kahane, G. (Eds.) *Enhancing Human Capacities*, Wiley-Blackwell.

Lichtenberg, J. 2010. "Negative Duties, Positive Duties, and the "New Harms," *Ethics*, 120, pp. 557–578.

Levy, N. 2009. "Culpable Ignorance and Moral Responsibility: A Reply to FitzPatrick," *Ethics*, 119, 4, pp. 729–741.

Levy, N. 2014. *Consciousness and Moral Responsibility*, OUP.

MacFarquhar, L. 2016. *Strangers Drowning: Impossible Idealism, Drastic Choices, and the Urge to Help*, Penguin.

Macpherson, I., Roque, M. V., & Segarra, I. 2019. "Moral Enhancement, at the Peak of Pharmacology and at the Limits of Ethics," *Bioethics*, 33, pp. 992–1001.

McCabe, S. E., Knight, J. R., Teter, C. J., & Wechsler, H. 2005. "Non-Medical Use of Prescription Stimulants Among US College Students: Prevalence and Correlates from a National Survey," *Addiction*, 100, 1, pp. 96–106.

Nagel, S. K. 2010. "Too Much of a Good Thing? Enhancement and the Burden of Self-Determination," *Neuroethics*, 3, pp. 109–119.

Nelkin, D. K. 2016. "Difficulty and Degrees of Moral Praiseworthiness and Blameworthiness," *Nous*, 50, 2, pp. 356–378.

Persson, I., & Savulescu, J. 2012. *Unfit for the Future: The Need for Moral Enhancement*, OUP.

Persson, I., & Savulescu, J. 2019. "The Duty to be Morally Enhanced," *Topoi*, 38, pp. 7–14.

Repantis, D., Schlattmann, P., Laisney, O., & Heuser, I. 2010. "Modafinil and Methylphenidate for Neuroenhancement in Healthy Individuals: A Systematic Review," *Pharmacological Research*, 62, pp. 187–206.

Santoni de Sio, F., Robichaud, P., & Vincent, N. A. 2014(a). "Who Should Enhance? Conceptual and Normative Dimensions of Cognitive Enhancement," *Humana.Mente Journal of Philosophical Studies*, 7, 26, pp. 179–197.

Santoni de Sio, F., Faulmuller, N., & Vincent, N. A. 2014(b). "How Cognitive Enhancement Can Change Our Duties," *Frontiers in Systems Neuroscience*, 8, 131, pp. 1–4.

Savulescu, J., ter Meulen, R., & Kahane, G. (Eds.) 2011. *Enhancing Human Capacities*, Wiley-Blackwell.

Schmid,Y., Hysek, C. M., Simmler, L. D., Crockett, M. J., Quednow, B. B., & Liechti, M. E. 2014. "Differential Effects of MDMA and Methylphenidate on Social Cognition," *Journal of Psychopharmacology*, 28, 9, pp. 847–856.
Singer, P. 1972. "Famine, Affluence and Morality," *Philosophy & Public Affairs*, 1, 3, pp. 229–243.
Smith, H. 2014. "The Subjective Moral Duty to Inform Oneself Before Acting," *Ethics*, 125, 1, pp. 11–38.
Spence, S. A. 2008. "Can Pharmacology Help Enhance Human Morality?" *The British Journal of Psychiatry*, 193, 3, pp. 179–180.
Strawson, P. F. 1962. "Freedom and Resentment," *Proceedings of the British Academy*, 48, pp. 1–25.
Tennison, M. N. 2012. "Moral Transhumanism: The Next Step," *Journal of Medicine and Philosophy*, 37, 4, pp. 405–416.
Terbeck, S., Kahane, G., McTavish, S., Savulescu J., Levy, N., Hewstone, M., & Cowen, P. J. 2013. "Beta-Adrenergic Blockade Reduces Utilitarian Judgment," *Biological Psychology*, 92, 2, pp. 323–328.
Unger, P. 1996. *Living High and Letting Die: Our Illusion of Innocence*, OUP.
Vincent, N. A. 2008. "Responsibility, Dysfunction and Capacity," *Neuroethics*, 1, 3, pp. 199–204.
Vincent, N. A. 2009. "Responsibility: Distinguishing Virtue from Capacity," *Polish Journal of Philosophy*, 3, 1, pp. 111–126.
Vincent, N. A. 2013. "Enhancing Responsibility," in Vincent, N. A. (Ed.) *Neuroscience and Legal Responsibility*, OUP.
Von Hirsch, A. 2001. "Proportionate Sentences for Juveniles: How Different Than for Adults?" *Punishment and Society*, 3, pp. 221–236.
Wasserman, D. 2014. "When Bad People Do Good Things: Will Moral Enhancement Make the World a Better Place?" *Journal of Medical Ethics*, 40, 6, pp. 374–375.
Weyandt, L. L., Marraccini, M. E., Gudmundsdottir, B. G., Zavras, B. M., Turcotte, K. D., Munro, B. A., & Amoroso, A. J. 2013. "Misuse of Prescription Stimulants Among College Students: A Review of the Literature and Implications for Morphological and Cognitive Effects on Brain Functioning," *Experimental and Clinical Psychopharmacology*, 21, 5, pp. 385–407.
Wong,Y. N., King, S. P., Laughton,W. B., McCormick, G. C., & Grebow, P. E. 1998. Single-dose Pharmacokinetics of Modafinil and Methylphenidate Given Alone or in Combination in Healthy Male Volunteers. *The Journal of Clinical Pharmacology*, 38, 3, pp. 276–282.
Wiseman, H. 2016. *The Myth of the Moral Brain: The Limits of Moral Enhancement*, MIT Press.

29
HUMAN FLOURISHING OR INJUSTICE? SOCIAL, POLITICAL, AND REGULATORY IMPLICATIONS OF COGNITIVE ENHANCEMENT

Iris Coates McCall and Veljko Dubljević

29.1 Potential philosophical and societal implications

In this section, we aim to provide readers with an understanding of the different lenses through which one can evaluate how the adoption of CE impacts society as a whole – namely those of "hype and hope" and "doom and gloom." Different types of enhancement exist, and the same intervention can be classified as enhancement or not, depending on our value framework (Savulescu, 2006). Julian Savulescu, a prominent pro-enhancement scholar, outlines three different tiers of enhancements: the medical treatment of disease, increasing natural human potential within the range typical of the human species, and then superhuman (also referred to as transhuman) enhancements that seek to bring the person's capabilities beyond what is typical for the species homo sapiens, for example gifting a bat's ability of sonar to a human (Savulescu, 2006). The key to understanding the differences between these categories is the concept of "species-typical functioning" introduced by Norman Daniels (Daniels, 1985).

These distinctions are important when deciding how to regulate enhancements and adjudicating when and in which forms they are permissible, mostly because of the commonly discussed treatment/enhancement distinction wherein medical intervention is deemed acceptable for those ailing or wishing to prevent disease (treatment) but frowned upon for those who are healthy but wishing for greater functioning (enhancement) (Buchanan, 2011, Daniels, 2000, 2001). Many, however, contest this dichotomy. For instance, Keisha Ray writes:

> For the sake of justice, disadvantages or some bodily or mental states obligate us to assist individuals with nondiseases. Daniels gives the example of offering abortions to women as a part of a national benefits package (i.e., medical insurance) as an example of a nondisease state that we may be obligated to assist with for the sake of respecting women's equal status. But if we rely on the treatment/enhancement distinction to guide our moral obligations, only those disadvantages or bodily or mental states created by poor health ought to be treated with medical resources. Daniels's objection to the treatment/enhancement distinction shows that the treatment/enhancement distinction does not always perfectly map onto our obligations. Well-being is an obligation that is neglected in the treatment/enhancement distinction if individuals are properly functioning.
>
> *(Ray, 2016)*

Further, this dichotomy tends to only come into play when it is medical (usually stimulant) intervention, ignoring other things that enhance that are widely accepted, such as education and caffeine. However, increasingly, technological enhancements, such as nanotechnology and information technology, will operate at a social level (Savulescu, 2006). What is considered an enhancement will inevitably depend on the action of others –

> the eagerness to gain an edge for one's children will be affected by whether many other parents are doing so; the willingness to use or forego medication for various sorts of psychic distress will be affected by the poverty or richness of private life, and the degree to which strong family or community support is (or is not) available for coping with that distress directly.
>
> *(Kass, 2003b)*

It is important that any and all discussions of the permissibility of cognitive enhancement occur at all levels – the individual, the community, and the societal.

29.1.1 Hype and hope

The moderate pro-enhancement argument hinges on the claim that CE is in itself neither a good nor an ill – its ethical nature lies rather in how it is used. And since it can be used for good, we should in fact do so: it can improve quality of life and productivity in addition to minimizing the effects of aging (Kass, 2003b). The main underlying argument for allowing cognitive enhancement is this: if there is good to be gained and improvement achieved, we should allow people to do so should they wish.

CE is good in that it helps empower people to meet the basic desires of our human nature for more and better than what we already have and are. In doing so, CE will also shape and change the form of those desires, for the desire for improvement is constant (Kass, 2003b). CE has the power to transform the notion of the possible, in the process enriching human aspiration and furthering human progress. Cognitive enhancements can be viewed as good because they are consistent with (and conducive to furthering) the fundamental American values of life, liberty, and the pursuit of happiness through offering the opportunity of longer life, enhanced abilities that can expand liberty, and further means/avenues to pursue happiness (Kass, 2003b). There is also a fundamental argument to be made from the point of liberty and autonomy: "mentally competent adults should be able to engage in cognitive enhancement using drugs" (Greely et al., 2008).

29.1.1.1 Superior performance

29.1.1.1.1 Performance enhancement

Performance enhancement refers to the use of CE that helps healthy adults achieve significantly better results on a given task than they would normally (Dubljević, 2012a). CE drugs can be used to enhance certain cognitive functions such as increasing concentration, promoting alertness, and improving memory retention and retrieval (Glannon, 2008). Depending on the substance used, attention (with modafinil), working memory (with methylphenidate), or verbal learning, vigilance, and inhibitory control (with amphetamine) can be increased (Dresler & Repantis, 2015). Some data is purporting to show that a class of Alzheimer's disease drugs, acetylcholinesterase inhibitors, increases performance in specific tasks in military settings (Dresler & Repantis, 2015). Additionally, computer training and brain stimulation techniques have been explored. For instance, transcranial direct current stimulation (tDCS) devices, when paired with brain training, purport to improve skill acquisition and specific cognitive abilities, such as solving mathematical problems (Coates McCall et al., 2019). Other forms of non-invasive brain stimulation, such as transcranial magnetic stimulation (TMS), have both therapeutic and enhancement effects. TMS is an FDA-approved treatment for drug-refractory major depression, migraine headaches, obsessive-compulsive disorder, and, most recently, nicotine addiction (FDA, 2018; Anonymous, 2020). At the same time, some early neuroscience studies with TMS focused on experiments unlocking savant abilities in healthy people (Snyder, 2009; Snyder et al., 2006). Even invasive forms of brain stimulation have been explored for CE effects: Deep-brain stimulation (DBS) offers the potential to improve episodic memory and mood to range significantly better than just "well" (Hamani et al., 2008; Coenen et al., 2009).

29.1.1.1.2 Performance maintenance

Unlike performance enhancement, performance maintenance simply keeps individuals functioning at their normal level but for a longer period than they normally could (Dubljević, 2012a). Usually, this takes the form of reducing the effects of fatigue and sleep deprivation. Such CE can be used in cases ranging from truck drivers driving long routes, physicians who have to stay awake while on night calls, and soldiers who have to perform under a range of adverse conditions (Dubljević & Ryan, 2015; Hamani et al., 2008). Most caffeine-based traditional enhancements (e.g., coffee) are understood to provide performance maintenance, including elevated mood, increased alertness, and increased sustained attention for individuals who are not fully rested (Dresler & Repantis, 2015).

29.1.1.1.3 Opportunity maintenance

Ray argues for a form of superior performance that falls outside the realms of treatment, that is, performance enhancement; and performance maintenance, that is, opportunity maintenance (Savulescu, 2004a). She sees CE with stimulant drugs as a "possible supplement for social disadvantages" (Ray, 2016) by using them as a potential remedy for underprivileged children who are not thriving in school, not because of any mental deficit of their own, but due to inadequate educational and socioeconomic situations. The argument goes that stimulants could be used to address these disadvantages by giving students the tools to better function within their disadvantaged setting (Ray, 2016). Ray argues that opportunity maintenance is a different kind of superior performance than performance enhancement and performance maintenance because it does not fall neatly within the treatment/enhancement dichotomy – it is not treatment because the people who would be taking the CE lack pathologies, and yet it is also not appropriate to call it enhancement as the users are not in a "normal" functioning range, rather they suffer abnormalities in socially relevant ways. "The dilemma that my argument poses for the treatment/enhancement distinction is that I want to explore stimulants' ability to remedy social deficits, not biological deficits, that impact well-being" (Ray, 2016). A counterargument is, of course, that since the source of these performance deficits is social/environmental, a better solution would be to alter the social cause through measures such as policy, social reform, educational reform, or other public programs. However, Ray argues that since these children have been clearly shown to not be a priority for those in positions of power, in the meantime "we have to be willing to consider stimulants as an option because we are not correcting students' disadvantages in other, more traditional ways" (Ray, 2016).

29.1.1.2 Better children

Nearly all parents want the best for their children – for them to be happy, to be healthy, and to flourish and thrive – and we employ a range of enhancements in an attempt to ensure these benefits. From education to vaccination against dangerous disease, to eyeglasses, to braces – we intervene in our children's biology out of concern for their best interest (Kass, 2003a). Yet these interventions are not those that people generally tend to think of when the topic of childhood CE is raised. Rather, what comes to mind are genetic enhancements and psychotropic drugs and so it is these that we will focus on here.

Savulescu argues for the principle of "procreative beneficence" – the principle of selecting the best child one could have of all possible children (Savulescu, 2004a). He argues that while we cannot place a value on a human life, we can know which traits or conditions contribute to a good life – which we most certainly want for ourselves and our children. Procreative beneficence is simply empowering humans to control their genetic fate and increase the odds of surviving well in an imperfect and oftentimes difficult and dangerous world.

The difficulty we run into is defining what constitutes a "better child." Not only will this vary by family and culture, but many different kinds of good could be sought to be maximized, often at the expense of another good (Bennett, 2009). For example, do you want your child to be well-rounded or a protégée in one area? Both are admirable aims and yet they are potentially mutually exclusive.

29.1.1.2.1 Genetic knowledge and technology

Existing genetic technologies have historically been used to prevent and treat disease. However, there are increasing instances where this technology could be applied to result in "better" children, and why not? Beyond reasons of parental pride, most parents want the best for their children and believe that acting to aid their kids in flourishing can only be a good thing. This is a perfectly honorable motive, and some might even find fault with parents who did not share this desire (Kass, 2003a). However, certain forms of enhancement sit differently with different people, and none is so contentious as when it takes the form of genetic enhancement. These existing genetic technologies can be divided into three categories: prenatal diagnosis (or "screening out"), trait selection ("choosing in"), and genetic engineering of desired traits ("fixing up") (Kass, 2003a).

Prenatal diagnosis, for example using amniocentesis, is commonly used in already established pregnancies to detect severe or fatal fetal abnormalities that would limit the quality or quantity of the life of the child or mother. In a sense, this could be seen as a possible form of enhancement through the "weeding out" of undesirable traits in an already existing pregnancy through selective abortion (Kass, 2003a). However, the potential to apply this technology to obtain a "better than normal" child is negligible – no genetic selection can improve upon what the parents have contributed to the fetus already (Kass, 2003a). At most, this "screening out" is enhancement only if you consider the prevention of suffering to be an enhancement.

"Choosing in" by selecting for desired traits relies on in vitro fertilization and preimplantation genetic diagnosis (PGD) – by screening several blastocysts for the presence or absence of genetic markers, one can opt to selectively implant only those in vitro embryos that have the desired genetic traits (Kass, 2003a). As is the case with prenatal diagnosis, when selecting among embryos one is still limited to what nature has created with what was given to it by the parents, rather than allowing a chance to determine which embryo shall be implanted (Savulescu & Kahane, 2009). Most often this ability is used to prevent heritable genetic illness by selecting out bad traits – if you have two embryos and one is sure to live a short, horrifically painful life while the other does not. Why should we leave it up to chance when we can reasonably reduce/prevent suffering? (Savulescu, 2007). But PGD has also been used for purposes beyond the health of the future child – namely, to select the desired sex of the offspring, and to select for a child who will have compatible bone marrow to transplant into an already existing very sick sibling (Kass, 2003b; Tur-Kaspa & Jeelani, 2015). But other forms of enhancement could utilize this technology for the benefit of the child. As Savulescu argues, no one is disadvantaged when the embryo with the best potential is selected: "Natural inequality exists – some people are born naturally smarter than others. Allowing selection would, in one sense, only level up. It would reduce inequality, especially if cheap and affordable" (Savulescu, 2007). There are of course limitations to the use of PGD for enhancement purposes. For one, it is difficult to select traits that are polygenetic in nature or rely on epigenetic processes to manifest, as will likely be most traits of CE interest (for example intelligence, memory, or appearance). A final issue is one of safety – fewer than 10,000 children exist as a result of PGD, and the technology is new enough that the safety implications of blastomere biopsy on the developing embryo are so far unknown. Such a risk is worth it to avoid a horrendous genetic disorder but potentially less defensible when employed in the search for improved native powers (Kass, 2003a).

Of the three genetic technologies presented, the one most likely to prove beneficial from an enhancement standpoint is the one that is mostly theoretical at this stage. The genetic engineering of desired traits, or "fixing up," involves improving in vitro embryos by introducing the gene or genes for the desired trait. Most of the traits for which parents might wish to engineer improvements in their children are almost certainly polygenic, that is, the trait (or phenotype) of interest depends on multiple genes or variants at several, potentially distant, locations on the chromosomes. The relationships and interactions between these genes (and between these genes and the environment) are certain to be enormously complex (Kass, 2003a).

29.1.1.2.2 Psychotropic drugs

Childhood temperaments are not always conducive to educational settings as children tend to be more energetic, fidgety, and lack a long attention span. And yet good educational performance and attainment are increasingly necessary to thrive in our society. For this reason, anything that could help a child succeed in their academic endeavors would surely constitute a benefit to that child. And yet, we run into the potential issue of medicalizing childhood itself – drugging our kids into submission to make them conform to a societal norm of a perfect child who is seen but not heard and to make them easier for stressed teachers and parents to control. On the other side of this argument, however, is that oftentimes these undesirable behaviors are in fact evidence of a more serious disorder that, rather than being a passing phase, could persist into adulthood and does indeed require treatment for the benefit of the child.

29.1.1.3 Leveling the playing field – justice/fairness

One of the most common objections to CE is that it will create inequality, injustice, and unfairness as a result of inequitable access (Annas, 2003; Fukuyama, 2009; McKibben, 2015; Savulescu, 2006). But many argue that one of the most intuitively appealing arguments in favor of CE is one of justice: CE can help us level the playing field and this establishes a moral obligation to enhance (Savulescu, 2006). Natural inequality is a reality and we frequently require social institutions to ensure that everyone has a fair go, a good enough chance of a good life (Savulescu, 2007). Why can't the same principle apply to biological interventions? Cognitive enhancement can be used as a means of helping us fulfill ethical/social goals related to alleviating inequality or helping those of lesser abilities to participate more fully in social and economic goods (Ray, 2016). As argued by Savulescu, justice requires enhancement as it requires as many people as possible a decent chance at a decent life (Savulescu, 2006).

> Justice/Fairness requires we get as many people as possible up to the minimum IQ necessary for a decent chance of a decent life… Far from being opposed to enhancement, justice requires enhancement. It is on these grounds that we choose to treat those currently with an IQ less than 70. But where we set the minimum threshold for treatment or enhancement is up to us. It depends on how we define a decent chance of a decent life in the way society and the world are likely to be.
>
> *(Savulescu, 2006)*

Indeed, as Ray argues, it is a moral requirement to pursue the possibility of stimulants being used as a means of remedying the negative impact social inequalities have on underprivileged children for the sake of increasing their chances of success and hence well-being (Ray, 2016).

Further, it is up to us how to allocate CE. A "hype and hope" lens does not necessarily mean supporting a totally free and open-access approach. We have the power to dictate policy surrounding the provision of CE in such a way as to promote justice – CE could be free, only made available to the poor or disenfranchised, or in other ways that would promote the betterment of society as a whole (Savulescu, 2006). By allowing not only those with medical deficiencies to access the benefits of CE, we can also remove the effects of genetic inequality and level the playing field. Far from being unfair, the proper utilization of CE promotes equality (Savulescu, 2004b).

Many argue against the use of CE with the argument that it constitutes cheating. But cheating is only defined by the rules we write. Thus, this cannot be the only argument against CE if changing the human-made rules automatically removes the immorality of CE use. By simply legalizing enhancement, all arguments from the standpoint of cheating are mitigated (Savulescu, 2006). A related argument based on fairness is this: it is unfair to the honest athletes who abide by the rules that they cannot enjoy the benefits of CE while the cheaters who do not abide by the rules do (Savulescu, 2004b). However, such arguments from the point of cheating are limited to competitive settings, whereas cooperative endeavors then seem to invite CE use. As stated by Kass in the PCBE:

> Drugs to steady the hand of a neurosurgeon or to prevent sweaty palms in a concert pianist cannot be regarded as "cheating," for they are in no sense the source of the excellent activity or achievement. And, for people dealt a meager hand in the dispensing of nature's gifts, it should not be called cheating or cheap if biotechnology could assist them in becoming better equipped-whether in body or in mind.
>
> *(Kass, 2003b)*

Allowing our lives to be determined by genetic lottery, chance, or wealth all lead to injustice (Savulescu, 2006). But judicious use of CE, based on a responsible, rational policy can ensure that each of us, regardless of chance, has "a fair go" (Savulescu, 2007). It is the spirit of humanity to seek to have a better life – doing so is not cheating but rather the moral endeavor to seek human flourishing (Savulescu, 2006).

29.1.1.4 The pursuit of a good life

Which effects of biotechnology and CE are determined morally permissible depending on which value we are seeking to maximize? (Savulescu, 2006). Across the board, it is safe to say that CE seeks to maximize the goodness of a person's life and/or her well-being (Savulescu, 2006). Just as with education, good health habits, and information technology, CE should be viewed as yet another way that our species uniquely tries to improve itself and the well-being of its members (Greely et al., 2008). Technology and human innovation already greatly increase the quality of human life. From homes to agriculture to biotechnology, our lives are made better by our innovative creations (Greely et al., 2008). Who is to say where the application of those innovations stops? If enhancement is understood as an intervention that increases the chances of a good life, it is hard to imagine a justifiable argument against trying to make people's lives go better – quite the opposite: beneficence would generate a moral obligation to enhance (Savulescu, 2006).

29.1.2 Doom and gloom

Few will argue that CE of all and any kind is bad. Indeed, the goal to cure and prevent physical and mental illness, as well as the search to improve ourselves, our children, our communities, and society in general are laudable (Kass, 2003b). However, the human imagination is limitless, and the very real possibility exists that just as we achieve what we originally sought to gain through biotechnology, we are presented with new possibilities and new desires. The potential of biotechnology is limitless, and so are human aspirations (Kass, 2003b). Unfortunately, we are not omniscient, and biotechnology ignorantly applied can lead to unexpected and unwanted implications. This is true too on a societal level – an individual empowered with CE may attain her desired goal to her benefit but to the detriment of society as a whole. It is for these reasons and more that we must be constantly cognizant of the potential future repercussions of novel CE and remain vigilant in its supervision as it is adopted.

As in the previous sections, we have adopted an adapted delineation of these concerns as they were presented in the PCBE, namely into issues of safety, justice/fairness, equality of access, liberty/coercion, unnatural means, and identity and individuality. The concerns identified related to hubris and humility, and identity and individuality will be discussed under the "Religious considerations" section below.

29.1.2.1 Safety

One of the core principles of bioethics is that of non-maleficence – do no harm. Thus, clearly, the moral permissibility of CE will be (or at least should be) dependent upon the safety profiles of these drugs and interventions. However, safety is a relative concept based on a risk-benefit analysis – indeed, nearly every medical intervention poses at least some small possibility of harm. Surgery to correct a broken bone or remove a tumor comes with the risk of infection. Most medicines have at least some small chance of a negative side effect. What we deem safe depends on what it is compared to, and in the context of CE, safety depends on the potential benefit gained (Greely et al., 2008). Greely and colleagues note that "a drug that restored good cognitive functioning to people with severe dementia but caused serious adverse medical events might be deemed safe enough to prescribe, but these risks would be unacceptable for healthy individuals seeking enhancement" (Greely et al., 2008). This is because, for the healthy user, this risk-benefit ratio does not favor intervention: "one should not risk basic health pursuing a condition of "better than well" (Kass, 2003b).

Further, little is known about the safety profiles of many CE interventions (Bennett, 2009). The challenge is even more difficult than simply whether something is "safe" or not because safety is context-dependent. Any medical drugs that come to market must have passed rigorous safety and efficacy testing for their therapeutic purpose – however, there is no such testing for unregulated "off-label uses" (Greely et al., 2008). This is troublesome, as currently much CE is achieved using therapeutics off-label (Glannon, 2008).

Finally, safety information is hard to come by, given that CE use of stimulant drugs is usually obtained by off-label prescription or obtained illegally, making it very difficult to collect public health information on its effects. Indeed, very little is known about the prevalence of CE use in healthy populations: the available evidence, which is mostly limited to college campuses, points to a prevalence rate between 1% and 35% (DeSantis et al., 2008; Jotterand & Dubljević, 2016). Additionally, not enough is known about the specific substances being used, even though Adderall, a form of amphetamine with high addiction potential, seems to be more commonly used than non-typical stimulants, such as modafinil, which may be safer (Hanson et al., 2013; Dubljević & Ryan, 2015). Further, neurotechnologies that purport CE effects, such as tDCS and EEG-based brain training, are often obtained through commercial products that to date remain unregulated by existing oversight bodies or self-manufactured through "do-it-yourself" communities, neither of which receive much if any oversight (Coates McCall et al., 2019; Ienca et al., 2018; Wexler, 2015). Good ethics requires good data and to inform responsible policy we must collect much more information on which CE is being used, by whom, in what situations, for how long, and to what effect (Greely et al., 2008).

29.1.2.2 Justice and fairness

When enhancement is understood as a means by which individuals can increase their chances of a good life, it is hard to see why its adoption is so controversial – however, there is a class of objections that argue that, while enhancements may be good for individuals, they introduce inequality, injustice, and unfairness (Savulescu, 2006). A main objection to the use of CE is that it gives its users an unfair advantage, especially in competitive or zero-sum situations (Kass, 2003a) – that CE is or will be used as a means for obtaining undeserved positional advantage (Maher, 2008; Dubljević, 2012a), or that it amounts to cheating (Greely et al., 2008). Many more argue that CE adoption will create injustice and exacerbate inequality (Greely et al., 2008; Dubljević, 2012a).

Under Rawls' final formulation of the principles of justice:

> (1) each person has the same indefeasible claim to a fully adequate scheme of equal basic rights and liberties, which scheme is compatible with the same scheme of liberties for all (the equal liberty principle); and (2) social and economic inequalities are to satisfy two conditions: first, they are to be attached to positions and offices open to all under conditions of fair equality of opportunity (the principle of fair equality of opportunity); and second, they are to be to the greatest benefit of the least advantaged members of society (the difference principle).
>
> *(Rawls, 2001)*

If advancements and technologies that were developed to, or could be used to, treat medical deficits or prevent disease, are used instead for purposes of enhancement, this would be a violation of the difference principle and distributive justice (Savulescu, 2007). Using CE technologies for performance maintenance or enhancement "is not an issue of providing basic necessities for those who are lacking, benefiting the least advantaged, or restoring citizens to a position of equal opportunity and liberty" (Dubljević, 2012a). Some authors even go so far as to say that treatments are obligatory and permissible while enhancements are not (Selgelid, 2007). "The threats of society-wide violations of equal rights and discrimination are questions of justice" (Dubljević, 2012a). In a society where resources are simply too limited to meet all treatment needs, justice requires that we meet all the health needs of the sick first – only if all health needs are met should resources be allocated toward enhancement (Dubljević, 2012a).

29.1.2.3 Equality of access

The issues of distributive justice and fairness, especially in competitive contexts, are especially acute when there are systemic disparities between those who will and those who will not have access to the life-improving powers of CE (Kass, 2003b). Much of the injustice discussed in the previous section would be caused by inequality of access – CE could perpetuate injustice if not everybody has access to it. To this end, Savulescu argues that objections to CE on the basis that it will perpetuate inequality by only being available to the rich miss the mark – it is not so much inherently an issue of justice but one of distribution (Savulescu, 2007). If CE presents a good to be sought, it should be provided equally. The injustice stems from our application of the technology, not the technology itself.

Whether or not CE is substantially unfair will depend on its availability and to what end it is used (Greely et al., 2008). If CE is expensive, only the wealthy and privileged will be able to access it and reap the benefits, thereby exacerbating existing disparities in health, performance, and quality of life (Kass, 2003b; Greely et al., 2008). As Leon Kass notes, this outcome is likely given certain core elements of American society, namely the existing inequalities in socioeconomic status, the belief in free markets to determine the development and distribution of goods, and libertarian attitudes toward unrestricted personal freedoms for all choices in private life (Kass, 2003b).

29.1.2.4 Liberty and coercion

Given the purported potential (short-term) benefits of CE, namely increased productivity, superior performance, and sustained functioning, many could stand to benefit from CE adoption beyond the individual using it. Corporate actors may see unlimited potential for increased profits if their workers were to enhance (Dubljević, 2012a). This has the potential to lead to widespread violations of rights and justice as direct and indirect coercion may result from utility calculations of corporate actors (Dubljević, 2012a). Truck drivers who take modafinil could work longer routes without sleep, increasing the speed of transit, productivity, and ultimately financial gains (Dubljević, 2012a). Performance maintenance in warehouses could function similarly. Members of the military may be required to enhance in ways that decrease reaction time and maintain heightened performance and vigilance for extended periods. Such pressure from an employer could amount to direct coercion to enhance if the employee does not want to enhance but is threatened with job loss. This is also a matter of fairness – in such a case it is the employer that gains all the benefits of enhancement while all of the safety risks fall only on the employee who is threatened with the loss of her job if she does not use it.

However, there is also the threat of indirect coercion wherein an individual feels compelled to enhance simply because everyone else does and thus feels that to perform competitively she must as well. If CE is freely permitted, accessible, and widely used, under certain circumstances its use may become practically mandatory (Kass, 2003b). If nearly all students are taking stimulant study drugs that allow them to study longer and retain information better, realistically other students who do not wish to enhance will still need to use them to perform competitively. If individuals' choices are dictated by external forces such as market forces or peer pressure that in practice make it only rational to pursue a limited range of options (i.e. to enhance), then the individual's status as a free and equal agent is undermined (Greely et al., 2008). This is well illustrated in Dubljević's application of the prisoner's dilemma model to the use of CE in a competitive environment: in all possible situations (i.e., when others do use CE and when others do not use CE) – the rational, value judgment-free decision will always be to enhance (Dubljević, 2012a). Thus, even if not directly forced to enhance, individuals' freedoms are limited by the widespread adoption of CE. There is some evidence bolstering such claims. For instance, one study found 132,099 unique Twitter users in areas close to major US universities mentioning Adderall as a "study aid" (Hanson et al., 2013).

These likely outcomes of direct and indirect coercion to enhance have implications beyond those for the individual user. Unrestricted, uncoerced use of CE may, in the aggregate, affect society as a whole. Widespread, self-selected, nontherapeutic uses of CE, while potentially beneficial for the user, may be used in the most common human wants and desires to the effect of leading us to greater homogenization of human society. As can be seen with cosmetic surgery, breast implants, Botox, and the like, these enhancements are most often used to achieve a society-wide adopted notion of what is desirable – it will provide yet more ability to adhere to socially defined notions of excellence (Kass, 2003b). Kass calls this reduction of freedom the "problem of conformity," with the effect of "perhaps raising the floor but also lowering the ceiling of human possibility" (Appel, 2008).

29.1.2.5 Identity and individuality

Enhancement necessarily involves some degree of changing the user – indeed, that is the point. We enhance because we seek to improve some element of ourselves that we feel is inadequate. However, "in seeking by these means to be better than we are or to like ourselves better than we do, we risk "turning into someone else," confounding the identity we have acquired through natural gift cultivated by genuinely lived experiences, alone and with others" (Kass, 2003c). And this is not just an existential consideration of what it means to be "ourselves" and what true identity is – it is a real biological phenomenon as well: certain CE drugs have listed "personality changes" as a side effect (Ranisch et al., 2013). Finally, as previously stated, the standards to which we hold ourselves are very often socially dictated – by coveting what is "popular" or "trendy" and empowered by CE, we run the very real risk of striving to be just like those around us. What is desirable will be determined by others. This brings us back to the problem of conformity and the homogenization of society. This is bad because our society's strength lies in our diversity – no one can be the perfect human who performs every task perfectly – we specialize to collectively leverage our potential. A threat to individuality is also a threat to our civilization.

29.2 Minority considerations

In addition to those concerns identified in the President's Council, certain subpopulations have identified issues of importance regarding CE as they relate to their particular worldview and experiences. We will discuss two of these – opinions on CE stemming from religious doctrine and those from the standpoint of disability ethics. We would like to make clear that there are many other subgroups with unique perspectives on CE, and those relating to religion and disability are in themselves rich in their diverse opinions and vast in the amount of scholarship already published. We do not claim to present the entirety of the opinions on CE of these subgroups, nor do we intend to speak on their behalf. Rather, we offer a cursory introduction to such approaches to CE and encourage readers to pursue further reading should these topics be of interest.

29.2.1 Religious objections

A 2016 Pew Research Center survey found that, in general, those who identify as religious are more opposed to enhancement technologies than their nonreligious counterparts (Lipka, 2020). When asked about genetic enhancement in a fetus to prevent serious illness, synthetic blood to improve athletic performance, and a brain-inserted computer chip to improve cognitive functioning, those who identified as religious were, across the board, opposed to such an intervention. The reasons given included themes relating to "changing God's plan," going against religious teachings, and the need to respect the limitations of life (Lipka, 2020). Religious objections to transhumanism include concerns about the point at which we can no longer even be considered physiologically or psychologically human (Masci, 2021).

The PCBE identified a set of concerns related to hubris and humility that for the most part boil down to a sense of unease that comes with humans "playing God." These concerns stem both from a sense of disrespect to a Creator in trying to improve upon His/Her/Their work, and from a sense of egoism that we somehow know better. Although couched in religious language, these sentiments also have secular counterparts. Arguments against enhancement based on hubris and humility revolve around one central tenet: that by intervening in that which has been perfected over eons of years of evolution or divine intervention, we wrongly believe that we can do better. This tenet can be formulated as humans "playing God," but it also has a secular version: not that you are messing with God's creation, but that you are interfering with such a complex and important entity as our bodies "in the absence of god-like knowledge": the hubris of acting with insufficient wisdom (Kass, 2003b). These sentiments have both a cognitive and moral component (Kass, 2003b): acknowledging the giftedness of life means recognizing that, despite our efforts to develop and exercise them, our talents and powers are neither wholly our own doing or even fully ours (Kass, 2003b).

The PCBE also recognized a subset of objections to CE that stem from the "unnatural means" by which enhancement is obtained. Arguments against CE based on "unnatural means" can be reduced to one notion: that to enhance is to cheat. However, if we find it morally permissible to use unnatural means for purposes of treatment, then it cannot be the unnaturalness itself that makes us uncomfortable (Kass, 2003b). Rather, it is some sense that by enhancing we are undermining the value of human effort (Farah et al., 2004). For while we value naturally given gifts – the innate ability and swiftness of a runner, or the ability to quickly perform complex math problems in your head – we also value those who, rather than being gifted those talents, have acquired them through sheer force of hard work (Kass, 2003b). By using CE, we are acquiring greater performance through biotechnological interventions acting on a passive subject – the resulting skill/performance being neither innate nor earned.

29.2.2 Disability ethics

Enhancement is, by definition, necessarily dependent on what is considered a "normal" performance or ability for a given function, with enhancement being an intervention that brings functioning beyond that threshold of "normal." But of course, what is normal is more often than not subjective – dependent on both others around you and the environment/context in which you are operating. There is a growing body of literature that argues that disability is a social construct rather than a biological reality (Wendell, 1996). As such, many disability advocates argue against enhancement measures as they intrinsically imply that a person's given state is somehow unacceptable (Wolbring & Diep, 2016). The deaf community is a particularly vocal example of this, with many arguing that deafness is not somehow a deficit to be corrected, but a different set of abilities, and as such are vehemently opposed to cochlear implants (Cooper, 2019). Further, as previously stated, many view enhancement measures as a means to impose socially acceptable "normalcy" on neurodivergent or differently-abled people, thereby decreasing the diversity and vibrancy of our communities. It threatens to medicalize human individuality and diversity into something that must be corrected (Kass, 2003b).

For this reason, many think enhancement will undervalue the life of a person with a disability and cause discrimination against the unenhanced (Savulescu, 2006) and are therefore against enhancement – genetic, technological, or otherwise. But others argue that if we have the ability to prevent suffering and promote a state of being that functions best in our given environment, we should indeed do so. On this account, "disability" does not refer so much to a given biological status but instead a reflection of the pairing between a person as they naturally exist and their environment. Savulescu argues for a biopsychosocial construction of disability, in which

> a disability is any state of a person which: (1) will reduce the goodness (value) of a life (disability in the intrinsic sense), in circumstances, C; and/or (2) reduces the chances of a person realizing a possible good life (disability in the instrumental sense), in circumstances in which the child will live, which we can call "C" ... that is, an impediment to the good life.
>
> *(Savulescu & Kahane, 2009)*

By such a definition, it is hard to see how one could argue against improving someone's life – either based on beneficence or even non-maleficence.

> *The mere fact that what constitutes a disability is partly socially constructed, does not imply that we cannot evaluate some states as disabilities relative to environment, or select children on the basis of the way our society is likely to be.*
>
> *(Savulescu, 2007)*

Concerns about discrimination rely on the idea that we have no control over social attitudes and practices – however, it is entirely up to us how we choose to use enhancement and treat both those who are unenhanced and enhanced (Savulescu, 2006).

> Whether someone is treated with concern and respect is completely independent of their biology – enhanced or unenhanced. It is a function of our attitudes and motivation to treat others with concern and respect. Discrimination is our choice – not written into biology.
>
> *(Savulescu, 2006)*

> When we are considering human enhancement, we are considering improvement of the person's life. The improvement is some change in state of the person – biological or psychological – which is good. Which changes are good depends on the value we are seeking to promote or maximize. In the context of human enhancement, the value in question is the goodness of a person's life, that is, his/her well-being.
>
> (Savulescu, 2007)

If we accept Savulescu's definition of disability, it would appear hard to argue against CE on the basis of disability rights. But it is paramount that we listen to the voices of those who identify (or are identified) as differently-abled and take their viewpoints into perspective when deciding how CE ought to fit into our society.

29.3 Potential ethical, legal, and regulatory frameworks

29.3.1 Laissez-faire approach

This approach essentially would permit free and unrestricted use of CE by any party in any way they choose, for whatever purpose, and to whatever end. People of any age and in any profession could use whatever form of CE they like. In contrast to genetic enhancements for children, if CE drugs involve competent adults making decisions that impact themselves alone, such an approach is potentially more ethically permissible (Dubljević, 2012a). While this approach most aligns with the widely valued principle of autonomy, the arguments against it are multiple, for all the reasons discussed under the "doom and gloom" section above: it could be unsafe, it could create unfair situations, and it could exacerbate existing inequalities. Ironically, however, despite being the regulatory framework that on its face most supports respect for autonomy, this is the approach most likely to create environments of coercion, thus eventually violating individuals' freedom to choose not to take CE by the fact its use has become the standard. This "chain reaction," as described by Dubljević (Dubljević, 2012a), will inevitably occur where the use of CE by some compels CE use by other unwilling parties simply to keep up. A laissez-faire approach to these methods would likely leave us at the mercy of powerful market forces that will surely, for example, pursue CE by employees to increase productivity and gain a competitive advantage (Greely et al., 2008). As stated by Dubljević:

> if these private or partial interests are to be fulfilled at the expense of public interest and/or drastically affect the very basic structure of society (by achieving monopoly, for example), principles of justice apply with full force, and autonomy is not violated, as justice is supposed to protect the autonomy and equal rights of those likely to be adversely affected.
>
> (Dubljević, 2012a)

The widespread, unrestricted use of biomedical CE that would follow a laissez-faire approach is unsupportable by those looking for a safe and just outcome of CE regulatory policy.

29.3.2 Prohibition

A prohibition-style approach would see the use of biomedical CE banned entirely for any purpose. This would be a challenge to implement in practice because the majority of CE use is currently pursued off-label, making a particular substance in itself very difficult to ban – you would have to ban the enhancement purpose for which it would be used rather than the substance itself. Most CE is not developed to be used as enhancements, but over time people come to find ways to use them for that purpose. It is very difficult to control how enhancement technology is used; people will always find ways to enhance, which brings us back to the chain reaction problem (Dubljević, 2012b). Further, the prohibition would require extensive, expensive enforcement measures (Dubljević, 2012b). As Greely and colleagues state, "Cognitive-enhancing drugs require relatively little effort, are invasive and for the time being are not equitably distributed, but none of these provides reasonable grounds for prohibition" (Greely et al., 2008).

29.3.3 Discouraged use

So, it would seem that the answer lies somewhere in the middle: because of the potential health and safety concerns and the potential threats to autonomy we do not want free-flowing CE, and yet, out of respect for autonomy, we cannot ban it outright. Therefore, we would want a regulation that would ensure that people do not use CE *too much*, yet are allowed to use it in certain circumstances. As stated by Greely et al: "Cognitive enhancement has much to offer individuals and society, and a proper societal response will involve making enhancements available while managing their risks" (Greely et al., 2008). Thus, a precautionary principle limiting CE use seems warranted – a reasonable middle ground is to warn those who choose to enhance that doing so entails risks (Glannon, 2008). This brings us to many discourage use policies that each, try to minimize CE use to only its most just and legitimate applications.

29.3.3.1 Gatekeeper model

Under this option, it is the prescribing doctor's decision whether or not a user's wish to enhance is justifiable and safe or not. However, this invokes a form of paternalism that does not favor autonomy – while doctors have the expertise to diagnose and treat disease, this is far from enhancement and every person should be able to decide for herself whether or not to enhance (Dubljević, 2012a). Most new biotechnologies, including CE that goes beyond therapy, will probably become ordinary/adopted through a medical setting (Kass, 2003c). If this is the case, the pursuit of happiness and self-improvement through CE may very well become yet another ordinary aspect of human life that has been medicalized and relegated to medical professionals (Kass, 2003b). This too could have deep impacts on the very nature of the medical profession and the doctor-patient relationship. When seeking to treat disease, a doctor's goal is clear and she is trained to have the expertise in how to reach that goal. But if the aim is to enhance, while still armed with the means, she has no special expertise in what an appropriate goal is, or even if it is desirable at all, and is left to navigate this clinical interaction in the absence of any established deep ethical norms (Kass, 2003c). A gatekeeper model would put doctors in the role of policing public policy, something beyond their mandate. Furthermore, in practice, such a policy would simply devolve into a laissez-faire approach as those who wanted to enhance would simply doctor shop until they found a physician who would prescribe (Dubljević, 2012b). A gatekeeper model creates issues of paternalism by putting all the power of CE distribution into the hands of physicians (Dubljević, 2012b) and raises issues of justice by limiting the number of prescriptions written and for whom they are written (Appel, 2008).

29.3.3.2 Taxation approach

A taxation model would see CE available for all but at an increased price to discourage its adoption. The model can take several forms. All work from the assumption that CE use is inherently bad and something to be reduced, a position not necessarily true and which must be argued for and ultimately accepted on a societal level before the adoption of these policies can be accepted.

29.3.3.2.1 Tobacco model

In this case, the government aims to impose high taxes/fees on CE products to decrease an undesirable activity that is nevertheless legal (Dubljević, 2012b), the point of such measures being to create financial burdens for both the users and producers of CEs. While this may indeed lessen any corporate incentive to push for the production or use of CE, it does little to address the justice issues: the rich will simply pay more for CE, while the poor cannot, exacerbating inequality.

29.3.3.2.2 Coffee shop model

Under a coffee shop model, limited use of CE is permitted providing it is consumed/applied on-site/at the point of sale. The legal sale of such CE must meet certain requirements, namely, designated places (for example, coffee shops or cafes), product (only specific enhancements can be sold – not alcohol), quantity, eligible users (adults only), availability of information (no advertisement of drugs is allowed) and the support of local residents (the local municipality must agree to the coffee shop and can give orders to close it) (Dubljević, 2012b). Along with regulating the use of CE, such a model provides the advantage of making it easy to collect usage trends/data for purposes of informing policy (Dubljević, 2012b). However, while effective for other controlled substances (such as cannabis in Amsterdam), such a model may not be ideal for CEs. For instance, with CEs we are looking for improved functioning (in whatever form) but avoid coercion, whereas cannabis is purely recreational and therefore poses a different set of problems (Dubljević, 2012b). A coffee shop model does little to stop undesirable side effects such as negative health effects and indirect coercion stemming from CE use (Dubljević, 2012b).

29.3.3.2.3 A regulatory authority for cognitive enhancements (RACE)

By this model, certain techniques are permitted under the license of a regulatory body – namely, the Regulatory Authority for Cognitive Enhancements (RACE) (BMA, 2007). The main idea is this:

> Many different professions have a role in dispensing, using, or working with people who use cognitive enhancers. By creating policy at the level of professional societies, it will be informed by the expertise of these professionals, and their commitment to the goals of their profession.
>
> *(Greely et al., 2008)*

The downside is, of course, that "the establishment of a statutory regulatory body is expensive, bureaucratic and involves considerable work and time from those regulated" (BMA, 2007) and shifts the decisions away from the using individuals to those who arguably belong to a certain prescribed/privileged class of persons.

29.3.3.2.4 The economic disincentives model (EDM)

Under this model,

> an already existing government agency (e.g., FDA or Ministry of Health) would offer a licensing procedure to pharmaceutical companies to market CE drugs for healthy adults. This way all citizens could have legal access to CE, but with the imposition of taxes, fees and requirements of additional insurance
>
> *(Dubljević, 2012a)*

thereby creating financial and regulatory burdens for their use. In order to use CE, adult-aged individuals would have to pay fees for a course about effects and side effects and pass an exam as proof of knowledge; additional medical insurance and obligatory annual medical tests would be required to obtain (and renew) a license to use CE; the prices of CE drugs would be regulated and contain the standard costs of production and distribution; the profit margin would be limited and an additional tax would be imposed. On the provider's side, the producing companies would be further taxed and the funds gained would be invested in providing medical necessities for the least well-off (Dubljević, 2012a). The idea is that "the imposition of licensing procedures, taxes, fees, and requirements of additional insurance should offset individual and collective positional advantage from using CED" (Dubljević, 2012a). Dubljević argues that "such a [economic disincentive] policy would be legitimate, as it is in accordance with the requirements of justice, and it does not undermine the autonomy of citizens any more than is done by taxes on alcohol and tobacco" (Dubljević, 2012a). The shortcoming of such an EDM, of course, is that it only offsets any financial positional advantage gained (such as for corporations who would like to compel their employees to take CE to boost their profit) while doing nothing to prevent coercion of the user, protect user safety, or offset any performance advantage.

29.3.4 Case-by-case basis

Rather than assuming an overarching positive or negative stance, some authors have proposed a case-by-case approach to CE. Just as "enhancing human vision" can be done by multiple forms of technology, from as innocuous as binoculars to as invasive as neuroprosthetics, such authors argue that it is the relative merits and demerits of technologies and their uses that need to be carefully assessed rather than relying on a broad categorization of "therapies" as good and "enhancements" as bad. Indeed, looking at the history of medicine and technology, one can find numerous examples of therapies that were very bad (e.g., lobotomy) and very good enhancements (e.g., microscope).

Thus, the therapy/enhancement distinction, if it has any normative force at all, draws it from the relative difference in the risk/benefit ratio in the use of, say, stimulant medication for someone with insufficient dopamine vs. normal levels of dopamine.

However, even though the case-by-case approach seems promising, many issues need to be resolved before they can be fully utilized in the enhancement debate. Namely the level of evidence for at least seven dimensions needs to be adequately empirically established to avoid undue speculation. These include prevalence, overall social acceptance, efficacy, an ideological stance of the regulatory regime, potential for misuse, long-term side effects, and the delivery of complete and clear information (Voarino et al., 2017).

The case-by-case approach boils down to a plea for closer attention to scientific and social facts and a more nuanced level of analysis by researchers and regulators. That said, four methodological guideposts guide the case-by-case approach, and these are (1) conceptual and normative transparency, (2) maximal scientific validity, (3) use of interdisciplinary methods, and (4) balanced interpretations of data (Racine et al., 2017).

Conceptual and normative transparency is achieved when a discussion of CE (conceptual or empirical) defines clearly how "cognitive enhancement" is understood and how it is (or can be) operationalized into a measurable entity. Additionally, transparency is achieved in empirical studies on CE by outlining the broader conceptual background and ethical positions underlying the specific study and its design.

Achieving maximal scientific validity in empirical CE studies is not easy and involves multiple aspects. First, researchers must ensure that the methodology and interpretation of results are not unduly biased by implicit ethical positions or stances (such as "hype and hope" or "gloom and doom"). A priori positions of the research team (which are impossible to eliminate entirely) should be explicitly stated and their impact limited by third-party opinion consideration. Second, researchers need to formulate clear and meaningful research aims and carefully select the adequate study design and methodological approach that will produce valid results. Third, studies should employ validated research tools to prove CE effects or validate their tools before use. Fourth, since the area of study is especially contentious, researchers should provide sample size and power calculations in advance, along with the criteria for the inclusion and exclusion of participants. Finally, researchers should attempt to replicate published results with new samples, and in different social contexts.

As noted above, CE as a phenomenon transcends disciplinary boundaries. Thus, researchers should use specific disciplinary methods, including but limited to conceptual (e.g., thought experiments), qualitative (e.g., CE user interviews), and quantitative (e.g., questionnaires about prevalence) approaches, but engage in interdisciplinary collaborations to strengthen research designs and calibrate data interpretation.

Last but not least, the danger of ideological conflicts buttresses the need for a balanced interpretation of CE data. Researchers should err on the side of caution in order not to draw premature conclusions, over-interpret, or overgeneralize the results across cultural differences. Additionally, researchers should strive to publish the results of CE studies in a neutral, modest, and balanced manner and avoid stimulating unrealistic hope and hype as well as gloom and doom, and distinguish *empirical results* from conclusions that may be extrapolated from them (especially those in the domain of social policy on CE).

As important as a case-by-case approach to CE may be, there are some counter-arguments to it. Indeed, such constriction of individual possibility could be the most important society-wide concern, if we consider the aggregated effects of the likely individual choices for biotechnical "self-improvement," each of which might be defended or at least not objected to on a case-by-case basis. For example, it might be difficult to object to an individual's choice for life-extending CE that would extend her life by three healthy decades – that is until everyone opts for such CE, their children come of age, and are now unable to find jobs, partners, or housing, as they are all still being used up by the super-aged. As we have suggested more than once, the aggregated social effects of individual enhancement choices, widely made, could lead to a Tragedy of the Commons, where the individual benefits gained are dwarfed by the harms that return to them from the social costs of allowing everyone to do the same (Kass, 2003b).

29.4 Conclusion

We hope we have shown here how CE use by healthy individuals is a complex and multifaceted issue, one that requires we consider the biology of the technologies themselves, the interests and inclinations of those that seek to use them, the appropriate level of oversight, and even what a desirable society as a whole looks like. As with most novel technologies, once released and if beneficial, it will be hard to stem the flow of CE adoption. Even now, CE drugs are being used off-label, and neurotechnologies are sold for CE purposes. If we are to avoid the pitfalls foreseen through a "doom and gloom" lens, and perhaps even achieve some of the good envisioned through a "hype and hope" lens, we must proactively define what role we want these technologies to play in our lives and society, stay abreast of current research into their health profiles and uptake trends, and pre-emptively devise evidence-based policy to steer CE adoption toward the good and away from the gloom.

References

Annas, G. (2003, April 21). *Cell Division*. Center for Genetics and Society. https://www.geneticsandsociety.org/article/cell-division.

Anonymous. (2020, August 24). *FDA OKs BrainsWay Deep TMS For Smoking Addiction*. https://www.mpo-mag.com/contents/view_breaking-news/2020-08-24/fda-oks-brainsway-deep-tms-for-smoking-addiction/.

Appel, J. M. (2008). When the boss turns pusher: A proposal for employee protections in the age of cosmetic neurology. *Journal of Medical Ethics*, *34*(8), 616–618. https://doi.org/10.1136/jme.2007.022723

Bennett, R. (2009). The fallacy of the principle of procreative beneficence. *Bioethics*, *23*(5), 265–273. https://doi.org/10.1111/j.1467-8519.2008.00655.x

Buchanan, A. (2011). *Better than Human*. Oxford University Press.

Coates McCall, I., Lau, C., Minielly, N., & Illes, J. (2019). Owning ethical innovation: Claims about commercial wearable brain technologies. *Neuron*, *102*(4), 728–731. https://doi.org/10.1016/j.neuron.2019.03.026

Coenen, C., Schuijff, M., Wolbring, G., Rader, M., Hennen, L., Klaassen, P., & Smits, M. (2009). Human enhancement. *Panel for the Future of Science and Technology*. https://www.europarl.europa.eu/stoa/en/document/IPOL-JOIN_ET(2009)417483.

Cooper, A. (2019). Hear me out: Hearing each other for the first time: The implications of cochlear implant activation. *Missouri Medicine*, *116*(6), 459–471.

Daniels, N. (1985). *Just health care*. New York: Cambridge University Press.

Daniels, N. (2000). Normal functioning and the treatment-enhancement distinction. *Cambridge Quarterly of Healthcare Ethics*, *9*(3), 309–322. https://doi.org/10.1017/s0963180100903037

Daniels, N. (2001). Justice, health, and healthcare. *American Journal of Bioethics*, *1*(2), 2–16. https://doi.org/10.1162/152651601300168834

DeSantis, A. D., Webb, E. M., & Noar, S. M. (2008). Illicit use of prescription ADHD medications on a college campus: A multimethodological approach. *Journal of American College Health*, *57*(3), 315–324. https://doi.org/10.3200/jach.57.3.315-324

Dresler, M., & Repantis, D. (2015). Cognitive enhancement in humans. In S. Knafo & C. Venero (Eds.), *Cognitive enhancement* (pp. 273–306). Amsterdam: Elsevier/Academic Press.

Dubljević, V. (2012a). Toward a legitimate public policy on cognition-enhancement drugs. *AJOB Neuroscience*, *3*(3), 29–33. https://doi.org/10.1080/21507740.2012.700681

Dubljević, V. (2012b). Cognitive enhancement, rational choice and justification. *Neuroethics*, *6*(1), 179–187. https://doi.org/10.1007/s12152-012-9173-5

Dubljević, V., & Ryan, C. (2015). Cognitive enhancement with methylphenidate and modafinil: Conceptual advances and societal implications. *Neuroscience and Neuroeconomics*, *2015*(4), 25–33. https://doi.org/10.2147/nan.s61925

Farah, M. J., Illes, J., Cook-Deegan, R., Gardner, H., Kandel, E., King, P., Parens, E., Sahakian, B., & Wolpe, P. R. (2004). Neurocognitive enhancement: What can we do and what should we do? *Nature Reviews Neuroscience*, *5*(5), 421–425. https://doi.org/10.1038/nrn1390

FDA Permits Marketing of Transcranial Magnetic Stimulation for Treatment of Obsessive Compulsive Disorder. (2018). *Case Medical Research*. https://doi.org/10.31525/fda2-ucm617244.htm

Fukuyama, F. (2009, October 23). *Transhumanism*. Foreign Policy. https://foreignpolicy.com/2009/10/23/transhumanism/.

Glannon, W. (2008). Psychopharmacological enhancement. *Neuroethics*, *1*(1), 45–54. https://doi.org/10.1007/s12152-008-9005-9

Greely, H., Sahakian, B., Harris, J., Kessler, R. C., Gazzaniga, M., Campbell, P., & Farah, M. J. (2008). Towards responsible use of cognitive-enhancing drugs by the healthy. *Nature*, *456*(7223), 702–705. https://doi.org/10.1038/456702a

Hamani, C., McAndrews, M. P., Cohn, M., Oh, M., Zumsteg, D., Shapiro, C. M., Wennberg, R. A., & Lozano, A. M. (2008). Memory enhancement induced by hypothalamic/fornix deep brain stimulation. *Annals of Neurology*, *63*(1), 119–123. https://doi.org/10.1002/ana.21295

Hanson, C. L., Burton, S. H., Giraud-Carrier, C., West, J. H., Barnes, M. D., & Hansen, B. (2013). Tweaking and tweeting: Exploring twitter for nonmedical use of a psychostimulant drug (Adderall) among college students. *Journal of Medical Internet Research*, *15*(4). https://doi.org/10.2196/jmir.2503

Ienca, M., Haselager, P., & Emanuel, E. J. (2018). Brain leaks and consumer neurotechnology. *Nature Biotechnology*, *36*(9), 805–810. https://doi.org/10.1038/nbt.4240

Jotterand, F., & Dubljević, V. (2016). *Cognitive enhancement: Ethical and policy implications in international perspectives*. Oxford University Press.

Kass, L. (2003a). Chapter 2: Better Children. In *Beyond therapy: Biotechnology and the pursuit of happiness*. essay, President's Council on Bioethics. https://bioethicsarchive.georgetown.edu/pcbe/reports/beyondtherapy/chapter2.html.

Kass, L. (2003b). Chapter 6: "Beyond therapy": General reflections. In *Beyond therapy: Biotechnology and the pursuit of happiness*. essay, President's Council on Bioethics. https://bioethicsarchive.georgetown.edu/pcbe/reports/beyondtherapy/chapter6.html.

Kass, L. (2003c). *Beyond therapy: Biotechnology and the pursuit of happiness*. essay, President's Council on Bioethics. https://bioethicsarchive.georgetown.edu/pcbe/reports/beyondtherapy/index.html.

Lipka, M. (2020, August 11). *The religious divide on views of technologies that would 'enhance' human beings.* Pew Research Center. https://www.pewresearch.org/fact-tank/2016/07/29/the-religious-divide-on-views-of-technologies-that-would-enhance-human-beings/.

Maher, B. (2008). Poll results: Look who's doping. *Nature, 452*(7188), 674–675. https://doi.org/10.1038/452674a

Masci, D. (2021, May 25). *Human enhancement: Scientific and ethical dimensions of genetic engineering, brain chips and synthetic blood.* Pew Research Center Science & Society. https://www.pewresearch.org/science/2016/07/26/human-enhancement-the-scientific-and-ethical-dimensions-of-striving-for-perfection/.

McKibben, B. (2015, February 21). *Designer genes.* Orion Magazine. https://orionmagazine.org/article/designer-genes/.

Racine, E., Dubljević, V., Jox, R. J., Baertschi, B., Christensen, J. F., Farisco, M., Jotterand, F., Kahane, G., & Müller, S. (2017). Can neuroscience contribute to practical ethics? A critical review and discussion of the methodological and translational challenges of the neuroscience of ethics. *Bioethics, 31*(5), 328–337. https://doi.org/10.1111/bioe.12357

Ranisch, R., Garofoli, D., & Dubljević, V. (2013). 'Clock shock', motivational enhancement and performance maintenance in Adderall use. *AJOB – Neuroscience, 4*(1), 13–14.

Rawls, J. (2001). In E. Kelly (Ed.), *Justice as fairness: A restatement* (pp. 42–43). essay, Harvard University Press.

Ray, K. S. (2016). Not just "study drugs" for the rich: Stimulants as moral tools for creating opportunities for socially disadvantaged students. *The American Journal of Bioethics, 16*(6), 29–38. https://doi.org/10.1080/15265161.2016.1170231

Savulescu, J. (2004a). Procreative beneficence: Why we should select the best children. *Bioethics, 15*(5–6), 413–426. https://doi.org/10.1111/1467-8519.00251

Savulescu, J. (2004b). Why we should allow performance enhancing drugs in sport. *British Journal of Sports Medicine, 38*(6), 666–670. https://doi.org/10.1136/bjsm.2003.005249

Savulescu, J. (2006). Justice, fairness, and enhancement. *Annals of the New York Academy of Sciences, 1093*(1), 321–338. https://doi.org/10.1196/annals.1382.021

Savulescu, J. (2007). In defence of procreative beneficence. *Journal of Medical Ethics, 33*(5), 284–288. https://doi.org/10.1136/jme.2006.018184

Savulescu, J., & Kahane, G. (2009). The moral obligation to create children with the best chance of the best life. *Bioethics, 23*(5), 274–290. https://doi.org/10.1111/j.1467-8519.2008.00687.x

Selgelid, M. J. (2007). An argument against arguments for enhancement. *Studies in Ethics, Law, and Technology, 1*(1). https://doi.org/10.2202/1941-6008.1008

Snyder, A. (2009). Explaining and inducing savant skills: Privileged access to lower level, less-processed information. *Philosophical Transactions of the Royal Society B: Biological Sciences, 364*(1522), 1399–1405. https://doi.org/10.1098/rstb.2008.0290

Snyder, A., Bahramali, H., Hawker, T., & Mitchell, D. J. (2006). Savant-like numerosity skills revealed in normal people by magnetic pulses. *Perception, 35*(6), 837–845. https://doi.org/10.1068/p5539

Tur-Kaspa, I., & Jeelani, R. (2015). Clinical guidelines for IVF with PGD for HLA matching. *Reproductive BioMedicine Online, 30*(2), 115–119. https://doi.org/10.1016/j.rbmo.2014.10.007

Veronica. 2007. *Boosting your brainpower: ethical aspects of cognitive enhancements. A discussion paper from the British Medical Association.* London: British Medical Association [BMA], 2007 November: 42 p.

Voarino, N., Dubljević, V., & Racine, E. (2017). tDCS for memory enhancement: Analysis of the speculative aspects of ethical issues. *Frontiers in Human Neuroscience, 10.* https://doi.org/10.3389/fnhum.2016.00678

Wendell, S. (1996). *The rejected body feminist philosophical reflections on disability.* Routledge.

Wexler, A. (2015). A pragmatic analysis of the regulation of consumer transcranial direct current stimulation (TDCS) devices in the United States: Table 1. *Journal of Law and the Biosciences.* https://doi.org/10.1093/jlb/lsv039

Wolbring, G., & Diep, L. (2016). Cognitive/neuroenhancement through an ability studies lens. *Cognitive Enhancement,* 57–75. https://doi.org/10.1093/acprof:oso/9780199396818.003.0005

30
CONTEMPORARY BIOETHICAL AND LEGAL PERSPECTIVES ON COGNITIVE ENHANCEMENT

Luca Valera and Vicente Bellver

30.1 Cognitive enhancement: Some previous philosophical concerns

We live in an age of technological civilization. We often interact and relate to others via technological platforms in which we exchange data. In this sense, technology has become our environment (Valera, 2020), one in which we are inserted at every moment – in most cases independently of our decisions – and which constantly surrounds us.

Clearly, such dwelling in technological environments has generated some ethical and legal concerns, to the extent that interactions between people have become more persistent and closer (Valera, 2021). If we also consider that technologies can affect or impact us from within, modifying us from our very organic constitution, other ethical and legal concerns emerge. This is the case with cognitive enhancement (CE), whereby we can intervene (through digital technologies or drugs) with our brain to enhance some cognitive faculties. A large body of international scientific literature has recently developed around this topic, both at the ethical and legal levels.

To further evaluate the legal issues that arise in this area, we will illustrate some of the significant elements of this debate, offering an interpretation from our perspective. However, before considering the ethical and legal discussion, it is necessary to clarify the terms of the debate: what is usually meant by the term "enhancement" and, more specifically, by "CE"? Roughly put, we may state that "every enhancement can be defined as an improvement, because there is a starting point (what do we want to improve?) and an objective/an end (what model do we want to pursue?)" (Valera, 2018, 9). In Buchanan's (2011, 76) words, "enhancement is capacity-relative: to enhance is to improve some particular capacity." The idea of enhancement, then, involves the possibility of improving the performances that we can achieve through our capacities. Since it is focused on achievements or outcomes, this term is strongly context-dependent:

> Usually […] the term "enhancement" does not serve to specify a certain method or technology but to specify the context of its use, for whether a certain method or technology is used as a treatment or as an enhancement depends on the concrete situation.
>
> *(Hildt, 2013, 2)*

Thus, when pursuing enhancement, we are moving our attention from the "status quo" of our capacities to a different and potentially better state of affairs. A distinction between treatment and enhancement is necessary – and does exist – and we should highlight that the aim of enhancement is to improve the current situation of the individual, and not to restore his/her condition. Indeed, as Grunwald (2013, 206) highlights,

> enhancement has no intrinsic limits or measures but opens up infinite possibilities [...]. Once a status has been achieved in human enhancement, [...] it serves as the starting point for the next enhancement, and so on. This feature radically distinguishes healing from enhancement: healing comes to an end when the patient is healthy, while enhancement does not come to an end even if it is successful but is driven ever onwards by the relentlessness of the technological imperative.

When talking about CE, thus, the theoretical background is quite similar to that of enhancement more generally understood. CE is also context-dependent since its aim "is not so much about an increase in cognitive functions per se but about an increase in cognitive functions that aims at an increase in mental performance in competitive situations" (Hildt, 2013, 6). Neuroenhancement's aim is, thus, to "improve the human knowledge situation by facilitating or accelerating knowledge acquisition, processing, storage, application, or range" (Hauskeller, 2012, 117), by means of the manipulation of the human brain (Cohen Kadosh, 2014). We may have, then, different kinds of CE depending on the means used; it is possible to distinguish between pharmaceutical, neurotechnological, and genetic CE[1] (Hofmann, 2017, 414).

All of these new possibilities have raised ethical concerns, both regarding the risks associated with neuroenhancement (e.g., risks of side effects, addiction, loss of efficacy over time, and overestimation of one's own abilities – Brukamp, 2013, 102–103) and "personal authenticity; quality of happiness; development of the character and self-awareness; accountability of achievement; fairness in competition; social pressure; social justice; changes of values and the idea of mankind" (Kipke, 2013, 147–148). Two main philosophical topics seem to be relevant when addressing the legal issue of CE: the difference between therapy and enhancement; and the search for perfection and the possibility of authenticity in the context of CE.

30.1.1 Treatment or enhancement: Where do we draw the line?

Most of the ethical concerns related to CE mainly pertain to the line between treatment and enhancement (Sandel, 2007); indeed, the same interventions that in many cases we consider ethically unproblematic because they are therapeutic, could generate concerns if they are used to enhance some cognitive skills. There are three main differences between treatment and enhancement: 1. The clinical condition of the human subject; 2. The aim of the intervention; and 3. The idea of "illness" or "pathology" employed (and, conversely, the concept of "normality"). These second and third issues are obviously more controversial than the first. The first one, indeed, is necessary to define whether the aim of the intervention is enhancement – i.e., to improve some capabilities – or treatment – i.e., to recover some functions of the organism – "In discussing the ethical issues arising out of the use of cognitive enhancement technologies, we need to distinguish between the use of enhancement technologies on healthy and unhealthy individuals" (Fenton, 2009, 48). A *caveat* should be made here: if it is true that any intervention on a healthy individual is an enhancement, it is not so true that any intervention on a sick individual – in relation to his/her disease – is a treatment. This point allows us to explore the aim of these interventions and, at the same time, the purpose of medicine. As Bostrom and Sandberg (2009, 324) point out: "One common concern about enhancements in the biomedical sphere is that they go beyond the purpose of medicine. The debate over whether it is possible to draw a line between therapy and enhancement, and if so where, is extensive." Depending on how we define the purpose of medicine, then, we may find a way to draw the line between enhancement and therapy.

Anyway, another two elements of complexity emerge here: when we recognize the (partly) historical and contextual features of the concept of health (Bellver, 2012, 87; ter Meulen, 2015, 88), the idea of medicine may naturally evolve. In this sense, the distinction between therapy and enhancement seems not to be necessary (Gilbert, 2013, 129), ever-changing, or, at best, non-existent. The two terms seem, indeed, to theoretically overlap to a certain extent (ter Meulen, 2015, 88). On the other hand, the distinction seems to have an important practical intelligibility: medical teams would be able to discern between the two simply by observing the current condition of the human subject, as well as the purpose of the intervention itself. In this regard, we do agree with Bostrom and Sandberg (2009, 312) that

> cognitive enhancement of somebody whose natural memory is poor could leave that person with a memory that is still worse than that of another person who has retained a fairly good memory despite suffering from an identifiable pathology, such as early-stage Alzheimer's disease.

Indeed, this same statement shows the different original clinical statuses of the two persons considered. To find the difference between the two approaches, then, it is useful to appropriately consider both the clinical condition of the human subject and the purpose of the intervention. In this regard, it would be nonsense to talk about CE as a therapy (Blank, 2016a, 4) and, conversely, to consider every treatment as "a form of enhancement encompassing therapeutic as well non-therapeutic effects" (Blank, 2016a, 7).

The distinction between therapy (e.g., a curative or palliative intervention) and enhancement (e.g., an "'improvement' to body, mind or performance" – Blank, 2016a, 8) does exist, at least in everyday clinical practice: the medical team knows where to draw the line.

30.1.2 Perfection, human nature, and the possibility of being myself

We can now evaluate what lies behind the idea of enhancement itself. Many authors (e.g., Sandel, 2007) have argued that this idea derives from that of perfection since every improvement is based on the desire to reach a model, which is almost always unattainable and extrinsic to the subject (Valera, 2018). Every enhancement, thus, entails a *telos*, but this *telos* is ever-changing, since the models of technological civilization are highly mutable, just like technology itself (Valera, 2018, 12–13). In this sense, the idea of perfection inherent in enhancement basically follows the models imposed by our current technological civilization, which point toward total corporeal flawlessness.

If the criticism of the "perfectionism" that lies behind every enhancement – including CE – is quite well-known, we should say the same for the critique against the arguments based on human nature to refuse almost any improvement to human beings: "Critics of neuroenhancement frequently refer to the value that lies in human nature. Key principles of such arguments are the maintenance of, or search for, authenticity, truth, originality, personality, and identity as a human being" (Brukamp, 2013, 106). These kinds of arguments imply that enhancement in some way prevents the human being from being authentically him/herself. The question should be formulated as follows: "Do individuals become categorically different persons when they transform themselves via enhancement?" (Maslen, Faulmüller, & Savulescu, 2014). The emphasis on the "categorically" seems to lead us to a negative answer to this question. Still, the idea that through CE we are changing something related to our "self" seems to be indisputable: "Neurological biotechnologies differ from others in that they ask us to explicitly consider the kind of 'self' we want to have; or, to put it less dualistically, perhaps, the kind of self we want to be" (Root Wolpe, 2002, 394).

The impossibility for the human being to "be able to be oneself" implied in CE emerges from the features of the models imposed by enhancement: they are unreal, extrinsic, and ever-changing (and, thus, unattainable) (Valera, 2018). How could we, then, authentically flourish when a project is extrinsically imposed on us? When we practice CE, are we self-realizing or are we only superficially adapting to models that society is imposing on us? Quite surprisingly, even among "bioconservatives,"[2] we may find various supporters of CE – not of all kinds of enhancement, though. This is the case of Jason Eberl (2014), who argues that some cognitive neuroenhancements might enable a larger number of people to develop a virtuous life. If the central aim of moral human life is to flourish according to her/his nature, "cognitive or physical enhancements may be licitly utilized in pursuit of augmented capacities that are conducive to human well-being as living, sentient, social, and rational animals" (Eberl, 2014, 307). Therefore, "Cognitive enhancement thus coheres with the Thomistic aim of human flourishing by means of actualizing our rational capacities in pursuit of truth or the accomplishment of practical […] endeavors" (Eberl, 2014, 300). CE, thus, would work as a "facilitator" (Fröding, 2011, 232), making us better at deliberating and assessing moral values, and being able to flourish according to virtues. A concern regarding these hypotheses, however, still remains: how can we be more virtuous, if our virtue depends on external – technological, pharmacological, or whatever – interventions? This question assists us in thinking about what kind of life is a good life, and how we should achieve it personally.

30.2 Personal or common choices? Fairness, the *laisseiz-faire* view, and the most vulnerable people

Nevertheless, the issue of CE not only affects our personal lives but also our idea of society: "One of the central and most controversial issues in the debate on cognitive enhancement concerns the relationship between individuals and society" (Hildt, 2013, 8). Thus, CE is one of the biggest challenges that public reason must face today, since it implies problems of social justice, concerning the relationship between personal freedom choices, on the one side, and vulnerable groups and social pressure, on the other. In this regard, CE challenges our idea of society, demanding better legislation and norms.

Here, the main concern is: should CE be considered only a matter of personal choice or not? The response to this question usually ranges from the *laisseiz-faire* view to one of solidarity, or, to put it more simply, between the idea of society as a market or as constituted by the human family (Patrão Neves, 2009; Marcos, 2016). The concept of vulnerability (Andorno, 2016; ten Have, 2016) plays a fundamental role:

> Although eliminating certain characteristics or increasing certain capacities might express nothing more than a personal preference, it could send the message that some people (the smarter ones, the stronger ones, the more competitive ones) are of greater intrinsic value than others.
>
> *(Blank, 2016a, 47)*

This idea of society implied in CE, thus, involves a fundamental question: who should we consider worthy of respect? Are we really creating a society based on equal rights and opportunities or are some people supposed to be more important than others? If, by highlighting the individual autonomy that characterizes the *laisseiz-faire* society, we allow that people may improve any characteristic they want to enhance, we are necessarily pointing out that the freedom to choose is the main principle in our lives. This fact implies that other features – i.e., solidarity and respect for the most vulnerable people – are necessarily less fundamental and second-order values. When we subordinate these values that characterize our humanity to the market, we are necessarily obeying the rules that regulate the market (Blank, 2016a, 244), and therefore entering a condition of perpetual competitiveness. In this sense,

> concerns are also raised about the societal implications of CE as it relates to distributive justice, that it will lead to unfair advantages for the best off. Will inequities in access to CE technologies exacerbate social inequality by adding to the advantages of elites?
>
> *(Blank, 2016a, 48)*

Indeed, in any society, personal options are never only individual choices, *strictu sensu*. They imply other choices since they strongly impact the public discourse, and even more if we are thinking of choices that concern the common future of humanity.

When considering CE we must thus think about the kind of society we live in: "In a society dominated by competitiveness, for example, it is clear that improved cognition will be perceived and evaluated differently than in a society where greater value is attached to solidarity" (Ferrari, Coenen, & Grunwald, 2012, 227). Otherwise,

> in a country with significant inequity, there will be an understandable concern that neurotechnologies are not inappropriately used to strengthen asymmetrical relationships between individuals and groups, while, at the same time, a range of enhancements are already being employed by those with more resources.
>
> *(Stein, 2016, 108)*

The potential commercialization of CE, together with some individual benefits, may provoke a huge disruption to the precarious balance of many social systems, particularly the most vulnerable ones: "CE could in fact create considerable social pressure, and that prohibition and laissez-faire types of policy would neither be effective nor justified" (Dubljević, 2019, 23). Together with the well-known problems concerning distributive justice, fairness, and cheating (Maslen, Faulmüller, & Savulescu, 2014), the implementation of CE may foster an indirect "coercion to enhance" (Dubljević, 2019, 14), particularly affecting the most vulnerable people. Indeed, the quest for perfection impacts the most fragile people and groups. This latest consideration explains why we need to regulate the use of enhancement in general, and more particularly, of CE.

30.3 Legal implications of CE

There are no specific regulations for neurotechnology at the international level, much less for CE. While genetic interventions, both in somatic and germline cells, have been subject to significant regulations, this is not the case for CE. It is true that there are important differences between the two types of interventions. The genetic ones can affect all types of living beings, human and non-human, present and future, while CE is initially directed only at individual human beings. Thus, genetic interventions can influence all present and future forms of life, while CE only affects human individuals who consent to the proposed intervention or even request it themselves.

Broadly speaking, there are two fields of regulation of genetic interventions depending on whether they are directed at humans or other living beings. The former has a main standard, which is the Universal Declaration on the Human Genome and Human Rights (UNESCO, 1996). At the regional level, there are also some relevant regulations such as the European Convention on Human Rights and Biomedicine (Council of Europe, 1997), which includes a reference to genetic interventions in humans. The field of biodiversity is regulated by the Convention on Biological Diversity (1992), and its two additional protocols of Cartagena and Nagoya.

As CE does not affect, in principle, either the environment or future generations, and it seems that it is limited to individuals who freely consent; it tends to be regulated just like devices or drugs to improve performance or personal well-being. Therefore, the United States regulations have to do mainly with the safety of the products. Laws do not pay attention to the individual and social impact of CE despite the fact that, in many respects, it is comparable to the worst effects of genetic interventions: it can lead to self-exploitation of the subject (Han, 2017), to the violation of privacy, to surveillance and oppression by governments or large corporations (Véliz, 2020), to the increase of social inequality, and even to the complete fracture of society.

From the perspective of national regulations, it is almost impossible to articulate a comprehensive policy on CE. Indeed, the regulation of devices, drugs, and procedures comes from different areas of law (health law, data protection law, consumer protection law, and criminal law) that lacks coordination (Ienca, 2021). Moreover, scientists tend to stress the importance of training in ethics to ensure that neurotechnologies in general – and CE in particular – "respect, protect, and enable what is best in humanity" (Yuste et al., 2017). But this call for self-regulation is insufficient in two ways: first, because it is not only a matter of pursuing what is best for humanity but also for individuals; and second, because the protection of individuals and their rights against possible harm caused by CEs is primarily the responsibility of law.

30.3.1 New neurorights and their critics

To mitigate the negative consequences that may arise from the unregulated development or application of novel neurotechnologies directed at CE, four basic recommendations have been proposed: 1. democratic and inclusive summits to establish globally-coordinated ethical and societal guidelines for neurotechnology development and application; 2. new measures, including "neurorights," for data privacy, security, and consent to empower neurotechnology users' control over their data; 3. new methods of identifying and preventing bias; and 4. the adoption of public guidelines for safe and equitable distribution of neurotechnological devices (Goering et al., 2021).

Of these four recommendations, the proclamation of new neurorights is the most directly aimed at laws of international scope. Neurorights can be defined "as the ethical, legal, social, or natural principles of freedom or entitlement related to a person's cerebral and mental domain; that is, the fundamental normative rules for the protection and preservation of the human brain and mind" (Ienca, 2021). The proclamation of these new neurorights, however, has been subject to three major criticisms, from the perspective of philosophy, human rights theory, and for its lack of conceptual precision.

Philosophers have argued that proposals to proclaim neurorights are in danger of embracing a reductionist theory of cognitive neuroscience:

> Thoughts and feelings are attributes of human beings, not of their brains – of the whole, not of just a part. A human being is a psychophysical unit, a sentient animal that can perceive, act purposely, reason, show emotions, use language, and be self-aware. It is not a brain inside a skull atop a body. As such, it is a Cartesian reductionist pretension to argue that creating new rights is essential to protect the brain, a specific part of the human body, as the purported seat of human identity.
>
> *(Zúñiga-Fajuri et al., 2021)*

It seems evident that CEs can violate fundamental human rights. Anyway, the protection against these new threats is not necessarily achieved by proclaiming new rights that shield access to the brain: there are already rights that protect the individual against these risks.

From the perspective of human rights theory, some authors argued that proclaiming new rights does not provide better protection. On the contrary, it can generate a rights inflation that diminishes its effectiveness as an instrument for safeguarding the fundamental goods of the individual. Rights inflation is an unjustified proliferation of human rights, since it spreads "scepticism about all human rights, as it dilutes them to mere moral desiderata or purely rhetorical claims" (Ienca, 2021).

Finally, the ambiguity of the concepts used in formulating the new neurorights has been largely criticized:

> Laws must be linguistically rational, e.g., the text of the law must send a clear message to the subjects bound by it. But to meet this criteria, proper use of the language matters. The proposed neurorights bills use terms such as "psychological and mental continuity," "mind," "thoughts," "neural connections" and "mental processes." The trouble with these

terms, evidently, is that they are so obscure and vague as to render the above requisite impossible to meet.

(Zúñiga-Fajuri et al., 2021)

In any case, if we finally consider useful or even necessary to enshrine some neurorights, they should comply with four principles (Alston, 1984; Bellver, 2004). First, the principle of coherence, which requires that none of these rights be in contradiction with human rights already enshrined at the universal level. This logically implies that they should bring those rights to development and concretion. Second, the principle of novelty, according to which these principles should contribute something new to what already exists. They can specify demands that appeared implicit in other rights already accepted, but they cannot be merely repetitive. Third is the principle of feasibility, so that the rights that are approved have a broad international consensus. It is useless to proclaim rights if there are not many governments willing to protect them. And fourth is the principle of utility, which requires that the rights enshrined do not consist of formulas so vague that they lack any requirement or admit the most diverse interpretations.

Ienca and Andorno (2017) have identified four new rights that meet the four conditions mentioned and may become highly relevant in the coming decades in the field of CE: the right to cognitive liberty, the right to mental privacy, the right to mental integrity, and the right to psychological continuity. According to Bublitz (2013), the right to cognitive liberty comprises two fundamental and intimately related principles: 1. the right of individuals to use emerging neurotechnologies, and 2. the protection of individuals from the coercive and unconsented use of such technologies. This cognitive liberty does not necessarily legitimize the subject's use of emerging neurotechnologies for improvement purposes. The right to mental privacy has a broader scope than the traditional right to privacy. It is the "recognition of a right to mental privacy, which aims to protect any bit or set of brain information about an individual recorded by a neuro-device and shared across the digital ecosystem" (Ienca & Andorno, 2017). The right to mental integrity does not aim to protect only against the risks of surveillance, interference, and conditioning against the will of the subject but also against those interventions even when they are protected by formally free consent. The degree of surveillance and conditioning that digital technology is exerting on individuals (Zubboff, 2019) can be achieved equally imperceptibly and with greater danger through neurotechnology. With the appearance of CE, total mastery over the individual mind can be achieved. Finally, the right to psychological continuity seeks to protect the individual from those alterations of psychological continuity that may harm the individual. The problem lies in the difficulty to determine when personality changes induced by neurostimulation, or memory-manipulating technology, constitute a violation of this basic human right.

By recognizing these rights, we are affirming that CE cannot be left exclusively in the hands of the market, nor of the states, but neither of the complete self-determination of individuals (Ballesteros, 2021). It is necessary to legally protect certain individual and collective goods which are not perfectly defined. For example, given the possibility of using effective techniques to enhance mental performance, should there be a prohibition, a permission-based paradigm, or a restriction on their use to minimize risks of adverse outcomes or to increase the likelihood of good outcomes? Who should make the decision: the market, the state, or the citizens, after deliberating on the advantages and disadvantages? According to some authors, "the availability of techniques that can enhance performance may in the future impose new duties on certain people under certain circumstances" (Santoni de Sio Faulmüller, & Vincent, 2014). It would be essential, then, that these decisions are made by citizens, with due respect for the aforementioned neurorights, and not by markets or public powers.

30.3.2 The Regulatory models

We can currently identify three regulatory models in the world that may address the concerns regarding CEs: 1. the Chinese model, which is open to incorporating CEs that produce collective benefits and increase the country's competitiveness even at the cost of limiting the freedom of individuals and invading their spheres of privacy; 2. the American model, which gives priority to individual freedom without paying particular attention to the social inequality that may arise depending on the type of access that citizens have to neurotechnologies; and 3. the European model, which is concerned both with the risks to cognitive liberty, mental privacy, mental integrity, and psychological continuity, and inequality in access to devices and drugs (Blank, 2016b).

As these three regulatory models are incompatible, it is currently impossible for the international community to adopt a convention enshrining the new neurorights. To date, two intergovernmental organizations – the Council of Europe and the Organization for Economic Cooperation and Development (OECD) – are debating and proposing the governance of neurotechnologies. In the absence of international tools in this field, the OECD Council adopted a Recommendation on Responsible Innovation in Neurotechnology (OECD, 2019) that begins to recognize the potential of this technology to improve mental health, well-being, and productivity. This recommendation outlines that neurotechnologies result from the convergence between neuroscience, engineering, digitization, and artificial intelligence (AI) and will alter the traditional boundaries between medical therapies and consumer markets. It doesn't address new neural rights but includes a reference to the Universal Declaration of Human Rights (1948) and recommends that actors involved in neurotechnologies may "avoid harm, and show due regard for human rights and social values, especially the privacy, cognitive freedom and autonomy of individuals."

The Council of Europe, for its part, adopted the Strategic Action Plan on Human Rights and Technologies in Biomedicine (2020–2025), addressing the governance of neurotechnologies. It doesn't take a definitive position on neurorights:

> Applications in the field of neurotechnology raise issues of privacy, personhood, and discrimination. It therefore needs to be assessed whether these issues can be sufficiently addressed by the existing human rights framework or whether new human rights pertaining to cognitive liberty, mental privacy, and mental integrity and psychological continuity, need to be entertained in order to govern neurotechnologies.
>
> *(Council of Europe, 2019)*

Because the Council of Europe approved in 1997 the Oviedo Convention, the only international legally binding instrument exclusively concerned with human rights in biomedicine, it is particularly interesting to know its opinion on the need or not of proclaiming new neurorights.

30.4 Unfit for the future?[3] The debate must go on

Throughout this brief chapter, we tried to present some ethical and legal questions concerning CE. Obviously, we did not expect to close or resolve the issues presented here but only to open a space for discussion by providing some possible interpretations.

As mentioned in most of the scientific literature concerning CE (e.g., Le Dévédec, 2018; Koch, 2020), the question of enhancement can open the way to transhumanist or posthumanist viewpoints, which seek to overcome human frailties and weaknesses. In this sense, CE invites us to think about our personal and common future, offering us a real opportunity to think about the image of the human being we are looking for. This allows us to rethink the possibility of being unfit for the future or not and, at the same time, understand our vulnerabilities and defects, and their role in our lives and potential self-realization.

Nevertheless, the mere existence of technology won't replace our philosophical or anthropological considerations: our society urgently needs new anthropological conceptualizations. The techno-fix mentality (Huesemann & Huesemann, 2011; Blank, 2016a, 9–11), with its extreme optimism and faith in technological potentialities, attempts to eliminate the deepest questions concerning our humanity, e.g., why should we enhance our cognition? Would we be better persons through CE? Is CE an effective means to help us flourish? All these questions need a philosophical and legal response, since what is at stake through the use of these technologies, in the words of the German philosopher Hans Jonas (1979, 43), is precisely "the image of man," not his/her existence. This "image of man" should be the basis for our legal and ethical future discussions about CE.

Notes

1 There are other possible classifications – which, for example, only distinguish between pharmacological and non-pharmacological CE (Kantak & Wettstein, 2015) – but we think that the one presented above is more capable of collecting the main and most frequent ways of improving the cognitive abilities of a human subject.
2 For more on this term and the differences from "bioloberals," please see Pugh, Kahane, and Savulescu (2016).
3 Obviously, the title of this section echoes the famous book by Persson and Savulescu (2012).

Reference List

Alston, P. (1984). Conjuring Up New Human Rights: A Proposal for Quality Control. *The American Journal of International Law*, 78/3: 607–621.
Andorno, R. (2016). Is Vulnerability the Foundation of Human Rights? (p. 257–272). In: Masferrer, A., García-Sánchez, E. (eds.). *Human Dignity of the Vulnerable in the Age of Rights*. Cham: Springer.
Ballesteros, J. (2021). *Domeñar las finanzas, cuidar la naturaleza*. Valencia: Tirant lo Blanch.
Bellver, V. (2004). ¿Existe una ética universal? Bioética y derechos. *Cuadernos de Bioética*, 55: 437–455.
Bellver, V. (2012). El debate sobre el mejoramiento humano y la dignidad humana. Una crítica a Nick Bostrom. *Teoría & Derecho*, 11: 82–93.
Blank, R.H. (2016a). *Cognitive Enhancement: Social and Public Policy Issues*. New York: Palgrave MacMillan.
Blank, R.H. (2016b). Regulating Cognitive Enhancement Technologies: Policy Options and Problems. In: Jotterand, F., Dubljević, V. (eds.). *Cognitive Enhancement: Ethical and Policy Implications in International Perspectives*. New York: Oxford University Press.
Bostrom, N., Sandberg, A. (2009). Cognitive Enhancement: Methods, Ethics, Regulatory Challenges. *Science and Engineering Ethics*, 15: 311–341.
Brukamp, K. (2013). Better Brains or Bitter Brains? The Ethics of Neuroenhancement. In: Hildt, E., Franke, A.G. (eds.). *Cognitive Enhancement. An Interdisciplinary Perspective*. Dordrecht: Springer.
Bublitz, J.-C. (2013). My Mind is Mine!? Cognitive Liberty as a Legal Concept. In: Hildt, E., Franke, A.G. (eds.). *Cognitive Enhancement. An Interdisciplinary Perspective*. Dordrecht: Springer.
Buchanan, A. (2011). *Better than Human. The Promise and Perils of Enhancing Ourselves*. Oxford: Oxford University Press.
Cohen Kadosh, R. (2014). *The Stimulated Brain. Cognitive Enhancement Using Non-Invasive Brain Stimulation*. London: Academic Press.
Committee on Bioethics (DH-BIO) – Council of Europe. (2019). The Strategic Action Plan on Human Rights and Technologies in Biomedicine (2020–2025). Available at: https://rm.coe.int/strategic-action-plan-final-e/1680a2c5d2.
Council of Europe (1997). *Convention for the Protection of Human Rights and Dignity of the Human Being with regard to the Application of Biology and Medicine: Convention on Human Rights and Biomedicine*. Available at: https://www.coe.int/en/web/conventions/full-list?module=treaty-detail&treatynum=164.
Dubljević, V. (2019). *Neuroethics, Justice and Autonomy: Public Reason in the Cognitive Enhancement Debate*. Cham: Springer.
Eberl, J.T. (2014). A Thomistic appraisal of human enhancement technologies. *Theoretical Medicine and Bioethics*, 35: 289–310.
Fenton, A. (2009). Buddhism and Neuroethics: The Ethics of Pharmaceutical Cognitive Enhancement. *Developing World Bioethics*, 9/2: 47–56.
Ferrari, A., Coenen, C., Grunwald, A. (2012). Visions and Ethics in Current Discourse on Human Enhancement. *Nanoethics*, 6: 215–229.

Fröding, B.E.E. (2011). Cognitive enhancement, virtue ethics and the good life. *Neuroethics*, 4/3: 223–234.

Gilbert, F. (2013). Nano-bionic Devices for the Purpose of Cognitive Enhancement: Toward a Preliminary Ethical Framework. In: Hildt, E., Franke, A.G. (eds.). *Cognitive Enhancement. An Interdisciplinary Perspective.* Dordrecht: Springer.

Goering, S., Klein, E., Specker Sullivan, L., Wexler, A., Agüera, Y., Arcas, B., Bi, G., Carmena, J.M., Fins, J.J., Friesen, P., Gallant, J., Huggins, J.E., Kellmeyer, P., Marblestone, A., Mitchell, C., Parens, E., Pham, M., Rubel, A., Sadato, N., Teicher, M., Wasserman, D., Whittaker, M., Wolpaw, J., Yuste, R. (2021). Recommendations for Responsible Development and Application of Neurotechnologies. *Neuroethics*, 29: 1–22.

Grunwald, A. (2013). Are We Heading Towards an 'Enhancement Society'? In: Hildt, E., Franke, A.G. (eds.). *Cognitive Enhancement. An Interdisciplinary Perspective.* Dordrecht: Springer.

Han, B.-C. (2017). *Psychopolitics: Neoliberalism and New Technologies of Power.* London: Verso.

Hauskeller, M. (2012). Cognitive Enhancement – To What End?. In: Hildt, E., Franke, A.G. (eds) *Cognitive Enhancement. Trends in Augmentation of Human Performance, vol 1.* Dordrecht: Springer.

Hildt, E. (2013). Cognitive Enhancement – A Critical Look at the Recent Debate. In: Hildt, E., Franke, A.G. (eds.). *Cognitive Enhancement. An Interdisciplinary Perspective.* Dordrecht: Springer.

Hofmann, B. (2017). Toward a Method for Exposing and Elucidating Ethical Issues with Human Cognitive Enhancement Technologies. *Science and Engineering Ethics*, 23: 413–429.

Huesemann, M., Huesemann, J. (2011). *Techno-Fix: Why Technology Won't Save Us or the Environment.* Gabriola Island: New Society Publishers.

Ienca, M., Andorno, R. (2017). Towards New Human Rights in the Age of Neuroscience and Neurotechnology. *Life Sciences, Society and Policy*, 13/1: 5. doi: 10.1186/s40504-017-0050-1.

Ienca, M. (2021). On Neurorights. *Frontiers in Human Neuroscience*, 15. doi:10.3389/fnhum.2021.701258.

Jonas, H. (1979). Toward a Philosophy of Technology. *The Hastings Center Report*, 9/1: 34–43.

Kantak, K.M., Wettstein, J.G. (2015). *Cognitive Enhancement.* Cham: Springer.

Kipke, R. (2013). What Is Cognitive Enhancement and Is It Justified to Point Out This Kind of Enhancement Within the Ethical Discussion? In: Hildt, E., Franke, A.G. (eds.). *Cognitive Enhancement. An Interdisciplinary Perspective.* Dordrecht: Springer.

Koch, T. (2020). Transhumanism, Moral Perfection, and Those 76 Trombones. *Journal of Medicine and Philosophy*, 45: 179–192.

Le Dévédec, N. (2018). Unfit for the Future? The Depoliticization of Human Perfectibility, from the Enlightenment to Transhumanism. *European Journal of Social Theory*, 21/4: 488–507.

Marcos, A. (2016). Vulnerability as a Part of Human Nature (p. 29–44). In: Masferrer, A., García-Sánchez, E. (eds.). *Human Dignity of the Vulnerable in the Age of Rights.* Cham: Springer.

Maslen, H., Faulmüller, N., Savulescu, J. (2014). Pharmacological Cognitive Enhancement – How Neuroscientific Research Could Advance Ethical Debate. *Frontiers in Systems Neuroscience*, 8: 107. doi: 10.3389/fnsys.2014.00107.

OECD. (2019). Recommendation of the Council on Responsible Innovation in Neurotechnology. Available at: https://legalinstruments.oecd.org/en/instruments/OECD-LEGAL-0457.

Patrão Neves, M. (2009). Article 8: Respect for Human Vulnerability and Personal Integrity. In: *UNESCO. Universal Declaration on Bioethics and Human Rights: Background, Principles and Application.* Paris: UNESCO Publishing.

Persson, I., Savulescu, J. (2012). *Unfit for the Future. The Need for Moral Enhancement.* Oxford: Oxford University Press.

Pugh, J., Kahane, G., Savulescu, J. (2016). Bioconservatism, Partiality, and the Human-Nature Objection to Enhancement. *The Monist*, 99: 406–422.

Root Wolpe, P. (2002). Treatment, Enhancement, and the Ethics of Neurotherapeutics. *Brain and Cognition*, 50/3: 387–395.

Sandel, M.J. (2007). *The Case against Perfection. Ethics in the Age of Genetic Engineering.* Cambridge (MA): Harvard University Press.

Santoni de Sio, F., Faulmüller, N., Vincent, N.A. (2014). How Cognitive Enhancement Can Change Our Duties. *Frontiers in Systems Neuroscience*, 8: 131. doi: 10.3389/fnsys.2014.00131.

Stein, D.J. (2016). Cognitive Enhancement. A South African Perspective. In: Jotterand, F., Dubljevic', E. (eds.). *Cognitive Enhancement. Ethical and Policy Implications in International Perspectives.* Oxford: Oxford University Press.

ten Have, H. (2016). *Vulnerability. Challenging Bioethics.* London & New York: Routledge.

ter Meulen, R. (2015). The Moral Ambiguity of Human Enhancement (p. 86–99). In: Bateman, S., Gayon, J., Allouche, S., Goffette, J., Marzano, M. (eds.). *Inquiring into Human Enhancement. Interdisciplinary and International Perspectives.* London: Palgrave Macmillan.

UNESCO (1996). *Universal Declaration on the Human Genome and Human Rights.* Available at: https://www.unesco.org/en/ethics-science-technology/human-genome-and-human-rights.

Valera, L. (2018). Against Unattainable Models. Perfection, Technology and Society. *Sociología y tecnociencia*, 8/1: 1–16.
Valera, L. (2020). New Technologies. Rethinking Ethics and the Environment (p. 29–43). In: Valera, L., Castilla, J.C. (eds.). *Global Changes. Ethics, Politics and the Environment in the Contemporary Technological World*. Cham: Springer.
Valera, L. (2021). Human Dignity in the Digital Age. May We Dwell (in) the Virtual? (p. 195–209). In: Puyol, J.M. (ed.). *Human Dignity and Law*. Valencia: Tirant lo Blanch.
Véliz, C. (2020). *Privacy is Power. Why and How You Should Take Back Control of Your Data*. London: Bantam Press.
Yuste, R., Goering, S., Aguera y Arcas, B., Bi, G., Carmena, J.M., Carter, A., Fins, J.J., Friesen, P., Gallant, J., Huggins, J.E., Illes, J., Kellmeyer, P., Klein, E., Marblestone, A., Mitchell, C., Parens, E., Pham, M., Rubel, A., Sadato, N., Specker Sullivan, L., Teicher, M., Wasserman, D., Wexler, A., Whittaker, M., Wolpaw, J. (2017). Four Ethical Priorities for Neurotechnologies and AI. *Nature*, 551/7679: 159–163.
Zubboff, Z. (2019). *The Age of Surveillance Capitalism: The Fight for a Human Future at the New Frontier of Power*. New York: PublicAffairs.
Zúñiga-Fajuri, A., Villavicencio Miranda, L., Zaror Miralles, D., Salas Venegas, R. (2021). Neurorights in Chile: Between Neuroscience and Legal Science. *Developments in Neuroethics and Bioethics*, 4: 165–179.

EPILOGUE

The perpetual quest for human enhancement

Marcello Ienca

As the Darwinian theory of natural selection elegantly explains, nature is in perpetual transformation. So, too, is human nature.

Unlike most other biological species, however, human beings have a distinctive additional capacity to modify their nature not only through inheritance ("descent with modification" (Penny, 2011), in Darwin's words) but also through so-called cultural processes such as the transmission of information (verbally and in writing), the production of technological artifacts, the transformation (in this case, anthropization) of the natural environment, as well as through activities such as medicine, sport, agriculture, engineering, politics, and many others (Henrich & McElreath 2007; Mesoudi & Whiten, 2008). The lowest common denominator of all these heterogeneous activities is a clear but non-teleological tendency toward the functional and structural enhancement of the human being at both individual and collective levels.

This perpetual process of enhancement is as old as the biological and cultural history of our species. However, it is only since the second half of the 20th century – with a few rare philosophical exceptions – that this process has become the subject of close moral scrutiny. This makes us wonder why the moral salience of this process has surfaced so prominently in the last century. A *prima facie* answer might be that the human enhancement that occurred prior to that time had milder effects in modifying human nature.

However, evolutionary-psychological and historical-archaeological studies show us that these enhancement processes had already led to changes in structural and functional characteristics that contemporary debates recognize as forms of enhancement. For example, the invention of writing or school literacy had a transformative impact on human cognition in a similar way to what is now termed "cognitive enhancement" (Bender, 2020). Similarly, the advancement of medicine and the increase in food production fostered by the invention of agriculture and the refinement of agricultural and industrial technologies had almost doubled human longevity by the mid-20th century compared to previous centuries (Riley, 2001) (a phenomenon that, as we saw in Chapter 12, is today referred to as "life span enhancement" or "life extension").

So what is the source of the greater moral significance of the human empowerment processes that have been made possible by the technological development of the last century and especially of the last five decades?

The contributions in this volume have given us a detailed and varied framework to answer this question. In particular, they have shown us how technological progress, and especially the technological convergence between biotechnology and information and communication technologies (Helbing & Ienca, 2022), has introduced at least three morally distinctive features.

The first is teleology. For the whole of biological evolution and for a large part of cultural evolution, human enhancement was not the primary goal of such processes. For instance, writing was not invented with the primary purpose of cognitive enhancement but for the storage and transmission of information. Therefore, writing-induced cognitive enhancement was what Stephen Jay Gould and Richard Lewontin have called a "spandrel," i.e., a phenotypic trait that is a byproduct of the evolution of some other characteristic rather than a direct product of adaptive selection (Gould & Lewontin, 1979). In contrast, the human enhancement made possible by the variety of modern technologies debated in this volume has its own intrinsic finality. This finality is morally significant because it places moral responsibility on the individual or group that makes decisions about the moral permissibility of a certain enhancement in a certain context.

The second feature is multi-modality. Current attempts at human enhancement involve multiple functional domains, from locomotion to physical strength, from sensory perception to cognition, from emotional states to morality. Therefore, they involve a selective and varied modification of human capabilities. This potential for multi-modal modification urges us to reflect on what it means to be a human being throughout this process of incessant and structural anthropological transformation. This meaning must necessarily be explicable in terms that are not fixist but transformative and dynamic.

Finally, the third characteristic is multi-scalability. Today's human enhancement processes and technologies operate at multiple levels of scale: from the very small to the very large, i.e., from the atomic level to the molecular, macromolecular, cellular, tissue, organ, organ system, whole organism, and even at the level of populations of organisms. This makes the ethical analysis of human enhancement extremely complex and diverse, as it must encompass numerous areas of applied ethics, from nanoethics to the ethics of molecular biology, from neuroethics to population ethics, and from medical ethics to public health ethics.

The contributions in this volume do justice to this complexity, offering a multifaceted analytical framework of human enhancement, the technologies that fuel it, and the philosophical, sociological, and legal implications raised by this socio-cultural-technical phenomenon. Furthermore, these contributions illustrate an avenue for ethical debate on future scientific-technological developments. Indeed, they highlight how the epistemic convergence between the life sciences and the computational sciences, thus also the subsequent technological convergence between biotechnology and ICTs, will increasingly blur the dividing lines between these domains. As a result, the ethical debate will be less and less able to afford to be fragmented across the various domains of applied ethics. On the contrary, it will have to acquire an increasingly unified theoretical posture to analyze human enhancement in the context of increasingly better integrated cyberbiological systems. And it is precisely in this context that the fundamental anthropological-philosophical question of what it means to be a human being will cease to be a rhetorical question. On the contrary, it will become the fundamental question for ethics, politics, and law.

References

Bender, A. The role of culture and evolution for human cognition. *Topics in Cognitive Science* **12**, 1403–1420 (2020).

Gould, S. J. & Lewontin, R. The Spandrels of San Marco and the Panglossian paradigm: A critique of the adaptationist programme. *Proceedings of the Royal Society B: Biological Sciences* **205**, 581–589 (1979).

Helbing, D. & Ienca, M. Why converging technologies need international regulation. Available at SSRN 4183791 (2022).

Henrich, J. & McElreath, R. *Dual-inheritance theory: The evolution of human cultural capacities and cultural evolution* (2007). In Barrett, L. & Dunbar, R. (ed.) *The Oxford Handbook of Evolutionary Psychology*, Oxford University

Press, Oxford (2007; online edn, Oxford Academic, 18 Sept. 2012), https://doi.org/10.1093/oxfordhb/9780198568308.001.0001,

Mesoudi, A. & Whiten, A. The multiple roles of cultural transmission experiments in understanding human cultural evolution. *Philosophical Transactions of the Royal Society B: Biological Sciences* **363**, 3489–3501 (2008).

Penny, D. Darwin's theory of descent with modification, versus the biblical tree of life. *PLOS Biology* **9**, e1001096 (2011). https://doi.org:10.1371/journal.pbio.1001096

Riley, J. C. *Rising life expectancy: A global history* (Cambridge University Press, Cambridge, 2001).

INDEX

4E cognition 94–95

acetylcholinesterase inhibitors 344
acquired psychopathy 256–257
addiction 239, 243, 254, 340, 342, 349; amphetamine 395; behavioral 241; defined 297; of kinds 297; neurochemical 127; nicotine 391; pathological behavior and 297; treating 303–304, 362
Advaita Vedanta 34, 92
Agar, N. 78, 82, 120, 123, 154–156, 158–159
aging 52, 54, 78, 107, 297, 314, 390; accelerated 171–172; altering 164–165, 167; biological 162, 165–166, 170–171, 173; challenges of 175–176; chronological 167, 170; as development issue 168; eliminating 34; ethical ambiguities of attenuation 175–182; healthy 168, 171; inequality 172; intervention 163, 164, 166, 168–170, 172–173; is universal 169; longevity and medical practice for 326; premature 171; status quo 162–164, 169–173; *see also* aging enhancement; slowing aging
aging enhancement 172–173; aging and natural 163–166; anti-aging pills for 172, 176; equality framework of 170; framing question of 163–173; metformin for 172; public health and 170, 172–173; within public health framework 172–173; rapamycin for 172; unequal death and 169–170; zero-sum games 170; *see also* slowing aging
Aikins, R. 207
Alighieri, D. 33
Allan, J. 83
Almodovar, P. 136
AlphaZero 191
alterity, importance of 91, 92, 268
American regulatory model 414
Anderson, F. 25
Andorno, R. 413
animalism 124, 125; psychological-continuity theory *vs.* 124

anticipatory ethics: adherence to scientific data 245; diverse stakeholder perspectives 246; empirical methodologies 246; recommendations for responsible 244–246; speculation in 244–245; unreflective 237–238
antihumanism 32
antisocial personality disorder (ASPD) 259, 263n3
Arendt, H. 327
Aristotle 121, 301
artificial intelligence (AI) 21, 177, 189, 224, 237, 241, 268, 303, 317, 414; advisors/"outsourcing" 191–192; authenticity and mental atrophy 196–197; brain-computer interfaces and 192–193; defining 190–191; development of 315; fairness 197–198; human-AI symbiosis 224–227, 233, 234n7; for intellectual augmentation 193–198; moral enhancement by means of 275–277; privacy and cognitive liberty 195–196; safety, coercion, and responsibility 194–195; technologies of relevance to prospect of IA 191–193
Artificial Moral Advisor (AMA) 275–277; advantage of 275; defined 275; functions of 275; moral standards of 275–276; self-learning algorithm 276; usage of 275
assembloids 56
attitude of mastery 80–81
Auer, M. K. 258
authenticity in human enhancement 26, 36, 120, 122, 204, 240, 274, 333; in cognitive enhancement 408; coherence 134–136; endorsement 136; ethics of 133–140; of genetic enhancement 145–151; and mental atrophy 196–197; narrative identity and 126, 127; relations 136–137; self-change 133–136; self-conception 125, 126, 135, 137–139, 325; self-creation 81, 133–138, 140; self-discovery 133, 137–138; self-knowledge 135, 138, 141n4; self-narrative 135–136, 138; self-presentation 138, 139, 141n4;

Index

true self, changing and creating 134–137; true self, expressing 137–139; value of 139–140
auxiliary moral capacities: core moral capacities and 376–377; hyperresponsibility for 380, 382–383

Baccarini, E. 254
Bacon, F. 178–181
Bagaric, M. 83
Baker, L. 121
Bard, I. G. 206
Barth, K. 180–182
Basl, J. 83
Baylis, F. 310
Bell, S. K. 239
Bernal, D. 99
Bernal, J. D. 19–22
beyond therapy 54, 64, 164, 165, 312, 401
Bezos, J. 326
Biedermann, S. V. 258
biohacking 30, 39–40, 175, 182n1
bio-psycho-social approach 303, 304
blastocyst complementation 53, 55–56, 392
blastoids 53, 67n29
Blitz, M. J. 363
Boethius 121
Bonhoeffer, D. 182
Bostrom, N. 78, 83, 123, 147–148, 267, 268, 309, 320, 408, 409
Bowles, S. 291
Brain-Computer Interface Race 321
brain–computer interfaces (BCIs) 190, 224–225, 233, 262, 341; authenticity and mental atrophy 196–197; human-AI symbiotic relationship 226–227; human-BCI agents 227–228; implants 228–229; implementations 230, 234n13; for intellectual augmentation 192–193; literacy 197; neurosurgical 241–242; privacy and cognitive liberty 195–196; removal 230; safety coercion and responsibility 194–195; self-monitoring 242; symbiosis 225–226; symbiotic companion 231–232; telepathic 241
Briken, P. 258
Brown, L. 158
Bruce, A. 381
Bruno, S. 259, 262
Bublitz, C. 224, 413
Buchanan, A. 78, 79, 150, 167, 290, 310, 407
Buchner, E. 48
Buddhism 34, 36, 97, 334–335; Mahayana 34; Theravada scripture 40n11; Tibetan 92–93; Zen- 92
Bush, George H. W. 26, 340
Butler, J. 91
Butler, R. 165–166

caffeine 124, 341, 343, 351, 359, 363, 390; based traditional enhancements 391; ethics of CE with 206, 208
Callahan, D. 165–167
Calment, J. L. 171
Campbell, F. 365

Campbell, P. 395, 401
Canavero, S. 259
capitalism: big data 30, 41; digital 21, 98; surveillance 41
Caplan, A. 121
Caplan, P. 121
Carter, J. A. 24, 214, 217
case-by-case approach 41, 151, 208, 403–404
Chalmers, D. 214, 217–219, 221, 222
Chan, S. 272–273
Chandler, J. 224
Chatterjee, A. 240
children 99, 137, 145, 146; cognitive enhancement of 365–366, 391–393; consent and choice 149; deaf 230; death of 163–164; desire to have best 103; see also sex selection; disability for 151; duty to protect 284–286; eugenics and collectivism 150; genetic knowledge and technology 392–393; genetic sex change 105; IVF 158; memory enhancement 25; moral dysfunctions 256; parental choices for healthy and equipped for life 327; parent-child relationship 323; protection law 359; psychotropic drugs 393; sexual urge toward 259; shaping genomes 335–336
chimeras 47, 55–56, 64; human-animal 55; human-macaque 56; human/nonhuman 128n9; neural 56, 57
Chinese regulatory model 414
Chorost, M. 331–333
Christen, M. 255
Christian theology 19, 26, 88, 177, 180–181; Baconian project 178–180; Christians resist life extension by slowing aging 176–178; Christocentric anthropology 180–181; Judeo-Christian tradition 25, 88
Church, G. 51
Clark, A. 95, 197, 214, 218, 220
cloning/clones 13, 47, 51, 60, 64, 65n10; animals 10, 48–49, 65n5; gestated 54; humans 10–11, 49, 51–52, 55
clustered regularly interspaced short palindromic repeats (CRISPR) 154–155; Cas9 52, 55, 125, 155–156, 158, 322–323; risk/benefit analysis 159; see also germline gene editing
Clynes, M. 23, 38
Cochrane, A. 83
coffee shop model 402
cognitive agency 217–219, 221–222
cognitive empathy 346
cognitive enhancement (CE) 15, 83, 122, 214, 217, 246, 261, 309, 316, 328, 359–360, 419; ambivalence on ethical issues 205–206; American model 414; blind spots of stakeholder engagement on ethics of 206–209; boundaries of ethical acceptability of 204–205; and caffeine 208; capacities and 376–378; case-by-case approach to 403–404; childhood 391–392; Chinese model 414; clinical practice and 324–326; coffee shop model 402; cognitive enhancers, varieties of 215–217; deep brain stimulation

for 240–241; defense of 221; defined 202, 407; dextroamphetamine for 214, 215, 219–220, 222; disability ethics 399–400; discouraged use of 401–403; economic disincentives model 402–403; empirical uncertainty about 203–204; equality of access 396; ethical controversy over 202–203; European model 414; extended mind hypothesis 217–218; gatekeeper model 401; genetic knowledge and technology 392–393; hyperresponsibility and 374–385; identity and individuality 397–398; internal enhancement 218–221; intervention *see* cognitive enhancement intervention; issues of ethical contention about 205; justice/fairness 393–394, 410–411; *laisseiz-faire* approach 400, 410–411; legal implications of 411–414; legal perspective 359–370; liberty and coercion 396–397; methylphenidate for 203, 214–216, 219–220, 222, 239, 254, 343–344, 378; minority considerations of 398–400; modafinil for 12, 203, 216, 219–220, 239, 254, 343–344, 378, 395, 397; moral enhancement and 272; opportunity maintenance 391; performance enhancement 390–391; performance maintenance 391; and personal identity 124–126; pharmaceuticals for 239–240; *see also* pharmaceutical cognitive enhancement (PCE); philosophical and societal implications 389–398; prevalence of 239–240; previous philosophical concerns 407–410; prohibition-style approach 400–401; proponents of 150; pursuit of good life 394; question about 209–210; regulation of 207–208; regulatory authority for cognitive enhancements 402; regulatory models for 414; religious objections to 398–399; representation in 207; responsibility for regulating 208–209; responsibility to interventions 378–380; safety 395; safety, efficacy, and prevalence of 203–204; stakeholder engagement on ethics of 204–206; stimulants for 219; taxation approach 401–402; transcranial direct-current stimulation for 243–244; transcranial electrical stimulation for 243; treatment and enhancement 408–410; vulnerability 410–411

cognitive enhancement intervention 360; cognitively enhanced person, responsibilities of 364–365; freedom 361–364; government regulation 368; intellectual property (IP) rights, owner of 367; international legal issues 368–369; law of armed conflict 368–369; makers, providers, prescribers, responsibilities of 365; obligation to not use 363–364; obligation to use 361–363; ownership 367; people toward dependents 365–366; responsibilities 364–366; rights of access to 366–367

cognitive enhancers 12–13, 208–209, 214, 221–222, 326, 351; argument in defense of 217; motivational to 324; pharmaceutical 341–342, 348–349; pharmacological 218–220; safety and efficacy of 239; varieties of 215–217

cognitive liberty 195–196, 198, 263n4, 359, 369, 413–414

coherence 48, 61, 85, 333, 413; diachronic 135–136; self-narrative 135–136, 138; synchronic 134–135, 141n2; of true self 134–136
collective action problem 146
collectivism 146, 149, 150
Collingridge, D. 238, 245, 368
Conan, G. M. 299
Conrad, E. C. 206
contrastive vignette technique 206
Convention on the Rights of Persons with Disabilities (CRPD) 366
core moral capacities: auxiliary moral capacities and 376–377; bioenhancement of 378, 384; defined 378; hyperresponsibility for 380, 382–383
COVID-19 164, 173, 290, 315, 317; aging populations and 173; concept of enhancement 310–315; duty to enhance 312–313; duty to perfect humanity 312–313; enhancement and improvement 311–312; and human enhancement 310–311; human predicament 313–315; mRNA vaccines and CAR-T cell therapies 159; self-discipline and 290; therapy and enhancement 312–313; vaccine 165, 172, 189, 316
creativity framework 270
Crick, F. 22
Crutzen, Paul J. 32
cryonics 30, 35–36, 41, 268
cybernetic enhancement 13
cybernetic organism 23
Cyborg Foundation 37–38
cyborg human 21–23, 27, 36–41, 124, 331–333, 338
cyborgization 20, 26, 99, 225

Dalai Lama 92
Damasio, A. 60
d-amphetamine 343–344
Daniels, N. 148–149, 389
d'Aquili, Eugene G. 94
Darby, R. Ryan 256
Darwinian theory 19, 147, 314
Davenport, C. 154, 159
de Beauvoir, S. 91
Deckers, J. 197
deep brain stimulation (DBS) 37, 98, 214–215, 218–221, 254, 258; closed-loop 242, 258–259; effectiveness of 216–217; future of 240–241; high-frequency 258, 259; of nucleus accumbens 127; in psychiatric neurosurgery 257
DeGrazia, D. 125, 136, 253–254, 261–262, 273, 274, 294, 295, 325
de Grey, A. 34, 326
de Melo-Martin, I. 272
Dennett, D. 380
De Ridder, D. 258, 259
De Salles, A. 258
Descartes, R. 88, 122
designer babies 50; autonomy of 334; parents, psychological and moral challenges for 334–336; partially designed 336–338

developmental biology 47, 158; biotechnology and human enhancement 61–65; and brain 56–58; brain, mind, and human freedom 60–61; cellular systems and gene editing 49–51; chimeras 55–56; clones 48–49; organoids 53–55; phylogeny and 57–60, 63; stability and change 58–60; stem cell-based embryo models 52–53; stem cells 51–52
Devolder, K. 150
dextroamphetamine 214, 215, 219–220, 222
Dinh, C. T. 207, 240
Di Paola, M. 326
direct-to-consumer (DTC) neurofeedback 242
disability 105, 110, 112, 123, 366; age-specific 162, 165–167, 172–173, 175, 176; biopsychosocial construction of 399; defined 399–400; discrimination 361; ethics 398–400; genetic enhancement and 151; intellectual and developmental 257, 259
double effect doctrine 15, 16
Douglas, T. 150, 253, 261, 271, 273, 274
Downie, J. 365
Drexler, E. 23
Drumwright, M. 163
Dubljević, V. 397, 400, 403
Duke University 364
Dunagan, J. 367
Dunn, M. 209
duty to non-maleficence 395, 399; duty to protect from 285; to future generations 284, 286, 289; violation of 283, 285
duty to protect 283–284; another person 285–287; discipline and 288–290; duty to non-maleficence and 285; features of 285; future generations 285–290; non-identity problem 283, 286; violation of 285; vulnerability model and 285–287, 289

Eberl, J. 79, 81–82
ecological situatedness 90, 95–96
economic disincentives model 402–403
electrocorticography (ECoG) 242
embeddedness: political 296; social 95–96
embodied cognition 93–95
embodied mind 61, 94, 129n20
embodiment 87–88, 122, 127, 177–182; attitude of mastery 80–81; body politics and 91–92; contemporary theory 96–97; embodied mind 61; enhancement and disembodiment 98–99; in human enhancement 97–99; "the other" in theories 91; phenomenological perspective on 97–99; phenomenological psychopathology 95–96; phenomenology and transdisciplinary approaches to 93–97; in philosophy and interdisciplinary research 88–93; philosophy of technology discovered 92; social (de)construction and 91–92; transcultural perspectives on 92–93
embryogenesis 51, 59, 63; mimicking 52–53
embryoids 52–54
emotion 13, 60, 94, 125, 138–139, 204, 267, 341–342, 362, 412; burden 166–167; capacities 202, 278n14, 312; cognition and 347–349; component of negative memories 325; countermoral 386n13; dispositions 126, 261; enhancement 26, 77, 138–139; facial 345; foundation of moral action 290, 302, 348, 351; integral and incidental 348; intelligence 255; non-negligible 342, 344; in pharmaceutical cognitive enhancement 347–351; positive states 242; pro-sociality and altruism, effects of 350; psychedelics for 346; reactions 272, 386nn11, 28; recognition 346; regulation 57, 193, 349; resources 380; roles of 57; states to morality 420; suffering 156
enactivism 90, 94–96
endorsement 58, 78, 120; authenticity 136–140; beliefs 219–221; enthusiastic 181; narrative 230–231
Engelbart, Douglas C. 23
equality of access 197, 395, 396
Erler, A. 135–136, 138
e-sports, competitive integrity of 363
eugenics 18, 20, 24, 27, 99, 149–151, 152n2; classical or old 149; genetic engineering 25; genetic enhancement and 149; goal of 154; inevitability of 114; liberal see liberal eugenics; Nazi 298, 322–323; parenting 80
examination of anomalous self-experience (EASE) method 93, 96–97
extended mind thesis (EMT) 197, 217–218

Faber, N. S. 205
Fabiano, A. 295
fairness see justice/fairness
Farah, M. J. 12, 395, 401
Faust, H. S. 253
female 83, 103, 107–108, 114–115, 168; benefits of being 109; biology of 104–105; fear of 109–113; moral significance of injustice 110; nature and norms 114; Parfitian reflections 109–110; plurality of good 111–112; reproductive life 54; see also feminism
feminism 92, 126; body politics and embodiment in 91–92; cultural studies 26; cyberfeminism 23; feminist theory 91
Fernandez, B. L. 123
Fitz, N. S. 206
flavor enhancer, defined 311
Focquaert, F. 273
Foot, P. 84
Forlini, C. 239
Foucault, M. 91
Frank, A. W. 231
Franke, A. G. 206, 208
Franken, C. 19
Frankfurt, H. 127, 134, 136, 274
freedom 59, 65, 80, 88, 196, 260, 269, 300, 397, 414; of aspiration 61; brain, mind, and 60–62; of choice 319, 410; common/garden 274; to engage in morally wrong behavior 262; to fall 274, 298; moral agent with 127; moral enhancement and 273–275; morphological 21, 119, 122, 225; obligation to not use cognitive enhancement

intervention 363–364; obligation to use cognitive enhancement intervention 361–363; restriction of 261–262; source of 57; of speech or religion 363; of thought 245, 363; violating 400; of will 273–274; of young people 327
Freud, S. 89
Fries, J. 171
Fuchs, T. 95
Fukuyama, F. 34, 267, 270
Fumagalli, M. 256, 259
Functional Electrical Stimulation Bike Race 321
Fuß, J. 258
FUTUREBODY project 27, 29n60
future generations 282–283, 323, 326–327, 411; collection of current individuals for 287; discipline and enhancement 287–290; duties to 283–285; duty to non-maleficence to 284; duty to not harm 283–284; duty to protect 285–288; germline gene editing of 159; obligation to 289; preserving a life for 35; self-discipline and 287–290

Gallagher, S. 95
Garasic, M. D. 326
Gasson, M. 39
gatekeeper model 401
Gawdat, M. 309, 315, 316
Gazzaniga, M. 395, 401
gender 32, 79, 105, 168, 177, 181; body politics and embodiment in 91; issues of 126; selection *see* sex selection; transgender 136, 139; *see also* female
gene editing 14–16, 52, 151, 161n29; bacterial-based 154; cellular systems and 49–51; enhancing people through 322–324; ethical guidance of tools 147; germline *see* germline gene editing; somatic cell 51; using bacteria-derived enzymes 145–146; *see also* CRISPR–Cas9
gene therapy 254; and enhancement 63; ethical discourse on 24–25; ethics of 25–26; germline 155, 156; memory enhancement by 25; somatic cell 155
genetic engineering 13, 22, 81, 145; of desired traits or fixing up 393; enhancement 25, 26; ethical discourse on 24, 26; eugenic 25; human 25, 299; in medicine 322–324, 327; playing God, notion of 24, 270, 398; in preimplantation genetic diagnosis 80; slowing aging process through 176; tools 322
genetic enhancement 11, 20, 26, 50, 79–81, 392; for children 400; consent and choice for 149; and disability 151; discourse on 24; ethics of 103, 145–152; eugenics and collectivism 149–151; in fetus 398; forms of 145–146; genetic immunization as 146; germline 110; impact of genes on phenotype and 104; inadvertent 15; liberal eugenics in 149; positional goods and inequalities 146–147; promoting 253; to treat disease 147–149
genetic immunization 146, 152n1
genetic pleiotropy 15–16

genetic sex change 105–106, 110; *see also* sex selection
germline gene editing 154, 161n28; animal studies 158; Chinese twins 51; clinical research with novel therapies 159; with CRISPR 154–160; inevitable 158–159; liberal eugenics argument for 156; objections prohibiting 157–159; risk-analysis response 156–157; risk/benefit analysis 157, 159; in vitro fertilization and 158
Gilbert, F. 242
Gillam, W. 242
Gintis, H. 291
Giubilini, A. 192, 194, 275
Glannon, W. 254
Glover, J. 316–317
God Machine thought experiment 273
Goldstein, K. 91
Goodin, R. 285–286
Google Glass 215, 217, 218, 259
Goold, I. 361, 362
gratitude framework 270
Greely, H. 365, 395, 401
Grunwald, A. 407
Gyngell, C. 150

Habermas, J. 80, 81, 323, 337–338
Hacke, W. 258
Haff, P. 39
Halbert, D. 367
Haldane, J. B. S. 19–22
Hall, W. D. 239
Hamlet, E. 362–363
Haraway, D. 23
Harbisson, N. 37–39
Harris, J. 78, 217, 261, 271–274, 276, 298, 320, 395, 401
Harrison, D. E. 172
Hauskeller, M. 83
Hayles, K. 23
Hays, R. 177
Heidegger, M. 36, 137
He Jiankui 15, 16
Hershenov, D. 124
Hitler paradox 30, 35–36
Hobbes, T. 163, 165
Hoeprich, Mark R. 259
Hofmann, B. 84
homosexuality 258
Howard, T. 24
Hughes, J. 254, 295–296, 301
human body 18, 87, 147, 165, 179, 267, 412; 19th century 89–93; Bernal's view on 19–22; deficiency of 88–89; despiser of 89; implant in 39; lived 89–91, 94, 96, 99–100, 100n9; as new starting point in philosophy 89–90; physiological condition 234n10; political, societal, and symbolic dimensions of 91–92; (re)discovering 89–93; self in 89, 93; sex, gender, and 91–92; as technological design space 331–339; *see also* cyborg human; designer babies; theory of a multi-layered

responsorium of 91; vision of changing 38; *see also* embodiment
human corporeality 27, 87, 89, 97; alteration of 21; between enhancement and disembodiment 98–99; intercorporeality 90–91; reflection of 88; transhumanist notions of 98–99
human dignity 77, 85; attributed 83–84; Bostrom's argument about 83; inflorescent 84; intrinsic 83; reception of arguments from 82–84; violating 51–52, 63–64
human duty *par excellence* 32
humane cyborg *see* cyborg human
human enhancement 1–2, 107, 110, 271–272, 363, 408; academic discourse on 26; age of 9–16; authenticity in ethics of 133–140; Bernal on flesh 19–22; better humans at the outset of 11–14; biotechnology, developmental biology, and 61–65; clinical practice and 319–328; core commitments of permissivist accounts of 78–79; COVID-19 and 309–310; defined 189; discourse on 18–27, 98; and enhancement 31–33, 312–313; ethico-political discourse on 24–26; functional enhancement and 277n9; genetic engineering 25; Hitler paradox 35–36; human predicament and need for 313–315; idea of enhancing humans 10–11; immediate forerunners of 22–23; and improvement 311–312; inadvertent, challenge of 15–16; and intellectual augmentation 189–191; limits to 320; moral marketing and problem of overselling 14–15; perpetual quest for 419–420; phenomenological perspective on embodiment and 97–99; philosophical advice for 9–10; posthuman take on 30–42; prehistory of concept 18–23; rules and principles to guide risk reduction in 79; to social evolutions 33–36; superhuman 389; in technology assessment and bioethics 98; through sex selection *see* sex selection; trade-offs and 9–10; transhumanism and 270; truly 127; types of 310; unintended or inadvertent 15–16; use and abuse of artificial intelligence for 189–198; violating nature 119–127; *see also* radical human enhancement
human enhancement technologies (HET) 77; human person as basis for evaluation of 81–82; permissivist analysis of 79
Human Genome Project (1990) 11
Humanity+ 128n2, 268
human nature 16, 19, 22, 27, 57, 61–64, 77–78, 180, 310, 409; alteration of 18; arguments from 84–85; cognitive enhancement and personal identity 124–126, 203; constituting 121–122; dangerous idea to leave 267–268; moral enhancement and narrative identity 126–127; need for 119–121; reception of arguments from 84–85; transhumanism and 122–124, 269–271; violating 121
human predicament 166–168, 310, 317; by conflict 163; and need enhancement 313–315; public health 169; of unequal health 170; Warnock's observations about 315; zero-sum 170

human rights 413–414; activism and social responsibility 35; instruments 366; law 360, 361–362; legislation 363; risks of crediting cryonics as 30, 35; treaties 368–369
Hume, D. 122, 124
Humphries, S. 240
Husserl, E. 89, 90
Huxley, A. 26
Huxley, J. 22, 34, 38
hyperperformance 326

identity-affecting technology 105–106, 110
Ienca, M. 224, 413
Ihde, D. 92
inadvertent human enhancement, challenge of 15–16
Indigenous people 32
individualism 150–151
injustice 84, 273, 383, 393–396; (global) structural 277n8; moral significance of 110–111; of Nazi medical experiments 159; social 103, 109, 126; *see also* justice/fairness
intellectual augmentation (IA); AI technologies of relevance to prospect of 191–193; artificial intelligence for 193–198; brain-computer interfaces for 192–193; human enhancement and 189–190
intelligence explosion 23, 192
International Olympic Committee 363
in vitro fertilization (IVF) 13, 106, 110, 145, 148, 392; societal acceptance of 154, 158

Jiankui, H. 323–324, 334
Jinpa, T. 92
Johnson, C. K. 224
Johnson, M. 61
Jonas, H. 327, 415
Jotterand, F. 83
Judith C. 177
justice/fairness: artificial intelligence 197–198; cognitive enhancement 393–396; *laisseiz-faire* view, and vulnerability 410–411; principles of 396
Jwa, A. 244

Kahane, G. 122
Kahneman, D. 162
Kant, I. 83, 119–121, 128n5, 276, 312, 313, 341
Kasparov, G. 191
Kass, L. R. 79–81, 83, 164, 217–219, 394, 396
Keenan, J. 120
Kernel 224
Kessler, R. C. 395, 401
ketamine 342, 346–347
Kierkegaard, S. 133
Kim, R. 84
Kirchhoffer, David G. 83
Kline, N. 23, 38
Kloosterboer, N. 379, 382
Kolber, A. J. 363
Kurzweil, R. 14, 122

laisseiz-faire approach 400, 410–411
Lakoff, G. 61
Langguth, B. 258
Lara, F. 197
Laughlin, Charles D. 94
law of armed conflict 369
Lederberg, J. 22
Leget, C. 168, 169
Levinas, E. 91
Levy, N. 137
Lewens, T. 84
Lewis, C. S. 19
liberal eugenics 149, 154, 155; argument for germline gene enhancement 156; benefit-risk assessment 157–159; in genetic enhancement 149; germline genome editing with CRISPR 155–156; risk-analysis response to 156–157
Lichtenberg, J. 380
Licklider, J. 23, 225–226
Liivoja, R. 369
Locke, J. 121, 124
Longevity Dividend Initiative Consortium (LDIC) 176
longevity science 162; aging and natural 163–166; equality 168–172; framing of 163–172; how long is enough life 166–168
Lovelock, J. 309, 314–316
Lucke, J. C. 239

MacFarquhar, L. 383
MacIntyre, A. 123
Mackie, J. 299
Macklin, R. 83
Maier, L. J. 204
Malatesti, L. 254
Maori people 33
Marcel, G. 231–232
Martin, L. 177
Marx, K. 19
Maslen, H. 361
Mauron, A. 168–171
McAllister, A. 369
Mccall, I. C. 198
McKenny, G. 122–123, 180–182
McManus, J. 94
Medawar, P. 165
memory 13, 15, 124–125, 138, 215–216, 242, 340–341, 347; acetylcholinesterase inhibitors on 344; caffeine and 343; *CCR5* expression associated with 66; coherence and 136; consolidation 243; deep brain stimulation 218–220, 240; dementia, progression of 344; of elderly people 324; by gene therapy 25–26; ketamine and classic psychedelic antidepressants on 346–347; memory-manipulating technology 413; memory-modulation techniques 325; nicotine and 342; non-psychedelic antidepressants on 345; psychostimulants on 344; retention 390; *see also* working memory
Menovsky, T. 258

mental integrity 196, 245, 369, 413–414
Merkel, R. 261
Merleau-Ponty, M. 89–91, 94
methylphenidate 203, 214–216, 219–220, 222, 239, 254, 343–344, 378
microphenomenology 93, 97
Mill, J. S. 12, 139, 140, 267
mind-body dualism 61, 87, 92, 94, 95, 267, 268; cerebral organoids and neural chimeras in 57; dominance of 89–93; importance of alterity 91; in Judeo-Christian narrative 88; overcoming 89–90
Minsky, M. 23
modafinil 12, 203, 216, 219–220, 239, 254, 343–344, 378, 395, 397
moderate human enhancement 78, 120, 127, 344
moral assertiveness (or moral resoluteness) 255, 260, 261
moral bioenhancement (MBE) 12, 126, 267, 287, 291, 293–294, 312–316, 350; case against 298–302; case for 294–298; concept of 271–272; context 300–301; defined 271; discourse 302–303; enthusiasm 299; and freedom 273–275; genetic 334; hyperresponsibility and 377–378, 381–382, 384; libertarian 295–296; by means of artificial intelligence 275–277; medical approach 271; and notion of morality 272–273; political embeddedness of 296; realistic 293, 296, 300, 303–304; salvatory 293, 296, 298–302
moral brain 256, 277n12
moral commitment 255, 260
moral compass 255, 260, 262
moral enhancement 26, 77, 119, 135, 268, 287–288, 295, 349–351, 376–378; behavioral improvement 273; biotechnological 126–127; classification of 273; ethically justifiable 260–262; improved insight 273; meta-ethical discussion about neurosurgical 261–262; motivational improvement 273; narrative identity and 126–127; neurosurgical 253–262; non-biomedical 290; numerical identity and 126; *see also* moral bioenhancement (MBE); neurosurgical moral enhancement
moral intelligence model 254–256, 260, 262, 263n1, 296
morality 192, 253, 261, 276, 294, 317; biologizing 301–302; brain network for moral behavior with 256; of cloning humans 10; common sense, vulnerability model on 285–286; demands 377; emotional states to 420; entanglement with 341, 342, 347–349; immorality 299, 394; mechanistic bioreduction of 299; moral enhancement and 272–273; nepotism enhancer and morality enhancer 254–255; in pharmaceutical cognitive enhancement 349–351; Warnock's view of 316
moral myopia 163
moral obligations 82, 150–151, 287, 291, 389, 393–394
moral pluralism 120, 156, 276, 296
moral problem-solving 255, 260
moral sensitivity 255, 260, 262, 348

Moravec, H. 23
More, M. 35–36
morphological freedom principle 21, 119, 122, 225
morphological intelligence 60
Murphy, P. 163
Musk, E. 12, 20–21, 193, 224, 241

National Institutes of Health 297
natural law 82, 156
NBIC (nano-bio-info-cogno) initiative 26
network effects 146, 149, 150
Neuralink project 21, 37, 224, 241–242
neurophenomenology 90, 93–95, 101n31
neurorights 245, 360, 369, 413–414; defined 412
neurosurgical brain–computer interfaces 241–242
neurosurgical moral enhancement 253–254; medico-ethical issues of 260–261; meta-ethical discussion about 261–262; model of moral intelligence 254–255; moral dysfunctions by brain disfunctions 256–257; reducing aggressiveness, neurosurgical interventions for 257–258; reducing psychopathy or sociopathy, neurosurgical interventions for 259; reducing sex drive, neurosurgical interventions for 258–259
neurotechnological enhancement 237; anticipatory ethics, impact of 237–238, 244–246; deep brain stimulation 240–241; future of 240–244; neurosurgical brain–computer interfaces 241–242; non-invasive brain stimulation 243–244; psychopharmacological enhancement 239–240; self-monitoring brain–computer interfaces 242
nicotine 341–343, 351, 391
Nietzsche, F. 89, 91, 133, 135
non-invasive brain stimulation 203, 237, 243–245, 390

ontological vulnerability 123
opportunity maintenance 391
Ord, T. 147–148
Organization for Economic Cooperation and Development (OECD) 414
organoids 47, 53–55, 60, 64, 67n42; cerebral 56–57; endometrial 54; intestinal 55; neural 56–57, 68n56; ovarian or testicular 54; parathyroid 67n43; patient-derived colorectal cancer 67n34; reproductive 54, 55; retinal 57; transplantable salivary gland/lacrimal gland 54
Orwell, G. 19
Otto 218–219, 221
Outram, S. 244, 365
Overall, C. 79
ownership 229, 360; of intellectual property 367; self-ownership 233

Page, L. 326
Palmer, J. G. 26
paradigm of availability 321, 328
paradigm of possibility of therapy 321, 328
Parasidis, E. 362
Parens, E. 26, 120, 270
Parfit, D. 109–110

Parnas, J. 96
Patterson, J. 33
Paul, A. 177, 230
Paul, Diane B. 19
perfectionism 165, 274, 298, 299, 323, 409
performance enhancement: academic 239; cognitive enhancement 98, 205, 390–391
performance maintenance 391
permissivism 78–79, 84, 85n4
person-affecting technology 105–106, 110
personal autonomy 273–274
personal identity 50, 95, 122, 228–229, 231, 337; cognitive enhancement and 124–126; narrative 124–127, 135, 138, 325; numerical 124–127, 325; psychological-continuity criterion of 124; synchronic and diachronic 268
Persson, I. 220, 253–254, 267, 272–274, 295, 376
Petersen, M. 208, 210
Petersen, T. 208, 210
Petitmengin, C. 96, 97
Pham, C. 242
pharmaceutical cognitive enhancement (PCE) 209, 340–342, 351; acetylcholinesterase inhibitors 344; caffeine 343; d-amphetamine 343–344; efficacy of 239; enhancement of 347–349; entanglement of emotion, morality, and context in 349–351; ketamine and classic psychedelic antidepressants 345–347; methylphenidate 343–344; modafinil 343–344; nicotine 342–343; non-psychedelic antidepressants 345; pharmaceutical policy 347–351; prevalence of 239–240; psychostimulants 343–344; public attitudes toward 240
phenomenological psychopathology 95–96
Pijnenburg, M. A. 168, 169
Pinker, S. 83
Pistorius, O. 320–321
planetary enhancement, social enhancement to 37–41
Plato 88, 121, 122
Plazier, M. 258
pleiotropy, genetic 15–16
Plessner, H. 89–91
positional good 146–147, 151
posthumanism 30–33, 36, 41, 120, 320, 414; academic 23; critical 32, 277n3; cultural 32; philosophical and existential 32; technological 268, 277n3; transhumanism vs. 268–269
Powell, R. 290
Powered Arm Prosthesis Race 321
Powered Exoskeleton Race 321
Powered Leg Prosthesis Race 321
Powered Wheelchair Race 321
preimplantation genetic diagnosis (PGD) 80, 105, 110, 112, 115n3, 392–393
preimplantation genetic testing (PGT) 145
President's Council on Bioethics (PCBE) 26, 29n57, 394–395, 398
Priori, A. 256, 259
prisoner's dilemma 146, 368, 397
Pritchard, D. 214, 217, 222

procreative altruism 150
procreative beneficence 149, 150, 392
product liability law 365
prohibition-style approach 400–401
Project Cyborg 37
Protestant-Jewish-Catholic coalition 24
psychedelic antidepressants 98, 342, 349–351; classic 346–347; non-psychedelic antidepressants 345; *see also specific antidepressants*
psychological-continuity theory 124–125, 127, 413
psychopathy 263n3, 382; acquired 256–257; developmental 256–257; neurosurgical 261; reducing 259
psychostimulants 342–344
psychotropic drugs 393
public goods problem 146
Pugh, J. 136
Putnam, H. 273

Racine, E. 210, 239
radical human enhancement 9, 77–78, 147; Agar's argument against 82, 85n6; attitude of mastery, emboding 80–81; ethics of 77–85; human dignity, compatible with 82–84; human nature, reception of arguments from 84–85; objections to 79–82; restrictivist and bioconservative criticisms of 77–78; social goods, undermining 81; valuable for humans and 81–82; vulnerability and finitude, repudiation of 79–80
radical life extension 30, 33–34, 41
Radner, E. 177–178, 182
Rakić, V. 274
Rand Corporation 175, 198
Raus, K. 273
Rawls, J. 396
Ray, K. 207, 389, 391, 393
Reade, W. 19, 99
regenerative medicine 52
regulatory authority for cognitive enhancements 402
Reimer, M. 256
reproductive autonomy 149, 151
Resnik, D. 148
reversal test 147–148
Ribas, M. 37, 39
Ricard, M. 92
Rifkin, J. 24
right to mental self-determination 263n4
Robert, J. S. 310
Romantics 133, 139
Rosch, E. 94
Rousseau, J.-J. 133, 137–139
Rueda, J. 123

Sadler, R. 83
Sahakian, B. 395, 401
Salles, A. 272
Sandberg, A. 122, 309, 408, 409
Sandel, M. 80, 81, 165, 217
Sartre, J.-P. 133, 137, 139
Savant Syndrome 70n86

Savulescu, J. 55, 122, 192, 194, 220, 253–254, 267, 272–275, 295, 320, 323, 376, 389, 392, 393, 396, 399–400
Schelle, K. J. 205, 209
Schermer, M. 273
Schopenhauer, A. 89
self-defense 262, 283
self-discipline 283, 288–291, 323
self-incurred immaturity 276
self-monitoring brain–computer interfaces 242
sexism 32, 104, 110–111
sex selection 91, 103–104; aggregate consequences of people 113; biology of sex 104–105; brain sex 109; as enhancement 106–109; ethics of 103; eugenics, inevitability of 114; for female 109–113; genetic sex change 105–106; injustice, moral significance of 110–111; lessons from 113–115; nature and norms 114; objections to claim 109–113; Parfitian reflections 109–110; plurality of good 111–112; policy of 112–113; sexism 32; wrong sex 106
Siegel, R. S. 25
SIENNA project 27, 29n59
Silver, L. 13
Singer, P. 383
singularity 14, 23, 192
sledgehammer approach 296, 301, 303
slowing aging 26, 176, 181–182; and Baconian project 178–180; Barth's Christocentric anthropology 180–181; Christians resist life extension by 176–178; *see also* aging enhancement
social animals, human beings as 123
social enhancement 37–42
Soekadar, S. 224
Somatic Cell Nuclear Transfer (SCNT) 49
Sparrow, S. 274, 310, 317
Specker, J. 273
Specker Sullivan, L. 210, 244, 246
Stapledon, O. 316
stem cells 51–52, 66n27, 113, 155; based embryo models 52–53, 54; embryoids 52–53, 54; embryonic (ESCs) 51–52, 106; human glial progenitors 57; induced pluripotent (iPSCs) 52, 56, 66n26, 106; integrated stem cell model 67n29; pluripotent 52–53; transplants 175; 2D cultures 55
Sterckx, S. 273
Stoermer, Eugene F. 32
Stoller, Robert J. 91
Strategic Action Plan on Human Rights and Technologies in Biomedicine 414
Strategies for Engineered Negligible Senescence (SENS) 34
Strathern, M. 309, 315, 317
substantial ambivalence 205, 206, 208
Sulmasy, D. 83
superhuman performance 18, 191–193, 310, 389
superintelligence 190–191
Swierstra, T. 12

Talbot, M. 12
Tanner, C. 255
taxation approach 401–402
Taylor, C. 139
technical mastery 80–81
test tube babies 13, 19
Thacker, J. 177
therapeutic enhancement 18, 189, 192–193, 320
Thompson, E. 94, 96
Thomson, J. J. 10
Tolkien, J. R. R. 19
transcranial direct current stimulation (tDCS) 194, 243–244, 259, 390, 395
Transcranial electrical stimulation (tES) 243
transcranial magnetic stimulation (TMS) 243–244, 259, 298, 390–391
transhumanism 22–23, 30–34, 98–99, 119, 267–268, 277nn3–4; aim of 268; Bostrom's 78, 328n1; critique of 122–124; democratic 32, 34, 42n10; history of 18–19; human nature improving 269–271; Huxley's 38; libertarian 32; posthumanism *vs.* 268–269; as radical visionary worldview 87; religious objections to 398; technological 268
Transhumanist Declaration 268–269
Transhumanist FAQ 268–269
translational neuroethics 246
transplants 53, 161n28; bone marrow to 392; brain 124; chimeras 55–56; chromosomal 105–106; organoids 54–57; stem cell 175; therapeutic 52; womb 104
Trotsky, L. 19
true self 133–134, 139–140, 141n5, 204, 270; changing and creating 134–137; coherence 134–136; endorsement 136; expressing 137–139; relations 136–137
Tversky, A. 162

"ultimate harm" argument 267, 271, 276–277, 294–295
Unger, P. 383
Universal Declaration of Human Rights 366, 414
Universal Declaration on the Human Genome and Human Rights 411
US Defense Advanced Research Projects Agency (DARPA) 23

Vallor, S. 83
Varela, Francisco J. 94
Vermersch, P. 97
Viana, J. 242
Vincent, N. 375

Waldenfels, B. 91
Walters, L. 25–26
Warnock, G. 313–317
Warwick, K. 37
Wasserman, D. 273
welfarist approach 272
Wells, H. G. 19
Wexler, A. 198, 210, 244, 246
Wieland, J. W. 379, 382
Williams, B. 14, 123
working memory 342, 346, 390; non-invasive brain stimulation on 203; spatial 215–216, 219, 347; verbal 347
Wu, K. C. C. 341

Yamanaka, S. 52

Zahavi, D. 96
Zamyatin, Y. 19
Zhou, M. 15
Zohny, H. 272
Zuboff, S. 41

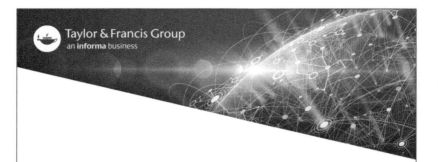